Anthony Seldon is the Head Master of Brigh[...]
biographer and historian. His many p[...]
authorised life of John Major and *10 Do[...]
History. He is also the editor of *The Blair Effect*, a collection of essays on
the first Blair government described by David Butler as 'essential
reading'.

Further praise for *Blair*:

'The architecture [of the book] is strikingly original [and] gradually the
structure draws one in, beaming fresh light on the familiar
personalities and news stories . . . This is an enlightening study of a
man who reached the top suddenly, before he was quite ready for it . . .
The book contains many revelations . . . Seldon is especially acute at
assessing Blair's limitations as policy-maker' Steve Richards, *TLS*

'Weighty . . . an impressively complete and up-to-date account of the
personalities and events that have formed Labour's longest-serving
prime minister. Although not authorised in the traditional sense – and
thus not constrained – many of those within Mr Blair's inner circle have
clearly trusted the author and his numerous researchers sufficiently to
talk freely and candidly . . . [the novel structure] helps to give a new
insight into what is perhaps Mr Blair's greatest political gift: his
extraordinary ability to make (almost) everyone who comes into his
orbit like him' *The Economist*

'The most readable of all the books this year on the Prime Minister
and/or the war was Anthony Seldon's *Blair*' Elinor Goodman, *Sunday
Telegraph* Books of the Year

'[Seldon] is serious in his verdicts . . . [Tony Blair] is judiciously and
movingly presented . . . Persuasive' Quentin Letts, *Daily Telegraph*

'Sharply-drawn . . . Reader-friendly' Andy McSmith, *Independent on
Sunday*

'Reflective . . . Entertaining . . . retains a healthy balance on a man who,
like Mrs Thatcher, can inspire excessive passions often because he goes
against the grain of British politics' George Walden, *Sunday Telegraph*

'It is high time we got a further full-length portrait of the Prime
Minister in office . . . [Seldon] shows himself a dab hand at detecting
personality flaws and character defects . . . Shrewd' Anthony Howard,
Evening Standard

'Honest and refreshing . . . Insightful' Howard Davies, *THES*

ALSO BY ANTHONY SELDON

Churchill's Indian Summer (1981)

By Word of Mouth (with Joanna Seldon, 1983)

Contemporary History (ed., 1987)

Ruling Performance (with Peter Hennessy, 1987)

The Thatcher Effect (ed. with Dennis Kavanagh, 1989)

UK Political Parties Since 1945 (ed., 1990)

Politics UK (joint author, 1991)

The Conservative Century (ed., 1994)

The Major Effect (ed. with Dennis Kavanagh, 1994)

The Heath Government 1970–1974 (ed. with Stuart Ball, 1996)

The Contemporary History Handbook (ed. with Brian Brivati, 1996)

The Ideas That Shaped Post-war Britain (ed. with David Marquand, 1996)

How Tory Governments Fall (ed., 1996)

Major: A Political Life (1997)

10 Downing Street: An Illustrated History (1999)

The Powers Behind the Prime Minister (with Dennis Kavanagh, 1999)

Britain Under Thatcher (with Daniel Collings, 2000)

The Foreign Office: An Illustrated History (2000)

The Blair Effect 1997–2001 (ed., 2001)

A New Conservative Century? (with Peter Snowdon, 2001)

Public and Private Education: The Divide Must End (2001)

Partnership not Paternalism (2002)

Brave New City (2002)

Old Labour New Labour (ed. with Kevin Hickson, 2004)

The Conservative Party: An Illustrated History
(with Peter Snowdon, 2004)

BLAIR

Anthony Seldon

with

Chris Ballinger, Daniel Collings
and Peter Snowdon

First published in Great Britain by The Free Press, 2004
This edition first published by The Free Press, 2005
An imprint of Simon & Schuster UK Ltd
A Viacom company

1 3 5 7 9 10 8 6 4 2

Simon & Schuster UK Ltd
Africa House
64–78 Kingsway
London WC2B 6AH

Simon & Schuster Australia
Sydney

www.simonsays.co.uk

A CIP catalogue for this book is available
from the British Library.

ISBN: 0-7432-3212-7

Typeset by M Rules
Printed and bound in Great Britain by
Cox & Wyman Ltd, Reading, Berks

*With gratitude for the inspiration I have received from
David Butler, Peter Hennessy and Dennis Kavanagh,
masters of contemporary British history.*

Contents

Contents

Introduction

This is not a conventional biography detailing chronologically every significant event in its subject's life. The obvious reason for this is that there have already been two excellent biographies of Blair: an early volume by Jon Sopel (1995) and another by John Rentoul (1995, updated in 2001). These books cover the ground extensively. They were both 'authorised' biographies in that their authors had a degree of consent from their subject when requesting interviews with family and friends. Although this book had very substantial access to those close to Blair, it is an unauthorised biography, and sees the subject through the eyes not of the mid-1990s, but through those of one writing ten years later. The concern of the early biographies was to explain how Tony Blair rose up to his exceptional hegemonic position. The objective of this book is to explain what he did with his power and how, by his tenth anniversary as party leader, he had lost the extraordinary authority that he had acquired. Whether the loss is temporary or permanent is yet to be seen.

I sought an alternative model to conventional political biography. Having written a book of some half a million words on Blair's predecessor as Prime Minister, I realised that I had produced less a biography of a man than a history of his government. My focus here is Tony Blair: what he thought, what he did, and why he did it. I decided to home in on the key events and the key people who have influenced him and made him who and what he is. Even here I had to be selective. I pared it down to twenty events and twenty people. Not all the episodes or people chosen are equally important, and the text indicates which are the seminal.

The 'people' chapters are not necessarily chronological, though their placing is roughly dictated by their relevance to an episode just discussed. The 'political' backbone of the book is provided by Chapters 10, 20, 30 and 40. The first of these is on Neil Kinnock, who was responsible for Blair's promotion but whose Labourite prescriptions were to be rejected by Blair. Chapter 20 is on Roy Jenkins, who offered him two ground-breaking ideas, neither of which he carried through. It was thus to be neither his Labour nor Liberal Democrat mentors who had the real influence on Blair: it was Margaret Thatcher, the subject of Chapter 30. Chapter 40, the last in the book, is on Gordon Brown, Blair's fellow architect of New Labour, but also the figure who repeatedly blocked Blair from carrying out his agenda once in power, and whose personal achievements after 1997 rivalled his own.

The 'episode' chapters are given odd numbers and are strictly chronological. Again, the chapter order follows a pattern. Those ending in seven thus see him at his boldest: Sedgefield (Chapter 7), seizing a seat against all reasonable odds; Clause IV (17), his most daring domestic initiative; Kosovo (27), where for the first time he risked isolation on the world stage; and Iraq (37), the decision on which he knew judgements on his premiership would turn. Some repetition has been inevitable to make each chapter comprehensible on its own, but it has been cut to a minimum.

More than many premiers, Tony Blair, like the barrister he once was, gave attention to one issue at a time, which makes the 'episode' approach, I hope, particularly appropriate. The focus on key people is also, I believe, peculiarly suited to the subject. Most premiers have been rooted in a party or body of thought. Blair, by contrast, has travelled lightly in terms of ideology and tribe, but has been influenced throughout his life by a series of powerful people. Each of the twenty individuals described in the 'people' chapters shaped his personality, his thinking, or his behaviour. My hope is that this approach helps make sense of my subject, even if it means important areas have inevitably had to be omitted.

The book was written while on a sabbatical in the last ten weeks of 2003 and was added to and revised in the first five months of 2004. It is based very largely on 600 interviews in all 'camps' and in many countries. Some 90 per cent of the book's content was derived from interviews: remaining sources in order of importance were unpublished diaries and papers, books and the press. The book has also benefited greatly from sending out chapters or parts of chapters to those who took part in events, and assimilating their comments as appropriate. This has also been essential in checking accuracy, and ironing out the very frequent differences over fact or interpretations. The practice is eschewed by most journalists and marks a clear line in the sand between journalism and contemporary history. Endnotes are another distinction between the two fields. All substantive points bar the most recent additions have endnote references. Where interviewees wished to remain confidential, the note is simply entitled 'Interview'. For those who might be interested in knowing the source, the full interview list will be placed in an archive library for consultation in the distant future.

The book addresses itself to the following questions about Tony Blair:

- Who have been the biggest influences on him?
- What have been the major turning points in his life?
- What are his main beliefs?
- What motivates him and his politics?
- Is he Labour; if so, in what form?
- What is the role of religion/morality in his life?
- When and why did he decide he wanted to be Labour leader?
- What have been the high and low points in his life?
- What does he think about Europe?
- What did he want to do as Prime Minister?
- How has power changed him?
- Who has he relied on most; when, why (and for what)?
- Why has he become so involved in foreign issues?
- What might be his legacy in history?

The biography also attempts to use images in a fresh way. Photographs are an indispensable aid to print journalism but have not sat as comfortably with biographies. In place of the traditional formula of grouping photographs together in a plate section, each chapter opens with a photograph which either sheds some light on or reflects the nature of the episode or relationship in discussion.

Longer and better biographies of Tony Blair will be written in the years to come. I hope to have provided a portrait of his personality and place in history on the tenth anniversary of his becoming leader of the Labour Party, as well as to have provided an alternative approach to the current model of narrative political biographies.

ANTHONY SELDON
May 2004

Introduction to the Second Edition

This edition contains new material, particularly in chapters 39 and 40, as well as a completely rewritten conclusion. The turning point in chapter 39 has been remodelled around Blair's 'wobble' in 2004. It examines how seriously he considered stepping down and why he subsequently chose to announce his intention to remain as Prime Minister for a full third term. Chapter 40 describes in detail the relationship and feelings between Blair and Brown and brings us up to date on their ten-year-long battle. The new conclusion spells out what I believe about Blair's character and leadership, and expands on why I chose to write the biography in its unconventional format, not as a narrative, but with alternating chapters focusing on key individuals and pivotal moments.

The first edition was concluded in the spring of 2004, when Tony Blair's authority and support was at its lowest level. By early 2005, with the Iraqi election successfully contested, with some improvements in public services beginning to be felt, Brown outflanked, the EU constitution referendum in 2006 looking winnable, and Blair's victory in the next British General Election almost certain, he is now in his strongest position since 2001. His standing has been transformed. He is bristling with radical ideas for his third term, which he sees as being far more successful than his first two. But, for all that, his achievements to date at home remain modest, aside from his startling success as an election winner, while his impact on Europe and the wider world is far from secure. Tony Blair knows this, which is why he is determined to stay on as Prime Minister to entrench his particular brand of neo-Thatcherite policy at home, oversee a 'yes' vote in the EU referendum and reap the rewards he is certain will flow from alliance with the United States abroad. We may well look back at Blair's power in the spring of 2005 as his last period of mastery. Or he may go on to achieve great things as Prime Minister. Political leaders, with prime ministers no exception, usually make their mark early on, or mid-way through their period in office. But Tony Blair has been full of surprises and may yet have a glorious Indian summer. No one should write off this extraordinarily feline politician. It is remarkable to note, nevertheless, that eight full years into his premiership, how little has yet been achieved, and that the verdict on him is still wide open.

ANTHONY SELDON
March 2005

BLAIR

Tony Blair at Fettes in about 1967. The photograph captures him on the turn from the biddable boy he was when he arrived at the school into the surly and knowing adolescent he was to become.

I

Father's Stroke, 1953–71

Very high achievers, the theory goes, often encounter difficulties in their early lives, difficulties which may help to forge their extraordinary drive and ambition. Tony Blair's childhood has often been raked over for clues to explain his later actions and character.[1] In reality, Blair's ambition only developed after the years covered in this chapter, and his exceptional self-belief after he became party leader. But what of his politics?

Leo Blair's stroke in July 1964 was the most important single event in the first eighteen years of his son's life. But did it propel the young Tony Blair into a life in politics? John Rentoul's first words in his thoughtful and well-informed biography are 'Tony Blair's political ambition began at the age of eleven, when his father Leo's ended'. Peter Stothard wrote during the 2003 Gulf War that the conventional wisdom is that after his stroke Leo transferred his political ambition to his son.[2] To understand whether this episode was indeed the formative personal and political experience that has been claimed, this chapter will look at the event in the context of Blair's first eighteen years.

His parents, Leo and Hazel, had grown up in Glasgow and were married there in November 1948. Their first child William, known as Bill, was born in March 1950, while Tony was born three years later, on 6 May 1953. Bill was born in Glasgow and Tony in Edinburgh, where Leo was working by day in the tax office. Leo's heart and mind, however, were elsewhere: by night he was completing a law degree and subsequently a doctorate at Edinburgh University, where he was also a part-time tutor. Leo was not only very bright; he was also unusually determined. He wanted his own family to be spared the insecurity and deprivation he had experienced, and he was set on taking his family up the social ladder. The law meant prosperity; and academia, status. No suitable openings then existed in Britain, so on Christmas Eve 1954, with Tony just twenty months old, he bundled the family on board the ocean liner *Iberian* for a journey to Australia, where he had secured a position as lecturer in administrative law at the University of Adelaide.

'My first real memories of my younger brother,' Bill Blair recalled years later, 'are from when the family moved to Australia ... The journey took about four weeks. I have a very clear recollection of leaving Glasgow, and our grandmother waving to us from the door of our house. I don't think she really expected to see any of us again, certainly not for a very long time.'[3] Their time in Australia was to be a golden period for the family. Leo prospered in Adelaide's law department, while Hazel bore her third and last child, Sarah, in July 1956, and Bill and Tony thrived in their new environment. One can imagine the stark contrast for the young family between South Australia in the 1950s, full of space, light and opportunity, and the dark north of Britain, full of memories for both Leo and Hazel of hardship. Although Tony was still young, Australia affected him deeply. Australian people, and culture, were to have a profound influence on him throughout his life.[4]

The idyll lasted three years. In January 1958, on the eve of the new Australian academic year, the family returned to Britain. A Qantas Constellation transported Hazel and the three children – a journey which took three days with an unscheduled stop in Athens because of engine trouble. Leo, meanwhile, travelled home via the Pacific and the United States. A lectureship in law at Durham University beckoned, meaning fresh opportunities for Leo back in the motherland; he was anxious also to develop a career in the Conservative Party. Not a natural choice, one might have thought, for a fostered child brought up by an active Communist in Govan, one of Glasgow's poorest areas, between the wars – but Leo was attracted now by the qualities of self-reliance and self-advancement which pushed his thinking firmly towards the right.

The family settled for a few months into an empty flat above The Chorister School, an independent prep school whose boys sang in the choir in the adjacent Durham Cathedral. Bill joined the school immediately, followed three years later by Tony (though neither was a Cathedral chorister) after a stint at Western Hill, a nearby 'pre-prep' school. These were to prove stable and increasingly prosperous years for the family. Characteristically, the academic world did not satisfy Leo's ambitions. Theorising about the law was no longer enough: he wanted to practise it and make some money. Leo was called to the Bar and soon built a thriving practice from chambers in nearby Newcastle. He also became chairman of the local Conservative Association, with excellent prospects of acquiring a parliamentary seat. Growing economic prosperity enabled a move for the family from the centre of Durham to a four-bedroom house on a new estate on the city's outskirts, with a double garage. The Blairs were an up-and-coming, well-to-do family – father working, mother at home, three children, popular with neighbours and respected in the city. There was no doubt who underwrote the family's fortunes. Charming, motivated, relentlessly ambitious and hardworking, Leo Blair had taken himself from a Glasgow tenement to a promising place in one of England's leading universities and most respected professions. But he had no intention of stopping there.

Happiness Punctuated

The day before American Independence Day, 4 July 1964, was a typical one. Leo had a long working day, the inevitable consequence of holding down two full-time jobs, with a dinner party in the evening – another key to stepping up the ladder. He and Hazel did not return home until 2.30 that Saturday morning. In the middle of the night he got up to go to the bathroom, but on the way he had a fall. Hazel immediately telephoned for an ambulance, which rushed him to hospital. At the age of just forty, he had suffered a severe stroke. Tony was woken by his mother early the next morning. He later recalled how he knew instinctively, the moment he saw his mother, that something 'terrible' had happened. 'My mother hadn't even spoken and I was in tears. Then she said: "Daddy's not very well, something happened in the night," and I knew it was dreadful and serious.'[5]

The next day Tony was, nevertheless, still sent off for his regular Saturday morning school. Staff were warned that his father was dangerously ill and to treat Tony gently.[6] He recalled kneeling down to pray with the Revd (later Canon) John Grove, Headmaster of The Chorister School. Fellow pupil James Fenton, later Professor of Poetry at Oxford University, had lost his mother some time before. 'Grove became very close to me. He would have been very understanding of Blair's predicament, and meticulous in paying attention to him.'[7] That afternoon, Hazel rushed from Leo's bedside to see Tony play in his Saturday rugby fixture. 'Dad is probably going to live,'[8] she told her anxious son. It had been a close thing. At the age of just eleven years and two months, Tony Blair had almost lost his father.

No one will ever know for certain the precise impact of this event on the young Blair's stable world. With his older brother Bill, a lifelong confidant, away at Fettes College, a boarding school in Edinburgh, his immediate sense of isolation must have been heightened. Anxiety too would not have been eased by the well-intentioned if common practice then of children not visiting seriously ill parents in hospital. Hazel wanted to protect her three children from seeing their once dynamic father lying 'full of fear and silent rage in hospital'.[9] When Leo eventually came home some months later, Tony had a 'terribly vivid' memory of going in to see him in his parents' bedroom. His father could ask for a cup of tea, and say 'good'. But that was about all. The man who had built his career through the power of speech could no longer talk.

Hazel spent the next three years nursing Leo back to health. Painstakingly, Hazel taught him to speak again. He kept his job at the university, and gradually returned to teaching duties. But Leo's ability to practise as a barrister was badly impaired and there was no disguising the reversal of fortunes. One of the cars in the garage had to be sold. The family was no longer sought-after in the local social hierarchy. Hazel also had to cope at this time with her daughter Sarah being hospitalised for two years with 'Still's disease', a form of infantile rheumatoid arthritis. But – and this is most important – Tony Blair showed no outward sign, then or later, of being severely disturbed by what had happened to his father. A period of introversion or other neurotic signs would have indicated that it had been traumatic for Tony. But he continued to be his usual smiling self. Teachers and friends at The Chorister School do not remember him becoming withdrawn, or suffering anxiety states. In the supportive, nurturing atmosphere of a small prep school, he had the best conceivable pastoral care. Bill, who has always been the calm one, returned soon after from school for the long summer holidays of 1964, and normality reasserted itself. Tony went on to have a happy final two years at Choristers, from 1964 to 1966. 'A. C. L. Blair', or 'Blair 2' as he was known, was popular, and contributed widely, though surprisingly he did not excel in debating, acting or music.[10] He featured prominently in school sports, particularly rugby and athletics. In the classroom, his strongest subjects were English and Latin.[11] Blair later said he looked back at the school with 'affection and gratitude' for the 'comfort, help and belief' it gave him.[12]

Hazel managed her recuperating husband and her sick daughter in her efficient and reassuring way. Economic concerns were not the least of her worries: income from the Bar in Newcastle dried up, and, but for the university, which maintained his salary, the family would have been in severe straits. William McLay, Hazel's stepfather, who had made a little money from butchers' shops in Glasgow, helped with school fees. Tony Blair later recalled, 'On an emotional level, I was suddenly made aware that nothing is permanent,' an innocent phrase that launched a thousand theses.[13] But, as Bill said, 'the family picked itself up, as families do'.[14] Tony looks back on his early life in Durham not as a place of anxiety and instability, but as a hugely happy grounding to his life. Above all, Hazel was the vessel who bore Tony through these turbulent waters, depositing him safely on the other side, onto the shores of adolescence. For young Tony, Leo's stroke was not happiness punctured: it was happiness punctuated.

Fettes College, 1966–71

'Butter wouldn't melt in his mouth' was how one teacher described the young Blair in his first year at Fettes College.[15] He had arrived from The Chorister School with an Open Exhibition. Fettes thought it had secured another pupil as accomplished as brother Bill, who was widely admired. One member of staff wrote, 'I liked his brother Bill. He was a thoroughly decent, responsible fellow, and a diligent, genuine scholar.'[16] For Tony's first year, indeed, all went well. He was charming, a keen sportsman who played in the school's 'Under 14' rugby and cricket sides, and was helpful to all. 'I remember Blair as very popular,' recalled the Upper Sixth-former for whom he 'fagged', 'running everywhere, very active, slightly immature, engaged all the time in some kind of activity.'[17] The notion of a boy, severely neurotic and disturbed, or one with his mind already fixated on a career in politics to achieve what his father now could not, does not fit the facts. The general impression of the early Blair at Fettes was 'an extremely cheery, dandy young boy, grinning away like mad with his attractive smile, very popular right from the word go, because he was so likable and enthusiastic'.[18]

Tony Blair was to spend five years at Fettes: three years to 'O' levels in 1969, and a final two years in the sixth form studying for 'A' levels, which he sat in 1971. The selection of Fettes was instructive about Leo. The popular choice from Choristers was Durham School, the local independent senior school. Fettes College, founded by a wealthy Edinburgh merchant in 1870, and built in imposing Victorian Gothic style with commanding views over Edinburgh, was regarded as Edinburgh's, and Scotland's, most prestigious boarding school. A pupil from Tony Blair's house at Choristers had won a scholarship to Fettes the year before him. A tradition existed.[19] But it was a school sought out by socially aspirational parents with Scottish roots, and regarded itself as the 'Eton of Scotland'. It was a big social step for Leo. Once he had chosen it for Bill, it was a formality that Tony should follow three years later.

While Choristers was, without qualification, a positive experience for Blair, Fettes most certainly was not. The boyish bonhomie of the first few terms soon gave way to a surliness and an increasing resentment of authority. One contemporary recalls, 'Tony was in the school fast track until about the age of fifteen. Then he fell off the Establishment ladder. He continued to climb, but on a different ladder, the anti-Establishment one.'[20] Was this abrupt change a belated reaction to Leo's illness? It is possible, but unlikely. Leo was well on the road back to health by the time Tony began to undergo this change, and was back at work, even making court appearances where strenuous advocacy was not required. Leo's story was an optimistic one. A much more likely explanation for Tony's change in outlook is a combination of three factors: adolescence, during which many become withdrawn and quarrelsome; his restless, questioning personality, which with growing maturity, he started to flex; and his being confined in a particularly conventional boarding school at the time of an explosion of youthful irreverence towards authority without precedent in post-war Britain.

Sport, at which he had excelled at Choristers, was a harbinger of the change. Still representing the school in his second year, by his third, he no longer wanted to play rugby and cricket, which were the 'Establishment' sports,[21] preferring instead the attractions of football and particularly basketball, which he captained, and where his height gave him an advantage. It was a highly effective and enjoyable way of putting two fingers up to the school's hierarchy. While not a top sportsman with a physique that would lend itself to first-team rugby, he had good natural ball skills and was thought to be 'very brave'.[22] He might easily have gone on to represent the school at second-XV level at rugby, and second-XI at cricket, a source of some adulation in the eyes of other schoolboys and of later pride that many carry throughout their lives. Blair forsook all this, and the approval of his masters, for basketball; one can, even today, sense his defiance shining out from the grainy photograph of the school's basketball team. It was an early example of him wanting to do things his own way, rejecting the conventional paths laid out before him.

Acting was one activity where Tony excelled, and was happy to excel. He had been in plays at Choristers, but only in minor parts, and he was fortunate that he went to a senior school with rich acting traditions. His name as a thespian was made when he played Mark Antony in Shakespeare's *Julius Caesar*, put on by his house in his second year.

Performances followed in a number of school productions or revues. But it was as Captain Stanhope, the tragic hero of R. C. Sheriff's First World War classic, *Journey's End*, produced in his final year, that he found his hour. It was his first experience of leadership, albeit acting, and he liked it. The play made a deep and lasting impression on him. On the eve of the war against Iraq, he recalled the plight of the whisky-sodden Captain surrounded by hostile forces: 'That play had a real effect on me . . . You have to isolate yourself when people are dying from what you yourself have decided to do.'[23]

Blair's two principal parts came in the two plays directed by his successive housemasters: Eric Anderson, an impressive figure who went on to become Headmaster and later Provost of Eton College, and who is discussed in Chapter 18; and the little-known but in his own way no less remarkable Bob Roberts, latterly Headmaster, poet and publisher. Anderson had become housemaster of a pioneering new house, Arniston, opened in September 1967. Blair had been exceptionally anxious to transfer to it, with its fashionable and liberal new master, and was delighted when his wishes were granted. One friend said, 'Fettes was incredibly tough, fagging and cold showers, but Arniston was comfortable and easy-going. It had duvets, unheard of at the time.'[24] Anderson, a subtle manager of wayward adolescents, eyed Blair's theatrical and histrionic talents, and though his protégé was only in his second year, gave him the major part of Mark Antony in the house play. Anderson later recalled that he had never known a pupil to change so much in front of an audience: 'He lit up, and became almost a different person.'[25] The school magazine described him as 'a very promising actor'.[26] The following year Anderson, alive to channelling his wandering energies into positive outlets, encouraged Blair and some friends to set up a society, named in self-parody 'The Pseuds', to perform vogueish modern plays.[27]

When Anderson left Fettes before Blair's final year, Bob Roberts also saw plays as a good way of instilling an *esprit de corps* into his new house. As an experienced director of schoolboy drama, *Journey's End* seemed the ideal choice – even if it meant that Blair, as the most experienced senior actor in the house, had to be cast as Stanhope. 'We all thought Blair agreed to do it so he could smoke on stage,' recalled one member of the house. 'When the curtain rose for one act, it looked like dry ice: you could barely see the actors for the clouds of cigarette smoke.'[28] Roberts found Blair predictably tricky to handle. During one rehearsal he repeatedly mimicked Roberts' attempts to direct him, but then he overheard one of his friends say from the shadows, 'For God's sake,

Tony, do what he says.'[29] From that point onwards he ensured everybody worked purposefully on the play. One recalled, 'He had made his protest and he wasn't going to allow himself to appear on stage unless he could give a very good account of himself.'[30]

Two different plays. Two different sides of Blair's emerging character. With Anderson in his second year, biddable, amenable, keen to impress both staff and peers, and with a growing independence of spirit and truculence. Mark Antony, loyal, self-sacrificing, upright, sways the crowd solely by the power of his oratory, altering the history of his country as a result. With Roberts in his final year, self-assured, dominant, knowing, his contemporaries eating out of his hands. Stanhope, a desperate, beleaguered and damaged young officer, trying to look after and protect those under his care from what he suspected would be the ultimate sacrifice. The seeds of much that followed can be found here.

Blair had outgrown Fettes long before he left. He felt constrained, under-appreciated and frustrated. What little affection he once felt for the school had completely drained by his final year. Looking back from Oxford, he complained that school had been grim, with fagging, petty rules and restrictions being his main bugbears.[31] Most people at university at that time probably felt similarly about their schools. But in Blair's case there was a real edge to it, which has not mellowed over the years. Some were surprised when he agreed to write the Foreword to the college's history in 1998, in which he omits to mention his own time at the school. In contrast, he had the warmest recollections of Choristers in Durham, where he readily returned to open a new building in 1993. Blair's frustration and anger burst forth with venom on the unsuspecting Roberts, who had trouble handling his wayward charge. Even with the positive regard Blair had for Anderson, and vice-versa, the relationship would almost certainly have come under great strain had Anderson remained his housemaster for that final year.

Roberts had not planned to take over the house. He was invited to do so unexpectedly by the Headmaster, Ian McIntosh, an abrupt but highly intelligent man who had a keen sense of the worth of the institution he headed. 'Suddenly McIntosh announced he wanted to come round to our house one Sunday. It was a very peculiar thing for him to do,' recalls Roberts. 'McIntosh arrived and declared, "Eric's got Abingdon." He said he wanted me to do the house. I wasn't certain I liked the look of it, and asked him for some time to think it over. As he was leaving he turned round and uttered, "House needs tightening up," and that was that.'[32] It was to be McIntosh's final year, and though he was a man of more intellect and subtlety than many pupils suspected, he was determined to maintain and reinforce the school's traditional values in what was to be its centenary year.

Roberts viewed his task as a hatchet job, tightening up the house after the pioneering Anderson. He used the cane, which was still a generally accepted form of punishment by Fettes housemasters – though not by his predecessor in Arniston – and beat Blair and two friends for 'persistent defiance'.[33] Taking over a boarding house is never easy for an incoming housemaster; the older pupils in particular resent the new man, their loyalties remaining firmly with the departed figure, for whom affection grows in hindsight. This typical pattern was heightened in this case by a particularly popular housemaster-and-wife team being succeeded by a proud traditionalist set on a course of discipline, and by the fact that a quirk of history meant a particularly large Upper Sixth (seventeen as opposed to the usual dozen pupils), with more than a fair share of disaffected boys. Roberts could be strict and inflexible, but he also had a sensitive side, revealed in his English teaching, his play direction and his own writing of poetry.[34] He either chose not to reveal this side to Blair, or Blair chose not to respond to it. Roberts felt that Blair had set the house against him, and that he pressured (bullied even) other boys into being anti-authority. Blair for his part bitterly resented the harsh way he felt Roberts had treated him.[35]

Blair decided he would read Law at university, as had Bill, and chose to apply to Oxford, where Bill had obtained a scholarship. Bill, probably no brighter academically than Tony, had been a more conscientious and consistent worker at Fettes and as a result proved better on paper.[36] Rather than sit for seventh-term exams (i.e. post-'A' levels) as did most pupils at the time, Blair, with the school's active encouragement, opted for the uncommon route of applying before his 'A' levels. He was offered a place by St John's College (which was deemed less difficult than Balliol), and was given an 'A' level target he passed with ease, achieving AAC grades in English, History and French. He might in fact have been expelled earlier that year had the Headmaster not been so concerned about losing numbers.[37] As it was, McIntosh was keen to get rid of him as soon as he completed his 'A' levels, while Blair wanted to make a point by leaving early of his own accord. Jack Mackenzie-Stuart, a distinguished Edinburgh judge (who later became Britain's first judge on the European Court of Justice), Fettes governor, and father of Blair's then girlfriend, Amanda, intervened to prevent his expulsion.[38] He persuaded Tony to stay, telling him that he would hurt his father by storming out in his last days at school. To neutralise a potentially explosive position, Mackenzie-Stuart arranged that Blair would spend his final week after 'A' levels away from school premises doing social work at a boys' camp on the East Lothian coast.

When he returned to Fettes to collect his books and possessions to take home, Roberts watched him unnoticed and mused on his future. 'I thought he would either go into the pop world and become involved with drugs, or become a disillusioned, out-of-work actor. But then I thought he's clever enough to avoid trouble and has the self-preservation to come out on top.'[39] It was a long way from his 'butter not melting' first impression and a sad but telling final verdict on Blair's schooldays.

The Fettes Effect: Blair at Eighteen

Who exactly was the young adult who returned to his parents in Durham in July 1971? Pictures show a handsome and outgoing young man. Though it had not formed him into the more conventional figure his father and the school might have expected, Fettes had secured him good 'A' levels and a place at Oxford. It had developed his acting and debating interests, and had overseen his development from an eager if naïve thirteen-year-old to a self-assured and rebellious eighteen-year-old, with his personality largely formed. He had already developed a particular charisma which was to be one his defining characteristics. When Tony Blair walked into a room, he naturally became the focus of attention. He was liked by both men and women. But Fettes had not brought out the best in him; neither did he make the most of what Fettes had to offer.

Religious interest, which had been stirred at Choristers, lay dormant at Fettes. He was not confirmed, as some of his school friends were at the age of thirteen or fourteen. School chapel appears not to have meant much to him, though he did not make chapel the target of his ridicule in the way he did, for example, the school's Combined Cadet Force. The school's Church of Scotland chaplain, the radical Revd George Buchanan-Smith, might well have touched Blair, in part because he related his spiritual beliefs to social issues, which struck a resonance in many. Blair was also taken up – indeed, championed – by Revd Ronald Selby-Wright (nicknamed 'Seldom-Wrong'), a senior Scottish cleric and larger-than-life figure who helped run the 'Fet-Lor' Boys' Club (run jointly with Loretto School, just east of Edinburgh).[40] Years later, Selby-Wright would still proclaim that 'it was a disgrace that the school had not made Blair a prefect', or made more of his basketball talent.[41] Why had Blair in fact not been given any leadership responsibility at school when he clearly had, even then, leadership aspiration and ability? It can be explained in part by a reluctance, in the eyes of his teachers, to say what he was in favour of as opposed to merely what he was against.[42] This trait would not just be confined to his views about boarding school life at the time. There was little evidence of interest in the social issues of the late 1960s and early 1970s, despite some hints of a developing social conscience and awareness. Political interest seems to have remained firmly unawakened, although one friend said that 'there was a streak of something that made his later conversion to socialism unsurprising'.[43] The problems of the Wilson government of 1966–70, trade union unrest, the General Election of June 1970 and the debate on entry into the European Economic Community in 1972 all seemed to pass him by. If he expressed views at the time, no one remembers them.

He definitely knew what he was against. His knocking on Eric Anderson's door and asking 'why he had to obey this or that school rule' has passed into folklore.[44] He would constantly probe and challenge the system. But he did not lead an anti-authority revolt, as happened at a comparable school in Kent in 1971,[45] or otherwise put his name on the line: 'He would stir up problems,' one contemporary recalled, 'and then blend into the crowd to see what happened.'[46] His nickname from Bob Roberts' wife was 'Macavity': he was always behind trouble, she felt, but 'Macavity wasn't there!'[47] One teacher said, 'He was a manipulator operating in the background, creating trouble.' He loved being the centre of attention, having a following. His grin was an absolute trademark, 'as was his aping of Mick Jagger'. 'He was definitely the leader of the "cool" gang, and people wanted to join it,' recalled a contemporary.[48] 'But he wasn't disliked by most staff because he was so engaging, and he wasn't seen as unpleasant.'[49] 'Most staff would have seen him as a smart-arse or as a prat, not as a destructive student,' said one pupil.[50] Staff and contemporaries contrast Blair with some of those with whom he chose to associate.[51] One in particular was deemed 'nasty, unpleasant, a bully and a thug. I am surprised he was so friendly with him.'[52] Blair always seemed to know what would be deemed unacceptable, and how far he could push things. For Blair, testing the boundaries meant smoking, drinking, breaking bounds, having long hair and mimicking staff and 'Establishment' pupils. Pushing the boundaries did not mean taking drugs or breaking the law (he was very clear about that), or doing anything he deemed immoral. But he enjoyed the company of those who had less scruples than himself, and always has. He possessed a marked ability to develop and sustain close friendships. The closest, by some accounts, was a quieter young man who subsequently became involved in hallucinogenic drugs. He killed himself at university while under their influence by crashing through the glass of Edinburgh's Waverley Station. Blair, deeply shocked, learned of the tragedy while at Oxford, and named his first son, Euan, partly in memory of his friend.[53] Nick Ryden believes it was a seminal event helping make him more serious and even perhaps explaining his turning to religion.

A lasting impression of Blair at Fettes is of his contrariness. He wavered between wanting to be accepted by the Establishment and wanting to destroy it. 'What I saw at Fettes,' said one fellow pupil, 'was a rebel without a cause: an outsider who wanted to come inside.' Because he found himself shunned by the Establishment, he decided to kick against it. 'Correctly harnessed,' recalls one who was a house prefect in his year, 'Tony Blair could have been Head of House and Head of School. The only real alternative that presented itself was to be leader of the opposition.'[54] Roberts himself acknowledges that 'Blair had the leadership qualities to make a very good prefect'. Roberts blames a difficult period at Fettes: 'The school was in transition when Blair was there. If he had been there a year or two later, when Tony Chenevix Trench was Headmaster, it would all have been very different.'[55]

Blair, by eighteen, had acquired the personal tools for his subsequent development, but he lacked the content. The rebel without a cause needed direction. He also still had to find the ideas that would shape his life, or any sense of mission. There is no evidence at all that Blair, by the age of eighteen, seven years after his father's stroke, envisaged a political career for himself; nor did he seem notably career-minded at all. The traditional explanation given for his political interest and purpose in life, namely his father's stroke in 1964, is therefore inadequate. The decisive events in his life were to lie in the future.

Leo and Hazel Blair in the late 1940s. Blair's physical resemblance to his mother is striking. Hazel provided him with his inner strength and was a much more dominant influence than his ambitious father, Leo.

2

Father and Mother

No influence in Tony Blair's life can compare with that of his parents, Hazel and Leo Blair. To them he owes his good looks and strong constitution. Without those looks he may not have become Labour leader, and thus Prime Minister; and without that strong constitution he would not have been able to endure with such apparent equanimity the extraordinary strains that are imposed on him as Prime Minister. To his grandparents he owes his height (he is much taller than his brother or sister, Bill and Sarah, and his parents): height was core to his self-confidence. To his parents finally he owes his intelligence: Bill and Sarah share the acute intellect, but not their middle sibling's ambition or self-esteem.

It is easier to see parental influence on nature than it is on nurture. Here we are in less certain territory. Explaining exactly how he was affected by his upbringing, and the precise influence of Leo or Hazel, may be ultimately impossible. But it is nevertheless important to try. Explaining why the same two parents produced three such different children, however, is beyond the scope of this chapter, and author.

We now know a fair deal about his father's background, but less about his mother's.[1] Hazel Corscaden was born in Ireland in 1923 into a staunch Protestant family, from Ballyshannon, County Donegal.[2] Her father, George Corscaden, died of appendicitis when Hazel was just six months old, and her mother, Sally, married another Ballyshannon man, Willam McLay. The family moved to Glasgow where William made a good living as a butcher. Tony Blair remembers visiting the Glasgow meat markets as a boy with his grandfather: 'He'd done something terrible to his leg once, so he had this stick. He was a very tough guy and he'd lash the meat with it.'[3] We do not know how close Hazel was to her parents, but she appears to have had a stable home. She left school at fourteen. During the war she joined up as a Wren, making it to Australia, and after the war went to work in government offices in Glasgow.[4]

The red-headed Hazel was bright, emotionally very strong and religious, though not church-going. We know she received little formal education beyond the minimum and that she never fulfilled her career potential (although few women of her generation did). We know she was quiet and steady, but with a hot temper if roused.[5]

Leo's story is remarkable. He was born in 1923, the same year as Hazel. Born to travelling music-hall actors, he was brought up in Glasgow by foster parents, Mary and James Blair. James was a shipyard rigger, but employment at the docks in the 1920s and 1930s was irregular, and money was scarce. These were the Depression years and living conditions were harsh. 'I remember my father telling me about being brought up in Glasgow in the 1930s, living in a crowded tenement, five or six families sharing a toilet,' recalled Tony Blair, 'foster mother finding it hard to make ends meet; his foster father a shipyard worker subject to the casual labour of those times.'[6] James died young, and after Leo left school he went straight into employment at the *Daily Worker*, the Communist Party's national daily newspaper, then enjoying something of a boom. Mary was a lifelong Communist, and Leo had become Secretary of the Govan branch of the Scottish Young Communist League in 1938 at the age of fifteen.[7] Steeped in politics, and a committed organiser, he had thoughts of becoming a Communist MP. In the polarised 1930s, with fascism on an upsurge, communism was a growing force in British politics, especially in Glasgow, where two Communist MPs were elected to Parliament in 1945. Entering the war in 1942 as a private, he finished as a lieutenant. Whereas the war made many young men left-wing, it had the opposite effect on Leo: he later attributed his conversion to the Conservative Party in pragmatic terms, to 'the great change from living in a tenement in Govan to life in the Officers' Mess'.[8] Privately he would say that he was surprised to find that men who were vilified in the name of the 'class war' turned out to be welcoming and normal.[9]

To the material deprivations of his childhood, which bred in Leo a restless desire for self-improvement, was added emotional turmoil and uncertainty. From the earliest age, Leo learned that Mary and James Blair were only his foster parents and that he had been born illegitimately in Yorkshire to two travelling variety actors, Celia Ridgway and Charles Parsons (whose stage name was 'Jimmy Lynton'). Celia was married to another man at the time and they asked the Blairs, whom they had met in

Glasgow on tour, to foster young Leo while they sorted out their affairs. This took them some time, and it was not apparently until 1926 that they married. While this was going on, the foster mother Mary came to love Leo as her own. It is not known if Leo's real parents immediately tried to have their three-year-old child returned, but at the age of thirteen there was an emotional battle with the Blairs, culminating in Mary Blair, who had had two miscarriages, barricading herself in her home and threatening to commit suicide if they took Leo from her.[10] Cards and letters from his parents to their separated son were secreted by him in a biscuit box under his bed until burned by Mary during the war: she told his parents that he was missing, presumed killed in action, and the communications ceased. 'I thought that they had lost interest in me,' Leo later confessed.[11] His real parents went to their graves thinking their son had died.

The exact effect of all this turmoil on Leo can never be known. But one can speculate with confidence that the feelings of abandonment, and the fight over who would bring him up, engendered in Leo a sense of insecurity and a determination that he had to rely on his own resources to get on in the world. Understandably, he did not want to discuss his parentage with his own children, though Tony confirms Leo thought his real parents had not wanted him.[12] The rejection was powerfully to impinge on his attitude to life.

The war not only cured Leo of communism; it also gave him status and confidence. Tony would say that the Army had 'transformed his life'.[13] Before being demobbed in 1947, Leo began work for the Ministry of National Insurance in Glasgow, where he met Hazel. They fell in love and married. She offered him the security that his life had so far lacked. He gave her a strength, a sense of fun and prospects for a much better life than she had ever known. The marriage certificate records Leo giving his name as 'Blair, formerly Parsons', having decided a few months before to change his surname from that of his real parents to that of his foster parents. This shows the debt he rightly acknowledged to Mary Blair. She had pushed him to achieve, and supported him in every way her limited means allowed. She adored him, and he regarded her as his mother.[14] But the attachment to his real parents remained. The deed poll records him taking 'Charles' and 'Lynton' as his middle names, a combination of his father's real (Charles Parsons) and stage (James Lynton) names. His first son, Bill, was then given 'James' and 'Lynton' as middle names, and Tony, the same middle names ('Charles' and 'Lynton') he had chosen for himself.[15] The name 'Parsons', his surname for the first twenty-five years of his life, was dropped for ever.

Leo was thus driven and intensely ambitious. He was an extrovert and a charmer, a workaholic and a ladies' man. He had taught himself to play the piano, and was accomplished in the popular music of his day. Leo's work and lifestyle meant he was rarely at home before Tony had gone to bed – a practice, consciously or unconsciously, Tony took care to avoid with his own children. Tony himself recalls seeing little of him in his first eleven years until the stroke: 'Dad had a flourishing legal business and was always lecturing around the country. He was also an astute self-publicist, appearing regularly on regional television.'[16] All the recollections speak of Leo as a man of immense charm and friendliness.[17]

His stroke in 1964 was a personal tragedy, coming at the very moment that his career was beginning to take off. Hazel admitted to finding her husband a lot easier to manage after his stroke.[18] The hectic round of social engagements, punctuated by prolonged absences, were difficult for her to juggle with three growing children at home. 'She never looked on ambition and success as of huge value in themselves,' recalls Bill Blair. 'She was more concerned with down-to-earth values such as family and friendship.'[19] Family holidays in the north of England, Scotland, Ireland and latterly in France were the main prolonged occasions when all five in the family would be together. When Tony was aged between eleven and thirteen, when most fathers are keenly involved with their sons, Leo was bed-ridden or recuperating. It cannot have helped them discover the closeness they do not seem to have had before.

The rock of his life was his mother, to whom he was much closer. It was she who gave him the inner strength and self-assurance which has endured all his life. The shape of his smile he might have inherited from his father, but the inner quality that made him want to smile came from his mother. She was the constant presence throughout his early years in Scotland, Australia and Durham. She was the one who comforted him through his father's stroke and reassured him that everything would be 'all right'. She was the one who held the family together through his father's incapacity, Sarah's illness and thereafter. It is probably with her that the roots of his faith can be found.[20] She chose not to clash openly with Leo on political matters. But her views were considerably different from his. Perhaps she saw the limits of self-reliance. At any rate, she did not share her husband's full-blooded, right-of-centre view of the world.[21]

Tony Blair grew apart from his parents in his teens. This natural tendency for any adolescent was heightened by his being away between the ages of thirteen and eighteen at school in Edinburgh for two-thirds of the year. Leo and Hazel were not regular attenders at Fettes events. School holidays would be spent partly staying away with friends: his social circle did not revolve around his home in Durham. His gap year, 1971–72, was spent in London, and the following three years at university in Oxford, two hundred miles away. Friends recall he rarely spoke of his parents. This did not mean he did not love them deeply, but neither parent seems to have been an active, formative influence on his life at senior school and university.[22] It was partly his self-reliance and developed sense of security that allowed him to cope so well on his own. On one occasion, he called in on Durham with a group of Oxford friends on their way north, by which time Hazel was seriously ill with cancer, and they were struck by the tangible love between mother and son.[23] Her son's love and admiration have remained undimmed: 'My mother had lovely, very red hair . . . she was tremendously loving to us, with a strong sense of discipline. She was just entirely without malice. I don't think I ever heard her say a bad word about anyone.'[24] Her inner strength, as seen when looking after her ill husband and daughter, or coping with her own illness, created a lasting impression: 'I didn't see her break down, never once.'[25]

Tony appears to have exorcised his angst against authority on his teachers at Fettes rather than on his parents. His long absences at school, and a sense that his father was still recuperating and should not be made angry, contributed to an apparent absence of the screaming matches between fathers and adolescent sons common in most homes, particularly at that time of a marked generation gap. 'Tory' fathers were often the objects of particular contempt by sons; but even his father's politics did not appear to be a cause of dispute. 'There was no serious political debate in the home,' he recalls, of any form, 'and no indoctrination.'[26] Tony Blair would latterly say, 'My father was Norman Tebbit!'[27] by which he meant a self-made man who had risen in life by his own exertions. He said his father rejected the Labour Party because it was not aspirational at the time, but, he felt, it also made those who wanted to improve their lot in life feel that the party was not for them.[28] 'My father quite liked Harold Wilson,' he said, 'but he felt the Labour Party was in the pocket of the unions.'[29] Leo's own political ambitions were killed by the stroke. After Hazel's death, Leo moved away from Durham in 1976 and settled in South Wales, where he later remarried. One senses that Tony has become closer to him after he himself became an adult. He admires his father hugely, and what he has achieved in life against the odds.

Tony's chosen careers in law and then politics owe much to his father's own experience and enthusiasms. Both Leo's other children, Bill and Sarah, followed their father's vocation in the law, which pleased him: Bill as a barrister in London and Sarah in legal publishing. Neither have opted for public careers and both have successfully fought to retain their privacy. It was Tony who inherited Leo's extrovert character and his natural charm.

Of the two siblings, Tony speaks far more often to Bill, who inherited his mother's inward personality. One close observer said, 'Bill is serious, steady, calm, reassuring, loving, sensible and strong. They are very close.'[30] Without being aware of it, the witness was describing the character of Hazel.

If Leo was not the major influence on his world-view and his politics, then who was?[31] The answer is Hazel. In the midst of the Iraq war, colleagues were startled when he started talking about his mother. An observer noted, 'The Prime Minister does not often mention his mother to his colleagues. His father . . . is a well-documented part of his official life. His mother, Hazel, is much less known.'[32] It is time for the official record to be adjusted and his mother to be written back into the centre of the story. Not only did she help imbue him with religious faith: it was her social conscience, commitment to others and sheer kindness which coloured his outlook. Hers was not an ideological nor a party political vision that she bequeathed her son, but she rooted in him a fundamental respect for others. Many people later in life came to dislike him, the inevitable fate of every top political figure. But few thought him arrogant or unkind. Women, in particular, he has always treated with respect, and even in his youth he was conspicuous in not taking advantage of them. Hazel was the most powerful figure who shaped his life. She is the unsung hero of his, and her family's, lives. In June 1975, Hazel died. This event, far more than his father's stroke eleven years before, was to change the course of his life.

Tony Blair in his official undergraduate garb shortly after he arrived at St John's College, Oxford, in 1972. The photograph records an impressionable and frivolous young man, lacking both gravitas and settled political or religious views.

3

Oxford and Loss of Mother, 1971–75

Blair left school in July 1971 with his outgoing personality largely established. He knew he would be studying Law at Oxford, and had thought of a career at the Bar. But he had not reflected much on what he would do with his life, nor on what he thought about the world, and his place in it. Some key milestones were passed in the four years covered by this chapter. In particular, he met someone who had a profound impact on him (the subject of the next chapter), and he became confirmed as Christian, which has affected the whole of his life. His religious faith and its impact on his political beliefs was to be a gradually evolving understanding, and does not compare with the dramatic single event which came at the end of this period. The years are often surprising for what did not happen. One might have expected someone who was to become a Prime Minister to have cut a major figure at Oxford. Instead, he occupied himself in these years doing much the same as every former public schoolboy. But, behind the frivolity, a metamorphosis was quietly taking place.

Gap Year, 1971–72

Many young men and women in the 1970s took a gap year between school and university, particularly if they were destined for Oxford or Cambridge.[1] The idealistic went to Africa or India on 'Voluntary Service Overseas', or similar programmes, to teach or work. Druggy types went off to Kathmandu and Marrakech. The conscientious took internships in law or medical practices, or whatever their chosen profession was to be. Those lacking a clear mission chose just to 'bum around', or did as Tony Blair, doing a bit of work here and there to raise some money before heading off for a long summer in search of the sun.

It is unclear what thoughts were in his mind as he came down from Durham to London in the early autumn of 1971. He had an idea of spending some time in France, utilising his 'A' level language in a country he enjoyed. He wanted to see more of the world, and to meet a wider range of people than he had so far encountered before settling into undergraduate life.[2] But a year was a long time to fill, and there is little evidence that he had a plan on how to fill it beyond coming down to London, a city largely unknown to him. He did not even appear to know where he was going to live.[3] In his pocket he had an address of an old school friend who had done badly at his 'A' levels and who was re-sitting at a 'crammer' college in London. The friend passed him on to a fellow student he had just met at the college, Chris Blishen, whose parents he knew were away. 'The bell rang and there Tony Blair was on the doorstep,' recalled Blishen. 'He had a small bag, a big grin and asked, "Can I stay a night?"'[4] He ended up staying two weeks, before he met Alan Collenette, a former St Paul's School chum of Blishen. Collenette warmed immediately to the amiable Blair and invited him to stay at his house in Kensington, west London. 'His entire possessions consisted of a tatty brown suitcase with a maximum of two changes of clothes, and a home-made blue guitar which he called "Clarence".'[5] He ended up staying most of the rest of 1971 with the Collenettes.

The gap year was spent predominantly in the company of others from public schools similar to Fettes: St Paul's, Westminster and Latymer Upper School. The New Year celebrations of 1971–72 were spent on a trip to Aviemore in Scotland to meet up with Nick Ryden and other Fettes friends. They stopped off at Durham on the way. Apart from this visit, and the usual family occasions, he did not see a great deal of his parents during the year, nor indeed of old school friends. This does not seem to have been because of any cooling of relations; it was a time in which he was determined to establish his own independence.

Collenette supplied Blair with a purpose, one which coincided precisely with what he enjoyed, and offered the promise of some income. Collenette's idea for his gap year was to promote rock bands in church halls and other venues in London, with sights ultimately on the big lights: Wembley Arena and beyond. Blair loved the rock bands of the time such as Cream and the Rolling Stones. They decided to form a partnership, to emulate the work of two top promoters, Jim and Tony Stratton-Smith, who showcased bands like Free and Led Zeppelin, an ambition they were not to realise. 'Our first few weeks were spent in the kitchen and at the hall table in Kensington phoning around church halls and clubs out of the phonebook, attempting to book venues . . . I recall Tony's attempts to convince men of the cloth that the events we had in mind were close cousins of chamber recitals.'[6]

A venue was found called the 'Vineyard' in Richmond, west London, which was overseen by a Mr Norman Burt, a retired school teacher who now ran Christian youth clubs in the evenings. Blair moved after Christmas into an upstairs room in Burt's house, paying a peppercorn rent in return for odd jobs, remaining there until the summer. He now had the ideal base from which to build and develop his fledgling career as a rock promoter, about which he was deadly serious.[7]

With a venue in the bag they now had to find someone to promote. Another St Paul's friend volunteered the basement of his parents' home near Kensington High Street to audition and rehearse bands, and they were away. The self-styled 'Blair–Collenette Promotions' promoted some eighteen 'happenings' between November 1971 and June 1972, a mixture of discos and live bands.

Too much has been made of Blair's role in forming or promoting these groups. The musicians remember him as a pleasant chap compared to the normal people they encountered in that 'demi-monde': 'He had this unique positivity, and was always making suggestions for doing things.'[8] He procured an old Thames van for driving the bands around, at a cost of £50. Here was something he could do well, and he took his band-ferrying duty very seriously. 'He would pick us up and was always very precise about timing. He was very keen to emphasise in advance that everyone should be ready to go when he arrived.'[9] But he was less secure in his role of rock impresario. 'Tony always wanted to be our manager, but didn't know enough about the trade really to be a manager. He was just a very friendly, very straight guy, unusually straight for the time. He never got drunk, never smoked marijuana, never abused women, wasn't predatory, and would sooner have died than tell a dirty joke.'[10] It is significant that Blair, who was at the centre of all that was 'cool' at Fettes, did not adapt to the metropolitan and loucher world of London youth in the early 1970s. If he did not wholly impress the budding rock musicians, he did at least become a hit with the circle of friends he met that year. 'He had immense charm and maturity for his age. He needed all that charm and interest in people because what he did wasn't easy, moving into a group of people who had known each other from various schools; you needed real skills to be accepted as readily as he was accepted.'[11]

Any income derived from rock promotion was pocket money, although one acquaintance recalls that 'he never had any money and was always borrowing it'.[12] One suspects that he received financial supplements from home, which he complemented by stacking shop shelves at Barkers of Kensington, whiling away the hours talking with Collenette of their grand designs. The serious musical breakthrough did not occur, and meanwhile any ambitious plans he had to travel and see the world evaporated. Oxford loomed, and university reading lists made him realise that his year of freedom was drawing to an end. He had had an enjoyable if not hugely productive (or commercially successful) time, and he made some friends who have stayed with him all his life.[13] His ability to form friendships with adults as different as Collenette's mother and Norman Burt showed unusual maturity for a young man of only eighteen. The growth in self-confidence was the most important facet of a fairly fallow year. He learned he could move to a big city where he knew no one, fend for himself and make his own way. The year did not see any noticeable development of his political, social or religious interest.[14] All that was still to come.

Oxford, 1972–75

Tony Blair was one of 107 expectant first-year undergraduates who arrived at St John's College in early October 1972, 28 of whom had been awarded scholarships and exhibitions. He sat his first-year law exams, called 'mods', in March 1973 and his Finals in June 1975. He passed his mods, a necessary requirement, and achieved a second-class degree in Finals (a degree class achieved by some three-quarters of Oxford students). He proved a good student, though not exceptional, who worked relatively hard, particularly towards the end of the course.[15] Reports on students were not always written at Oxford, but in their place tutors give oral comments each term, which were summarised by Sir Richard Southern, the President of St John's, thus:

Early 1973: 'Well organised. Apt to leave things till the last minute. But a strong interest in many things.' June 1973: 'Pleasing structure to work, but some weakness in content.' February 1974: 'Seems extraordinarily happy.' December 1974: 'Signs of really understanding the principles of the subject.' March 1975: 'Needs to be tougher in thinking through his ideas.'[16]

For the first two years he lived in college, and for the last he lived 'out', in a house in east Oxford with four fellow students.

These are the bare bones of Blair's Oxford years. They would have described the lives of 90 per cent of Oxford undergraduates in the early 1970s. But none of the others was to become Prime Minister of the United Kingdom. Benazir Bhutto, who became Prime Minister of Pakistan, was a contemporary. But she was a huge presence at Oxford, flamboyant, much talked about and obviously destined to go somewhere. Blair, in contrast, was almost invisible. He did not become President of the Oxford Union, nor a leading actor, nor a sportsman, nor well-known young legal blood, nor a debater. He did not join the University Labour Club, still less become its head. One searches long and hard to find clues at Oxford to his future career and interests. It is quite normal for the very high-achieving in life not to have made much of a mark at school or in gap years, if they took them. But one generally finds surges of activity or other harbingers of later greatness at university.

Acting was one of his greatest sources of pleasure and success at Fettes. Oxford was awash with student drama, with five or more plays in most weeks. In his first year he must have decided not to audition for any plays: if he had, with his ability and skill as a mimic, and his self-confidence, he would have been offered parts (though it is always possible that he tried and was rejected by a student director, and did not want to risk another rebuff). But it still seems a puzzle, as there were so many plays on offer that even students with no previous experience, or talent, were offered parts. He was still very interested in acting. His housemates saw acting as a possible career for him.[17] 'I enjoyed acting tremendously,' he said, 'particularly at school, but for some reason it never quite worked out for me at Oxford.'[18] He even speculated that if his parents had been wealthier and provided him with a safety net, he might have 'taken a gamble in trying to be an actor'.[19] But he also said, which rings truer, that 'I don't think I was ever serious about being a professional actor.'[20] In his second year he instigated a small revue for his college drama society, *Déjà Revue*, performed in the Newman Rooms from 5 to 8 December 1973. Attendees were particularly struck by his Monty Python-inspired sketches, a humour that always appealed to him,[21] and the student newspapers also praised 'the superb spoof philosophy lecture by Geoff Gallop'.[22] Nicholas Lowton, who wrote the music for this and another impromptu dramatic production with him, and who directed him as 'Matt' in Brecht's *Threepenny Opera* at the Oxford Playhouse in June 1974, said, 'He was always more comfortable acting in revues, because he could create his own characters. I don't

think he ever felt particularly happy with the formality of acting in a play.
I think that he felt awkward on stage, having to stick to a set script.'[23]
This might help explain why acting never worked for him at Oxford. He
is always happier doing things his own way, and it may well be that he
felt that the constraints of acting a character with set lines and set
movements impaired his natural creativity and joy in performance.

The revues at least led on to another artistic venture. A fellow student
had seen him act in one of the shows and was struck by his animated
stage presence.[24] The embryonic band he was forming needed a
frontman. Was Blair their man? He certainly had the interest in music,
as seen in his gap year. To his enjoyment in listening to music,
essentially rock, was added singing, and playing piano and guitar
(classical music, interestingly, has been a lacuna all his life).[25] He passed
their audition, and his membership of the student rock band, Ugly
Rumours, has gone on to become the most widely-known fact about his
youth.[26] All this exposure of Blair's rock career is largely nonsense,
because the band, in which he was always, by his own admission, never
more than a moderate performer,[27] put on barely half a dozen gigs
altogether, in the summer and autumn terms of 1974. Off-stage he was
even less comfortable than he was on stage. A fellow band member
recalls, 'Tony was never really on our wavelength. He had long hair, he
sang the songs well enough, but he didn't share our views about things.
He was always controlled and contained. I really didn't know what drove
him to want to join the band when he really wasn't getting a lot of
friendship from it, but it was obviously important to him.'[28] Another
member of the band said, 'To be honest, we saw Tony as "a bit straight".
My overwhelming impression of him is that he was a nice guy, very easy-
going, very flexible about the songs we prepared, always cheerful and
friendly, but straight.'[29] A disagreement over religion is remembered as
indicative of the gulf between Blair and his fellow band members. Blair
must have been disappointed that no more came of his musical career
than his acting one. He has continued to play the guitar and sing all his
life. But mostly alone.

If he was disappointed by his failure to shine at drama and music, he
didn't let it get him down. He threw himself into everything else one
would expect an energetic Oxford undergraduate to do. He played
football for the college; he smoked cigarettes but there is no evidence
that he smoked even the odd joint, or tried other drugs; he drank but
never became drunk; he grew his hair very long and wore flamboyant old
clothes; he gave parties, including one which was reported in the
fashionable diary in the *Cherwell* student paper;[30] he took part in a joke

eight-man rowing team; and he went to the Oxford Union but once, to hear Michael Heseltine.[31] He had a 'string of very attractive girlfriends' according to Marc Palley,[32] but he always treated girls well, said former female friends. One of them, Sally Brampton, said, 'Oxford was very public-schooly at that time. The students' culture patronised women and tried to get off with them. Tony just saw girls as people.'[33] His rebellious side was satisfied by doing a stint 'occupying' the Examinations School in the autumn of 1973 as part of a student protest; his Establishment side by his attendance at the ultra-traditional Archery Club, a heavy drinking St John's College society.[34] The members would wine and dine and shoot some arrows. 'You had to be elected by members. It was full of public school types. TB was a typical ex-public schoolboy. He was a likable, fun guy,' recalls the Club Secretary.[35]

His ability even then to appeal to all different types was seen in the friends he made on the far left of political life, in which he had a growing interest. This was the first important development for Blair at Oxford: the growth of a political perspective. Geoff Gallop, an Australian on a Rhodes scholarship at St John's, and a revolutionary Marxist at the time, became a key influence on Blair. Gallop became a lifelong friend, and later a successful politician, rising to Premier of Western Australia. At Oxford, though, he was a firebrand. David Aaronovitch, a student rebel later sent down by the university, recalls a typical Gallop moment. Cigarette in mouth, in his long sheepskin coat and leggings, and looking very way out, Gallop declaimed in the Examinations School's 'occupation' by students, with all the fervour of a communard at the barricades in Paris in 1871, 'The university is shitting its dacks [a pair of Australian trousers].'[36] Gallop, a lead figure in the occupation,[37] was also a prominent member of the St John's 'Left Caucus', a group of hard-left students founded by undergraduate Colin Meade. Blair skirted around its fringes, but never fully joined: 'He was very conscious of keeping his nose clean,' said Meade,[38] who must be the first hard-left figure to have become cynical about him. Blair did deliver a paper to the group on 'Marx's "Economic and Philosophical Manuscripts"',[39] and talked of reading modish if largely indigestible far-left writers like Antonio Gramsci. But how deep were his left-wing leanings at the time? Gallop thought he started to 'flirt with Marxism but never really got into it'.[40] Laura Mackenzie, a third year house-mate, thought, however, that Tony was 'more left-wing then than he later became'.[41] For Blair, though, the interest was in political ideas and debate, not in playing student politics. He was never involved, nor displayed any interest, in student politics and disapproved of the kind of person ('hacks' as they were known) who took part in university politics societies. 'Were you involved in politics at Oxford?' he later asked Tim Allan and James Purnell at their interview to join his staff twenty years later. They were embarrassed to admit they had not. 'I'm relieved,' said Blair. 'That is precisely the kind of person I want.'[42]

Gallop was also significant in introducing Blair to Peter Thomson, the Australian priest discussed in the next chapter, who was also a student at St John's from 1972 to 1974. They belonged to an informal discussion group, around Thomson, containing, among others, Marc Palley, Blair's great friend; David Gardner, later a journalist on the *Financial Times*; and Olara Otunnu, a Ugandan refugee. They met in Thomson's room in college, in pubs or the Randolph Hotel, often consuming large quantities of cigarettes and coffee. The conversations were more searching and sustained than the general run of student chat, and focused, said Gallop, on topics such as 'Labour Party reform versus revolution'; 'What does socialism mean?' 'The relationship between Christianity and Marxism' and the relevance of 'liberation theology' to the world today. One thinker in particular illuminated their discussions.[43]

'If you really want to understand what I'm all about you have to look at a guy called John Macmurray. It's all there,' Blair blurted out on the eve of being elected Labour leader in July 1994.[44] For Thatcher there was F. A. Hayek and Milton Friedman, well-known figures. But who was Macmurray? He was born in 1891 and fought in the First World War, the event which made him realise there had to be a higher purpose in life than pleasure. Macmurray had the misfortune, as Samuel Brittan put it, to write in simple, understandable English, a quality distrusted by serious philosophers.[45] Whether for that reason or another, Macmurray fell from vogue in the 1950s and was little noticed until Blair's remark shot him centre stage in 1994.[46] He has become the subject of so much criticism since his connection with Blair became known that it is important to observe that he had a distinguished career: Jowett Lecturer in Philosophy at Balliol College, then Grote Professor of the Philosophy of Mind and Logic in London before finishing his career as Professor of Moral Philosophy at Edinburgh University.[47] His concern above all was the relationship of individuals to society: which should predominate? Neither alone was his answer. In sum, he opted for a 'third way'; to him, ultimate reality was neither the individual nor society alone, but could be fully formed only in personal relationships.

The ultimate quality of Macmurray's thinking is irrelevant, as is whether Gallop/Thomson/Blair made a correct reading of it. What matters is that Macmurray's writing greatly stimulated a young man whose mind had hitherto engaged little with such issues. 'I don't think

Tony had any political leanings when he came to Oxford,' said Gallop. 'But he became really fired up by the ideas we were discussing. He was someone who wanted to change the world for the better and suddenly he saw that he could do it through politics. I think many of his life's beliefs were formed in that period.'[48] Macmurray helped crystallise in his mind the central importance of 'community'. Here was the genesis of the first plank (community) of the five policy platforms he developed over the next twenty years. It found later expression, for example, in the reworded Clause IV of 1994, which opens with the assertion, 'By the strength of our common endeavour, we achieve more than we achieve alone'. It is not that far from Thomson's favourite Macmurray quotation: 'All meaningful knowledge is for the sake of action, all meaningful action is for the sake of friendship.'[49]

Just before his two friends returned to Australia after the end of the summer term of 1974, Blair hired a car with Thomson and his wife, and Gallop and his partner (later wife) to go to Scotland for a final holiday, calling in on his family in Durham en route. In Edinburgh, sitting in a café, they wondered if Macmurray was still alive. A check in the telephone directory revealed he was, and Thomson called in to see him: 'Having waited for years for this opportunity, when I was in front of him I was tongue-tied, and couldn't think what to say,' recalled the normally loquacious Thomson.[50] The guru was deemed too frail to see more than one person, and Blair and the others remained, tantalisingly, in the car outside. The visit had been just in time. Macmurray, already eighty-six, died soon afterwards.

Macmurray's thoughts, and the heated conversations with Thomson, Gallop and others, also made Blair's mind turn increasingly to religion. Another member of the Thomson–Gallop group, Olara Otunnu, was a practising Christian: most were not. He and Blair discussed Christianity together. Otunnu regularly attended college chapel, and Blair, who had shown no great interest in religion in the first twenty years of his life, began to attend too, being introduced to the college chaplain, Graham Dow, by Thomson, who said Blair wanted to be confirmed.[51] The process was intensely private. Blair had long conversations with Dow, who was struck by his excitement at his discovery of God: he was 'full of vitality, warm and politically aware'.[52] The process of working out for himself his own understanding of God was very important to him. Close friends did not even know that he was being confirmed.[53] His was no evangelical conversion, and he never, as far as one can tell, tried to convert anyone else to Christianity: he was thus at the opposite end of the spectrum, spiritually and socially, from the so-called 'God-squadders', the evangelical Christians in the college and university who wanted to make a show that they were 'batting for Jesus'.[54] For Blair, religion was something very private; it also had a mainly practical content.[55] The God he was discovering now was an active force in the world who wanted followers to build a good society.[56] 'I had always believed in God but I had been slightly detached from it,' he later said. 'I couldn't make sense of it. Peter [Thomson] made it relevant; practical rather than theological. Religion became less of a personal relationship with God. I began to see it in a much more social context.'[57] Matthew d'Ancona, who has written persuasively on the subject of Blair and religion, believes that 'Blair's religious awakening at Oxford was the defining moment of his life'.[58]

Oxford became a different place for Blair in his final year, 1974–75, after Thomson and Gallop departed for Australia. Third-year undergraduates at St John's lived out, and Blair and Marc Palley were invited to share a house in Argyle Street by three lively and independent-minded young women from St Anne's College: 'We always thought of Marc and Tony as the boys and as a very close pair. Marc had a very dry sense of humour, very funny, but was the quieter one. Tony was the more extrovert, good fun, amusing, easy to have around. It was a very good-humoured household.'[59] Alan Judd, the writer, was a frequent visitor to the house. 'I remember him as quite left-wing, and laughing a lot, but never that earnest about politics.'[60] Others, however, remember the stirrings of an interest in party politics and, in particular, his disquiet over the influence of the far left on the Labour Party. One, Delia Rothnie, recalls him saying, 'People like me will get into the Labour Party and change all that.'[61]

Blair did become much more serious about his work, though his academic subject never fully engaged his interest. He later said that law only began to become meaningful to him when he fell under the influence of Derry Irvine at the Bar.[62] To Roy Jenkins he said, with real passion, '"I wish to God I'd read history instead of the boring Oxford School of Jurisprudence!" It was an absolute *cri de coeur*.'[63] Many students who went on to practise as lawyers read other subjects at university. Blair had wide intellectual interests which were not engaged by the narrow way law was taught at Oxford, and it constrained him.[64] Jenkins felt that history would have been more engaging for him but also more practical. 'He is interested in history rather than particularly knowledgeable about it. Suddenly he will seize on something in history, but his knowledge is vague.'[65] He worked hard,[66] hard enough to secure his second, the same degree as all the other St John's candidates: none from the college achieved a first in law, and only 20 out of 217 lawyers in his year at Oxford achieved that distinction.[67]

The young man who packed his bags and possessions together for the last time in June 1975 was more focused than the one who had arrived in Oxford in 1972. He had become both a practising Christian and seriously interested in political and social discussion. He had broken outside the public-school circle that had dominated his school and gap years, and had befriended vital figures from the British Commonwealth, like Otunnu, and Anwal Velani, an Indian postgraduate, as well as the two Australians, Gallop and Thomson. And what of his future plans? Friends thought he was as likely to have a career in the church as in politics: his ideas were very inchoate. He looked forward to a career at the Bar but without noticeable relish or a clear idea about which branch of law he should specialise in. He saw it just as the inevitable next step on a ladder that was leading up to he knew not where. As Thomson put it, 'I think his life lacked purpose and direction. Beyond getting a degree, I don't think he really knew what he was doing at Oxford.'[68] Hardly any of those he met at Oxford marked him out as a future national figure, still less the re-shaper of the Labour Party and long-serving Prime Minister.

Hazel's Death, 1975

Hazel Blair was diagnosed with cancer of the throat when Tony was in the sixth form at Fettes. 'I don't know why on earth I didn't realise how serious it was. But I suppose you think your mother is indestructible. It never occurs to you that she can die.'[69] She was sent to hospital for treatment, calmly reassuring her family as ever. 'She very much downplayed it. She just said she had a lump on her throat and she had to get it removed.'[70] Her condition stabilised for a few years, but worsened dramatically during Tony's final year at Oxford. He did not witness the decline and his parents decided to hide her deteriorating condition from Tony, so as not to distress him. Their concern above all was to avoid distracting him from work on his Finals, which they saw as the passport to a secure future for their headstrong son – they felt no such qualms with the far steadier Bill, successfully starting in practice as a London lawyer, nor about Sarah, now recovered from the worst of her illness, and with success at school behind her.[71] Leo met Tony at Durham station on his return from Oxford. 'He said, "I'm afraid Mum's a lot more ill than we thought." I said, "She's not going to die, is she?" He said, "Yes, she is," and that she would only last a few days.'[72]

Suddenly Oxford seemed a world away. It was a cruel homecoming.

She had indeed just days to live. He saw her every day in hospital. In his words, 'It was terrible how she had suddenly aged at the end. She knew she was dying but she was very, very lucid. She saw each one of us in turn and went through things with us. She was extraordinarily unselfish. She was very keen as to what type of future life we should lead. She wanted to make sure that the rest of the family was looked after.'[73] She died in her sleep in hospital on 28 June, aged just fifty-two.[74] Her worries had been primarily for Leo: she knew how much her husband had depended on her; more than he realised. '"She's a real lady," Dad always used to say about my mum. Yes, he did adore her, it's fair to say he did.' The couple had bought a house the year before which they were renovating: they never spent a night together there.[75] Leo went through a very bad time after Hazel's death. He sold the dream house and moved to Wales. Friends said how tender Tony was with his father, and the shared loss brought them closer together – perhaps closer than they had ever been before.

But it was Tony who was the most affected. He may or may not have been his mother's favourite child, but he certainly felt he had a unique bond with her. Her removal from his life, the suddenness of it, and coming at such a critical juncture in his life, caused him to re-evaluate his world.[76] He adored his mother. For some time he felt very bleak. When he went to Edinburgh that summer he called in on an old friend, who was deeply touched by the way he talked about his mother.[77] The summer over, he went down to London a changed man to study for the Bar. Marc Palley, who came down from Oxford at the same time and moved into a house with him in London, noticed a more serious and brooding side to his closest friend. He would be intensely focused on his work, up at dawn, back from his studies late, then sit up in bed reading his Bible.[78] His mother's death had stripped away from him the secure comfort of the certainty of the love that he had worn all his life.[79] Her death left him alone in the world, with Oxford over and no cycle of academic routine to return to, no close girlfriend, and no job. It left him exposed to the sole parental influence of his father, an utterly different figure from his mother: intensely ambitious, driven, and political. Out with the long hair and student clothes went the carefree youthful days. He was alone aged twenty-two in an adult world. Time was not infinite. A steel entered his soul.

Although this picture dates from 1995, it still shows Peter Thomson's energy and charisma and Blair listening to him intently. He was the first 'teacher' Blair had in his life who truly connected with him, and opened his mind.

4

Peter Thomson

Peter Thomson is a man of middle height, an engaging manner and a religious faith which is far from conventional. He was more important to Tony Blair than any other adult he met at school or university. Whereas he bonded with some – not many – teachers at school, perhaps the Revd John Grove at Choristers Prep and Eric Anderson at Fettes, it is notable that no tutor at Oxford became particularly close to him, and none kept up with him afterwards. The relationships with Grove and Anderson were very much master–pupil. The relationship with Thomson, despite the age difference of seventeen years, was one of equals.

Thomson was born in Australia in March 1936. At the age of seventeen, he realised that he wanted more in life than to run his father's estate agency, and became drawn to the church. 'I know it sounds corny, [but] that is what grabbed me. I just had to make sense of it. That meant I needed the theology,' so he went off to study for the priesthood at Ridley College, a 'conservative evangelical establishment', in Melbourne.[1] While at the college he became captivated by politics as the way of fulfilling the social obligations of the church. Thomson's words, which give a valuable insight to his exuberant personality, were: 'I had never been politically challenged before and it just blew my mind – here was a basic rationale for faith that was not about personal salvation or being perfect. I could see there was a job to do.'[2] After a series of jobs in Australia and England, he discovered his vocation was working with the young, and in 1969 he went as chaplain to Timbertop in Victoria, the outward-bound section of the famous Geelong Grammar School, best known in Britain for educating Prince Charles. After three years there and two years at Oxford as a mature student between 1972 and 1974, he returned to Timbertop as Head from

1975 to 1983 before becoming Head of St Mark's Anglican College at
the University of Adelaide. He retired in 1991 aged fifty-five, but quickly
became bored, and busied himself in a number of jobs including working
in universities and as a priest and charity worker in England.

Thomson has always been a restless spirit: a seeker, a noisy iconoclast
challenging the status quo. When working as a priest in Melbourne, he fell
foul of the Bishop over claims that he was a Communist: Thomson claims
he 'wasn't and never [has] been a Communist', which is true. But the label
of agitator stuck, and in some ways it is surprising that an independent
school as close to the Establishment as Geelong Grammar sought to employ
him. Equally, it is surprising in some ways that he decided to spend so much
of his career looking after privileged, fee-paying children. Thomson was a
big hit with the pupils. Boris Johnson, Conservative MP and editor of the
Spectator, who worked for a period at Timbertop, said, 'He was direct,
approachable and very fair. He was famed for his sermons, which were
funny but had a note of sternness about them. He was very good at
inspiring kids and getting them to understand the difference between right
and wrong.'[3] While Thomson enjoyed teaching the young, he wanted to
tackle bigger questions, and deepen his own reading and thinking. He had
encountered a series of writers who had inspired him, including the Jewish
thinker Martin Buber; the Christian, Dietrich Bonhoeffer and John
Macmurray. He fell on the last, and devoured his every word. For him it
grounded Christian thinking not in the abstract, but in action, and human
relationships. His pop résumé of Macmurray captures Thomson's free
manner of speech: 'I'll tell you, mate, Macmurray is the classic. He changed
philosophical thinking. All his philosophy had a practical relevance; he
changed the reference from the idea to the real. What he was on about was
community. It's about fellowship, friendship, brotherly love.'[4] Macmurray
provided Thomson with the perfect riposte to what he saw as the bloodless
tradition that had dominated so much of twentieth-century philosophy –
logical positivism and the linguistics of Wittgenstein, which he deemed a
'lost half-century'.[5]

Thomson's mind was buzzing with all these ideas when he arrived in
Oxford in September 1972. He wasn't certain what it would be like, and
dreaded a repetition of the arid tutorials he had experienced at theological
college. He couldn't believe his good fortune therefore when he discovered
himself playing court to a lively, intellectually acute and responsive group
of undergraduates. Enticed initially by his hospitality, students began
congregating in his room in Canterbury Quad at St John's from late in his
first term for two-hour lunches over pies and HP sauce. They could hardly
believe their ears, or their luck. Here was an adult who, in gathering them

in, managed 'to mix a four-letter word, rolling a cigarette and a sermon into one sentence'.[6] He had met Blair through Gallop, and began talking to him at breakfast in college. Thomson would come for breakfast after chapel, while Blair, unusually for an undergraduate, was an early riser: breakfast was not a popular undergraduate meal. 'I met him quite early on in that Afghan coat. He was particularly drawn to meeting people from overseas and he liked the openness of Australians, like Geoff Gallop and me.'[7] Thomson found his protégé responsive: 'He wasn't notably political or religious when we met, but whereas Geoff had had some bad experiences of religion, Tony had had a couple of good ones – at Durham, and Selby-Wright in Edinburgh: he would talk about the impact that he had on him. But like most public school kids, their experiences of school chapel and chaplains hadn't inspired him.'[8] But neither had Fettes totally killed religion in him. Thomson found him 'just alive'. Tony had never heard theology spoken of in this way and he was enthused.[9]

Thomson could easily have exploited his position with his group of eager acolytes. It is an easy lot to play guru to a group of bright and impressionable young men who as yet know little of the world. It can be very gratifying and rewarding to become a cult figure: many teachers at schools and universities have fallen into the trap. It is to Thomson's credit that he does not seem to have succumbed to the temptation. His quirky manner of speech and ideas could be easily dismissed as hippy chic or new age psycho-babble, and he was not without his detractors at this time or later. But he did not strike this exceptionally bright group of students as a charlatan. Former St John's pupils as diverse as the journalist David Gardner, the diplomat Olara Otunnu and the cleric Nicholas Lowton found him an impressive, sincere and stimulating man, with an extra-ordinary energy and passion for life, and with an infectious ability to com-municate to anyone willing to listen and engage with him.[10]

Blair had already shown a propensity in his acquaintance with Selby-Wright and Norman Burt (from his gap year) to be drawn to older churchmen who became protective of him. But his relationship with Thomson was of a completely different order. Thomson challenged him to think. His law tutors and lecturers failed to make him do that. One should not perhaps blame them. Blair did not choose to respond to them, and they were no doubt frustrated by his failure to give of his best to them. It may even have made it harder for him to enjoy law tutorials: how could they compete with the intensity of Thomson's fizzy 'tutorials' laced with cigarettes and coffee, with passionate debates on subjects that had begun deeply to interest him and his friends? Thomson kept the conversation going, interspersed with hilarious laughter, in the quads, in pubs or on the tennis court, never letting up. His was an extraordinary energy. Blair described him as 'one of the most inspiring, honest and decent people I have ever met in my life . . . There's nothing soft about him. He's tough, he's courageous. His Christianity is instructive.'[11] Thomson was a breath of fresh air in Blair's life. 'It's difficult not to imagine Tony, or anyone else aged eighteen or nineteen, falling under his spell,' said one observer. 'Peter was a mixture of missionary and rock star, combining religion and counter culture in a unique way.'[12]

Thomson's explosive brand of Christianity brought him into conflict with the college. His incendiary sermons in chapel, in which he'd typically complain that the college chapel was a meaningless charade, and would only have value if it engaged with the lives of ordinary people and 'the agenda of socialism', came to the attention of the college President.[13] Words were spoken, although he departed on good terms at the end of the summer term in 1974.

Blair mourned Thomson's departure greatly, as did others in the circle. It marked the end of the first and very intense phase of their relationship, which lasted just two years. There followed a twenty-year period when they saw each other rarely. The death of Tony's mother came and went: 'It must have been terrible for Tony, losing his mother. When I met her, I thought what a fantastic darling she was. But of course, by then I was back in Australia.'[14] They did not meet again until 1982, when Tony visited Australia with Cherie, then his relatively new wife, who he proudly introduced to Thomson, and with whom they stayed at Timbertop as part of a month-long tour of the country. 'He was the same as he was at Oxford,' said Thomson, 'except now he was a Labour Party boy and on his way.' They spoke about Blair's emerging credo – he gave an important speech at Murdoch University in Perth where Gallop was teaching politics. 'Tony's basic position was "if we get the vision right, everything else will follow". And he's spot-on.'[15] Another eight-year gap followed before their next meeting in Adelaide, where they had dinner together in 1990 when Blair visited Australia on a fact-finding tour with Gordon Brown.[16]

Blair's election as Labour leader in 1994 ushered in a new phase in their relationship. In the early 1990s Blair began casting around for intellectual roots for his embryonic policy platform, and began recalling the influence of Macmurray. He also began to seek out Thomson again, wanting to recapture the political discussion of their St John's days. Thomson and his wife Helen came over for a month in June 1995, and had long conversations with Blair.[17] The exchanges went well, and at Christmas that year, the Blair family, accompanied by the Palleys, flew to Australia for an idyllic ten-day holiday at Thomson's 200-acre farm near Timbertop in Victoria, touring the area together in a hired eighteen-seater camper bus. It was to be one of the best and least disturbed family holidays the Blairs were to enjoy together.

In May 1996, Thomson returned to England to work as a priest at St Luke's Church in the tough inner-city London parish of Holloway. The move was at Thomson's instigation because, as he said, 'things were happening for Tony and I wanted to be part of it'.[18] Stories started to appear in the press that Thomson was 'the older friend the Blair family needs as it heads towards Downing Street',[19] before becoming, it was said, 'Blair's priest at Number 10'. This was embarrassing to both sides. Some started jumping on the bandwagon, and saw Thomson as a conduit to his powerful protégé: Thomson, not well versed in such manoeuvring, was on occasion put in an awkward position. Thomson came under great pressure, not least from journalists, who kept probing him on all subjects including: would Macmurray have thought Blair had 'sold out'?[20]

Their relationship entered a final phase after 1997. If Blair did indeed think he needed to have his old mentor close by, he rapidly realised, once in Number 10, that he could cope on his own. Thomson moved jobs in 1997 to work in the developing field of 'social entrepreneurship' in London. He still saw Blair, in London or at Chequers.[21] But the regular personal meetings declined, and in 2001 he left to settle back in Australia with his family on his farm in the Victorian highlands. He still aims each week to leave a heartening message at Number 10 for his old friend and they talk periodically on the phone.

Thomson's impact on Blair was greatest at Oxford. It is difficult to exaggerate the importance to Blair of meeting an adult (older than many of his law tutors) who was fascinating, irreverent, anti-Establishment, and genuinely interested in him and his ideas. Thomson himself plays down his influence on Blair's development.[22] To Charles Leadbetter, however, who knows both men very well, 'He, more than anyone, explains Blair.'[23]

The Impact of Peter Thomson

One can trace the impact of Thomson on Blair on a number of levels. Thomson introduced him to the ideas of Macmurray, which, as we have seen, fed, through a long filter process, into Blair's espousal of 'community' which flowered twenty years later. 'I didn't work these things out very clearly at the time,' Blair later admitted, 'but they were influences that stayed with me.'[24] In Thomson, Blair at last encountered someone whose ideas seemed to be a sensible explanation of the human condition, 'which meshed two strands of thinking that he had become swept up in by his second year at Oxford, namely Christianity and left-of-centre politics'.[25] One can also trace Blair's undoubted commitment to Africa and to alleviating poverty to the discussions in Oxford on the Third World and liberation theology.

Thomson's quintessential Australian identity was another powerful factor, for which Blair's happy early childhood experiences in that country might have prepared the way. As Thomson said, with paradoxical truth, 'the thing about Tony is that he is an Australian'.[26] To another shrewd observer of the Blair–Thomson relationship, 'Peter helped Tony stand outside England and the English ways of thinking on the English class system. He has helped open Tony's eyes to fresh ways of looking at things which are outside the box of conventional British party political thinking.'[27] Had Oxford locked Blair into a rigid intellectual channel of convergent thought, as legal training can do, he would not have had the freedom of mind to think through the divergent channels that he has.

Would Blair have been a Christian or a Labour politician without Thomson? Thomson certainly gave Blair a powerful impetus towards taking Christianity seriously. 'What I took from Peter Thomson is the idea that your religious beliefs aren't something that shut you away from the world, but something that meant you had to go out and act.'[28] No one can know, and perhaps he himself does not know, why he became a communicant Christian. But it seems likely that, whereas Thomson helped prepare the ground, his decision ultimately followed his realisation of the finality of his mother's cancer: Hazel had taught him to pray and in her way was a religious woman. As he gazed ahead at the uncertain world beyond Oxford, he sought to deepen his spiritual roots. Interestingly, not only did he keep his closest friends like Palley in the dark about his confirmation, he did not invite Thomson to the confirmation service.[29] Without Thomson Blair may well have joined the Labour Party; but it would probably not have happened so soon. A lifelong friend of Blair's said, 'Peter made Tony much more serious. The seriousness of purpose translated into his joining the Labour Party.'[30] Ultimately, we can never know what Blair would have done without Thomson. The likelihood is that Oxford would have been a much more frivolous time for him, as it was for most of the undergraduates.

Thomson's greatest importance to Blair, however, lies in none of the above areas: rather, it was in giving him, for the first time, a sense of worth as a young man with valuable and serious views of his own on life. He forged Blair's raw talent and energy into some kind of shape. Before

Thomson, Blair's ideas were a series of inchoate thoughts; after Thomson, they were more coherent, and with a distinctively left-wing hue. Thomson gave Blair the confidence to be the person he was feeling his way towards becoming.

*A seat at last. A newly determined Blair in May 1982, having secured
the nomination at Beaconsfield, standing proudly alongside
Labour leader Michael Foot.*

5

Commits to Labour, 1975–82

The pace of life for Blair accelerated quickly after he came down to London in September 1975 to begin a one-year course reading for the Bar at the College of Law, Chancery Lane. These seven years from the ages of twenty-two to twenty-nine saw him qualify and launch himself enthusiastically as a barrister, and then become disenchanted with it; they saw him join the Labour Party, fail to become a local councillor and lose a parliamentary by-election; then saw him meet and marry his wife; and they saw a change from him being an amiable if somewhat aimless student into an ambitious, serious and focused man.

It is in these years that the questions and myths about his political life begin to accumulate. Could he have joined the Social Democratic Party (SDP), formed in March 1981, had circumstances been different? Was it Cherie Booth who made him join the Labour Party, or at least made him much more left-wing than he naturally was? Did he just 'fall into' politics and out of the law, or was it part of a long-term game plan? The core 'event' in these seven years was his decision to forsake the law, the only career he had ever seriously countenanced, for an uncertain and difficult life, working his way up from the bottom of the Labour Party, then in the grip of the hard left and far from sympathetic to people from his social background. With Labour under Callaghan crashing out of office in May 1979, it was in many ways a perverse career move for one so ambitious. It was a huge mental and emotional leap of faith, and one which, in bleak periods in the years to follow, he would occasionally question.

It was a very sober and saddened Tony Blair who arrived in London in September 1975. Continuity and comfort at least came from living with Marc Palley, his closest Oxford friend and former housemate. The two settled in a basement flat in Earls Court, west London. The one-year course was particularly demanding, and he had to work hard all week, interspersed with periodic train journeys to Durham at weekends to see his father and sister. Bill, who had followed the same route as him three years before, was living in London and acted as mentor and guide to his younger brother. The work he found a chore and no more stimulating than he had found the law at Oxford, but it was still a surprise, given his application and intellect, that he only received a third-class degree in the summer 1976 Bar final exams. But it was a pass, and he was duly called to the Bar at Lincoln's Inn. Having lost his summer holidays the year before because of his mother's death, he was determined to get away. A College of Law friend, Bruce Roe, offered him a room in a flat in Paris, and together they went off for a couple of months, supposedly to develop their French and meet the locals. In practice 'we went to bars and restaurants and ended up meeting American tourists and girls who were in Paris, and were easier to communicate with'.[1] It was space in his life he badly needed, free from pressures and unhappy memories.

The key task for any candidate sitting Bar finals is to secure a pupillage in a set of chambers for the following year, a position leading to the expectation of a tenancy, a permanent place in those chambers.[2] Unlike many former public school pupils in the mid-1970s reading for the Bar, neither Blair nor his family had connections in London chambers, and Blair had to fend for himself. Places in prestigious 'sets', as they were called, were at a premium. Through a chance meeting at a wedding, Blair received an introduction to Derry Irvine, head of a well-known set and already a controversial figure, who was later to split acrimoniously with his chambers colleague and partner, Michael Sherrard.[3] The set had a good standing among fellow barristers, and had close contacts with the Labour Party, stemming from Irvine's close friendship, dating back to university days at Glasgow, with the senior Labour front-bencher, John Smith. Irvine, after some jibbing at Blair's public school background, took him on. Irvine was to prove a most powerful force in Blair's evolution as a lawyer and thinker, and helped groom him as a budding politician. Blair was a late starter, and without Irvine's patronage he would not have risen so speedily: he may well, indeed, not have risen to become Labour leader at all. Under Irvine's watchful eye as a pupil in 1976–77, Blair grew visibly in stature and confidence. Law began to make sense to him. Irvine was a very demanding task-master, but Blair could relate to him, unlike his Oxford tutors and his lecturers at the College of Law. He rose to the challenge.

Despite Blair's third in Bar finals, Irvine was impressed with his qualities as a mind and advocate: '. . . absolutely excellent. I have no doubt that he would have been a QC . . . Very keen sense of what was relevant . . . Very good at getting to the point . . . a fast gun on paper, possessing an excellent facility with the English language.'[4]

Irvine's personal backing was decisive in persuading member barristers in the chambers to award Blair a tenancy in 1977. Over the next five years he specialised in employment law, a branch which chimed with his sense of social justice in looking after the individual against powerful corporations or the state: it was also one which allowed him to build up an extensive range of contacts among key figures in trade unions and in the Labour Party, which would be of considerable help to him in the future. He began to shine. 'Law only came alive to me when I started to practise it,' he later said. Rather than spending hours in the library poring over law cases, he was now 'dealing with practical problems in people's lives and finding solutions to them'.[5] Friends and associates speak of him as a hard-working and ambitious young barrister, with a strong streak of human compassion.[6]

While he found the practising of law a big improvement on the theory, and was earning real money for the first time in his life, Blair began to question whether he was made to be a career lawyer. Bill was, and still is; but they are different characters. His younger brother needed a bigger stage, more variety and greater excitement than even being a leading QC would ever have afforded him. He later reflected on his career, with rather too much hindsight, 'Law is a very, very good discipline for politicians, providing you don't stay too long at it,' adding, 'If you stay too long, you become a lawyer.'[7] But at what point, and why, did he decide to *give up* the Bar, where he was beginning to enjoy greater personal success and greater financial security than he had ever known, in favour of politics?

Blair's Commitment to Labour

Although the details remain elusive, Blair joined the Labour Party in the autumn of 1975, before he met Cherie, and before he met Derry Irvine. The two certainly shaped his political thinking, and his career in the party, but they are not responsible for him joining the party. It was his own decision, as Marc Palley confirms.[8] Charles Falconer, a loose acquaintance since before university, explains his thinking: 'During Oxford and immediately after he became utterly immersed in a sort of

Christian spiritual approach for the solutions of social problems . . . He concluded the only way forward was by political action within the confines of conventional politics.'[9] It is thus entirely consistent with his thinking at the time that he should want to take that decision to join Labour. He was also conscious of something missing in his life in London. With so much of his attention spent studying arid law, he wanted to recapture the excitement of the political discussion and debate which had made his life at Oxford so worthwhile. Nothing in his life had made him so animated, and he wanted the same energy and purpose badly. In his first working year in London, so utterly different from the frivolity of his London gap year, he was anxious to meet other like-minded young people. He did not, at the time, visualise a career in politics: he merely sought alternative stimulation. He registered initially with the national party, whose headquarters were then at Transport House, and was told to contact his local party, which was the Redcliffe branch of the Chelsea Labour Party.

He found a hollow shell. The local organisation had all but disappeared, and the constituency chairman wanted it revived, an exercise in which Blair participated enthusiastically. Though he had minimal short-term effect, the experience implanted a seed in his mind about the importance of mass membership for the party. Sandy Pringle, one of those charged with overseeing the renaissance in Chelsea, found Blair 'had a strong sense of social justice – that's what motivated him. We had very left-wing people in the local party who he'd take on: I'd have said he was on the centre-right of the party at the time, but definitely still anti-Establishment.'[10] Blair displayed his appetite and perhaps also naïveté in allowing himself to be co-opted as branch Secretary, by common consent a dogsbody's job.

This early interest in Labour dwindled after he and Palley moved in early 1977 to St John's Wood, and he devoted all his energies to making his mark as Irvine's pupil. Marylebone was now his local constituency party, but he seems to have played little or no part. With his tenancy secure, and income beginning to flow, he then moved in early 1979 to a house near Wandsworth Bridge and became a tenant of Falconer, who had, after Cambridge, also joined the Bar, and who went on to become a lifelong friend. It was a Labour enclave, with everyone in it subscribing to the Fairfield branch of Battersea Labour Party; but neither Blair nor Falconer proved much good at the hard graft of local politics – delivering notices and canvassing was not for them, despite it being a time of intense activity with the Tories, elected to Wandsworth Council in May 1978, busy cutting services. This became the source of some resentment among fellow party members, not least because of Blair's lack of roots in the Labour movement.[11] Blair was up very early and off to his work at the Bar, arriving back late exhausted, leaving little time for his political interests. Nevertheless, it would appear that it was during the 1979–80 period that he first began thinking of a career in politics. First, he wanted to climb up the local party hierarchy. This meant making an impression on fellow members. The surviving branch minutes record how on 9 July 1979, Blair 'gave an interesting talk on democratic control, in the work place, in Parliament and in the Labour Party'. At the AGM on 14 January 1980, he was elected Assistant Secretary. In order to become eligible for the parliamentary candidates list, he had to join a trade union, and caused amusement when he asked a Fairfield member how to do so.[12] Cherie was certainly a factor in his decision: 'I suspect that before Cherie, he put the Bar first and politics second,' recalled Oxford contemporary, David Fursdon. 'After he became serious about Cherie, it would have been the Bar second and politics first.'[13] Geoff Gallop, who had done so much to interest him in politics, had returned to Oxford after a gap of three years to study for a doctorate, was another voice to encourage him to believe in himself as a politician. They would discuss their joint hopes for political careers.[14]

After his marriage to Cherie in March 1980 (discussed in more detail in the next chapter), they moved to Hackney, and that November they attended their first party meeting together – a significant statement of their shared interest and intent – at the Queensbridge branch of the Hackney South Labour Party.[15] Few Labour wards in the country contained more talent. Branch members included neighbours Barry Cox (later deputy chairman of Channel 4) and his then wife Katie Kay, later to work in Number 10, who became friends and regular holiday companions of the Blairs,[16] and who introduced Blair to many television figures, including John Birt, Melvyn Bragg and Greg Dyke. John Carr and his wife Glenys Thornton; Ben Pimlott, the historian and biographer; and his wife, the academic Jean Seaton, were also prominent figures. Katie Kay describes the easy relationship she and Barry Cox had with the Blairs: 'We were in and out of each other's houses for a glass of wine and some food.'[17] Another notable figure in Hackney was Charles Clarke, fresh from being President of the National Union of Students (1975–77) and now education adviser to the rising front-bench star, Neil Kinnock; while next door in Islington was Margaret Hodge, who went on to lead the Council. John Lloyd, later editor of the *New Statesman*, and Alan Haworth and his wife, Maggie Rae, a close friend of Cherie's, also came to know Blair well during this period. This was a new generation of highly ambitious, middle-class activists who were determined to challenge the orthodoxies of the old-style party in Hackney.[18] Records from branch meetings show that Blair would support and propose motions that failed to chime with the views of many traditionalist Labour councillors.[19] Glenys Thornton recalls, 'They were really quite advanced and modernising arguments for the time – on issues to do with racial and sexual equality, which presented problems for "Old Labour" in places like Hackney.'[20]

By 1980, Blair's politics had settled into a 'soft left' groove, which was beginning to find its voice in a London Labour Party dominated by the hard left. Following encouragement from Charles Clarke and Alan Haworth, the Blairs became delegates to the Labour Co-ordinating Committee (LCC), which, after initially siding with Tony Benn, now sought to disassociate itself from the hard left represented by Ken Livingstone.[21] Despite Blair's attempts to resolve differences between the soft and hard left,[22] the bitter divisions within the London party had left him disillusioned.[23] He also realised that the protracted and overly bureaucratic proceedings of local party politics would continue to turn many away from Labour. A fellow branch member recalls that 'he was very impatient with the silly rules and routines you had to go through to be part of the party, which were so off-putting to ordinary people. He articulated this long before the rest of us did.'[24]

Blair was supportive in public of Michael Foot, the left-wing leader who had succeeded James Callaghan in 1980, and was in favour of high public spending and tax, against the European Economic Community (EEC), pro-CND, and unashamedly anti-privatisation in any form, then in its infancy under Mrs Thatcher. Blair was clearly identified as opposed to the far-left Militant Tendency and to Tony Benn, who had become the champion in Parliament of the party's drive for a purer form of socialism. Blair also identified with those who made clear their opposition to the views of Roy Hattersley, the leading centre-right figure in the Parliamentary Party, despite coming to admire him once elected himself.[25]

Some believe that Blair could easily have left the party to join the newly-formed SDP, which highlighted its threat to Labour when it formed an electoral alliance with the Liberals in September 1981 and which was attracting widespread interest from right-wingers in the party.[26] Blair was certainly disillusioned with the left of the party, which he thought was wrecking its credibility and electoral prospects locally and nationally. His stand at the Bar made his outright opposition to the far left abundantly clear: the best-known legal advice of his career was his counsel to the party on the expulsion of Militant Tendency.[27] But does that imply he was so much on the right of the party that he was prepared to abandon it?

The period when he might have come under the greatest temptation to jump ship and join the SDP was when he was finding it hard to find a seat to contest in 1981. Blair is so ambitious, and his roots in Labour so shallow, that surely he would opt, some believe, for whatever party was most likely to get him into Parliament? Stories have circulated of screaming matches with Cherie and her pulling him back from the brink. Others recount an occasion at this time when he announced that he wanted to become an MP and a friend and party activist, whose advice he had sought, responded, 'Really, which party?'[28] If his later close ally, Peter Mandelson, came so close to joining the SDP (it is alleged) then surely Blair himself must have been close to joining at a time so many reasonable, like-minded people were doing so?[29] Melvyn Bragg acknowledges that this was the thinking at the time. 'It was assumed that people like Tony Blair and me would be natural fodder for the SDP, but it never occurred to me to join them, nor, as far as I could tell, did it ever occur to him either.'[30]

So what really happened? No evidence can be found to suggest any truth in the SDP thesis. If Blair had discussed the possibility of defecting to the SDP with friends, the story would have leaked by now. Besides, since his second year at university, Blair had seen himself as a man of the left. It is quite implausible that he would have gone back on his commitment and the ideas of Thomson and Macmurray, and on all he had done and said, increasingly in print, since the mid-1970s.[31] His relationship with Cherie was grounded in part on a shared commitment to Labour. His personal attachment to Labour was strong: it gave him a sense of belonging, which he never had before. Friends and associates regarded defectors to the SDP, such as Hackney South Labour MP Ron Brown, whom they had fought hard to save from de-selection, as treacherous: staying with the cause, even through hard times, brought companionship and affirmation. He would not have sacrificed that. Blair's legal cases representing trade unions and his relationship with Irvine further bound him into Labour. Blair, moreover, is an unusually loyal person, loyal to people and to institutions. He was increasingly impatient, certainly, but he wanted to change Labour from within.

Ultimately, one can never know what was in his mind from the frustrating period of 1980–81 until he became locked into Labour following his adoption as the party's candidate for the Beaconsfield by-election in early 1982. But defection to the SDP, one must conclude, was never a serious possibility. At the core, Blair had made a commitment to an organisation, the Labour Party, but not to its policies. In practice, he had yet to work through his own position on many issues. He articulated the views he did to advance his career, not because he believed in them deeply, but because he was pledged to fulfil his ambition in the Labour Party. That explained his fury when he thought Labour were getting it wrong. His *instincts* were Labour: he was only now just beginning to work out for himself what these instincts meant in terms of doctrines and policies. Charles Clarke says, 'It would never have been anything else than Labour for Tony. He was from the libertarian-lawyer tradition of the party, but he was always a moderniser.'[32] Typical of Blair, he was not going to accept received wisdom, but was going to work policy through in his own way and his own time.

Search for a Seat, 1980–82

Blair's ambitions for a parliamentary seat crystallised in 1980. Cherie had the same aspiration. They discussed their hopes and plans together, and came up with their famous 'pact' that whoever won a seat first would become the career politician while the other would remain at the Bar and become the breadwinner. Blair's decision to become involved again in local politics, which he found necessary but dull, had much to do with his parliamentary ambitions and the need to show his serious credentials as a committed party member. Some in Hackney were surprised, if not a little bemused, by his intention to find a seat so soon after becoming involved in local politics. 'I remember laughing when he said he was going to go for a seat. I think we all thought he wasn't very political at all, but perhaps it was the influence of all of us that made him want to go for it,' recalls Margaret Hodge.[33] Others, though, remember a more determined young man: 'He didn't hide the fact that to change things you needed to be in Parliament, and that's where he was going to be.'[34] He applied for his first seat in December 1980, just one month after attending his first Queensbridge ward meeting. The seat, Middlesbrough, appealed to him because of its proximity to his home town, Durham, and he was nominated by the electricians' union (the EETPU). In the event, the union covertly switched its support to another candidate, Stuart Bell, who was successful: Blair failed even to make the shortlist.[35]

Once the Middlesbrough route closed, he had little choice but to do the hard graft in Hackney. The dislike he had already formed for the hard-left, Bennite wing of the party was only deepened by what he now saw. The minutes of his first meeting of the Queensbridge ward on 6 November 1980 record Blair supporting 'one-member-one-vote' as the method of electing the party leader, a seemingly modest democratic stance, but then viewed as right-wing.[36] The ward's hard left won the day with their support for an 'electoral college', the system which was duly adopted by the milestone Wembley Conference two months later, provoking the breakaway of the SDP that March. Encouraged by like-minded friends, Blair decided to take on the hard-left, and in February 1981 ousted the Bennite branch Secretary by a vote of seventeen to fifteen.[37] Hard work and much persuasion and hospitality by both Blairs had paid off. '

To broaden his contacts and build his profile – desirable prerequisites, he was told, for finding a parliamentary seat – he began writing for political weeklies. Heavily informed by his work at the Bar, articles duly began to appear with the by-line 'Anthony Blair' on subjects ranging from the legal rights of illegal immigrants to the freedom of the press. His first of two articles for the *Spectator* appeared in August 1979,[38] and he wrote eight articles for the *New Statesman* in the years 1979–81. They make dull reading today and shed no great light on the evolution of his thinking. Alexander Chancellor, then editor of the *Spectator*, thought his pieces technical and dry.[39] But they are important as evidence of his growing ambition to build a reputation.

Blair continued looking for a seat during the course of 1981, and befriended the former footballer and Labour MP (and friend of Cherie's wayward father) Tom Pendry, taking him several times to the fashionable Gay Hussar restaurant in Soho to discuss his increasingly desperate search. Pendry found Blair 'very eager and keen to learn': he invited him for what was his first visit to the House of Commons, which he gazed at in awe.[40] Blair was busy networking among leading trade union figures and in the party, meeting John Smith (via Irvine) and befriending Denis Healey,[41] who became deputy leader in 1981. But it was not an easy time for someone of Blair's persuasion. The hard left were carrying all before them, while the soft left and centre-right were suffering from their perceived failure to deliver while in government under Harold Wilson and James Callaghan from 1974–79.[42] Blair was nominated but not shortlisted for a northern seat, Teesside Thornaby. There was a growing suspicion that he was having his applications rejected because he was not on the hard left which dominated so many constituency Labour parties[43] and because he was a public-school barrister who had been to Oxford. He came to resent this bias in the party.[44] At a lunch with Patrick Wintour, the journalist, he complained, 'I've finally realised I'll never get a seat and I'm going to give up politics. They don't want people from my background.'[45] Cherie, even with her working-class background, fared no better with her search for a seat in 1981: she tried unsuccessfully to win the Labour nomination in the by-election in her home town, Crosby: the Labour candidate was defeated by one of the founders of the SDP, Shirley Williams, ironically a childhood hero of Cherie's.

Despairing of finding a parliamentary seat by the end of 1981, and fearing the next General Election to be only fifteen months away (and so it proved), he determined to swallow his pride and become a humdrum councillor for a few years to broaden his curriculum vitae.[46] Local elections were due in May 1982, and early that year wards in Hackney held selection meetings to choose their three candidates. He decided he must be one of them. Blair was not universally popular. 'He was regarded by some people in the ward as a bit of a "toff": he certainly had to try harder than some to gain acceptance,' recalled John Carr, a fellow student of Cherie's at LSE. Some also had doubts about the sincerity of his political beliefs.[47] He could not be present at his selection meeting in February because his legal work took him on his first trip to the United States.[48] Cherie spoke on his behalf and gave a brave and persuasive performance, beginning, 'I'm not only saying this because he's my husband, but . . .' before going on to extol his virtues and predict what a fresh and energetic councillor he would make for Hackney. In the event, her efforts failed to move members. Whether this was because he had been in the branch for only a year, or because his absence on the evening was deemed cavalier, or because of his centre-left politics, no one can be sure.[49] It was a painful rejection. He had failed even to become a local councillor. But on such small quirks of fate do great political careers turn. Had Blair secured the nomination, he would have felt duty-bound to fight the May 1982 Council election in Hackney, and would not have continued to search for a parliamentary seat, one of which came up just a couple of months later. Friends in Hackney believe it was Ben Pimlott's vote, together with his wife, Jean Seaton's, which lost him the nomination. If that is indeed the case, Pimlott – biographer of Harold Wilson – was indirectly responsible for helping Blair on his way to become a future Labour Prime Minister.

The death of Ronald Bell, a far-right Conservative MP for the ultra-safe seat of Beaconsfield, on 27 February 1982 meant a by-election had to take place. It also created a vacancy for Labour, which had yet to select a candidate for the approaching General Election. The media interest, however, was not on Labour's travails, but on the SDP–Liberal Alliance, which was in full flood, and ready to cap Shirley Williams' famous victory at Crosby in November 1981 with a victory for Roy Jenkins at Glasgow, Hillhead in the by-election to be held on 25 March. With the Tories fighting to defend a safe seat and the Alliance the interesting challengers, the Labour fight was of little consequence. Derry Irvine, John Smith and Tom Pendry nevertheless advised Blair to go for the nomination. Pendry told Blair that Betty Bell-Smith, the constituency secretary and Pendry's girlfriend, would 'assist his nomination'.[50] Bravado or not, one of Blair's rivals certainly believed the local party had manipulated the selection for Blair, who was duly selected as Labour candidate on 1 April.[51]

For all the talk about the Labour fight being irrelevant at Beaconsfield, and the Falklands War a further distraction, it was nevertheless the moment when Blair's name first came to the attention of the political world. Cynics wryly commented that there was something peculiarly appropriate in Blair fighting a seat deep in the heartlands of Tory Buckinghamshire. He campaigned on a safe pro-leadership platform, which included pledges to take Britain out of the EEC and was supportive of nuclear disarmament ('unilaterally if necessary').[52] One should not read too much into this, although inevitably he has been criticised for cynically articulating positions in which he did not believe. He was a young man keen to impress the party leader, who had been elected just two years before and, for all he knew, would remain in the saddle for many years to come. It would have been political suicide for him to challenge the leadership on core positions. He was happy to say in public that he opposed Tony Benn and far-left politics, and told the local newspaper, 'I'm basically a centrist in the party, and want to see it united.'[53] In private, he remained critical of the party, its tolerance of the far left and its failure to espouse policies which would bring it back into the political mainstream. But he was not yet ready, or sure enough of his thinking, to say so in public.[54]

Blair knew Beaconsfield gave him a superb opportunity – not to win, which was never a possibility, but to make an impression: a springboard for him to obtain another seat, perhaps even a winnable one, before the General Election. He pulled out every stop to create a good impression, contacting all his friends asking them to canvass for him, as well as bringing in celebrities through Cherie's father, the actor Tony Booth. Cherie laid aside her busy Bar practice to turn up in the constituency to support him. The FA Cup Final replay (between Queen's Park Rangers and Tottenham Hotspur) the evening of election day reduced still further the turnout of the pitifully small numbers of working-class voters in the constituency: 'People were almost violent when we knocked on their doors,' recalls one campaigner.[55] Labour's share of the vote fell from 20 to 10 per cent, and, as predicted, Labour fell to third place, with Blair losing his deposit.

But the result, as he had hoped, was not what mattered. What his campaign had done was achieve his real objective: to be noticed. Most significant for his future was to have Michael Foot's endorsement during the campaign on BBC 2's *Newsnight*: 'We're very proud of everything he's been saying here and, whatever the result, we believe he is going to have a very big future in British politics.' Healey, Smith and Kinnock came up to campaign for him, and all were impressed by this eager, well-heeled young man, as were the other big beasts who trooped down the M40 to Beaconsfield in the hope of putting a halt to the Liberal–SDP bandwagon.[56] The Alliance, which achieved a respectable second place, barely paused to take heed of Blair, so insignificant did it regard Labour's challenge. Richard Holme, who managed the Alliance campaign, said, 'All we noticed was that Labour had come up with a personable young chap who was pro-CND. He just didn't register with us.'[57]

What was it about Blair that led the Labour leadership to form such a favourable impression? By-election candidates, even in hopeless seats, are often relentlessly energetic, for obvious reasons – not least being the attention by-elections receive from the top party brass and the media. So being highly dynamic does not in itself explain it. His strikingly civil and personable manner in relationships gets us further. Hattersley thought him 'unusually polite'. His youth, good looks and plausible sincerity won over not only the local Beaconsfield party, who initially did not know him, but won him admirers across the political divide.[58] His Bar experience had honed his latent thespian skills to make him an even more effective orator and communicator. For all that, had it not been a by-election fought close to central London, and in the run-up to a General Election, and with intense political interest in the rise of a new third force in British politics, it would not have been so noticed. Above all, he showed a genius, at a highly divisive time for the party, for not saying anything that would upset any faction of the party (even offering an olive branch to the Bennites when he said, 'I do agree with some of Tony Benn's views'). He later claimed he was unlucky to have had to fight Beaconsfield. In fact, it was a brilliant campaign for him to have fought. And he played it perfectly.

Where did he go from here? Beaconsfield convinced him that his destiny was to be in Parliament.[59] He had felt more excited and alive fighting in this campaign than ever before. Law had lost whatever lustre it once held for him. Hackney had given him and Cherie political soulmates who were to become friends for life, but the local party also disillusioned him with parochial politics, and with the antics of the far left. When the lights went down on Beaconsfield, his ambition was far more focused, but concrete hopes of a career in national politics remained uncertain.

Blair with Cherie in the library of his chambers in about 1980.
His studied confidence contrasts with her innocence and
self-consciousness in front of the camera.

6

Cherie Blair

Cherie was to be an ideal if demanding partner for Tony Blair. As a good-looking young man, never short of female interest, he could have married any one of a number of very pretty, not especially able girls, who would have doted on his every word. Instead, he chose the most formidable legal intellect of her generation, and one with uncompromising views of her own. Cherie is indeed both brilliant and immensely ambitious; but she is also fiercely loyal, and was prepared to project her own ambitions on to him so he could advance his career. Her interests in law, politics and the Church chimed with his own; they are both gregarious and like the same kinds of people, enjoy the same holidays, and talking about the same kind of subjects. She was as keen as him to establish and nurture a large family, which became the bedrock of both their lives. She combined the roles of being an independent person with that of a devoted wife, without losing herself in either. She has remained throughout the marriage his touchstone, a person of independent views, who, as one friend who has always known them put it, is his 'reality check'.[1]

Difficult Start

Cherie Booth was born in Bury, an old textile town on the northern outskirts of Manchester on 23 September 1954. Her father, as is well known, is the actor, Tony Booth, who became a household name in the 1960s as the angry young man in the television comedy series *Till Death Us Do Part*. Hard-drinking, a philanderer, and self-indulgent, he was often absent and failed to give his daughter the security and affirmation that attentive fathers give their growing daughters. Countless girls who grow up to become confident women have never known fathers in their lives, and too much can be, and has been, made of the negative effect on Cherie of having such an errant father as Tony Booth. But his fathering certainly did not contribute positively to her childhood or development.

Why was Tony Booth such a wayward adult? One searches for clues to his behaviour. If one goes back in his life, following Philip Larkin's famous epigram,[2] does one see a man fucked up by his mum and dad? The answer is 'no': one finds George and Vera Booth, decent types who gave birth to Tony in October 1931 and who reared him in a comfortable if modest terraced house they purchased in Crosby, Liverpool. George suffered an accident in the docks, and was shoddily treated afterwards by his employers, which Tony claimed made him a lifelong socialist. That aside, it was a normal childhood, and after school Tony drifted on to the stage.[3]

Tony married an aspiring actress, Gale Smith, in March 1954, six months before Cherie's birth. For the first few months of Cherie's life, mother and child toured the country following Tony's acting performances around different provincial theatres. It was not much of a life for Gale and Cherie. A succession of affairs, and Gale's second pregnancy, led to a re-think of their itinerant lives, and they decided mother and daughter should settle down with Tony's parents in Crosby, with a promise from him to visit as often as he could. Lyndsey, Cherie's only full sister, was born shortly after in 1956, and the two girls grew up with their mother and paternal grandparents in the terraced house. It was to be Cherie's only childhood home and she still retains fond memories of it.[4] Money from Tony Booth's acting was sparse, and he gave them even less, so Gale had to resort to working in fish and chip shops and other jobs to support her daughters. When Cherie was nine and Lyndsey seven, Tony Booth walked out for ever. As McDougall notes, by this time, he had fathered two more girls, Cherie's half-sisters, by another woman. A further three half-sisters were sired by Booth over the following few years, by another two women.

Security for Cherie and Lyndsey came partly from their grandmother, Vera, but above all from their mother, Gale, a fiercely strong and capable figure who did not let her sadness at being abandoned distract her from giving her daughters as normal and happy a childhood as she could manage. Cherie was a shy, determined young girl, who worked hard at her Catholic primary school and earned a place at Seafield Convent School, a selective grammar run by nuns. So bright was she that she had already been pushed up a year, and arrived at Seafield for the autumn term in

September 1965 aged just ten. In every way, she became a serious convent girl: she worked hard, and her Catholicism deepened. She joined the Labour Party aged sixteen, shortly after joining the sixth form, from which she emerged with four A grades at 'A' level in the summer of 1972. Her degree subject, Law, was chosen in part by her grandmother, and in part by the nuns, who thought it appropriate (after it was clear she would reject their first option, teaching) because of her skill at debating.

The London School of Economics (LSE) was a bold choice. But Cherie was attracted by its fame, then at a high point, and by its outstanding academic reputation. No gap year for her, which meant she caught up in age with the more leisurely pace pursued by Blair. This genuinely working-class girl arrived at LSE in September 1972, with a County Major Scholarship to ease her financial position. Her move from the small protected world of a convent school close to home to a bustling international university in London could not have been starker. She might have been shy, but she was strong, and she coped. Fortified by her academic success and plaudits from her teachers in this new and very different environment, she blossomed. According to fellow student, John Carr: 'She was already a minor celebrity at the LSE by the time I met her. Everyone knew who her father was, a cult figure on the left-wing, and she was ferociously bright. People were in awe of how she did in the first-year exams.'[5] Her performance continued at this high level after her fresher year. With few non-work activities to distract her – the Labour Club was one – she could focus on her law studies.[6] Unlike Blair, she enjoyed academic law. In her Finals in the summer of 1975, she was one of only four students to gain a first, and came top of her year of sixty-one students, with one of the highest marks the LSE law department had awarded in many years. Against the odds, and wholly through her own endeavours, she had emerged by the age of twenty-one as one of the outstanding young law students in the country.

Courtship and Marriage

Cherie could very easily have gone to Oxford in the autumn of 1975 to study for a one-year Bachelor of Civil Law (BCL): part of her always hankered after Oxford. It was tempting. But she opted for the more practical route, to take the one-year course for Bar finals, which would lead more directly to her earning an income. Another scholarship helped ease her path. Fiercely serious and ambitious, she set herself the task of carving through the traditional male domain of the Bar, and emerging one of the top female lawyers in the profession. She set about the task at the Inns of Court in the autumn of 1975 with her customary industry, crowned by her coming top in the country in the Bar finals in the summer of 1976. Quicker off the mark than Tony, she arranged her pupillage, and was delighted to be taken on by the prestigious Irvine, who could not fail but be impressed by her brilliant academic success as well as by her obvious Labour Party zeal.[7] She was subsequently thrown to learn that Irvine had agreed to take a second pupil: one was the norm, and a second pupil would bring her under greater pressure to achieve the tenancy in the chambers when her pupillage ended. As she told CBS *Sixty Minutes* in 1998, in one of her very rare interviews, news of Tony's pupillage 'didn't please me at all, because I had been assured I would be the only one'.[8]

Her courtship with Tony Blair, which began gradually during 1976, has been often retold. Cherie's initial reservations about the public school, upper-crust Tony Blair; the Christmas event where they played party games; the lunch given for them by Irvine at an Italian restaurant and his quiet withdrawal, leaving them both alone together . . .[9] She was a departure for him in one respect: hitherto, his girlfriends had not always been noticeably intellectual.[10] Certainly none had been as sharp as Cherie. He was attracted to her in part, as he put it, 'because she was so different. She's a one-off, unusual and totally her own person.'[11] In all his life, he had never met anyone remotely like her. She also had glamour, as the daughter of a cult, working-class actor. Religious faith was another pull, as was her interest in the Labour Party, a growing interest of his. Cherie was just the kind of young lady his mother, who had died only six months before they first met, would have wanted for her son – steady, serious, strong, as she herself was. Gale, Cherie's mother, felt similarly, saying, with a warmth not all mothers-in-law can match, 'I love him. He's just like a son to me. I don't see him as a politician at all.'[12]

Tony and Cherie both had mothers who were all-important in their lives, and they also had headstrong, charismatic fathers – though in Cherie's case to a far more extreme and undermining extent. Cherie settled Tony emotionally, and he provided her with a stability she had never known from any significant male in all her life. Like her father, this Tony was charming and good-looking – but unlike her father he was also solid and dependable, and her instincts told her what has indeed been the case: that, unlike her father, her husband would never be unfaithful to her, nor let her down. If that experience of errant fathering has inclined her to an over-protectiveness over the years, it is a personality trait that is understandable.

Cherie still took some convincing, which explains the length of their courtship. He would have preferred to have married earlier. It was not only that her mother's experience had taught her to be cautious of men: she and Tony were still not settled in their careers. They were also rivals for a prize tenancy – a job, they believed at the time, for life. It is known that Irvine had high praise for the talents of both his pupils. Which to choose? His dilemma was understandable. They were both outstanding, Cherie for her razor-sharp intellect and glittering academic success; Tony for his polished manner and exceptional presentational skills.

Tony got the nod. Irvine recommended his chambers to take him on over Cherie in part because of his gender, in the opinion of a senior barrister: 'Sexism is not as much of a problem now as it was then.'[13] Irvine later claimed that it was Cherie who pre-empted the choice by looking for chambers elsewhere: not so. She only sought out an alternative tenancy because it was obvious that she was not going to secure one with Irvine, and she didn't want to be left high and dry.[14] Besides, she was a formidable catch, and was duly snapped up by a good set, which shortly after became gilded when it was joined by George Carman QC, who had built a personal reputation as an experienced crime (later libel) advocate but who was to become renowned as a drinker, philanderer and a bit of a chancer.[15] Cherie was happy enough with her tenancy, even if it was not ultimately to prove the right chambers for her. In his lifestyle and his contempt for convention, Carman bore some similarities to her father, Tony Booth.[16]

Tony's and Cherie's professional futures settled, they set off in the summer of 1977 for a two-week holiday together in a rented apartment in Italy. It was to be a make-or-break trip. 'I'd come to the complete conviction in my own mind that this was the person I wanted to marry,' he recalled. 'I was very nervous. Then, quite near the end of the fortnight I suddenly thought: "Right, it's now or never."'[17] She accepted the proposal and, after an unusually long engagement, they were married on 29 March 1980 in the Chapel of St John's College where, just six years before, Tony had been confirmed. Oxford was a natural choice for the wedding: Cherie's mother now lived in the city. St John's Chapel had happy memories for Tony. And it avoided awkward choices about whether they should be married in a Catholic (her) or Anglican (his) church.

Guests at the wedding recall a lovely spring day. Irvine gave Cherie away – Booth was absent, recuperating in hospital from severe burns suffered during a drunken escapade. Not that she let it spoil her day. Tony's father was absent also, but through no fault of his own: he had had a (second) stroke. Cherie and Tony were both unduly proud to have as the father figure for the day, Irvine, who made a short, witty speech, in which he teased Blair for writing for the right-wing *Spectator*.[18] 'They stood out because they were so devoted to each other,' commented the Revd Anthony Phillips, who married them, and who had also presided during Blair's confirmation service. His words here are unsurprising; he was almost bound to comment in this way. But he added that they stood out for being 'so devout in their Christianity'.[19] Their religious commitment and shared moral views have continued to underpin their marriage.

Political Wife, 1980–97

Cherie was not at the outset more left-wing than Tony: as we have seen, he had yet to develop fully his own political thinking. It was a very different experience of life that had led her to subscribe to the Labour Party, forged in a relatively poor and working-class area of Liverpool. With vivid memories of the damage the Militant Tendency had done to Labour in parts of Merseyside, she had no illusions about them and fought to have the faction ousted from the Labour Club at the LSE.[20] Cherie was more focused on practical politics than Tony. From their shared conversations came the impetus for him to develop his political ambitions, first in Hackney and then in his quest for a parliamentary seat. Cherie in her turn was bolstered by the confidence her relationship with Tony gave her, and by the success of her own flowering career at the Bar, and, though still very green, she felt emboldened to start looking for a seat herself.

They operated conspicuously as a team, and were a popular and attractive couple. They joined the Queensbridge branch together, they were elected to the branch General Management Committee together, and they sought seats together in 1981–82. He was the first to be successful in the quest, at Beaconsfield, but she was the first to obtain a seat to fight at the coming General Election. Cherie's perch was Thanet North. A safe Tory seat, but a parliamentary seat nevertheless; and, if she did well, it could lead on to a safe Labour constituency afterwards. With the Beaconsfield by-election over, there was a period of just a few months when her career ran ahead of his. She had a seat to fight, he didn't, and there seemed precious little chance of him finding one before the General Election. Tony would come down to Thanet to support Cherie while she got to know her constituents, but local party officials found him bumptious and intrusive. He was definitely not comfortable in the capacity of 'spouse of candidate'.[21] His worst fears of being left high and dry were confirmed when Mrs Thatcher, flushed by success in the Falklands War, and with an improving economy, announced that the General Election would be held on 9 June 1983. When he did hear eleven days later that he too had a seat, and a safe Labour one, he telephoned Cherie in Thanet. Even between newlyweds and loving couples there can be jealousy. If she felt it, she did not show it. Her chairman in Thanet recalls her leaning on the desk in his office when she took his call. 'When he told her that he had won [the nomination], she let out a great whoop of joy.'[22] Still in the midst of her first parliamentary campaign, the phone call in fact signified that her own political career had come to an abrupt end.

Cherie settled far more comfortably into the role of parliamentarian's spouse than Tony would have done. Their agreement about the one who did not become an MP becoming the family breadwinner notwithstanding, it is almost impossible to imagine Tony happily settling down as Cherie's consort. It is also hard to imagine him being content with life just at the Bar, even if he had become a celebrated lawyer in the mould of Anthony Lester or Michael Mansfield. Had Cherie in fact been offered a winnable seat and entered Parliament, it seems unlikely that their pact would have endured. Far more likely is that he would have entered Parliament too at the earliest opportunity. He had had his eyes opened to the excitement of a life in politics, and there could be no going back.

The ground, anyway, was changing: Cherie was now pregnant, and their first son, Euan, conceived as the General Election campaign was declared, was born in January 1984. If Cherie had pangs about not being elected to Parliament, they were soon submerged in her delight at the prospect of becoming a mother. Both she and Tony determined that they would give their children the normal, stable upbringing which she had conspicuously lacked, and he made it plain that he was going to be more involved with bringing up the children than his own father had been.[23] Nicholas ('Nicky') followed in December 1985 and Kathryn in March 1988. He attended the birth of Euan ('took ages, a day more or less, and had to be induced'), missed Nicholas ('he was early') but was there for Kathryn ('a Caesarean and all over in forty-five minutes').

These were busy years for Cherie. A conscientious and relatively well-organised mother (although 'she is constantly late', according to one friend[24]), she devoted all the attention she could to her legal practice, battling her way through the glass ceiling for women barristers that still existed in the 1980s.[25] She travelled the 250 miles up to Sedgefield many weekends to stay in their second home, Myrobella, a comfortable Victorian house they purchased in 1984, which was and remains their base in Tony's constituency. She had their home in Hackney to run, and she continued with her political interests in the Hackney South constituency and with the Labour Co-ordinating Committee, being elected to the Executive in late 1983 and again in 1984 until she bowed to the inevitable and took a break from her political interests at about the time of Nicky's birth in December 1985.

In one sense, at least, Cherie was the senior partner in these years. While his salary was £20,000 per annum as a backbench MP, she was earning far more at the Bar. He toyed with keeping up work at the Bar, but gradually let it go, sacrificing a course followed by many barrister MPs, who earned substantial sums if they picked their cases carefully. So his pace of life eased after 1983, and he was meticulous about going home early in the evenings to put the children to bed. He did not do this because Cherie insisted he play his part, though she did: he went home when parliamentary life permitted it and looked after the children because he wanted to. He is naturally affectionate with his children: he hugs and kisses them often and calls them names like 'darling' and 'chick'.[26] He is much more 'new man' than his restrained father was to him. That said, it was her income that enabled him to spend the time with the children and paid the mortgages, which became heavier when they moved from Hackney to Islington in 1986. Her money also paid for a succession of nannies, a big feature of their lives, and paid for family holidays in France and Italy, spent typically with Barry Cox and Katie Kay, or with Alan Haworth and Maggie Rae. Bringing up a family and juggling so much in their lives brought its stresses, and they would argue openly. As one friend said, 'They are close enough and secure enough together to have a testy relationship and to fight with each other in the company of others.'[27] These were also immensely happy years for Cherie: she was content and fulfilled, and her essentially easy-going temperament could cope comfortably with the pressures she was under. She was in control.[28] Feeling in control is central to her make-up. Later, she was to lose that ability to be the mistress of her life.

By the late 1980s, Cherie had become disenchanted with life in George Carman's New Court chambers. She had spent much of the time on employment law, plus her share of crime and matrimonial cases, but she now wanted to specialise much more in family law, which was not the speciality of his set, and she felt marooned. While quite brilliant at academic law, she was not seen as filling that potential to the same stellar extent as a practitioner at the Bar.[29] At Irvine's suggestion, she moved over to work in Michael Beloff's chambers in Gray's Inn Square in 1991. Her child-bearing days were over, she thought. Now she would give the Bar her all. She learned to take some hard knocks in the early and mid-1990s. Press intrusion she found very difficult to take, never more so than in a profile by Barbara Amiel in the *Sunday Times* in July 1992.[30] Flattering about her husband, it painted her as prickly, awkward and far more left-wing than she was. The furore over their choice of the London Oratory School for Euan in 1994 was described by a friend as 'the worst thing that had happened to them' up to that point.[31]

Cherie gradually learned to adjust to these new strains and she re-focused her efforts seriously on her legal work. Her career began to take off as a result, and in April 1995 she took silk, the top rank in the Bar and the aim of every barrister, becoming 'Cherie Booth QC' (not Cherie Blair). This meant the world to her, and she was tipped to become a High Court judge, and to be appointed to the House of Lords, on her own merits.[32] Friends noticed how much more relaxed she became after taking silk. The press too spoke about there being 'a carefree confidence about her that would have been unthinkable five years ago . . . She walks these days as though on air.' The increase in self-esteem that resulted from her success at the Bar and the sense it gave her of her own importance as an individual, separate from Tony, were profoundly significant. Comments also began to appear about 'the most celebrated power couple in the country'.[33] Harold Wilson's, Jim Callaghan's, Margaret Thatcher's and John Major's marriages to their spouses had never been discussed in such equal terms. Neither had Cherie ever been written about before as an equal. But just as she was reaching this position of great personal satisfaction and happiness, Tony had moved up the ladder too and was upstaging her again. She was now married to a particularly celebrated Leader of the Opposition.

The Impact of Cherie Blair

Cherie's importance to his personal and political life is clear to see. On a personal level, she glided almost seamlessly into being the core woman in his life with the briefest of gaps following the death of his mother in 1975. She settled him when he was in his early and mid-twenties, and has remained the emotional constant all the way through his life. They are not a couple who have grown tired of each other. Friends tell how, at dinner parties, they are more interested in each other than anyone else, a telling sign. She has remained in love with him: when she announced publicly at her fortieth birthday party in 1994 that she 'loved him', it struck guests as utterly spontaneous and sincere.[34] One aide who works closely with them at Number 10 said, 'They are more in love than any middle-aged couple I know.'[35] She provided him with the family he craved and which has been such a source of happiness and balance for him. Then, in his late forties, when he was beginning to realise the hard knocks of life at Number 10, she gave birth to another child, Leo, born in May 2000, who brought him great solace through difficult times. She kept the news of her pregnancy to herself until she broke it to him at the Labour Party Conference in October 1999. 'He was shocked beyond belief when she told him,' recalls one observer. He told the Queen excitedly about the news. 'Oh, oh, gosh', she is said to have replied. One aide noted, 'He was bowled over with joy at the birth.'[36] Leo gave him the same grounding experience in deep human relationships beyond the world of politics that his three earlier children have given him. Once, in the middle of the 'foot and mouth' crisis in early 2001, he saw Leo in the garden; he left his colleagues in a meeting mid-sentence, went out into the garden, and held him, coming back a changed man.[37] At the height of the Gulf War, it was Leo, it was said, who 'keeps everything in proportion'.[38] That remark could equally have been extended to Cherie's role in his life.

Politically, Cherie crystallised his views, rather than formed them, and she shaped his political ambition, rather than engendered it. She rejoiced in his gaining a parliamentary seat, stood loyally by his side all the way through his rise through the ranks, affirmed his belief that he could make it to the very top, stiffened his resolve to stand as party leader against Gordon Brown in 1994, made his enemies her enemies, and once in Number 10, helped him build allies at home and abroad. She was important in cementing the relationship with the Clintons, through her close friendship with Hillary, and also with Liberal leader, Paddy Ashdown, through her relationship with his wife Jane.[39] She also makes it clear who she does not like, above all Gordon Brown, about whom she can be venomous.[40] As one senior minister explained, 'She shared none of the good memories that Tony had of Gordon. All she ever saw of him was ambition.'[41]

John Rentoul, in the second edition of his biography, highlights Cherie's pivotal role in putting 'iron in his soul' in Blair's decisions over the leadership in 1992 and 1994, and concludes that she has been a key player in his premiership.[42] There is much in this, but one can overstate the position. For all her dislike of Gordon Brown, above all for his disloyalty, he retains his influential position. She was never comfortable with Blair's assistant Anji Hunter, but Anji remained with him for fifteen years until 2001. While Cherie might have shaped his thinking, to some extent, about people, she has barely influenced his policies. The platform he put together for the party leadership in 1994, the changes he introduced in the period leading up to 1997, and his policies as Prime Minister, bear little or no Cherie imprint. She cared far more that he obtained power, and survived all its pressures and onslaughts, than about the detail of the policies he pursued. According to one former minister, she never bustled into his meetings or intruded into policy discussions even when they were taking place in her kitchen or sitting room, as they often did. But she was keen for him to be able to have time on his own to relax and regenerate.[43] This led to some tension with his diary keepers, together with the difficulties when, as she perceived it, the Number 10 machine – under media pressure – tried to close her down and keep her silent.[44] She wanted to be her own woman. For a proud and energetic professional, the almost unimaginable constraints and pressures she was under ultimately proved too much. But that is the subject of another chapter.[45]

Blair in Sedgefield in 1983, thrilled to have acquired a safe seat, presenting a certificate to a constituent for sixty years of membership of the Labour Party. Members of the Sedgefield party were to transform Blair's thinking about Labour's policies.

7

Sedgefield, 1983

For Tony Blair's thirtieth birthday on 6 May 1983, Cherie organised a surprise party. As we have seen, Cherie had secured a seat to fight for the coming General Election, Thanet North, and he had not. Underneath his surface bonhomie on that milestone evening lay a profound and brooding despondency. The Labour Party was looking for good women candidates, and if Cherie put up a good fight in Thanet North, she would be a front-runner for a safe seat that came up after the election. He, in contrast, had no immediate political prospects. The idea of being consort, much though he loved Cherie, filled him with gloom. It was a very bitter-sweet party for him that night.

Just five weeks later, he was Labour MP for Sedgefield, with a cast-iron seat for life ahead of him. It was the most dramatic change in political fortunes of his career until 1994. And it happened against all the odds. A chance set of circumstances coincided to lead him to win the Sedgefield nomination. If he had not procured it at the eleventh hour, he would in all probability have secured a seat later, to be elected to Parliament in the 1987 or 1992 General Elections. That would have been much too late to have made his mark to be the front-runner to succeed John Smith on his death in May 1994. If the Sedgefield Labour Party had not backed him in 1983 he would, in short, never have become Prime Minister in 1997. What happened in Sedgefield in the days and weeks after his thirtieth birthday was to change his life for ever.

A Difficult Year, 1982–83

The euphoria of Beaconsfield gave way to anguish in the months that followed. After all the activity, the cameras, the big names and the focus on him more than ever before in his life, came the void. Tony Blair had committed himself emotionally to giving up the Bar and to a life in politics, and the weekly grind of work as a junior barrister began to pall. The party leadership in Westminster was firmly left-wing, party activists in the country even more so. The SDP–Liberal Alliance was the enemy, and Labour positioned itself firmly to the left of it. Would there be a place in such a party for someone with his profile?

He knew he should have been pleased for Cherie with Thanet North, and he was, but he felt uncomfortable going down to the constituency. At a rally in Margate, Cherie and the local party arranged an event to upstage one organised by the SDP, which had planned a meeting with Roy Jenkins as the keynote speaker. Cherie's event attracted more public interest, and she boasted from the stage of her pride in sharing a platform with the 'two Tonys' who had inspired her in her quest for socialism.[1] One was Tony Booth, her father, and the other . . . Tony Benn. Tony Blair, an unknown figure in the party, could hardly have expected to be on the platform or to be singled out by Cherie; but the irony rankled.

He found himself making more pro-left noises than he believed in, as did Cherie, which helped spawn the idea that she was a serious left-winger, or at least on the centre-left of the party. On both their parts it was sheer opportunism: she, like him, was highly ambitious, and she, like him, sang the tune of the day, though from her mouth the song was less discordant. In the run-up to the 1997 General Election, her utterances from this time were pored over by the right-wing press in an attempt to show that in her past she had been an extremist. In desperation rather than commitment, he even joined the Campaign for Nuclear Disarmament (CND). He was not comfortable about such tokenism, but felt that if he were ever to make progress in the party and find another seat, such genuflections were required.[2] All the time he was getting angrier at what he saw as the party's hijacking by the left. But as yet he had no alternative to offer.

To make matters worse, his journalism career, which had flowered earlier with articles in the *Spectator* and *New Statesman*, appeared to be stalling. Editors felt that, beyond angles on some legal issues, notably employment law and civil liberties, he did not have much that was fresh to say, and they thought his writing style rather ordinary. He penned periodic pieces for other outlets, including the *Guardian* and *Labour Weekly*, but was disappointed not to be able to do more to keep his name in the public eye and not to be more in demand as a pundit.

One bright episode in his wilderness year was his trip with Cherie in August 1982 to Australia. Blair had kept up with Geoff Gallop, who had returned to Oxford in 1977 after an absence of three years. After studying for a doctorate at St John's, Gallop moved on to Nuffield, a postgraduate college in Oxford, where he was elected a research fellow. He kept in touch with Blair, enticing him to come up to Nuffield to give a lecture on trade union law, which Blair had made a specialism.[3] Gallop and his wife also saw a great deal of Cherie's mother, Gale, now living in east Oxford, and they celebrated two Christmases with her. When Gallop returned to Australia in 1981, to take up a post at Murdoch University, he invited Tony and Cherie to visit. They were only too pleased, and stayed with the Gallops in Perth, where Tony delivered the first major statement in his life outlining his own thinking. There followed a holiday on Rottnest Island, off the Western Australian coast, before they flew over to the other side of the country where they stayed with Peter Thomson at Timbertop.[4]

Blair's lecture, delivered to Gallop's weekly seminar group, offers a shrewd analysis of Labour's predicament, buttressed by carefully judged references to the political science literature of the day. The reasons for the failure of the left-wing in Britain, he said, were its viability to appeal to the working-class voter, its slavish adherence to Marxist thinking at a time when communism in Eastern Europe looked increasingly discredited, and chronic division. He was more confident on diagnosis than prognosis. But he did offer important pointers to what he thought Labour's strategy should be in the future: an appeal to all 'sections' in Britain, including those living in the south-east, and the young; 'one-member-one-vote' democracy, with genuine party members rooted in their local community, rather than the Bennite vision of 'political activist democracy' as enshrined at the Wembley Conference in 1981; and a willingness to listen to voters and to be pragmatic (which he said the left regarded as a 'dirty' word) and to connect with the aspirations of ordinary voters.

Labour must appeal, he said, to the lower-middle- to middle-income people who were attracted to the SDP because it offered 'some compromise between the callousness of Mrs Thatcher and the old-fashioned collectiveness of Labour . . . Labour needs these middle-ground voters to be sure of defeating the Tories.' And what should those policies be? Tellingly, he does not say, but he does suggest that the party must look to its political philosophy and visions, 'something more sensitive, more visionary, in a word more modern, than Marxism'.[5]

This paper is enlightening about Blair's thinking for the analysis it offers of what had gone wrong for Labour, and what the party needed to do to find its way back to power. It differs little from what he was saying and doing ten year later. The hole is its failure to espouse positive policies (though he did suggest, disingenuously, and ludicrously, that 'Labour can achieve this [middle-ground] support without altering its policies at all'.) He is more convincing when saying what he is *against*: he warns against the party continuing to support re-nationalisation without compensation, and barring the sale of council houses. There is much more Gallop (political analysis) than Thomson (Christian socialism philosophy) in the speech. One could speculate why he does not propound middle-ground policies and say he did not want to offend Gallop, who had sobered but was still on the far left. He might not have wanted to risk saying anything that, if reported back home, would make him sound like an SDP member, which would have been death to his chances of finding a Labour seat. But the real reason he did not articulate the centrist policies the logic of his argument was leading him towards was because he had not yet worked them through in his mind.

Once back in the northern hemisphere, life returned to being much more prosaic. He continued to extend his relations with trade unions, and became a TGWU delegate on the Hackney South General Committee. He lost no opportunity to represent trade unionists on redundancy cases, and famously won a claim of unfair dismissal against British Steel on behalf of thirty Birmingham steelworkers. He milked Irvine and the practice for all the cases where he could work with or represent the Labour Party or unions. But it did not seem to be getting him anywhere.[6] He became so disillusioned with London that he discussed with Cherie whether they should move up to the north of England after her Thanet election was over. He made enquiries of his father's old chambers in Newcastle. He could enter politics in the north-east area, work his way up through being a councillor – he had despaired of finding a council seat in Hackney after his rejection – and find a parliamentary seat in the region, a part of the world he had always liked. Meanwhile, he and Cherie would work in chambers in Newcastle.[7] He became quite reconciled to bidding London farewell and to the new future ahead of them. Change was indeed to come, but in a way neither he nor anyone else envisaged.

Serendipity in Sedgefield

Blair's eleventh-hour acquisition of the safe seat at Sedgefield has been often told, and told well.[8] Ironically, it was the old Labour politics machine backfiring that gave him his opportunity. Blair had heard several months before that a new seat would be created in the county of Durham, which immediately interested him given his affection for the city of Durham, where he grew up.[9] But after the initial euphoria, months passed and he heard no more about it.

Then, in March 1983, he suddenly received some exciting news. Not only had a seat been created in Sedgefield, next door to the Durham City constituency, but it had yet to select a Labour candidate.[10] He immediately went up to the north-east to campaign in a by-election in Darlington at the end of March and to have a sniff around. The initial intelligence was disappointing. A phone call to the Secretary of the constituency party produced a brush-off: tired of calls from a stream of hopefuls, he was told there would be 'no information given out until the formal selection began', and that was still a few weeks away. It looked as if Ernie Armstrong, another County Durham MP, was lining up his daughter, Hilary, for the new seat. The greater challenge was to come from the hard-left MP, Les Huckfield, who was eyeing the seat because he feared for his own, Nuneaton in the Midlands, due to boundary changes. It did not look encouraging.

In early May, the Sedgefield Labour Party at last began its selection procedures. Without particular expectations, Blair put in for it. He had first to be nominated to go before the General Committee for final selection, and so he made use of a contact he had made with Giles Radice, MP for Chester-le-Street and a leading Labour Party figure in the north-east. Radice, who had been impressed by Blair at a dinner in Hackney with John Lloyd in March, thought Blair could make use of his TGWU credentials.[11] Traditionally on the right of the Labour movement in the north-east, the TGWU had already spurned Huckfield's advances to seek its nomination.[12] On Radice's recommendation, Joe Mills, head of the TGWU's Northern Region, helped secure Blair the union's nomination. It would not be enough though: the TGWU was affiliated to very few branches in the constituency. If Blair was also able to find a branch to nominate him, he would not have to rely on the single thread of the TGWU nomination. In the following few days, Blair phoned around all the branches and was repeatedly told they already had their nominee in place. He discovered that there was only one branch left in the constituency, Trimdon, which had yet to put forward a nomination.

On 9 May, Mrs Thatcher called the General Election for 9 June. This news gave sudden urgency to the deliberations of the Sedgefield Labour Party; it was now the last Labour constituency in the country to select a candidate.

The Trimdon branch Secretary, John Burton, was growing weary of all the phone calls he was receiving from hopefuls. But there was something in particular about Blair's voice which caught his attention when he spoke to him on Tuesday 10 May, and he invited him round to his house the following evening: the branch had already interviewed the other aspirants, including Ben Pimlott from Hackney.[13] Blair knew little about what to expect when he turned up at Burton's house that evening. What he did find was a group of four or five young men from the local Labour branch engrossed in a European football match on television.[14] Blair accepted the *status quo*, waited until the game was over, then pitched himself in just the right way, speaking about his views and answering their questions. What particularly struck home was what he said about power in the party residing in unrepresentative groups in 'smoke-filled rooms', and how the party needed to be opened up to a larger membership. This was his hobby horse, forged by his experience of London Labour activists, and given a full outing in his Australian lecture, and it played well in Trimdon too.

What won them over most, however, was not his views but his manner. 'We quickly realised that here was someone who was different to a lot of people in the party at the time,' recalled one activist. 'His warmth and his charisma and his personality shone through right away. We were quite taken by him.'[15] Blair told them he realised that he would be sacrificing a big, 'possibly six-figure' salary at the Bar to become an MP, and, yes, he did realise how little MPs earned, and, yes, he did realise Labour might be out of power for a long time. Burton's endorsement was to be all important: 'My first impression was that he was obviously intelligent, a pleasant personality, young, good-looking. There was something about him that said to me "I can trust him".'[16] After Blair left at about 11 p.m., they discussed what they thought of him. They liked him, but thought that Burton himself would be a better and safer nominee from Trimdon. Burton had been tempted, but to put himself forward would ignite local rivalries. Selflessly, he declared: 'You're never a prophet in your own land . . . I think we should give Blair our support.'[17] The others then rallied behind Blair, who they thought better by far than any other candidate they had met over the previous few days. Paul Trippett, one of those present, summed up their feelings that evening. 'There he was, charismatic, good-looking, easy to get on with, articulate, about our age. How on earth could we not gravitate to someone like that?'[18]

Four of the five present in Burton's house that night were to become Blair's key team, not just in the fraught few days that lay ahead, but over the following months and years: apart from Burton himself, there were the three 'Ps', Peter Brookes, Paul Trippett and Phil Wilson.[19] With their backing and canvassing, others in the branch rapidly fell in behind Blair. Critically for Blair, the then branch Chairman, George Terrans, with Burton's encouragement, also fell in behind Blair. Terrans was not only Chairman of the Trimdon branch, he was Chairman of the entire Sedgefield Labour Party and of its General Committee, and a big political figure in the constituency and in the north-east. Blair was duly nominated by the Trimdon branch on Saturday 14 May, winning by twelve votes to three. 'I suppose we hadn't realised just how many links and contacts we had between us locally,' said Peter Brookes.[20]

Blair was far from home. The next battle, and it was to prove a far more difficult one, was winning the backing of the Executive Committee of the Sedgefield Labour Party. Here his Trimdon friends' persuasive skills counted for little, as the Executive Committee was dominated by the left and the powerful Trades Council. Its principal task was to draw up the shortlist. For some days, the Executive Committee had been receiving names from branches of their nominated candidate, almost all of whom were better known than Blair, and indeed the favourite, Les Huckfield. They included Joel Barnett, the former Cabinet Minister; Hilary Armstrong, Ernest's daughter; Reg Race, the Labour MP; and Sid Weighell, recently retired General Secretary of the National Union of Railwaymen.

By the time the list closed, it included sixteen nominations. The Executive Committee met on Monday 16 May and rejected ten names. Out went big names like Barnett and Weighell. The list was chosen, Burton felt, with one express design, to favour Huckfield's chance of being selected. Blair's name was not there. That should have been the end of it, but there was one final opportunity to have his name inserted on the shortlist. A meeting of the larger General Committee, which contained a broader cross-section of the constituency party, with proportionally fewer trade union and party activist members, was to be held on Thursday 19 May, to ratify the shortlist selection. Burton was furious at the naked favouritism, as he saw it, of the Executive Committee, which told its members to vote against making any additions to the shortlist. The General Committee meeting is often a formality, as the Executive Committee's judgement is usually accepted on the composition of shortlists. Could Burton still add Blair's name? All the sixteen candidates were read out at the General Committee, where some eighty voting delegates were in attendance. When it came to Blair's name, Burton jumped to his feet and waved a piece of paper, shouting out, 'I've got a letter from Michael Foot saying he wants him in the House as soon as possible.' Critically, Terrans was in the chair, and he allowed Burton to make his point. The 'letter' was in fact merely a standard 'thank you' letter that Foot sent Labour candidates after by-elections, and which Blair had kept after Beaconsfield. But Burton made it sound like a personal endorsement from the party leader, backing Blair as the future star the Parliamentary Party badly needed to have in the House, which was transparently not the case.[21] Burton was not certain his intervention would carry the day, but he had no further tricks to pull.

Blair was waiting for the verdict in the Red Lion pub in Trimdon with his loyal backers, who had by now all become desperate to see their man win through. Cherie was in the midst of fighting her own seat in Kent and, unusually for their marriage, Blair had to endure the tension that Thursday evening alone. There were no mobile phones back then to get the news through early: they had to wait. Burton, ever one with a sense of drama, burst into the pub door, looking glum. 'They only added one name to the shortlist,' he said. 'And that was Tony Blair.' Wild jubilation broke out. They still talk today about Burton's arrival at the Red Lion as the key moment in the whole selection drama.[22] Just one vote out of eighty had decided it and when one of the Executive Committee protested at Blair's inclusion on the shortlist, Terrans from the chair dismissed the point. The Executive's wish to exclude all additions from the shortlist was thus thwarted. By a margin of just one vote (42 to 41) on that Thursday evening, Blair's candidacy was still alive. Had that one vote gone the other way, had Burton not spoken as he did, had Terrans not been in the chair, Blair would not have been added. He would never have become the Sedgefield MP, and his whole political life would not have unfolded as it did.

One final hurdle remained: to win the selection against the other six candidates. The General Committee was the body charged with making the decision. As Sedgefield was such a safe Labour seat, whoever they chose would effectively become the MP on 9 June. The decisive selection meeting of the General Committee was to be held on the night following the cliff-hanging meeting, Friday 20 May, in Spennymoor Town Hall at 7 p.m.

Before the meeting, Blair drove to Durham Cathedral to pray. The cathedral was the religious building that had always meant the most to him. Before major events in his life, he had invariably tried to pray. The selection meeting was now all down to him. Securing the nomination from Trimdon, and having his name placed on the shortlist at the eleventh hour, was largely due to the work of others. This speech was to be the biggest political test of his career. He had to stand up in front of all the delegates, and talk for ten minutes. Being a southerner did not help, but he managed to avoid the perception that he was a carpetbagger, which was how Huckfield had begun to appear to some, with a groundswell growing against him and against the Trades Council for acting as if he had secured the seat already.[23]

Blair spoke with passion and conviction, talking without notes about his family roots in the north-east, and what he would bring the constituency – though no record of what he actually said seems to exist. He may have lost some ground by mentioning Europe positively in the speech (there was great sensitivity about losing jobs in the north-east to the continent) but overall his presentation was thought to have won him far more support than it lost. When it came to questions his supporters again came to his aid. Burton planted questions with friendly delegates devised by his team to put Huckfield on the spot. Terrans in the chair helpfully called them from the floor. Burton still has one of the planted questions which he wrote on the back of an envelope: 'Don't you think, Mr Huckfield, it counts strongly against you that you deserted Nuneaton when it became a marginal, allowing the opposition parties to say Labour couldn't win because the sitting MP had defected?' This was politics in the raw. Blair had seen it in Hackney and elsewhere being used by the left to advance their cause: now it was running in his favour. Three of the questions Burton had in store to embarrass Huckfield came from none other than Moss Evans, General Secretary of the TGWU. The union didn't want Huckfield because of his 'connections' with Militant Tendency, and one of the questions probed his connections with the faction in Birmingham. Huckfield lost his temper and responded that he had no connections with Militant in Birmingham. But the delegates were left thinking, as one put it, 'Holy shit, maybe there's something in this.'[24]

After the speeches, the first round of voting saw Blair win with 39 votes compared to Huckfield's 27, in second place. By the fifth round, just Blair and Huckfield were left in the race. Delegates were left in the air, lacking confirmation for some time who had won. All Terrans announced was, 'We've got a new MP: let's give him our congratulations.' All seven candidates were brought up on to the stage and it gradually emerged that Blair had won it over Huckfield by a margin of 73 to 46 votes.[25]

The news failed to make much impact on the national stage because the General Election was in full swing, having just finished the second full week of campaigning. Labour was also in the middle of tearing itself apart over its policy on defence. Some of the senior figures in the party, however, noticed the selection: Denis Healey, the deputy leader, was convinced that it was the unions who had fixed it for Blair.[26] Others single out the Fire Brigades Union as swinging it for Blair, which is unlikely as their candidate, Bill Griffin (once described by former FBU General Secretary Ken Cameron as 'an absolute head-case'), secured only nine votes on the first round, insufficient to have been decisive.[27] The vote seems to have been won for him not by the unions, still less by the left, who voted for Huckfield: the message Blair took away was that it was won by the votes of the ordinary delegates. It was a powerful message for him.

There were just nineteen days left to polling day, on 9 June. Blair's election address had to be hastily put together. It advocated withdrawal from the EEC (contradicting what he had said at the election meeting), nationalisation, scrapping Britain's nuclear weapons, reversing council house sales and other left-wing policies in line with the party's election manifesto. Much has been made of the address, on top of his left-wing statements at the Beaconsfield election, to suggest either he was genuinely left-wing at the time (which he wasn't) or that he was a hypocrite. There is more substance in this hypocrisy point. But it is not a serious charge, as he was following the party line and did not want to provoke controversy, least of all mid-campaign in his first parliamentary election. Roy Hattersley, nevertheless, is one of those to hold the purist line: 'I don't buy this "he had to conform" business. It never occurred to me as an aspiring candidate to pretend to believe things I didn't believe in. It's the only way to behave if you want to have any self-respect.'[28]

Practicalities now took centre-stage. Blair had nowhere to live so moved in with the Burtons for the campaign. After all the political machinations came the pageantry. For the constituency, the highlight was the visit of Tony Booth and his partner Pat Phoenix (whom he married on her deathbed), adored in the north for her playing of Elsie Tanner in *Coronation Street*: Blair had mentioned them both in the curriculum vitae he presented to secure the nomination, and, like Cherie, he was set on using them as much as he could. 'Our Elsie wows the voters down the street' was the headline to a gushing report of her visit in the local newspaper the *Northern Echo*.[29] Booth's and Phoenix's support helped win the unknown Blair fame and popularity in the constituency in what everyone viewed largely as a coronation, with the SDP and Conservative challenge of little serious interest. Blair, however, refused to believe he would win until the result was announced.

Blair grew increasingly apprehensive as polling day approached. At the count, 'He was dead nervous, he was a wreck.'[30] At one point a local headmaster and Labour councillor took Blair aside to offer him a whisky.[31] His anxiety was heightened by the polling boxes from the few middle-class Tory districts in the constituency being the first to be counted. He saw vote upon vote going on the Conservative piles. His supporters reassured him, largely in vain, that the balance would change as soon as the boxes from the safe Labour areas were opened. There were indeed to be no surprises that election night, at least not for the Blair family. Cherie secured 6,482 votes in Thanet North, coming third behind the Conservatives and SDP, which obtained over 12,000 votes – many of which would have gone to her. Two hundred and fifty miles to the north, in Sedgefield, the SDP candidate came third with just over 10,000 votes, the Conservatives came second with around 13,000 and A. C. L. Blair was the clear victor with 21,401 votes.

The clouds that surrounded him for a year had been blown away in the most conclusive and sudden fashion. Blair had his seat, and in the very part of Britain to which he felt the strongest attachment. He also had a constituency party and a new ally in Burton, who would powerfully shape his thinking about the future of the Labour Party.

*Blair with John Burton, father figure and mentor throughout his
parliamentary life. The ease in their physical proximity suggests
the intimacy of their relationship.*

8

John Burton

Photographs taken that night in Sedgefield on 9 June 1983 reveal an elderly, bespectacled figure, slightly stooping, with moist eyes. What thoughts must have been going through Leo Blair's mind that evening? Here was his son achieving the very ambition he had sought for himself until his stroke nineteen years before. Leo was moved, and intensely proud of his son for achieving this pinnacle, and on the very same stomping grounds where he had once envisaged his own parliamentary career being launched.

It was to be John Burton, however, rather than Leo, who was to become Blair's father figure in the north. 'I'm very proud of him. He's almost like a son,' said Burton of Blair.[1] 'John is very, very close,' said Nick Ryden, one of Blair's oldest friends. 'John is like a father figure to Tony.'[2] 'On the day he won the leadership I was in tears all day. I thought I had helped him achieve this': Burton's words burst with a parental pride.[3] Their relationship indeed mixed elements of a father–son relationship with that of a school teacher and pupil, with Burton the mentor – perhaps not surprisingly, given that Burton spent most of his career teaching in schools.

John Burton, a busy, energetic man, with a big moustache and growling voice, was born in Trimdon village in 1939. He trained as a teacher, rising to become Head of the Physical Education Department at Sedgefield Comprehensive School. He became a local councillor in 1976 and Secretary of the Trimdon branch of the Sedgefield constituency when it was reformed for the 1983 General Election. He remained in teaching until 1994, when he gave it up aged fifty-four to become full-time agent in the constituency: when Blair became party leader he needed to have someone he could trust running the constituency full-time. Married with two children, Burton is a keen sportsman and footballer (he scored seventy goals for Stockton in one season) with an avuncular, optimistic manner, and was a perfect companion to Blair. They had much in common, including Christianity, the importance of family, enjoyment in playing sport and music, and central to both of them, a Monty Pythonesque sense of humour and outlook on the world.

Burton and Sedgefield

Burton is the personification of Sedgefield. He remembers growing up in the austere post-war years with children running around with no shoes on their feet. To understand Burton one has to understand Sedgefield. Mining was the life-blood of the area: 'You left school and you got a job down the mine,' said Burton, recalling his youth. 'If you were fortunate,' he added, 'you got an apprenticeship [for skilled work] down the mine.'[4] The powerbase in the community was the National Union of Mineworkers (NUM), which chose the Labour MP in Sedgefield as in all other County Durham constituencies. Communal life was strong, with working-men's and other clubs and pubs being the centres of life. The mining industry, which had faltered in the intervening years, went into steep decline after the Second World War as demand for coal fell. But the galas and strong communal traditions survived. Blair remembers being moved by them when he was a young boy in Durham in the early 1960s.[5]

In Burton, one can hear distant echoes and reverberations of Thomson: 'People here are sensible, hard-working, and their politics have been formed over the years by their way of life,' said Burton. 'Their socialism was the way they lived: helping neighbours.' Rolling down off the hills up in the north-east of England is a neighbourly vision of community which is a cousin of Thomson's vision formed on the other side of the world.

The heart of the constituency were the mining villages whose pits were closed in the 1960s and 1970s, which, together with pay disputes, sparked the miners' strike of 1971–72: feelings of loss and abandonment were still raw in the early 1980s when Blair became MP. The villages, some of which date back to the tenth century, included the 'Trimdons' (Trimdon Grange, Trimdon Colliery and Trimdon Village itself, where Burton was raised), West Cornforth and Ferryhill. The villages are a mix of Industrial Revolution terraced cottages and new council houses, separated by hills and green countryside. Sedgefield village, a market town since the fourteenth century, looks as if it could be in the Cotswolds. Spennymoor, where Blair's selection took place, is the one industrial town in the constituency, to be replaced by Newton Aycliffe, a similar town, in the 1995 boundary revision. The constituency was to enjoy an industrial revival in the 1990s, with Fujitsu and other companies putting up plants in Newton Aycliffe, and factory workers making up half the workforce. But in 1983 it was a community in the midst of a long and painful transition into an uncertain future.[6]

Burton was actively keen to find someone to represent the constituency not as it was, but as he thought it should be in the future if it was to survive and prosper. Trade union and old Labour candidates represented the past. In Blair, he saw someone young and energetic who articulated, however sketchily, ideas for the future. Blair's thinking about mass party membership, in contrast to caucuses of the left, was music to his ears. Burton's biographer, Keith Proud, puts it clearly: 'John was already talking about the need for a new Labour Party before Tony Blair arrived on his doorstep in 1983. When they met there was a remarkable synthesis of views and values.'[7] Together with Blair, Burton and the Trimdon team set out to create nothing less than a mass membership party in Sedgefield. When the constituency was re-created for the 1983 General Election, the party had only about 400 members. 'Even back then, Tony Blair was saying that if we wanted to reflect the views of ordinary men and women, we just had to broaden the party,' Burton recalled.[8] 'We have to do something about membership: we've got to do it from the bottom up,' Blair indeed said at the time. He knew mass membership was not only the way to defeat the hard left in the party and the unions in Sedgefield; more importantly he wanted the party to reflect the pluralist, communitarian society he aspired to create in the constituency.[9]

Blair, Burton and fellow party workers battled hard in the 1980s to increase membership at a time when the national party under first Foot and then Kinnock was still unpopular. In their room in the House of Commons, Blair and Gordon Brown spoke about it at length and Brown produced a pamphlet for *Tribune* on increasing membership just before the 1987 General Election. By the end of the 1980s, Blair was saying, 'If I'm going to change the Labour Party, I've got to prove what I mean by doing it in my own backyard. If I can't do that we can't win.'[10] Disappointed in the early 1990s with the rate of increase in membership, he charged Phil Wilson, who worked full-time in the constituency office until 1994, to devise new methods, including one-member-one-vote for all key decisions. Numbers edged up to 1,200 by 1991[11] and in 1993 they introduced a new scheme which allowed members to pay as little as £1 per year for belonging to the party (with the hefty balance being raised through innovative fund-raising schemes) rather than the standard £15, which was then the full fee per member paid to Labour's national headquarters. Within two years, membership had risen to 2,000, some four times the average in Labour constituencies. Sedgefield moved into the limelight.[12] In 1994, Blair said, 'I see the Labour Party here as the model of what the Labour Party [nationally] should be. It's a big party, with roots in every part of the community. It's one of the things I'm proudest of in my political career.'[13] His leadership bid that summer was based in part on highlighting the virtues of mass membership, linked to internal party democracy and the extolling of Sedgefield as a beacon for the way ahead.[14] More emphatically, Phil Wilson claims, 'I think Sedgefield helped shape the modern Labour Party. I think New Labour started in 1983 in Trimdon.'[15]

Wilson is partly right. What Burton and Sedgefield gave Blair was an education not only in the traditional Labour Party, but also in the mentality and aspirations of the working class. As Blair never tired of saying, the working classes of Sedgefield are utterly different from, and have no time for, hard-left political agitators with their Marxist policies. What they are interested in is a secure job, social justice, and economic stability. In its attitude to crime and criminals, Labour had traditionally shown little obvious empathy for the victims of crime: the focus was very much on the evils in society which spawned crime, and, in London in particular, the Labour-controlled authorities regarded the police with deep suspicion. But what Blair was hearing in his Sedgefield constituency in the 1980s was much more about the damage that crime was causing individuals, families and businesses.

If community, informed by Peter Thomson, was the first plank in his credo, and direct democracy channelled through political machines was his second, a tough line on crime and personal responsibility was gradually emerging as a third plank. Blair acknowledged that the uncompromising policies he articulated as Shadow Home Secretary had their origins in his experiences in Sedgefield. His constituents, as he put it, 'don't believe that you can ever allow the identification of causes of crime to become an excuse for not having an effective justice system'.[16] Or, as Phil Wilson put it more bluntly to journalist Beatrix Campbell: 'Tony Blair knew from Sedgefield that law and order was a working-class issue.'[17] With all these influences, one can understand why Blair said of Sedgefield: 'It's the centre of my political life.'[18] The deep grounding he found, and finds, in the constituency can be heard in what he said to a party meeting at a time of acute international pressure in 2002: 'Every time I come here I feel a weight come off me . . . I feel I regain my own fundamentals, what I am trying to do and what I believe in. You have no idea of the support, succour and help you give me.'[19] The words were of course chosen to flatter a local party that had seen little of him of late, but they also came from deep inside him. Blair might not love the Labour Party, but he loves the Labour Party of his homeland.

In other ways, Burton's influence on Blair has been more personal. Blair's friends and observers have high praise for him. 'John Burton is a working-class auto-didact. Tony is fantastically lucky to have come across such a person as John Burton,' says journalist Martin Kettle.[20] 'John is very shrewd. He wouldn't have let just anyone into Sedgefield,' says Nick Ryden. 'He had a strong sense he was on to a real winner in Tony – John has made an enormous difference to Tony.'[21] When the *Mirror* pressed Blair in 1996 on who he turned to in a crisis, the one name he volunteered was John Burton.[22] 'I trust his political judgement almost more than anyone else,' he said.[23] Hidden largely from the public gaze, Blair places Burton's judgement on common-sense issues on a par with that of Alastair Campbell, Anji Hunter and Peter Mandelson.[24] Periodically, Blair seeks broader opinions in Sedgefield and consults others in the group, especially Wilson, Brookes and Trippett. But Burton's is the voice he most wants to hear.

By the time the 1983 General Election campaign was over, Burton and Blair had forged a close bond. As Blair drove back from the count in his brown Mini Metro, he said to Burton, 'I just want to say this to you John, and I'll only say it once. I can never thank you enough for what you have done for me.'[25] It was not long before he needed Burton's support and affirmation again. The hard left, furious about being thwarted over Huckfield, sought revenge. Their opportunity came in an open meeting they organised in Spennymoor Trades Council. Blair has always believed in his ability to sway even hostile audiences, and agreed to speak on a platform with the left-wing MP Dennis Skinner, renowned for his sharp tongue. Blair spoke first but the audience was not with him. He was then rounded on by Skinner, who let rip, accusing him of betraying socialist principles. Blair was made to look, as one attendee recalled, 'like the new boy on the block'.[26] Les Huckfield, who was in the audience, was seen to be vastly enjoying the humiliation of the man who had vanquished him. Burton thought the whole meeting was a put-up job to unnerve Blair as a first step to win the seat back for Huckfield. Blair was hurt, angry and upset with himself for falling into the trap. Burton stopped him blaming himself and pointed his still very inexperienced charge towards the future: 'You mustn't move towards the party,' he said, 'the party must move towards you.'[27] The personal humiliation, though, and the exposure to the brutality of the hard left, were to leave a deep scar on him.[28]

Burton's importance to Blair over the years has indeed been fundamentally one of reassurance that his convictions were right, above all on reform of the Labour Party, and on the policies 'ordinary voters' needed. When Blair was pushing through Clause IV and reforming the Labour Party in the mid-1990s, he said, 'The best advice was from . . . John Burton, a wise and shrewd man. He always said, "Just keep doing what you're doing because people know that it's right."'[29] When Blair was under attack for his choice of school for Euan in the mid-1990s, Burton said just 'press on'.

When the Blairs' children were in their teens, they wanted to spend their weekends with friends in London; foreign demands also dictated that regular weekends in the constituency (as many as three out of four in the 1980s and early 1990s) began to decline. He was acutely conscious of this and his decision to include Sedgefield in President Bush's visit in November 2003, the first State visit by a US President in over eighty years, was in part a signal to his constituency about how highly he valued it. Membership in the constituency had been falling for some years, from its highpoint 2,000 to some 900 in 2003.[30] Reports coming in to Number 10 that Blair was losing touch with 'middle England' coincided with this decline in visits to the constituency, and regular conversations with Burton. Criticisms of his absenteeism and of Cherie, never a favourite in the constituency, began to be heard. The flagship flexible payment membership scheme was quietly ditched after receiving insufficient support from party headquarters.[31] Cracks in Blair's once invincible public stature began to grow, as the mood swung against Labour nationally. But the Sedgefield edifice still stands, buttressed as ever by his allies in the Trimdon Labour Club. Of everyone he has ever met in the Labour Party, there is no one more loyal to him than Burton. When Blair is in his final ditch, it will be Burton, father-figure, mentor, choreographer of his political career, who, together with Wilson, Trippett and Brookes, will be by his side.

Blair speaking to the TUC annual conference. His stance on the closed shop was the first time he stood out and became a figure on the national stage. Indicatively, he was attacking traditional trade union rights.

9

The Closed Shop, 1983–90

Tony Blair arrived in the House of Commons in June 1983, aged thirty and one month, the youngest Labour Member of Parliament. He had made no significant impact on the Labour Party up to that point, either at university or local government, or as a special adviser, speechwriter or on party bodies. Beaconsfield had given him a fleeting exposure, and he was regarded as the very lucky beneficiary of Sedgefield. But he had no standing or base in the Labour Party. He was a blank slate. No one knew what he thought. By 1990, however, he was being spoken of as future leader, with some clear, uncompromising ideas on how to take the party forward. The speed of his advance in these seven years is all the more remarkable given the slow start to his political life and his lack of any deep commitment to any group in the faction-riven party at the time. The seminal event that brought him to the attention of those inside and beyond the Westminster world as a man of substance occurred at the end of the seven years covered by this chapter – the end of Labour's support for the 'closed shop', which had been regarded up to that point as an undeniable right of the trade unions.

Up the Ladder, 1983–89

The House of Commons Blair entered in 1983 saw Labour at a very low ebb. Its share of the national vote had fallen in the General Election to 27.6 per cent, its lowest figure since the election of 1918. The Liberal–SDP Alliance, hot on Labour's heels, secured 25.4 per cent and became widely favoured as a serious challenger to take Labour's place as the principal opposition to the Tories. Labour had only 209 MPs, many of them distinctly unimpressive. Mrs Thatcher was dominant, and not even at the height of her power, and led a party largely united around her. Labour, in contrast, had become increasingly fractured under Michael Foot's leadership (1980–83), and was split between supporters of Tony Benn and the 'Campaign Group' on the left and Roy Hattersley and John Smith backed by the 'Solidarity Group' on the right, with the centre-left 'Tribune Group', Neil Kinnock's political base, located somewhere in between.

One of the first challenges for the party, which it set about even before the election results were known, was to elect a new leader to replace the amiable but obviously unsuitable Michael Foot. Four candidates immediately put themselves up for election: Eric Heffer on the left; Peter Shore, the anti-EEC candidate, on the centre-left; Neil Kinnock, the choice of Foot, on the centre-left; and Roy Hattersley, on the centre-right wing. Blair went to listen to all the different candidates, reminding one colleague of 'being an Oxford undergraduate at a "societies fair", travelling round to see what was on offer'.[1] And so he was, testing the water, being seen and meeting people. Blair chose to support Kinnock, the front-runner, who was joined by Hattersley for deputy leader – the so-called 'dream ticket'. Blair's choice was a statement of his centrist beliefs as well as a shrewd calculation about backing a winner, and being seen to do so.

From the outset, Blair was seen as highly ambitious. Politics was now his life. The Bar was all but over. Apart from his family – Euan was born in January 1984 – he had no outside interests or distractions. According to Charles Falconer, he had far more time on his hands when he entered Parliament than he had ever had at the Bar.[2] He could now focus single-mindedly. He took every opportunity to meet people of influence in the party and to help them if he could. He listened intently to the way the political winds were blowing. Tom Sawyer, then a senior official with the trade union NUPE, recalled him as 'unusually ambitious. He looked for people with influence in the party. I am sure I was one of a long stream of people who got a call from his office: "Would I like to come and have a cup of tea with Tony?" So I did. I saw him in public-school mode, middle- to upper-class, not someone born to Labour but obviously someone who had made a choice. He was all rather "gosh, golly".'[3] So upper-crust indeed was he that Tory grandee Edward du Cann stopped him in the corridor and had a long conversation with him before realising he was not one of their new Conservative intake.[4] Blair never tried to dress or talk down. 'This was the time when in the Labour Party you had to take your tie off, or wear your shirt with the top button undone,' said Peter Kellner. 'He never did. He always looked smart. He never tried to disguise who he was.'[5]

Nineteen eighty-three proved an ideal year for an ambitious MP to join the Parliamentary Labour Party.[6] Every party has its golden years for new members – the Conservatives in 1950, Labour in 1997. But it is much better for an ambitious MP to join in a poor intake. Only thirty-two Labour MPs joined the House in 1983. Gordon Brown, Clare Short, Tony Banks and Chris Smith were some of the ablest, as were Derek Fatchett and Sean Hughes, future front-bench stars who both died early.[7] But overall the influx of fresh blood did little to refresh a Parliamentary Labour Party with less talent than at any time since 1945.

Blair elected in 1985 to join the Tribune Group, the centre-left group.[8] But this was in part a guise. 'He played the part of someone on the left mainstream of the party. But he was never ideologically of the left. He was never properly committed to our camp,' recalled a senior Tribune member.[9] Blair's core beliefs were not the received party doctrines, nor were they influenced by Labour's great canon of approved thinkers but ones he himself had thought through, namely community and party democracy. However, he made little progress in developing either strand. A draft proposal for a pamphlet on 'community' was rejected by the Fabian Society[10] – attempts to trace it proved abortive – while his efforts to convince the party as a whole of the benefits of mass membership were viewed by some as impertinent and naïve.[11] His maiden speech on 6 July 1983, into which he put considerable effort, was banal, and contrasted tellingly with Gordon Brown's more impressive first performance on the floor of the House.

Blair's impatience with the failure of Labour to engage with the electorate and to respond to its aspirations was clear from the start. After the euphoria of victory in 1983 and the initial excitement of being an MP wore off, he began to worry that he might be doomed to a long period in the vacuum of opposition in a party that was asleep. 'I think a real sea-change in Tony's attitude to things [came] after 1983,' said Falconer. 'In the period after the 1983 election [he] became aware that here was a party that could not begin to cope with what was happening politically.'[12] This belief came across in his first television appearance, just after the 1983 election: BBC's *Newsnight* interviewed some of the new intake of Labour MPs in a Westminster pub. 'The image of the Labour Party has got to be more dynamic, more modern,' opined the young Blair. 'Over 50 per cent of the population are owner-occupiers – that means a change in attitude that we've got to catch up to.'[13]

This is the authentic Blair, but one heard too little of it in public over the next few years, in part because he was not yet sure enough of himself and what he should say, but also because front-bench duties from 1984 precluded him talking outside his narrow portfolio. Roy Hattersley, then Labour's deputy leader, formed the impression that 'he had no lodestar to guide him because he hadn't thought about politics very much until right at the beginning of his political career'.[14] Instead, one hears a histrionic tone, the language of a young man eager to please who doesn't yet know what he thinks. Blair was fiercely critical of Tory policy to restrict trade union powers, labelling the 1984 Trade Union Bill 'a scandalous and undemocratic measure'. This is a reprise of Blair, the young barrister in Irvine's chambers, fighting employment cases on behalf of the unions rather than an indication of where his thinking was going.[15] On the miners' strike of 1984–85, he was notably restrained and in step with Kinnock's stance.

As Blair matured politically, he acquired insight and knowledge of Labour's workings principally at the feet of his roommate, Gordon Brown. When Blair first arrived at Westminster he shared an office with MP Dave Nellist, who was later expelled from the party for his support for Militant. Much has been made of this odd couple: was it a perverse joke to put together two such diverse MPs?[16] There were reports of animosity between them and clashes over politics. Nellist contests this. 'There was no bad feeling. We didn't have time to form any real relationship.' What about the political gulf? 'He certainly didn't appear a moderniser at that time,' Nellist retorts.[17] Blair quickly moved out of this tiny windowless room into a marginally larger windowless room with Gordon Brown. Brown simply was everything Blair wasn't. While Blair had been nothing much at Oxford, Brown had finished as Rector of Edinburgh University; while Blair struggled to have articles and pamphlets published, Brown had already written or edited three books on Scottish policy and devolution, and had been a current affairs editor on television; where Blair had failed to make a significant mark anywhere in the Labour Party, Brown had been Chairman of the Scottish Labour Party. Blair had several acquaintances in high places; Brown had senior friends in the party. Brown had no family and worked flat-out and obsessively; Blair wanted to get home in the evening to be with his young family, and worked moderately hard and unobsessively. Brown knew where he was going. Blair, as yet, did not.[18] For all that – indeed, because of all that – they became the closest of allies. Blair was, as Falconer put it, 'mammothly dazzled by Brown's power'.[19] Blair realised that, of everyone he had so far met in politics, it was Brown who would give him the most.

Blair's various patrons may not have regarded him as of the same quality as Brown, but they liked his freshness and intelligence. Neil Kinnock, as party leader, was clearly the figure on whose decisions Blair's rise most depended. John Smith had become acquainted with Blair through Irvine before he entered Parliament, was impressed, and selected Blair (and Brown) to serve on the committee to examine the Trade Union Bill in 1983–84.[20] Roy Hattersley had observed Blair's performance at the Beaconsfield and Sedgefield elections, thought he was 'brilliant', despite having 'no idea' of his politics. He recounts a revealing conversation with Michael Foot, who said, '"Good young lad, Blair," and I said, "Yes, he's on my wing of the party." "No, he's not," said Michael. "I've had a long conversation with him. He's on the left of the party."'[21] Blair was to become the first of the 1983 intake to be offered a front-bench job and one shadowing the most powerful government department, the Treasury. (Brown is said to have turned down a job at this same time, though Kinnock denies he offered him one.)[22] Blair was delighted to accept. 'He was literally overwhelmed with thanks,' Kinnock recalls. 'He was so nervous when he came in to my room. It was quite touching. He left with a smile the width of his face.'[23]

Blair owed his first preferment in large measure to Hattersley: 'Roy did everything he could to promote Tony,' recalled a close observer,[24] although they were later to grow apart. The Kinnock–Hattersley combination may have succeeded in bridging divisions within the party, but the two men never worked very closely together. Hattersley thought Kinnock might fall during the 1984–85 miners' strike, and again when he failed to impress during the Westland crisis in January 1986 when Mrs Thatcher was on the ropes. Had Kinnock fallen, Hattersley was the obvious successor, and his influence was never quite the same after Kinnock weathered the storm. With MPs falling to some extent into either the Kinnock camp or the Hattersley camp, Blair knew that identifying too closely with the latter could damage his prospects of further promotion.[25] Blair was nevertheless fortunate to have Hattersley as a mentor. Although promoted to the shadow Treasury team, Blair had never studied economics; nor did he then, as now, have any natural feel for its technicalities. Hattersley was no economic specialist, but he knew more than Blair and shared his knowledge freely: 'Roy was a powerful tutor to Tony into the world of economics and finance,' said a close aide at the time.[26]

Already Blair was thinking outside the established way of doing things. In 1984, through a mutual friend, he had met Arnab Banerji, then at the investment bank Schroeders. Banerji, who had been in the Labour

Party in his student days, had let his membership lapse in protest at the party's economic policy. When Banerji met Blair, he explained his points of disagreement. Instead of responding by parroting the party line, Blair decided that he wanted to hear more. A few weeks later, the two began to meet regularly to discuss economics. 'He thought that not enough time and attention had been given to the issue of wealth creation,' recalled Banerji, who echoed this critique of Labour Party policy.[27] Documents discovered in the Labour Party's archives in Manchester show that, from early 1985, to supplement his tutorials from Banerji, Blair hit upon the idea of establishing an 'economic advisory group'. The membership included economists such as Alan Hughes and Ken Coutts from Cambridge University as well as John Eatwell, Kinnock's economic adviser. In his inaugural letter to the group, in March, Blair was candid about the problems that had prompted him to act: 'I have found two constraints since becoming a front-bencher on economic affairs.' 'First, we just don't have the reserves of back-up and expertise; and secondly, there are very few forums where MPs can gather, test out, and exchange ideas about economic policy and gain the confidence that is vital in a parliamentary debate.'[28] Revealingly, Blair went on to highlight the 'fragmented' nature of the economic debate in the Labour Party and suggested that he was keen to explore new ground: 'People are happy enough talking about how bad unemployment is and its social effects, but not about how we obtain growth in the economy.'[29] This was one of the challenges he set for the new group.

Blair acted as chairman for the series of meetings that followed in 1985 and 1986. Held in the Commons or sometimes at a college in Cambridge, Blair allowed the experts to lead detailed economic discussions, beginning with a paper on the relationship between macro- and micro-economics. Titles for subsequent discussions included 'Protection and Devaluation' and 'Industrial Policy Issues'.[30] For Tony Blair, listening to and then testing out his ideas with these prominent economists proved invaluable. He was learning all the time. As he developed a solid grounding in contemporary economic issues, so his confidence grew.

Hattersley described Blair as one of the two most outstanding sub-ordinates he ever had.[31] Backed by his growing economic knowledge, Blair was able to capitalise on his barrister's training to master his briefs, and to understand complex legislation. He managed to sound convincing enough for MPs on both sides of the House to notice this new well-spoken MP, admiring his polished manner and his obvious intelligence. Nigel Lawson, Chancellor of the Exchequer, was one of those who respected his ability, but saw through him. Privately, Lawson's verdict was, 'I don't think he's a socialist.'[32] Some enemies were made on the way up the ladder. One Labour front-bencher found him 'overly ambitious and resentful of any competition, especially competition from women. You got the impression that he did not think a woman should have the nerve to compete with him. And you just didn't feel he wanted to be a team player – he would hog whatever media opportunity came up, cherry-picking the best for himself.'[33]

Blair's growing reputation was reflected in his being asked to appear on BBC's *Question Time* in May 1985, a big opportunity for someone who had only just celebrated his thirty-second birthday. In the mid-1980s he also began to meet a tight-knit group who, with Brown, were to become his closest allies. The National Executive Committee (NEC), on the basis of Kinnock's proposal, appointed Peter Mandelson as the Labour Party's Director of Communications in October 1985. Mandelson was arguably the first to spot and exploit Blair's media appeal. Labour-friendly journalist Alastair Campbell, who was very close to Kinnock, was another he met at this time. He also had his first fleeting glimpse of Philip Gould, the pollster and election guru who was to shape his thinking, though did not get to know him well until later. In June 1986, he drafted Anji Hunter, whom he had known since his teenage years, into his office. Initially she joined only for the summer, but she became full-time from June 1987, having obtained a first in the degree she had taken as a mature student.[34] These five – Brown, Mandelson, Campbell, Gould and Hunter – would, in very different ways, prove indispensible to Blair's rapid rise and political career. Having met remarkably few political soulmates in his first thirty years, he now met in the space of just four years those he would rely on most heavily on the road to Number 10 and beyond.

Blair was challenged and excited by these new figures who began to come into his life. But he was still prone to the periodic despondency he had experienced in 1982–83, exacerbated now by loss of sleep, with his second child Nicky born in December 1985, and Kathryn on her way. To close friends he would confide that he did not feel his career or the party were making the progress he had hoped for, and he had thoughts of looking elsewhere.[35] Part of this reaction was a psychological safety valve: it has always been important to him – he says it often enough – to remind himself that his life is about much more than politics. But he also feared in material and personal terms that the career he had chosen might for him, in contrast to his contemporaries, be a blind alley. He was passionate about making rapid progress, and took reversals badly.

The June 1987 General Election, the first he fought as a sitting MP, saw the Tories under Thatcher riding high. He thus viewed the election less with excitement than with trepidation. Blair was greatly distressed when his one high-profile foray into the national campaign, an attack on Mrs Thatcher at a news conference for having 'an unchecked and unbalanced mind', was seen, despite Mandelson's efforts to play it down, as an error of judgement. The main consolation for Blair in the election was his personal majority rising by nearly 5,000 to over 13,000 in Sedgefield. For the party as a whole it was another grim night. The national share of the vote increased to just 31.5 per cent, the second worst result (after 1983) for over fifty years, and Mrs Thatcher was returned to power with a majority of 102.

The defeat made him even hungrier for radical change. Less than two weeks after election day, in an important article in the *Guardian* headlined, 'Picking up the pieces: how to become the people's party once more', Blair called for a drive to boost party membership accompanied by a 'broad sweep of new ideas and thinking'.[36] He also became more focused on his own advance. Colleagues noted a change in his relations with parliamentary colleagues. From 1983 to 1987 he had been personable, always, but slightly detached – superior, even, some thought. After 1987 he began assiduously to court friends. His praise of the maiden speeches of new members who joined in 1987, as discerned by the journalist Andy McSmith, illustrates this new zeal: John Reid, he said, had made a 'witty, brilliant speech', Rhodri Morgan's was 'absolutely superb', Bruce Grocott, his future Parliamentary Private Secretary, was 'excellent', while Calum MacDonald was nothing less than 'fascinating'. Anji Hunter proved a most adept ally in his quest to build up new friends. To continue their advance in the party, Blair – and Brown – were both told by Kinnock that they should also run for the Shadow Cabinet and the NEC and Kinnock began to work actively for both of them, using his authority as leader to garner support. 'I remember Gordon was always keener on the NEC than Tony, partly because Gordon had always been more of a party man than Tony,' Kinnock recalled.[37] Running for election to the Shadow Cabinet obviously ran the risk of defeat and possibly humiliation, but the prize of being placed in the top fifteen and gaining a front-bench role could not be ducked if further advances were to be made.

Even with Kinnock's support Blair still had much work to do. Somewhat nervously, and after seeking reassurance from colleagues that he would not make a fool of himself, he put his name forward in the summer of 1987. He did well, especially for a first attempt and after only four years in the House, and was placed seventeenth with 71 votes (Brown, who was elected, received 83 votes). Kinnock promoted him to City and Consumer Affairs spokesman, number two on the shadow Trade and Industry (DTI) team. After nearly three years, he was therefore no longer working for Hattersley. 'I paired him up with Bryan Gould because they were both very smart guys,' Kinnock said, 'working in an area of industry and the City where we needed to make serious progress.'[38] Kinnock saw more of him now than before, and they would travel around the country together meeting businessmen, in a regular series of seminars organised by Kinnock's office, to give reassurance and win friends. His well-spoken, smartly dressed young companion, he thought, did the job 'very nicely'.[39]

Blair's first significant success in his new DTI post came in an obscure case in the summer of 1988. Blair knew that to earn the respect of both sides of the House of Commons one had to be commanding speaking at the Despatch Box.[40] Bryan Gould, who was a generous boss to him, allowed Blair to take the lead on behalf of a group of pensioners who had lost their life savings with an investment group, Barlow Clowes. Labour's angle was that the government had failed to regulate the group adequately and had given bad advice to the pensioners about their investment. Blair put huge energy into the case, which came at the end of a long summer session when the government's guard was down, and he sensed he could make a killing. 'We stayed up all hours trying to get the figures to work out,' recalled Phil Wilson, who worked in Blair's office at the time.[41] With his mastery of argument and arcane detail, Blair struck with deadly effect. His performance was described as 'excellent' in the *Guardian*, and in glowing terms in the financial press.[42] One of his new close circle made a particular impact advising him during the Barlow Clowes debate. 'I remember that I said: "Do not go over the top. Be reasoned. Don't become hysterical. Be factual, precise and lethal" . . . I remember him just looking: "I'm going to learn from him. I am going to lock into this person."'[43] This person was Peter Mandelson, who was delighted by how responsive his new pupil proved to be. The advice worked. Bryan Gould was in no doubt that Barlow Clowes was 'the issue which made Blair's name'.[44]

Blair's performance may have woken up the Westminster village to his talents but not the nation at large. That would come. Immediate payback came in the shadow Cabinet elections in November 1988, when he shot up from seventeenth to ninth, with 111 votes. Gordon Brown retained his lead over him, topping the poll for the first time with 155 votes. There was no stopping Brown, who had stepped faultlessly into

John Smith's shoes as shadow Chancellor when the latter had a heart attack in October 1988. Blair himself now qualified for a place in the shadow Cabinet, a considerable achievement after just five and a half years in the House. Kinnock had earmarked him for shadow Employment, to utilise his specialist knowledge of employment law possessed by few others on the Labour side, and in an area in which Kinnock was anxious to see more progress towards modern practices and standards. But at the last minute he switched him to Energy because the privatisation of electricity had just been announced in the Queen's Speech that November. This would be a major Bill and he thought Blair's knowledge of the City would help him land some blows on a flagship government policy.[45] To John Prescott's chagrin, he was moved out of the Energy post after just one year, a further sign of the high confidence Blair had inspired in Kinnock – and an indication of Kinnock's view of Prescott.

Blair rose to the challenge. Mrs Thatcher had put her favourite, Cecil Parkinson, back in Cabinet in 1987 charged with this major item of legislation: both party leaders had thus put up their champions, the old trooper against the young turk. Although it was always inevitable, given the size of the government's majority, that Parkinson would win the votes, it was Blair who carried away the honours. His success was due again to his mastery of detail, his debating skills and a growing skill at parliamentary tactics. His contacts in business and in the City proved helpful. From them he received much insider advice which he used to devastating effect against a surprised Parkinson. But he also deployed two fresh weapons. He had built up a coterie of good contacts in the press, including Alastair Campbell, Patrick Wintour and Peter Riddell, to whom he gave exclusives and stories (here again one sees Mandelson's influence): according to Rhodri Morgan, his junior shadow at Energy, 'the media community covering Parliament now began to take him very seriously indeed'.[46] There are parallels with John Major's rise on the other side of the House: like Blair, he too had built up good press contacts during this period. Blair secondly made use of a tactic Brown had been exploiting since he first came into Parliament, namely leaks of sensitive and embarrassing material to the government from Labour-friendly civil servants. It disarmed Parkinson on several occasions. The Conservative side of the House had rarely seen a Labour spokesman give such an effective performance, and they were scared.[47]

For Blair the process of embarrassing the Tory government, and doing well for himself, was more important than the actual substance under debate. He possessed none of the visceral hatred of privatisation of those on the left of his party. What did he truly think about ownership of industry aside from the point-scoring? Was he against privatisation or not? Deep down, and as yet not articulated by him in public, he was coming to accept that a regulated free market economy – as opposed to state control – should be the way ahead for Labour. That state ownership was not the panacea. But he kept such views hidden. A revealing illustration of the contortions in his thinking at this stage came when he was selected as one of four front-bench spokesmen to appear in a party political broadcast for television. When filming his profile, he was asked why had he joined the party. An eminently reasonable and easy question. But he was so rambling that his comments had to be edited out.[48] Perhaps he did not want to think too much – at least in the open – about the substance of what he was debating so skilfully in Parliament. The hour demanded just that he try to pummel the Tories over privatisation, and he threw himself into the task with relish and without pity.

In the Limelight, 1989–90

For all his success since the 1987 election, Blair was still only a coming man. Brown's triumphant stewardship of the shadow Chancellorship, while John Smith recovered from his first heart attack until the spring of 1989, easily eclipsed Blair's achievements. Brown was the stronger performer on television and in the House and, more to the point, the public had some idea what he stood for.

It was at this stage that Blair emerged from the chrysalis of the Westminster village. When he did so, it was not carefully planned. It looked to the world outside like a brilliantly conceived piece of strategy. In reality, it was a piece of bravado: a high-wire act that he feared could end his career. In the autumn 1989 shadow Cabinet elections, and on the back of his performance against Parkinson, Blair moved up from ninth to fourth place in the polls (behind Gordon Brown, John Smith and Robin Cook). Kinnock saw this as the moment to appoint Blair shadow Employment Secretary, replacing Michael Meacher, whom he felt had gone as far as he would in reforming industrial relations policy. Some union leaders were also irritated by Meacher, and wanted a minister with a fresh approach.[49] On his appointment, Kinnock gave Blair wide licence: 'If anyone asks, "Are you speaking for Kinnock?" you should answer "Yes". Then, if you are not sure whether I'm with you on anything that you are doing, come and see me and I'll make it abundantly clear to anyone that I am behind you.'[50] Few shadow Ministers are given *carte blanche* to this degree, but Kinnock wanted to move further and faster on reforming the party's industrial relations than many people realised at the time. Again, Blair was his man to carry out his wishes, but this time there were no ideological gymnastics for Blair – he believed in what he was doing.

Blair saw his task at Employment as 'neutralising the negatives' in the electorate's minds associated with over-mighty trade unions and union bosses, the focus of so many damaging folk memories and so skilfully played on by the Tories since the 'winter of discontent' in 1978–79. Blair's class background, which had earlier been useful in reassuring the business community and City, was again seen as a positive factor, rendering him less likely to 'go native' with the union bosses, and less likely also that 'the brothers' would want to claim him as one of their own.[51]

Blair realised the scale of the challenge, and consulted the best industrial relations authorities including a young post-doctoral student, Jon Cruddas, who was to help him considerably over the coming months.[52] Blair rapidly realised the major opportunity the post offered him to move the party far forward in an area of great historic and emotional importance to the whole Labour movement. His own lack of emotional ties with the party, not for the last time, allowed him to take steps a more conventional Labour politician might have baulked at. Undisturbed by what he had said in 1983–84 about the state having no right to interfere in union affairs, he was now ready to jettison all sacred cows, including even the party's deep-rooted support for closed shops, the arrangement whereby trade unions insisted that all employees in a firm or plant joined a union. If successful, he would change the relationship between the unions and the Labour Party irreversibly, and move it on from the mire of the trade union–party dispute which had dogged the party for twenty years. If he failed, he could ruin his career, or so arouse the unions' ire against him as to damage his whole standing and credibility. He realised that finding the right springboard would be crucial.

His opportunity came the month after his appointment to Employment. On 29 November the House of Commons was debating the European Union's Social Charter, just a week after Parliament began to be televised. Labour's front bench were keen to embrace the Charter, partly because it gave positive rights to workers, but also to show that it was Labour, not the Tories (who had under Heath taken Britain into the EEC in 1972), who were now the true party of Europe. Blair was needling the government for its failure to embrace the Charter when he was interrupted by Tory MP Timothy Raison, who asked for Blair's response to the Social Charter guaranteeing an individual's right *not* to belong to a trade union.[53] Blair fudged an answer but was in a dilemma. The Tories sensed they had Labour on the run. Blair knew that a new Employment Bill was about to be brought forward quickly by Norman Fowler in the Commons, and that the government would taunt Labour relentlessly until it said, unequivocally, what its position was on the closed shop in the light of its support of the Social Charter. Blair's mind worked overtime and he suddenly saw a way out of the impasse.

Tony Bevins, the sympathetic journalist then on the *Independent*, led the press questioning – in collusion with Blair's office – about what exactly Labour's policy was on the closed shop in the context of the Social Charter.[54] This was useful because it forced Labour to make up its mind early on, and Blair's mind was already reaching a conclusion. Blair, working in close contact with Peter Mandelson, who encouraged him to be bold, decided he would challenge the unions to take him on[55] and say that it was the closed shop that had to be rejected rather than Labour's support for the Social Charter. Early on, he took his conclusion to Kinnock and the deputy leader, Hattersley – more as a courtesy, telling them what he wanted to do, rather than seeking their permission.[56] Next call was on John Monks, Deputy General Secretary of the TUC, who was becoming increasingly influential and close to the leadership. 'In Blair's own mind, the Social Charter had to win out because it was looking forward, not looking back,' recalled Monks. 'I told him I agreed with him, and suggested who he should see in the unions to get the key people on side.'[57]

Over the next week, Blair made a frantic round of calls to the union bosses including Ron Todd, Bill Morris, John Edmonds and Brenda Dean, the last being particularly sensitive as her union, SOGAT, representing print workers, was still reliant on a closed shop. Some bosses he saw several times. His pitch was the same: Labour had to decide between the Social Charter, which had benefits for working people, or the closed shop, and there was next to no time to take the decision. Most leaders were sympathetic to the dilemma the party was in, and felt that they would have to bow to the inevitable. Not all were impressed, however, by the argument or by the tactics he employed. 'He challenged us to disagree with him,' recalled John Edmonds. 'I think he could have got what he wanted by discussion and by negotiation rather than by this pre-emptive strike. The result was a substantial legacy of mistrust.'[58] Blair did not consult Labour's General Secretary, Larry

Whitty, nor the NEC (a body of which he was still not a member) nor the NGA print union, all of whom were angry when they heard about his plans in which they had not been involved.[59]

By 6 December, just one week after the Tories' ambush in the Commons, Blair was ready to announce that Labour accepted the Social Charter 'in its entirety', a fairly heavy hint of what was coming. On 12 December, he went further, commenting to the *Financial Times* that Labour would not 'pick and choose' from the Charter. For the *coup de théâtre*, he chose to deliver his unequivocal statement in his constituency. On Sunday, 17 December, he gave the key speech to the Sedgefield Labour Party (on which he was advised by none other than Brenda Dean) spelling out Labour's abandonment of the closed shop.[60] It was the biggest move of his career to date, and Blair was exhausted and highly wrought. One aide recalled the long hours Blair spent in his office in the Commons, regularly consulting Mandelson, Campbell and Brown in particular, and going over and over the speech as he worried about what it might do to his future career prospects.[61] Peter Mandelson and Labour press officer Colin Byrne briefed the media heavily over the next twenty-four hours. Media management was critical, and it proved extraordinarily effective. Dropping the commitment to the closed shop became a major national, and indeed international, news story. The *Guardian*, for example, opened its report: 'Thousands of Labour members will have been surprised to learn from their newspapers, yesterday morning, that their party is no longer in favour of the closed shop,' and it concluded, 'A rigid insistence on total union membership offends against both civil rights and the temper of the times. Mr Blair is right to say it ought to be jettisoned.'[62]

A backlash was perhaps inevitable. Blair (and Kinnock) had to endure some anger and muttering from union leaders and from the NEC. One of the NEC members wrote a formal letter to the party's General Secretary to complain that Blair had abrogated the authority of the NEC to determine the content of party policy.[63] John Prescott was irritated that Blair had not got the unions fully behind the policy before he announced it, though he supported Blair's decision in the shadow Cabinet.[64] Overall, however, the applause from the party far outweighed any negativity. The union bosses continued to splutter for much of 1990 and beyond, with much of the venom directed personally at Blair. One of Kinnock's aides thought 'they behaved appallingly, because privately they all acknowledged the closed shop was history. Being hounded by the union leaders and listening to all that bullshit for that year was a formative exercise for him.'[65] The TUC, impressed by a speech by Jacques Delors, President of the EC, was becoming much warmer and less fearful of the European agenda all the time, which helped reduce criticism of Blair's decision on the closed shop. The issue was eventually put to bed at the Trade Union and Labour conferences in the autumn of 1990, when, after a lot of coalition-building and arm-twisting behind closed doors, union bosses agreed to back the proposals.[66] But Blair's relations with union leaders overall never recovered.

Blair's handling of the closed shop issue was very much his own – he had called for Kinnock's support only twice in the whole process. Charles Clarke, who had become Kinnock's Chief of Staff, admits that, tactically, 'Tony moved faster than I think Neil might have done.'[67] Blair had been braver than Kinnock would have dared to be, but when his gamble paid off, Blair went up significantly in Kinnock's eyes.[68] The minutes of the meeting of the Labour Parliamentary Committee on 20 December 1989 record Hattersley's view also that 'Tony Blair had carried off an almost brilliant coup'. Reflecting years later, Hattersley felt that 'this was the second thing after his selection [at Sedgefield] which demonstrated his steel'.[69]

Blair took other important decisions as shadow Employment Secretary between 1989 and 1992, notably his support for the minimum wage, but none of these decisions were anywhere near as crucial as his struggle over the closed shop. David Aaronovitch articulated a growing view when he said, 'This was the moment I realised he was going to be leader.'[70] No one seriously thought of him in that way before 1989. It was the closed shop that marked him out. Why did he suddenly emerge at this point as a trenchant fighter, prepared to take huge risks and tackle head-on the almost inviolable trade union leaders? With Barlow Clowes and electricity privatisation, his task had been much easier because his argument had been against the Tories. The confidence he took from those earlier successes was important, as was the inspiration he gained from the network of advisers now coalescing around him: the advice he already received from Irvine was re-doubled by his interactions with Brown and Mandelson and later with Campbell and Gould. The key to the closed shop, though, is that Blair did not fully have his heart in the issues he had fought before. Now, at last, he had found an issue – the rights of the individual worker against over-mighty trade unions – on which he could articulate his own voice.

Blair and Kinnock after the second electoral landslide in 2001. Kinnock's face is like a setting sun slipping down behind the horizon. His obvious delight in their embrace does not seem shared to the same extent by Blair.

10

Neil Kinnock

Captain Stanhope's closest relationship in R. C. Sheriff's play *Journey's End* is with Lieutenant Osborne, an older man and a schoolteacher in civilian life, whom he calls 'uncle'. Osborne watches over his young and rapidly promoted friend, until towards the end of the play he dies in a raid, leaving Stanhope to fight on alone. The analogy can be pushed too far, but it reveals something of the personalities, and also captures something of the relationship between Blair, who played the part of Stanhope at school in Scotland, and Kinnock who played Osborne at his school in Wales.[1]

On paper, Kinnock might not have been the most promising figure for Blair to have served under in his early years in Parliament. Clement Attlee or Harold Wilson might have been more likely to respond positively to someone from his background, and Hugh Gaitskell or Jim Callaghan more likely from the first to have seen him as a political ally. Why did Kinnock, still identified with the left of the party in the early 1980s, warm to Blair so readily?

Kinnock's Early Life

Kinnock's background could not have been more different to Blair's. Born to a coal-mining father in Tredegar, south Wales in 1942, and educated in state schools, he joined the Labour Party aged fifteen. He entered Parliament in 1970, supported the miners' strike of 1972–73 and was elected to the NEC in 1978. Something of a back-bench rebel in the dying days of Callaghan's minority administration, Kinnock declined several offers to join the government, but did agree to join the Opposition front

bench as shadow Education spokesman after Mrs Thatcher's victory in
1979. When Callaghan stood down in October 1980, it was Kinnock
who, despite early doubts about his suitability, crucially backed Michael
Foot, then sixty-seven, to stand for leader. During his three-year reign,
Kinnock detached himself from the hard left, urging fellow left-wing MPs
not to support Tony Benn, who was trying to unseat Denis Healey for
deputy leader in October 1981. Healey just survived, and Kinnock
increasingly became identified as a principal bulwark in the battle against
the hard left. His succession to Foot as party leader after the 1983 General
Election defeat was a popular choice, achieved that October with a 71 per
cent vote. Kinnock thus set out on his leadership role at the same point
Blair launched his career in Parliament.

Kinnock's nine-year spell saved the party from the disaster to which it
had been heading under Foot. He saw the party climb from 209 MPs in
1983 to 271 in 1992; he saw off the challenge from the Alliance and he
did much to modernise the party to prepare it for office. His first major
act as leader was to reverse Labour's policy of withdrawing from the
European Community. Second, he repositioned Labour into accepting the
free market system, i.e., capitalism, rather than advocating the opposite, i.e.,
state socialism. A third change was the ousting of extremism from the
party: first he marginalised Militant, memorably achieved in his annual
Party Conference speech in Bournemouth in 1985. The next day, in an
even more courageous speech, which Blair recalled as a seminal moment
(and indeed one that might have been in the back of his mind when
reforming Clause IV), he attacked the trade union equivalent of Militant,
Scargillism, named after Arthur Scargill, leader of the NUM, who had
spearheaded the year-long miners' strike of 1984–85.[2] In 1986 he also
attempted to change Labour's policy of unilateral nuclear disarmament,
though it took until 1989 to achieve it. This was a formidable body of
work, mostly achieved before Blair had become even a middle-ranking
shadow minister in June 1987, and before he was senior enough to play
any significant part in it.

After the 1987 election, Kinnock set up a series of policy reviews to try
to maintain his drive for reform and make the party electable. Blair only
became involved, albeit pivotally, in the fifth and final Kinnock change,
ending Labour's support for closed shops. Kinnock has always believed
that the miners' strike in 1984–85 cost his leadership a year, and critically
slowed the reformist momentum he had been eager to advance. He had
certainly wanted to tackle such issues as the party's policy on trade union
relations, including the shibboleth of the closed shop, earlier. Had he done
so, Blair would not have been senior enough to have been the figure who

executed the policy. The closed shop success aside, however, the 1987–92 Parliament was less creative for Kinnock, and the reviews failed to drive policy forward as he had hoped, losing him the confidence of his shadow Cabinet colleagues in the process. Kinnock himself did not therefore oversee the two final major pieces of modernisation of the party, 'one member, one vote' (OMOV) and the reforms to Clause IV, although he supported both changes. OMOV was introduced in 1993 under John Smith's leadership, but had been proposed unsuccessfully at conference back in 1984 by Kinnock; the replacement of Clause IV was achieved by Blair in 1994–95, but found support from Kinnock in a TV essay in early 1994.[3]

Kinnock relied on a close-knit team centred on his office. Charles Clarke, his political secretary until the 1987 General Election, when he became Chief of Staff, was the key figure in the whole 1983–92 period underpinning Kinnock, marshalling all the events and delivering Kinnock's modernisation strategy.[4] Peter Mandelson, who became Director of Communications in October 1985, was principal architect of the re-launch of Labour's image and its media relations. He was valued highly by Kinnock, although in December 1989 the latter was frustrated that Mandelson found a seat to fight in the 1992 General Election, and could not bring his skills to bear as he had done in previous elections. Patricia Hewitt was his press adviser from 1983 to 1988, before becoming policy co-ordinator and then departing as a founding member of the IPPR think-tank in 1989. From the IPPR she continued to advise Kinnock on policy on an *ad hoc* basis right up to the 1992 election. Kinnock's principal source of economic advice from 1985 to 1992 was John Eatwell, the academic and writer.

Kinnock was selective in his use of shadow Cabinet ministers, and never felt that he could trust them entirely to support his modernising agenda. 'Kinnock relied on key individuals to carry out important tasks in the reform process, if necessary bringing in fresh blood to keep the momentum going,' said Martin Westlake, Kinnock's biographer. 'By a combination of threats, persuasion and sheer application, Kinnock sought to integrate Labour into the mainstream.' [5] Healey stayed on as shadow Foreign Secretary until his retirement in 1987, but was no longer the creative force he once was. His successor, Gerald Kaufman, brought fresh vigour and Kinnock relied on him heavily to ease the party towards abandoning demands for unilateral nuclear disarmament and for advice on handling the first Gulf War. Hattersley, despite his shrewd intellect and experience, was less of a force after the mid-1980s, though he combined being deputy with shadow Chancellor until 1987, then shadow Home Secretary. One member of the shadow Cabinet in the 1987–92 Parliament upon whom Kinnock particularly relied was Bryan Gould, because he appreciated Gould's ability to provide answers rather than just identify problems.[6] Kinnock's model of using close advisers for key advice rather than shadow Cabinet/Cabinet colleagues was one which Blair, albeit perhaps subconsciously, was to follow himself as leader.

Kinnock was far more important to Blair than Blair ever was to Kinnock. Hattersley was Blair's first vital patron. Bryan Gould thinks that it was not until 1985 or 1986 that Kinnock began to view Blair seriously, and they had yet to develop a personal rapport.[7] By 1987, however, Kinnock was personally recommending Blair to Gould as the City spokesman in his DTI team,[8] and was working to have Blair elected a member of his shadow Cabinet.[9] Kinnock joked with Gould when discussing Blair's eagerness for promotion: 'Oh yes, young Tony, *very*, *very* keen!'[10] But it was Kinnock who pushed Blair up the greasy pole, and gave him the challenging jobs that were to make his name. Kinnock, increasingly impressed at Blair's handling of electricity, then the closed shop, grew fond of him by the end of the 1980s. 'I think almost a paternal relationship sprang up between Neil and Tony,' said one colleague who worked closely with both men. 'He became, rapidly, a favourite, someone Neil thought he could rely upon to deliver.'[11] The Kinnock archives at Churchill College, Cambridge are indeed full of evidence about their deepening relationship, as when Kinnock wrote to Blair in April 1990 to help him draft a speech to 'steal the last shreds of the one good idea the Tories have had'.[12] Kinnock, however, claims he never saw the relationship in these terms. He valued Blair and liked the fact that, unlike some of his colleagues, he did not take himself too seriously. He invited Tony and Cherie to dinner a couple of times, but for Kinnock, the idea that the relationship became paternal is palpably absurd.[13]

Kinnock was under great pressure for much of the period from 1987 through to 1992. Labour had only advanced 20 seats in the 1987 General Election, and although the party fought a brilliant campaign in the eyes of many, his strategy since 1983 was blamed by his detractors for the disappointing electoral progress. His office was becoming divisive, and first Hewitt and then Mandelson departed. Some of the blame fell on Kinnock. Some also fell on Clarke, for eschewing the opportunity to embrace Campbell, who would have sharpened Labour in the 1992 election.[14]

In 1988, Benn challenged Kinnock for the party leadership on a hard left-wing agenda. Benn's humiliating defeat, and a strong Labour showing in the June 1989 European elections, beating the Conservatives handsomely, bought Kinnock time. But he suffered from continuous speculation about his leadership. He became periodically tired and depressed, not the least by the criticism: he is a very emotional man with a surprisingly thin skin that has never hardened. Most vituperative among his shadow Cabinet was John Smith, who had a barely concealed contempt for his intellect and grip.[15] After the 1987 General Election the 'mantle of *dauphin*' passed from Hattersley to Smith. Some believe that Smith was pondering a challenge to Kinnock in the autumn of 1988, but if so, he was prevented by his heart attack.[16] Kinnock's team certainly believed that Smith was jostling for power, but after Smith's return to work in early 1989, any thoughts he had of contesting the leadership before a General Election were effectively ended. Smith told Robin Cook in 1990 categorically that he would not challenge Kinnock.[17]

Smith continued, however, to quarrel with Kinnock's leadership, and felt it was undermining his economic policy. The nadir came in January 1992 when Kinnock appeared to be reformulating economic policy during a dinner with journalists at Luigi's, an Italian restaurant in Covent Garden, without consulting Smith.[18] Smith's biographer, Andy McSmith, says the Luigi's episode was the angriest that Smith was ever to be with Kinnock,[19] while according to Martin Westlake, it was the 'last straw' for Smith, whose 'resentment continued to burn throughout the campaign'.[20] Open warfare with briefing and counter-briefing broke out between the rival camps, until the imminence of the General Election brought them to their senses. Kinnock's team were increasingly dismissive of Smith, who they believed had not been supportive on the 'difficult' issues, such as Labour's support for the war in Kuwait in 1991, or earlier over Militant and reforming the relationship with trade unions. The anger of Kinnock's supporters against Smith burst into the open in a letter to the *Guardian* by Colin Byrne, who had resigned as Labour's chief press officer the previous autumn, just after the 1992 election.[21] It later became known that Byrne's letter was written without Kinnock's knowledge and that it had caused him great discomfort.[22]

The Impact of Neil Kinnock

Where did Blair stand in all this? Despite the growing appreciation that Kinnock undoubtedly had for Blair, the feelings were not, at this time, fully reciprocated. Blair's success with the closed shop bolstered his confidence about what he could achieve by himself, and made him restless for change more radical than anything Kinnock was achieving, a feeling Brown fully shared. Jealousies were aroused when Mandelson repeatedly pushed Brown and Blair in the media over more senior figures in the shadow Cabinet.[23] But it seems very unlikely that Blair and Brown plotted to have Kinnock removed before the General Election, as some believe.[24] They were frustrated and irritated with him, but they were not seeking to unseat him. Their frustration was evident in their attitude to shadow Cabinet meetings: 'They didn't always turn up,' recalled a shadow Cabinet colleague. 'It was quite noticeable actually.'[25] Their high-handed attitude raised eyebrows in the leader's office, who felt the real problem lay in Blair and Brown's failure to engage with their colleagues and work to remedy the problems they perceived.[26]

Labour's lead in the Gallup poll peaked at 24 points in March and April 1990. The Conservatives regained their lead from the point Major took over as Prime Minister from Mrs Thatcher that November, although from March, the parties were nearly level in the polls up to the election.[27] Kinnock's personal standing in the country and media was not high, and both Blair and Brown became despondent about the party's prospects. Kinnock himself believed the removal of Thatcher in November 1990 hugely damaged Labour's prospects.[28] Privately Blair was willing to admit to friends and even journalists such as Robert Harris that he did not think the election would be won.[29] However, there was certainly no enthusiasm for precipitating a leadership election when a General Election could be called at any time: it was widely thought that Major would go to the country in the spring or autumn of 1991. And who, anyway, would replace Kinnock? Smith was the obvious successor, but Blair and Brown were having growing reservations about whether he would be an improvement. Their thoughts turned increasingly to the future after the election, to the merits of skipping a generation, and to what they would do if the party were to fall into their hands.[30]

After Kinnock's departure following the April 1992 General Election defeat, Blair's annoyance and irritation with Kinnock rapidly evaporated, but he gradually became disenchanted with the pace of change under his successor, John Smith. Kinnock, Blair and Brown had offices on the same floor in the Commons, and Blair regularly sought Kinnock's perceptions on his new portfolio, the Home Office, and on his own position in the party.[31] Blair's frustration with Smith was not helped by the deep resentment felt by the Kinnock team towards Smith, and the new leader's wholesale clear-out of Kinnock's confidants. Charles Clarke headed off to start his own business, while Peter Mandelson and others such as Colin Byrne and Julie Hall were banished to the wilderness. The foundations of discontent had been laid, and the different forces might well have coalesced into a move against Smith before the next General Election had he not died in May 1994. Kinnock was studiously even-handed between the merits of Brown and Blair in the ensuing leadership question, and then rapidly fell in behind Blair once Brown dropped out. Tellingly, one of the first groups to flood to Blair's office to offer support when Smith died in 1994 was the Kinnock clan, including Clarke and MP Adam Ingram.[32]

Kinnock resigned as an MP in January 1995 to become a European Commissioner, but Blair continued to have regular meetings with him. Kinnock in private was critical of what he thought was the party's emphasis on appearances. The term 'New Labour' was particularly disliked by him: 'What is deemed "new" can become "old",' he was heard to mutter.[33] He was critical of the promise of a referendum on the Euro (and even more of Blair for delaying it).[34] Kinnock's irritations were muted in public because of his determination to stay loyal, having seen the damage done to John Major by the bitter snipings of his predecessor. It also helped that he and Glenys enjoyed a very close friendship with Alastair Campbell and his partner, Fiona Millar.

Blair's respect for Kinnock grew once he was in the leadership himself. Interestingly, when he became embattled, Blair identified more and more with Kinnock. He told Peter Kellner during the Clause IV debate that 'only now am I realising how much Neil achieved and how difficult it was for him'.[35] Kinnock played no public role in the 1997 election campaign. He made it clear well in advance that public campaigning would be considered incompatible with his new post on the European Commission. He knew the Labour Party was 'no longer his show' and was sensitive to doing anything that might be seen as interfering.[36] But he could not eliminate his emotion after nine years of fighting to change the party ended not in victory but in humiliating defeat. When Kinnock paid a visit to party headquarters during the election, Peter Mandelson made a speech, which was followed by cheers and applause from all round. Kinnock was overwhelmed, and unable to hold back the tears.[37]

Once in office, Blair was generous in acknowledging Kinnock's contribution to his success. His highest public praise came during the 1997 Party Conference, when Blair was notably more fulsome towards Kinnock than he had been towards John Smith: 'The mantle of Prime Minister was never his,' he said of Kinnock. 'But I know that without him, it would never have been mine.'[38] They remained fairly close over Blair's premiership years, and Kinnock was again fêted at the 2003 Party Conference.[39] On one level, the Kinnock legacy can be seen in the return to centre-stage of his former aides, Clarke and Hewitt, and also John Reid; while Kinnock's distrust of Mandelson has meant that he lobbied for Mandelson not to be appointed a European Commissioner. From time to time, Blair has solicited Kinnock's view on specific problems. In 1997, for example, Blair shared his concerns about the obvious desire of Ken Livingstone, Kinnock's old nemesis, to become a candidate for the newly proposed elected Mayor of London. As Blair took careful notes, Kinnock stressed that Blair needed to remind the media of Livingstone's political record and build up an image of him as a disloyal publicity-seeker who had done great harm to the party in the past.[40] Kinnock was not pleased by Livingstone's readmittance to the party, but a far more serious issue was the war in Iraq. Kinnock disapproved strongly of Britain's involvement, and Glenys even more so, and he battled very hard with himself to keep his views private.[41]

So what has been the overall 'Kinnock effect' on Blair? Margaret Beckett is unequivocal: 'Neil Kinnock was overwhelmingly the patron of Tony Blair. He was responsible for Tony Blair's promotion.'[42] In one sense this is obviously correct. Kinnock, initially on Hattersley's prompting, gave Blair his first job, and then of his own accord pushed him rapidly upwards, cleverly exploiting his class background rather than being deterred by it, and coming to see him, by 1987–88 as a fellow crusader in his effort to modernise the party. Charles Clarke agrees that Kinnock's patronage was important, but stresses that Blair would have risen quickly under any leader. To Clarke, Kinnock's importance was less as patron and more as political tutor.[43] However, while Blair certainly listened to and watched Kinnock, he reached his own conclusions about what he needed to do. He admired him but was never in awe of him, and always saw his limitations. Blair shaped his own strategy and tactics much more from listening to Brown, Mandelson, Campbell and Gould. Kinnock's ultimate importance to Blair then was his work in reforming the party in the 1980s. Blair would not have put in the graft that Kinnock did, and was not exhausted nor compromised by the in-fighting in the 1980s as Kinnock was. Kinnock's work let Blair stand on his shoulders. But it was Blair who determined what he would do once on those shoulders. And as Kinnock, from his dugout in Brussels, surveyed the actions of his subaltern on the front line, on the whole he took avuncular pride in what he saw.

Clinton's election strategist James Carville in the 'war room' at Little Rock, Arkansas, in November 1992, the month of the presidential election. Bill Clinton's success gave great heart to a demoralised Labour Party, and above all to Blair and Brown. The Clinton and 'New Democrat' influence on them has been all-pervasive.

I I

United States Visits, 1991–93

Tony Blair and Gordon Brown both realised that the Labour Party would not move beyond the stasis that had befallen it without fresh thinking and ideas being injected from outside. If the Labour Party were to rely solely on its own resources and traditions, it was doomed never to advance. Both Blair and Brown had a deep empathy for the United States, which was regarded by the hard left at the time as the arch-capitalist country and the epitome of evil. Influences from the United States were to change Blair's and Brown's thinking, which in turn changed the Labour Party and therefore Britain. The US had never had a socialist party in its two-party system: the UK was ceasing to have one too. If Australia was the first country outside Britain to have been a major influence on Blair, the second and only other country to have had a serious impact on him is the United States. For all his love of France and Italy, neither country, nor their thinkers and politicians, were to shape him to any significant degree.

Early Visits

Blair's early political visits to the US came in 1986.[1] The first was a now well-known three-day stay that June as part of an all-party delegation to Washington to lobby on behalf of the Unified Tax Campaign: the trip (which included flights on Concorde) came to the attention of the media in 1995 when it transpired that Blair had not recorded it in the 'Register of MP's Interests'.[2] Blair was technically in error and suffered some short-term embarrassment. Of much greater interest is the second trip that year, for the whole month of August, which was paid for by the US government and has not come to light before. Blair saw a trip to the United States as a chance to study its economic policies. Such an experience would enhance the contributions he could make to the shadow Treasury team. The US government had different ideas about what they were paying for, and were keen to inculcate this young Labour MP with the benefits of nuclear deterrence and the Strategic Defence Initiative (SDI) at a time when Labour was only just beginning to move away from unilateralism. As journalist Michael Elliott put it rather cynically, 'Blair's trip was one of those "study tours" that are meant to convince you what a Big Country America is.'[3]

The trip began in Washington with heavy briefings at the Pentagon on Nato and SDI before he moved on to Sacramento, San Francisco, Denver and Chicago, and then back to Washington. The briefings became increasingly focused on what interested him – economics and welfare – and he also held several meetings with Democrats, both at federal and state levels. Cherie and the children joined him at the end of the trip, his itinerary lodged in the State Department reveals, 'for a long weekend in Virginia'. In total, he had about fifty 'briefings' during the four weeks.[4] It would be wrong to suggest that the trip made him an America-phile overnight. But the cumulative impact of meeting so many people in so many locations would have had a powerful effect in opening his mind to a country he hitherto barely knew.

Gordon Brown's knowledge of the United States' history, politics and society never ceased to impress the Americans. He likes to holiday there. His love affair with the country dates back to even before his trip to the 1984 Democratic National Convention in San Francisco,[5] and his long-standing contacts included the well-connected Democratic consultant Bob Shrum. Brown had met Clinton long before he secured the Democratic Party's nomination for president.[6] It has been assumed that Brown introduced Blair to the US, but the evidence of the August 1986 trip would suggest that, while Brown may well have been the more enthusiastic of the two, Blair had already been bitten. Their first trip together came in 1988, when they visited the Democratic National Convention in Atlanta, Georgia. Here, they saw the Democrats choose Michael Dukakis as their nomination for president and witnessed at first hand the growing tension in the party between the traditionalists and modernisers.[7] Dukakis' defeat at the hands of Republican George H. Bush, after he failed to appeal beyond his core liberal support base, underlined the importance of building a broad-based electoral coalition. As Blair and Brown came to realise, this lesson extended well beyond America's shores.

The two men were at the height of their closeness. In 1990 Neil Kinnock had sent Brown and Blair to Australia to witness a successful Labor government in action, and see what they could learn. They met with the Labor Prime Minister, Bob Hawke, who stressed the importance to a Labour government in Britain of both formal and informal union relations. Blair also met his Oxford friends, Gallop and Thomson, and 'struck up a particularly good rapport with the then Treasurer [the Australian equivalent of the UK's Chancellor of the Exchequer] Paul Keating in a long and lively meeting'.[8] Buoyed up by the success of this trip together, Blair and Brown decided to return to the US together the following year, not least to get away from the pre-election squabbling in the party.[9] They had no money, however, so they turned to Philip Morris, the tobacco company, which paid for public figures to visit the US in return for a speech to businessmen in New York. The trip lasted from 4 to 7 December 1991: one aide recalled, 'Both Tony and Gordon were like excited schoolchildren going over to the States. They really relished the space to talk to each other twenty-four hours a day without the constant distraction of being in London.'[10] They were still too junior to see the big names in American politics, and the most important gain of the trip was a contact made in the British Embassy. Anji Hunter discovered that visiting MPs could use the Embassy free of charge. She was particularly struck by one of the young diplomats she encountered, 'who was just incredibly calm, helpful and friendly'. She made a note of his name: Jonathan Powell.[11]

Nineteen ninety-two was the first year since 1964 when the British General Election and the US Presidential election coincided. Blair's focus was on British politics in the first half of the year but he began to take increasing note, as the year progressed, of the emergence of Bill Clinton as the Democratic candidate to challenge the incumbent Republican, George H. W. Bush. Blair's visits to Australia and the US had been distilling some fresh thoughts. Was there common ground between Labour in the UK, the Democrats in the US, Labor in Australia and left-of-centre parties elsewhere? In mid-1992 he wrote, 'We should go out of our way to build common cause with other parties around the world in searching out the way forward.'[12] On the opposing side, the Republicans in the US had reached a similar conclusion about collaboration. They caused great offence in 1992 by asking the Tories if they could root out any damaging stories about Clinton from his Oxford days. They had also begun to seek direct advice on how John Major, despite a recession and disenchantment with a long period of right-wing rule, had managed to win the General Election. Tory help began to drift across the Atlantic to the Republicans. The Clinton campaign panicked, and in September reached out to Philip Gould for his advice on how the Tories had won against the odds, and what techniques they had used. Clinton's aides were grateful for his input, which they felt gave a boost to their campaign, and this helped significantly in cementing a strong relationship between the Democrats and the Labour Party.[13]

In January 1993, Blair and Brown returned to the United States on a three-day visit arranged for them by Jonathan Powell at the British Embassy. Robin Renwick, then ambassador, fixed meetings for them with Alan Greenspan, Chairman of the Federal Reserve, and other key figures from the economic Establishment. Renwick's hidden agenda was to convince them of the benefits of depoliticising the interest rate in Britain.[14] However, the Embassy encountered problems in trying to secure meetings with many senior figures in the administration: Tony Lake, National Security Advisor, didn't want to see them. Enquiries were met with the response, 'Who are these guys? They are not even the leaders of the party that isn't in power?'[15] Although there was a gratitude to the Labour Party in some sections of the new administration, it was not associated with Blair himself, who was a complete unknown in Washington. The administration was also keen not to upset the Conservative government by appearing too friendly with the Opposition.

Powell, nevertheless, managed to arrange some political meetings with leading Democrats. In this quest, he was helped by friendships established when he had been following Clinton's campaign trail for the Embassy the previous year: many of the President's staffers had formed a very high opinion of him.[16] Powell developed these relationships further after the election, exchanging papers with the Americans on the latest progressive ideas for public policy.[17] Key figures Blair and Brown met included Clinton's pollster, Stan Greenberg; Al From, President of the Democratic Leadership Council (DLC); and Elaine Kamarck from the Progressive Policy Institute (PPI). The DLC and PPI had been key in articulating ideas that would bring the Democratic Party back into the American mainstream, something Blair and Brown hoped to repeat with the Labour Party in Britain.[18] They eagerly lapped up the details of how Clinton had repositioned himself and his party. Elaine Kamarck recalls, 'I was invited with Al and Stan to the British Embassy to meet Tony Blair for tea. We had no idea who he was, but we all went to the Embassy because it was so neat to be invited. We'd been out of power for twelve years and no one had invited us to embassies for a long time. Tony Blair looked like a kid to us. He took out a small notebook and asked us some questions about how we had begun in 1989 and we talked him all the way through it. He took furious notes about everything we said. He was very courteous, very humble, very focused.'[19] Blair also learned about modern campaigning techniques from Paul Begala, one of Clinton's leading political strategists, and had lunch with the journalist Sidney Blumenthal, who was later helpful in developing Blair's American contacts.

Blair and Brown returned at the end of the week to a one-day conference entitled 'Clinton Economics: Can Britain Learn the Lessons?'. Initiated and organised by Philip Gould, this was held at the Queen Elizabeth II Conference Centre in Westminster on Saturday, 9 January, and was sponsored by the *Guardian* and the TGWU. Stan Greenberg, Paul Begala and Elaine Kamarck from Clinton's team all spoke. The messages they put over were the same Blair and Brown had heard in private conversations during the week in Washington: discard the old images of being obsessed with history and associated solely with the poor, the unions, minorities and special interests. Instead, forge a populism of the centre, which is a prerequisite for electoral success, broaden class appeal beyond the working class and use the media to the fullest and most professional extent.[20] Delegates also heard how, to distance himself from the negative associations of his party in the past, Clinton had styled himself leader of the 'New Democrats'.[21]

All this razzmatazz went down predictably badly with the traditionalists in the Labour Party. John Edmonds went and complained privately to John Smith that the highly publicised visit was an obvious bid for control of the future direction of the party and that only one of the pair should have been allowed to go. 'I was enthusiastic that we should learn from the Clinton campaign, but not the way they used their visit to imply Smith was behind the game and rather out of touch.'[22] John Prescott and Clare Short were openly hostile, speaking in the vein of Labour's traditional deep anti-Americanism.[23] Prescott was particularly vocal, criticising the modernisers for wanting to 'Clintonise' Labour and turn it into a social democratic party, cutting away from traditional values and the trade unions.[24] The publishing of Paul Begala's seminal advice to Blair and Brown in Washington, that everything else was 'strictly secondary to the necessity for a good candidate', further inflamed tensions by pointing a finger at Labour's new leader, John Smith.[25] While the duo were still in the US, Smith had summoned Mandelson to his office to vent his anger. 'All this Clintonisation business, it's just upsetting everyone. Stop boat-rocking with all this talk of change and modernisation,' Smith is reputed to have said.[26] He was more tactful later when he saw Stan Greenberg in London. The meeting was positive but Greenberg was not convinced Smith 'had the right style for a leader of a modernising party'.[27]

Shortly after Blair's return from the US, one of his aides reminded him that there were hazards in appearing too closely linked to a new president's administration, when their success in office was far from guaranteed. His response was unequivocal: 'Clinton? I've just studied him. The guy's a winner and he's going to do really well. I know there's a danger in becoming too associated, but I'm convinced he's a winner.'[28] The attitude to Clinton and the New Democrats marked a real divide in the Labour Party in the 1990s, albeit less potent than the clashes over militant trade unionism earlier in the 1980s. Smith tried to bridge the passions on both sides, but temperamentally he was in the opposing camp to Brown and Blair. One observer highlighted the stark contrast between the clinical visit paid by Smith's deputy Margaret Beckett to Washington in 1992, when she met leading Democrats and members of Clinton's victorious election team, but no great enthusiasm was aroused on either side, with the Brown/Blair visits, which were 'packed with energy, excitement and genuine warmth'.[29] Smith dutifully saw Clive Hollick, who had written a paper after a visit to talk to the Clinton team, in which he argued for a 'new Labour Party, new policies on tax and on trade union links'. Smith listened in silence and then responded along the lines of, 'This is all very interesting, but I think you'll find that it will be our turn next time.'[30] This vignette perfectly illustrates the *kulturkampf* in the Labour Party, the fault line between the two very different visions of the party's future.

Blair returned to the US in November 1993, this time without Brown, to meet policy-makers in the administration and explore some ideas that he was developing as shadow Home Secretary. Sidney Blumenthal, who regarded himself as the key power-broker, invited Blair to a dinner party: 'His name was virtually unknown; his status, to be generous, minor. I invited the then Speaker of the House, Tom Foley, and a number of other Democratic notables,' he recalls. 'They were sceptical but turned out anyway.'[31] For Blair the chief interest of this trip was a visit to New York to observe US law enforcement efforts close up. On his return to the UK, he wrote an article about his experiences. 'When you see New York you see what London could become . . . I visited the 72nd precinct in Brooklyn . . . As the commander of the precinct put it: "The problem is drugs, drugs, drugs."' The solutions, he said, are to be found in combining punishment with prevention, rebuilding local communities, and tough gun laws. He concluded that 'crime is perhaps the number-one issue in the USA'.[32] He was to write almost the same words about Britain to Number 10 aides ten years later.

The next time Blair visited the United States, in April 1996, he was party leader, and it was to see Clinton himself in the White House. By then he had become a figure of real status: Americans were now battling to see him. But it was the early contacts in 1991–93 that were to prove the transforming experiences. John Rentoul aptly wrote that the January 1993 trip 'marked a turning point in his development as a politician'.[33] The Blair team made much in public, in the mid- to late-1990s, of the US influence. In part this was a ploy because, as one aide admitted, 'It played better for us to make out that the fresh thinking came out of the United States because the British media outlets we wanted to impress were financed by US interests and were in love with America, not Europe.'[34] But the seminal influence of the United States on Blair and Brown was real, and made its mark before the spin machine got to work in earnest after 1994.

Impact of the Early US Trips

So why were the trips in 1991–93 turning points for Blair? Critically, the United States exposure reminded him and Brown that Labour could never win until it attracted the middle-ground voters, and the Clinton campaign in 1992 gave them a road map for how to achieve this; it also gave the modernisers in Labour the confidence, palpable at the Westminster conference in January 1993, that they could indeed win.[35] After four defeats in a row this was a message of great importance. Blair and Brown used the radical repositioning of the Democratic Party by Clinton as a stick to beat the traditionalists in Labour. Look, they were saying, left-of-centre parties *can* win, but only if they offer a forward-looking platform, transform their image and put their message across to the electorate in a dramatic new way. On occasion, Blair appeared to take this lesson rather too much to heart. The uncanny resemblance of a whole series of phrases used by Blair in his 1994 address to the Labour Party Conference (such as 'with opportunity must come responsibility') to the words used by Clinton at the 1992 Democratic National Convention (such as 'we offer opportunity. We demand responsibility') generated considerable – albeit short-lived – embarrassment when uncovered by the media.[36]

The 1991–93 exposure engendered or affirmed a host of other changes in the minds of Blair and Brown. Blair found further evidence that his 'tough on crime' message was the right one, in electoral and policy terms, and it was useful to him to cite US experience.[37] Brown's transfer of control of interest rates to the Bank of England in 1997 'owed much to advice [he] had received from Mr Alan Greenspan, the Chairman of the US Federal Reserve'.[38] This decision also reflected the influence of the Harvard economist Larry Summers who, as with Greenspan, Brown and Blair had first met on the January 1993 trip. The meeting with Summers was arranged by Ed Balls, who, after being taught by Summers at Harvard had kept in touch. Balls was one of Brown's contacts and would later become his chief aide. Summers stressed the need for Labour to be market-oriented and suggested the phrase: 'Not the invisible hand, not the heavy hand, but the helping hand.'[39] Blair and Brown were reminded during these exchanges of the supreme importance for Labour of economic competence once in power, something all previous Labour governments had failed to sustain in the long term.

Brown's team, notably Geoff Mulgan and Ed Balls, deepened their existing contacts in the US with individuals, with the administration and with think-tanks. The 'third way' conferences were one of the eventual fruits of these contacts. In March 1995, through an invitation initiated by Mulgan, Blair met Amitai Etzioni, a sociology professor at George Washington University and a communitarian thinker, who was misleadingly trumpeted in the British press as the 'father of Tony Blair's big idea'.[40] Etzioni's communitarianism, which stressed that the West's focus on individual rights had been at the expense of responsibilities and communal values, struck a deep chord with Blair: Etzioni left their meeting delighted that he had finally met 'a major British leader who understood and cared about our message'.[41]

On the strength of their encounters over the early trips, Blair invited Jonathan Powell to leave the Foreign Office and join his team. Powell chose to be called 'Chief of Staff', emulating the White House title, providing just one example of the American model of government permeating Blair's approach to leadership. As Peter Riddell has pointed out, the reorganisation and expansion of Blair's Downing Street operation has left Number 10 looking like a scaled-down version of the Executive Office of the President. In addition, Blair has 'adopted a deliberately presidential style, trying to stay above the fray: no longer first among equals, but rather first above equals'.[42] Many of the seeds of these changes were planted in Blair's mind during these early US visits and were then nourished by his continued fascination with American politics. Contacts established in the early 1990s, often through Philip Gould, whose influence is discussed in the next chapter, also proved crucial to the evolution of New Labour's campaign techniques. Discussions followed with a stream of Democratic political consultants, who made specific contributions to the New Labour campaign and message in the run-up to the 1997 General Election and after. These included Paul Begala, James Carville and, most crucially, Stan Greenberg, who was hired as the Labour Party's official pollster.

The US trips and contacts in 1991–93 were indeed defining for Blair and Brown. Their visits came at the very moment when the Democrats had re-found their way after twelve years out of power, and the Labour Party was still struggling to re-find it after thirteen years out of power. It was a most significant historical conjunction. Brown may have been more of an instigator than Blair, and was certainly treated as the more senior of the two in the US, but both were changed profoundly by the experience.

Philip Gould, mercurial and brilliant strategist behind New Labour in and out of power. The picture suggests Gould as the figure at the centre of a large web.

12

Philip Gould

A man who has had one of the most consistent influences on what Tony Blair has done with power is neither a Labour politician, nor a socialist philosopher, nor does he represent any previous strand of Labour's history. He is a process man. Herein lies not only a key to how Blair has managed to break out of the chrysalis of orthodox Labour Party thinking, but also the key to the hostility towards him harboured by so many traditional Labour figures.

Philip Gould was born in Surrey in March 1950, the son of a primary school head. He suffered from dyslexia, failed the eleven-plus exam and was educated at a secondary modern school in Woking, Surrey. Fascinated by politics from an early age, he joined the Labour Party in the year of Harold Wilson's great landslide, 1966. 'I was a bit anoraky. I was rather shy, rather lonely. But I just loved politics, the smell of the halls where they held meetings, everything about it.'[1]

He did not have the same enthusiasm for his academic work and left school with one 'O' level, in Geography. His sense of rejection and failure as an adolescent helped shape his sympathy for the excluded, and he spent the next two years on building sites, working with the disadvantaged, going to rock concerts and marching on anti-apartheid and anti-Vietnam war protests.[2] Dissatisfied, he went back to college, passed his 'A' levels to read Politics at Sussex University, where he met Gail Rebuck, later his wife and Chief Executive of publishers Random House. He went on to take an MSc in the history of political thought at the LSE from 1974 to 1975 (Cherie's final year; they did not meet). He then spent ten years in advertising, but yearned for more from his life: he later claimed that reading David Butler and Dennis Kavanagh's general election books helped fire his passion to spend his life working on political campaigns.[3]

Blair and Gould

Gould's subsequent life and relationship with Blair can be divided into three phases.[4] In the first phase, 1985–92, he helped change the Labour Party, but only towards the end of the period did he and Blair interact significantly.[5] In the beginning, Gould was one of a group of hugely able young people of similar outlook and lifestyle who coalesced around Kinnock. The others included Peter Mandelson, Patricia Hewitt and Charles Clarke. By the later 1980s, Gould, together with Mandelson and Alastair Campbell, became part of an overlapping but distinct group that gathered around Blair and Brown. These groups are similar in their impact, if not their ideas, to the New Right cohorts who coalesced around Mrs Thatcher from the mid-1970s.[6] Gould met Mandelson fleetingly in 1984. When the latter was appointed as Labour's Director of Communications in September 1985, Gould wrote him an eleven-page letter explaining why he should hire him to work for the party.[7] Mandelson, impressed, commissioned him to write an audit of the party's communications. Gould was contemptuous of the existing apparatus, which he thought archaic, and his 64-page report, delivered in late December 1985, was damning.[8] He concluded that Labour 'had too many committees, spent too much of its time speaking to its diminishing number of activists . . . and spurned new communications methods'.[9] He reinforced Mandelson's belief that there were a large number of Labour sympathisers working in the advertising and communications industries who would be only too willing to help bring the party up to date. Indeed, a group of these sympathisers, known as the 'Tuesday Group', already met informally and offered advice.[10] What was lacking was a structure or a formal system into which their advice could be fed. The traditionalists in the party, for whom the slick world of advertising was anathema, were nervous. But Kinnock, nevertheless, supported the establishment of a Shadow Communications Agency (SCA), proposed in Gould's report, which utilised the brains of these media specialists who gave their services to the party gratis.

The SCA swung rapidly into gear. Under the chairmanship of Chris Powell, brother of Jonathan and of Thatcher's aide Charles, it reported to Mandelson, and helped facilitate one of the biggest overhauls of Labour's communications since the party's foundation in 1900. The red rose emblem was a striking early result of their work. Labour received widespread plaudits for its 1987 election campaign, though it did not prevent Mrs Thatcher handsomely winning her third successive victory. Defeat left Gould even more determined to make Labour electable. He continued to work closely with the SCA, undertook extensive opinion polling and began an intensive programme of 'focus groups', a technique common in advertising and public relations where the views of small groups of voters were carefully probed and their reaction to ideas, words and phrases closely monitored. Using these techniques, Gould was able to build up a clear picture of what current Labour voters, and, very significantly, potential Labour voters, liked and did not like about the party. Properly used, it was a potentially transforming tool for a party in need of reconnecting itself with voters, after years of the hard left dictating what Labour voters wanted, or rather, should be wanting. As Dennis Kavanagh put it, 'Conventional opinion polls provided the numbers but focus groups enabled Gould to "understand the mood behind the numbers".'[11]

Gould's work helped show how the five changes that Kinnock and his lieutenants in the leader's office pushed through the party in the 1980s were being received by voters. Independently, Gould was reaching the same conclusions as Kinnock about what Labour needed to do. Gould put it graphically: 'In these years what I did was to argue not only that Labour had to change but it had to change emphatically. I was obsessive. I banged on and on about the only way of doing this being to change radically and emphatically. There could be no going back. I battered away about modernisation and renewal until my view eventually prevailed.'[12] The reach of all this work on presentation was extensive: it affected the party's advertising, television broadcasts, themes, logo, image and style.[13] His obsessiveness won him admirers but also detractors. The journalist Anne McElvoy wrote: 'His personal manner is eccentric, at times endearingly positive, at times verging on the wearying. You would know if you were in a restaurant with Philip Gould because he becomes so passionate in pursuit of his subject that his voice rises to an unignorable crescendo.'[14] More serious than those who objected to his manner were those in the party, the traditionalists on the left, who regarded Gould as an interloper, encouraging the leadership down avenues which would ultimately destroy everything they believed the Labour Party stood for, however sacred. They saw him as a kind of evil witch doctor, using sinister devices to destroy the purity of their cause.

Gould first met Blair properly during the 1987 General Election campaign.[15] In 1988, Blair appeared in two consecutive television broadcasts, and in 1990 he and Gordon Brown were interviewed in a ten-minute film directed by Hugh Hudson. It was when Gould listened to Blair's speech at the 1990 Party Conference that he first thought Blair had the potential to go all the way to the top.[16] As Gould's pessimism mounted as the 1992 General Election approached (his research was showing that

Labour would not win as long as it was seen as the high tax party), his thoughts began to move in fresh directions. Gould came to believe that Kinnock's grand 'policy review' exercise launched after 1987, although a brave initiative by the leader, was moving much too slowly.[17] Kinnock's failure to prevail over Smith on tax, which Gould saw as fundamental, disillusioned him, as it did the other modernisers. However, Gould stuck firm to the belief that the key to electoral success was the root-and-branch reform of the party. The best hope for achieving these reforms, Gould came to realise, lay with Blair and Brown, two people who understood his concerns about tax and everything else the party needed to do to make itself electable.

The second phase of Gould–Blair relations, 1992–97, sees the two men move closer together. The 1992 election result was for Gould and the modernisers the terrible experience they had feared. He, Mandelson, and others in the SCA, were to be scapegoated by the new Smith leadership team for the alleged failure of their high-tech communications strategy to deliver victory. Gould believed that the election was lost not because of too much but too *little* modernisation – above all on tax, where Labour were fatally weak to resist the full brunt of the Tories' negative campaigning about high taxation. Traditionalists like Prescott readily seized on the defeat as evidence that the party abandoned its core left-wing values and traditional methods at its peril. The Smith years, 1992–94, were not a happy time for any of the modernisers. Gould saw more of Brown than Blair early on in this second period, finding Brown the more congenial company.[18] A vignette of Gould in the 1992–94 period is provided by the playwright, David Hare, who shadowed Labour's campaign in 1992 as research for his play *The Absence of War*. He described Gould as 'quick, in an adman's baggy suit, with long curly hair. He's given to rambling, energetic sentences which die suddenly in mid-air.'[19] It was a bleak time for him. He felt his career and his aspirations had 'died in mid-air'.

The SCA was closed down in mid-1992, and it seemed as if Labour under Smith (the next Prime Minister, everyone assumed) would have little use for Gould. Then a faxed message came for him to visit Clinton's campaign in Little Rock, Arkansas. As discussed in Chapter 11, this contained a plea from the Democrats for help in combating Republican attacks that appeared to have been heavily influenced by strategists from Conservative Central Office. 'For me, at that time,' Gould later wrote, 'dejected, depressed – this fax was like water in the desert . . . arriving at that campaign was like leaving the shadows and coming into the sunlight.'[20] Once in Little Rock, he wrote a number of memos, one of which had a particular impact on Clinton's campaign. 'It's the last week that counts,' he wrote. 'Forget the plaudits, concentrate on the smears; fear builds slowly, and only shows in the vote; tax and trust are the only issues that matter.'[21] But Gould was learning too, as Clinton's campaign with its innovative strategy and cutting-edge techniques was played out before his eyes. His four weeks with the Clinton campaign re-energised him and transformed his morale.[22] Back in London in November, he spoke excitedly about the two main lessons he had learned. The key was 'winning on the economy. Nothing else matters.' Second, 'Clinton had targeted the middle class, by articulating their concerns.'[23] 'Lessons from America' spelled out his conclusions in an article he wrote with Patricia Hewitt for the first issue of a sympathetic new magazine *Renewal*, launched in January 1993. Gould and Hewitt pulled their punches so as not to overly upset the Smith camp, but the message was clear. 'The lessons which the British left can learn are not so much about *content*,' they wrote, 'as about *process*.'[24] The path for Labour would have to be one of radical change.[25]

Gould was now back in business. He spoke tirelessly about 'instant rebuttal', 'war rooms' and all the other paraphernalia from Little Rock that was to find its way into Labour's arsenal. Smith's failure to respond positively to this new tide of ideas swept Gould even further into the arms of Blair and Brown, and the embrace, at least with the former, never faltered over the next eleven years. As long as Smith was in the saddle, though, Gould's meaningful relationship with both men would be constrained because neither sat in the leader's office. By 1994 his admiration for Brown was undimmed, but he had reached the opinion that Blair would be the more effective messenger in carrying the modernising agenda to the country at large. Gould had time on his hands, and devoted some of it to politics in Europe, but kept focused on the domestic scene and wrote a memo on 9 May 1994 distilling his thinking over the previous two years. He took the memo to Blair two days later. Blair was preparing to fly up to Aberdeen to campaign for the European elections later that day and was distracted and impatient. He readily agreed with Gould's call for radical change, but their doubts remained about how far the leadership had the will and the understanding to make the changes.[26] The next morning John Smith was dead.

One of Anji Hunter's earliest actions was to call Gould and invite him to join them. On Monday 16 May he spoke to Blair who was in the kitchen of his Islington home, and reinforced his instinct to stand as leader, no matter what decision Brown might reach about his own participation.[27] The next day Gould typed a seminal document, 'Strategy for the Election for Party Leader and Beyond'. Labour, he said, must stand for community, democracy and opportunity, and at the appropriate point they had to say to the public — and to the party — we are a *new* Labour Party.[28] It reprised part of the 9 May memo, but it also articulated many of Blair's personal themes, as well as describing much that came to pass. Gould's core point was that unless the party appeared to be new and different, the electorate would never believe it had changed.

Gould joined Blair's campaign team and helped toughen his image and sharpen his message. On 6 June, he began to conduct focus groups for Blair, concentrating on those who voted Tory in 1992 but who might now switch. This research was relied on heavily by Blair for the leadership election campaign. On 21 July, the day following the election, Gould handed Blair a 25-page memo entitled 'Consolidating the Blair Identity: Rebuilding Labour; Demolishing the Conservatives'. This is Gould's other seminal document from the 1992–97 period. Blair's, and Labour's, weaknesses were fully dissected — Gould has never pulled back from hard truth. Blair, he wrote, was seen as 'over-smooth', 'too soft' and 'inexperienced', and he suggested how his protégé might overcome these handicaps. On the party, 'There is still a lurking fear about unions and the loony left . . . they've no idea what Labour stands for.' The memo reiterated Gould's cry that only a profound overhaul would reconnect the party with both working-class and middle-class voters. In a long passage he wrote: 'Labour must say that it is a new Labour Party, that it is left of centre, but which has moved beyond old left–right boundaries.'[29]

Blair was impressed by his holiday reading, and once back in London in September he asked Gould to work with him (as long as the memos were shorter). The importance of Gould to Blair over the next three years was to remind him he had to reassure voters that on the key issues — tax, law and order and the family — Labour could be *trusted*. Gould's insistence on re-branding the party begat New Labour, and the need for 'shock therapy' affirmed Blair's instinctive desire to re-write Clause IV. Gould described the changes to Clause IV as 'a huge symbolic shock which led to a sense of liberation'.[30] Throughout these years in opposition, Gould was remorseless, worrying away at the party and at Blair himself. After sharing in one of these conversations in January 1996, Dennis Kavanagh wrote, 'Philip does the intellectual spadework for Tony Blair. He saw himself as a person who was able to articulate what Blair would be writing if he had time.'[31] This contemporary evidence says much about the Blair–Gould relationship.

In September 1995, one of Gould's memos, in which he advocated a unitary command structure 'leading directly to the party leader', was leaked to the press.[32] Blair's leadership both before and after 1997 has indeed been distinctive for its central command structure.[33] But this memo, which caused much excitement, reflected only one of many themes that Gould was scooping up and firing at the leader. His influence on the opposition period was to make Blair more cautious – in March 1995 he wrote, 'support for Labour' could collapse 'at any point'. His impact on the 1997 Labour campaign was extensive: phrases such as 'one nation' and 'renewal' (a favourite Gould phrase), as well as soundbites like 'the future not the past', 'the many and not the few', 'Britain deserves better' all owed their origin or shaping to Gould.[34] (The five election 'pledges' were in fact Peter Hyman's idea, though they have often been attributed to Gould.) Trust, he had always said, could be gained by making small promises, delivering them, and then telling the electorate you have delivered them. Gould's access to Blair, and the prominence given to his views, aroused inevitable jealousy. The big beasts in the shadow Cabinet – Cook, Prescott, Beckett, as well as Blunkett, Cunningham, Dewar and Straw – all felt they were being excluded from the inner sanctum, and so indeed they were.

Success, however, mutes dissent, and harmony prevailed after the May 1997 election (in sharp contrast to the dissent after April 1992). The third phase of the Gould–Blair relationship now began, lasting from May 1997 until the present day. Gould's influence waxed and waned after Blair went into Number 10, as one might have expected from a figure who had no formal post in Downing Street. Physical proximity to Blair matters: influence was often measured by how close someone's office in Number 10 was to Blair's own. Gould's importance was mainly *ad hominem*: on average he would meet with Blair once a week while in government (more often during election times) and in addition they would talk to each other on the phone regularly. Gould's influence was also played out through his very close friendship with Campbell, a similarly driven man welded to the success of the New Labour project, as well as through his presentations to senior ministers at 'Political Cabinets' (without civil servants) or to Number 10 staff on 'strategy' days. He was influential in the repositioning of the *Express* newspaper, owned by Clive Hollick, into a New Labour-sympathetic tabloid. That foray into high journalism aside, he devoted all his attention to his tried and trusted conventional channels.

In May 2000, he spent several hours ensconced in Downing Street with Blair on paternity leave, watching over baby Leo, and told him that he was seen to be hiding behind the gates in Downing Street and Chequers, and the electorate found him out of touch. 'You are not focusing on the domestic agenda and your language is wrong,' he told the Prime Minister.[35] In the run-up to the 2001 General Election he warned Blair that he was seen to lack conviction, that he was overly identified with spin and presentation and saying things just to placate people.[36] Blair at the time was far from willing to accept Gould's strictures.

After 9/11 and the Afghan war, however, Blair turned again to Gould for help on how to address the criticism that he was giving insufficient time to domestic policy.[37] Gould's memos have kept pumping out the same messages about the electorate's concerns about public services and crime and, from 2001, asylum. The drip, drip, drip of the memos to Blair has continued unabated to the present day. They have been a constant dose of sober psychoanalytic reality to a man who is often dangerously optimistic. Gould has brought Blair down to earth. At times, he would not come down, to his loss, because hot air could not sustain him forever. At other times Gould has been overly depressing. In the 1994–97 period he grossly underestimated Labour's strength, and made Blair far more cautious and defensive than he needed to be.

The Impact of Philip Gould

Gould is a phenomenon. There has been no figure quite like him in British political history. Bob Worcester, the chairman of the MORI polling organisation, has some similarities as a public crusader for the importance of polling to politics, and had been Labour's pollster before being fired by Mandelson after the 1987 election.[38] The Tories have had their Gordon Reeces, Tim Bells and Maurice Saatchis. Only Maurice Saatchi continues to have a significant influence (as party co-chairman), but none has had the continuity of influence nor the same degree of penetration on the Tory leadership that Gould has had on Labour's. Since 1985, for twenty years, Gould has had an almost unbroken influence on the party he helped re-create. The austere figure of Michael Fraser, *éminence grise* to Tory leaders in the 1950s and 1960s, runs Gould a close second for influence. Gould has elements of Brendan Bracken in his influence on Winston Churchill, Arnold Goodman on Harold Wilson, or Norman Tebbit on Mrs Thatcher. But he is much more than a frank friend, a sounding board and a trouble-shooter. He is more than just a pollster who provides research: he is a tireless proselytiser for what that research means. He inspired and encouraged Labour's change from a doctrine/tradition-driven party to a values/market-driven one. A political advertising man has taken the place of generations of socialist philosophers. His closest equivalents are to be found best in US politics – Pat Caddell to Carter, Dick Wirthlin to Reagan and, more recently, Dick Morris to Clinton.[39]

Blair has listened to him because, unlike many he has encountered, Gould does not shirk from telling him hard truths, which are rooted in what the working class, lower middle class and middle class think. For all Gould's manic behaviour, and his changing his opinions daily, hourly even, but always passionately expressed, he is an immensely sympathetic listener and discussant. And he is utterly fixated on Blair. Their relationship has grown ever closer during the years in government, although it has not taken on a social dimension.[40] Gould has also remained, rare in Blair's immediate circle, close to Brown, and has helped to patch up some of their disputes. Given the opportunity, he would want to continue working for Brown if he became leader: not many in Blair's court might be offered that opportunity. By the summer of 2004 he had become a key intermediary, and a major strategist planning the next General Election. Gould does not care what anyone in the government thinks of what he writes or the difficulties that what he says might cause other ministers. His focus is solely on the big picture, and the big picture is always winning the next election.[41]

Gould himself says, 'With Tony Blair everyone has a place. My place? Basically, it is to tell him what the public think.'[42] The moot point remains how far Blair, as with Kinnock before him, does what he does because of his own inner convictions and values, which chime with Gould's research, and how far he is shaped by that research. The truth is that Blair's own values have always been a core driving force: 'What Philip does is to reinforce Tony Blair's gut instincts,' said a senior official.[43] The criticism that Blair has been influenced wholly by focus groups is thus misplaced. As Blair himself said to Martin Jacques in 1994: 'I see the Labour Party as a vehicle for certain key values, principles and beliefs rather than as a movement which is about class or sectional interest.'[44] Ultimately, therefore, it has been Blair's own values and beliefs which have shaped his thinking, whether on crime, public services, Northern Ireland or terrorism and abuses of human rights. But Blair is also a highly political politician who has always been fixated on winning elections. For the most of his twenty plus years in politics, his instincts chimed with 'what the nation thinks'. Where they did not, as over Iraq, he became unstuck.

Gould is New Labour's guru, explaining the outside world to his client, and his client to the outside world. Tony Blair found the perfect man to help him articulate what he believed needed to be done. Gould paved the way for Blair to come to, and remain in, power. He is both foreman in the electoral engine-room as well as court strategist of New Labour.

Blair addressing the Labour conference in 1992. The photograph shows a man who has discovered new powers and confidence within him, and who will be stopped by no one in his ambition for the party.

13

General and Leadership Elections, 1992

The election defeat in 1992 and the decisions taken in its immediate aftermath concerning the leadership and deputy leadership elections were the decisive events for Blair of the years 1992–94. He had expected Labour to be defeated, but the extent of the party's failure still came as a shock. He had lost faith in Kinnock being the future, and in Smith, his anointed successor, having the commitment to 'modernisation' he deemed so vital. Since his closed shop triumph he had been reappraising his ideas about his own future. Salvation lay in his and Gordon Brown's hands. Exactly how, he was not yet sure – and so he allowed the chance for them to stand for either deputy or leader just after the General Election to pass by. But after it went, a new determination entered his soul. He set about carving out his own niche in the party, and profile in the media, with a single-mindedness and ruthlessness he had not displayed before. The gnawing concern – how he and Brown would reach the summit, and, far more fraught still, in what combination – was on temporary hold with Smith firmly ensconced in the leader's office. But frustration was mounting all the time.

Blair Comes of Age, 9–11 April

Blair was unhappy with the way the General Election campaign was fought, and with the issues the leadership had selected as the principal battlegrounds. Mandelson's departure to stand in Hartlepool had meant that Brown and Blair and their modernising cause were no longer promoted in the media as much as they would have liked. Other than informal advice to Philip Gould over the phone, Mandelson played little role in the national campaign. A reaction against the three modernisers, particularly Mandelson, had set in among Kinnock's senior shadow Cabinet colleagues – Jack Cunningham, Bryan Gould, Roy Hattersley, Gerald Kaufman and John Smith. 'They would not touch [Mandelson] with a barge-pole,' admitted a Kinnock aide.[1] 'Blair was seen as an asset,' insisted Charles Clarke,[2] but Kinnock's aides felt compelled to make greater use of more senior figures. Outside Kinnock's circle, many were fed up with the threesome, were irritated by Kinnock's continuing empathy with them, and even tried to outmanoeuvre him over them.[3] Relations had been notably poor between Bryan Gould and the modernisers; Gould's handling of the Tories over the poll tax earned Blair's derision;[4] Brown was even more critical.[5] Jealousy lay at the heart of it, as Gould wanted to be leader after Kinnock, and believed that Mandelson was working for the succession of Brown and Blair.[6] Kinnock still regarded Bryan Gould highly, but he was also full of praise for Brown, and from time to time mentioned him as a preferred leader over John Smith.[7] The rivalry and jockeying was fierce, and continued up to election day. The modernisers were particularly angry about Smith's tax policy, which ignored all the advice from Philip Gould – and the United States – that Labour would never win as a tax-and-spend party. Kinnock was frustrated that Smith presented the Shadow Budget just a month before the election, which left far too little time to refine and explain Labour's tax message against the deafening barrage of Tory election propaganda.[8] Smith was equally angry at the way he saw his plans and statements being undermined by the leader's office.[9] All in all, it was a very unhappy time at the top of the party, and one can only speculate how fractious life might have been had Kinnock won.

Brown and Blair had not been included in Kinnock's 'Leader's Committee', which was set up to oversee the campaign as it had in 1987. In addition to representation from the trade unions and the NEC, Kinnock selected shadow Cabinet members Hattersley, Smith, Bryan Gould and Cunningham, whom he appointed campaign co-ordinator – an idiosyncratic choice in the eyes of some of Kinnock's senior colleagues.[10] Kinnock claimed that his determination to limit numbers on the committee meant that he had no room for anyone else.[11] Others thought too much was being made of their exclusion, as the Leader's Committee was largely a nominal body, of no particular significance. It was still seen though as a rebuff. 'Surprise has been voiced among some Labour MPs,' wrote Philip Webster, one of their allies on *The Times*, 'that Gordon Brown . . . and Tony Blair, two of the party's fastest rising stars, are not on the Leader's Committee.'[12] Brown, Blair and Mandelson all felt strongly that the job of overseeing the campaign should have been given to Brown, and they disagreed with decisions taken by the new Director of Communications, David Hill, formerly Hattersley's aide.[13] Kinnock achieved his wish to give Blair some prominence during the election, however: 'I started the campaign with Tony in Swansea, where he spoke, and I finished it in Barry, where I asked him to deliver the warm-up speech,' he recalled.[14] Kinnock was privately both shocked and amused that Blair gave almost the identical speech at both occasions. 'Bloody hell!' he joked. 'If I could have got away with doing that, my whole life would have been different.'[15]

How did Blair react to the subordinate role he was given in the election? His staff acknowledge that he felt excluded and that he was cross not to be doing more nationally. He spent a lot of time during the campaign languishing in Sedgefield musing on radical thoughts about the future.[16] David Hill's appointment in particular was read as an important signal:[17] it indicated the way the leadership was thinking. What role would a moderniser like him have in the future if they didn't make a start now? He took great care not to let his disappointment and frustration show, and was typically jokey and good-humoured with staff working on the national campaign: few perceived his churning below the surface.[18] He did not even share his private thoughts about the future with Brown or Mandelson. Nor with Anji Hunter, who had been temporarily drafted in to help Kinnock's campaign. There was no one he could trust with whom he could talk it over.

Blair gave the journalist and writer Robert Harris lunch on 3 March at L'Escargot restaurant in Soho, just before the campaign opened, and was despondent about the party and its anti-metropolitan (i.e., its pro-Welsh and Scottish) bias.[19] He had resigned himself early on in the campaign to Labour losing.[20] He had some fleeting periods of optimism during the campaign: one evening he arrived back at Myrobella, having spent the day with BBC's *Newsnight* team touring constituencies, to find the latest polling coming through on the fax machine. The headline numbers showed Labour seven points ahead: 'My God, maybe we can win this,' Blair exclaimed.[21] But the euphoria was short-lived. On election day he told John Burton that the Conservatives would win by twenty seats.[22] He was one out. The Conservatives won 336 seats to Labour's 271, with the Liberal Democrats receiving just 20: the Conservative majority was 21. Labour's defeat became evident as Blair watched news of the early results in silence at his count. He felt desperately sorry for Kinnock: the frustration with him which had grown over the past year was rapidly replaced by compassion – he knew he would be suffering terribly.[23] After his own result was announced – his majority showing a modest increase of around 1,800 to 14,859 – Cherie, Gale and the children headed home. Blair went on to thank his party workers, who had gathered at the Black Bull in Trimdon. 'He was really angry that we lost,' recalled Trimdon aide Phil Wilson. With his campaign loyalists Blair was defiant. 'Reform doesn't stop,' he declared. 'We've got to go on. We've got to change.'[24] He then headed home, stone cold sober, to think about what he was going to do next.

'The result in 1992 was bitter. It hit him particularly hard,' said Paul Trippett, who had also spent election evening with him. 'I came down early the next morning to find him pacing around downstairs. I don't think he'd slept,' recalls Clive Russell, a young aide, up from Blair's London office for the election. 'Blair was working out in his mind what he was going to say to the media.'[25] Most of the shadow Cabinet were still asleep or resting on the Friday, or too depressed to appear on the media. It was Blair who seized the opportunity to become effectively the senior Labour spokesman, and the man to explain the defeat to the public. 'Blair was conspicuous as the first person to pick himself up and get down to work. He was the only one who came out fighting,' said one.[26] Those who worked with him noticed a transition. Former aide Roz Preston said, 'The first time I realised Tony could become leader was when I saw how strong he was the day after the election. He was very commanding and powerful.'[27] Blair spoke all over the media about how he did not think Labour had changed enough, and how it had to change much further to win next time. From the outset, as his speech in the Black Bull showed, he was alert to how traditionalists would try to portray the defeats, repeating their mantra that it was the result not of too little modernisation, but of too much. From the very dawn of the new government, before John Major had even gone to Buckingham Palace to see the Queen, Blair had set out his stall firmly against those who felt the party could just sit back, the 'one more heave' school, and wait for the electoral pendulum to swing and knock the Tories from power. The first after the 1992 election to assert that Labour would not automatically win power next time, he was almost the last to believe in May 1997 that the party was indeed at last safely home.

Blair saw that the 1992 result, despite being relatively close in terms of seats, gave a misleading impression of the true extent of Labour's plight. After five years of work Labour had advanced only 3 per cent on its 1987 result, and its 34.5 per cent of the popular vote was still 3 per cent behind the result in 1979 when the Conservatives, under Mrs

Thatcher, first defeated Labour. The party would also have to achieve a bigger swing to defeat the Tories than any party had managed since 1945, and by persuading more than one million voters to switch directly from Conservative to Labour. (Blair had a keen eye for election data, as his Australian lecture in 1982 and regular comments since revealed.) Blair told the BBC on that Friday that he regarded Labour's failure to win seats in the south-east of England and in London as 'very important': if the party were ever to win again, it had to appeal more to the middle classes.[28] When not in studios he spent much of the Friday on the phone. He was, characteristically, almost the only shadow Cabinet member to phone Kinnock to offer commiserations, and he spoke several times to Brown and Mandelson.[29] The immediate future dominated the conversations. Blair had some explosive ideas he was bursting to share on which he had been ruminating, and which now demanded urgent decisions. It is unclear how far Blair had finalised his plans before the election defeat, and whether he shared his thoughts with anyone beyond Cherie (and one or two friendly journalists with whom he tested ideas). What is beyond doubt is that immediately the result was known, Blair's thoughts exploded to the surface. Brown arranged to meet him at Myrobella the next morning.

That Saturday, Brown tellingly brought with him to Sedgefield his close ally Nick Brown, and the three met again at Nick Brown's home in his Newcastle East constituency and for a third time, with Mandelson, in County Hall, Durham.[30] The core question they addressed, given Kinnock's and Hattersley's almost certain resignations, was, should they themselves make a bid for the leadership now? And, if so, should it be Gordon or Tony? The media had been airing Brown as a leadership candidate in the run-up to the General Election. Ever since he had stood in for Smith in 1988–89, he had the look of a future leader. Before the election, Brown's and Smith's staffs were fighting almost a virtual leadership contest. Kinnock's staff knew about their boss's preference for Brown as his successor over Smith, and Brown knew of it too.[31] Brown had topped the shadow Cabinet poll three years in succession, a clear indication of his popularity in the party with MPs. And he was deeply ambitious for the job. As rumours of mutual hostility began to spread throughout the PLP in 1991, Smith and Brown agreed to meet in Edinburgh in August to bring matters to a head. Smith was blunt: 'What the hell are you doing?' he demanded of his former protégé. Brown assured him that he would do nothing to harm Smith's interests, especially his leadership prospects: 'When the time comes, I won't stand in your way,' Brown fatefully promised.[32] At Brown's request, Mandelson ensured this pledge found its way into the press.[33] But not everyone was convinced by his pledge. Blair, for one, confided in Robert Harris at L'Escargot in early March 1992 that he still expected Brown to stand against Smith for the leadership if Labour lost. He also said he would stand for deputy, and he made Harris believe he would be interested in him joining their team.[34] Harris wrote it up obliquely in his *Sunday Times* column.[35]

At their meetings on Friday and Saturday, 10 and 11 April, Blair tried hard to persuade Brown to stand for leader.[36] Despite later denials, Brown flirted seriously with the idea, and received considerable encouragement from inside his office and beyond to go for it. But he pulled back, offering this explanation later: 'I felt I owed a debt of gratitude to John Smith. I felt I had to be loyal. It was for no other reason.'[37] Brown had indeed agreed a pact with Smith. But there *were* other reasons for his decision. Brown thought his time would come: he was still aged only forty-one and Smith, not a young fifty-three and with a history of heart problems, would likely retire early. Why hurry, especially with an expected four or five years of slog in opposition immediately ahead? Brown was also deeply cautious: everything has to be clear in his head before he makes a move. And everything was not clear. Above all, he was not clear that he would win. Smith had very few enemies, and many in the party were looking forward to the day when he would lead them to Number 10.[38] To be the losing candidate who had turned on his popular mentor might end his leadership prospects for ever.

Later, Blair's supporters justified his standing for the leadership in 1994 on the grounds that 'Gordon had had his chance in 1992 and he ducked it'. This line led Brown's side to deny even more strongly that he ever thought of standing: 'I never thought for a minute of standing against John Smith,' he told his early biographer, Paul Routledge.[39] But he did think of standing against Smith, seriously. Because Brown backed down, people began to ask why. They heard the official reason his supporters gave, but they suspected there was more to it, a sub-text, and baseless rumours began to spread about his sexuality. It was distasteful and it was unfair. And it damaged him.[40]

In the immediate term Blair had to accept that Brown had made up his mind not to challenge Smith. Blair thought seriously about standing for leader himself and discussed the possibility with close friends, but he realised he was not a credible candidate: a *Sunday Times* snap leadership poll among Labour MPs put Smith first with 64 and Brown second a long way behind with 16. Blair received no votes:[41] standing for the leadership would risk humiliation. He was still not even a member of the NEC (he joined later in the year) and he also saw himself in 1992 very clearly as subordinate to Brown. 'He just didn't feel comfortable leapfrogging Gordon,' said a friend with whom Blair worked through his options at the time.[42] But what about the deputy leadership? Blair's first preference was for Brown to stand for deputy, which would put a moderniser in the number two position. If Brown saw any merits in this idea, Smith most definitely did not. He had already promised Brown the shadow Chancellorship. That was prize enough. Without Smith's endorsement, Brown did not want to stand. 'Having two Scots with constituencies seventy-five miles apart makes no sense,' Smith told Brown.[43] The party would expect a more geographically balanced leadership ticket. Yet if Brown decided to stay out of the race, Blair felt he should consider his own chances. He could offer Smith the geographical balance that Brown could not and senior colleagues, such as Gerald Kaufman, urged him to run.[44] But Brown saw things very differently. He was adamantly against Blair standing, even for a job reckoned to be the graveyard for leadership aspirants – Clement Attlee was the only deputy leader (1931–35) to go on to become Prime Minister (1945–51), almost fifty years before. Brown's great fear was that Blair might make something of the job, outshine him, and establish himself as Smith's clear successor ahead of him.[45] Brown was in a quandary: should he run against Smith's wishes, or should he quit the field in favour of his junior partner?

Publicly, Smith had been giving out mixed messages about his favoured deputy, but when the post-General Election speculation had peaked, he had come to the conclusion that his best and safest option was to support Margaret Beckett, who would provide him with the much sought-after balance: not only was she English, but she was a woman.[46] Smith was just as unenthusiastic on a Blair candidature as Brown, despite what his staff later said.[47] He thought it would be divisive for Blair to stand and it might have provoked Cunningham, who saw himself as the senior north England MP, to come into the ring.[48]

Smith worried that matters were getting out of hand. The news was accordingly leaked to the media that Margaret Beckett, who was on the left of the party, would be standing as deputy. She first heard about it listening to the radio that weekend: 'I was quite horrified,' she said. 'I rang both Gordon and Tony and said, "I'm not running for deputy leader. And I assume one of you will be."' But she changed her mind, she says, after a deluge of phone calls from all sections of the party, as people recognised that she would balance John Smith's ticket. By the

Monday evening she decided to stand.[49] Kinnock formally resigned the leadership the same day. Brown's nightmare was resolved for him when Blair decided, on hearing of Beckett's decision, that he would not put his name forward. He also saw the logic of having a woman as Smith's deputy.

The principal reason why Blair pulled back was not because of Brown's feelings but electoral arithmetic. He was particularly concerned about gathering support from the trade unions, which under the Electoral College then held 40 per cent of the vote.[50] Brown had asked Nick Brown and Doug Henderson to 'do the arithmetic' and count up those who would vote for Blair: their findings, which Brown presented to Blair, were that he would not even carry the Parliamentary Labour Party.[51] Brown's obvious hostility, though not decisive, also weighed with Blair: he did not want, at this stage, to do anything that would seriously upset his great friend and partner.[52] Roy Hattersley, who had held the post for the last nine years, told Blair it was a 'nothing job' although he thought Blair was 'very torn about standing as deputy'.[53]

By pulling back Blair and Brown faced the certainty that neither the party's leader nor deputy leader would be modernisers: Bryan Gould was Smith's only challenger for leader (Kinnock failed to persuade him not to stand). Gould, Prescott and Beckett were the three deputy contenders. Of the three, the one who was most committed to modernisation was Gould. However, his brand of modernisation, firmly rooted in the soft left of the party, differed considerably from Blair's,[54] and both Blair and Brown were highly critical of Gould's political judgement. 'They also saw Gould as a major threat in the glamour stakes,' said one close contemporary.[55] Pulling back only made Blair more resolute that the next time the opportunity beckoned he would seize the moment. Blair's supporters were frustrated, none more so than Cherie, who had wanted him to stand for deputy, and who blamed Gordon Brown and Nick Brown for talking him out of standing, as she saw it, for their own selfish advantage.[56] Her frustration was partly with Gordon Brown – but it was also with Tony for his assumption that he had to make way for his friend.

The General Election defeat thus had deepened Blair's belief that only profound modernisation would lead to electoral success; the drama about the leadership and deputy leadership over the period 10–13 April made him realise how much he craved power himself. The ERM débâcle that was to irrevocably damage John Major's government five months later would serve to heighten the stakes for him and his party. His relationship with Gordon Brown, while remaining close for another two years, was never quite the same again.

Plugging His Gaps, 1992–94

From 14 April 1992, Blair was clear he would stand either as deputy or leader of the Labour Party the next time the opportunity presented itself, although this was not a belief he shared beyond the tightest circle. Those working in his office, for example, were not yet brought into his confidence.[57] Over the following months, his desire for the top job grew, and by the end of 1993 he was absolutely convinced, as was Cherie, that he should go for the leadership when the moment came. He was aware that he lacked the key attributes of a leader, notably a clear agenda of his own, sufficient allies in the party and unions, and a profile with the media and in the country. He set out on a path of deliberately plugging these gaps.

Blair's pronouncements and actions since he joined the Labour Party in 1975 had been guided, more than anything, by the opportunities that arose along the way. He may have read deeply at Oxford, but, if he had read much Labour history or left-wing philosophy in 1983–92, his utterances bore little mark of it. 'Community' remains a mantra, but one sympathetic journalist who tried to tease out what exactly he meant by it, and whether it was a geographical or social concept, found him 'ludicrously vague, even incoherent'. 'Modernisation' was another mantra, but modernisation to Blair was a means to an end: a united Labour front that would deliver an election victory. However, he still had not seriously thought through the policies that a modernised party would need to enact when it achieved power. He was aware that his platform was wafer-thin. In the *Guardian* Melanie Phillips described interviewing him as 'a bit like talking to a man without a shadow, a man with no form . . . a pleasant man with a pleasant family living in a pleasant North London house'.[58] It was a common perception.

His first serious attempt to bring his ideas together had come the year before the election. He had offered an article to Martin Jacques, editor of *Marxism Today*, a monthly journal at the cutting edge of thinking about policies and society. Jacques usually turned down unsolicited proposals from politicians as of little interest, but he accepted Blair's offer – 'I thought he was the first person who fully understood the extent of Labour's crisis.'[59] Jacques went to Blair's Islington home to discuss the article, and they grew friendly for a time. 'I gained the distinct impression that Cherie was the *Marxism Today* reader,' he later said. 'She was the thinker, he the politician.'[60] The article went through three or four drafts – Blair took immense pains over it – and it appeared in the October issue. In embryonic form, Blair articulated what were to become the five strands of his lifelong credo. First, community: 'Citizenship . . . without community is empty rhetoric.' Second, direct democracy: 'Our political system is a conspiracy against reason.' Third, and new, social moralism: society needs to recognise 'rights and obligations'. Fourth, the primacy of wealth creation, rather than a focus just on redistribution: 'A thriving competitive market is essential for individual choice. It is not a threat to ordinary people.' Finally, modernisation in an international context: Britain requires 'a modern constitution and modernised government' linked 'with Europe and the broader world' and 'in Europe we should be leading events'. He even began talking the language of the third way: in the future, the traditional debate of market versus the state should be superseded by an effort to 'make the state and market subject to the public interest'.[61] Underlying everything he said was the sense of Blair defending the individual in society, the patient against the NHS, pupils against teacher unions, the victim rather than the criminal.

Blair lacked the cast of mind, the knowledge and the contacts, to flesh out these five positions further himself. Martin Jacques highlighted this when he turned on Blair in July 1992. He wrote about his disappointment at the failure of any one of Labour's leaders to address or indeed fully understand the party's crisis. He thought Blair, 'frequently cited as the leader Labour needs', was better than most, and he 'spoke' a good game about how Labour had 'got into its present mess'. But when required to speak about plans and policies for the future, Blair tended towards 'waffle and cliché'.[62] Blair made a careful note of some of Jacques' prescriptions for the way ahead: talk to the Liberal Democrats, leading to an electoral pact; abandon the idea that state is the universal saviour; and learn from non-Labour thinking in Britain and abroad.[63] Blair absorbed the *Marxism Today* language quickly enough, declaring in the *Guardian*, 'Winning the next election for Labour requires . . . a project. A project of renewal.'[64] *Marxism Today* readers liked the word 'project'. But the hard content was still missing in Blair's thinking.

Another big opportunity to set out his stall came when Barbara Amiel, a *Sunday Times* journalist, offered to write a profile on him, which was to be his biggest newspaper exposure to date. 'Huge consideration was put into exactly what he would say,' recalls one in his office. 'We spent two weeks agonising over it.'[65] Amiel had agreed to write the piece on set terms. 'I agreed to do it as long as I could stay a weekend with them. Islington was ruled out (I later found out due to Cherie, who was relentlessly hostile to me) and I stayed with them in Sedgefield.'[66] The profile is remembered less for her difficult chemistry with Cherie –

which she largely excluded from the finished piece – nor for what Blair said, though his determination to change the Labour Party by ending block votes received its most emphatic statement to date, nor for Amiel's forensic cross-examination of what exactly Blair meant by 'community'. Rather, the article is remembered for the headline added when it appeared in the 'Magazine' section on 19 July, the day after Smith was elected leader: 'LABOUR'S LEADER IN WAITING', with the sub-heading 'Yesterday Labour elected a new leader. Some feel the party should have skipped a generation and gone for Tony Blair. At the very least they believe he should have stood for deputy leader.'[67]

The leadership election on 18 July had produced no surprises: Smith received over ten times the vote of Bryan Gould for the leadership, and Beckett won the deputy leadership election with 57 per cent of the vote. Prescott came second with 28 per cent and Gould a poor third with 15 per cent. Blair may not have been a candidate but his quick response after the General Election defeat had at least helped shape the debate over the party's future in the terms he, Brown and Mandelson intended, delineating the two sides as 'modernisation' against the 'one more heave' school. Even traditionalists like Smith realised over-identification with the latter would be perilous, and his leadership manifesto *New Path to Power* had a modernising timbre. The three arch-modernisers played some role here, drafting various sections of the manifesto, which led Mandelson to spin the line that Brown and Blair had 'ridden to the rescue' of the Smith campaign.[68] The principal author of the Smith manifesto was his campaign manager, Robin Cook,[69] and his big idea was the Social Policy agenda put together by Patricia Hewitt – then with the IPPR – after consultation with Kinnock.[70]

The shadow Cabinet elections the following week saw Brown top the poll and Blair come second, his highest placing so far. Brown received from Smith his promised shadow Chancellorship and chairmanship of Smith's newly created Economic Policy Commission, comprised of shadow Cabinet and NEC members, while Blair was given the job for which he had lobbied, shadow Home Secretary. Kaufman and Hattersley were the two principal figures of the old guard whom he liked to regard as his mentors, and they both told him to go for the job: it was a senior post and a clear area in which the party needed to rethink its policies.[71] Ironically, had Kinnock won the election, Blair would have been given a lesser post (albeit in government), Secretary of State for Employment and Training and Brown would have been given Trade and Industry. 'These were what I'd pencilled in,' Kinnock later wrote, 'just in case things had gone better than I expected.'[72]

The shadow Home Secretaryship from 1992 to 1994 gave Blair the chance to develop the third plank of his credo: 'responsibilities as well as rights', and social moralism. As he often did, he spent the first few weeks in his new job thinking and not committing himself.[73] He discovered he had a real interest – unsurprisingly, perhaps, for a barrister – in crime. His first real mark in the post came six months into his job, with the words 'tough on crime and tough on the causes of crime', spoken to Nick Clarke on Radio 4's *The World This Weekend* on Sunday, 10 January 1993. 'It was probably the cleverest political slogan any Labour politician had hit upon in fourteen years of opposition,' wrote Smith's biographer, Andy McSmith.[74] Blair was speaking on the weekend after his return from his important post-Clinton election trip to the US with Brown, where he had been fired up in part by the success of Clinton's tough line on crime. Blair's Sedgefield constituency had also helped shape his view that crime was a Labour and a working-class issue, and that the party had become too identified with blaming society, rather than law-breakers, leaving the ground open for the Conservatives to be the 'tough on crime' party. Clinton had reclaimed crime as a Democratic Party issue: Blair now wanted to do the same for Labour. His thinking also owed something to his Christian beliefs, rooted in personal responsibility for one's actions. The words themselves that Sunday have had their paternity claimed by the rival Blair and Brown camps,[75] while Mandelson suggests they originated with Bill Clinton.[76] In fact the precise words were Brown's: 'I heard him utter them.'[77] But the more important point is, was there substance to underpin the words? Admiration for the cute phrase distracted attention from the fact Blair had to flesh out the words he spoke.

Blair visibly expanded into his theme. In the *Sun* two months later he wrote, 'It's a bargain – we give opportunity but demand responsibility. There is no excuse for crime. None.'[78] Blair had also absorbed another lesson of the Clinton campaign as mediated to him by Philip Gould – don't have too many messages, keep them simple, repeat them often. The opportunity for the biggest realisation of the formula came after the shocking murder of two-year-old James Bulger on 12 February 1993. The killing, by two adolescent boys, horrified and traumatised the nation. Blair himself was deeply moved, and decided to use the platform of a speech he was to give to the Labour Party in Wellingborough a week later to air his feelings. It was to be one of the most personal and heartfelt speeches of his career. Displaying a growing confidence and felicity with his use of language, he wrote every word himself, and he travelled alone to the unlikely venue of an upstairs room in a pub.[79] 'The news bulletins of the last week have been like hammer blows struck against the sleeping conscience of the country,' he told the Wellingborough Labour Party. 'A solution to this disintegration doesn't simply lie in legislation. It must come from the rediscovery of a sense of direction as a country . . . not just as individuals but as a community.' Responsibility for bringing up children, he said, rested firmly with parents. 'We cannot exist in a moral vacuum. If we do not learn and then teach the value of what is right and wrong, then the result is simply moral chaos that engulfs us all.'

Blair masterfully caught the mood of the nation, as he was to do four years later following the death of a young princess in Paris. He received his biggest postbag to date, as well as, in the words of journalists Michael White and Patrick Wintour, 'mass media attention for the first time since taking the Home Affairs brief after the 1992 election'.[80] The most important impact, though, was on his self-confidence.[81] For perhaps the first time he articulated in public thoughts coming from deep within himself, and the fact that they struck a chord in the nation gave him an immeasurable boost. He was beginning to find his voice.

There were to be no other comparable events during his shadow Home Secretaryship, a role he played to perfection. The appointment of Michael Howard to replace Ken Clarke as Home Secretary in May 1993 proved hugely beneficial to Blair. This was not because he found Howard an easy opponent: he did not. However, unlike Clarke, Howard brought an activist approach to the Home Office and was determined to shake up policy, making radical changes as necessary. 'Prison works,' Howard declared as he unveiled twenty-seven points of reform at the Conservative Party Conference in October 1993.[82] The controversy that this generated ensured that Blair's clashes with Howard earned considerable public attention. Blair decided not to oppose the government on all its measures, persuading Smith, for example, to co-operate with the government on the Prevention of Terrorism Act, and instead focused all his energies on just a few areas. His stance won him new friends and admirers: David Blunkett and Jack Straw were very supportive, and became allies.[83] Blair developed his 'family' theme in a speech that June: 'Out of a family grows the sense of community. The family is the starting place.'[84] This kind of line did not go down well with *Guardian* liberals: 'I don't want some pol like you telling me that I represent social disintegration because I'm separated from my wife and children,' fumed Will Self later.[85] But it played well elsewhere, especially on the centre and right. Melanie Phillips pricked up her ears at talk of family, a particular interest of hers, and she responded to a request to see him. 'There is a hole at the heart of Labour voting,' he told her, 'and it is called "the family".' She felt he was exploring the kind of Labour leader he wanted to be and was casting around for roots: he was reading a biography of Keir Hardie at the time, and was looking for historical parallels. Over a series of discussions, he and Phillips ranged over ethical socialism and antecedents in Labour thinking on the importance of the family.[86] She remained suspicious of Blair in other areas, however, and became thoroughly disillusioned when he failed to take the steps she deemed necessary to strengthen the family when he entered Number 10.

Blair was relentlessly working to heighten his profile. In support of his bid to join the NEC in the autumn of 1992, a step he reluctantly believed was now necessary, he campaigned heavily on Labour becoming a party 'not just of activists, but of ordinary voters'.[87] He came fifth in the poll. He wrote powerful rallying articles such as 'Why Modernisation Matters' for *Renewal* and 'A Battle We Must Win' for the *Fabian Review*.[88] Blair seemed particularly incensed by claims that his 'project for renewal' did not sit well in the Labour tradition. His message, as expounded during an interview for the BBC's *On the Record*, was a radical one: 'It's anti-elite, it's anti-Establishment and it is the fulfilment of our values, not the shedding of them.'[89] He was as keen to win friends in the oldest organisations on the left as in brand-new ones like *Renewal*, which was founded in 1993 by Neal Lawson and Paul Thompson.[90] The Blairs' Islington home became a social centre that drew in politicians and thinkers of all parties. Blair spread himself in entirely new ways too. In April 1993, he attended a four-day 'Bilderberg' conference in Athens, a glitzy international event attended by leading international figures, including Amiel's husband Conrad Black, Chairman of the Telegraph Group, and Andrew Knight, Executive Chairman of News International.[91] He attended the exclusive 'Other Club', founded by Winston Churchill and F. E. Smith in 1911, where Robin Day introduced him to Robin Butler, the Cabinet Secretary, with the words, 'You are sitting next to a future Prime Minister.'[92] A speech at the INSEAD, the prestigious business school outside Paris, boosted his confidence and connections.[93]

The press was cultivated assiduously, a role in which Blair was enthusiastically helped by Mandelson as well as Anji Hunter. He was pushing at an open door. Andrew Neil, editor of the *Sunday Times*, was perhaps his most influential convert:[94] as early as 1990 he had spotted Tony Blair as a future leader, and thought that Brown in contrast lacked the language to communicate beyond the party faithful.[95] Neil prompted the pieces by Jacques and by Amiel, and wrote the provocative headline to her July 1992 profile. Alastair Campbell, a former political editor at the *Mirror*, the party's loyalist newspaper, and then at *Today*, was also promoting Blair, and was similarly convinced of his merits over Brown's. Philip Stephens of the *Financial Times* became another to be convinced of his strengths: 'The party's "foremost moderniser" or "the next Labour leader" are the epithets most commonly applied by political commentators to Tony Blair,'[96] Stephens wrote in September 1993. Philip Webster of *The Times*, Patrick Wintour of the *Guardian* and Andy Grice of the *Independent* were others who were impressed by him, and in whom he confided.

Building up his office was another prerequisite for his advance. He had fought the 1992 election with just Roz Preston and James Purnell (helped by intern Clive Russell). Anji Hunter returned in September 1992, Purnell and Preston left soon after, and Tim Allan joined. It was a strong team, but it failed to match the numbers and firepower of Gordon Brown's office, which, from 1993, had been strengthened by the formidable intellectual presence of Ed Balls and the media savvy of Charlie Whelan.

Blair had thus begun to put in place during 1992–94 many of the elements he would need if he were to become leader. But he was very far from ready. He had come to believe that he was the best-qualified figure to take over from Smith, but that eventuality, he assumed, was a long way off. Fatally weakened by Black Wednesday in September 1992, it was already clear by early 1994 that the Tories would lose,[97] and that within two years, or at the most three, John Smith would become Labour's first Prime Minister since James Callaghan almost twenty years before. Ample time was thus available, he believed, to build up further his platform, his staff, his allies in the party – and to talk over the succession with Gordon Brown and persuade him that he would make the better leader.

*Peter Mandelson watches Blair intently over his shoulder. Like a ventriloquist,
Mandelson's mouth is shut. He has spent twenty years monitoring
Blair's every move.*

14

Peter Mandelson

No other influence on Blair has been so controversial as Peter Mandelson. He polarises opinion more than anyone else Blair can count as a friend. He is the most intuitively brilliant of all Blair's entourage, yet his sporadic misjudgements have left Blair intensely frustrated. Many of those sympathetic to Blair, when contemplating his dependence on Mandelson, respond with one word: 'Why?' The difficulty of writing about Mandelson and his importance to Blair is heightened by his pervasive presence in the literature and press, which is not always accurate, or even half true, and because people speak about him with such passion – sometimes positively, often not. Mandelson's biographer, Don Macintyre, highlights this core difficulty when he says, 'The Mandelson, Blair, Brown triangle is fundamentally impenetrable to anyone outside. When you try to understand these things, or anything to do with Peter, it is very much a case of "through a glass darkly".[1] This chapter, nevertheless, endeavours to gaze through that glass and to assess his importance to Blair, and less directly, to the modern Labour Party.

Mandelson: Finding His Mission, 1953–85

Peter Mandelson was born on 21 October 1953 in a comfortable north London suburb. His father, George, was advertising manager for the *Jewish Chronicle*; his mother, Mary, was a one-time office worker. Peter had always been intensely proud of the fact that her father was Herbert Morrison, a great folk figure of the golden years of Labour under Clement Attlee, having been leader of the London County Council before the war, Home

Secretary during it and Deputy Prime Minister after it. Harold Wilson lived close by and young Peter and his older brother played with the Wilson children. When Wilson became Prime Minister in October 1964, Mandelson visited them at Number 10, went to garden parties, toured the Cabinet and state rooms, and saw the Trooping of the Colour. In his early years, the Labour Party permeated Mandelson's life. He passed the 11-plus exam to enter Hendon County Grammar School, where he was rebellious and politically active, joining the party formally at the age of sixteen, then the Young Socialists and, for a time, the Young Communist League.[2]

Unlike Blair, Mandelson had an altruistic gap year, spending it partly on community work in Tanzania. And unlike Blair, but like Brown, he was active at university in the Labour Club. Mandelson's interests dictated his degree subject, Philosophy, Politics and Economics, which he read at St Catherine's College, Oxford from 1973 to 1976 (he later quipped that he didn't know Blair at Oxford, where they overlapped for two years, because he was interested in politics).[3] Mandelson became president of his college's Junior Common Room and also National President of the UN Youth and Student Association. The second-class degree he earned on leaving university failed to do justice to his intellectual ability. This was due less to his active political and social life and more to illness (a tropical bug from his time in Tanzania), which forced him to miss most of two terms of his final year.

Mandelson left Oxford even more focused on politics than when he had begun. Two particularly influential experiences followed. Shortly after leaving Oxford he joined the TUC's Economics Department and worked as researcher to Shadow Transport Minister Albert Booth. His duties included taking notes at the meetings between the TUC General Council and senior Labour politicians, during which he witnessed the appalling relations between the unions and the Labour Party at first hand. In 1978 he became chairman of the British Youth Council, where he met Charles Clarke, then still President of the National Union of Students. Mandelson's second formative experience came later that year when, at the age of just twenty-four, he was elected to Lambeth Council, where he met his lifelong ally (and co-author of *The Blair Revolution*)[4] Roger Liddle. Liddle later joined the SDP (at the time it was wrongly alleged that Mandelson was himself tempted to join), but rejoined Labour when Blair became leader and went on to work on policy in Number 10. The Labour group in Lambeth was led by Ted Knight, a determined hard-left figure, who helped inspire in Mandelson a distaste and loathing for the extreme left-wing of the party.

In 1982, amid widespread despair at the state of the Labour Party nationally, Mandelson joined London Weekend Television (LWT), working on the current-affairs programme *Weekend World*, described by Anthony Howard as 'that great Blairite kindergarten'.[5] Mandelson began as a researcher but was soon promoted to producer. Colleagues said that he had the talent to branch out beyond current affairs. Mandelson, however, was not planning on a lifelong career in television: politics remained his real love. At LWT he met many key figures who would be of great importance to him later, including John Birt and Barry Cox, and he studiously absorbed lessons about the way in which the media, specifically television, operated, and how to present an individual or an argument in the best possible light. Without this grooming, Mandelson would have been just another young hopeful who wanted to work for the Labour Party. With it, he was a figure of real skill and knowledge.

In October 1985 came his critical appointment as Director of Campaigns and Communications, aged only thirty-two. Charles Clarke, who had been initially reticent about Mandelson applying,[6] eventually warmed to the idea and helped him secure the post.[7] 'Steel first entered my soul when I realised what I had taken on,' he said. 'I had never done a job like that before. I was young and found it a colossal strain.'[8] The organisation he joined had a deep suspicion of modern communications and associated techniques. Ex-General Secretary, Jim Mortimer, encapsulated the prevailing atmosphere when he pronounced: 'The Labour Party will never follow [advertising] in its presentation of politics . . . We are not presenting politicians as if they were breakfast food or baked beans.'[9] Mandelson clearly had a mountain to climb, and he also found a party in disarray having suffered in 1983 'its greatest defeat since 1931'. He imagined his role as comparable to the task faced by those, including his grandfather, after the terrible trauma in 1931 under Ramsay MacDonald. 'I'm very much my grandfather's grandson,' he said. 'My grandfather was a key figure, along with Clement Attlee, Ernest Bevin and Hugh Dalton. He rebuilt the Labour Party from the ashes of the 1930s . . . Now I see the Labour Party rebuilding from the ashes of 1983.'[10] Bringing in Philip Gould, and setting up the Shadow Communications Agency, were key steps in realising his goal.

Mandelson and Blair, 1985–97

Mandelson was like a film mogul in his new post. He picked his cast, wrote the polished scripts and promoted them where and when he wished. As he said in his first interview in the job: 'Communication means throwing your net much wider than publicity. It means deciding what we say, how we say it and which spokesman and woman we choose to say it.'[11] Although he had a high opinion in the mid- to late 1980s of Bryan Gould, Mandelson's two enduring stars were Brown and Blair.[12] Hattersley and then Kinnock were the first to spot, and then to promote, Blair, but it was Mandelson, with Kinnock's backing, who gave him exposure on the national stage. The Parliamentary Labour Party was so small, and so low in talent, that only Brown and Blair filled Mandelson's exacting requirements of looking good on television, being bright and sounding intelligent, and having the right modernising instincts. To Mandelson they were of an utterly different class to others in the party. Mandelson's activities soon aroused resentment on the Labour front-bench team: Oonagh MacDonald from the shadow Treasury team was an early figure to complain about Mandelson's preference for Blair over her.[13] More serious were the 'big beasts'. Mandelson had little or no time in his work for many of the party's senior figures, such as Michael Meacher and John Prescott, particularly after the latter challenged Hattersley for the deputy leadership in 1988.[14] These feelings were fully reciprocated.

The first phase of Blair's relationship with Mandelson lasted from 1985 to 1990. Mandelson became to both Blair and Brown a mixture of casting director, coach and mentor. His protégés had immense talent, without which they would never have progressed, but Mandelson honed their performances and made sure they were noticed in the places that mattered. He watched over them giving interviews, and then immediately phoned them afterwards to give them feedback. Their trust in him was complete. They were in awe of him. The prestige media slots, above all the weekend radio and television slots, and choice print interviews would be pushed in their direction. Mandelson talked up both men relentlessly to friends in the media. Few could deny that Brown and Blair had talent, and many journalists were happy to print most of what he told them.[15] 'By 1987 it was pretty clear that he'd got a way with reporters,' said one senior aide from the time. 'They were either eating out of his hand or they were terrified of him, and he had a clique who were prepared to take almost everything he said and use it.'[16] An increasingly self-confident Mandelson would lash out verbally at editors, broadcasters and writers who attacked or talked down his protégés. Senior figures in the party would increasingly find themselves briefed against, though Mandelson insisted this only happened when they stepped out of line with party policy and with Neil Kinnock's full knowledge.[17] Most of the shadow Cabinet were indeed utter innocents in this world and the circles in which Mandelson operated, and he exploited that fact to the full. He was five steps or more ahead of most of them.

Mandelson was also playing a growing part in shaping not just Labour's presentation but also its policy. Mandelson was devoted to Neil Kinnock and later said that he was the politician he admired most for 'guts and courage'.[18] Kinnock needed both of these qualities in abundance as he struggled to wrestle control of the party from the radical left and put it on the path to modernisation. Together with Clarke, Mandelson helped form a 'ring of steel' around Kinnock, knocking back the attacks and shoring up his position in the media when necessary.[19] Mandelson is rightly given much of the credit for Labour's presentation as well as policy being so improved in the 1987 General Election. His personal fame was also growing. 'Ah, the red rose man,' Prince Charles greeted him at a reception at Kensington Palace.[20]

The Mandelson–Brown–Blair relationship took off fully only in 1987, during, but mostly after, the General Election,[21] and by 1988 they were seeing each other and talking to each other on the phone several times most days. Mandelson was the most confident figure of the three on presentational matters, and the other two deferred regularly to him. 'I helped Tony to air his plans and anxieties, test his ideas and I provided reassurance,' said Mandelson. 'I did all this in continuous conversations with him.'[22] However, at this stage Mandelson was closer to Brown and spent more time with him, not least in the evenings after Blair had gone home to his family.[23] At the outset Mandelson regarded Brown as unquestionably the senior and the more capable of the two. The identity of interest between the three, the shared sense of mission and their companionship, was rare in politics. The only other people who came close in the late 1980s to penetrating the clique were Philip Gould and Alastair Campbell. But in 1989, to Kinnock's amazement and Clarke's horror, Mandelson decided that he wanted to become an MP. This made perfect sense to him and he was encouraged in his decision by both Brown and Blair. From his Sedgefield base, the latter was instrumental in helping Mandelson win a nomination in the north-east.[24] He no longer wanted to be in the wings or in the studio barking out instructions: he wanted to be on the stage himself, in the limelight. Mandelson left his post in late 1990, shortly after he secured the Hartlepool nomination. 'Peter was sick of making other people into stars,' said one of his staff. 'He wanted to be a serious politician in his own right.'[25]

'Triumvirate' best describes the second phase of the relationship, from Mandelson's standing down as Director of Communications until John Smith's death in 1994. Mandelson continued offering periodic advice to the party in 1990–92, but his heart was focused on his Hartlepool constituency, on which he lavished great attention, and on building his career in the north-east.[26] With Brown and Blair taking a back seat in the national 1992 election campaign, the three spent even more time together and became almost inseparable. When Mandelson entered the House after the 1992 General Election, they continued to bounce ideas off each other, and fire each other up. Mandelson remained Blair's and Brown's promoter and defender in the media, and their adviser on presentation. 'I was driving Mandelson in my car one day in the early 1990s and he spent the whole journey on the phone to Blair, going through a speech with him line by line, pointing out the elephant traps,'[27] recalled Richard Stott, then editing the *People*. Towards the end of this period Brown, unlike Blair, acquired his own specialist media adviser (Charlie Whelan – ironically, given their later deep hatred, on Mandelson's recommendation). Brown, Blair and Mandelson had their differences, principally over the leadership and deputy leadership issue in 1992, and the hidden and never discussed issue of the succession. But, at least on the surface, harmony between three extraordinarily close friends returned. Mandelson helped on Blair's campaigns for the NEC elections in 1992, he worked with them both on the prolonged OMOV debate, with Brown on the new economic policy and on the Clintonisation thrust.[28] Smith suspected that Mandelson was acting as spokesman for the modernisers in the media, spinning the line that the leadership was not moving fast enough. So antagonised did Smith become with Mandelson that in the end he resorted to a ploy, unsuccessfully, of persuading him to come to work for him as media adviser, as a way of keeping him quiet. Mandelson asked for time to think about it, then declined Smith's offer.[29] He preferred being associated with Brown and Blair. Tim Allan remembers how relaxed the three were in each other's company: 'The three of them would spend just hours together, sitting around drinking tea.'[30]

Blair delighted in Mandelson's company. Clive Russell, who worked for both men from 1992 to 1994, said, 'I'd never in my life met anyone quite like Peter. Neither had I ever seen a relationship like his and Tony's. I've never witnessed any two people so close as Tony and Peter. I used to think Peter was like Merlin, with this incredible ability to see into the future, and Tony was King Arthur.'[31] For all that, Mandelson still saw Brown as closer to him. Another observer explained why. Both men were more 'political' than Blair; and Mandelson admired Brown's energy and obvious work capacity more: Brown was available in the Commons more often while Blair had gone home to be with his family, and both men were far more emotionally committed to the Labour Party than Blair ever was. The greater closeness is illustrated by Mandelson asking Brown to draft ideas for his selection speech at Hartlepool, and by Sue Nye, one of Brown's staff, hosting Mandelson's fortieth birthday party in October 1993.[32]

Extraordinary heat has been generated over whether Mandelson had decided before May 1994 to support Blair rather than Brown. Mandelson's friends are firmly of the opinion that Mandelson remained loyal to Brown until some days after Smith's death: 'It's just rubbish to say Peter was promoting Blair over Brown before Smith's death.'[33] Brown's supporters think that Mandelson abandoned Brown far earlier. According to Paul Routledge, 'although initially closer to Brown, [Mandelson] had discreetly gravitated to Blair, the man most likely to advance his ill-concealed ambition'.[34]

The truth lies halfway between these notions. Mandelson was in a terrible dilemma: as one close friend says, 'he admired Blair but he loved Brown'.[35] But Mandelson, by 1993, was coming to appreciate, as were many, that Blair was developing into a formidable political personality who could take the party forward. He would not, however, admit it to himself, still less to anyone else, that Blair was the better candidate to win the General Election, and found it extremely difficult to detach himself from Brown, the closest friend he had ever had in politics. He continued to work closely with both men while pushing the question of where his ultimate loyalty lay firmly to the back of his mind.[36] All of this would have been academic so long as Smith was leader. But Smith's sudden death precipitated a crisis. Mandelson's ambivalent position was no longer tenable. In the immediate aftermath of the death, he made a point of talking up Brown as the preferable successor.[37] But then he began to bow to the overwhelming feeling that it had to be Blair, at which point his concern became how to persuade Brown to withdraw without losing face. What is clear is that by the weekend immediately after Smith's death, Mandelson had decided that a Brown candidature would be difficult to mount, and that he should be persuaded to make way for Blair.

What Mandelson was trying to avoid was precisely what happened, a ferocious response from Brown and his entourage, which has shown no signs of abating even ten years on. As the next chapter demonstrates, the Brown camp felt Mandelson had been treacherous. Why did they care so much? It was more than a personal betrayal. Brown (and Blair) ascribed to Mandelson almost legendary powers to sway the media and public opinion, and in effect deliver the leadership. They thought that Mandelson was the kingmaker. Blair himself did not need Mandelson to advise him to run: he made up his own mind. He played an important role advising Blair on strategy and his use of the media throughout the campaign, but Blair kept his role secret so as not to antagonise the campaign team (and Brown) and then compounded this deceit by naïvely disclosing his role (and nickname, 'Bobby') after the victory was announced.

After Blair's election as leader, his relationship with Mandelson entered a new phase, which lasted until 1997. The triumvirate was no more. When the three were together, tension took the place of laughter and suspicion the ready trust of the past. Shouting and slamming of doors became commonplace. Campbell, who joined Blair's staff in September 1994, announced before one meeting, 'I'm off to see the children.'[38] The final break between Mandelson and Brown was cemented at the Chewton Glen Hotel seminar convened by Blair in September 1994 to plan the way ahead. Brown is alleged to have said to Mandelson in the penumbra of the seminars that if they worked together, they could prevail over Blair and effectively run the party. Mandelson replied that he would always work closely with Brown, but that ultimately Blair was leader. Brown paused. 'You make your choice,' he is said to have retorted before storming off.[39] From that moment on, the intense friendship the two men had was replaced by a quite extraordinary and destructive froideur.

Blair, on becoming leader, had his profile as Prime Minister-in-waiting massively increased overnight. He was in a very new world, and did not have the army of helpers he would find on entering Number 10. Blair thus relied on Mandelson more intensively in the 1994–97 period than at any other time in their twenty years of knowing each other. Mandelson was initially concerned that being cast as the 'leader's little helper' would help neither Blair nor himself.[40] Both men recognised that the gap between Mandelson's junior position (Opposition Whip in 1994 and then Opposition spokesman on the Civil Service in 1995) and his role as one of Blair's most powerful advisers would produce unfavourable comment and cause resentment in the party. But Blair could see no immediate alternative. Despite the difficulty of the situation, Mandelson's willingness to accede to Blair's wishes was beyond doubt. He committed himself to Blair with an ardour some found surprising: 'There is no question of me ceasing to act as your friend and adviser,' he wrote to Blair in mid-1995. 'I am always thinking of you. I will do anything you ask of me.'[41]

Blair capitalised on these sentiments to the full. For Blair's first six months as leader (until Jonathan Powell arrived from the British Embassy in Washington) Mandelson was de facto chief of staff, and he advised heavily with appointments. There were few of Blair's major decisions between 1994 and 1997 in which he was not closely involved. Blair was obsessed about raising enough money to fight the coming General Election on equal footing with the Tories, and while Michael Levy was in the lead as fundraiser, Mandelson would help by giving presentations to 'high value' donors. The 'big tent' strategy was very much a shared enthusiasm. He and Blair were both enthusiasts for the 'third way' and, on a much more practical level, he worked closely with Blair on policy formation. He was particularly influential in Blair's positioning on the Euro, on the minimum wage and the windfall tax, and advised on how to manage Whitehall once in office. Mandelson's book, written with Liddle, *The Blair Revolution*, was conceived as a broad statement of Labour thinking, and advocated electoral reform and a coalition with the Liberal Democrats. But a much watered-down form was published in February 1996 so as not to clash with Labour's official policy. One of its ideas, however, for a stronger, streamlined powerhouse for the Prime Minister in Number 10 and the Cabinet Office, was brought into being. Mandelson helped induct Campbell, and then worked with him closely if not always harmoniously on day-to-day media management. He also managed relations with the BBC through liaising with John Birt and his subordinates. By 1996 he was installed full-time at Millbank in the run-up to the General Election. He chaired the weekly planning meeting and performed a role for the party similar to that in the 1987 General Election. He worked closely with the Liberal Democrats' leadership exploring various plans for co-operation during and after the election.

Mandelson was also a principal architect of New Labour. Philip Gould provided the research evidence that showed that Labour had to appeal to the middle ground. If Gould was the technician, Mandelson was the strategist who saw that 'Old' Labour was fatally torn between two wings, which had crippled it in power in the 1960s and 1970s. Trying to reconcile both wings was pointless. The only viable way forward was to reject both the old left and the old right and to re-brand the party as, in effect, a new party: New Labour. Mandelson was disappointed in one major area only: he harboured a desire to be made officially responsible for policy towards Europe,[42] but instead, after the election, Blair appointed him Minister Without Portfolio at the Cabinet Office, albeit with several European responsibilities. Six months later Mandelson suggested to Blair that it would be much better if he took over increased responsibilities for Europe, but Blair disagreed.[43] He had other plans for Mandelson.

Blair and Mandelson, 1997–2004

The 1997 General Election ushered in a new phase of the Blair–Mandelson relationship, and their relationship never again found the same groove it had rested in before 1997. Mandelson was no longer the only strategist and fixer. Instead, Blair was surrounded by a small army of helpers at Number 10, and had a far wider range of issues to cover as

Prime Minister, for many of which Mandelson was not in the loop. In this phase, their relationship thus shifted: they saw less of each other, but they still talked on the phone most days, often several times.[44] Mandelson might not have wanted to have been stuck in the Cabinet Office, without a department of his own to run, but Blair had Mandelson exactly where he wanted him, adjacent to Number 10, through an internal door, allowing him to meet with Mandelson without drawing attention to his presence, still relying on him as a sounding-board. He was also placed on more Cabinet committees than any minister except John Prescott.

Mandelson was bitterly disappointed in October 1997 when Blair lost control to Brown over the timing of entry into the Euro. Mandelson helped Campbell restructure government communications, but the latter rapidly established his own domain and there was always rivalry between them: sometimes they clashed on presentation, but often Campbell resented Blair seeking media advice from anyone other than himself.[45] Campbell and Mandelson had been close socially before 1997, but became more distant after Blair entered Number 10.[46]

In late June 1997, Blair gave Mandelson the Millennium Dome to oversee. Many had counselled against proceeding with the highly expensive project in London's Docklands even before Labour came to power, but Mandelson rose to the challenge. One of Blair's friends suggested that this was 'typical of Peter and Tony taking a huge risk together and ignoring others' reservations, which had often been successful in the past'.[47] With hindsight, however, given the critical response and costs associated with the Dome, few would agree that it was a risk worth taking. Mandelson was also heavily involved in the problems over welfare in 1997–98, and would be consulted by Blair when crises came up, as over Ecclestone in November 1997. Indeed, although Mandelson was not yet in Cabinet, he had more influence on Blair in 1997–98 than any Cabinet minister except Brown. His relations with the latter remained very difficult. Their relationship was generally a negative force within the government, yet on occasion it also worked to Blair's advantage. A senior official observed the way in which, when dealing with particularly controversial issues, Blair could play the two men off against each other and then seize the initiative himself.[48]

Despite his many roles in 1997–98, Mandelson was not satisfied, and he was said to have 'bombarded' Blair and Richard Wilson, the Cabinet Secretary (in succession to Robin Butler) with requests to be moved to a department of his own.[49] He was desperate to show that 'he was not the "prince of darkness" but that he was someone in his own right,'[50] as one of his officials put it. Mandelson had been someone's man all his political life: first Kinnock's, then Brown's, now Blair's. He wanted to be his own man.

Mandelson's wish was finally granted one year into the Parliament. In July 1998 he was appointed Secretary of State for Trade and Industry, a department he badly wanted. His officials quickly developed an extraordinary admiration for him: they liked his energy, warmth and verve, and the whole department felt lifted. 'He was a fantastic success,' said a very senior DTI civil servant.[51] He worked hard, particularly on the competitiveness white paper on building a 'knowledge-driven' economy and on the future of the Post Office. Now it was Mandelson who was very busy, and he and Blair saw less of each other as a result. When they did meet, their conversations were as much about Mandelson's work at the DTI, which impressed Blair considerably, as about political strategy.[52] Mandelson was well on his way to being one of the first-rate departmental ministers Blair badly needed in his first term. Mandelson, for the first time, was showing the world what he could achieve entirely on his own.

It all unravelled in December 1998 when Mandelson's house loan from Geoffrey Robinson, Paymaster General and Brown's key ally in the Treasury, was made public. The background to the story is well known. In 1996, before accepting ministerial office, Mandelson accepted a loan from Robinson to buy a house in Notting Hill. While the two men agreed that the loan would be considered a strictly private matter, the information controversially fell into the hands of Brown's top lieutenants. It was duly noted and stored away.

Frustration with Mandelson in Brown's camp, notably from Ed Balls, Nick Brown and Charlie Whelan, had been growing throughout 1998. The very reshuffle that saw Mandelson promoted to the DTI witnessed Brown's camp suffer. Mandelson's confident demeanour, and policies, in the second economic department (to the Treasury) irritated the Chancellor. Now Brown's supporters had the means to destroy him.[53]

Mandelson's problems began when the DTI looked into Robinson's past business activities. As soon as Mandelson became aware of the inquiry he had himself removed from all contact with it and with Robinson, avoiding, in his mind, any possible conflict of interest with the person to whom he owed so much money. He admitted to his officials that Robinson had been a friend of many years' standing, but, rightly or wrongly, he chose not to disclose the loan. Mandelson's conscience was clear, but his failure to declare the loan at this stage, even in confidence to his officials, risked the *perception* of a conflict of interest arising, should the loan ever become public. It is a significant failing on Mandelson's part that his acute political antennae did not foresee this possibility and act accordingly. Mandelson obviously hoped that the loan would remain private. His enemies, however, had different ideas.

Given the animosity between Brown and Mandelson, and Brown and Blair, news of the loan was bound to come out eventually, and it found its way into a critical biography of Mandelson by Paul Routledge. Suspicion for the leak fell on Whelan. On Thursday, 17 December, having been tipped off that the loan was about to become public, Mandelson asked his assistant, Ben Wegg-Prosser, to call Campbell and break the news to Number 10.[54] Realising the gravity of the situation, Campbell told Blair immediately, interrupting his frantic last-minute preparation for a Commons statement about action in Iraq.[55]

The next day, Michael Scholar, the Permanent Secretary at the DTI, went to see Richard Wilson, the Cabinet Secretary, to brief him about the loan. Wilson then went to see Blair and told him that day, and again on Sunday, 20 December, that he would find it very hard to defend Mandelson. Although there was no evidence that the home loan had led to a conflict of interest, the Ministerial Code, which lays down strict rules for ministers' conduct in office, requires that ministers not only ensure that no conflict of interest arises, but also that no conflict 'appears to arise'. The growing fear in Number 10 was that Mandelson had not done enough to avoid the *appearance* of a conflict of interest. And the media was scenting the blood of a man many had distrusted and reviled for his 'spin-meister' work since the mid-1980s.

When the story broke on Tuesday, 22 December, in spectacular style, these fears seemed justified. 'MANDELSON MUST GO' roared the *Evening Standard*, while the *Guardian* revealed the details of the 'secret' loan and several commentators began to call for Mandelson's resignation.[56] As the media spotlight intensified throughout the day, the need for Blair to come to a swift decision heightened. Blair and his Number 10 team spent Monday and Tuesday, 21 and 22 December, trying to save Mandelson. The Tories launched their own tangential attack, questioning whether or not Mandelson had declared the loan on his original mortgage application form. Mandelson's predicament deepened when Charles Falconer and Lance Price, a Number 10 press officer, learned from Wegg-Prosser that Mandelson had not told his building society about the loan.[57] Yet as the crisis began to grow, few recognised this charge as a red herring. Anything irregular seemed to be part of a picture. In fact, there had been no need for Mandelson to declare the loan when he filled in his mortgage application form, a fact confirmed in January 1999 by the conclusions of an investigation by his building society.[58]

By Wednesday morning, Blair very reluctantly concluded that the perception of a conflict of interest had now become too commonplace to deny. There was nothing more he could do. Campbell and Price were deputed to go to tell Mandelson the game was up. Price's diary records the drama of the day. 'Very traumatic and emotional . . . I got to No. 10 about 9.45 and AC [Campbell] came about 20 minutes later. He said he was pretty clear that P [Mandelson] would have to resign and that was TB's view too. I went to the Private Office and Jonathan [Powell] was already working on the reshuffle with Byers in line for the DTI.' Campbell and Price then went to the DTI office. 'AC said straight away that P should talk to TB [on the phone] and the rest of us left the room. Ben [Wegg-Prosser] started talking about the mortgage but I told him it had got beyond that. He asked me what I meant and I drew a line across my throat. He visibly blanched and tears came to his eyes – the first of several people to react in that way.' Mandelson broke off the phone call with Blair to think. He'd tried to persuade Blair that a severe reprimand would suffice. He was in a terrible quandary. 'P said "What do you think I should do?" I said I think you have to resign, but say you've done nothing wrong but that you're not prepared to see the government and the party damaged. He said "Yes." I gave him a squeeze on the shoulder and he had tears in his eyes too. He got on the phone to TB and said, "You've clearly made up your mind and there is no point trying to change it." AC started to draft the resignation letters . . . P said he didn't want to go at the same time as GR [Geoffrey Robinson] and Charlie [Whelan] "like some pack of thieves".'[59]

Because they knew that William Hague, the Tory leader, was booked to appear on the media that lunchtime and would call on Mandelson to resign, the press office concocted a story that Mandelson had told Blair the night before that he was going to leave the government. 'We did it because we didn't want to see the Tories get the credit for forcing his resignation,' one aide later said, 'and we wanted to contrast Labour's ministers speedily resigning with the lingering death of Tory ministers under Major.'[60]

Blair had acted decisively but also felt guilt about sacking his old friend. He assuaged it by inviting Mandelson and his partner, Reinaldo Avila da Silva, to spend that Wednesday night with him and Cherie at Chequers. Blair gave his former mentor some advice. 'He wrote out for me in his own hand . . . what I needed to do to put things right for myself,' Mandelson recalled, 'what changes I needed to make to my life, my persona, how I dealt with the media, my relationships – the whole lot.'[61] Blair urged Mandelson to reconnect with the public, become more of a 'team player' in the parliamentary party and be more open about his personal life.[62] Blair also confided in him that there was more he wanted him to do, but for now he must bide his time.[63] Mandelson left Chequers that Christmas Eve less burdened than he had been for many days.

The wilderness period for Mandelson lasted until October 1999. What is significant is that, during it, it was Blair who contacted Mandelson more than the other way round. Within two weeks of the resignation, which some thought, or hoped, would end Mandelson's political career for ever, Professor Anthony King, the academic, was writing: 'The Prime Minister clearly missed Peter Mandelson,' and he went on to list fairly accurately the benefits Mandelson brought him – 'company', 'moral support', 'candour', 'loyalty to his major political projects . . . who [else] can now look after New Labour?' and 'a capacity for strategic political thinking unrivalled in his generation'.[64]

Valuable though phone calls were, Blair missed Mandelson's presence. As King identified, Blair missed Mandelson's support in advancing his own, New Labour, agenda, which was not always his ministers' agenda. Nor, increasingly, was it Brown's agenda. Mandelson helped Blair keep on track, and in 1999, with disappointment beginning to mount at the government's failure to deliver, Blair needed his presence back in the government badly.[65] But he had problems. Mandelson was associated in the public's mind with 'sleaze', the sin for which Blair had lambasted the Major government. Derek Draper, Mandelson's former aide, had embarrassed Mandelson by boasting of his ability to achieve access to the heart of government in return for hard cash. Blair's own 'whiter than white' image had been damaged by the Ecclestone affair.[66] Bringing Mandelson back prematurely would bring 'sleaze' back to the top of the agenda. It would rekindle the growing concern about the government's obsession with spin over substance, with Mandelson (and Campbell) clearly identified as 'spinner in chief'. It would ignite concerns in the public's mind, highlighted not least by Philip Gould, that Blair was too keen on spin and not a resolute leader. An early return to office would make Blair appear to be weak, and also beg questions about why he was so dependent upon a damaged subordinate.[67]

Mandelson followed some of Blair's Christmas advice and kept a relatively low public profile for the first half of 1999, co-operating with Don Macintyre in his detailed biography, which Mandelson hoped would help rehabilitate him.[68] The road for his return was paved by the report of the House of Commons Select Committee on Standards and Privileges in the summer, which after a lengthy investigation found that Mandelson had acted 'without dishonest intention' and decided not to take any further action. Mandelson's name – not that many noticed – was cleared. A stigma remained, however. The whole loan affair had highlighted the intensity of the opposition to Mandelson. For all his qualities, Mandelson has always had an uncommon propensity to make enemies and it is this, more than anything else, which has hampered his political career.

Blair considered long and hard bringing Mandelson back into the government in the July 1999 reshuffle, but in the end deemed it too early. Instead, in October, he appointed Mandelson as Northern Ireland Secretary. Blair hoped that criticisms about his return after just ten months might be lessened because he was given a job that few ministers wanted, and its work was largely isolated from Westminster. Blair was also very keen to move Mo Mowlam, the incumbent, out and to put in someone he trusted, who would reduce the amount of time he was still having to devote to Northern Ireland once the glamour of the Good Friday Agreement had faded, for so little political reward.[69] Mandelson was thrilled by the new assignment, delighted to be accepted back, and relished the return to ministerial status.[70] Few ministers enjoyed their jobs as much as Mandelson. Some months later he was invited to chair Labour's General Election planning group. The wheel had turned.

Mandelson put the same effort into Northern Ireland that he had into the DTI, perhaps even more, because he now not only had a reputation to build but a reputation to salvage. He told the press, 'I made a mistake and paid a heavy price . . . I feel that I've come through it a chastened and a stronger person.'[71] Mandelson's closeness to Blair was a useful asset in the new post because Gerry Adams and David Trimble were willing to work through him, rather than insisting on talking directly to Number 10 as had often happened during Mo Mowlam's time in the job.[72] His presence in Northern Ireland for much of the working week meant he was less involved in the course of 2000 in Blair's strategic thinking: 'He's still doing his time,' one insider said.[73] Another questioned whether, with all his departmental responsibilities, Mandelson had managed to keep up with the latest developments in campaigning.[74] But as 2000 wore on Blair turned increasingly to him. Regular early morning phone calls to Belfast became an established feature. Away from his portfolio, Mandelson's biggest concern was to keep Blair's eye fixed on joining the Euro, to the consternation of Brown. Jealous eyes also noted that Blair would often invite Mandelson to remain behind for a talk after Cabinet meetings.[75]

Ironically, it was the imminence of the General Election, and perceptions of Blair in the build-up to it, that tipped the scales in Mandelson's second and final ministerial dismissal. The background to the story concerned the Hinduja brothers, Indian businessmen who had donated money to help fund the Millennium Dome, but by January 2001 were facing possible corruption charges in India.[76] Back in December 2000, Norman Baker, a Liberal Democrat MP, had submitted a Parliamentary Question to the Home Office, asking whether representations had been received from Mandelson in relation to the request for British citizenship by Srichand Hinduja. In the course of their research into this question, the Home Office contacted Mandelson's office, who acknowledged that they made enquiries about Mr Hinduja's eligibility, but reported that Mandelson had no recollection of any personal involvement. The problem came when this information appeared to conflict with the suggestion that Mandelson had, in fact, personally made a telephone call about the matter to the Home Office.

On Wednesday, 17 January 2001, Jack Straw, the Home Secretary, spoke to Mandelson, and told him that Mike O'Brien, a junior Home Office minister, had said he remembered a conversation with Mandelson about Srichand Hinduja's ongoing request for citizenship.[77] Despite this, Mandelson insisted that he still had no recollection of the phone call ever taking place.[78] There was no suggestion that Mandelson had acted in any way improperly in what he did. The only disagreement was over whether or not Mandelson or Mandelson's office had made enquiries into the future status of the Hinduja application. In the end, the answer released to Norman Baker by the Home Office stuck to O'Brien's recollection that Mandelson had made 'enquiries' relating to an application, but stressed that he 'did not make representation that an application be granted'.[79] This, they hoped, would be the end of the matter. Little did they realise what lay in store.

On Sunday, 21 January, the *Observer* ran a story in which it claimed that Mandelson had lobbied for Srichand Hinduja to gain a British passport after the brothers had agreed to give £1 million to the Dome, which was then Mandelson's responsibility. When asked for a comment prior to publication, Mandelson stuck to his line with Straw, and told the newspaper that the matter had been dealt with officially, not by him but by a Private Secretary, and that 'at no time did I support or endorse this application for citizenship'.[80]

Campbell spoke to Mandelson on the Sunday, and he verified the role of Mandelson's office in contacting the Home Office. Campbell then told the morning lobby briefing on the Monday that Mandelson had nothing to do with the matter. The Home Office, when they read the report of the lobby briefing, phoned Number 10 to point out that Campbell's line was at odds with their own version of events: there had been contact and, what is more, it had been Mandelson himself, they insisted, not his Private Secretary, who had spoken about the issue of citizenship to Mike O'Brien. Campbell, puzzled and increasingly angry at the possibility that he had misled the lobby, called O'Brien. He verified that he had spoken to Mandelson and read Campbell a note of the alleged conversation.[81] At this point Campbell organised a conference call between himself, O'Brien and

Mandelson, the conclusion of which was that Mandelson was persuaded to accept that his memory was at fault. Very reluctantly, Mandelson agreed to go along with the Home Office story.[82] He was in the middle of an intense series of meetings concerning the shaky Northern Ireland peace process and 'did not realise the elephant trap he was dropping himself into'.

The next day, Campbell announced to the lobby that a mistake had been made, and Mandelson had in fact spoken to O'Brien himself, something he had now remembered. Mandelson, after agreeing this line with Campbell the previous evening, tried to adhere to it but when confronted with his faulty memory in a television interview that Tuesday evening, baldly declared that he had forgotten nothing.[83] Straw, irate, phoned Number 10 to tell Blair and Campbell, 'Mike O'Brien remembers a phone call and, what is more, I told Peter about it last Wednesday.'[84]

Blair now became directly involved. Back on Monday he had asked Richard Wilson to investigate whether the rules had been broken in any way over Mr Hinduja's passport application. His report arrived at Number 10 on the Tuesday evening confirming nothing irregular had happened. Blair phoned Wilson in his car shortly after 11 p.m. while he was being driven back to his Buckinghamshire home. 'I think there is a firestorm developing,' he told the Cabinet Secretary, and said he thought an inquiry was needed to resolve the confusion. Could he think of some likely chairmen? At that point Mandelson's job was still safe. Jonathan Powell was clear, at midnight that Tuesday evening, 'that sacking Mandelson was not on the Number 10 agenda'.[85]

The next morning, Wednesday, Wilson went straight in to see Blair, who was in the Number 11 flat with Campbell, Powell and Hunter. Wilson suggested that if Blair wanted to establish an inquiry, Sir Anthony Hammond, the former Home Office Minister and Treasury Solicitor, who was free at the time, would be a suitable chairman. He was duly appointed: Mandelson could remain in his post for the duration of Hammond's investigation. But Blair's line had now hardened. 'There is an alternative,' said Blair. 'Peter goes now.' With O'Brien's recollection of the call with Mandelson gaining currency, the growing perception was that Mandelson, through his insistence that his Private Secretary had made the call, had misled Campbell, who had then misled the lobby. Furthermore, Culture Secretary Chris Smith had also used the Private Secretary story in the Commons on the Monday, which had led to accusations that Parliament had also been misled.[86] Irvine, who arrived at the Number 11 flat at about 9.15 a.m., has been blamed for adding to the pressure on Blair to sack Mandelson. But the die was already cast by the time Irvine joined the discussion that morning.[87] Irvine had to read himself into the story by looking at the pile of papers that had been collated by Clare Sumner, a junior Number 10 official. For once, the great lawyer was initially unable to make sense of a brief.

The meeting in the flat broke up, and reconvened downstairs at about 10 a.m. in Blair's office, the 'den'. Blair was told soon afterwards that Mandelson had arrived to see him, and everyone promptly went out through the double doors into the Cabinet Room. As he was leaving, Powell turned to Blair and asked, 'What are you going to say?' Blair replied, 'That he's got to go.' Everyone was very emotional, none more so than Hunter. In tears, she said, 'This is the end of New Labour. It was all created by Tony and Gordon and Peter and me, and now Peter is going.'[88]

Campbell was due to meet the lobby at 11 a.m. He paced around outside Blair's office and kept interrupting the meeting with Mandelson, wanting the latter to say that he had resigned so he could then tell the press that he was departing with dignity. But Mandelson was immovable. He insisted he had done nothing wrong, and he knew that after a second resignation he could never come back. Why not wait for the result of the inquiry? he asked Blair.[89] 'Are you going to destroy my entire political career, if not my life, on the basis of one morning's newspaper headlines?' Mandelson pleaded. 'I'm afraid I don't think I have any alternative,' responded Blair.[90] But he was evidently reluctant finally to pull the trigger on his old friend.

Campbell arrived at the lobby briefing, over ten minutes late, without Mandelson's resignation in his hands. The delay had further heightened the lobby's suspicions. Campbell, clearly flustered, announced to them that the Prime Minister was still in conversation with the Northern Ireland Secretary, and that it might be in the lobby's interests if he could return as soon as possible to put them in the picture. Some of the papers had been vitriolic about Mandelson that morning. 'How many more lies Mr Mandelson?' was spread across the Daily Mail, while Trevor Kavanagh, a persistent critic of Mandelson's, wrote in the normally pro-Blair Sun, 'Deceit is second nature to him – a tried and trusted weapon in his political armoury.'[91] Many in the lobby had little sympathy for Mandelson, and what they took from Campbell's words and body language in his brief appearance before them that morning was that Mandelson was finished. 'As we walked away from the lobby we all felt Peter would be gone within the hour,' said Philip Webster of The Times. 'Alastair was so evasive, we just knew it.'[92]

Back in Blair's office the Blair–Mandelson meeting was drawing to a close. Blair persisted that to hang on for an inquiry to report would be worse for him – and for the government. Mandelson suddenly crumpled; denied the opportunity to think it over or phone a friend, the fight went out of him. 'I saw Peter standing there in the den looking very distraught. He was terribly, terribly emotional,' recalls one observer.[93] Mandelson walked out of Downing Street after 1 p.m. and announced his resignation with the words: 'I do not accept in any way that I have acted improperly . . .'[94] When the Hammond Inquiry reported the following month it vindicated Mandelson's view, finding no evidence of wrongdoing.

The vitriol about Mandelson in the Wednesday morning's press, and the likelihood of it escalating in the run-up to the General Election, proved fatal for Mandelson: an early morning meeting that Wednesday between Blair and Campbell, gazing at the grim headlines, and the prospect of days more of similar press bile, was what finally made up their minds. Mandelson's friends firmly believe that this second resignation would never have happened without the first: 'The first resignation had so sensitised Number 10 that the first whiff of a problem the second time around led to very precipitate action.'[95] At the time, Mandelson was utterly furious, especially with Campbell, but also with Blair, whom he felt had betrayed him in his hour of need.[96] Campbell, who had not been having a good spell with Mandelson, was clear he had to go, but it is Blair alone who took the decision – even more so than over Mandelson's first departure. How did Blair feel after taking the decision? 'Emotionally very upset at first,' recalled a close aide, 'but then liberated.'[97] It showed a ruthless side to Blair which had been little in evidence in the first term – no one, not even his old friend, was going to jeopardise his second General Election victory. Blair had demonstrated beyond all doubt that he was truly the master of their relationship.

There was to be no overnight stay at Chequers this time. Mandelson remained angry for several weeks, and briefed fiercely against those he felt had dragged him down. Within Number 10 and elsewhere rumours ran wild that he was threatening to write his memoirs telling his side of the story (although in fact these rumours were unfounded).[98] Blair worked hard in 2001 to ensure that Mandelson did not go sour, and to keep him within bounds. This concern, as well as guilt,[99] explains the time he lavished on Mandelson.

Mandelson spent much of 2001 in the political cold; his new free time was spent travelling. By 2002 he was staging a comeback. After about a year, he had a *rapprochement* with Campbell, and they began to talk again.[100] Mandelson later claimed that his relationship with Blair never had to heal because 'it never missed a heartbeat',[101] but this is difficult to believe. Mandelson has a wide range of acquaintances and is also a popular choice as godfather for the children of many of his friends.[102] But he has few whom he would call intimates: Blair is one of them and Mandelson was not going to sacrifice him, betrayed though he felt he had been in January 2001.

But what role could he fill as an active man not yet aged fifty? He toyed with the idea of a job in Brussels, or at the UN, returning to his undergraduate interest in international politics.[103] More productively, he worked on a restatement of his traditional social democratic principles, including tackling poverty and encouraging redistribution, which was published in 2002 as the preface to *The Blair Revolution Revisited*, a new edition of his earlier book with Roger Liddle.[104] Mandelson continued to press the case for closer relations with the EU, and joining the single currency, to the intense anger of Brown, with whom relations remained icy. Pro-Europe remarks to journalists in May 2003 caused particular reverberations in the Treasury, and Blair himself was reported to be 'livid'.[105] Mandelson's interest in the 'third way' debate culminated in him convening and chairing a two-day international meeting on 'Progressive Governance' in London in July 2003, attended by Blair, German Chancellor Gerhard Schröder, and left-of-centre leaders and thinkers from around the world.

By 2003, however, Mandelson was no longer a voice on the outside. Although few outsiders picked up on it at the time, by the summer, Mandelson was back in Number 10, working directly for Blair at the heart of government. In July, Blair had offered him the chance to return to Downing Street to carry out a major overhaul of the internal structure, processes and personnel in the Prime Minister's office. This was partly in response to Campbell's impending departure and to concerns voiced during the Iraq War and after the botched reshuffle earlier that month that Number 10 operated too much in 'silos', with insufficient internal communication.[106] As Blair made clear to Mandelson at the time, if he accepted the job, he would have no formal position, no office and no official status.[107] History made these impossible. But Blair wanted him back and Mandelson accepted immediately.

In August, having cancelled his holiday plans, Mandelson held lengthy discussions with Jeremy Heywood and John Birt in Number 10. The three worked together on the reorganisation, which was implemented in September. With this task completed, Blair, with Prescott's input, asked Mandelson to chair a weekly political strategy meeting, bringing together his top lieutenants to take a look at the big picture and work out where Blair's premiership was heading. The meetings, which continued into 2004, were held every Monday afternoon and regular participants included Jonathan Powell, Sally Morgan, Pat McFadden, Geoff Mulgan and Philip

Gould. The group also planned to meet with Blair every Wednesday, although diary commitments sometimes made this impossible. As with so much that Mandelson has done, this work has been controversial. Some consider his contribution to have been 'brilliant'[108] and stabilising whereas others feel that a major source of tension returned to the heart of government.[109] By mid-2004, his continuing presence was as controversial as ever.

The Impact of Peter Mandelson

Blair would have become party leader in 1994, and Prime Minister in 1997, without Mandelson. Blair believes that Mandelson's importance has been as his 'strategic thinker'[110] developing the concept of 'New Labour' from the earliest stages. Others in the court see Gould as more the strategist, with Mandelson the tactician, 'brilliant at knowing where a story would go, how to position the party'. Mandelson's time of greatest practical importance to Blair, however, was between 1994 and 1997, when Blair was desperately short of expertise in handling the media and on presentation. It is suggestive of the limits to Mandelson's influence that once Blair became Prime Minister, many of the former's flagship policies, such as the single currency and a progressive realignment in British politics, did not come to pass. In the second term, although Blair's enthusiasm for another of Mandelson's favoured causes, the 'third way', faded, many of the ideas live on in government. If the third way is considered less as a political philosophy, which evidently it is not, and more as a vehicle for debate about the purpose of social democracy in a global economy, then its influence appears more pervasive. It is through his contribution to this debate, which has helped New Labour to occupy the middle ground between old Labour on the left and the Thatcherites on the right, that Mandelson's strategic influence has been at its strongest.

Blair also sees Mandelson as the 'keeper of his moods and feelings'.[111] This takes us to the heart of the personal relationship between the two men. If Mandelson's practical importance declined after 1997, Blair's emotional need for Mandelson did not diminish, partly because of the stresses of coping with disappointment (almost unknown in his political life from 1985, when he met Mandelson, until 1997) and because of the effective loss as a friend of the erstwhile intimate of both men, notably Brown, and then Campbell, who left in September 2003. Blair feels that no one cares for him as single-mindedly or can help him navigate his way as much as Mandelson. 'Peter is there night and day for him. He's incredibly sensitive and responsive to him twenty-four hours a day,' said one. Cherie also likes him. When in December 2002 the couple were at their lowest as the 'Cheriegate' scandal raged, it was to Mandelson that they turned. As Mandelson put it, 'I'm always there for him, even when he's wandering off and spending his time doing other things with other people, we just pick up where we left off. I believe in him and what he's doing in the Labour Party and for the country.'[112] Mandelson has a love for Blair, and it is reciprocated. Blair's love explains his blindness to the despair many feel about the relationship. Blair built his political career from the 1980s through a network. Mandelson is one of the very few of the original network still remaining and Blair will not, cannot, let him go.

Blair with Margaret Beckett, the acting Labour leader, in June 1994. Blair gazes confidently ahead, utterly assured that victory would be his.

15

Leadership Election, 1994

Only when Blair heard of John Smith's death on the morning of Thursday, 12 May 1994 did he realise that he had been mentally preparing himself for this day for several months. Within a few moments of registering the shock and sadness, he knew what he was going to do. He would stand for the leadership. How to handle Gordon Brown did not enter his head at this stage. He just knew that this was something he had to do.

Changing Relations, 1993–94

In the months after John Smith's death, out of respect for the man, and with the wish to unite all strands of the party, the extent of Blair's frustration with the Smith regime was glossed over. Andy McSmith, John Smith's biographer, now acknowledges that the judgement he would most want to revise ten years after writing his book is the extent of the antagonism between the two men.[1] Blair became, for the first and only time in his career, contemptuous of a boss. Journalists he trusted would be told in ever more thinly veiled form that he thought Smith complacent, conservative and lazy.[2] He complained to journalists on the way back from the 1992 Party Conference in Blackpool that the leadership had not been sufficiently focused.[3] At a dinner at English's restaurant in Brighton during the 1993 conference he expressed his exasperation at the pace of progress to a group of journalists from *The Times*.[4] Tony Howard (who was not present at the dinner) is convinced that 'what Blair was doing was spreading disenchantment, much more so than Gordon Brown'.[5] Mandelson mirrored Blair's exasperation and briefed the press accordingly. 'Blair never bad-mouthed Smith in a way that could be traced,' said one observer. 'He didn't need to, because Peter was already doing it.'[6]

After meetings of the shadow Cabinet and the NEC, Blair would return to his office in the Commons, 'so frustrated that he would repeatedly bang his head on the desk'.[7] He treated the shadow Cabinet in a cavalier fashion: 'He'd arrive late, leave early, sit in the corner with Gordon, pass notes to him and make in-jokes,' said one attendee.[8] 'It was obvious he did not have time for John's style, which was to give everyone a chance to have their say; Blair never concealed his dislike for listening to some, who he found dull and boring.'[9] He displayed a similar attitude to PLP meetings. Alan Haworth, the PLP secretary, as well as his old friend, had to write to Blair reprimanding him for his poor attendance.[10] Smith initially hoped he could make light of Blair's behaviour, and jolly him along. But when Blair's media profile in the autumn of 1992 caused shadow Cabinet eyebrows to be raised, Smith grew increasingly frustrated: 'I've just given him a huge new job,' he confided to Margaret Beckett. 'What I want him to do is to master that first. There'll be plenty of time for his "philosophising" about the party later.'[11] Smith's attitude toughened further in early 1993 and he became concerned that Blair's approach to punishing crime was too hard-line and likely to unsettle the liberal wing of the party.[12] The only reaction Blair received from the leader's office on his celebrated Wellingborough speech after the Bulger tragedy was 'stop hogging the limelight'. It made Blair very angry.[13]

Another Smith strategy for handling Blair was to try to detach him from Brown: divide and rule. His favouring of Brown, by offering him the chairmanship of the joint shadow Cabinet and NEC Economic Commission, and giving him a major say in the oversight of the party in Parliament, was one part of this.[14] 'Smith regarded Brown as a very bright but hair-brained student. He would burst into meetings late with piles of paper spreading everywhere,' said union leader John Edmonds. 'Smith was very much closer to Brown than to Blair. He regarded Brown as his protégé.'[15] Smith had always liked and admired Brown, and had not been troubled by his obvious outshining of him in his command of economics, and was prepared to put the rivalry in the run-up to the 1992 election behind him. But Smith grew increasingly wary of Brown's ambition, and even became worried that his own chief of staff, Murray Elder, was too close to Brown.[16] But Smith was not an insecure man, and he realised that his own jibbing against Kinnock meant he had no grounds for complaint when others were bumptious about him.[17] Both Smith and Brown were Scots; they enjoyed long talks over late drinks together, and had many close friends and experiences in common. 'Smith had his own "Scottish mafia",' said Margaret Jay, 'many of whom were hard-drinking men, whisky drinkers, late-night people: Blair was simply not part of that life. Brown, on the other hand, relaxed in their company.'[18] Smith was a man's man, in contrast to Kinnock and Blair, who enjoyed the company of women. Patricia Hewitt was one of Kinnock's women Smith particularly disliked, although he had no time for many of Kinnock's people, including Clarke, who rapidly departed from the leader's office.[19] Smith's team consisted of David Ward, Murray Elder and David Hill, but to a far greater extent than Kinnock or Blair, Smith ran policy in a collegiate way through the shadow Cabinet. One reason he was less reliant on a close core was because, unlike Kinnock and Blair, he was in less of a hurry.

Blair was now identified squarely at the head of the modernising faction. Every six weeks or so, at Blair's or Margaret Hodge's house, a group of modernisers – Blair, Mandelson, Hodge, John Carr, Sally Morgan and Jack Dromey (of the TGWU, and regarded then as the modernisers' great hope in the unions) – met to discuss the way ahead.[20] The group had no name and kept no records, and Smith never learned of its existence. Brown was nominally a member, but never attended in case, it was said, Smith found out. Instead, he sent along a supporter to ensure he stayed in the loop: he wanted 'wiggle room' was how one attendee quaintly put it.[21] These modernisers were not impressed by Smith's one major move in their direction, 'one member one vote' (OMOV), passed at the annual conference in the autumn of 1993.[22] Smith had put Blair on to a sub-committee of the NEC looking at the issue, in the hope that he could bind him to his own more modest vision of OMOV. However, Blair (openly) and Mandelson (behind the scenes) pushed very hard throughout 1992–93 to see OMOV adopted in a pure form for the selection of party leader and deputy leader as well as for selection of candidates in constituencies, and a final end to the manifestly undemocratic 'block vote'. Smith, backed by the unions, who had been overwhelmingly supportive of his own election, pushed for a form of OMOV leaving the trade unions an important voice. His compromise only just squeezed through the Party Conference, folklore has it because of a stirring speech from Prescott.[23] Blair could claim a partial victory on OMOV, but it was won only at the cost of creating still more resentment among union leaders. John Monks, then TUC General Secretary, believed that OMOV was the factor which more even than

Clause IV enraged union leaders and lost him their support: 'They saw Blair as the figure who had forced Smith to go through with it.'[24] Yet Blair felt Smith had far from gone through with it fully. His frustration found a voice in an Andy Grice article in the *Sunday Times*: 'Modernisers fear Smith may have damaged Labour's long-term prospects by offering too many sweeteners to the trade unions and the traditionalists.'[25]

Blair had pressed more strongly than Brown on OMOV, and it was noticed. 'Blair's stand on OMOV for me and for many people was when he really rose above the crowd. The despair he felt was palpable. He was alone on that committee fighting for whole-hog reform. What impressed me was his bravery,' said one.[26] Blair's firmness of intent on the issue won new supporters in the press: 'The succession is decided . . . Step forward Tony Blair. Give way Gordon Brown,' wrote Toby Helm in the *Sunday Telegraph* at the end of 1993.[27] Blair's relationship with Smith deteriorated badly after the 1993 conference. Smith 'really couldn't understand what the hell Blair was still banging on about. John had only just got OMOV through conference, and risked his leadership to do so. Why on earth should he risk a bust-up with the party and unions by continuing to drive ahead? The General Election was in the bag: the only risk would be further division,' was how one of his former aides summed up his thinking.[28] According to McSmith, Smith felt sad and angry that 'Blair and the Blairites never acknowledged he'd risked his political future on OMOV'.[29] Blair, on his side, became even stonier. He told close friends, 'John will lead us to defeat, and I will challenge him after we are defeated.'[30] A conciliatory dinner convened for Smith and Blair in January 1994 led only to a temporary improvement in relations.[31] Failure to change the party's image on the economy away from a tax-and-spend party was Blair's particular bugbear in early 1994. Blair viewed the impact of 'Black Wednesday' in September 1992, when Britain had been forcibly ejected from the Exchange Rate Mechanism (ERM), as a disaster for Labour: it was the start of Labour's long-term lead in the polls, and thus it fortified Smith, he felt, in his complacency.[32] For Brown, 'Black Wednesday' was a disaster in a different way: he had been closely identified with support for the ERM, so had little leeway to attack the Tories, and his continued support for the single currency angered colleagues, precipitating Bryan Gould's resignation from the Commons.

'Black Wednesday', in another sense, was a great boon for Blair, because it was the single event that turned Rupert Murdoch, head of News International, and Andrew Knight, its executive chairman, away from the Conservatives under John Major, for whom they had, by now, utter contempt. In this judgement, Murdoch shared the views of Mrs Thatcher, whom he idolised. Murdoch signalled the change in his thinking by appointing Richard Stott from the pro-Labour *Mirror* to edit his new newspaper, *Today*. Murdoch had noted with interest Andrew Neil's backing for Blair in the *Sunday Times*. News International was as yet uncertain how to jump politically: it knew who it was against – Major – but had yet to decide to support Labour, a huge leap. The company viewed Smith sympathetically, but as too 'old' Labour, especially on tax. Blair, however, excited and interested them as the coming man – Labour, certainly, but shorn of the adjuncts to Labour they found unpalatable. Brown on the other hand was viewed, tellingly, as a figure of no great interest.[33]

Sadly for Brown, it was not only News International who felt his star was fading by 1993–94. Brown found his period as shadow Chancellor far less rewarding than his earlier brief tenure standing in for Smith. After a honeymoon period in 1992, he became depressed, for three principal reasons. The 1992 election had been lost, Brown thought, primarily on the tax-and-spend issue, and he was determined to reverse the party's position in this area. However, Smith, as shadow Chancellor from 1987 to 1992, had been the principal architect of the tax-and-spend policy. This explained, in Brown's eyes, why Smith did not support him against difficult colleagues, above all Robin Cook and Peter Hain, whom Brown believed were actively undermining him in the parliamentary party and in the press.[34] He blamed them for his disappointing position in the shadow Cabinet elections in autumn 1993, when he came fourth, behind Dobson, Cook (his old foe), and Prescott, who was emerging as a leader of the traditionalists. Brown became frustrated secondly because the corollary of reversing the tax-and-spend policy was telling colleagues that he could not assent to their spending demands. This would be a difficult position for any shadow Chancellor but was aggravated in this case by Brown's abrupt manner with colleagues, which needlessly lost him support and friends.[35] To many he came across at this time as 'bad-tempered, demanding, driven and unlikeable'.[36] Finally, Brown was suffering because, in contrast to his own difficulties, Blair was attracting unprecedented applause for what he was doing as shadow Home Secretary. It was Peter Mandelson – ironically, given the later twists in their relationship – who helped Brown out, planning a better structure for his office in 1993, which involved bringing in Charlie Whelan to improve his battered image. Ed Balls, Brown's brilliant policy adviser, was recruited by Mulgan as his successor. Yet these changes would take time to make a difference to Brown's prospects. In Smith's last few weeks, some claimed he had decided Blair would be better placed to succeed him than Brown. However, according to Roy Hattersley, who recalls a conversation with Smith just days before his death, Smith felt confident that Brown would overtake Blair again, certainly before the moment came for the next leadership election.[37] Elizabeth Smith, his widow, meanwhile has revealed in the authorised biography of Smith by Mark Stuart (2004) that he had no definite favoured successor, but deliberately played one off against the other. This 'divide and rule' only heightened tension in Blair and Brown's fraying relationship.

While Blair's star may have been rising above Brown's, this did not alter his root problem: John Smith. Yet Smith was so securely placed in the party and the unions that there was no prospect of a successful coup.[38] Unseating a Labour leader, as Blair had reason to reflect happily in later years, was difficult, as it had always been in a party famed, unlike the Tories, for not jettisoning their pilot. Blair later said that by the time of his death Smith was coming round to the need for urgent reform: 'I actually think John would have done a lot of what I've done, if he had lived,' he told Robert Harris.[39] If Smith was indeed on the verge of a giant leap into the modernising dark, the evidence is that Blair felt no lift at the prospect. In April 1994, Blair's old friend Cathy Ashton confided in Paddy Ashdown that Blair was 'thoroughly fed up' with Smith.[40] He talked with growing frequency of leaving politics altogether.[41] 'I don't still want to be stuck as an opposition MP while friends at the Bar are getting on with their careers,' he told another acquaintance.[42] On the weekend of 7–8 May 1994, he and Cherie abandoned London to stay with friends in the West Country. His mood was down, but very focused. 'I will not go on doing this job for ever,' he told them. 'The party has to change fundamentally if we are ever to be electable.'[43] Blair's gloom about the leadership's continuing resistance to change was evident on Wednesday, 11 May, when he saw Philip Gould to hear more about what his research revealed, and about the mountain Labour still had to climb to make it electable.

Blair's Emergence, 12 May–1 June

When Blair was told about Smith's heart attack, 'He went incredibly silent and simply said, "Oh, my God."'[44] Blair took the call while being driven from Dyce Airport to a speaking engagement in Aberdeen for the European election campaign that was just getting under way. His first call was to Brown, with whom he had a long conversation: their first thoughts were for Elizabeth and her three daughters. They did not talk about the succession, but arranged to meet in private later that day. Brown was the more emotional,[45] by personality as well as by dint of the greater length and intimacy of his relationship with Smith.[46] When they finished speaking, Blair spoke to Cherie. They agreed he would fly back early and she would meet him at Heathrow. Blair, meanwhile, went ahead with the first part of his visit. Outside the Labour Party office in Aberdeen he gave a short tribute to Smith for television. 'He had the extraordinary combination of strength and authority, humour and humanity: I think the whole country will feel his loss,' he intoned on that cold May morning. No one can watch the television pictures of him delivering those words and not see either a man deeply moved and on the verge of tears, or the performance of a master actor. Perhaps there were elements of both. As he flew down south alone, he 'felt the mantle of office fall on his shoulders'.[47] Cherie was absolutely fixed on what he had to do. Her husband had been thwarted by Brown in 1992, she felt, and she was determined he would not lose out to him this time. This time he must not defer. But Blair had made up his mind on his own.

Anji Hunter was travelling up from Sussex by train that morning and knew nothing of the news of Smith's death until she arrived at the top of the lift in Blair's office at 1 Parliament Street, to be greeted by one of their aides, Peter Hyman, in tears. She froze. 'Tony's plane's crashed' was the first thought that entered her head. Hyman told her the news and she rushed along the corridor to Blair's office. Donald Dewar was talking to Blair on the phone; Robin Cook was there in tears, as was Kate Garvey, whom Hunter had recruited to help in the office.[48] One MP who tried to see both Brown and Blair that afternoon said, 'I went to Gordon's office, and it was silent. I went to Tony's and it was like a lunatic asylum, with everyone queuing up outside along the corridor.'[49]

The *Evening Standard* was the first newspaper to phone Hunter, just minutes after she arrived.[50] Sarah Baxter, formerly of the *New Statesman* but now on the London paper, had been asked by Sarah Sands, the deputy editor, to write a piece on the death for that day's paper. Sands was impressed by Blair's case to be the next leader: 'It was blindingly obvious that it had to be him,' she recalled.[51] When Baxter phoned Hunter, Baxter already knew that Smith was dead. The news given out at the time was only that he had had a heart attack: the Smith family wanted to hold the full truth back until one of their daughters, then in the United States, had been told. Baxter asked Hunter if Blair would stand. 'We haven't even thought about that yet,' Hunter replied.[52] A little later, Baxter revealed her bottom line. 'I'm really sorry and I hate to say this, but I have to write an opinion piece today,' she told Hunter, 'and I am going to say that it should be Tony.'[53] When Blair arrived at Westminster from Heathrow, the *Evening Standard* was already on sale on the pavement. Inside, Baxter's article began: 'There is only one potential successor to John Smith who is streets ahead of all other candidates. He is Tony Blair . . . an unabashed moderniser with the mission to make the party electable – whatever it takes . . . The Labour politician the Tories fear most . . . When Brown did not stand against Smith, it seemed as though he had missed his moment. Almost subconsciously, people stopped talking about Brown–Blair . . . and began talking about Blair–Brown instead.'[54]

The biggest myth in British politics in the 1990s must surely be that Brown was still the front-runner for the Labour leadership when Smith died. The *Evening Standard* shows what two independent-minded journalists, Baxter and Sands, one on the left, one more on the right, thought instantaneously.[55] These views were shared by the vast majority of the political world. John Major was working in the Cabinet Room preparing for Prime Minister's Questions when confirmation came through of the death. One of his aides summed up what went through everyone's mind at Number 10: 'Our first thought was, "How awful, a man only in his mid-fifties." Another second later, the next thought followed, "Well, that's stuffed Hezza" [Heseltine, then jostling for position with Major, who had just suffered a heart attack himself] – a moment of satisfaction. But then a new thought struck. "Oh, my God, it'll let in Tony Blair. He'll be even more difficult."'[56] William Hague recorded in his diary for 12 May that within two minutes of the news, Tony Blair was the overwhelming favourite.[57] Robin Cook, who was himself tipped to stand, and who was eventually to throw in his lot behind Blair, said by noon, or by 4.00 p.m. at the latest, that day, the Tea Room had decided Blair was the preferred candidate of the parliamentary party.[58] Gerald Kaufman put it precisely: 'When John Smith died it was clear to *everyone* that Tony was the obvious leader. Politics is about timing. Gordon's moment didn't coincide with the chance for the leadership: Tony's did.'[59]

The one main group that had not yet reached this conclusion was Gordon Brown and his principal lieutenants, Ed Balls, Nick Brown and Charlie Whelan. Indeed, ten years later they still have not yet reached it, which has given rise to myths which are recycled repeatedly by those who would have preferred to see Brown as leader, and by those for whom the truth is not the prime concern, such as the makers of a widely promoted television drama entitled *The Deal*, which caused a brief stir when screened in September 2003.[60] Mandelson was made into the scapegoat by Brown's camp for allegedly turning the press against their champion and denying him his natural inheritance, for which they believe he was uniquely qualified. The *Evening Standard* story which led the news, however, was not spun by Mandelson. Andy McSmith, who spoke nationwide on the BBC television news that evening and tipped Blair, had not been spun by Mandelson.[61] Alastair Campbell, who backed Blair on BBC *Newsnight* that night, had not been spun and neither had Philip Webster, who wrote in *The Times* that 'Blair emerged last night as the favourite to succeed John Smith'. Webster had not been spoken to by Mandelson,[62] nor had Ian Hargreaves, who drafted the leader in the *Financial Times* the next day that favoured Blair as the moderniser candidate.[63]

The two principal reasons why Brown lost his position to Blair, neither of which make it any more palatable for Brown or his supporters, are that while Brown had been making enemies in the parliamentary party from 1992 to 1994, Blair had been making friends; and Brown had let himself be portrayed in the media as a gloomy, remote, rather negative figure, who seemed happiest playing it safe. By contrast Blair appeared adventurous and a risk-taker. He came across as young, personable and, in his response to the Bulger death, able to touch the nerve of the nation.

Blair's resolution to stand at all costs lasted throughout the first day. Harriet Harman spoke to him that day and he told her he would definitely stand.[64] In the evening, Blair received a steady stream of calls urging him on. 'You have to seize the moment,' Clive Hollick insisted,[65] while Blair's old friend John Carr tackled the key issue head on: 'Don't under any circumstances let Gordon talk you out of it,' he counselled. 'Don't worry,' replied Blair, 'I won't.'[66] But a conversation with Brown at Bill Blair's house that Thursday evening indicated that Brown would indeed try to talk him out of it. 'There is no question that Gordon thought that he had an agreement with Tony that Gordon would succeed John Smith,' said one Brown intimate.[67] But had there been an agreement or merely a tacit understanding that Brown had convinced himself was a firm and inviolable pledge? Brown at first simply could not believe that Blair was proposing to stand. Brown told Blair that he had every intention of standing himself. Blair did not want to stand against his older and closest friend, nor risk splitting the moderniser vote and let in Prescott.[68] He had not anticipated Brown reacting so negatively. 'Gordon wants it more than me,' he would say to Hattersley and a select few when Smith was still alive. He had always worried he might react very strongly but thought – in as far as he gave it deep thought in Smith's lifetime – that he could win him round like he always won people round in the end.

By the Friday, Blair's initial fire had been spent in the face of Brown's utter determination. Blair talked to aides about backing down. Was he sincere, or was it a guise to test reactions? Almost certainly it was the latter. He received overwhelming support to stand with Cherie the most steadfast of all: 'She came over as very strong and very determined that he had to go for it,' recalled one close observer.[69] A growing group of parliamentary colleagues, including Mo Mowlam, Jack Straw and Peter Kilfoyle, added their voices of support. Hunter reinforced the message by asking Alastair Campbell to do what he could to stiffen Blair's resolve. Campbell had already set off for North Wales to attend the funeral of Glenys Kinnock's mother, who had died the day before John Smith: he spent much of his drive on the phone to Blair, shoring up his determination to stand.[70] Derry Irvine also weighed in heavily, pushing him to stand in private, and in public, declaring with the added weight of his being asked to speak at John Smith's funeral, that Smith regarded Blair as his 'natural successor'. Such statements, at best only half true, merely added to the climate of intrigue.

Blair's resolve, if it ever genuinely wavered, had fully returned by Sunday, 15 May. Blair spent that day in Islington with Cherie, their nanny and the three children. The phone was ringing incessantly, and Tim Allan was asked to come to the house to help field calls. On that same day, Brown spoke to Philip Gould, a close friend of both men. Gould steeled himself to convey the painful news to Brown that he thought Blair was the better candidate because he not only 'met the mood of the nation [better], he exemplified it'. Gould's argument was bolstered greatly by polls in the newspapers that Sunday, which had hit Brown badly. A MORI poll of the general public had Blair on 32 per cent, Prescott 19, Beckett 14 and Brown on just 9 per cent. The only consolation for Brown was that Cook was on 5 per cent. Gould also gave Brown critical advice: he should only stand down if he could 'live with the consequences'. Brown did not respond directly, other than to say poignantly that he wanted to have the chance to implement his ideas which 'he had spent a lifetime developing'.[71]

Blair and Brown spoke to each other on the phone that Sunday and also met again in person. Brown, heavily pressed by his aides, was in no mood to yield. Blair acknowledged Brown's point, that he had strong support in the trade union and constituency sections of the party's Electoral College, but he was adamant about the point Gould had made forcibly to Brown: that it was he who would stand the better chance of maximising the vote in the General Election. Brown realised he was not going to be able to put Blair off. But should he stand also? The meeting broke up inconclusively.[72] An agreement that campaigning should not begin at least until after the funeral was completely ignored. Nick Brown was Brown's major parliamentary champion testing out his support, while Beckett, Cook and Prescott were all assumed to be likely to stand.[73] Hunter spoke to the elder statesmen in the party, Hattersley, Kaufman and Cunningham, to try to win them over for Blair.[74] Beckett meanwhile, who had immediately become acting leader on Smith's death, fought an increasingly forlorn battle to try to stop all the campaigning until not only the funeral but the European elections on 9 June, in which the party had made a great investment. Her fear was that a party divided into rival camps would damage their showing at the polls.[75] In the feverish atmosphere, some read her actions as advancing her own prospects of obtaining the leadership.

What of Mandelson in all this? Smith's death suddenly shone a spotlight on his dilemma. Mandelson, as we have seen, was emotionally committed to Brown, and wanted to see him lead the party, a position he knew would be the fulfilment of his close friend's lifetime dream. At this point we reach a critical juncture, at which facts no longer seem black and white, but burst forth in glorious technicolour. Brown's camp claim to have been incensed that Blair's team started their campaign so early – in fact, while Brown was still in mourning for John Smith: according to Charlie Whelan 'he was only interested in writing obituaries'.[76] Mandelson was the first person to visit Brown in his flat after news of Smith's death.[77] He reports that he discussed the succession in some detail with Brown that morning, and claims that Gordon Brown met with Nick Brown afterwards to begin planning his campaign. The clear assumption on Brown's part, which Mandelson apparently made no attempt to alter, was that he, not Blair, would stand as the modernisers' candidate.[78]

Ultimately, scraps over which camp started its campaign first are not of great historical importance. The salient, and probable, facts are that within hours of Smith's death the popular view was that Blair was far ahead; and that this view had developed quite independently of any campaign or bandwagon. 'It was like standing in front of a herd coming towards you,' recalled Mandelson. 'It was inescapable.'[79] By Sunday Mandelson was edging towards Blair's camp, but could not quite let go of his original hopes for Brown. The result was that he gave out mixed messages, which included his comments to Irvine on the Friday that he was not persuaded that the leadership was Blair's, and then a TV interview on Saturday in which he spoke about the need for a leader who would reach out beyond Labour's traditional base and 'play well at the box office'.[80] He finally acknowledged that weekend that it had to be Blair. His tortured position was finally spelled out in a text he sent to Brown on Monday, 16 May, in which he tried to analyse the current state of play. He outlined Brown's weaknesses against Blair and offered two courses of action: to reverse his downsides, which he would help him to do, or 'exit with enhanced position, strength and respect'.[81] Mandelson says that he wrote the letter in consultation with Brown's Scottish ally Donald Dewar, and at Brown's request, as they were both concerned to give their friend an 'exit strategy'. This letter has become the holy text the Brown camp cites as evidence of Mandelson's double-dealing and betrayal: it was 'the most treacherous and devious letter I have ever seen,' said one.[82] Mandelson says that Brown expressly did not see the letter as 'treacherous' or even disloyal at the time. It is hard ten years on to see quite why the letter provoked such controversy. Brown is all about loyalty, and he read Mandelson's actions as those of a man changing sides and not being candid about it. It seems that, because the news was unwelcome, and because Mandelson would not be able to procure some 'secret weapon' to transform Brown's standing, he was to be condemned, and insincerity was the stick that would be used to beat him with. Beyond this, there is little else of interest to note about Mandelson's role in the leadership affair. Mandelson, as we have seen, was a key figure in Blair's life, but his importance to this part of the story, the leadership election, has been overestimated and vastly over-written. It is a tribute to Mandelson that so many ascribed to him king-making powers. But in this particular scene of the play, the two princes are alone at the front of the stage with Mandelson merely a foot soldier hovering by the exit.

Brown was in a trap, and could see no way out. The message from most of his supporters was that he would win against Blair, but it would be close, which explained why they were so prickly about premature lobbying of MPs and attempts to spin the media towards Blair and against him. Some of his followers believe that rumours were being spread deliberately by the Blair camp about Brown's unsuitability for the top office because he did not have children, with implications that he might be gay and had secrets to hide. They believed in particular that this speculation helped tip Scottish MPs against him. But these baseless rumours began to circulate, as seen in Chapter 13, from when Brown did not stand in 1992. Blair himself was extremely unhappy about the smears.[83] It is inconceivable he personally gave currency to such nastiness. While it is not provable whether any of his more ardent followers were involved, what matters is that the Brown camp *believed* Blair's supporters to be responsible. As the week beginning on Monday, 16 May, wore on, his followers began to realise that it was possible Brown might not be able to beat Blair. But he was absolutely not going to concede. He knew that Blair, for personal and political reasons, was desperate to avoid them both standing, which could risk all they had striven to achieve. For the time being he resolved not to disclose his hand.

Blair's confidence grew throughout that second week. He knew that his support was firming up day by day, that he was the favoured 'moderniser' candidate, and he began to feel calmer about his prospects. His one all-pervading anxiety remained Brown, and what he might do. Blair's aides were doing the back-room work with MPs and the press, which allowed him to present a dignified position above the fray. A weekend poll on 28 May of party members gave Blair 47 per cent, Prescott 15 and Brown 11. Behind the scenes, Anji Hunter and Sue Nye, close friends throughout, and the one remaining rope-bridge between two increasingly hostile sides, worked overtime to ensure their bosses kept in touch. But Blair's and Brown's meetings (whose secrecy was guarded 'like lionesses' by Hunter and Nye[84]) still produced no way ahead.[85] Smith's funeral was held on 20 May at his parish church, Cluny, in Morningside, Edinburgh. Kaufman memorably observed of Blair at the funeral that 'the mark is on him already'.[86] Blair had stayed with Nick Ryden in Edinburgh when he had visited Smith's widow, Elizabeth, immediately after the death. He stayed again with his old school friend after the funeral. 'My house was commandeered,' Ryden recalled. 'Tony was with us overnight and Gordon turned up. There was wine in the fridge. I gave them the number of the Indian takeaway and just left them to get on with it.'[87] As Brown's prospects of winning declined, his team seemed to become more entrenched and bullish. Brown's line to Blair that evening was 'so you are a bit more popular than me now but, so what? Fortunes ebb and flow. I'm much the better qualified for leadership and, anyway, it's been agreed it should be mine.'[88]

Brown sat down with his closest advisers to plan out the course ahead. One recalled the situation as they saw it: 'By the end of the first full week, our expected supporters were only lukewarm. We argued that the only way to beat Blair would have been for Gordon to launch an extreme *ad hominem* attack on his person – Gordon couldn't attack Blair on his policies because broadly he shared them. As Brown's acolytes saw the prize slipping away before their eyes, and with it their chances of high office and power, their disappointment had turned venomous. And their venom was focused on the one person of Blair, for whom Balls and Whelan in particular had already developed a profound dislike. But Gordon wouldn't make that personal attack.'[89] Some in Brown's team wanted to play hardball and to portray Blair as having been in reality a closet SDP person all along, non-Labour and anti-trade union. They were stilled by Brown.[90]

But could Brown still outflank Blair by garnering support on the left? His last show of strength came two days after the funeral, at the Welsh Labour Party in Swansea on Sunday, 22 May. Sabre-rattling under great duress is a periodic Brown resort, seen in his provocative speech at the 2003 annual Party Conference. The Blair camp were shocked when they heard the news, and one later described the Swansea speech as the worst moment. They read it as Brown deliberately abandoning his modernising stance to see if he could bolster his support with votes from unions and the left. Brown's words themselves were deliberately careful, to allow him to retreat if necessary, but Blair's camp thought Whelan had spun the speech to make it appear to be the opening public shot in a Brown bid for the leadership and a lurch to the left.[91] When the bandwagon failed to roll, and when another speech a week later at Luton (calling for 'an assault on inequality') failed to arouse much interest on the left (the hard left favouring Prescott or Beckett and the soft left largely sticking with Blair) they realised the ploy had failed.

So the Brown team knew that they would have to change course. But how? Blair could not be made to stand down. Brown would be defeated if he stood against him, quite possibly humiliatingly. A *Scotsman* poll on 27 May showed ambivalent support for Brown even in his own heartland, while a BBC *On the Record* survey on 29 May showed Blair had a solid lead over Brown among voters in all three sections of the Electoral College, i.e., MPs, unions and party members in the constituencies. Brown indeed was placed third behind Prescott.[92] The palpable truth of Brown's weak position at the time has been obscured since by Brown's supporters, who argued that such polls meant nothing. 'Brown genuinely believed – and still believes – he could have won the leadership,' insisted Paul Routledge. 'As soon as the "upper-class, public school-educated" Blair came under serious fire from Brown's more conventional Labour credentials then he would be in trouble.'[93] But would Blair have been 'outed' in a straight fight against Brown? It is very unlikely, as Blair's momentum was simply too great. Brown's advisers counselled that his best course of action was thus to try to extract as much as he could out of Blair as the condition or 'deal' for his not standing against him. This became Brown's theme in the final week of their discussions.

The two men met several more times in the lead-up to the famous dinner at the fashionable Granita restaurant in Islington on Tuesday, 31 May. They were intensely difficult meetings for both men, with hurtful things said on both sides. 'Tony had to battle Gordon into submission. It was incredibly tense. Incredibly emotional. There were moments when Gordon gained the upper hand. He made Tony feel like a younger brother.'[94] It has entered folklore that the dinner was the forum when the two men hammered out the agreement that Brown would not stand against Blair in return for certain very significant, if contested, concessions. The Granita dinner, as we can see, was in fact merely the culmination of a series of some ten meetings and countless conversations between the two men over the previous nineteen days.[95] And what exactly was decided? In brief, no one knows. Worse for history, no one will ever know for certain, because Brown and Blair left the restaurant with two very different ideas of what had been agreed, and their understandings have since been elaborated and recast many times over. Two particular issues are contested. Was Brown granted quasi-leader autonomy over tracts of economic and social policy? What exactly, if anything, was said about when Blair would stand down for Brown?

Brown believed that he had his wish granted to be the central figure over economic and social policy in the future Labour government. The hard negotiations over this issue can be seen clearly in a draft of the private 'line to take' briefing note, which came out into the open in 2003 as part of the continuing war between the camps. Originally drawn up a few days before Granita, the aim of this document was to enable Blair and Brown to present a unified view to the press on what they had agreed.[96] Time and time again, the two men went over the draft as they argued and bargained over the 'deal' between them. In the leaked draft, the original typed text reads, 'Gordon has spelled out the fairness agenda – social justice, employment opportunities and skills – which he believes should be the centrepiece of Labour's programme and Tony is in full agreement with this, and that the party's economic and social policies should be further developed on this basis.' However, using a black felt-tipped pen, Brown has scribbled out 'Tony is in full agreement with this' and replaced it with 'Tony has guaranteed this will be pursued'.[97] Despite Brown's repeated efforts to extract this 'guarantee' Blair stood firm, and the words 'in full agreement with' remained.[98] This left considerable room for uncertainty as to the exact degree of control that Blair had ceded to Brown over economic and social policy. The extant written evidence is thus no more reliable a guide than the recollections of the conversations. But there is no doubt that substantial if imprecise control was granted to Brown, and Blair believes he has delivered on this promise since 1994. Prescott's understanding was 'that Gordon would run everything domestically and Tony would be Prime Minister – which he didn't like one bit because he didn't trust the Treasury and what Gordon might do from it', said one close to Prescott.

There is much less consensus about what, if anything, was said about the second issue: Blair standing down. The Brown camp assert a firm undertaking was given and are quite specific: it was agreed that Blair would be Prime Minister for no longer than seven years. 'Brown and Blair saw eye to eye on this,' claimed one Brown intimate. 'They knew that the relentlessness and intensity of office would mean that after seven years it would be sensible for Blair to stand down.'[99] Such an undertaking is dismissed by the Blair camp as pure fiction: 'The seven-year story was just something constructed by Charlie Whelan,' said one. 'There was no deal in 1994.'[100] The most they are prepared to concede is that, accepting Blair's propensity to be vague when it suited him, he might have said something like 'I won't be there for ever. Of course I'll back you for leader when the time comes.'[101] Blair does indeed have a history of letting people come away with an impression that he supports what they are saying.

The history of the next ten and more years turned on the differing understandings of 'the deal'. So what exactly was agreed? The most one can say is that there were clearly words spoken by Blair about allowing Brown to have a lead role over part of domestic policy, and a less certain undertaking to back Brown's candidacy as leader at a future point. Had a secretary been present to take a precise note, history might have been very different. But had a secretary written a precise note both men would never have agreed to the record. It was the very vagueness that carried the day.

Squabbling about what had been agreed broke out between both camps the very next day, Wednesday, 1 June, over the 'line to take' briefing note. Brown had gone on from Granita to a second dinner at the Rodin restaurant in Millbank with Balls, Nick Brown and Whelan and, as ever, they whipped up his sense that he had been cheated. As his team saw the apparent final draft of the briefing note, they yet again sought agreement from Blair that Brown had been 'guaranteed' control over economic and social policy. Blair refused once more to take this on board, but this did not stop Brown's camp using the word in discreet lobby briefings. Peter Riddell in *The Times* picked up on this, and reported on the accord that 'guaranteed Mr Brown that [his] fairness agreement, broadening employment opportunities and improving training and skills will be the centrepiece of Labour's economic and social programme'.[102] This clarified nothing and left both factions to believe whatever they chose.

Home Straight, 1 June–21 July

Blair had been exceptionally tense about Brown – as he has always been since – so when he secured his agreement to stand down, successfully portrayed as an act of self-sacrifice in the interests of the party, he relaxed hugely. For Blair, the tough battle for the leadership was thus over even before the campaign officially opened. He knew he would win the actual contest rationally, but part of him still doubted it, and the campaign team had to provide regular reassurance. With Brown squared, Blair turned his attention to the lesser concerns of building a team, raising the money, producing a manifesto, and deciding who he would like to have as his deputy. He knew he would win, but he wanted to win 'well', in a way that would build for the future.

The official launch of the leadership campaign was on Friday, 10 June, the day after the European elections. As expected, Beckett and Prescott each stood for both deputy and leader, while Cook, after the discouraging opinion polls, decided to bow out. Beckett and Prescott held their news conferences in the House of Commons, but Blair deliberately chose the parochial venue of the Trimdon Labour Club in Sedgefield, where he spoke about how he wanted to reproduce his constituency's huge boost in individual party membership across every constituency in the nation. His campaign team were announced on the same day; Robin Cook declined Blair's invitation to be his campaign manager,[103] and he chose Straw and Mowlam jointly instead. Other members in his team were Barry Cox, John Carr, Hunter, Kilfoyle and Brown's ally Andrew Smith, to ensure liaison with Brown's team. Behind the scenes, and against the express wishes of Mowlam, Straw and Kilfoyle,[104] Mandelson advised Blair on an *ad hoc* basis on strategy and communications. 'It was the easiest campaign imaginable and all we had to do was make sure things didn't go wrong because he was plainly going to win,' said Jack Straw.[105] One reason why they felt so secure of victory was because his campaign team had been at work stealthily for three weeks before their official launch. Indeed, so assiduous had they been that on the day of the launch they leaked to the *Guardian* a list of all those MPs who would support Blair – amounting to over half the PLP. 'It was game, set and match to us before the campaign had even started,' said Kilfoyle.[106] The press carried the names of 135 out of 268 MPs, to climb three days later to 154, including 13 out of 18 members of the shadow Cabinet. Prescott could muster just four members of the shadow Cabinet, none front-rank, while Beckett had none. Not all Blair's support came from those who fully endorsed his modernising views: much came from MPs who simply wanted to back the winner – as he rather tactlessly highlighted in his acceptance speech.

Money had to be raised quickly, and in significant quantities, as this was the first time the party was to elect a leader on a broad one-member-one-vote basis. US electoral experience, with great effort put into 'primaries', where parties selected their candidates, helped point the way to a new approach. Blair has always been concerned to have enough money to do what he wanted and so great effort was put into fundraising. Barry Cox, by now a millionaire, was chief fundraiser, and he asked media friends like Melvyn Bragg, Greg Dyke, David Puttnam and Ken Follett to help with the funds. Bragg said, 'After a period when the party didn't seem to know exactly where it was going, Blair was a leader, his principles were strong and I agreed with his modernising ideas. I was happy to help them raise the money.'[107] Michael Levy, who had sold his large independent music business and had already worked with the Labour Party to raise funds, thought Blair represented the best hope for the future, and he helped to procure a substantial percentage of the money raised.[108] Levy also had particularly strong connections with the business world in which Blair had yet to meet many people: David Sainsbury was one donor to the leadership campaign. The sum of £88,358 was declared for his campaign,[109] though some commentators, like Nick Cohen and Paul Routledge, have queried the methods used and have argued that this figure underestimates the real amount,[110] which eclipsed easily that raised by Beckett (around £17,000) and Prescott (around £13,000).[111] Cox said raising the money was easy because donors 'were eager to back the favourite'.[112] The sums involved, and the perception that this style of fundraising was out of sympathy with the party's traditions, raised unfavourable comment, as later did the granting of peerages, albeit for very different reasons, to many of those who gave, including Birt, Bragg, Levy, Puttnam and Sainsbury. It helped prepare the ground for the perception of Blair once in power for being over-enamoured with celebrities and plutocrats.

While Cox and Levy set about filling the campaign's bank account, Blair charged his old friend, John Carr, with overseeing the establishment of his campaign office and associated organisation. Carr began work immediately, identifying suitable premises in Abbey Orchard Street, installing a computer system and recruiting the core administrative staff.[113] Work also began on Blair's manifesto, which was deliberately designed to signal change without giving out specifics that might alienate individuals or groups. Blair drafted in the intellectually brilliant David Miliband and James Purnell from the IPPR think-tank, and Liz Lloyd to help on policy and speeches. Speeches were drafted by Derry Irvine on the constitution, Peter Hyman on welfare, professor of education Michael Barber on schooling, Arnab Banerji on the economy and Liz Lloyd on law and order.[114] All these were figures who were already playing, or were about to play, important parts in Blair's life. Campaign funds paid for a glossy leaflet for party and union members, 'Principle, Purpose, Power', with the text drafted by Alastair Campbell and the title from Chris Powell of the now defunct SCA.[115] Blair's leadership manifesto 'Change and National Renewal', launched at Church House in Westminster, was a mixture of current Labour policy and breezy rhetoric. It was as safe as Blair's speeches and media interviews in the campaign. Yet they achieved precisely what he needed to achieve: confirming him as the clear 'change' candidate without upsetting anyone. After long and hard discussions, Blair pulled back from giving hostages to fortune by providing details of what he might do in the future.[116] An inclusive electoral strategy was certainly one reason for Blair's failure to spell out his future plans. As important was that he did not yet know what his precise policies would be. This was something he still had to work through; something he always saw coming at some more favourable point in the future.

Confident of the MP and party member sections of the Electoral College, the unions, the third element, were the Blair team's only real concern. One factor that greatly eased their anxieties was that individual union members, not the union bosses, would be voting. John Edmonds of the GMB, no Blair friend, explained how Blair carried the day: 'Union leaders were confused and demoralised. They might not have liked Blair personally but there was no concerted effort to stop him because it became very obvious to us after John Smith's death that he was going to win, and when Brown withdrew, it indicated this even more strongly. What else could we do? Most of us thought Labour could not win under Prescott. Bill Morris and I tried to hold it together for Margaret Beckett, but it didn't make much difference. Just as there had been an overwhelming feeling that Smith was the winner in 1992, so there was this feeling Blair would be the strongest candidate now.'[117]

One of the very few wobbles came at the start of the official campaign when Brown nominated Beckett as the candidate for deputy leader.[118] Blair's team were anxious to maintain harmony between all the candidates, on which Anji Hunter had in particular worked so hard. Blair was genuinely torn between Beckett and Prescott for the deputy position. In the end Blair's team chose to support Prescott, partly to balance Brown's support for Beckett, but also because they sensed Prescott would be more useful to them. To explain this choice to the party, Mandelson helped promote a sense that Prescott would be to Blair what Bevin had been to Attlee[119] – thinking more, no doubt, of their appeal across the Labour movement than their corpulence. The principal issue on which Prescott had chosen to challenge Blair in the campaign, jobs, was one where he was happy to concede some ground. Blair thus went into the campaign with Prescott the arch-traditionalist as his bed-fellow – and the author, if maverick MP George Galloway is to be believed, of some spikey words about Blair at the time. It was to be one of the shrewdest personal judgements of his political life.

The leadership election results, declared on 21 July, produced few surprises. Blair achieved 57 per cent of the total vote, doing best with MPs (and MEPs), 65 per cent of whom voted for him, and he secured the backing of 58.2 per cent of party members and 52.3 per cent of trade union members, his smallest percentage, but a very significant majority nonetheless. This union support was despite the fact that the leadership of all bar two of the twenty-six trade unions affiliated to the Labour Party nominated Beckett or Prescott. Blair was indeed the first Labour leader to be elected without the support of union bosses, and was thus not beholden to them. Blair derived particular satisfaction from securing almost three times as many union votes as Prescott, allegedly 'the friend of the unions'.[120] Prescott came ahead of Beckett for both leader and deputy leader in two close contests. Blair was duly elected leader, aged only forty-one, and just eleven years after entering Parliament. His acceptance speech was typically bold in rhetoric and vision, but airy on substance: 'We can change the course of history and build a new, confident land of opportunity in a new and changing world.'[121]

Blair had achieved exactly what he wanted. He had risen above Brown and had him where he wanted and needed him to be, or so he thought at the time; he had won the election with a comfortable majority on a modernising but vague agenda, and had done so by utterly outflanking the left and the unions, his two *bêtes noires*; and he had the team around him, Hunter, Mandelson, Campbell (shortly to join officially), Gould and Miliband, who he knew would see him through into Number 10 and beyond. After months and years of frustration and anxiety in a party he felt was going nowhere, he was finally happy, and he had at last found exactly what he wanted to do with his life.

Derry Irvine, who launched Blair's legal career, groomed his intellect and became his political godfather – before ultimately, all usefulness over, he was sacked by Blair.

16

Derry Irvine

'He has a brain the size of a planet,' Tony Blair would boast about his great mentor Derry Irvine.[1] In his new job as party leader from 1994, Blair would not contemplate appointing anyone senior nor would he take any major decision without first running it past Irvine. In these critical years, 1994–97, when his confidence was growing, there was no one, not even Mandelson, in whose judgement he had more confidence and respect. Blair revered him: he was the man who had forged his own career and who had been the dominant figure at his wedding; no one seemed more a rock-like feature of the Blair landscape than the granite figure of Irvine. Yet their relationship was to end in 2003 by Blair peremptorily dismissing him. Tony Blair rarely parts company with anyone after they have been admitted to his inner sanctum. What went so right for twenty-five years only to go so wrong?

Derry Irvine: The Life

An only child, Alexander Irvine was born in June 1940 into a working-class family in Inverness. His father was a roof-tiler by trade who was away at war for the first five years of his life, and his mother was a waitress.[2] She never liked his first name, which her son shared with her father and husband, and called him 'Derry' instead, which has remained with him all his life. After the family moved south to Glasgow, he won a scholarship to Hutchesons' Boys' Grammar, a well-known public school, and from there he won a further scholarship to Glasgow University. Law was his passion, and although he became close friends at university with John Smith and

Donald Dewar, and joined the Labour Party in 1958, he was not yet passionate about politics. At Cambridge University he was awarded firsts for both his BA (top out of 220 in the law tripos) and LLB law degrees, from where he went on to study for the Bar, during which time he also lectured on law at the LSE to pay his way. This was the time when he was most radical politically. For representing the NUS President against the LSE authorities, students elected him one of two honorary life presidents of their union: the other was Mao Zedong.[3]

For all of Irvine's intellectual brilliance it was perhaps surprising that he failed to secure a tenancy after completing his pupillage in 1967 and being called to the Bar, but he was subsequently taken on by Morris Finner at his chambers at 2 Crown Office Row. Irvine's first foray into politics came when John Smith persuaded him to stand as parliamentary candidate for Hendon North in the 1970 General Election. The country swung to the Conservatives, with Heath replacing Harold Wilson, but even taking account of the national swing, Irvine was felt not to have performed well in a potentially winnable seat, and failed to appeal to the working-class vote. Irvine does not like losing and the experience, coupled with his failure to secure the safe Labour seat of Aberdare in 1974,[4] resolved him to turn his attention fully to building his reputation at the Bar. A further reversal at the time was the breakdown of his first marriage, and the beginning of his relationship with Alison, the wife of Donald Dewar, for whom he had been best man.

Irvine later had two sons by Alison, who became his wife in 1974 (he chose not to mention his first wife, Margaret, in his entry in *Who's Who*). Irvine rapidly became a senior figure in Michael Sherrard's chambers, but became even better known for his work for the Labour Party than for his qualities as a barrister (a subject on which opinions differ widely). In 1978, he took silk, in Labour's last year in office, becoming at thirty-seven the youngest QC in the country. In 1981 he parted acrimoniously with Sherrard, who felt he had brought Irvine on and now felt betrayed by him.[5] Irvine, determined to become a head of chambers, set up at 11 King's Bench Walk, taking nine star pupils with him. A 'benevolent despotism' is a kind description for the way he ran his new set. Blair quipped at the time, 'Does the principle of one-person-one-vote apply in these chambers? Yes, I say. And Derry has the vote.'[6] For all that, the new chambers were one of Irvine's proudest achievements. All his pupils went on to become QCs, except one – Tony Blair.

Irvine's Labour Party connections were to be useful to him in building up his practice, described by one as 'very much a champagne socialist set'.[7] His shift in emphasis from criminal law to employment and then to commercial law disappointed some on the left, who had hoped he would be more of a champion of the underdog rather than becoming, as they saw it, a member of the Establishment. In recognition of his service to Labour, most notably his advice on legal action against Militant,[8] he was appointed a life peer by Kinnock in 1987. As Lord Irvine of Lairg he became spokesman on Legal and Home Affairs in the Lords until 1992, when Smith appointed him shadow Lord Chancellor.

Blair's relationship with Irvine is one of the most intriguing, and had five distinct phases. Irvine's choice of Blair as a pupil in 1976 is paradoxical. Irvine prided himself on recruiting young talent with Oxbridge, and preferably Bar, firsts (though Blair had neither), and Irvine made a big play of not appointing public school pupils — though he himself had been to one, he sent his children to another and several of those he selected were ex-public school. He growled at Blair for attending Fettes, but he was clearly impressed by Blair's energy and exuberance. 'He bowled me over with his enthusiasm,' he later said.[9] Charm, to which Irvine is always susceptible in men and women, won Blair his support over the rather intense Cherie Booth. Irvine decided his confidence was well placed and he frequently chose Blair as his junior over the next six years. Blair had to work hard: Irvine was renowned for being quite exceptionally demanding. The contrast in their styles was notorious: Blair has 'a beautiful, easy manner in court and was charming outside court', said one contemporary. Irvine, in contrast, was 'a disagreeable opponent, as disagreeable as Tony was agreeable'.[10]

Irvine may well have exaggerated when he described Blair in the mid-1990s as 'a brilliant lawyer. A complete natural.'[11] Other lawyers regarded Blair as a good and a thorough young barrister, but not exceptional. Irvine was nevertheless sufficiently impressed to include him in the nine he took to 11 King's Bench Walk in 1981, at the very time Blair was coming to the conclusion to leave the Bar for a career in politics. Blair's debt to Irvine in this first phase of their relationship, 1975–83, is prodigious. Irvine alone picked him for a far more prestigious set than his academic track record might have warranted; he then groomed him intellectually, teaching him how to think and develop the gravitas his law tutors at Oxford had conspicuously failed to bring on; he made law both interesting and practical for him; he helped give him both polish and edge as a performer; he introduced him to key figures in the Labour Party and trade unions; he encouraged him to look for a seat and advised him against fighting Beaconsfield again when asked to stand for the 1983 General Election; and he helped bring him together with Cherie. Very few young people receive so much in so many years from just one mentor figure. It is a formidable list, which left Blair very greatly in his debt.

Blair saw much less of Irvine in the 1983–94 period, when the relationship moved from being master–pupil to one, by the end, of equals, but with Irvine still *primus inter pares*. 'Tony can say "no" to Derry and Derry can say "no" to Tony,' said Maggie Rae of their relationship in this period. 'It is a partnership of equals.'[12] As a mark of their esteem, the Blairs asked Irvine to become godfather to Nicky, born in 1985. Blair and Irvine spoke frequently on the phone, for advice on people and on his line to take, early on in his parliamentary career, and on the closed shop and employment issues when he was shadow spokesman from 1989 to 1992. When Smith took over and was nettled by Blair, Irvine would help smooth relations, and he may well have helped convince Smith to give Blair the shadow Home Secretary job in 1992.[13]

The premature end of Smith's leadership in May 1994 ushered in a third phase of their relationship, which lasted until the General Election in 1997. Now Irvine and Blair are truly equals: Blair deferring to Irvine's intellect and shrewd judgement; Irvine to Blair's undeniably senior position. In the immediate aftermath of Smith's death, Irvine worked behind the scenes to have Blair elected, spoke more warmly of Blair as Smith's favoured successor than the facts strictly justified, and helped fundraising from sympathetic lawyers. Once elected party leader, Blair immediately sought out Irvine's counsel and spoke to him virtually every day on the phone or in person for the next three years.[14] Irvine advised Blair on the wording of the revised Clause IV and on all main policy statements up to and including the election campaign. He went through the election manifesto line by line with David Miliband, its principal author, his main brief being to ensure it concealed no hostages to fortune, though in the process he caused exasperation by being, some thought, excessively pedantic.[15]

A quality Blair particularly admired in Irvine was his ability to get to the heart of any issue, cutting through complexity, and identifying weaknesses and threats. For this reason, Blair consulted him over handling John Major at Prime Minister's Questions. Blair found him a uniquely reassuring presence: he knew if he gave Irvine a job, it would be done meticulously.[16] He knew also that if Irvine said someone would be good in a job, he could rely on that judgement.[17] Blair's personal office, however, did not share their boss's stellar opinion: 'During meetings with Alastair, Peter [Hyman], Liz [Lloyd] and others, he would always address Tony Blair directly. It was as if we were not there. He is very good at making others around him feel intellectually inferior.'[18] His lack of grace and humour were much commented on.[19] For the time being, Blair turned a blind eye, but he showed Irvine that he was aware of the offhand way he treated people when he kicked open the door to his office in Millbank mimicking his behaviour: 'Come on, Irvine,' he shouted, 'haven't you finished the work I gave you last night?'[20] 'Melon head' was his nickname among Millbank staff, after Blair had said he had a brain 'the size of a melon'.[21] Irvine's supporters deny he is rude or offhand: they ascribe his manner rather to shyness, and say he adopted a bombastic manner as a way of overcoming his inhibitions with people. They also ascribe the fact that some felt intimidated by him to his relentless quest for the truth and use of cross-examination techniques, which unsettled those not used to his manner.[22]

Irvine hosted a key secret dinner in May 1995 for senior figures in both Labour and the Liberal Democrats. 'I do what he tells me, including making my house available at the drop of a hat,' Paddy Ashdown's diary recalls Irvine saying. Ashdown thought, 'He seems to act as a kind of godfather to Blair.'[23] Irvine became a key adviser to Blair on the issue of a possible link with the Lib Dems, which caused so much difficulty with their senior colleagues in the shadow Cabinet. Reform of the constitution was another area on which Blair involved Irvine. This large agenda included House of Lords reform, on which Blair had modified his position considerably since he had advocated, as recently as 1993, having only elected representatives; incorporation of the European Convention of Human Rights, to which Irvine had been converted by Anthony Lester; and the fraught subject of devolution.[24] This last had been the main unfinished business of the Callaghan government of 1976–79, and had been a particular enthusiasm of Smith's. After Blair became leader, several senior voices, including Jack Straw, advised him to drop it as a distraction from New Labour's prime focus on the economy and improving public services. They argued that it was not an important issue for the English electorate, and that vital parliamentary time should not be sacrificed for it in the first two sessions.[25]

Blair turned to Irvine, who was committed to fulfilling Smith's legacy, to chair a secret committee in late 1995 looking at the various devolution issues.[26] Blair's senior Scottish colleagues – Brown, Cook, Dewar and George Robertson – made it clear they would never allow it to be dropped; and the Liberal Democrats, whom Blair was courting, were also very keen, so he agreed, after consultation with Irvine, to let it go ahead. Blair's one major input into the debate was to insist that a referendum, deemed essential by Dewar and Robertson to ensure smooth passage of the bill through both Houses, should be specifically mentioned in the draft manifesto (which was to be put to an all-party vote in early 1996) and that in Scotland there should be a separate question about its tax-varying powers.[27] When the referendum commitment was announced, it was seen as a U-turn and as a way of delaying devolution indefinitely, and for a time it created considerable bad feeling in Scotland.[28] But even critics later agreed that the decision to be open about the referendum, held in September 1997, had been the right one. Blair was even less enthusiastic about Welsh devolution. But he allowed it to go ahead, though he was adamant that a Welsh Assembly should not have full legislative powers.[29]

Irvine was an enormously happy and fulfilled person in the 1994–97 period. He hugely enjoyed having the ear of the Labour leader, to a far greater degree than he had ever had under Kinnock or Smith, and he revelled in the various tasks he was called on to do for Blair. He was also utterly secure about his own future: the *New Statesman* observed in 1996, 'His is, without exception, the surest appointment in Blair's first Cabinet, in which he would be Lord Chancellor.'[30] This position had already been heralded by Cherie when she introduced her former pupil-master in public the year before as 'the next Lord Chancellor'. Irvine was reported to be earning £500,000 a year at the Bar in 1996/97, he had bought a large home in the Scottish Highlands, where the Blairs were infrequent visitors, and he boasted at his elegant West Hampstead house an impressive collection of paintings, including works by Walter Sickert, Stanley Spencer and Paul Nash.[31] Blair was in awe of Irvine's taste in art, so much so that he boasted to Paddy Ashdown, at a dinner party at their home in Islington, that 'Derry Irvine is my art consultant'.[32] 'I envy the Medicis their taste,' Irvine told Don Macintyre just before the 1997 General Election, 'and the sensible use of their great wealth in accumulating their treasures.'[33] If he was aware of hubris at this point in his life, it was not a concern he shared with others.

After the 1997 election, the Blair–Irvine relationship moved into its fourth phase, which lasted until about 1999/2000. They were no longer equals: Blair was clearly the master. Irvine never fully recognised a change of status he felt uncomfortable with. It is not easy to accept a reversal of a master–pupil relationship, especially if one is proud, and Irvine is pride personified. Blair's faith in Irvine remained undimmed, and he appointed him to eight of the twenty Cabinet committees set up in 1997, asking him to chair three of them. Irvine was thought to be the most skilful committee chairman in the government: with Blair's disregard for taking decisions in Cabinet and its committees, Irvine's were indeed almost the only Cabinet committees that functioned properly.[34]

Irvine's most important contribution in the first term was his chairing of the Cabinet committees on constitutional reform, on which he coaxed or bludgeoned through the agenda (depending on viewpoint), taking a minute interest in every detail, aided by ministers and officials, knowing he was carrying the full authority of the Prime Minister. 'Derry had a mission with the John Smith legacy,' said one aide. 'He had a directive from Tony to get it through as quickly as possible so it didn't block anything.'[35] Opposition to the proposals came particularly from Prescott and Straw, with the latter as Home Secretary becoming Irvine's foe on legal issues, notably over the Freedom of Information Bill. The Human Rights Act (for whose passage Straw claimed credit), reform of the legal aid system as well as reform of the House of Lords (on which he opposed elected peers) and a Freedom of Information Act (albeit considerably tamer than he wanted) were all issues that Irvine drove through in these early years in power.[36] Chief credit for the constitutional changes, one of the seminal achievements of the first Blair government, is due to him.[37]

Irvine's other government interventions were less happy. After the first few weeks, Blair thought his Prime Minister's Questions team was missing a vital ingredient, and he believed Irvine could provide it. His addition did not impress the team, not because they were jealous of an interloper, but because they thought it did not play to his strengths. 'He would get an idea of what he thought Hague might lead on, and he would be very pleased with himself. But often he was wrong. He would say such silly things,' said one official.[38] 'What Blair was really after was a small number of telling facts that he would want to repeat again and again once he'd found them. Derry had no political brain and his meandering, discursive style didn't help us find them,' said another.[39] After a while, Charles Falconer began to attend these sessions and Irvine was gradually eased out of the picture.

By 2000, the Blair–Irvine relationship was entering its fifth and final phase. A series of 'gaffes' had been made by Irvine soon after the 1997 election, of which much was made by the media partly, his friends felt, as a way of getting at Blair. Best known were his support for the refurbishment of the Lord Chancellor's residence, including the choice of £300-a-roll wallpaper (costing £650,000 in total); asking his staff in the Lord Chancellor's office to peel his oranges for him and his comparison, at a private function at the Reform Club in October 1997, of his own position to that of Cardinal Wolsey: 'It is true that I have a closer relationship with the Prime Minister than, I believe, any previous Lord Chancellor has had,' Irvine said. 'The Lord Chancellor is not the King's conscience any longer, nor is he the Prime Minister's conscience. But he is, once again, one of the principal advisers of the political leader of our country.'[40] This last episode, which Irvine had intended as a joke, was the most damaging because it reinforced his reputation for self-importance and boastfulness – providing further embarrassment for Blair.[41] None of these were hanging offences, but at worst lapses of judgement by a man unused to the intense media scrutiny that comes with a top political job. The assumption was that political antennae would develop. Blair was inclined to this view, and was relieved when Irvine was persuaded to accept a special adviser, Garry Hart, a City solicitor who was a close Islington friend of his and Cherie (and godfather to Kathryn). Hart was an adept and diplomatic presence who helped acclimatise Irvine to the very different world of ministerial life, and modify some of his 'quirks', as did Alan Percival, who joined as his press secretary. Alastair Campbell, a man who matched Irvine for bluntness, achieved the same end in a less subtle way. He gave him trenchant instructions to stop talking to the media.

The man with the shrewdest judgement in the world in Blair's eyes was in danger of becoming, within just two or three years, a source of regular and embarrassing headlines. Far more important to Blair, who was never unduly perturbed by the press stories about gaffes, was that he was discovering he did not need his old mentor so much. Irvine's disappointing performance on the Prime Minister's Questions team was an early indication in Blair's eyes of his fallibility. Blair found that others could fill Irvine's shoes without the collateral damage. Jonathan Powell more than anyone provided him with Irvine's 'wise counsel' role, on appointments as well as on policy; Straw's authoritarian stance on legal issues chimed more with Blair than Irvine's more libertarian views; and Blair turned increasingly to his old friend Charles Falconer for the kind of advice, legal and personal, he had hitherto sought from Irvine. When Blair was appointing Robin Butler's successor as Cabinet Secretary in 1997, Irvine was an essential figure interviewing the four candidates: when Richard Wilson retired in 2002, Blair did not even think to call on Irvine's assistance.[42] After the first main tranche of constitutional reforms were enacted, Irvine had fulfilled much of his purpose. What role was there for him beyond his specialist legal work as Lord Chancellor? Not much, Blair was reluctantly concluding. Yet Blair did not dismiss him in the 2001 reshuffle, still less did he think about it in earlier reshuffles, as some had tipped him to do (Lord Williams of Mostyn was mentioned as a successor, and latterly Lord Goldsmith who became Attorney General). The 2001 reshuffle aroused particular surprise because it followed one of Irvine's most publicised alleged errors of judgement, when he wrote to Labour lawyers asking them to attend a Labour Party fundraising event, seen by some as an abuse of the neutral aspect of his position as Lord Chancellor. It came to be dubbed the 'cash for wigs' scandal. Irvine roundly rejected the charges, claiming the role of Lord Chancellor also involved a party political element. He had done nothing wrong.

Irvine insisted that he still had much to do in Blair's second government – the second stage of reform of the House of Lords, reform of the criminal justice system and promotion of the Community Legal Service. Blair, who was thinking through a second tranche of constitutional reform for the new term of office, let him remain. As always, he did not want a confrontation, which he knew would follow if he moved Irvine. He was content for him to stay as long as he avoided embarrassments and supported his programme. After a subdued first year,[43] concerns resurfaced that Irvine's political nous had not developed as hoped and about his lifestyle ('There's no doubt he had a keen appreciation of fine claret and malt whisky, but he also had a huge capacity for long hours, and the former never adversely affected the latter,' said one friend).[44] This background noise distracted attention from the contributions he was still making, not least his standing up for the independence of the judiciary, which had won him plaudits from many in the legal profession, if not in Number 10.[45] He successfully persuaded peers in the House of Lords to Blair's view that a wholly elected second chamber would be an error (Blair feared an all-elected House of Lords could be very disruptive to the government's legislative programme).

But the second term proved more turbulent for Irvine than the first. The turning point for Blair came when Irvine appeared on the BBC's *Today* programme in January 2003, saying that people were happy to see burglars kept out of jail even for second offences, which provoked the right-wing press to predictable uproar. Irvine was defending guidelines from Lord Woolf, the Lord Chief Justice, on the sentencing of burglars, which were extremely unpopular with many in Number 10, who feared appearing 'soft' on crime. Fury resulted, and Blair convened a meeting in February at Number 10 to find a 'way forward' (the common form of words when a crisis meeting was called). 'Blair was really irritated,' said one attendee. 'You could hear it in his voice.' Blair thought Irvine had been politically inept, and that his remarks undercut the government's policy of pushing for tougher sentencing. Blair surprised those present by how strongly he stood up against Irvine, who defended himself equally robustly. Shortly after, Irvine accepted a £22,000 pay rise, and greatly enhanced pension rights, which led to a weekend of hostile press comment and a recirculation of the 'trouble with Derry' stories.[46] He refused to cut back or reform his department, or his methods of operating, which were arousing concern in Number 10.[47] It all raised further questions in Blair's mind about whether Irvine's political skills had in fact developed over time, as he had hoped.

The catalyst that spelled the end for Irvine, however, apart from Blair realising he could live without him, was that Blair decided that he wanted to go ahead with a second tranche of constitutional reform in the second term. He wanted it done quickly and he became convinced that Irvine was not the man to carry through the changes, which centred on the abolition of the position of Lord Chancellor – the appointment of judges was to be given to a new recommending body, a separate Supreme Court and a new department for constitutional affairs.[48] Academics and lawyers had been talking about abolishing the post of Lord Chancellor for thirty or more years: many thought it inappropriate to still have one person fulfilling all the roles of the Lord Chancellor. Irvine himself saw the case for reform, and had produced and introduced monitoring of judicial appointments and other innovations. In part, he saw the sense of what Blair wanted to do in modernising his ancient and anachronistic post.[49] 'Why on earth do you sit on the Woolsack in the House of Lords every day?' Blair chided Irvine, 'That's a complete waste of your time.'[50] But Blair thought it would be completely wrong for Irvine himself to preside over the abolition of his own post and the introduction of the reforms. There were extraordinarily difficult meetings between Blair and Irvine in Number 10 in early June 2003. Blair found them 'harrowing' and 'exhausting'. It was as bad as – worse than – he had feared, and was exactly the kind of confrontation he had worked hard to avoid. Irvine's vision of a legal department was very different from Blair's. Irvine favoured a 'rights' department, as did most of the legal profession. Blair, however, was much closer to Blunkett (and Straw before him) favouring a less liberal and more authoritarian solution with a clearer separation of the role of judges and politicians. Crime became one of Blair's top priorities in his second term, and he did not see Irvine as embodying the values he now wanted to espouse. Irvine showed no sign of tempering his line following the furore over his *Today* remarks at the start of the year. Blunkett clashed with Irvine, as had Straw before him, but the personality issues, though significant, mattered far less than the real clash of visions that Blunkett and Irvine articulated. In the end, Blair saw Irvine as both an institutional and philosophical block to what he now wanted to do as Prime Minister. In the June 2003 reshuffle he dropped him, and the post, in a media storm that utterly eclipsed any of the squalls caused by Irvine's gaffes.[51] Irvine was not the only person to be angry about the abolition of the Lord Chancellor's post: neither Lord Woolf, nor the Leader of the House of Lords, Lord Williams of Mostyn, knew about it until the day of the announcement. Nor, indeed, did the Queen know; she was said to be 'hopping' about it.[52]

Irvine had made himself such an isolated figure that few in the government or the Labour Party mourned his passing. That knowledge heightened his despondency. Irvine's stock began to rise, however, from the moment he stood down. Many began to talk about not only his brilliant intellectual gifts but also his very substantial service to the legal profession and to the government. Those who disliked what they saw as an increasingly illiberal government mourned the passing of his steadying presence. He received several hundred letters on his retirement, many from lawyers or from those who had worked for him. And all four private secretaries who had served him at the Lord Chancellor's Department combined to invite him to dinner, which touched him greatly. Praise from fellow barrister Lord Alexander of Weedon that he was 'the most influential Lord Chancellor of the twentieth century', while welcome, was scant consolation.[53] Number 10 briefed that Blair was 'very troubled' about having to dismiss Irvine and that he found it 'as traumatic as sacking Peter Mandelson'.[54] 'Blair realised that he had left Derry *in situ* for much too long,' said a senior Number 10 figure, 'but at the same time was looking for any way out other than having to sack him. In the end he bit the bullet.'[55]

Blair had spent many years listening to Irvine, but Irvine was less happy to listen to advice from Blair, or to alter his way of conducting his department and his affairs. Like Ted Heath, another only child, Irvine was happiest when communicating with others when he was the figure in authority asking the questions or giving instructions. The fact that he survived so long in Blair's government is a measure of the very profound debt of gratitude and affection Blair felt for him. Unlike Gordon Brown, who also displeased Blair, or Prescott, who also made gaffes, Irvine had no political constituency, so he could be disposed of in the certain knowledge there would be no backlash.

Blair felt he had needed Irvine 'there' every time he rose up the political ladder (in 1983, 1989, 1994 and 1997). Then, over the space of two or three years, he realised he no longer needed Irvine's judgement, or his presence to give him self-belief. Irvine's referring to him as 'young Blair', while partly just banter, was also an indication of his inability to adjust to the changed realities. Most Lord Chancellors, reared in the law, also find it hard to adjust to the very different world of politics. Some, like Lords Kilmuir (1954–62) and Hailsham (1970–74 and 1979–97), were far more autocratic and patrician than Irvine. Irvine, nevertheless, was happiest when he was master of his destiny. He liked doing things his own way, winning arguments and being the boss. Another lesson Blair learned from Irvine was how to be a boss and how to be tough, as we shall see in the next chapter.

A delighted and very relieved Blair at the Clause IV conference in Westminster on 29 April 1995. Not for another eight years was he able to take a similarly bold stand on a domestic issue.

17

Clause IV, 1994–95

'The core difference between Tony Blair and Bill Clinton,' said veteran US election pollster, Stan Greenberg, 'is that when Clinton beats someone, he wants to hug them and take them along. Tony Blair wants to stand on their neck and then move on to the next battle.'[1] Much has been made of Blair's eagerness to be liked and his dislike of confrontation. His actions on beating Brown and becoming leader – whether over the leader's office, the party organisation or the party's constitution – were the opposite of a politician who is sentimental or eager to please. If Greenberg's comment is correct about Blair, it would apply to 1994–95, after which he was never again so decisive or ruthless. 'Don't forget, you'll never be as strong as when you are first elected,' was the advice proffered to him by John Birt, then BBC Director-General. It was counsel he heeded in 1994 more than in 1997, 2001 or 2004.[2] The defining moment in this period indeed came early on in his three years as Leader of the Opposition: his full-frontal assault on the very totem of everything he disliked about old Labour, the revered Clause IV of the party's constitution.

Coup d'Etat, July–September 1994

Blair had existed with a small and shifting office since he entered Parliament, the most constant figure, there for seven of the eleven years, being Anji Hunter. With his election as leader, however, he resolved to have a stable as well as a high-powered team which would carry him over into Number 10, and he determined to find the money he would need to establish and run it. Michael Levy, who had helped out with his leadership campaign, now helped him raise funds so he could have a properly staffed office. He also helped raise money for Gordon Brown's office, a role later taken over by Geoffrey Robinson. Blair was very concerned that the funding be beyond reproach, and so appointed three unimpeachable trustees for the 'Leader's Office Fund', Baronesses Dean and Jay and Merlyn Rees.[3]

Margaret Beckett, when acting leader from May to July 1994, had retained John Smith's core office, but Blair swept many of them aside. However, he always found it easier to be tough in speeches than in personal encounters: when staff were to be informed that their contracts would not be renewed, or worse, they were fired, Blair would often call upon his trusted Anji Hunter.[4] Smith's confidant, Murray Elder, stayed on to assist with union relations and to provide continuity with the Smith era, but proved unable to diminish the resentment the Smith family and supporters felt towards the new regime.[5] He left for a new job as a lobbyist in January 1995.

The heart of the new office was Hunter herself, with the title 'head of private office', and Alastair Campbell, who became press secretary, providing continuity with the Kinnock leadership by dint of their close friendship. Beneath him were three in press relations: Hilary Coffman, who had worked for both Kinnock and Smith and was the partner of David Hill; Tim Allan, who had already worked for Blair; and Peter Hyman, who was given speech-writing duties. Head of policy was David Miliband, who had been working with Patricia Hewitt at the IPPR think-tank and on the Commission of Social Justice, and who had edited a book, *Re-inventing the Left* (1994), which Andrew Rawnsley later described as the 'set text for New Labour intellectuals'. Pat McFadden was brought in to work on union relations, and Liz Lloyd remained as a researcher. Jonathan Powell was to join as chief of staff and Sally Morgan as head of party liaison in early 1995. A post that was still empty by the time the bulk of the appointments were announced in early September was that of 'economics adviser', a position he was never to fill satisfactorily with a figure of Ed Balls' stature or influence – although it would have made for an even more turbulent relationship with Brown if he had found such a person; reminiscent of the struggles between Mrs Thatcher's economics guru, Alan Walters, and the Treasury.[6]

To help oversee his office, Blair, with Mo Mowlam's enthusiastic support, tried to recruit his old ally from the closed shop debate, Tom Sawyer.[7] He turned the position down but accepted Blair's next offer, to become General Secretary of the Labour Party. This meant sacking Larry Whitty, who had been in post since 1985. To some like Alan Haworth, it was 'one of the worst things that Tony ever did. It was unnecessary and it suggested utterly the wrong relationship with the party.'[8] To others, however, Whitty was a trade unionist who had been disloyal to John Smith, conspicuously failing to support him over OMOV.[9] Whitty was stunned, and thought of resisting; if not quite splitting the party, it would nevertheless have created great turbulence during Blair's honeymoon. Whitty was encouraged to fight because only the NEC, not the party leader, is entitled to dismiss a General Secretary. But he backed down, not wanting to cause dissent, and received a peerage and later a place in the government.[10]

Blair's determination to make a 'clean sweep'[11] resulted in many other senior Labour officials departing and being replaced by those more sympathetic to Blair's mission. This met with some resentment even from those who came from a similar background within the party. 'He seemed to have surrounded himself by people who were far too keen to take on the party rather than to work with it and win it round,' said one senior figure.[12] Selling party headquarters at Walworth Road, described by Campbell as 'fuck-awful', and finding new premises for the party organisation was part of the same clean-sweep approach.[13] Blair also wanted to sack various figures from Smith's shadow Cabinet like Tom Clarke, Ron Davies and Derek Foster, and had to be reminded that the shadow Cabinet was elected, and the leader had no power to hire and fire at will.[14] Blair was in a hurry, and gave the impression of either not understanding or more probably not sympathising with the time-honoured rules that governed the functioning of the party in and outside Parliament.

On policy he felt no such hurry, and was content to bide his time until he had a chance to talk matters over with his new team after the summer. He realised his policy platform had been indeterminate during the leadership campaign, but he had no wish to make policy on the hoof. He wanted, however, to give some early signposts and create a tone. Thus he said 'two parents' were better than one; business was as important to his Labour Party as trade unions; high tax days were over, and Labour could be trusted to run the economy better than the Tories. The most important indication he gave of Labour's future style and intentions came on 26 July, just five days after his election, when he openly contradicted the shadow Education spokesman, Ann Taylor, saying that the party was in favour of publishing league tables on school examination results, which went expressly against what Taylor, the unions and the left had been saying for some years.[15] He was told he could not have the shadow Cabinet he wanted. Very well. He would take them head-on one by one if he did not like what they were saying.

Clause IV: September 1994

Blair was looking for a symbol (a 'shock' in Philip Gould's words) which would visibly demonstrate to the country how much Labour had now changed. 'We had seen change below the surface before 1994, but now it needed to blossom out into the open,' he later said.[16] Or as David Hill put it, 'It was a classic rebranding exercise. Announce that you are new and different, then demonstrably *show* that you are new and different by a very high-profile act. Clause IV was the perfect device.'[17]

Blair knew relatively little of the history of the Labour Party when he became leader; and what little he did know, he did not like. The only administration he looked back on with anything approaching admiration was that of Clement Attlee from 1945 to 1951,[18] though even here he believed that Attlee had left unresolved 'fundamental issues of ideology and organisation'.[19] Attlee's successor as Labour leader, Hugh Gaitskell, had tried in 1959 to change the manifestly out-of-date words of Clause IV of the Labour Party constitution of 1918, which had begun to appear on the membership cards of Labour members that very year, but was defeated. The clause, which famously committed the party to the 'common ownership of the means of production, distribution and exchange', was an irrelevance to the party from the outset, and had only been included seventy-five years before to keep middle-class socialists happy. Wilson, when party leader from 1963 to 1976, did not agree with Clause IV, but argued that no one had to believe it any more than a Christian did the literal truth of Genesis.[20] Callaghan (1976–80) lacked the opportunity and Foot (1980–83) the inclination to change the clause. Kinnock wanted to and paved the way with his and Hattersley's 'Statement of Democratic Socialist Aims and Values', which was debated at the 1988 party conference. Their statement, and the 1989 Party Review, formalised the abandonment of nationalisation as Labour policy, but without expressly repealing the totem of Clause IV. In 1991, Kinnock had printed thousands of membership cards without the Clause IV words, but backtracked when the left cried 'traitor' and the cards were shredded. Kinnock could get no further down the track before the 1992 General Election. Thereafter, Smith felt he had gone as far as he wanted to go with 'changes' with OMOV in 1993, though he had been planning to introduce his own statement of Labour's aims and values at the 1994 conference which, he hoped, would quietly supersede Clause IV, in a characteristically unostentatious way.[21]

Blair did not want 'quiet'; he wanted the opposite of unostentatious. He had mulled over abandoning Clause IV initially with his Trimdon team in the 1983–87 Parliament.[22] He had then been preoccupied with other front-bench matters until he began to think seriously in 1991–92 about what he might want to do if he became party leader. In his 1991 *Marxism Today* article, 'Forging a New Agenda', he firmly distanced himself from public ownership.[23] Barbara Amiel remembers on her visit to interview him at Sedgefield in the early summer of 1992: 'Everything hinged for him on getting rid of Clause IV. I was very struck by his determination and by the promise his determination held out.'[24] Pressure for change to Clause IV also arose from other quarters under Smith's leadership. The Fabian Society published the findings of the Archer Committee in 1993 entitled 'A New Constitution for the Labour Party', calling for a replacement of Clause IV.[25] Jack Straw published an influential pamphlet, 'Policy and Ideology', calling for the party to adopt a new constitution. 'Touching Clause IV had become a taboo. Someone had to break the log-jam,' Straw later said. 'Tony and I did not see much of each other before the 1992 election, so I was surprised and gratified when he gave me a bit of encouragement with what I was writing.'[26] But Smith told Straw to 'back off' and then made sure everyone knew that he had told him to do so. Will Hutton summed up the views of many progressive Labour thinkers when he wrote in *Renewal* in 1993 that Labour will be ready to contest the Conservative legacy 'if it can amend Clause IV to express the aims and values of a modern socialist party'.[27] The groundwork had been laid. Or so Blair thought.

He deliberately avoided talking about Clause IV during the leadership campaign, as we have seen, saying on *Breakfast with Frost*, disingenuously, that 'no one' wanted it to be 'a priority for the party'.[28] David Frost had put the deliberately searching question to Blair after talking to Peter Kellner, one of the pundits he consulted before his flagship show. As Kellner predicted, it put Blair on the spot.[29] Blair ducked at the time, but over the summer his mind increasingly turned to it as providing the ideal 'defining moment' at the start of his leadership. He discussed it with Brown, who did not share his enthusiasm, but raised no objections.[30] Brown had been impressed on one of his many US trips by a conversation over dinner about Clinton's attack in 1992 on 'Sister Souljah', a black rap singer who had made inflammatory remarks about whites – it was an emblem, Brown was told, of the Democratic Party under Clinton being prepared to attack unacceptable forms of speech even from the ethnic minorities, whom few Democrats had dared criticise. Brown's American interlocutors suggested that Clause IV could be 'New Labour's Sister Souljah'.[31] The conversation may have moved Brown, though his simmering anger left him ill-disposed to any Blair initiative at the time.[32] He did not set out to undermine Blair, though some still speculated that, if Blair was weakened, or even if he fell because of it, then Brown would be the beneficiary.

Blair worried away at Clause IV over August, which he and his family spent in France and then at Tim Allan's parents' Tuscan villa.[33] Campbell, who he saw en route in France, was attracted by the boldness of the move, and still more by the mover, thinking 'this was someone who wasn't going to mess about'.[34] Mandelson was keen, as was Gould, and by early September Blair decided he had the support he needed. But first he wanted to secure his home-base. He resolved that he should thrash out the issue, and much else besides, at an 'away day' as soon as his team were back from their holidays. He wanted to plan out his path all the way up to the General Election, and, more immediately, think through how to play the party conference in Blackpool in early October. Blair turned to Colin Fisher, a corporate strategy consultant and Labour sympathiser, who for several years had hosted confidential dinners in his Clapham home with Brown, Blair and Mandelson. Blair had as yet to build up the party's coffers. Would he pay for the event?[35] Fisher was only too happy to be 'in at the creation', and selected the opulent and discreet Chewton Glen Hotel in the New Forest.[36] But it was not to be the happy coronation seminar Blair had envisaged. Prolonged agonising followed as to who should attend. The first real indication Blair received since the leadership election that Brown had not fully accepted the result was when he pressed for 'his people' to attend. 'We didn't know what he was talking about at first. We said it was Tony's conference and he didn't need his own staff present. But he insisted he did,' said a Blair aide.[37] Eventually a compromise was struck. Campbell, Mandelson and Gould would go, but not Hunter or Miliband.[38] Brown brought with him Michael Wills, a young protégé, then a television producer, whom Brown lobbied to become Deputy General Secretary to balance Blair's choice of Sawyer. Mandelson brought with him Roger Liddle.[39] The principal absentee was Prescott, deliberately omitted in the face of Campbell's protestations.[40] When Prescott found out about the meeting he was 'incandescent'.[41] It confirmed his then suspicions of Blair as a double-dealer whom he could not trust.

On 8 September, the night before the main party joined, Blair, Brown and Mandelson dined alone in a private room with Fisher. According to Fisher, the atmosphere was extremely tense, in stark contrast to their convivial dinners of old. Brown produced a list of ideas on domestic policy, which Blair was happy enough about, and some thoughts on organisation, which created more difficulty. The main animosity was between Brown and Mandelson, and Brown, it was noted, refused to look him in the eye. Blair went to bed before midnight. Brown, Mandelson and Fisher remained talking for half an hour.[42] According to Mandelson, as they walked back to their rooms in the hotel, Brown demanded to know why he had not supported him on all his proposals for party organisation, including the appointment of Wills. Mandelson believed it was at this moment that their friendship cooled irrevocably:[43] to Brown's camp, the key moment came earlier, with Mandelson's actions in the leadership election in the summer.

The next day the remaining seminar attendees arrived, oblivious of the excitements of the night before. They had all been furnished with a long Gould and a short Fisher paper to facilitate their discussions, which were dominated by questioning about what New Labour should stand for. As one present recalled: 'Brown's focus then, as now, was on opportunity . . . Blair was anchored in community.'[44] In terms of giving Blair a road map for the future, and building an *esprit de corps*, Chewton Glen was to prove a damp squib. It resolved nothing important – Blair's policy platform, the conference theme and the final decision over Clause IV were all left up in the air. What it did reveal was that Brown was not going to be easy to handle. He had brooded over the summer, as was his wont. His team had encouraged his belief that he could dominate Blair, with Brown's (disputed) attempt to pull Mandelson away from Blair a first step.[45] Chewton Glen, their first multilateral meeting since the election, revealed to Brown that Blair would be tougher than he thought, and Blair realised that Brown would be less biddable than he hoped. Blair also realised that he would not treat Prescott in the semi-detached way that Kinnock had his deputy, Hattersley. Prescott would be far more trouble to him 'outside the tent pissing in, than inside pissing out' as L. B. Johnson, oddly not one of Blair's favoured presidents, had famously said about handling colleagues.

The sheer euphoria of victory in July and Blair's summer holiday now seemed far away. The four weeks that followed Chewton Glen were nervous, unsteady times. The conference slogan was still not decided on Monday, 25 September, a week before it began. Campbell came up with the line 'New Labour, New Britain'. After some difficult conversations with party officials, who feared it might backfire against them, the slogan was adopted.[46] The conference can thus be considered the official launch date for 'New Labour', though the term had been in frequent use by Gould and others, especially after the success of Clinton's 'New Democrats', for two or more years. But, emblazoned above the stage to be picked up by the television cameras, this was the first time the general public became aware of 'New Labour', and it did not arouse the dire consequences the cassandras had predicted.

Blair and Campbell discussed what to do about Clause IV when they drove together on the Saturday from Manchester Airport up to Blackpool for the conference. They failed to decide whether Blair should tackle the issue. With twenty-four hours to go, Blair's speech on the Tuesday was still not completed, and the decision to announce any change to Clause IV was still not made. Blair was torn. His instincts told him it was the right moment to make a bold statement saying that the anachronistic constitution was going to be rewritten. But it was his first speech as leader; the party was deeply divided between modernisers and traditionalists. Were the traditionalists, even if only a few still believed in wholesale nationalisation, really ready for this symbolic step? He even found himself wondering at times whether Smith had not been right after all, that the General Election was in the bag as long as the party did not tear itself apart beforehand.

Blair and Campbell decided that the key to deciding this issue was Prescott. Campbell said, 'There was no way we could have done it without John Prescott – not just John reluctantly agreeing, but John actually giving his blessing to it.'[47] Prescott was initially hostile to the idea and was still sullen about the Chewton Glen rebuff: it would ruin Blair's delicate relationship with the left of the party, he argued, and he did not favour the party being bounced into anything. Campbell, for whom Prescott had a respect he did not extend to Mandelson or some others in Blair's camp, was to prove crucial in bringing Prescott on side.[48] Campbell saw the successful delivery of his master's wishes on Clause IV as his first test in his new post. The conference speech was on Monday, 3 October, and even hours before it the issue had still not been resolved. 'I was up practically all night,' said Campbell, 'up and down the stairs to John's room.' Prescott was told very clearly that this was to be the loyalty test on which his new partnership with Blair would be built.[49] He was 'hammered away at' until at last he relented, though he demanded as a concession that Blair give his agreement to have a veto on the revised wording.[50] 'If you are going to do this,' he eventually agreed, 'you have got to say it, you can't bugger about.'[51] The agreement was finally reached in the early hours of Tuesday morning.

When Campbell briefed senior party officials in strict secrecy about the plan, some thought it would spell the end of Labour. Blair anxiously received the reactions while he worked in his hotel room on final drafts of his speech that morning. Up to this point, the possibility of him announcing a change to Clause IV had been discussed in only the closest circles: the reactions from party officials were unnerving. He began to wonder whether he would still be in a job by the following evening. This was more than him indulging his tendency to overdramatise: Gould, in 1998, described the next few hours as 'the most uncertain in his political career'.[52] He also displayed a rare petulance, which he mostly had learned to master.

They decided that it would be better before he gave the speech to forewarn the shadow Cabinet on the Tuesday morning. Blair saw them one by one, and they were told of Prescott's backing, though he subtly changed the message depending on the individual. According to one party official, Blair held various sections of the speech in his hands, making a careful note of how they responded to what he said.[53] None openly objected, but several were clearly unhappy. Particular effort was put into winning over the left – Beckett, Blunkett and Cook – the latter seen as the left's main star. Blair also saw selected union leaders, again changing his pitch depending upon whom he was seeing. To Edmonds he tried to appeal to his better nature, arguing that whereas John Smith had been a long-established and respected figure at the top of the party, he, Tony Blair, needed to do something dramatic to gain attention and respect. But he fell short of telling him specifically about Clause IV.[54] While he spoke to them, finishing touches were being made to the speech by Campbell, David Miliband and Peter Hyman.

The significance of having Prescott on board was the message it gave that even traditionalists like him were prepared to adapt their principles for the sake of achieving power under Blair's leadership. But ultimately Blair's team were not sure whether Prescott's endorsement would be enough to carry the day. Neither, in the last analysis, were they totally confident about Prescott.[55] Robin Cook, who would have been the favourite left candidate to succeed Blair if he fell, was yet to be won over.[56] Cook later recalled, 'I was surprised how little thought had gone into what might take its place.'[57] The incomplete and uncertain support explained why they decided at the last minute not to go for the 'whole-hog' option, i.e., with Blair telling the conference directly that Clause IV was being dropped, in favour of a 'half-way house'. Under this plan, Blair was to conclude his speech by suggesting that Labour required 'a modern constitution that says what we are in terms the public cannot misunderstand and the Tories cannot misrepresent', and saying that he and John Prescott would prepare a new statement of the party's objectives to 'take its place in our constitution for the next century'. Unlike the failed attempt of Gaitskell, Blair promised a wide debate in the party on the new proposals. Campbell decided to leave out from the copies of the leader's speech circulated to the media the all-important conclusion, so he could himself put the construction on it he wanted, tuned up to the last moment by final conversations and by listening to how the speech had gone down in the conference hall. As soon as Blair finished talking, and he and Blair judged it had been well enough received, Campbell went frantically to work telling the media what it 'really' meant, while Blair and Prescott prepared for their joint press conference in the press centre. Only at the very last minute did they finally commit to saying that the reference referred expressly to Clause IV.

As the audience rose to applaud the speech, many failed to realise the significance of what their leader had just said. 'The party was taken completely by shock,' said Peter Hain. 'I was commenting live on Channel 4 and Elinor Goodman, the political editor, said the last page of Blair's speech was missing and there's a rumour that he's going to ditch Clause IV. I said on air, "You must be joking".'[58] John Monks, General Secretary of the TUC, was listening to the speech on the radio and had no idea Blair was talking about Clause IV. 'It was very odd,' he said. 'I heard the audience clapping rapturously and in the same state of ignorance of what he meant about Clause IV as me.'[59] Blair knew that the unions, already raw about his remarks in July about their having no more access to him than business, had at least to be neutralised. He concentrated his one-to-one efforts on winning over leaders of the larger unions. He was under no illusions about what the leaders thought of him: they had made their views clear in the leadership election. In addition to Edmonds, he worked hard on Morris (TGWU) and Jinkinson (Unison), but ignored those like the rail unions and firemen whom he knew he would never win over.[60] His principal opposition was to come from Rodney Bickerstaff, General Secretary of Unison, who became an outspoken critic of New Labour.[61] In general, union leaders were not impressed. One said, 'It sounded to us like the closed shop again. He was putting us into a position where he was saying, "You can either defeat me and divide the party, with all the damage that will cause, or you can support me and acquiesce."'[62]

Union leaders aside, Campbell's first spinning operation was a minor triumph. 'Mr Tony Blair has begun his leadership of the Labour Party by seeking a fresh statement of mission,' said the *Financial Times* in its leader the next morning. 'It is clearly his intention to follow that through with a thorough modernisation of every aspect of Labour's work.'[63] It was exactly the line that Campbell had pushed with the press, and most papers wrote in similar terms. Delegates on the floor, however, were not so convinced. Traditionalists took note that they were no longer addressed as 'comrades' but as 'friends' and 'colleagues', they heard his uncompromising rejection of repealing Thatcher's 1980s trade union legislation, and his levering down of expectations concerning the dividend that the unemployed and low-paid might reap under a Labour government.

When it came to the vote on retaining Clause IV, the conference rejected Blair's proposal by a margin of 50.9 per cent to 49.1 per cent, a victory for the left, though by no means a humiliation for the new leader.[64] Blair's team blamed the result on Robin Cook seeking revenge for not being consulted about the move earlier and using his position in the chair to call speakers who supported Clause IV.[65] Campbell laid the blame in press briefings on unions voting in accordance with mandates.[66] One senior Labour official thought that 'it was very foolish to have gone ahead with the announcement without checking whether they were going to win the vote the next day or not'.[67] But the die had already been cast. The party was told that the matter would be returned to later: the conference vote was not the end of it. Delegates left Blackpool realising that the timid voice that Blair had offered in the summer had barked, and barked loudly. Where it would all lead, no one was sure.

Blair's team clearly had much work to do. The delegate moving the resolution reaffirming the retention of Clause IV said it was 'a symbol of our commitment to the working class'.[68] Arthur Scargill, who was overheard damning Blair just after his speech, later said, 'We are fighting for the very soul of the party.'[69] Scargill defined the battle correctly. Blair had unleashed a battle royal for the soul of the party. Win it, and he thought he would finally vanquish the hard left, or at least beat them into submission for many years. Lose it, and his prediction that he might be out of a job would be realised: the victim of the left, the unions and his poor judgement, with plenty of contenders lined up to stoke the flames and inherit the crown, notably Brown and Cook.

Clause IV in the Country: October 1994–April 1995

After all the tension of the conference in early October, Blair was relieved to take his foot off the accelerator. As Campbell later admitted, 'We got a bit complacent.'[70] The future of Clause IV now lay in the hands of Blair's least favourite and least supportive party body, the NEC. Blair had earlier bounced it over the closed shop and on parts of the modernisation programme, and leading members of it felt hostile and resentful, notably those who represented trade unions.[71] Tom Sawyer, Blair's new choice of Labour General Secretary, had lost goodwill with unions over OMOV the year before, so this was when Sally Morgan offered her first major support to Blair. As Director of Campaigns and Elections for the party, she set about bringing the NEC and constituency parties round to supporting their leader on Clause IV. 'First of all I had to get them on board to support modernisation,' she said, 'so we had to win a majority of them over to start being part of the solution, rather than being in opposition.'[72] With great difficulty, and helped significantly by her advocacy, the NEC was by December willing to agree a timetable for a special Labour Party Conference to vote on Clause IV in the spring of 1995.[73] Blair's team made two particular contributions: they insisted on the special conference being held before the big union conferences, whose leaders they feared would try to turn their members against the leadership on Clause IV as they had over OMOV; they also lobbied for the NEC to urge all constituency parties to ballot their members, to reduce the risk of left-wing activists deciding the matter. The special conference vote would still be held, however, on the existing rules for party conferences where 70 per cent of the votes were held by unions and only 30 per cent by constituency parties. Hence the nervousness.

After his initial honeymoon in the summer, opposition to Blair had been growing apace. The Blairs' decision to send Euan to London Oratory, an 'opt-out' Catholic state school rather than their local 'community' comprehensive in Islington, became a public issue in December, and offended many across the party, although it did not stop Labour winning the Dudley West by-election that month with the largest swing to Labour since 1933.[74] In early 1995, attacks on his leadership came in quick succession. On 10 January a majority of the party's MEPs sponsored an advertisement in the *Guardian* defending Clause IV. On 13 January, one of the signatories, Ken Coates, said Blair had no understanding of the mentality of the Labour Party. On 15 January, Roy Hattersley said that the party did best when it avoided rows and was at peace with itself, a clear attack on Blair's judgement in opening up an 'unnecessary' battle over Clause IV. On 21 January, Bill Morris, one of the more supportive of union leaders, said he had yet to hear anything from Blair which satisfied what trade unions wanted. More worrying still was the fact that initial ballots of constituency parties revealed a lack of enthusiasm among the membership to change the clause.

Blair decided he had to move on to the front foot and take the argument to the country. He has always believed in his ability to persuade people of his point of view through meeting them face to face. The NEC had settled on the date of 29 April 1995 for the conference on Clause IV. Blair asked his two most senior women, Hunter and Morgan, joined by a third, Margaret McDonagh, to put together a nationwide campaign. Launched at a joint press conference with Prescott on 25 January, the 'New Labour, New Britain' roadshow aimed to secure backing across the country for the change to Clause IV. It consisted of two or more meetings a week nationwide over the following three months, calling at twenty-two towns and cities,[75] and was the biggest consultation exercise he launched until late 2003. It was to prove the making of his relationship with the party. The party in the country saw him at his reasonable best, in shirt sleeves and willing to listen and engage, and it soon became clear that he thrived on this kind of direct interaction. He learned more about the views and fears of party members across the whole country than he had done in his eleven and a half years as an MP. He also learned how to reshape and hone his arguments with audiences who were not altogether receptive to his message. Margaret McDonagh saw him change as the tour went on: 'At the beginning he wasn't so sure of himself, but he rapidly found his measure and came over as funny and clever, and also passionate.'[76] This was the side of him that only his Sedgefield constituents had seen before. Labour voters the length of Britain, he realised, were not so different from his beloved constituents in Sedgefield. He admitted in an interview after the debate was over that, until he became leader, he did not really know the party. The nationwide meetings made him realise the party did not want to fight the class war, but was full of 'basically rather decent and honest people'.[77]

As the roadshow wore on, Blair sensed that the balance was beginning to tilt in his favour. He announced that Brown and Cook were to help selling his message; they had been a significant omission before, and they now gave this quest a vital extra ingredient. Cook's compliance had come at a price. He let it be known that he was playing the role of 'critical friend' and that he would ensure that the redraft did not contain any overly prescriptive statement about the family, a particular fear among a section of the party.[78] Campbell thought that Cook's support, coming in an article in the *New Statesman*, was a key turning point.[79] Sceptics began to fall into line, realising that Blair would carry the day and that they could only damage themselves by continuing to oppose. Some sought concessions, notably union leaders who demanded Blair's commitment on the minimum wage.[80] But while all this haggling was in train, and before he himself became sure of the outcome, he had endured a worrying start to 1995. 'Support for Labour is highly fragile,' Gould wrote to him in March. 'It could collapse at any point . . . commitment to Labour is based on no real knowledge of the party or what it will do. No one has any idea of Labour's policies.'[81]

With support starting to go their way, the text of the new Clause IV now became a priority. Blair's office began to work on it shortly after the conference, but by January they were still not satisfied. Drafts circulated from Miliband to Gould to Irvine, who would then send it over to Brown, who would then tear it apart and redraft it with his advisers.[82] Then the text would go to the shadow Cabinet, union leaders, and back to Blair's office again for redrafting. Rarely can so much effort have been put into words that, as with the original Clause IV, were symbolic rather than a plan of action. Blair had to deliver his final text to the NEC on Monday, 13 March. Eventually, he rewrote it on board a plane coming down from Glasgow, and finalised it in his bedroom in Islington on a Sunday afternoon in early March with Campbell, Miliband and Powell. The final text was substantially Blair's own.[83] He wanted to write a statement which would endure, embracing the market economy, and one which was a meaningful symbol of values and beliefs. The final words, speaking of individuals being advanced by strong communities, where rights and responsibilities are balanced, were his, though the line 'power, wealth and opportunity in the hands of the many, not the few' came from Hyman.[84]

A huge test came north of the border on Saturday, 10 March, when the Scottish Labour Party voted on amending Clause IV. Blair's team did not take anything for granted, making sure they rallied all the support they could muster ahead of the conference in Inverness.[85] When it looked the day before that the vote would be lost because of union block votes,[86] Blair was brought under great pressure to make concessions, including inserting a commitment to full employment, which he resisted. It was touch and go. 'Almost everyone in the unions and the party believed that he would lose the Scottish vote,' said senior Scottish MP, George Robertson.[87] Blair's speech was ironically helped by a computer problem which obliged him to make an unscripted but very effective direct appeal to delegates. Some believe his abandoning his notes and his eye-to-eye contact swung the vote for him. A passionate debate ensued with powerful speeches from George Galloway, on the left, and from John Reid, who rallied behind Blair and helped tip the vote in support of the leadership. 'Winning the Scottish vote helped tip the balance,' thought

Robertson, an opinion with which most would agree.[88] The 'Yes' gave Blair's spirits a great boost, and meant he looked forward to the special conference on 29 April with a new confidence. Symbolically it was held in the same venue, Westminster Methodist Central Hall, where the original Clause IV had been adopted over seventy-five years before. The conference was portrayed as the bookend to Labour's wilderness years, which had begun with the special conference in January 1981, precipitating the breakaway of the SDP. The months of work were to pay off. Blair carried the day with a 65 per cent vote, despite the leaders of two of what he thought were sympathetic unions, the TGWU and Unison, casting their block votes against the change without consulting their members. Behind the scenes, Prescott, Morgan, Pat McFadden and others had worked tirelessly to carry the majority of unions with them. It had been close. Had the GMB not voted for the change, it would have been on a knife edge. Edmonds, its leader, said, 'the argument that swung it was that defeating him could lose us the General Election. Typically, Tony never said "thank you".'

After the result was announced, Blair spoke powerfully without notes, but with words he had thought about deeply. 'I wasn't born into this party. I chose it. I've never joined another political party. I believe in it. I'm proud to be the leader of it and it's the party I'll always live in and I'll die in.' He then said, acknowledging the feelings of those who had felt bounced by him, that he realised he could be overhasty, but then came the artful admission that if he had erred, it was because of only one reason, his anxiety to destroy their common target: 'I can't stand these people, these Tories, being in government over our country.'[89] The device of unifying the party against the Conservatives was useful, though he was not specific, then or later, about what it was about the Tories that he found so repugnant, and which policies would be so very different under him. Not that anyone asked the question at the time. The key fact was that he had won.

How had he managed to do so, and reverse the conference vote of six months earlier? The unions had provided the main opposition, with even moderates like Morris fearing that the demise of the traditional Clause IV could be the first step towards a complete divorce of party and unions.[90] The more that far-left leaders like Scargill spoke out, however, the more it suited Blair's cause. The unions' ability to be destructive has been reduced by organisational reforms introduced since 1987, but not removed. In the Parliamentary Labour Party, some on the left, like Chris Mullin, had already sided with Blair in his leadership election on what was to become a common argument, that the party stood the best chance of defeating the Tories with Blair at the helm. Critically, no leader emerged with the authority of a Nye Bevan (Gaitskell's nemesis) to challenge the leadership. Tony Benn was too old to lead a fight: 'You can't embarrass the leader.' 'Nobody wanted it, though,' he later said.[91] Diane Abbott and Dennis Skinner, leading opponents on the NEC, bowed to the inevitable and made sour remarks. Blair won where Gaitskell had lost ultimately because of 'more favourable political circumstances' coupled with 'greater tactical and strategic skills,' as one academic put it.[92]

For Blair, the victory on Clause IV was a huge personal success. To have changed a manifestly redundant policy which had thwarted Gaitskell, a respected and courageous leader, and to have seen off a challenge from the left and the unions, greatly bolstered his position and his self-confidence. 'We are not going to be pushed around,' Blair told the *Mirror* just after the vote, in a very direct message to union bosses.[93] It was not to be for another eight years, in the war against Iraq and in the battle with the party over his education and health reforms, that he took a similarly audacious stance. Victory at the special conference in April was as important to him as his victory in the leadership in July 1994. The first gave him a title, the second the confidence to take the party forward in his own direction. Had he lost the vote, he would have resigned as leader, and returned, in all probability, to the Bar. He chose to fight the party to see if it would be led: it would and he was now its master – he would find the annual conference, and to a lesser extent the NEC, easy to dominate. The PLP for the time being were quiescent. His relationship with trade union leaders and the left remained a source of mutual (and growing) suspicion and tension, but the Clause IV episode had clearly stamped his authority on them for the time being. 'The legacy was a renewed feeling Tony and his people would never be straightforward,' said one disgruntled union leader. He had also carried out the most daring and significant move with virtually no advice from Gordon Brown. He had, on this issue at least, learned to live without his old friend. The intriguing historical questions are what did he do with his new-found power and independence; and had the battle over Clause IV in any way made him averse to taking similar risks, at least on domestic policy, in the future?

Eric Anderson with Blair in Number 10, October 1997. The former teacher
stands over his famous pupil, and both men smile uneasily at the camera.
Anderson once described Blair as the most difficult pupil he had ever taught.

18

Eric Anderson

With his hold over the Labour Party base camp now secured, Tony Blair
sought out new converts to ease his journey to the summit. With a
discredited Tory party offering barely any challenge, he set out to bring all
who held influence in British public life within New Labour's 'big tent' –
businessmen, the Tory press, leaders of the arts world, royalty, the Liberal
Democrats, leading academics and thinkers. Hardly anyone was left out.
Mention began to be heard at this time of a new name, Eric Anderson,
who had appeared in a feature article in the *Daily Telegraph* titled 'Tony
Blair . . . who's really in his kitchen cabinet?'[1] The Establishment boasted
fewer more illustrious, unimpeachable figures than Eric Anderson, teacher
and mentor to Prince Charles and later celebrated Headmaster of Eton
College. In Blair's quest as Leader of the Opposition to show solid
credentials to reassure middle England that they were safe to give him their
trust, Blair discovered that he had been influenced in his early life by no
more reassuring and respected a mentor figure than Anderson.

Anderson: The Mentor Reality

Eric Anderson was born in May 1936, a fifth-generation member of an
Edinburgh family firm of kiltmakers – 'Kinlock' Anderson. He attended
George Watson's College in Edinburgh, leaving one term before Ian
McIntosh, who later went on to head Fettes in 1958, became Headmaster.[2]
Anderson remained in Scotland to attend St Andrew's University, where
he met his wife, Poppy, both taking firsts in English. Anderson's initial
teaching post was at Fettes in 1960. McIntosh's plans for Anderson to take

over as Head of English and director of school plays were blocked by the
continuation in both posts of Blair's schooldays nemesis, Bob Roberts.
Anderson, intensely driven to get on, sought promotion elsewhere and
went to Gordonstoun in 1964, the year in which he published his first
book, *The Written Word*. It was during his two years at the remote and
spartan Scottish school that he met Prince Charles. Charged with reviving
school drama, Anderson selected *Henry V*, where he cast Charles as the
Duke of Westmorland, which he performed so well that Anderson cast
him as Macbeth the following year.[3]

McIntosh was desperate to have his protégé back at Fettes, the more so
because he wanted a top Housemaster for his prize new house, Arniston.
Charles was leaving Gordonstoun, and with him, the attraction of
remaining in the remote school five hours' drive from Edinburgh. Flush
with his reputation as the future king's mentor, Anderson returned to
Fettes to begin planning and recruiting for Arniston. McIntosh's pleasure
at his return was not echoed by all in his Common Room, some of whom
thought Anderson was playing the system and should not have come back
so soon.[4] Anderson's tangible success at setting up and overseeing the new
house was helped greatly by Poppy, who compensated for a certain
gaucheness of his by her very considerable warmth and hospitality. But the
success aroused new suspicions among the old guard, who viewed him as
dangerously liberal. Few institutions in Britain are more inward-looking
and judgemental than the traditional boarding schools. But secure in the
patronage of McIntosh, Anderson could press on untroubled with his
humanising agenda, including abandoning personal fagging (where younger
pupils waited on senior boys) and the cane.[5]

Blair's inclusion for Arniston, which opened in September 1967,
transformed his outlook at Fettes after the fairly bruising end to his first
year. For a time, Blair and Anderson related well together, as during
Anderson's direction of *Julius Caesar* in the first year of the new house. But
as Blair became increasingly truculent the following year, during which he
took his 'O' levels, the relationship came under strain. Anderson tried hard
to channel Blair's energies into positive outlets, such as debating or
producing 'new-wave' plays with the acting group 'The Pseuds'. Blair also
benefited greatly from Anderson's English teaching: 'Eric's English lessons
were more like university tutorials than a conventional school lesson, and
Tony liked being in them because he could argue and debate rather than
be told what the answers were,' said Alastair Singleton.[6] Nick Ryden
concurred: Blair liked the lessons because 'Anderson was far more liberal
and laid-back than most teachers at the time'.[7]

But in the house, matters grew worse, and in their last year together, when Blair was in the Lower Sixth, Anderson found him very difficult.[8] Anderson told Roy Jenkins that whenever anything went wrong in the house, 'I expect it is A. C. L. Blair who is behind it again.' He once told a friend, 'He was one of the most challenging boys I ever encountered.' Anderson now looks back with affection to their days together at Fettes, but there is no doubting that the relationship was difficult at times on both sides. He thought that Blair took advantage of the liberal regime and the trust he showed in him. Behind his back, Blair would mock and be contemptuous of Anderson, and mimic him in front of his peers.[10] It is an open question as to whether Anderson would have been more successful than Roberts in handling Blair in his final, Upper Sixth year. It is at best doubtful whether he would, and it was Anderson, not Roberts, who decided in the summer term of 1970 not to appoint Blair as one of the first batch of house prefects for the coming year. There was no love lost then between Anderson and Blair when the former parted to head Abingdon School at the end of the summer term in 1970. The relationship had soured, and Anderson's attempts to civilise Blair, and to encourage Blair to meet him, and the school, half-way, had failed.

It is hard to see that Anderson had much impact on Blair beyond encouraging him in acting, and in developing a love of English, neither of which were to become interests that endured, at Oxford or beyond. Almost all the former pupils and teachers from Fettes interviewed said Anderson had a 'big' or 'major' influence on Blair, but when asked to be specific they were less sure what precisely that impact was. Anderson readily admits in all his newspaper interviews that Blair had no interest in politics at Fettes, so he made no impact there, nor on encouraging him to study law, nor to go to Oxford, where Blair followed the path already laid out by his brother Bill. Nor did he reconcile Blair to even the 'enlightened despotism' of his own rule, nor to the school. Nor, though Anderson is a firm Christian, did he open Blair's eyes to religion. Compared to the enduring influence many boarding housemasters have had, who see much more of their charges in those adolescent years than parents, Anderson's impact on Blair, intellectually, emotionally, socially and spiritually, was modest. When they parted in July 1970, bar the occasional meeting or card, they had neither regular nor significant contact for twenty-five years.

Anderson: The Mentor Myth

In July 1994, the month that Blair became leader, Anderson stood down as Headmaster of Eton College after fourteen years, to become Rector of

Lincoln College, Oxford. The relationship now became important to both of them. Following an invitation from Anderson to speak to the Politics Society at Eton in early 1994, Blair reopened the dialogue and sought out Anderson's advice on a number of matters including managing his relationship with the royal family and Prince Charles in particular.[11] Neither Blair nor Anderson protested when the media perhaps made more of the relationship of close confidant than the facts would justify. Blair, who had mostly negative feelings about his Fettes years (as Charles had about Gordonstoun) did not want that knowledge nor his chequered time at school to become the received wisdom. To have attended Scotland's 'Eton' as a preparation for Oxford, and to have been the protégé of Eric Anderson was just what he wanted.

So when Rosie Boycott asked him in the *Independent* if he had a 'special teacher', Blair replied, 'Eric Anderson, who was my housemaster and my English teacher, had a very big impact on me. He gave me a love of literature.'[12] When Blair chose *Ivanhoe* as his book on Radio 4's *Desert Island Discs*, it was Anderson, the press assumed, who had been responsible for instilling the love – not unreasonably, because Anderson is a Walter Scott scholar.[13] But Anderson denied any influence, saying of Fettes, 'I don't recall seeing *Ivanhoe* on the syllabus.'[14]

In the run-up to the General Election in 1997, Anderson sent Blair a postcard on which he drew a sketch of a ladder, alluding to the time at Arniston when Blair was caught late at night by a policeman shinning his way up a ladder to get back into the house. 'On that occasion you only got half-way,' Anderson wrote deftly. 'This time I hope you will get to the top.'[15]

In October 1997, Blair was one of eighteen 'celebrities', including John Cleese, Ben Elton and David Seaman, asked by the Teacher Training Agency to nominate their 'favourite teacher' for a series of advertisements the agency was running to recruit young people into the profession.[16] Blair nominated Anderson and they were 'reunited' in a meeting at Number 10 to boost the campaign. To his credit, Anderson said that being singled out in this way had been slightly embarrassing and 'beyond belief in some ways'.[17] The idea that Anderson had been a seminal figure in Blair's life was given added currency when the *Scotsman* described Anderson as 'the most influential person in his life'.[18] The media frenzy crescendoed when, in April 1998, Blair appointed Anderson chairman of the National Heritage Memorial Fund to succeed Lord Rothschild (less noticed was that John Major had appointed Anderson a trustee in 1996).[19] It was the appreciation of the royal family, however, rather than Blair, who lay behind the conferring of Knight of the Thistle, Scotland's highest honour, on Anderson on St Andrew's Day, 2002.

Blair's relationship with Anderson was blown out of all proportion by the media, with Blair's encouragement and somewhat to Anderson's embarrassment. Anderson was not the mentor figure he was made out to be. Blair was simply not in the frame of mind at Fettes to let himself be seriously influenced by someone, however enlightened and stimulating, whom he thought part of the Establishment. But something of Anderson's *style* did rub off on him. When Blair began to build his career after Oxford, he scouted around for examplar figures, and Anderson came back vividly to mind, personable, smartly dressed, a writer of 'thank you' letters and notes. It was a role model that Blair, consciously or not, absorbed, to significant effect when he wrote the letter to thank Michael Foot and Roy Hattersley for canvassing for him at Beaconsfield. Hattersley commented that 'it was one of the very rare occasions in our long careers in politics when either of us had been thanked by letter'.[20]

When Blair became party leader he again cast around for role models, and looked at Anderson once more. His reopening of the dialogue was partly the action of a 'rebel come good' wanting to renew acquaintance and seek approval from the schoolteacher whom he felt he had slighted. To Anderson, too, it was a surprise that, of the many hundreds of boys who had grown up under him as a Housemaster or Headmaster in four schools, it was Tony Blair who had become the leader of his party. Blair had not even made it to house prefect, the merest first rung of responsibility. Indeed, Blair and Campbell had a trace about them of naughty sixth-formers who had stolen in uninvited and taken over the prefects' study. There was also an element of Blair wanting to wrap himself in the clothes of a doyen of the British Establishment, and show how inclusive was Labour's 'big tent'. But there was also something about Anderson's manner – personable, concerned to reach out to individuals, lacking in cynicism – to which he was attracted and on which he modelled himself. During the Gulf War in 2003, Sir Michael Boyce, Chief of the Defence Staff, and Britain's most senior military figure, was struck by Blair's 'exceptional manners, his politeness, his willingness to listen. He was very charming but also very informal.'[21] He could have been describing Anderson. Blair's courteous manner won him countless friends during his premiership, not least abroad. Anderson's importance to Blair was principally his tone and persona, in public and private. Given that there was no other teacher at Fettes, and certainly none at Oxford, who had a lasting influence on him, Anderson's influence becomes all the more significant.

Blair with Cherie and their three eldest children, waving to the cameras on the morning after the May 1997 General Election. Blair and Cherie had achieved the prize for which they had both yearned for five and more years. Neither of them had any idea how going through that door would change all their lives for ever.

19

General Election, 1995–97

Tony Blair is 'like a man with a very large, utterly priceless crystal bowl', Roy Jenkins memorably said in 1996, 'condemned to walk miles and miles down slippery passageways . . . His role in history was to get to the other end without dropping the bowl.'[1] Blair's insistence that everything in 1995–97 had to take second place to winning the General Election, and his almost neurotic anxiety about whether Labour would achieve victory, conditioned everything that happened in these years. Opinion polls were watched over with an ever increasing anxiety. The obsession was partly a tool to ensure the party kept in step, but it was also born out of the very real traumas of four successive defeats, and the fear that, as happened in 1992, the party could destroy its own chances at the eleventh hour. A fifth defeat, he believed, would sound the death-knell for the party. The Conservatives, under Stanley Baldwin, went into the 1929 General Election on a 'safety first' policy. For Blair, it was safety first, second and third. As the election approached, Blair's team devised the mantra: reassure (the party really had changed), remind (about the Tories) and reward (with what Labour could offer).[2] Every word and deed would have to count with an electorate which, in the past, had deserted Labour in their millions. The defining moment in this chapter is less the election victory itself than the two years before it, when decisions taken on the need for caution and not jeopardising success were to affect the whole tenor of Blair's premiership.

Many of the foundations needed to make Labour electable had been laid by the time Blair became leader. Abandoning unilateralism, opposition to the European Community and to the market economy, and jettisoning Militant, the closed shop and the block vote (in part) had all taken place. Clause IV had provided 'the shock to the system' to demonstrate how far Labour had changed and announced Blair had arrived. But what Philip Gould's research showed Blair very clearly was that, for all these massive changes over the last ten years, the party was still not properly trusted. Blair's chief concern in the run-up to the General Election was to reassure the media and the electorate that on all the key issues – tax, trade unions and patriotism – New Labour *could* be trusted, and to ensure that rogue voices did not resurface to remind the electorate about what old Labour had been like. Blair focused attention in 1995–97 on three main areas: producing a policy platform, entrenching his personal domination of the party, and bringing within New Labour's orbit as much of the media and of intellectual and popular opinion as he could.

Taming Policy

Tony Blair was fortunate in having time to plan policy for power. His predecessor, John Major, found himself elevated suddenly to the premiership in late November 1990 with no such opportunity to prepare for office: he sat down in the Cabinet Room on one of his first evenings in power and wrote down a list of what he might hope to achieve.[3] The last Labour Prime Minister, James Callaghan, similarly had no clear time to think ahead before he took up the job in April 1976. Unsurprisingly, both premierships are seen as reactive and lacking in coherence.[4]

Blair went into the 1995–97 period with three of his five core principles already clearly established (community, direct democracy and social responsibility), and he developed the last two (wealth creation and modernisation) in these years. He had jettisoned Clause IV and produced some fine words to take its place, but he had yet to work out what it meant in terms of practical policy. Blair's aspiration did not come from Labour thinkers, factions or the party's history. But these five principles gave him nevertheless a very solid platform from which to build. He had identified very clearly what he was against – the hard left, militant unionism, party caucuses, socialist economics and liberal morality. He was also, largely for tribal rather than deep doctrinal reasons, against the Tories (although he admired Thatcher), and against the Liberal Democrats (although he wanted to do a deal with them). He now had the golden opportunity to deliver his own unique policy agenda.

No Labour leader since Wilson in 1963 had been afforded such an opportunity. What Blair never did in 1995–97, however, despite periodic efforts, was to sit down and devise policies 'bottom up' out of his five principles. Rather he adopted a 'top down' approach, making all policy subservient to the 'three Rs' (reassure, remind, reward). It was a decision he was later to regret, because, as he was to realise, formulating policies is much easier while in opposition than in government. These years saw, after an initial period of interest, a turning away of Blair's mind from the intellectuals and currents of thought which had so fascinated him in the early and mid-1990s, when he came under a wider range of influences. Blair said that arguments had to be won from government and could not be won from opposition, and promised, 'I'm going to be a lot more radical in government than many people think.'[5] There can be no doubting that he meant what he said.

Blair's failure to develop more fully his own distinctive platform in the period 1995–97 can also be explained in part because he did not want to intrude too far into what Brown saw as his own domain, domestic policy. After all the traumas of the leadership election, he did not want to risk further upsets by tackling Brown head-on. A senior Blair aide confirmed that, 'Above all, Tony's priority in these years was to ensure that he and Gordon remained close.'[6] But there was more to Blair's deference to Brown on policy than simply wanting to avoid confrontation. Blair respected and, to a large degree, relied upon Brown's expertise in policy development between 1995 and 1997, as he had done before 1994.[7] The first policy initiatives New Labour enacted – Bank of England independence, the New Deal and the Working Family Tax Credit – were thus the product of Brown's endeavours in opposition, not Blair's. Apart from education, and crime, on which Straw had put in much work, the other main 'non-Brown' area where policy was successfully hammered out in order to be executed fairly speedily after the election was constitutional reform. Tellingly, it received no great enthusiasm from Blair, although without his positive backing, the agenda, including devolution, would never have transpired.

Brown was aided by a formidable team in his policy preparation, and Ed Balls' policy input was now strengthened by advice from Geoff Mulgan, the director of the think-tank Demos, and described as 'the brain of Britain' in an article in the *Independent on Sunday*.[8] Blair's office by contrast was smaller, and had to focus much more widely.[9] Jonathan Powell assembled a small group to advise Blair on the emerging policy platform,[10] including Mandelson, Hewitt and David Miliband, the last having been appointed as Blair's head of policy in the summer of 1994. Miliband was described by one aide as 'personifying Tony's kind of values, a sparkling intellect yet also very gregarious and touchy-feely'.[11]

What he did not achieve, however, was to impose on Blair the discipline to work out detailed and precise policies across the board. The defence case is that, underlying the manifesto preparation was the fear that if they produced a 'laundry list of commitments', the party would fall into the same trap they fell into in 1992, when the Conservatives took apart their programme by costing every single commitment.[12] That is true in part, but it does not account for why Brown's team managed to come up with a detailed list of policy ripe for enacting once in power.

Critically, Blair never found a big hitter to fill the economics adviser post in his office. He would have liked Gavyn Davies to have taken the job. A veteran of the Policy Unit under Labour before 1979, Davies would have brought badly needed expertise into the heart of the government. His wife, Sue Nye, worked in Brown's office and would have helped defuse tension. But Davies was locked into a lucrative job at Goldman Sachs, and ruled himself out, although he made himself freely available to Blair whenever he could, and drafted several of Blair's economic speeches.[13] Davies would have compensated for Blair's lack of understanding of economics: Blair did not make the impact with economic speeches one might have expected of him as Leader of the Opposition, which was indicative not only of his lack of expertise and ideas in the area, but, critically, also of Brown's predominance and his understanding that this was not Blair's domain.[14] Blair did not ask for help from Andrew Graham, who had advised three of the previous four Labour leaders, nor did he seek counsel from a host of other economists who would have made themselves available.[15] He did call on the part-time support of Derek Scott, deliberately chosen from the City rather than academia, in part to give out a clear message. Scott was a gifted economist (and former SDP candidate in 1983) but not someone who was ever going to keep Brown and Balls awake at night.[16] The result was that Brown was allowed to make all the running on economics, and on thinking about the single currency. The potential for conflict was shown in May 1995 when Blair delivered the Mais Lecture, written by Scott, which gave a tough message on control of inflation. Brown's office disliked its old-style monetarist tone, and its straying onto their own territory. Blair shied away from such controversial statements in future. There is no doubt that Blair allowed himself to be underpowered on economic advice. A Prime Minister is critically weakened if he surrenders total sovereignty of such a portmanteau area as economics to his Chancellor, however brilliant – indeed, especially if as brilliant as Brown.

One of the qualities Blair most liked in Miliband was his drawing in of thinkers whom he felt Blair might like to meet, including Will Hutton, author of the bestseller *The State We're In*, published in January 1995, and John Kay, author of *Foundations of Corporate Success* (1993) and *Why Firms Succeed* (1995).[17] Blair became enamoured by Hutton's writing, who had become a cult figure in Britain after the publication of his stake-holding book. He and Blair talked regularly about how increased public investment and a less short-termist financial and business culture could transform wealth creation – complete with a new role for trade unions.[18] For a time, above all when Blair gave his 'stake-holder' speech offering his vision of a revitalised British economy in Singapore in January 1996, it looked as if Hutton had become Blair's economics guru. Blair spoke of the need for another buzz-word, 'trust', in firms and within society, and advocated an economy in which opportunity is available to all, 'advancement is through merit, and from which no group or social class is set apart or excluded'.[19] Was stake-holding to be the big idea, it was asked, to replace Clause IV socialism? But Hutton was unceremoniously dumped and then found himself briefed against. He believed that Mandelson disliked the degree of influence he was having on Blair, and the risks it ran of him being seen to be unduly influenced by a journalist on the left (Hutton was to become editor of the *Observer* in 1996). It was also claimed that Brown thought Hutton's approach to be too inflexible and anti-private sector.[20] Hutton formed the view that 'they would jettison anything that Conservative critics would say was favourable to trade unions, anti-business or likely to increase taxes even if it was not. Rightly, they wanted to put winning the General Election first; wrongly, they made no calibration of what was negotiable and non-negotiable in policy.'[21]

Blair's Singapore speech in fact reflected John Kay's ideas far more than Hutton's.[22] Blair was attracted by Kay's ideas about a compromise between *laissez faire* and a highly regulated environment for business. 'When I read the Singapore speech,' Kay said, 'I thought I had written it because he was echoing my ideas and my very words.'[23] Kay was also to find himself summarily dropped. Brown thought that talk of 'stake-holding, with unions being given a new voice, was too aggressive for the City'.[24] Perhaps Brown did not want Blair to be setting the agenda on any economic subject – especially with an idea he had not himself mediated into the bloodstream of their thinking. Derek Scott poured cold water on the whole stake-holder idea also. In any event, stake-holding was not to be Blair's big economic idea. Blair never developed a big economic idea.

Blair's major contribution to the economic sphere was 'reassurance'.

He was utterly determined to convince the electorate that Labour could be trusted on the economy. One of his key statements on this theme was at the National Film Theatre in London in September 1994, when he set out in a speech, written for him by Brown and by Miliband, to ditch Labour's 'tax, spend and borrow' image.[25] Blair went on the rampage to bury preconceptions about Labour's policies, and challenge entrenched beliefs that it was the Conservatives who were the party best placed to run an enterprise-based, low-inflation, low-tax economy.[26] In his Mais Lecture on the economy in May 1995, he gave a resounding endorsement to the 'crusade' against inflation, for which Labour governments in the past had been justly criticised.[27] Blair and Brown believed that one of the great post-war Labour thinkers and politicians, Tony Crosland, had over-emphasised the debate about how to redistribute wealth: they wanted the emphasis to be much more on how to create wealth in the first place. The task of reassurance was made easier because, after the devastating 'tax bombshell' attack by the Tories before the 1992 election, even the left of the party saw the argument for extreme caution on tax, and all the more so after the Conservatives lost the nation's trust in the 1993 budget, which raised taxes in the wake of 'Black Wednesday'. To be absolutely certain that the Tories and the press would not damage them on economic policy, Blair and Brown agreed on the seminal commitments not to increase income tax rates (Brown had to be persuaded by Blair, following months of discussion, that he should not increase taxes for the top income earners) and to retain Conservative spending plans for the first two years in power.[28] Brown trailed the announcement on the *Today* programme on 20 January 1997, before making a speech on the party's new tax policy at the QEII Conference Centre in Westminster. The calamitous 1992 Shadow Budget, with its tax increase proposals to pay, in particular, for commitments on child benefit and pensions, had etched itself deep on to Brown and Blair's consciousness, as seen in these decisions: the ghost of Smith lived on.

Blair's principal policy interest in Opposition was education. It was also the main area in government associated directly with him where considerable progress was made in the first term, 1997–2001. Blair's interest stemmed from different roots. He saw education paving the way to a more inclusive society, a theme echoed strongly by the Social Justice Commission's 1994 report, written by Hewitt and Miliband, and described by one insider as 'the single most important influence on policy between 1994 and 1997'.[29] The subject was informed, naturally enough, by his experience as a thoughtful parent reflecting on the state primary education his three children were receiving. He was indeed the first Prime Minister with children of primary school age in more than a century. He saw education as the main unreconstructed 'Old Labour' area of domestic policy, where Labour's thinking was still very much 'producer' driven (i.e., by the unions, specifically by the National Union of Teachers), rather than 'consumer' driven (i.e., by parents).[30] As we have seen, Blair saw Ann Taylor, the shadow Education Secretary, as the embodiment of this old thinking. Educational policy, apart from skills and employment policy, was not an area Brown was much interested in, so Blair had a free run. Blair chose Blunkett as Taylor's successor in October 1994. Blunkett was not New Labour, but he was moving in that direction, and Blair knew he had the right instincts and would give a strong lead on standards. He admired Blunkett for a number of reasons, not least because Blunkett had pushed himself through the education system against considerable odds, especially his blindness, and had a traditional approach to pedagogy.[31] One of Blunkett's first actions was to pledge Labour to continue with league tables, which were spurned by trade unions, and which gave a powerful signal of his future intent to be his own man.

In December 1994 the Blairs were embroiled in the media and political storm over sending Euan to London Oratory School, but, as one aide said, 'I'm quite certain that he was happy with the message that it sent out, that parents should choose what they consider to be the best school for their children.'[32] Others, like Alastair Campbell, were not at all happy with this message.[33] In January 1995, Miliband convened a small education seminar for Blair in the leader's office in the Commons, attended by Blunkett, Conor Ryan (his education adviser) and Michael Barber, who gave a paper in which he said the critical theme for the party should be that 'standards matter more than structures'. This approach was duly adopted because it shifted the argument away from the mire of the abolition (or not) of grammar schools and on to focusing instead on the standards schools were achieving, regardless of their structure, thus letting them off the hook of what could have been a hugely difficult debate for Blair. Blair was impressed by the seminar and told attendees, 'I want to be a Prime Minister who has education as the centre of his agenda.' 'But that is exactly the aspiration of John Major, George Bush and Bill Clinton,' Barber replied.[34] He went on to suggest what Blair must do to turn his aspirations into reality, which included ensuring that the Education Department was given a high status in his future government, not moving secretaries of state after a short time in the post, and signalling his own personal commitment by giving several speeches each year on education.[35] Blair followed the advice, and Blunkett was the only shadow Cabinet member (apart from Brown) to be publicly promised their job after the election.

Blair duly gave education the highest personal priority in speeches, most memorably in his 'education, education, education' phrase (penned by Jonathan Powell) describing his priorities in his party conference speech in 1995. At Southwark Cathedral in January 1996 he had to speak in the wake of the major row over Harriet Harman's decision to send her son to St Olave's Grammar School, a highly popular selective school, which he described as giving him 'the worst week of his life'.[36] Blair's theme was raising education standards and placing a new emphasis on responsibilities at the heart of his programme for restoring social cohesion.[37] His education speeches were drafted by Miliband or Barber, but he was content to leave the detail of education policy to Blunkett, whom he backed to the hilt. Blunkett worked closely with Barber and Ryan to produce the literacy and numeracy strategies and a range of other policies which were duly enacted after 1997. One can only wonder how different Blair's record might have been in his first term as Prime Minister if he had given similar attention to other areas while still in Opposition.

Improving the National Health Service was high on New Labour's campaign agenda, but largely neglected by Blair in terms of policy preparation. He had thought about decentralising and 'loosening up' the NHS as a way of releasing new energy, while still retaining a nationalised system, but detailed thinking was mostly absent. The gap was not helped after the election by the fact that the Health Secretary, Frank Dobson, was not expecting to be given the job. Brown's decision to adopt Conservative spending plans for the first two years of the new Parliament would inevitably delay a large increase in investment, but some planning went into promoting a set of national standards, which led to the establishment of the National Institute of Clinical Excellence (NICE) and National Service Frameworks. Transport was an even more neglected area, while pension policy was left in a muddle. On crime, Blair had powerfully set the tone during his two years as shadow Home Affairs Spokesman (1992–94), and his successor, Straw, in typically business-like fashion, fleshed out policies in tune with the social moralism agenda. But Blair did not give the area the personal impetus he had earlier, or as he did once in power, when he discovered being tough on this 'working-class' issue was also electorally popular.

Foreign and defence policy was an area on which Blair had gained no experience nor showed any marked interest before becoming leader; yet it was to be an area where, paradoxically, he was to make his profoundest impact as Prime Minister. Jonathan Powell was very aware of his lack of knowledge, and in discussion with David Gillmore, a former permanent under-secretary at the Foreign Office, they arranged some six 'seminars' for Blair in 1996 and early 1997.[38] Gillmore, Robin Renwick, recently retired Ambassador to the US, and David Hannay, former Ambassador to the UN, attended all of them, with senior retired diplomats, Nicholas Henderson and Michael Butler occasional attendees. Held mostly on Friday mornings at Blair's Islington home, the sessions covered Russia, the US, the Balkans, Europe and the Euro. The attendees were impressed by Blair's open mind and by the quality of his questioning. Some positions were already beginning to crystallise. On the Balkans Blair had wanted to know why Britain's involvement had not been more effective in the past, why the United States were regarded as so critical to the region, and whether it was possible and sensible for Britain to play a bigger role there. On the United States he was on stronger ground, and indeed had already met President Clinton at the White House in April 1996. He was clear he did not see the choice as between being Atlanticist or European, and was already groping towards the idea that Britain's role under him should be to act as a 'bridge' between the US and Europe.[39]

His acute nervousness about jeopardising the election result by appearing enthusiastic about the EU dictated a few chosen press stunts for the benefit of the tabloid press. It also meant that no one in Whitehall was clear of what the incoming government's policy would be on the Euro, with the Treasury thinking up to the last forty-eight hours before the election that they should be in a position to prepare for early entry.[40] Officials in Whitehall were surprised to discover after the election that Blair's detailed thinking, still less planning, on the Euro and the EU, had not been put in place. Blair fell back on inviting Hannay and Renwick to join him in Number 10 for his last *ex cathedra* seminar, before he left for the EU's Inter-Governmental Conference in Amsterdam in June 1997.[41]

When Blair appointed Miliband in the summer of 1994, his express brief to his new policy chief was that he wanted to go into government with a set of very clear policies in specific areas, and it was Miliband's job to give him those policies.[42] We have seen that, despite Miliband's best efforts, this did not happen. Miliband was co-author of the wide-ranging *Social Justice Commission* but found problems in enacting much of its agenda. The lack of coherence in the party's emerging policy platform was much commented upon at the time. David Marquand said 'there is a curiously makeshift air about it. No coherent vision informs it,' while Hugo Young's view was that despite 'being honed over many months and years it is interesting . . . how little [Labour's programme] changed in all that time.'[43] Martin Jacques, who was having increasing worries about the man he had so enthusiastically cheered on in the early and mid-1990s, was not the only one now asking, 'Who is Blair? What does he really believe in? What is the Blair Project?'[44] As if in acknowledgement of this line of thought, Blair convened a meeting in February 1996 for some eighty academics and thinkers 'to help him come up with ideas for a new political vision'.[45] Then, in response to these criticisms, and as an attempt to bring together all his thoughts and statements over the previous months, Blair wrote *New Britain: My Vision of a Young Country*, published in September 1996. Despite efforts to produce an imaginative and cogent personal manifesto, the book was disappointingly bland.[46] Blair fell back on the line that lack of detail across the policy spectrum was a positive asset, partly because he wanted 'to avoid giving any hostages to fortune once we were in government'.[47] This was a judgement that he would come to regret after his first year in office.

Taming the Party

Blair 'believes quite simply that the only way to power lies through him: the party has to realise they are either with him or against him and those who fail to fall in with his modernising "project" need their heads examined,' concluded the *Observer* in a pre-conference interview with him in September 1995.[48] Blair's dislike of unrepresentative party activists, the block vote and other manifestations that obstructed his 'one member, one vote' vision of party democracy dated back twenty years. 'Democracy' in the Labour Party had long been regarded by many as a sham: Robert McKenzie in his classic book *British Political Parties* (1955) described Labour as a 'living lie' because of the gap between its supposedly democratic constitution and the reality of the undemocratic way it took decisions.[49]

Gaitskell had, forty years before, identified that activists were taking the party away from the middle ground to an unrepresentative left enclave, and were also, through accusations of 'betrayal', creating a climate of unrealistic expectations of what Labour could achieve once in power (Blair was to reprise the 'betrayal' thesis when under fire in 2003). Harold Wilson suffered badly at the hands of the left, especially in his latter years, while under Foot's leadership, activists increased their say over party policy, the selection of candidates and the election of the leader.[50] Kinnock and Smith both attempted to wrest back some control from activists, but much was left to Blair, who increased the membership and extended one member, one vote, established the National Policy Forum (chaired by Robin Cook) which effectively undermined the role of the annual party conference in policy-making and reduced the power of the NEC.[51] Many of these changes had been developed by party officials, like Sawyer and McDonagh, and were inspired by experience abroad, such as the Swedish social democratic model.[52] They were of the greatest importance: had Gaitskell, Wilson or Callaghan faced an NEC and annual party conference as biddable as Blair had after these reforms, they would have had a very different experience of leadership. Blair repeatedly used the dichotomy of Old and New Labour in performing this feat. Old Labour was everything that was bad: the destructive influence of the trade unions, the dominance of the block vote at party conferences, the scourge of the hard left and Militant and the pettiness of the radical party activist. These were facets of the 'bad' Labour Party, when the leadership had been unable to do its job effectively. In contrast, New Labour was streamlined, modern in outlook and method, participatory, and loyal. Blair was never to be the complete master of the NEC, still less the PLP, that he might have wished to be. The fact that his concept of Old Labour was also fundamentally ahistorical did not seem to matter: the dichotomy was an idea that worked. 'New Labour' had first been unveiled as a name at the 1994 party conference and the phrase was entrenched in 1996 with the Conservatives' advertising campaign 'New Labour, New Danger'. The 'danger' was more obvious to the Conservatives than to the electorate.[53]

Arch symbol of the bad old past were the headquarters in Walworth Road (though the party had in fact only moved there in 1983 from the real 'old' Labour symbol, Transport House). 'Tony really didn't like Walworth Road at all. He thought the building was "crap" and everything about it was "crap". So did Gordon. It was associated with failure and defeat. It was small, cramped and stuffy,' said Tom Sawyer, the new party General Secretary.[54] 'Tony said, "We needed to create the most modern campaigning party the world had ever seen," which represented an entire break with the past and all it stood for,' stressed Jon Cruddas.[55] The search for a new head office led Labour to Millbank Tower, into which the party moved in January 1996. Occupying one floor, they now had a base in a modern building only five minutes along the river from Parliament. Millbank boasted the famed 'Excalibur' computer, which had been developed by John Carr for instant rebuttal, and was partly inspired by a trip to the US to meet senior Clinton officials in 1994. It soon became a highly effective weapon in Labour's armoury, notably aiding the party's response to the Scott Report in 1996.[56] Criticised for its 'control freakery' and dark electoral arts, Millbank was also a widely admired and much copied headquarters by political parties abroad. Ironically, Millbank was erected in the 1960s on the site of the homes of Sidney Webb, author of the original Clause IV, and the Old Labour elder statesman, Tony Benn.[57]

What was given with one hand – greater say for the ordinary party member – was thus taken away by the other. Discipline was the key to New Labour. An appeal to the bad times in the past, the 'winter of discontent' or Militant in Liverpool, was the ready reason given for power being focused on the leader's office. 'If people seriously think by going back to where we were ten or twelve years ago we are going to win power,' said Blair in 1995, 'then they require not leadership but therapy.'[58] The comment was seen as partly a rebuke to Hattersley, who finally broke with New Labour after he ceased to be an MP in 1997, though he sat on the Labour benches in the Lords. He was a rarity. Most stayed in 'the project'. The party in general accepted the disciplined regime like pupils who suddenly arrive at a new school and dare not challenge a system they do not truly comprehend. 'The discipline that was imposed on the party by the leadership in the period 1994–97 was formidable,' said Helen Liddell. 'Shadow Ministers and backbench MPs equally had to be consistently "on message".'[59] The desire for power, the fear of a return to the anarchy of 'Old Labour' and a belief that this would really be the party's last chance to win was enough to keep the PLP and activists in line.[60]

The most manifest jibbing in 1994–97 came not from the troops, but from within the Officers' Mess, from Brown, Cook and Prescott, who were constantly jockeying for power and interpreting every signal from the leader's office in terms of the position they would have after the General Election.[61] These three, together with Blair, made up the 'Big Four', who officially met each week before the shadow Cabinet, though the meeting did not always take place.[62] Cook was unhappy about being moved from shadow Trade and Industry to shadow Foreign Secretary, and used his chairmanship of the new Policy Forum to challenge his old foe Brown. Prescott was emerging as the staunchest supporter of the three for Blair's new regime, and he had no time for Brown's or Cook's empire-building. Brown was very jealous of Prescott's title, but was assuaged in part by Blair's promise that Brown would chair the Economic

Policy Committee of Cabinet, a function usually reserved for the Prime Minister, but which Brown saw as his right under the 'deal'. Blair was not too distressed by the creative tension.[63] It was useful to him in the same way Blair's and Brown's jockeying had suited Smith.

An early fruit of Blair's zero tolerance of disloyalty was his second party conference as leader, in October 1995 in Brighton, when for the first time since the 1960s the leadership was not once defeated. In January 1996, the NEC established the 'Party into Power' project, which published a year later *Labour into Power: A Framework for Partnership*, setting out the changes the party would have to make to ensure a 'united and co-operative approach in the future'. The measures were needed, it was claimed, because the last time Labour had achieved a proper working majority, under Wilson in 1966, he was unable to capitalise fully because the party was not sufficiently attuned to the need for discipline and loyalty to the leader.[64]

Sweeping away old faces from the party was as important to Blair as changing habits, structures and buildings. Out with Larry Whitty went the top echelon of party officials – comparisons were made, rather absurdly, to Stalin's purges – and in came the Blairites, notably Margaret McDonagh, Head of Campaigns (and Sawyer's successor as General Secretary) and Matthew Taylor, who became Director of Policy for the party. 'Blair was obsessed by getting in the right people. It really preoccupied him,' said Sawyer.[65] To the unions' surprise and relief, given Blair's statement that they could expect no favours from a Labour government, there was no organised attack on them, but there was regular briefing against them, and the unmistakeable impression that emerged was that the unions were now outsiders.[66] Of most concern to Blair was his desire to change the perception among many in the media (and the electorate) that the leadership was in the pocket of trade union leaders.[67]

The distancing of the party from the unions meant that it now had to find alternative sources of finance. Ken Follett, the millionaire novelist, had been in the vanguard of fundraising from 'high value' donors until the Blair camp reacted badly to a private dinner in January 1995 at his Chelsea home.[68] The press, who had been tipped off, filmed the Blairs arriving, resulting in a flurry of media stories about the Blairs' alleged high living in 'luvvie-land'. With the Clause IV debate in a delicate stage and a difficult month for Labour with opinion polls and the press,[69] 'Campbell was told to torpedo Ken Follett in the media'.[70] Dismayed by what he thought was a gross over-reaction, Follett immediately walked out of his fundraising role, after a meeting with Blair which the leader clearly found awkward and embarrassing.[71] Follett's departure left the space open for Michael Levy to step in, and by 1997 he had raised between £10 and £15 million. The money allowed Labour to have a full advertising campaign in the run-up to the 1997 election, one of the key facets in the new communications strategy, along with its key seats policy and 'pledge cards'. Transforming the image of the party and impressing Blair's own personality on voters and the media was at the heart of the strategy of New Labour, by giving presentation and media management a higher priority than the party ever had before.

Taming the Media

The ferocious and personal attack on Neil Kinnock by the *Sun* during the 1992 General Election campaign, epitomised by the headline on election day, 'If Kinnock wins today, will the last person to leave Britain please turn out the light?', deeply scarred Blair's and especially Campbell's thinking.[72] Indeed, the paper had not pulled its punches for most of Kinnock's time as leader. Might Blair be the subject of a similar right-wing attack?[73] Much that happened in 1994–97, and much that did not happen, was due to the perception of the damage that could be caused if the press turned against them. Campbell advised Blair from the outset that he needed to bring another tabloid on board, and with the party confident of the *Mirror*, that meant going for the prize of the *Sun*. To detach the *Sun* from the *Daily Mail*, the arch Tory papers which had worked together to such devastating effect to attack Major, and to make the *Mail* less hostile, would be an additional boon.[74] If some titles could not be brought fully on side with New Labour, at least they could be tamed: 'To make a paper 10 per cent less bad,' was the aim, said Campbell.[75]

The greatest effort was put into winning over News International, which owned the *Sun*, *News of the World*, *The Times* and *Sunday Times*. Some progress had already been made before Blair became party leader. Rupert Murdoch was open-minded towards Labour, even under Smith, because of his contempt for Major, and when Blair succeeded Smith, the floodgates opened. Shortly after he became leader, Murdoch invited Blair to one of his twice-yearly parties in St James's and was impressed.[76] Powerful voices were advising Murdoch to take Blair seriously, including Irwin Stelzer, his guru, and Woodrow Wyatt, the former Labour politician and journalist. Murdoch's enthusiasm was fickle, however. Richard Stott, editor of *Today*, advised Blair to be cautious: 'The thing you have to understand about Murdoch is that his first, second and third priority is News Corporation [the parent company]. That's all he cares about.' If Michael Portillo had replaced Major in 1995 and re-injected a dose of Thatcherism into the Tory government, Murdoch would, in all probability, have swung back behind the Tories, dumping Blair unceremoniously.[77]

But the success of Major's 'back me or sack me' leadership re-launch in mid-1995, which secured his place as the Tory leader up to the election, came at the cost of Murdoch focusing even more single-mindedly on Blair. 'Rupert likes controversial people and he thought that Blair would challenge the perceptions of his London newspaper staff, who were still mostly locked into thinking that they had to support the Tories,'[78] said Irwin Stelzer. Stelzer was partly responsible for the invitation to Blair to speak at a conference hosted by Murdoch for senior executives of News Corporation at Hayman Island, a resort off the coast of Queensland, Australia in July 1995. After many years of hostility between the Labour leadership and News International, the invitation was a real news event. Blair was surprised and delighted when the invitation arrived and readily accepted. He realised the opportunity it would provide to show News Corporation employees worldwide that he was a serious person who could be trusted to run the British government and the economy. But there were high risks. Some in his own party would accuse him of 'selling out', and his acceptance would also backfire if he failed to impress Murdoch sufficiently. 'Frankly, I did not believe he would accept the invitation for political reasons,' said Jane Reed, Director of Corporate Affairs at News International. 'We were amazed that he accepted.'[79]

Blair decided to take Campbell,[80] who was known to the News International group (as an employee up to the time he joined Blair), and Anji Hunter. A close aide described the trip as 'the biggest single step up for us we were ever to experience before 1997'.[81] The trio left after Prime Minister's Questions on Thursday, 13 July, and, for the first time, flew first-class, arriving in Sydney on Saturday morning. They spent the day at Kirribilli House, the official residence of the Australian Prime Minister, Paul Keating, usually reserved for visiting heads of government. Blair's Oxford friend Geoff Gallop joined them for lunch. Keating was determined to be very welcoming to his fellow left-of-centre leader, and loaned Blair his official jet to fly them up to Cairns in Queensland, and then he piloted the plane himself on to the lavish conference.[82] Blair's speech, over which he laboured particularly hard, was one he found difficult to pitch: too friendly and it would have created (even more) problems at home; insufficiently accommodating to News Corporation's values, and it would backfire. Blair opted for a strategy of criticising Thatcherism (risky), but for failing to provide social and economic stability (better); and alighted on the Establishment as a common target that the News Corporation executives and New Labour shared. He made 'no discernible concessions to the Murdoch world-view', wrote Michael White, to their relief, in the *Guardian*.[83] Murdoch found his views stimulating, and expressed himself well pleased by his new friend. Mission accomplished, the party left the island to fly back to Britain in time for Prime Minister's Questions on Tuesday, 18 July, to accusations that they had been 'supping with the devil'.[84] Blair weathered the storm over the free plane tickets and the 'toadying' to the hated Murdoch: he judged it a journey well worth making. Blair's attendance, far more than his speech, made its mark. 'I think Rupert and the company took it as a sign of courtesy and also [found it] rather flattering that he had flown half-way round the world to be there,' said Stelzer.[85] Crucially, at the same time Blair started moving Labour towards a more liberal stance on ownership of the media, which News Corporation wanted, and this further paved the way for a warmer dialogue.[86]

The *Sun* was the prize that Blair and Campbell sought, because of all the News International titles, it carried by far the most weight with voters, as Philip Gould's research clearly showed. The *Sun*, and to a lesser extent the *News of the World*, was also Murdoch's only British paper that he himself sought seriously to influence.[87] As the General Election approached a big debate took place over the *Sun*'s line: would they now back Labour? Kelvin MacKenzie, editor until 1995, was an ultra-Thatcherite (and anti-Major) Conservative and would never have agreed to back Labour. But he was succeeded as editor by Stuart Higgins, who was more open. Higgins, nevertheless, was against a total switch to supporting Labour, as were Chris Roycroft-Davis, the leader writer, and Trevor Kavanagh, the political editor.[88] Against them stood Irwin Stelzer, who was advising that it should back Labour: 'One, because the Tories were awful; two, Blair had restored Labour to where it could be a worthy part in the two-party system; three, although Blair was left he was sensitive to the needs of business and the market; four, we had nowhere else to go.'[89] Les Hinton, News International's new chairman, was also with Stelzer, and was swayed by the argument Blair and Mandelson put to him that the Labour Party was not a 'sheep in wolf's clothing' and that the changes on the economy, defence and crime were genuine.[90] The balance shifted in their direction. Trevor Kavanagh's own job with the paper came under threat for a time, which he believed was the result of pressure from Peter Mandelson. Murdoch decided in the end to override the *Sun*'s senior staff and the paper endorsed Labour. When he asked to see the first edition, and saw how lukewarm the paper's support was, he called in the deputy editor, Neil Wallis (Higgins was away), and insisted that if they were going to back Labour they wanted to see them win with a massive majority. He instructed Wallis to strengthen the *Sun*'s endorsement.[91] The news of the paper's switch was timed with deadly effect for 18 March, the day after Major announced the election.[92] Blair and Campbell only heard about it on a train to Gloucester and were surprised and hugely gratified.[93] Campbell said that he regarded getting the *Sun* to endorse Labour in 1997 as his biggest achievement in politics.[94] Mid-campaign, the *News of the World* also came out for Labour.

Murdoch had not liked it when Andrew Neil of the *Sunday Times* had earlier backed Michael Heseltine over his great hero, Mrs Thatcher, but let him do it and was not unduly put out by it.[95] He was much more 'hands off' at the broadsheet end of his papers, and was content to let the *Sunday Times* be supportive of Blair and *The Times* neutral for the 1997 election. Peter Stothard, the *Times* editor, flirted with the idea of backing Blair.[96] Stothard confirms he came under no pressure from Murdoch, and says his reason ultimately for not backing Labour was because he did not think that Blair, whom he interviewed just before the General Election, was capable of delivering on his promises.[97] *The Times*'s senior editorial team debated the issue in private at the Reform Club in January 1997. Michael Gove put the Tory case and Mary Ann Sieghart Labour's case. In the end *The Times* opted to advise its readers to back the most Eurosceptic candidate in their constituency regardless of party.[98]

After the *Sun*, the paper Blair tried hardest to woo was the *Daily Mail*, which Philip Gould always believed was possible. Almost as an act of bravado, they started to court this arch-Tory paper, which was thought to have more influence over its readers than the heavyweight pro-Tory *Daily Telegraph* and *Sunday Telegraph*. In great secrecy, Anji Hunter contacted Viscount Rothermere, the proprietor, and David English, the editor-in-chief, and Blair began to meet them for periodic discreet lunches in a room at London's Claridge's Hotel.[99] The Daily Mail and General Trust (DMGT), the group which owned the *Daily Mail*, had never persuaded Kinnock to come and have lunch with them, but succeeded with Smith, whom they felt had given quite a good account of himself. After the ice had been broken with Blair, he accepted an open invitation to lunch, when, in contrast to Smith, he impressed them by coming on his own. He made the very noises they wanted to hear: opposition to high taxes, pro-family and anti-sleaze.[100] The last was the issue that above all had turned the *Daily Mail* against the Conservatives, and the paper had enjoyed rising circulation while the pro-Major *Daily Express* continued to decline. This interested Rothermere, for whom commercial concerns were the first priority. English was more interested in the politics of New Labour, and also in honours. He enjoyed advising Labour on the media in secret, and was rewarded with a peerage on his deathbed. 'It was absolute love-bombing,' said one DMGT senior executive.[101] Scoops on education, for example, would be fed by Campbell to the *Daily Mail*, to the annoyance of the *Guardian*, which did not unduly worry Blair. For all this effort, however, Paul Dacre, the new editor, and later *bête-noire* of the Blairs, did not back Labour in 1997: 'I would have thought it incredibly expedient to have changed our traditional position so rapidly,' he said.[102] But all the effort did succeed in making the *Daily Mail* for a while less hostile to Labour than it had been for many years.

The two dailies Labour were most secure about were the *Guardian* and the *Mirror*. Alan Rusbridger, the *Guardian* editor, would call in regularly for talks with Blair, and in Patrick Wintour and Martin Kettle, in particular, they had two senior journalists they knew who were well disposed. The *Guardian* maintained, however, to Campbell's dislike, a fiercely independent line and regularly ran stories embarrassing to the Labour leadership. The *Mirror* was politically more of a worry when in November 1995, Piers Morgan came in from the *Sun* and *News of the World* as its editor. Campbell had stormed out from the *Daily Mirror* in 1993, and his relations with David Montgomery, the chief executive, were not good. Just before he took up the post, Morgan went in to see Blair in the Commons, accompanied by David Seymour and John Williams, the political editors, to reassure him that 'a Morgan *Mirror* would be a Labour-supporting *Mirror*'. Morgan initially liked Blair – they were both young, dynamic, and there was no significant ideological divide between them.[103] Morgan had also grown up in the same Sussex village of Newick as Anji Hunter, another point of contact.[104] The *Observer* was also courted. Blair made a great feature of telling its editor, Andrew Jaspan, when he was interviewed in September 1995, that it was 'the paper that most Labour Party members read on Sunday', and repeatedly stressed, almost over-anxiously, how much the paper mattered to him.[105] Jaspan's *Observer* was supportive towards Blair and little changed when, in 1996, Will Hutton was chosen to succeed him as editor.

Hollinger Inc., then owned by Conrad Black, also received Blair's attentions, out of damage limitation to Labour and damage maximisation to the Tories. Neither the *Daily Telegraph* nor *Sunday Telegraph* would ever be persuaded to back Labour, however deep their dislike of Major.[106] Charles Moore, editor of the former, says lobbying was never as intense as with the *Mail* and News International, but in 1994–97 there were 'lunches, handwritten notes, Alastair Campbell being matey'.[107] Black himself was also courted, the first contact having been through his wife, Barbara Amiel, in her *Sunday Times* piece in 1992. On the *Sunday Telegraph* approaches were made to editor Dominic Lawson and deputy editor Matthew d'Ancona, helped by both being Major-haters. Campbell was pleased that their efforts meant that both *Telegraph* titles were 'moderately friendly' in the last six months before the election.[108] Everything seemed to be running Blair's way: two of Major's last-ditch supporters as editors had left their posts in 1995 to be replaced by editors better disposed to Labour: Stewart Steven was thus replaced by Max Hastings at the *Evening Standard*, and Nicholas Lloyd by Richard Addis at the *Daily Express*.

The Blair–Campbell net was cast far beyond editors and proprietors. 'We wanted to try to persuade every journalist who was taken seriously in a spectrum from Hugo Young to Simon Heffer,' said Anji Hunter.[109] With right-wing writers, the task was aided considerably by Blair's admiration for Mrs Thatcher and a shared loathing of John Major – above all for Maastricht and Major's pro-Europeanism. Peregrine Worsthorne, William Rees-Mogg, Simon Heffer and Paul Johnson all, to differing degrees, declared themselves impressed by Blair as Opposition leader.[110] Johnson was particularly targeted. Religion was a big issue for him and he thought that Blair was a 'moral force' and a man of the future.[111] Johnson wrote enthusiastic columns supportive of Blair in the *Mail*. For him, as for Heffer, Rees-Mogg and Worsthorne, Blair's own pro-Europeanism was the major stumbling block, so when he moderated his tone as the election approached, it removed another obstacle to their support, as it did when their heroine, Mrs Thatcher, made some lukewarm remarks about the Labour leader.

Blair was also fortunate that a number of senior journalists on the centre or centre-left had formed favourable impressions of Blair and what he had achieved with the Labour Party, most notably Phil Webster at *The Times*, Andy Grice at the *Sunday Times*, Patrick Wintour at the *Guardian*, Andrew Marr, Ian Hargreaves, Donald Macintyre and John Rentoul, all at the *Independent*. Many other heavyweight journalists in 1995–97 were well disposed towards Blair and what he was trying to do to make Labour electable, with criticism of him coming mostly not from the right, but from the left. A huge investment had been made in

winning over a favourable press for the General Election. The task had
been brilliantly successful. But victory had come at a price.

The General Election

Major announced on 17 March that the election would be held on 1 May.
The election itself will be discussed here briefly, less because it has been
exhaustively covered in so many books,[112] more because it reveals very
little that is new about Blair. We know he was obsessed not only about
winning, but about winning with a very large majority: 'I wanted to slam
them,' he later said.[113] He even had hopes that if the defeat were large
enough, the Tory party might turn in on itself and split into a moderate
pro-Europe party and a right-wing ideological party.[114] His ambition for
a landslide was not admired by all. 'It was typical of Blair that he wanted
to go out and completely smash the opposition,' said Paul Routledge.
'He wanted to humiliate his opponents. It's indicative of his lack of self-
confidence that he wanted to win by a mile.'[115]

Having the *Sun* on board from the start of the campaign gave the
Millbank team its biggest boost, compensating for an unconfident start
in the first week. The *Sun*'s support came with a small price attached:
having to feed them positive stories and regular articles by 'Tony Blair'
(written mostly by Campbell or Tim Allan). Although freed of the grind
of writing articles, Blair still found the campaign a strain. As seen in Roy
Jenkins' remark at the beginning of this chapter, he was petrified of
something going wrong. Blair's calling in of Derry Irvine was symbolic
of the importance he attached to avoiding anything which could rebound
against Labour: he felt hugely comforted by his old mentor's picking
through the manifesto, launched on 3 April, line by line. The manifesto
offered 177 promises and opened with Blair's personal message:
'Education will be the Number 1 priority.' It was, in some ways, a clever
document in that it suggested major policy change while avoiding the
specifics and hostages to fortune of the flawed 1992 manifesto. As one
of its authors also admitted, 'We were so petrified that we would be seen
to lack credibility if we promised too much.'[116] Hubris was to be avoided
at all costs. Memories of the Sheffield rally in 1992 meant that all signs
of triumphalism were stamped on, which explains the downbeat, almost
puritanical tone Blair adopted throughout the campaign.

Blair found it a strain also because of continuing tension between
Brown and Mandelson, which had bedevilled the three years of electoral
preparation since the Chewton Glen conference. 'Though Gordon

would never trust him again,' says Whelan, 'it didn't stop Gordon working very closely with him right up to election night.'[117] Irvine's arrival at Millbank was partly to act as 'go-between' and keep the peace (and an eye out) in Blair's absence.[118] As a result of this tension, which was more about personality than substance, Blair had to maintain a tighter, strategic grip on the campaign than he would ideally have wanted. At the start of the campaign, the 8 a.m. meetings between Blair, Mandelson, Campbell, Powell and Brown would unleash some of the friction that had built up between Brown and Mandelson. The former blamed Mandelson's scheming, the latter claimed that these meetings were largely preoccupied with trying to get Brown to agree to the strategy that had been put in place before the campaign.[119] Brown and Mandelson hid the tension well from staff in Millbank; as one insider remarked, 'Gordon and Peter were very courteous towards each other and worked well in meetings during the campaign.' Only after the election, when a briefing war broke out, did they discover the truth.[120] The difficulties between his two senior lieutenants drew him closer to Campbell and to Jonathan Powell, who remained largely above the fray. Brown himself was also a worry to Blair. *Esprit de corps* was not improved by the belief of some senior staff that 'the Brown team always had their own press meeting'.[121] Blair himself maintained good relations with Brown on the surface, but he worried about what he might be planning, and about what it might mean once they were in government. For the time being, though, he refused to believe ill of Brown, despite what his aides were reporting to him, and directed his angst on to Brown's team, especially Whelan. As soon as the campaign was over, he spoke to Brown in an abortive attempt to persuade him to sack his errant press secretary for the sake of good relations in the future.[122]

Blair also had worries about whether he would be able to manage the job. Leo, his father, had identified this anxiety and on election night 'kept saying to me . . . "You will do it well". He understood what I was worrying about.'[123] Robin Butler had also detected a certain diffidence when they first started to meet, in early 1996, after Major had authorised official discussions between the Civil Service and the Labour Opposition.[124] When he and Cherie went to dinner in Dulwich with the Butlers in the early summer of 1996, he found that Blair knew little about government (despite Roy Jenkins' best endeavours to teach him). Butler gave Blair a folder containing a list of staff positions he would need to fill, and a floor plan to Number 10 and Number 11 Downing Street. Cherie asked whether 'the children would be able to practise the piano'. Butler suggested the family buy a 'people carrier' so they could all travel in one car.[125] The security dimensions of the job were just one facet that the Blairs had not by then fully assimilated. Realising that their and their children's lives would never be the same again, not just when they were in Downing Street, but for the rest of their days, was a major adjustment: as Leader of the Opposition he and his family had been able to live relatively normal lives, not hemmed in by the constant surveillance of Special Branch police protection.[126]

When Blair and Cherie focused more on the more immediate, day-to-day realities of what their lives would be like, however, they appreciated that the flat above Number 10 in which Prime Ministers traditionally lived would be too small for the five of them. After some considerable pressure from Cherie, which created some bad feeling, Gordon Brown agreed to move into the Number 10 flat releasing the larger private residence above Number 11 (and 12) for the Blairs.[127] Blair's fears about his ability to cope rapidly disappeared after he became Prime Minister and he discovered 'his life was more enjoyable' and that in contrast, 'leading the party in Opposition was hell'.[128] But when he was still fighting the campaign, the future for him, for Cherie, and for the children, often looked daunting.

A further strain in the run-up to polling day was that he was not absolutely certain that Labour unity would hold. Major had called a six-week campaign in the hope, partly grounded on research, that fear of Labour was growing and that it might become divided during a long campaign, as its policies came under the spotlight. Labour's leadership, however, thought the Tories had made a 'big mistake', and that the long campaign helped them in three ways: it showed that it was the Conservatives who were divided and not governing the country properly; it provided ample time for Labour to repeat its mantra of no more income tax, keeping the trade unions under control and maintaining a strong pound and economy; and it showed that Labour could provide a united front, even under intense pressure. 'We could have fallen apart,' Blair said in private soon after the election. 'People were prepared to give us the benefit of the doubt, but we had to come through the campaign.'[129]

Finally, Blair found the campaign stressful because of his anxiety about whether the result would go wrong. Blair is a periodic pessimist, who imagines the worst partly as a way of warding it off. Soon after the election he admitted: 'I believed in Labour's victory a bit more than I let on. The public dislikes politicians who tell them they are certain to win the election. It seems like taking them for granted. In 1997, I was prepared to envisage a narrow Labour win.'[130] The moment he finally realised that the Tories had lost the election and that he would definitely become Prime Minister was when one of Major's own ministers, John Horam, seemed to depart in a *Newsnight* interview from the Tory party's agreed line on Europe. Blair was spending the night of 15–16 April at the Grand Harbour Hotel on the seafront in Southampton, as the campaign was entering its final two weeks.[131] Campbell burst into his room to tell him the news about Horam. Blair replied, 'They can't come back from this. They are becoming a joke.'[132] Blair said to himself, 'That's it. These people can't run the country.'[133]

Some stresses eased as the campaign went on. 'I had the whole weight of the thing on my shoulders,' he confessed to Robert Harris early on in the campaign.[134] Excitement at the prospect of power built over the weeks. His conviction that he had only entered politics to 'do things' became a dominant factor in his mind. 'I could write a Ph.D. thesis on the politics of opposition,' he told Hugo Young on 30 April, with obvious relish that it was about to end: 'I know every single thing there is to know about it.'[135] Blair spent 1 May, polling day, in Trimdon, in the company of his close aides. With Powell he discussed ministerial appointments, while Campbell spent much of the day on the phone to the media. Mandelson drove over from Hartlepool for a talk, Anji Hunter and Sally Morgan were a constant source of support, while the local Trimdon team including Burton were on hand to help him keep a sense of perspective.

By early afternoon he realised from exit polls that the lead was holding up, and by 7 p.m. Campbell told him that Labour had a sixteen-point lead. That evening, the family congregated at Myrobella, with Leo, brother Bill and sister Sarah, Cherie's mother Gale and her daughters, and Tony Booth. Blair worked mostly alone in his study but came into the sitting room at 10 p.m. to hear the BBC and ITN exit polls, predicting a Labour majority of 180 and 150 respectively. 'I don't believe it. This isn't real, you know. Don't pay attention,' he said. He thought the majority was likely to be about 70 at most. The talk was of the exit polls in 1992, which predicted Labour doing much better than proved to be the case. When the BBC news predicted an even bigger margin, he said, 'This can't be real. Can it?' As the rest of the room exploded in joy, he felt 'oddly calm. I'm thinking ahead. I know what I want to do.' They left for the count at Newton Aycliffe Leisure Centre, arriving just after midnight. Robert Harris recorded his words as each result was announced: 'My God. It's a landslide.' 'This is getting ridiculous.' At one point he turned to John Burton, while watching the television screens at the count – which were still showing a Conservative seat tally of 0 compared to Labour's 100 – and said, with a degree of pity, 'I hope they've won *some* seats.'[136] When at 12.43 a.m. all three television networks predicted a Labour majority of 150, he uttered, 'This is crazy!'[137] His lack of euphoria in public was understandable, but his remarks in private showed that a big part of him was still shocked at how well Labour had done. Despite what he had been told for days, and from early afternoon onwards on 1 May, he only fully accepted the results of the landslide after midnight.

Jonathan Powell told him that President Clinton wanted to phone him to congratulate him, but that the State Department had forbidden it until Major officially conceded. At 1.30 a.m., Major phoned Blair at the Leisure Centre to congratulate him with these words: 'It is a testing job, unique and sometimes enjoyable. You have a big majority, you should enjoy it.' [138] Major remembers him being very 'gracious and very human'. Blair thanked him and wished him luck.[139] Shortly after, the convoy of cars left for Teesside Airport. The party flew south in two chartered jets: in Blair's sat Cherie, Hunter, Campbell, Fiona Millar, Powell, Burton and the photographer Peter Stoddart. Blair maintained his studied thoughtfulness, the cabin hushed except for Hunter's regular forays to the toilet for a cigarette.[140] One moment of relief was when Campbell's pager went off to say that Labour had won genteel Hove, which seemed so implausible that Blair momentarily let his guard drop.[141] They arrived at London's Stansted Airport, and were driven to the South Bank for the victory celebration, where Jonathan Powell for the first time addressed Blair as 'Prime Minister'. As Blair took to the stage at 5 a.m., the sun was rising, remembered by all there as an intensely symbolic moment. In a downbeat speech his seminal words were: 'We have been elected as New Labour and we will govern as New Labour.' After a brief rest at Islington, Blair was driven to kiss hands with the Queen at Buckingham Palace, and then on to the gates of Downing Street. His staff had been among the crowds of Labour supporters outside the door of Number 10. 'I listened to John Major talking about the curtains falling,' recalls Margaret McDonagh, 'and wished he'd just go away so we could get on with it. But then I remember thinking, "This will be us one day – what a brutal world politics is."'[142] When Blair entered the building at midday, he was surprised to find a bottle of champagne from Major on a table in the flat upstairs, accompanied by a note that read: 'It's a great job – enjoy it.'[143]

The Significance of 1995–97

The character of Blair's whole premiership was dictated by the two years covered by this chapter, from the end of the Clause IV debate to the General Election. All the roots of his premiership were to be found in these years. He would run his premiership as he did his Opposition leadership, relying on his close team – Campbell, Powell, Hunter, Morgan, Mandelson and Gould – rather than on his senior political colleagues, whom he would by-pass as much as he had in Opposition. Those six were added to by a small number of officials after he entered Number 10 and met regularly in his room ('the den') at the end of the Cabinet Room: they became the 'denocracy' that effectively ran the country during his premiership. The breezy way Blair had treated advice on the mechanics of running government meant that he did not use the official machine to best advantage once he arrived in power. He relied heavily on Jonathan Powell as his guide to Whitehall: but Powell had been a relatively senior official in just one department, and reliance on his close circle precluded him listening to officials as effectively as he might. Some seasoned commentators like Peter Riddell believed that Blair never understood how government worked.

Blair's wariness of Brown became entrenched in these two years: significantly, his first conversations with Brown in Downing Street on 2 May (about Whelan) were acrimonious: another leitmotif of his premiership. Blair's almost perverse failure to countenance that Labour would have a very big majority prevented him fully exploring what he would do with the quite extraordinary power, personal and governmental, this landslide had given him. The caution displayed from 1995 to 1997 over policy had meant that, with the notable exception of education, all too little of his own agenda had been addressed seriously in Opposition, with the result that too little of it was enacted in government. Blair's intimations of radicalism just before the election were soon followed by overtures in office about making the most of the groundswell of support that had accompanied the landslide.[144] He warned advisers and officials in Number 10 that now would be the time to introduce daring and, if necessary, unpopular measures. But it soon emerged that a top priority from day one in power was acquiring a second full term with a large working majority, which meant daring policies were ruled out. Watching the press obsessively, another feature of 1995–97, became entrenched, with too great attention being given to the next day's headlines to the detriment of long-term policy thinking. Labour's media-management operation, which was so effective from

Millbank, was transferred to Whitehall, less appropriately and with less success. Philip Gould's memos to Blair after 1997 repeatedly highlighted 'the media' as a real threat to him: to some extent this was payback from a press corps rebelling at the way they felt manipulated. Blair's claiming of the high moral ground in 1995–97 ('morality' came up frequently in his speeches) and his derision of the Tories' effectiveness at running public services aroused almost impossible expectations which his own government, still less his ministers, were to find hard to fulfil. All these were to come back to haunt him in later years.

Blair had achieved a majority of 179, the largest landslide in the history of the Labour Party, out-doing in scale Attlee's famous victory of 1945. Blair had indeed carried the crystal bowl safely down the miles of passageways, in the phrase of Roy Jenkins (whose influence is examined next). That task, Jenkins said, would go down as Blair's 'role in history'. The question in the second half of this book is whether his 'role in history' would be much more than cautiously leading his party to great election victories.

Roy Jenkins at a press conference on electoral reform in Westminster in October 1998. Jenkins asked questions of Blair, and offered him two answers which would have transformed his premiership had Blair listened to them.

20

Roy Jenkins

Tony Blair's life intertwined with Roy Jenkins' at Blair's time of greatest historic opportunity, 1995–98, when he was best placed to make major strategic shifts in policy. For three years their minds locked together, to the huge enjoyment of both men, the senior at the end of his long career of thirty years at the top of British politics, seeing in his young protégé the opportunity to fulfil dreams for which he had fought all his life. The other at the very start of his career as leader of the Labour Party, having just rejected its creed of the last seventy-five years, and avid for the ideas which would shape his 'new' Labour party and mark him out as one of history's great Prime Ministers. Blair knew all too well after the Clause IV debate that he had defined far more clearly what he stood against than what he was for. The 'third way' offered one set of ideas that he could pursue; Roy Jenkins offered him another avenue that, if followed, would have changed the Labour Party, the mould of British politics and Britain's place in Europe – and perhaps the world – decisively. For three years the Jenkins candle burned bright. Then it dimmed, and the two men, although still friends, went their own ways.

How serious was Blair about the Jenkins agenda? Why did he not follow it, and what did Jenkins think about it after their opportunity had passed? These questions are all the more important as, with the passage of time, the Blair premiership is considered not to have made the agenda-changing impact that Blair himself so ardently sought for it.

Roy Jenkins: The Promise

Roy Jenkins only encountered Tony Blair in the seventy-fifth year of his life. His father's and his own political life spanned almost the entire history of the Labour Party in its first century. Arthur Jenkins was politically involved as a miner before the First World War. He became Labour MP for Pontypool from 1935 to 1946, and finished his career as Parliamentary Private Secretary to Clement Attlee. Roy was his only son, and he fully imbibed his father's love of politics and the Labour Party, and wrote an authorised early biography of Attlee. His father's hope that they would sit together in Parliament was not to be: Roy's first parliamentary contest in 1945 was unsuccessful, and his father died before Roy won a by-election in 1948. He was on the liberal and centre-right wing of the party and was one of a generation of Labour politicians, including Anthony Crosland and Denis Healey, who were at Oxford together and then went on to dominate the party in the 1960s and 1970s. To many on the centre and left of Blair's party, Roy Jenkins had become a figure of hate, a claret-soaked hypocrite. He had led the Labour faction that gave Heath the votes to take Britain into the EEC in 1971. Worse still in the eyes of the left, he was one of the 'gang of four' who founded the SDP ten years later, which fatally undermined Labour throughout the 1980s.

After the collapse of the SDP's dream of remoulding British politics, Jenkins saw Blair as the man to complete his task of destroying the old left. He was also flattered by the attention of this eager, enquiring young man,[1] who had none of the hang-ups of traditional Labour politicians about 'supping with the devil'. As his relationship with Peter Thomson and Derry Irvine showed, Blair had a penchant for older mentor figures, and recognised in Jenkins a profound and good man, which cannot be said of all those to whom he was to listen. Given Blair's hostility to 'old' Labour, there was little chance of him turning to elder statesmen in his own party, such as Wilson, Callaghan or Healey, for advice. Instead, he looked to Jenkins.

Tony Blair would later share with friends the heresy that when Roy Jenkins was elected to Parliament as an SDP member at the Hillhead by-election in March 1982, just before his Beaconsfield by-election, he identified much more with what Jenkins was saying than with the Labour candidate.[2] Jenkins remained the MP until the General Election of 1987, when the SDP–Liberal Alliance star had begun to wane. Elevated to the upper House, as Lord Jenkins of Hillhead, he settled down to a life of writing and periodic interventions in politics. But he imagined his days of power and real influence were behind him.

Then, 'out of the blue' as he put it, Tony Blair wrote to him, before he had become leader of the party, asking for Jenkins' advice on economic policy.[3] The approach was all the more remarkable because of Blair's sensitivity (until he had secured the leadership) to allegations that he was a closet SDP sympathiser, or that he and the modernisers were trying to make Labour into SDP Mark II. But his obvious interest in Jenkins personally and his belief that he could learn from him overcame his qualms of consorting with the 'arch-traitor'. The thought of working with the Liberal Democrats as a way of defeating the Tories had been in his mind since conversations with Martin Jacques and others in 1991–92, as part of an anti-Tory alliance to prise them from office. The first of many private meetings between Jenkins and Blair came in mid-1994.

Blair had earlier met Paddy Ashdown, leader of the Liberal Democrats, at a private dinner hosted by Anthony Lester and his wife in July 1993.[4] Lester, a lawyer and a friend of Ashdown, had been keen for both men to meet, and felt that from the outset 'they fell in love'.[5] To continue their dialogue, they agreed to meet again over dinner at Ashdown's flat that December. During the evening together, Blair vented his frustration with Smith's slow pace of reform, and expressed his wish to work with Ashdown to reformulate the politics of the left around Blair's hobby horses of 'community' and a new contract between the citizen and the state.[6] 'He was absolutely clear about what he wanted to do,' recalled Ashdown. 'He had the whole strategy worked out.'[7] Ashdown, who was similarly free-thinking and who had been contemplating abandoning the Liberal Democrats' policy of 'equi-distance' between the Conservatives and Labour, was most interested. Both men were struck by how, after Labour's policy changes of the mid/late 1980s and early 1990s, their parties now had far more uniting them than dividing them. Blair, however, remained powerless to do anything practical about these thoughts while Smith was leader, and he had no significant contact with Ashdown until after July 1994. Three of the four SDP leaders – Jenkins himself, Bill Rodgers and Shirley Williams (but not David Owen) – all endorsed him almost immediately, which was symbolically important because of the bitter feelings still between Labour and the SDP's founders thirteen years after the split.

As Blair reflected on his opportunities over the summer of 1994, the idea of bringing about a progressive left-of-centre realignment in politics rose to the top of the pile. Now he, not Smith, held the reins. He knew from his earlier conversation that Ashdown was open to dialogue, and he now sought out Jenkins too. A new thought entered Blair's mind, providing another incentive for the dialogue. From the moment he became leader, he focused with utter single-mindedness on winning the General Election. An alliance with the Liberal Democrats could help him achieve this end, and it would also allow him to sideline his left wing once in government.[8] Blair held separate meetings after his summer break with Jenkins and Ashdown and sought to overcome their understandable suspicions that he was consorting with the Liberal Democrats in private merely to convince them to turn their fire away from New Labour in public. Blair insisted his efforts were genuine: 'You can trust me on this,' he told Ashdown. Both Jenkins and Ashdown concluded that Blair was serious about some form of co-operation but felt he did not yet know exactly what he wanted. They also agreed that one option Blair remained deeply sceptical about was the Liberal Democrats' holy grail, proportional representation (PR).[9] Other currents that were shaping Blair's co-operative thinking at this time were the Democrats in the US, who had 'rediscovered' the progressive politics of Theodore Roosevelt, President at the start of the twentieth century, and Philip Gould, whose research was driving Blair to pitch his appeal to the middle ground, the territory also occupied by the Liberal Democrats.[10]

Blair was preoccupied over the months following September 1994 by the Clause IV debate, which only heightened his enthusiasm for finding a way to prevent Labour's left wing neutering the party once it won office. He met Ashdown in early May 1995, four days after the special conference which settled Clause IV, for a 'secret' dinner with senior Labour and Liberal Democrats, which gave birth to the 'Cook–Maclennan group' to take forward joint constitutional reform discussions (Cook in the lead for Labour, Robert Maclennan for the Liberal Democrats). Since their meeting the previous September, Blair had 'changed quite a lot', Ashdown recorded in his diary. 'He has grown in self-confidence.'[11] Blair's conversations with Ashdown meandered on for the rest of the year and by November 1995 he felt their relationship had become 'very friendly and relaxed'. He chronicled every twist and turn of their discussions at great length in his diary, later published, which provides a remarkably accurate record according to other witnesses.[12] It is also the only complete written account of the discussions, as Blair did not make any comprehensive notes himself.

On Sunday, 3 September 1995, the Blairs and the three children went for Sunday lunch with the Jenkinses at their home at East Hendred near Oxford (Roy, ever meticulous, recorded in his diary that the Blairs stayed from 1.20 to 4.55 p.m.).[13] They spoke about the possibilities of a relationship between the Liberal Democrats and Labour. Blair gave him the unequivocal statement that he would prefer to have a government in which Liberal Democrats were present than a government made up entirely of the

Labour Party. Jenkins later confided in a friend that he would never have left Labour if it had been led by Blair, 'but it's too late go back now'.[14] Jenkins' vision rather was to reunite the left-of-centre forces that had split first in 1900 when the Labour Party was formed (in competition with the Liberals) and then again with the SDP breakaway from Labour in 1981. He wanted to re-create the politics of the nineteenth century, when the Whigs or Liberals were the progressive force in British politics, and the principal opposition to the Tories. Jenkins told Blair that the key to unlocking the door to reunification was PR, which would be absolutely critical for the Liberal Democrats if there was to be an enduring relationship in the future. So he was naturally disappointed to find Blair unmovable on this issue. In November 1995, he reported to Ashdown that Blair's view on PR was 'very, very cautious. It is extremely disappointing.' 'Of course, I will do what I can to put pressure on him. It is a ridiculous position. He must realise how much is at stake here.'[15] Jenkins had lunch with Mandelson at the end of 1995, who was very keen on seeing discussions with the Liberal Democrats pushed ahead, and he told him that Blair was moving from a neutral position towards welcoming PR.[16] This helped explain Jenkins' belief that, in time, Blair would be persuadable. Blair certainly did nothing to disabuse Jenkins of the notion, and began to seek his advice on a wide range of matters.

Jenkins was settling into and hugely enjoying his role as mentor to Blair. 'I think Tony treats me as a sort of father-figure,' he said. 'He comes to me a lot for advice, particularly about how to construct a government.'[17] Jenkins became concerned, however, as to how little Blair (or indeed any of his front-bench team) knew about the practicalities of government; Labour had not been in office since 1979, before most of his shadow Cabinet had even entered Parliament. Jenkins thus conceived the idea of a dinner at his Kensington flat to which, on 16 January 1996, he invited Robin Butler, the Cabinet Secretary, and other mandarins – including two who went on to become Cabinet Secretaries, Richard Wilson and Andrew Turnbull – to meet Blair and Jonathan Powell.[18] Blair appreciated the idea but his mind was not yet engaged on the business of running the Civil Service. Management had never been an interest of his and he would probably have preferred to have spoken to Jenkins about politics all evening.

The opportunity for a confidential discussion came on the doorstep after the great and good had departed. Jenkins pressed the PR case again hard on Blair, saying that a commitment on PR before the election, even in private to Ashdown, would open the door. Jenkins thought that Blair was 'becoming convinced intellectually' but was worried that if he adopted it, it would split Labour.[19] Blair also had another concern in mind. Within two weeks of that dinner, he was saying very explicitly and honestly that 'my main reason for not wanting PR is because I understand the power of Murdoch and Black', the owners of News International and the *Daily Telegraph* respectively, who were vehemently opposed to such a change.[20]

Blair's worry that many of his colleagues were opposed to any relationship with the Liberal Democrats, 'the project' as Blair, Jenkins and Ashdown termed it, was very real. Brown and Prescott were the main opponents, with Margaret Beckett, Nick Brown, Jack Straw, as well as Alastair Campbell, all antagonistic. Gordon Brown and his advisers were fiercely opposed to any formal deal with the Liberals, and viewed with deep suspicion Blair's talk of the Liberals as helping to guarantee 'ten years of progressive government in Britain'. Prescott 'fumed and giggled' at the mention of the name 'Liberal Democrats', while Brown pointedly referred to them in public as 'the Liberals' to nettle them.[21] Opponents in the shadow Cabinet and below far outweighed supporters for Blair's big idea, so he kept his talks and musings as close to his chest as he could. The only shadow Cabinet 'big beast' who was an active enthusiast for the 'project' was Robin Cook, who was personally committed to PR, and who was active with Maclennan in taking forward the joint constitutional reform agenda.[22] The other principal conduit for discussions in the Blair–Jenkins–Ashdown triangle was between Mandelson and Richard Holme, a long-serving Liberal stalwart and strategist with still-raw memories of how the Liberals had been taken advantage of in the Lib–Lab Pact of 1977–78. Mandelson's fellow enthusiast was Roger Liddle, who had left Labour for the SDP in 1981 but returned to the fold in 1995. They wrote enthusiastically about realignment and PR in a draft of their book *The Blair Revolution* (1996), but after parts of it were leaked, potentially inflammatory passages were greatly toned down.[23] Irvine was another prepared to look positively upon talks, but the combination of him, Cook, Mandelson and Liddle was not the most propitious for winning over Labour doubters to the cause.

Blair had dinner with Jenkins on Friday, 26 April 1996, at Jenkins' Kensington flat. After his warm encouragement, Jenkins was thrilled to hear Blair respond that, if Labour won a majority, he would form a coalition government, inviting two or three Liberals to join (he most wanted Ashdown and Menzies Campbell, both of whom were canvassed as Foreign Secretary).[24] If there were no overall majority a full coalition would be the result as not even the most opposed Labour politicians would seek to resist it. His desire to go for a coalition, he told Jenkins, was because he felt he could rely on Liberal support better if it were tied in with a formal structure. Jenkins told him that he did not have a high opinion of Blair's shadow Cabinet below Brown and Cook, and this played to Blair's thinking that his Cabinet would be stronger with some of the best Liberal minds in it. Blair again said that he was 'moving' towards PR[25] (although he focused on the Alternative Vote [AV] model, a variant of PR, which was not so favoured by the Liberal Democrats, since it did not produce a strictly proportional outcome).

The stumbling blocks remaining from spring 1996 were whether Blair would change his mind again on PR, and whether he could take his party with him on any coalition with the Liberals. Another piece of Jenkins' advice was for Blair to build a very close relationship with one person in his Cabinet, on whom he could always rely for support.[26] In this context Jenkins reminded Blair what a rock Ernest Bevin had been to Attlee when Stafford Cripps attempted a coup during the post-war Labour government.[27] This thought may have generated in Blair's mind the notion that Prescott should be such a figure (who indeed rode to his rescue in 2003–04). Meanwhile, with a General Election possible at any time, Ashdown wanted to seek more concrete understandings on a pact and he tackled Blair on the matter when they had a long meeting in the Commons on 8 May. Would he be able to carry the party on a coalition government, Ashdown asked? Ashdown was worried in particular about the antipathy of Gordon Brown, who was convinced neither about the merits of a coalition nor PR.[28] Ashdown and Brown subsequently had a meeting, which was described as 'amicable', but neither brought the other round to their point of view.[29]

By mid-1996, Jenkins, the strategist with a direct line to Blair's imagination, and Ashdown, the tactician concerned with the day-to-day realities of parliamentary life, were working a pincer movement on Blair. Jenkins offered the carrot of a realigned centre-left in Britain, keeping the Tories out of power for many years; Ashdown the stick, saying that unless a referendum on PR were to take place in the first year of the government, and with Blair's personal support for a 'yes' vote, talks of partnership were over. Jenkins sent Blair away to Tuscany in August 1996 with a pile of history books to read, including the speeches of Keir Hardie and David Lloyd George. This was to broaden his reading beyond the biography of Henry Campbell-Bannerman, Liberal leader from 1899 to 1908, the time of the splitting of the centre-left in Britain into two opposing parties, which was once described by Robert Harris as 'the only political biography Tony Blair ever seems to have read'.[30] Blair returned from Italy fired with a new zeal and soon after arriving back went to Sunday lunch at East Hendred with the Jenkinses. Blair was now at his most enthusiastic, lyrical even, about building a 'radical centre' force in British politics. Blair had utterly persuaded himself about the new era shortly to dawn. But, as Jenkins wrote to Ashdown, 'It is the nuts and bolts which pose the problems, e.g. PR. But I think he will ultimately subordinate them to the wider strategy.'[31] 'The real shame is that our two parties weren't able to stay together in the early part of the century,' Blair told Ashdown, when he saw him five days after his lunch with Jenkins. 'It was such nonsense that Keynes and Bevan and Beveridge were all in different parties . . . we have to bring these two strands back together again.'[32] But Blair's new-found command of history had shallow roots.

The Jenkinses went to dinner with the Blairs in Islington on 19 January 1997.[33] The euphoria of the late summer had evaporated in the chill winter winds of political reality in Westminster and Fleet Street. Blair's principal concerns were opposition from his own party; his personal doubts about PR, which had resurfaced; and concern that an announcement about a change to the electoral system would unite the Tories and media with a force that could still lose him the election.[34] For the first time since their special relationship began, Jenkins began to feel dejected. 'I'm going to find it difficult even to incorporate the Liberal Democrats in the next government,' Blair told Jenkins at the dinner. Blair mused on the idea of just offering Ashdown a seat in Cabinet, as Churchill had done to the Liberal leader, Clement Davies, in 1951; but Jenkins told him it was out of the question. Jenkins was so taken aback by Blair's new coolness to the grand design that it was only the next day that he thought of a plan offering himself as 'honest broker' between Blair and Ashdown, as the last shot in his locker. Ashdown ruled out this option.[35] He too was getting frustrated, and for the first time was becoming angry with Blair, whom he felt was reneging on undertakings he had given, leaving Ashdown terribly exposed with his party.

Blair's overriding concerns with the Tory press and internal divisions, with Brown and Straw in the early months of 1997 the most vocal opponents, damaged the prospects of a closer formal agreement before the General Election, although when Blair and Ashdown spoke on the Sunday before polling day, they agreed that plans (specifics undefined) were still 'on track'.[36] At the last minute the idea emerged of the Liberal Democrats serving not in full Cabinet but on Cabinet committees, as occurred in the inter-war years when Baldwin, the subject of one of Jenkins' biographies, was Prime Minister.[37] Remarkably, Blair phoned Ashdown on election night, 1 May, to say he was still keen on exploring links together. Ashdown put the new proposal to Blair specifically, suggesting that Liberal Democrats served on committees on constitutional reform, a project dear to the Liberals. Blair was immediately receptive, and repeated to a not entirely convinced Ashdown, 'I'm absolutely determined to mend the schism that occurred in the progressive forces in British politics at the start of this century.'[38] It is hard to know exactly what was in Blair's mind. Was he still worrying that Labour would not win a working majority so he needed the Liberal Democrats as a safety net? Robert Harris was with the Blairs that night and when the magnitude of the victory became clear he saw Cherie touch Blair on the arm and say, 'Don't let this shake you in your resolve.' Only later did Harris hit upon an explanation for the remark: Cherie, he believed, had been advising her husband not to let the size of the majority be used by those opposed to collaboration with the Liberal Democrats as a pretext for jettisoning it.[39]

The next morning, 2 May, Jenkins joined Ashdown, Holme, Tom McNally and others in Ashdown's office for an early morning meeting about how to play the new Prime Minister. A call from him was expected at any moment. Jenkins argued that they should hold out for at least two seats, and ideally three, in the Cabinet, and also insist on some changes in policy.[40] Blair phoned just after the meeting broke up and before he went to Buckingham Palace to see the Queen. As the immensity of his victory sunk in overnight, he had cooled, and he did not ask, to neither their surprise nor particular disappointment, for the Liberal Democrats to join a coalition with Labour. With a majority of 179, he could not conceivably have persuaded hostile colleagues that a coalition was in any sense necessary or sensible. Ashdown also reluctantly concluded that this was not the moment to win round his own unreceptive colleagues after his equally unexpectedly high tally of 46 seats, the largest number since Lloyd George had been leader in 1929.[41] The strong performance of both parties, which had ruled out a partnership, ironically had been helped by their close contact during the campaign. Daily conversations had taken place between senior strategists on both sides to ensure fire was turned on the Conservatives rather than each other; 'The election was fought as if we were in coalition already,' said Richard Holme.[42]

After the election victory Blair did not want the 'project' to wither and die. He had also developed a thicker skin. He could now afford to ignore those in his party who were outraged by the idea of talking to the Liberal Democrats. Indeed, he positively relished going against the party over it: 'He enjoyed the feeling almost more than anything else,' one close aide told James Naughtie.[43] With his huge majority, he may not now have needed Liberal Democrat support any longer to keep his left wing in check. But he did not want to disappoint Jenkins, or other partnership enthusiasts in his party and outside, and this became an important factor in keeping the dialogue open. So the dinners and conversations kept going, much to the disgust of Brown and Prescott and, indeed, most of the Cabinet – especially when Blair appeared to be heralding a new wave of co-operation possibilities in his party conference speech in September 1997. 'Division among radicals almost a hundred years ago resulted in a twentieth century dominated by the Conservatives,' he said, in words that could have been written for him by Jenkins. 'I want the twenty-first century to be the century of the radicals.'[44]

Blair was indeed anxious to show that he had not cynically used the Liberal Democrats only to dump them. Liberals could point to PR for the non-Westminster elections as a tangible fruit of the two years of talks. He also assented to the Joint Cabinet Consultative Committee, announced before the summer and which met first in September 1997. Blair and Ashdown were both in attendance, but, tellingly, neither Brown nor Prescott was. Supporters could boast that Liberal Democrats were now involved in government. The discussions never amounted to much, however, and were spoken of dismissively by Charles Kennedy after he succeeded Ashdown in 1999, boasting that he had little time for the committee because 'I'm not blinded by the lights of Number 10 Downing Street and I'm not in favour of meetings for the sake of it.'[45]

The Commission on Electoral Reform, as promised in Labour's 1997 manifesto, was in particular Blair repaying his debt to Jenkins, whom he asked to chair the body against the angry protests of some in his party but to the delight of the Liberal Democrats.[46] When Blair offered him the job, Jenkins wanted to be sure that he was getting more than a consolation prize. He therefore asked for Blair's Private Secretary to be sent out of the Number 10 study and asked Blair frankly if he was serious about electoral reform. Only when he received that reassurance, did Jenkins agree to take up the offer.[47] Jenkins then set about what was to be his swansong in public life with a quite remarkable vigour, relishing the views of his talented committee, which ranged from David Lipsey on the left to Bob Alexander on the right. The Commission's aim was to come up with the best alternative to Britain's first-past-the-post electoral system to put before the public in a referendum. All the members of the Commission had praise for Jenkins' skill and tenacity, especially when it became obvious that the moment for real change had probably passed, and it would have been all too easy to have lost heart. Lipsey thought 'his stamina, humour, patience and drive would have been extraordinary in anyone; in a man of seventy-eight they were beyond belief'.[48] Jenkins 'was very careful not to be too purist, but to seek a solution that the government might find acceptable and workable', said Bob Alexander.[49]

Even before the report was published in October 1998, Blair was back-pedalling and the prospect of an imminent referendum on the voting system was fading rapidly: 'I'll have huge problems getting my lot to agree to it by November,' Blair told Ashdown that July. 'There are too many people to get on board and I am faced with a real possibility of splitting my party.'[50] Prescott, Brown and Straw were the principal figures who killed the report; it sank without trace, and with it the last vestiges of hope of seeing any pledge to PR in parliamentary elections. 'Roy was terribly disappointed when, having pushed through a watered-down compromise report, nothing came of it,' said Matthew Oakeshott, his former special adviser.[51] 'Roy is very dispirited with Blair himself,' Ashdown recorded at the time.[52] But Blair had other fights which were preoccupying him, so he turned a blind eye and let his head, which had always had doubts about PR, rule his heart, which had momentarily convinced him it was a price worth paying for the greater objective of political realignment. The 2001 Labour manifesto barely mentioned electoral reform, and the issue was effectively dead. Ashdown's successor, Kennedy, despite Blair's continuing positive comments, conclusively ended any meaningful co-operation between Labour and the Liberal Democrats.

All was not lost in Jenkins' mind, however. He still nurtured hopes that Blair would respond positively on the other great enthusiasm of his life, Europe. He had spoken to Blair less often, but with no less ardour, about the importance of Britain joining the Euro. Jenkins, who had been trying since the 1950s to encourage Labour to embrace Europe positively, saw his task as coaxing Blair further down the European road. It is 'crucial that the government gives the impression that it wants monetary union to succeed', he told Blair in September 1997, and thus he hoped that 'a formula would be worked out during the British Presidency in the first half of next year that will commit us to early, if not immediate, entry'.[53] Had Liberal Democrats joined the government, they too would have pushed for an early entry.[54] Chapter 23 examines in detail what happened to Jenkins' dreams on the Euro.

The Impact of Roy Jenkins

Was Blair sincere about a coalition with the Liberals? 'Tony took Paddy Ashdown for all he was worth. He used him mercilessly and then dumped him after the election when he realised he was no longer needed. It shows what a hard bastard Tony is,' said one close Blair aide.[55] However, while Blair cannot have been ignorant of the short-term electoral benefits of co-operating with the Liberal Democrats, this view is too cynical and misjudges his primary motivation. Blair's vision was broad, grand and vague. He was utterly sincere in his desire to see a partnership with the Liberals, and would ideally have liked a full merger. In his more euphoric moments he even countenanced bringing in Europhile Tories like Ken Clarke to smash the Tory party asunder.[56] Blair's was a pragmatic vision about power, and stopping the Conservatives dominating the new century. But this vision, which was always high on grandeur and short on detail, differed from Jenkins' vision, which was always *ideological*, concerned with reconnecting progressive parties and forces. It differed too from Ashdown's vision, which was focused on delivering PR and on agreeing a specific programme between the Liberal Democrats and Labour, which would avoid the pitfalls of the Lib–Lab Pact.[57] Without ever fully acknowledging it, the three were pursuing different, and incompatible, ends.

As the premiership ground on, Jenkins became increasingly frustrated with Blair's performance. In November 1999, he ruefully told an old friend, 'I have three great interests left in politics – the single currency, electoral reform and the union of the Liberals with Labour. And all three are languishing.'[58] Other disappointments began to accumulate. As Chancellor of Oxford University, Jenkins helped sell the idea of 'top-up' fees to Blair, but was disappointed, says Jenkins' successor, Chris Patten, that Blair would not agree to a larger figure.[59] He was furious too about the 'Laura Spence affair', and about attempts to push Oxford further towards positively discriminating in favour of students from less advantaged backgrounds, although his ire here was directed mostly at Gordon Brown.[60] He became critical of Blair for being over-anxious about press barons, and for following, not leading, the newspapers' agenda. He began to give mildly critical speeches and to write articles in the same vein.[61] In mid-2000 he told the *Spectator*'s Boris Johnson that he thought Blair had a 'second-class mind', although he soon regretted this outburst and phoned Blair to apologise.[62] He later penned a long survey of Blair's first three years in power which concluded thus: 'He has clearly shown himself a competent Prime Minister. Whether he will be a great one remains to be seen. But I am not unhopeful.' He warned against premature judgement: 'It is unwise to tip the waiter until the meal is over.'[63] In 2001, however, he thought Blair squandered the opportunities of a second landslide. He and his wife Jennifer were to have had dinner with the Blairs over Christmas 2002. Jenkins felt very strongly about Iraq and the Bush administration and thought that going to war would be very risky for the country, the government, and for Blair himself. He would certainly have raised his doubts at the dinner, Jennifer believes.[64] But there was to be no

Christmas meal; they were never to meet again. Roy died on 5 January 2003.

So Jenkins was unable to offer a final 'tip to the waiter'. Yet Jenkins lived long enough to see his two greatest ambitions dashed, the reuniting of progressive, centre-left parties and a serious renewed commitment to the EU in the shape of joining the Euro. It is no coincidence that Gordon Brown opposed both Jenkins' great projects. While responsibility for the decisions on both lies ultimately with Blair, it is nevertheless true that if Brown had supported Blair on either, as opposed to fighting him, the outcomes would have been very different. In these two great issues, Blair was sincere in his interest, but ultimately not sufficiently convinced to overcome the forces ranged against him. Jenkins thought Blair's most important personal trait was that he is 'a man on a journey who hasn't yet arrived at his destination'.[65] Jenkins met Blair at the time of his greatest opportunity, and gave him a destination, which chimed with his own convictions. Jenkins, like Blair, was an iconoclast who had no time for the left, and who saw political parties as a means to an end, not the end itself. They were political soulmates. Neither the 'third way', nor New Labour, nor Blair's own five core beliefs provided him with an alternative destination. Jenkins' *potential* importance was as great as any of the nineteen other figures described in this book. However, Blair declined Jenkins' agenda, and thus he was almost the least important. Whether Jenkins' projects were right or wrong is not the issue. What is clear is that had Blair followed his frustrated mentor's advice, his place in history, and that of the Labour Party, would have been very different.

OWEN HUMPHREYS/PA

Blair delivers the 'People's Princess' speech in Trimdon churchyard on the morning of Diana's death, 31 August 1997. Rarely has a Prime Minister so captured the nation's mood.

21

Death of Diana, 1997

The high point of Blair's premiership in terms of popularity and authority came just four months after the 1997 General Election. In the immediate aftermath of Diana's death, he captured the mood of the nation as well as any Prime Minister since Churchill in 1940. Blair's remarks in Trimdon about the 'People's Princess' on the morning after the fatal crash and his reading from Corinthians at the memorial service in Westminster Abbey six days later were the performances of a leader with very finely honed instincts of heart and intellect. He became, said a *Guardian* leader, 'more dominant than any Prime Minister since Margaret Thatcher following the recapture of Port Stanley' – the conclusion of the Falklands War. That was one of the more measured tributes he received from the press during that extraordinary week in early September 1997.[1] His approval rating soared to over 90 per cent, making him the most popular Prime Minister since records began. New Labour also appeared, in that highly wrought time, to personify the same kind of glamorous, touchy-feely but also vulnerable promise that Diana herself had offered.[2] Very few Prime Ministers enjoy a defining moment where they are seen to embody the spirit of the nation. Blair's decisions during that week are all the more remarkable for being unpremeditated and touching on areas that were largely new to him.

The First Hundred Days

Tony Blair set out deliberately after 1 May to 'hit the ground running'. He wanted some controversial measures executed quickly to satisfy the party faithful. Advice from the Democrats in the US to 'do everything that we did up to the election then do nothing that we did for two years after it' also weighed with him.[3] (The Democrats had gone wrong by reverting to type rather than remaining in the middle ground, hence Blair's desire to stress that 'we would govern as new Labour'.) At the back of his mind also was the advice he said his mother would have given him had she been alive: 'Remember it won't last, and somebody will come along after you, so make the most of it while you can.'[4] The requirement for the first seventy-two hours, when they were all recovering from the exhaustion of the election, was for clockwork efficiency, facilitated by Jonathan Powell's mapping-out of everything they had to do in Number 10, and an avoidance of dissent, helped by Blair's long-deliberated decisions to leave his 'big beasts' in their portfolios and abide by the tradition that the shadow Cabinet would make up the Cabinet. That got Blair through the first weekend and Bank Holiday Monday.

At the start of the first full week in power, he signalled his core determination to build a new relationship with the EU by dispatching Doug Henderson, Minister for Europe, to Brussels and signing up to the European Social Chapter. In the second week, the Queen's Speech saw education and law and order top the legislative programme, highlighting the work that Blunkett (Education) and Straw (Home Office) had put in to prepare for office. At the end of the second week, to signal his commitment to the peace process, Blair flew to Northern Ireland to an orchestrated statement of intent from Sinn Féin to work towards a new ceasefire. On 23 May, he spoke at his first EU summit at Noordwijk, lecturing his fellow leaders enthusiastically on the relevance of the 'third way' to European politics. At the end of the month, Blair's most valued foreign friend, President Bill Clinton, visited him in London and addressed ministers in the Cabinet Room, entrenching a relationship that was to be predominant in the first few years of his premiership. In his first month, Blair had thus deliberately highlighted what he wanted to be the key themes of the premiership: education, crime, Europe, Northern Ireland, and the primacy of the special relationship with the US.

More important by far for the government in its first month was the move with which he had been only tangentially involved: Brown's decision that the Bank of England would take over responsibility for setting interest rates, and that it would lose its regulatory powers over the City, to a new body, the Financial Services Agency. Blair was told by Robin Butler that there would be no time for a Cabinet meeting before the announcement on Bank of England independence. 'Does it matter?' Blair asked. He was told that a decision of that magnitude should be discussed with Cabinet. 'Oh, they won't mind. We'll ring round,' he replied breezily.[5] Thus was signalled at the outset another key theme of Blair's government, an impatience with the traditional methods of governing in favour of a personalised system which had worked well in Opposition since 1994 and which, it was believed, could be translated from Millbank to Whitehall.

June saw a slightly gentler pace. Powell's tight schedule lasted for the first thirty days, and, after it ran out, Blair had an opportunity to adjust to the fact that his landslide on 1 May had enhanced his opportunities as Prime Minister. In mid-June, Blair attended the EU Inter-governmental Conference in Amsterdam, where he was treated like a celebrity. This helped underline the fact that a new era in Britain's relations with Europe had begun, with Britain again having a powerful leader able to speak with the authority that comes with having a large majority in the House of Commons and a united party. Blair's agility when filmed riding a bicycle and his youthful and fit demeanour succeeded brilliantly in creating a fresh, purposeful image. One week later, his star status was projected on to an even bigger canvas when he flew by Concorde to the G7 meeting in Denver, calling in on New York on the way home to speak at the UN summit on the environment. Comparisons began to be made with the charismatic and handsome young President Kennedy, who was also forty-three when he took office. The announcement on 17 June to continue with the controversial Millennium Dome was significant as it demonstrated Blair's primacy over his Cabinet, as a majority were opposed,[6] and his boundless optimism that he could transform it into a commercial success that would define the age. A leader in the *Independent* commented harshly on Blair's first three months, that 'the one big decision directly attributable to the Prime Minister was presentational – the go-ahead for the Millennium Dome'.[7]

This judgement was made despite his taking some tough decisions, notably in July. On 9 July, Blair announced that he endorsed the ban on fox-hunting, the day before an estimated 100,000 pro-hunt campaigners converged on Hyde Park to protest against the anti fox-hunting bill. On the same day it was announced, to the fury of many in the PLP, that the government would not relent on cuts to lone-parent benefit. On 23 July he announced the establishment of the Joint Cabinet Committee with the Liberal Democrats, a move of constitutional and potentially political importance, disliked by most of his Cabinet; and the following day Blunkett announced the government's backing for student tuition fees, bringing to an end universal free access for all to higher education. Blair later said he found this the 'hardest' decision of his first three months. His 'other tough call', he said, was sending in SAS troops to intercept Bosnian war criminals, the first time in his life he took a decision that could have resulted in loss of life. 'I thought long and hard about that,' he told Sedgefield's local newspaper, the *Northern Echo*.[8] He rapidly developed a thick skin about taking such decisions.

July concluded with white papers outlining proposals for the Scottish Parliament and a Welsh Assembly, and the government announced plans to create a Greater London Authority with the innovation of a directly elected mayor and an assembly. Brown's July budget announced an extra £1.3 billion for schools and £1.2 billion for the NHS, his 'welfare to work' scheme and a cut to the public spending deficit. Again, Blair received the positive headlines he sought for his bold announcements.

Blair felt pleased with the first hundred days – the phrase originally referred to President Roosevelt's frenetic first hundred days in 1933 – which concluded on 9 August. There had been no significant hitches to distress him or to end his honeymoon period prematurely. Blair visibly relaxed as the weeks passed. He began to enjoy being the youngest Prime Minister since 1812. Cherie and the children had settled happily into the flat above Number 11, and the family followed Robin Butler's advice and acquired a people-carrier, a Ford Galaxy. As the novelty of living in Downing Street wore off, the family had to come to terms with the restrictions on their lives, but they all seemed to be adjusting well. Blair had established his own style of running Number 10, which was casual but smart. 'Call me Tony,' he famously said to his first Cabinet on 8 May. 'He was told that he ought to give ministers notice of issues under consideration,' said one senior official. 'But he took no notice. He made it clear from the outset that he had no particular time for agendas and briefs, but he wanted to use Cabinet to give his ministers a message.'[9] Instead of standing on ceremony, Blair wanted to be an open, friendly and accessible Prime Minister; many were charmed by it. The old left were not, and the unions regularly complained 'that New Labour isn't interested . . . any more'.[10] Blair was happy for them to complain because they were powerless to damage the government and their protests advertised how much he had changed the party. The first months had proved he could handle the job at home and abroad, and his lingering doubts about himself had disappeared; sceptics who had highlighted his being the first Prime Minister since Ramsay MacDonald in 1924 with no previous ministerial experience were silenced. He was pleased and surprised by the quality and impartiality of the officials at

Number 10, above all Alex Allan, the Principal Private Secretary and John Holmes, the Foreign Affairs Private Secretary, both of whom he inherited from John Major. Allan left in July but Holmes stayed on until February 1999, a man of seminal importance to Blair, inducting him into the ways of government, Northern Ireland and foreign policy.

While his standing remained generally very high, some irritating comments appeared in the press before the summer about his personal agenda. Before the election Blair had deflected criticism that it was vague and modest by retorting that 'the project' would only become fully clear when '[we] are in government and . . . doing things'.[11] He was now in office and had started 'doing things', but the overall coherence and direction of his 'project' still seemed unclear. What exactly, it was asked, did 'governing as New Labour' mean in practice? The *Economist* said that the most striking feature of Blair's first hundred days was that 'in some ways Britain's strongest government this century is acting as if that strength were an illusion – as if, indeed, this were a weak administration, not a powerful one'.[12]

Number 10's concern with presentation was commented on adversely from the very dawn of the government. One early example was the attempt to deflect attention from Robin Cook's marital difficulties by leaking a story about an MI6 investigation into Chris Patten, Governor of Hong Kong. The *Economist*'s suggestion that 'Campbell bad-mouthed those who dared to voice criticism, just as he did during the election campaign', was an early harbinger of what was to come.[13] The *Daily Mail* as well as some among 'old' Labour disapproved of Blair giving former Tory minister David Mellor responsibility for overseeing football, as they did his populist gestures such as inviting Noel Gallagher of Oasis to a reception in Number 10.[14] To moralists and traditionalists, such gestures were tacky, and reminiscent of Harold Wilson's courting of celebrities. Blair's populist gestures provoked differing reactions. His decision to campaign in the Uxbridge by-election on 31 July was seen by some as a positive and visible indication of a Prime Minister not hiding away in Number 10; but to others it seemed to be lacking in the dignity and detachment expected of a Prime Minister. His promised monthly 'talk to Tony' public meetings, and some publicised focus groups, were seen by some as heralding a new responsiveness by government to public concerns, but to others they appeared indecisive and indicating a government 'in a permanent election campaign'.[15] Concerns began to be expressed within Number 10 that presentation was taking precedence over policy, but, as we shall see in Chapter 29, these concerns went largely unheeded.

Blair was in good humour when he left with his family for a three-week holiday in the Midi-Pyrenees and then at Geoffrey Robinson's villa in San Gimignano in Tuscany. Here was his opportunity, after months of stress and many thousands of miles of travel, to relax and to take stock. As he would always do on summer holiday, he would think, plan his conference speech and make notes of all he wanted to achieve. Turbulence back in London – Cook's announcement of leaving his wife for his secretary, Gaynor Regan; Clare Short, International Development Secretary, saying after a volcano eruption in Montserrat that the local government would be demanding 'golden elephants next'; squabbling between Prescott, who was left in charge, and Mandelson, whom he compared to a crab – barely disturbed his summer idyll.

When the family returned to Britain towards the end of August, Blair was full of excitement about the enthusiastic way his arrival in May had been greeted on the world stage, and he was brimming with new ideas about how to capitalise on this (rather than on how to clarify and implement his domestic agenda, or the pressing issue of what to do on the Euro). He gave an interview to his press secretary manqué, Andy Grice, for the *Sunday Times* on 31 August in which he said he wanted to launch 'New Britain' on to the world stage, which would be the 'long-term goal of his premiership'. Warming to his grandiose theme, he said, 'I believe there is a new era of confidence in this country and about it abroad. People see Britain as the go-ahead country which has regained its confidence and stature.' He wanted to change the lingering perception that Britain was still too rooted in the past, and his task was to project Britain as a 'model for a twenty-first-century developed society'. There were echoes here of what his role model, Mrs Thatcher, had achieved for Britain's standing in the world in the 1980s. How exactly would he effect this transition? Blair had plans to use the British Presidency of the EU in the first half of 1998, its forthcoming chairmanship of the G7 and his planned visits to Russia, the United States and Germany to project this new image.[16] But the readers of the interview that Sunday morning had little opportunity to absorb the Panglossian vision he offered, because their attention was drawn, along with the rest of the nation, away from their newspapers to the radio and television.

In Touch With the Nation

The Blairs were spending a few days at Myrobella, their home in Sedgefield, at the end of August. When the phone rang at two in the morning, at first they did not hear it. Angus Lapsley, a Private Secretary from Number 10, had received news of a car accident in the Place de l'Alma underpass in Paris, where the Mercedes in which Princess Diana was travelling with her lover, Dodi Fayed, had crashed just before 12.30 a.m. It is always the task of the Private Secretary who is 'on duty' at Number 10 to decide whether or not the Prime Minister should be woken on any issue. Lapsley was in no doubt. When the Blairs did not answer their phone, he had to persuade the reluctant police protection officers who are on twenty-four-hour guard duty at Myrobella to go into the house and wake up the Prime Minister. Blair had been sleeping deeply, but immediately wanted to know how Diana was. Lapsley did not know details at this stage, but he believed that Diana was seriously injured and Fayed probably dead: 'As far as we know she is still alive but very badly hurt,' he said. Blair was shocked and upset and found it hard to comprehend the news.[17] Lapsley promised to keep him in touch with developments: he then spoke to Michael Jay, British ambassador in Paris, who by now had heard that at 4 a.m. (3 a.m. UK time) Diana had stopped breathing at La Pitié-Salpêtrière hospital.[18] Lapsley had the task of telling Blair the news, which he broke to a very shocked Prime Minister at 3.30 a.m.[19]

Blair got out of bed, went downstairs, made himself a mug of tea and paced around the study, thinking through what it all meant. His first conversations were with Cherie and Campbell. 'Fucking hell. What do we do with this?' Campbell is reported to have said. 'It is just too big. It's just too big a story.'[20] Blair saw at once that there would be an extraordinary public reaction to the news: 'This is going to produce real public grief on a scale that is hard to imagine.'[21] But should he say anything? Was it his place to say anything? If he did, what exactly should he say? The shock, the early hour – it was still not light – his detachment from the bloodstream of London in the stillness of his home, all combined to heighten his sense of unreality.[22] With dawn breaking, he began to sense that he should say something, a conviction only strengthened when he spoke to the Queen and was told that none of the royal family would be saying anything by way of praise.[23] Sure enough, from Buckingham Palace later that morning came just the bald statement registering the Queen's and Prince of Wales' deep shock, but no expression of regret nor tribute to her life and work. One of the tasks Blair found hardest was breaking the news to his own three children, who had met Diana and Prince William just weeks before, when they had come to Chequers.[24] Blair's most recent experience of Diana had thus been wholly positive. The Queen's, in contrast, had been wholly negative. To the revulsion she and the Duke of Edinburgh felt at Diana's attacks on Charles and the Palace and her disloyalty in the media, were added their revulsion at the most recent images, just days before, of Diana, semi-naked, cavorting in the Mediterranean with her 'playboy'.[25] Their feelings towards Diana, even in death, were very raw and bitter.

'Tony was absolutely shocked and shattered. He was deeply affected,' said John Burton, who arrived at Myrobella at about 9 a.m. 'Yet he was able to focus – that is one of his great strengths.'[26] By 10 a.m. the nation were glued to their televisions absorbing the most stunning and shocking news since President Kennedy's assassination in Dallas in November 1963: television and radio programming had been cleared to keep everyone abreast of developments. Shortly after 10 a.m. the channels all switched to a slightly dishevelled and obviously emotional Prime Minister arriving at St Mary Magdalene church in Trimdon. Phil Wilson, one of the Trimdon four, had been deputed to ensure Michael Brunson of ITN asked Blair just one precise question, 'On this sad day is there anything you would like to say, Prime Minister?'[27] Visibly moved, Blair turned to camera and said: 'I feel like everyone else in the country today, utterly devastated. Our thoughts and prayers are with Princess Diana's family – in particular her two sons, her two boys – our hearts go out to them. We are today a nation in shock, in mourning, a grief that is so painful . . . how many times shall we remember her in how many different ways, with the sick, the dying, with children, with the needy? With just a look or a gesture that spoke so much more than words, she would reveal to all of us the depth of her compassion and her humanity.' They were his words; for the finale he chose the words that resonated over the following week: 'She was the People's Princess and that is how she will stay, how she will remain in our hearts and our memories for ever.' The phrase 'People's Princess' was suggested by Campbell, though it had been used earlier to describe Diana by authors Julie Burchill and Anthony Holden. Blair's eulogy – simple, direct, honest – touched the nation as nothing else he has said as Prime Minister. It helped to set her death in context and give it a national significance. While the Blair family went on to Trimdon church, the Queen went to Crathie's parish church in Balmoral, where, as Rawnsley noted, the visiting preacher Adrian Varwell may have been the only preacher in the country that morning not to mention Diana's name. This lack of empathy, and the cool official statement from the Palace, were rapidly to become the subject of widespread adverse comment.

While Blair was still reeling, Campbell, always less sentimental, was seeing the media potential of the tragedy. The royals, whom (apart from Diana) he disliked, were badly misjudging the public mood because of their anger over Diana's behaviour. Very well. Tony Blair and New Labour, he decided, would fill the vacuum. The Queen, backed by the Spencer family, led by Diana's brother, Earl Spencer, argued that Diana should have a purely private family funeral.[28] Blair and Campbell disagreed. With the Queen at Buckingham Palace in the opposing camp, Blair fell back on Prince Charles, with whom he had established a good personal relationship dating back to 1990: indeed, Charles had developed such close links with New Labour that one tabloid ran a story entitled 'Charles joins Labour'.[29] Diana too had attracted support from across New Labour, with her championing of the underprivileged and her campaigning against landmines. Blair had seen in her a kindred spirit, and was keen to let her play the role she sought as 'roving ambassador'. When he became Prime Minister, Blair was very clear that he wanted to play an even hand between Charles and Diana.[30]

That groundwork now paid dividends. When they spoke later that day he found Charles was of a like mind regarding the huge impact of her death. Charles agreed that, to meet the public outpouring of grief, so evident from the immediate reaction already that Sunday, there needed to be a 'unique funeral for a unique person'. The Spencers' wish for a private service had thus to be overruled. Despite his differences with his estranged wife, Charles showed himself to be far more in tune with the national mood than the Queen, who was falling headlong into one of the greatest misjudgements of her reign. Charles also insisted, against the Queen's wishes, that he fly to Paris to accompany Diana's body back to England. Blair himself flew south from Sedgefield to be present at RAF Northolt, west of London, when the aircraft bearing Diana's coffin arrived back on English soil.

While waiting for the plane, Blair discussed the funeral arrangements in Northolt's VIP lounge with Lord Airlie, the Lord Chamberlain, the senior courtier charged with overseeing major royal occasions. Airlie said, to Blair's great relief, that the event would have to be 'a mixture of the traditional and the modern',[31] and announced, with masterly understatement, that it would be a 'very, very difficult funeral'. He explained to Blair, still new to such matters, that if the Queen or Queen Mother were to have died, the Palace would know exactly what to do because they had long had plans in place. Indeed, guest lists had been decided and were regularly updated; in the Queen Mother's case, the funeral procession was practised at least once a year in the early hours of the morning.[32] Plans for royal funerals are code-named after bridges –

Tower Bridge for the Queen Mother, London Bridge for the Queen. But, in those terms, Diana had no 'bridge'. This was virgin territory. No plans were in place for the death of one so young, to which was added the complications of her divorce from the Prince of Wales, her being stripped of the HRH title, preventing it being a royal funeral, and the tawdry stories about her various affairs, most recently with Dodi Fayed. Airlie asked Campbell, who was accompanying Blair, 'to come to the Palace tomorrow'.[33] Calls were made from the Palace that evening to the Dean of Westminster Abbey asking him to clear any bookings for the Abbey that Saturday. Blair and Campbell had made strong representations that the normal nine-day rule between royal death and funeral be shortened to six because of the disruption to the major devolution elections in Scotland and Wales to take place the following week.

Over the next few days regular planning meetings took place in the Chinese Room at Buckingham Palace. Blair was represented variously by Campbell, Anji Hunter and Hilary Coffman from the Number 10 press office. Tension was high at these meetings between the courtiers and the Number 10 team, who argued with increasing force the case for the Queen to leave Balmoral to come down to London, and for the flag to fly at half-mast above Buckingham Palace.[34] 'Number 10's feeling was that the most famous person in the world had died and the British Establishment was utterly at sea and that we had to come in to take control.'[35] Deep divisions were also evident between the royal representatives themselves. Three separate agendas became clear early on: Buckingham Palace's, which sought to protect the Queen and the monarchy as an institution; St James's Palace, whose task was to represent the interests of Prince Charles; and Kensington Palace, who sought to defend Diana's reputation.

Too much can be made of Number 10's influence during this week. Most important decisions on the funeral arrangements were taken by the royal officials themselves. 'Tony's whole aim that week,' said a close aide, 'was to mitigate the opprobrium towards the Queen and Prince Charles. He is very pro-royal and he was worried for them.' The imploring of Campbell in particular for the Queen to be seen to be empathising with the national mood of grief was significant. It helped nudge the Palace towards an obvious conclusion, not least because of the picture being painted by the press of the contrast between the young, in-touch head of government, and the old-fashioned, unfeeling head of state. Had the Queen not relented, and remained rigidly away from London, without any sign of recognition of Diana, untold damage would have been done to the monarchy. A crisis point came on the Wednesday, when Campbell tried again to budge Buckingham Palace on the symbolically important step of its flag being flown at half-mast. Blair shared his concerns with Charles that day that if the Queen were to come back to London from Balmoral without making any concessions, she might well be booed. Blair himself went out on to the street outside Number 10 and said, 'All our energies are now directed to trying to make this [the funeral] as tremendous a commemoration as possible . . . I know these are very strongly the feelings of the royal family as well.'

Blair's words, however, merely highlighted the stark contrast between his warm response to Diana in death and the Queen's cold formality. The following morning, Thursday, the press were the fiercest yet, calling on the Queen to respond sympathetically.[36] That morning, Robert Fellowes, her Private Secretary, phoned Number 10 to say that there had been a complete re-think on the Queen's position: she would now be leaving Scotland for London, the Union flag would fly at half-mast above Buckingham Palace, and there was a possibility, later confirmed, of the Queen making a special television broadcast. Campbell argued that it should be a live broadcast from Buckingham Palace, at 6 p.m. on Friday, to capture the most attention. When he saw a text of what she intended to say he inserted the humanising phrase 'speaking as a grandmother' to improve a wooden script.[37] The pressure from Number 10 had played its part. At the eleventh hour, the Queen had pulled the monarchy back from the brink. At the funeral the next morning at the Abbey, it was more the 'modern' than the 'traditional' elements that caught the nation's imagination, especially Earl Spencer's highly charged oration and Elton John's rendition of 'Candle in the Wind', rewritten not to commemorate Marilyn Monroe but another female icon. Blair had shown very clearly that he was the better judge of the national mood than the monarch, and to the Palace's chagrin the impression was clearly created and recycled that Number 10 had helped guide the Queen in her hour of need. It only served to enhance Blair's good name further.

After the funeral, the Queen and Buckingham Palace were left in a state of shock. This was less because of their resentment that Number 10 had helped them out; some were grateful that Blair and Campbell had intervened and offered good counsel, though some others suspected that Number 10 was either trying to take over the Palace or at least deliberately to upstage it. Blair was not in fact motivated by a desire to score points against a Queen of whom he was still in some awe: Campbell, a republican, and deeply suspicious of the Establishment, may have had different priorities. What traumatised the Palace far more

than any irritation at Number 10 was the realisation of how far public
opinion had turned against them. 'The shock at the Palace was realising
how much hostility there was and how they only just turned it round in
time,' said one insider.[38] Relations between Number 10 and some in the
Palace never fully recovered after Diana's death. They resented stories
comparing Blair's role in coaxing the Queen into modernising her role to
that of Disraeli, who encouraged a mourning Queen Victoria from
Osborne House on the Isle of Wight back on to the public stage.[39] On
the first anniversary of Diana's death, Simon Heffer spoke for this
patrician tendency in the Palace when he wrote of the distaste he felt at
seeing 'the Queen being ordered about by this lackey of her Prime
Minister' and at the institution of the monarchy being 'prostituted for
the political gain of the government'.[40] Poetic justice, as some saw it,
came when the Queen Mother died in April 2002 and the government
was accused of trying to muscle in on an event which, to the Palace's
delight, saw an outpouring of emotion no less exceptional for being more
understated than for Diana's death. But 'Tower Bridge' had been
planned by the Palace for many years.

This later turbulence did nothing to ruffle the extraordinary lift Blair
gained in the immediate aftermath of Diana's death. His ability to
combine strength with emotion (much more affecting when fairly
spontaneous in Trimdon churchyard than in his overly mannered reading
from Corinthians in the Abbey) struck many across all ages and parties
as deeply impressive. The contrast with the lamentable response of
William Hague, in his televised comments on the death from his
constituency in Yorkshire, was palpable. The whole experience boosted
not only Blair's self-confidence, but also that of Number 10. 'Diana's
death brought people in Number 10 together as nothing before had
done,' said one senior official. 'It showed Number 10 that it could run
events. My impression was that people became much bolder
afterwards, whereas before they would worry about doing everything by
convention.'[41] Blair's Number 10 in fact never worried unduly about
convention: what the 'Diana week' did was to affirm the already strong
conviction that they could write their own rule book.

Blair travelled to Brighton for his first party conference as Prime
Minister on an extraordinary personal high. His pre-eminence over the
political scene had been bolstered still further by 74.3 per cent voting in
favour of establishing a Scottish Parliament on 11 September and 50.3
per cent for a Welsh Assembly a week later. His conference speech on
30 September spoke about his aim for Britain to be nothing less than 'a
beacon to the world . . . we can never be the biggest and may never again

be the mightiest. But we can be the best.' He outlined his hope to lead 'one of the great, radical, reforming governments of our history'. His ambition was breathtaking: he promised to create a coalition of left-of-centre political forces to dominate the twenty-first century; to provide 'modernising leadership' in the EU; to re-found the welfare state; and to secure peace in Northern Ireland.[42] The driving force for this revolution would come from the real modernisers, 'the British people', who by nature are 'innovators, adventurers, pioneers'. His language was more Christian than socialist, in marked contrast to Brown the day before. Blair spoke of 'compassion', 'soul', 'duty' and 'love'. Martin Jacques was temporarily won back round, and wrote 'towering above everything – party and nation alike – is the figure of Tony Blair . . . New Labour was Blair's creation. It was he whom the people voted for in such numbers on 1 May.'[43]

Amid all the euphoria, Blair was aware that there were tough choices lying ahead. He had yet to announce what would happen on the Euro, on which a statement had to be made before the end of the year; in the absence of income tax increases, the cash for the NHS and education would have to be found from elsewhere, which would mean some tough decisions; several Cabinet ministers, disproportionately Brown's allies, were clearly not up to their jobs, and blood would have to be spilled; and the rejection of Mandelson in the NEC elections in favour of Livingstone showed that 'old' Labour still had life. The 1997 party conference nevertheless marked the point of Blair's greatest influence and power. That is why this period has been selected as a turning point. If Tony Blair had realised that he was never again to have so much authority, would he have done anything differently?

Alastair Campbell on the day before the 1997 General Election. For nine years he shaped New Labour's and Blair's image.

22

Alastair Campbell

Alastair Campbell, the man who had come improbably to the rescue of the monarchy, spent more 'face time' with Tony Blair from September 1994 until he resigned in September 2003 than any other man. For nine years Campbell watched Blair's back and oversaw his every move forwards. To Prescott's and Brown's chagrin, he was dubbed the 'real Deputy Prime Minister'. Campbell and Blair were not only professionally very close: they were also the warmest of friends, almost like brothers. Campbell filled some of the intense friendship role that Blair had so enjoyed with Brown until their personal relationship soured in 1994 – the very moment Campbell took up his post. Campbell's supporters praise his extraordinary capacity for hard work over those nine years, his fierce loyalty to Blair, his tenacious handling of an increasingly difficult media pack, his decisive mind and his charm. Philip Gould sums up how the Blair team regarded him: 'It was like a football team with five players in a particular position rather than just one.'[1]

His detractors see him variously as a yob and a bully, the destroyer of the traditional relationship between government and media, as the prime person who encouraged Blair to be fixated on short-term headlines rather than long-term issues, and spin over substance. They say that under his powerful tutelage, Blair became almost a journalist himself, whose governing obsession was not losing the support of Murdoch. Campbell's critics further allege that a personal vendetta against the BBC was the driving force behind the damaging row in the summer of 2003, which precipitated the death of the government scientist, Dr David Kelly, and threw the government massively off course. Campbell's diaries, when published, will powerfully shape the way the Blair premiership is seen in history in the same way that his work in Number 10 powerfully affected the premiership itself. The author of Campbell's entry in the sober *Dictionary of Labour Biography* describes him as 'arguably the most influential journalist that there has ever been in British politics'.[2] To assess Campbell's importance to Blair accurately is thus vital to understanding Blair himself.

Alastair Campbell: The Man

Born in May 1957 in Yorkshire, where his father was a vet, Campbell attended junior school and then spent a term at Bradford Grammar School (then direct grant, now independent) between the ages of eleven and twelve, before his family moved south to Leicester. He won a scholarship to Cambridge where he studied Medieval and Foreign Languages (French and German), finishing with a 2:1, but he did not enjoy Cambridge much, and felt at odds with what he saw as the pretensions of university life in the late 1970s. After leaving, he trained at the *Tavistock Times* in Devon in the early 1980s before joining the *Daily Mirror* as a reporter in 1982. After an unhappy period at Eddie Shah's *Sunday Today* from 1985 to 1986 he had a nervous breakdown. 'It was a bad time, and it ended up badly,' he later said.[3] 'What I discovered from all that was a sort of inner strength in myself and a political core that up until then I had been coy about.'[4] The experience culminated in him giving up drinking, and a return to the Mirror Group, finishing as the *Daily Mirror*'s political editor from 1989 until 1993, when he left to rejoin Richard Stott, who had been his editor at the *Mirror*, now at News International's *Today*.

The two principal influences in his life until he met Blair were Fiona Millar, from a staunch Labour family, who became his partner and mother of his three children, and Neil Kinnock, to whom he became close early on in Kinnock's period as leader and who proved an enduring friend. Fiona and Glenys Kinnock are also close. The relationship with the Kinnocks, and the inside track it gave him, was critical in his rapid rise as a journalist. Nothing beats inside knowledge in journalism, and Campbell had it from the very fount. Critics have highlighted Campbell's weakness for powerful men: Robert Maxwell (who accepted him back at the *Mirror* in 1986), then Kinnock, then Blair. Campbell was certainly attracted to power and was intensely ambitious. He has also been fiercely loyal and protective to his three mentors, famously hitting fellow journalist Michael White when he made light of Maxwell's death in November 1991.

Like Blair, Campbell was raised in a comfortable, right-of-centre middle-class family, and remained inactive politically until after university.

Like Blair, he also found a partner for life who was exceptionally determined, at least his intellectual equal and more political at the time than he was. Fiona's father, Bob Millar, was a much-loved Glaswegian and journalist, latterly on the *Daily Express*, from whom Campbell learned much about politics and people: 'A lifelong socialist and political to his dying breath' was how Campbell described him on his death in June 1994.[5] Alastair and Fiona became a very tight-knit couple, possessing a strong moral streak, and a particular dislike of privilege, especially in education. They also harboured a hatred of most Tories, whom Campbell considered elite, arrogant and imbued with the belief that they had a divine right to rule.[6] As Joe Haines, one of Campbell's patrons at the *Mirror*, and earlier press secretary to Harold Wilson, said: 'Fiona would not want to be seen to be stronger than Alastair, but there's a greater clarity of mind. Alastair is not a deep political thinker. His gifts are elsewhere, as a networker, an operator, a tactician. She is more than that and she is also more of a socialist.'[7] But Alastair is the more driven, obsessive figure. He is also physically very strong, as seen in his running the London Marathon in 2003 in an impressively quick time. He needed all his physical strength to keep going for nine years with Blair. Ruggedly good-looking, he was also given to uttering profanities, as the world learned during the Hutton evidence in the summer of 2003. He is a man's man, with some of the same iconoclasm that had appealed to Blair in his school friend Nick Ryden.

Campbell and Blair

Campbell's relationship with Blair has gone through four phases. The first lasted from the mid-1980s until Smith's death in 1994. Campbell first met Blair in the Members' lobby of the House of Commons shortly after he had first been elected, and found him 'open, funny, engaging . . . and absolutely sure what Labour should be about'.[8] They saw each other socially, and Campbell was also impressed by Blair's mind: 'He was one of the politicians I would go to for insights into politics,' he later said. When, in 1987, Campbell became political editor at the *Sunday Mirror*, he had a direct line to Labour's energetic Director of Communications, Peter Mandelson. 'It was a necessity for *Mirror* political staff to get close to senior Labour figures, and vice-versa,' said Richard Stott. 'The *Mirror* papers were the only titles steadfastly for Labour, so Alastair became friendly with Peter and found they thought very similarly.'[9] Campbell, influenced heavily by Kinnock, knew who he wanted to identify with, and it was definitely not the traditionalists like Hattersley, Smith and Prescott.[10] In the late 1980s, with Fiona, he began to write a series of portraits in the *Sunday Mirror* – in a style described as a blend of *Hello!* magazine with the *Soviet Weekly* under Stalin – of the figures he most admired in the party.[11] The first columns were, tellingly, about Kinnock, Brown, Blair and Mandelson. Brown, to whom Campbell was particularly close at this time, he imagined as the future Prime Minister, 'with Blair a very likely Chancellor'.[12] As Blair moved up the Opposition ladder, he increasingly sought out Campbell for advice. When shadow Employment Secretary, Campbell was one of the voices he wanted to hear on how to handle the trade unions.[13]

Campbell's importance increased markedly when in 1989 he became political editor of the *Daily Mirror*. In October 1990, he wrote 'Labour's young guns took the party conference by storm yesterday,' referring to Brown, Blair and Straw. 'Their speeches showed off the emerging A-team of young shadow ministers Labour leader, Neil Kinnock, hopes to present as an exciting alternative to the current Tory Cabinet.'[14] When Mandelson left as Director of Communications, Campbell's name was mentioned enthusiastically by some of Kinnock's aides as a possible replacement. Kinnock, however, was not keen: 'We didn't have enough papers with fully supportive journalists or political editors on them,' he explained, 'and we couldn't afford the luxury of losing Alastair from the *Daily Mirror*.'[15] But Campbell was losing his appetite for political journalism, and wanted to be on the inside track himself. He readily acknowledged that by the late 1980s his interest had moved away from trying to write objective journalism. 'Tony Bevins [the political journalist and a close friend] once described me as a brilliant propagandist and I don't deny it,' Campbell said. 'I have much more time for frankly biased journalism than for people who just pretend they are reporting objectively.'[16]

Had Kinnock won the election in 1992, he would have appointed Campbell his press secretary at Number 10.[17] With Kinnock's fall from power, Campbell was one of several whose star faded under Smith. 'He started attaching himself increasingly to Tony Blair, and they became very friendly together,' said Haines.[18] Tim Allan described the Campbell–Blair relationship in 1992–94 as 'more friendly than just journalist and politician, and Alastair was clearly totally committed to the modernising project'.[19] After 1992, Campbell and Brown began to drift apart, particularly when Whelan started as the latter's press adviser: they were to fall out very badly. With Mandelson also still very close to him at the time, Brown had little need of Campbell. On holiday in Majorca in the summer of 1993, Campbell sided with Gould in backing Blair above Brown as the next leader, and tried to wean Mandelson off promoting Brown.[20] Campbell and Millar had both concluded that Brown was too idiosyncratic to ever become a successful leader.[21]

Campbell's association with the modernisers notwithstanding, John Smith realised that the political editor of the *Daily Mirror* was far too important a figure to be kept at a distance. Smith's biographer said, 'John talked to Alastair and developed great respect for him. I once heard him, albeit jokingly, describe Alastair as a future Lord Campbell. But Alastair was never as impressed with John as John was with Alastair.'[22] Indeed, Campbell shared Blair's criticism of Smith's 'one more heave' approach and became highly critical of the leadership at this time.

When Smith died, Campbell's response was electric. 'He still remembers the place where he was driving on 12 May when he heard the news . . . He says he knew then . . . that Tony Blair would be leader. He also knew that he would work for Tony Blair.'[23] He was one of the first to back Blair in public, on *Newsnight* on 12 May. Campbell then worked tirelessly for his election. Routledge, Brown's biographer, claims that Campbell was 'briefing heavily and continuously against Brown',[24] although this is vigorously contested by those close to Campbell, who insist that everything he did during the campaign was done openly rather than from the shadows.[25] It is a puzzle, as Peter Oborne, Campbell's unofficial biographer notes, that Brown never developed the resentment towards Campbell that he did towards Mandelson. The answer is that Brown never regarded Campbell as one of his closest political friends, so there was no similar sense of personal betrayal. Campbell had never told Brown that he would support him when the moment came. There was also a respect for Campbell from the Brown camp, whose mainstream Labour views they found far more congenial than Blair's.

The second phase of the Campbell–Blair relationship, from September 1994 to May 1997, was Campbell's most creative and important to Blair and to the Labour Party. Campbell was not Blair's first choice as press secretary. There was some nervousness about how the *Mirror* would take it, with relations still raw after his departure on bad terms in 1993. Mandelson also was unhappy at the prospect of such a powerful figure coming into an area he regarded as his own domain, and persuaded Blair first to approach Andy Grice of the *Sunday Times*, to whom he was close.[26] Grice, however, declined, 'Partly because of the effect on my family, but also because I am a journalist, not a propagandist.'[27] Another possibility was Phil Bassett, then industrial editor on *The Times*, who had strong contacts with John Edmonds and other union leaders,[28] who later joined Number 10 in a different guise. One person Blair knew he did not want was David Hill, whom he regarded as suspect for being too close to Hattersley and the Smith camp.[29]

Blair hedged his bets because he was uncertain whether Campbell, very clearly the front-runner, and widely acknowledged to be Labour's best propagandist, would accept. Blair spoke to him in July before they both went off for their summer holidays, aware that Campbell admired 'his reckless determination to move ahead'. Blair spoke to Campbell in excited terms about his plans for Clause IV and on rethinking Labour's entire media strategy.[30] Despite Campbell's flash of insight on 12 May, he had yet to be fully convinced. The Blairs stopped over in August at the house where Campbell and Millar were staying at Flassan in Provence, en route to Italy.[31] 'Fiona was basically hostile, she felt it was too much. Neil [Kinnock] was totally hostile . . . saying it will completely ruin your life. It will ruin your family's life. It will ruin your health.'[32] Other factors weighed too, the drop in salary, the ending of his career on breakfast television just as it was taking off, his daughter Gracie being just one, the media raking over details of his private life: they would never have any privacy again. On the other hand, his job was not going anywhere on *Today* (it folded in 1995) and he could not go back to the *Mirror*, with chief executive David Montgomery, his reason for leaving, still there. Kinnock had dangled the enticement – not so appealing to the moderately Eurosceptic Campbell – of joining him in his Commissioner's office in Brussels.[33] 'What persuaded Alastair to work for Tony in the end,' said Kinnock, 'was his exasperation with the media and his desire to do something about it.'[34] The other key factor was being able to take the Tories apart and see Labour elected.

So Campbell accepted the job of Press Spokesman, announced in September 1994 at the TUC conference in Blackpool. From the very outset, he was determined to get the media exactly where he wanted them. The degrading treatment Kinnock received at their hands was an utterly formative experience for him, not only up to the election in 1997 but all the way through until he left in 2003. This sense of injury combined to devastating effect with his natural pugnacity and desire to get the better of the Establishment, in his case in the form of the powerful media corporations and their outlets in the press and broadcasting. 'The press,' he said 'were complete bastards to [Kinnock]. [But] I hold the view that, however bad the press is, you have to work at it all the time.'[35] From the minute he took up the job in 1994, he made it clear to the media and the party that he alone was managing Blair, and that absolutely no one would have access to him without his permission.[36] Campbell is nothing if not single-minded. His impact was immediate and resonated everywhere.

Campbell was important in this opposition period for three reasons: he moulded Blair, he remoulded the party's media operation and he built an entirely new understanding between the Labour Party and the press. In his relationship with Blair, he was the junior in rank, obviously, and also in age, by four years. Yet in some respects he began immediately to act as Blair's senior. In September 1994, Blair was still naïve in his outlook. Campbell taught him to be more savvy and street-wise, and to be crisper and more decisive. Campbell watched him like a hawk, all the time. Unlike Blair, he knew how low and underhand the press could be, and he knew the very worst it could do and say. Campbell took Blair down to their level and opened his eyes to very different sides of life and to less generous interpretations of people's motives. Campbell taught him to be guarded and careful in all he said. He saw traps where there were hidden traps and where there were no traps; but vigilance at all times was the lesson Blair absorbed. Michael Brunson of ITN talked of a lunch with both men in late 1994, and he noticed, as did everyone else they encountered, how 'Blair was visually and verbally checked over by Campbell constantly. It was clear that through eye-contact Blair was deferring to Campbell's instructions and guidance.'[37] Paddy Ashdown, who had not spoken at length to Blair since the autumn of 1994, wrote in his diary for May 1995 that he was 'especially struck that Blair is suddenly using rather cruder language than I remember from him before, with quite a few "bollocks" thrown in. All part of a leader becoming a leader,' he supposed.[38] Perhaps. But it was also the Campbell effect.

Campbell remoulded Labour's media operation. He was responsible for the 'New Labour' slogan appearing at the 1994 party conference.[39] His first major spinning operation was after Blair's speech foreshadowing the change to Clause IV, and his first major act of persuasion was the crucial step of helping Blair bring Prescott on side.[40] When briefing for Blair's speech at the conference he realised he was facing two other rival briefing operations. There was David Hill, Labour's chief media spokesman, whom Campbell swiftly fixed, making the party's media operation subservient to the leader's office. And there was Mandelson. Inevitably, and as Mandelson had already sensed, there would be a clash over territory. When *The Times* suggested that Mandelson had written part of Blair's 1994 conference speech, Campbell exploded, and vented his anger in one of his last columns for *Today*. 'Having been a close friend of his since the days before cufflinks,' he began, before going on to belittle Mandelson's writing skills, saying that when Mandelson had contributed a regular newspaper column 'he had to look to his friends to help him out. Know what I mean?'[41] It was vulgar, but it warned Mandelson, still clearly the senior of the two in

Blair's eyes, that Campbell would play hardball. Both men had complementary skills, which is why Blair worked so assiduously to keep the peace. Mandelson was the better strategist, more feline, and better on the big picture; Campbell was better on day-to-day matters, with demonstrably better people skills. He had worked in the lobby and he knew and understood it in a way Mandelson never could. Campbell was better at the tabloid end of the media, and better at handling individual journalists, and understanding what they needed. That was why at this stage, for all his strong-arm tactics and brusqueness, so many admired him.

Not all did. The risk of the high-profile role he carved out as Blair's minder, of course, was that he would arouse unfavourable comment. As early as January 1995, the *Daily Mail* wrote that he 'has hardly missed an opportunity to raise his personal profile. [He] has often outshone shadow ministers with outspoken performances on both radio and TV.'[42] Although he enjoyed aspects of his TV profile, particularly the power it gave him to move people and events forward, such comments caused him resentment with Blair's political colleagues and it was decided that it would be wise to phase out his TV appearances. He worried away obsessively at putting Labour's message across more effectively and belittling his hated Tories. Campbell made a particular project of undermining Major, whom he despised. 'Spoiling' stories would thus be put out to upstage Major's trips. The acme of his success humiliating Major was thought to be the tip-off about the Prime Minister's sartorial habits he gave Steve Bell, cartoonist at the *Guardian*, which resulted in his portrayal of Major wearing his Y-front pants outside his trousers. (Bell insists that Campbell was not his source, although it was the kind of ploy people associated with him.) Underhand? 'Fair game,' he would say, with Blair occasionally raising his eyebrows.

When Millbank was set up in January 1996, and when the money began to flood in to the party, Campbell was at last able to build what he wanted: the most modern, the most combative, and the best resourced operation any political party had seen in Britain. The work flowered fully in the General Election, during which Campbell's skill at managing the media to ensure favourable stories for Blair was at its height. Never again would Labour allow itself to be pushed around by the media as it had been under Kinnock. There was now a level playing field.

Campbell's final achievement in Opposition was reversing Labour's traditional antipathy to dealing with Tory-supporting newspapers. To the surprise of many, he proved he could be as effective with the broadsheets as with the tabloids, though his particular forte remained in handling the *Sun, News of the World*, and the *Mirror*, as well as Sky, the BBC and ITN. He was happy to let Anji Hunter deal with the smarter end of the press, and with proprietors and editors. Hunter would arrange for senior journalists such as Andrew Marr, Peter Riddell and Michael White to come in to see Blair, but Campbell would always arrange the big interviews and release of stories. Hunter would also liaise with News International and other media groups. She was the queen smooth-talker, with a charm and silver tongue that Campbell would never claim he possessed.

Campbell's relationship with Blair was not always easy. In this period, the most serious division came over the choice of schooling by the Blairs and by Harriet Harman, which made him so angry he was on the verge of resignation.[43] There were other bleak moments and he would phone his old friend Philip Gould, to whom he had spoken before he took the job, for reassurance that Labour really was going to win:[44] that prize alone justified all the downsides of the job. As the election approached, Campbell began to think about how he would run the media operation once in power, and held lengthy conversations with former press secretaries at Number 10, including Joe Haines, and also with Gus O'Donnell and Christopher Meyer, who served Major. He thought of speaking to Bernard Ingham, Thatcher's press secretary, but decided he was too *parti pris*.[45] As Ingham became increasingly vitriolic, Campbell, who had an admiration for his work at Number 10, found it difficult to take him seriously.[46]

With success at the election in 1997 came a new phase in the Blair–Campbell relationship. Campbell now had three main roles. The first was his official capacity as Chief Press Secretary, briefing the lobby journalists twice a day and co-ordinating the work of the press officers across the Whitehall departments. To strengthen his power, a special 'Order in Council' was approved by the Privy Council to give Campbell (and Powell) the authority to issue instructions to civil servants; a controversial move, it was not claimed by Campbell's successor, David Hill. While still in Opposition Campbell had formed a poor opinion of the Government Information Service (GIS) and felt he had run rings around it while Major was still Prime Minister. His first weeks in office after 1 May confirmed his worst fears about its quality.[47] In particular, he thought the GIS was insufficiently active in anticipating the demands of a twenty-four-hour news media, it was slow in correcting 'errors' in circulation, it failed to harmonise policy with the effective presentation of that policy, and it failed to prioritise information, so the seminal could be swamped by the merely routine.[48] At an early meeting with information officers, Campbell declared that he wanted them to be able to predict what would be on the front page of the *Sun* the next day and to help write it.[49] In September 1997, he wrote to all Whitehall departments saying Labour's election had provided 'a real opportunity for the GIS to raise the game'. What he was saying in private was that it was 'crap', in much the same way that Walworth Road in 1994 was 'crap', because it simply was not sufficiently sharp, hungry or single-minded.[50]

To address Campbell's concerns, an inquiry was set up under Robin Mountfield, which resulted, among other changes, in the creation in January 1998 of the Strategic Communications Unit (SCU), accountable directly to Blair and Campbell, bringing in as special advisers two journalists with strong Labour sympathies: Phil Bassett from *The Times* and David Bradshaw from the *Daily Mirror*. The SCU aimed to replicate Millbank's communications regime at the heart of government, with an emphasis on 'key messages' across all government departments and a co-ordinated approach to the wide range of media outlets. Wednesday lunchtime saw a meeting in Number 10 when a 'grid' was agreed for the phased timing of all government announcements, which then went up to Cabinet on Thursday.[51]

Campbell was mostly pleased by the changes he had wrought but the media focus on him personally was causing him, and increasingly Blair, concerns. Campbell's appearance on the BBC's *Any Questions* was judged a mistake. Romula Christopherson, who left her post in 1999, one of many who lost their jobs as part of the 'great purge' of senior GIS figures in 1997–99, dubbed Campbell the 'monarch of all he surveys'. She wrote that Blair 'turns to him on policy as much as presentation. He is more at the centre of the "big picture" than anyone else in the Cabinet.'[52] In September 1998, Blair had told Paddy Ashdown that he feared his government was now 'suffering more from "spin doctoring" than benefiting from it'.[53] Blair's worries about the damage being done to the government's standing and integrity by the frequent stories about New Labour's reliance on spin and 'control freakery' continued to grow. The birth of his son Leo on 20 May 2000 gave him time while on paternity leave to reflect, and he returned to work intent on renewing his connection with the electorate in a more 'wholesome' and un-spun way.

'I think we in government – and that means me – have to trust people more. We don't need to fight over every headline,' Blair told the Women's Institute on 7 June 2000. His audience, however, felt they were being treated as a party political audience and his speech was heckled. The cameras homed in on a man at sea as his genuinely heartfelt comments were thrown back in his face. In the press, the spin-doctors took the blame: 'A cynically stage-managed event inspired by the belief that spin can conquer all,' thundered the *Daily Mail*.[54] 'All a bit ironic,' Campbell's political deputy Lance Price recorded in his diary, 'as AC [Campbell] was at the forefront of those telling [Blair] the speech was crap.'[55] Worse followed on Sunday, when the second of Philip Gould's leaked memos appeared in the *Sunday Times*, which spoke of a perception of Blair lacking conviction and being 'all spin and presentation'.[56] Campbell's own role was highlighted in a BBC film by Michael Cockerell, *News from No. 10*, broadcast in July 2000, to which Campbell assented ironically in an effort to demystify his role – 'I wanted someone to come in and take a look at what I actually do,' he told Bill Hagerty in an interview in *The Times*,[57] but the idea backfired by focusing attention even more heavily on him, as even Campbell later realised. Rory Bremner, the television impressionist, parodied his relationship with Blair mercilessly.[58] 'If you turned the sound down,' it was alleged, 'you couldn't tell which was the Prime Minister and which the Press Secretary.'[59] Books by the BBC's Nicholas Jones and Peter Oborne, and radio and television programmes all pointed the finger at him for 'spin', and excessively heavy-handed management of the media.

Campbell decided himself the time had come to rethink his role. His twice-daily briefings had attracted particular criticism from lobby journalists, mainly for the blunt way in which he would conduct them.[60] Blair himself had concluded that Campbell was spending too much energy fighting day-to-day battles with the press and that he should spend more time working on longer-term strategy.[61] In July 2000, Campbell duly announced that the lobby briefing (which, following Mountfield, were on the record) would in future be mostly given by a career civil servant, Godric Smith: his own briefings were cut to around two a week, rising to about three that autumn. The change did not, however, greatly alter the perception that he was the behind-the-scenes puppet master. Nor did it free up much more time for Campbell to focus on longer-term strategy.[62] Campbell himself felt that he was being punished for the fairly brutal first two years at Number 10, and that his role and importance were being trivialised. Neutral officials at Number 10 held him in high regard, however: 'I always felt that the Press Office under him was the most successful part of Number 10,' said one of them about this period.[63]

Relinquishing the lobby briefings did not alter his second role, adviser to Tony Blair. On a range of issues in the 1997–2001 period – the response to Diana's death, the Good Friday agreement, the war in Kosovo, the fuel protest of 2000 and foot and mouth crisis of 2001 – he was at Blair's side, counselling and guiding him on how best he should respond.[64] Policy and the presentation of that policy, Campbell always argued, were inextricable: 'Everything has a communication angle,' he would say.[65] He had the right to attend almost all meetings at Number 10, Cabinet, Cabinet Committees, Blair's meetings with individual ministers. 'He would walk into the middle of something, sit down, listen, then walk out,' said one official.[66] 'We were all scared in Number 10 before he arrived,' said another. 'We were worried he'd think we were all Tories. But in fact Number 10 quickly came to respect his judgement. He was always very straight in his advice to Blair – accurate and bold. He had no agenda of his own separate from the Prime Minister's that I saw.'[67] At morning meetings in Blair's office, the 'den', Campbell would talk the most after Blair. His is a domineering presence. Whoever else was in the room, it would be Campbell's voice and opinion people would most fear, and want to hear. His interventions, yet another civil servant said, were 'ruthless, brutal, cutting through argument. In a way, he was the "grown-up" of that group.'[68]

Appointments were another area where he had influence in his 'adviser' role. Campbell had very sharp and clear judgements on the kind of people he rated. 'Competence, speed, confidence, accuracy, communication skills, getting the decision right,' were what one official said Campbell valued.[69] One of the few Tories he respected was Alan Clark, because he was so forthright; another was the streetwise David Davis. Prescott, Beckett, John Reid, George Robertson and Jack Cunningham, along with ex-Kinnockites Clarke and Hewitt, were all ministers he admired. Chris Smith, on the other hand, he considered ineffective.[70] Campbell was always heavily involved with dismissals – as with Mandelson, Geoffrey Robinson, Ron Davies, and also with the fall-out from Cook's separation from his wife, Margaret.[71] Obviously Campbell's opinions, freely expressed, would have affected Blair's own, though his evaluation of people, he would say, was made on the basis of how well or badly they served Blair and Labour. When Campbell told Irvine to stop talking to the press, when he was brutal with Frank Field, when he spoke bluntly to Robin Cook as his marriage disintegrated, it was assumed he was speaking with his master's voice. In fact, his views rarely differed from Blair's. His highly critical view of Whelan, who was eventually sacked in January 1998 after ceaseless implorings from Campbell, reflected Blair's own opinion.

Campbell's gift for words, as a drafter of speeches and articles, was another facet of his adviser role. The suggestion of the phrase 'the People's Princess' after Diana's death was his (although the words had already been used elsewhere). He helped draft Blair's conference and other big set-piece speeches. He worked closely with speech-writing team Miliband, Hyman, Bassett, McFadden and David Bradshaw and was especially valued for highlighting passages that would be newsworthy.[72] Chameleon-like, Campbell could write what Blair would have written sometimes better and certainly quicker than Blair himself. Journalists would note how words and phrases that Campbell uttered in the Wednesday lobby meeting would often be repeated verbatim by Blair at Prime Minister's Questions that afternoon.

Campbell's dislike of Chris Smith had nothing to do with Smith being gay, although he was prone to make throwaway anti-gay (but never racist) remarks.[73] He shared the same sense of humour as Blair: very dry and disparaging, often self-disparaging. The third facet of their relationship then is the extraordinary personal closeness that the two men had built up over many years, but which only consolidated fully when they entered Number 10. 'Campbell was the closest Blair had in Number 10 to having a "buddy",' said one insider. 'They were like two undergraduates. They would sit together for an hour or more, drink tea, and just "chew the cud".'[74] Campbell uniquely was capable of putting Blair at ease. 'He would take Blair out of himself,' said another.[75] On trips abroad, Blair would usually share his car with an official or minister to brief him, but 'when he was tired or wanted to switch off,' said Helen Liddell, 'he would always share a car with Alastair. Alastair enabled Tony to relax and unwind.'[76] Campbell would be merciless in making fun of Blair, on high or mundane issues. When Blair met Paul McCartney, or when Cliff Richard visited Number 10, Blair would, in an almost childlike way, be star-struck. It would be Campbell who had to prick the bubble.[77]

Campbell's obvious empathy with Blair was a source of envy from others, who felt excluded from the relationship. Mandelson was an obvious loser, both as a media authority and as a source of personal friendship. Campbell's decisive role in Mandelson's second dismissal in January 2001 was the most severe blow to their relationship. Campbell viewed Mandelson as a figure of major importance, in particular for the work he had done for the party under Kinnock, but his patience wore thin as the crises and status-seeking mounted over the years. 'The Secretary of State for Smugness,' said Campbell as he watched Mandelson walk down Whitehall following his first promotion to Cabinet. While neither Campbell nor Mandelson have much in common personally, they both appealed to a different part of Blair's character: with Campbell it was the male laddishness and the grit, with Mandelson it was the more cerebral and sensitive side of his nature. Campbell was one of the very few who would tell Blair difficult truths: 'I remember Anji Hunter saying, "Why do you have to undermine him like that?"' Campbell recalled. 'I'd say I don't like everyone saying we're perfect when we're not.'[78]

For all the bonhomie, and the sense of being on the very inside track of a historic period for the Labour Party, by 2000 the work and the hours were beginning to tell on Campbell. He had been working non-stop since

1994 and there were occasions when he would boil over with the stress of the job. Fiona, who had joined Number 10 as a special adviser in the press office, had moved across to advise Cherie. But she too wanted him to give up, and they both wanted to see more of their three children.[79] Campbell also realised that, even after his re-designated role, he no longer carried the authority he once did. So he decided he would leave at the election in 2001. Blair froze when Campbell told him, and he asked Richard Wilson to see what he could do to dissuade him. Blair was adamant that he still needed him by his side. Following discussions in February and March 2001, Campbell relented, and it was decided that he would have a new role as 'Director of Communications and Strategy' with an increased salary, that a new structure would be instituted with Godric Smith and Tom Kelly becoming joint spokesmen, and that various proposals would be put in place to allow him more time away from work.[80]

The fourth phase of the Campbell–Blair relationship began after the election in 2001. His last two years until his departure in the early autumn of 2003 were the least happy of all his nine years with Blair: 'He would say endlessly that he wanted to leave,' recalled a close adviser, 'but everyone in Number 10 wanted him to stay on.' The last two years were also Campbell's least successful. Several factors explain why this is the case.

The first problem was that Campbell never properly mastered the new job, whose specifics were always somewhat vague. A long period away after the 2001 election might have refreshed Campbell and given him the space to think through his ideas as director of strategy. But there was no time, and as soon as the election was over, Campbell was sucked back into the daily treadmill at Number 10. Strategic direction was what the second term singularly lacked. Campbell had shown his flair and interest in strategy from the earliest days of Blair's premiership, but trying to give Blair's mission by 2001 strategic clarity was going to require much more than giving Campbell a new title, and there is little evidence that anyone in Number 10 fully took on board the challenge of importing a new strategy from 2001 onwards to invest his leadership with the momentum they so obviously had after 1994. Campbell's skills at communicating, however, remained undiminished. Stothard's book *Thirty Days* reveals clearly Campbell's central role advising on communications before and during the Iraq war. A memo to the Hutton inquiry revealed that Blair's words about seeing the smiling faces of Iraqi children on his first post-war visit were scripted by Campbell.

What knocked the government off any kind of strategy more than anything was 9/11. The attack on the United States, and the ensuing wars in Afghanistan and Iraq, put an almost intolerable strain, physical, mental and emotional, on Campbell, as it did on Blair. It ground down two exceptionally fit, middle-aged men. Six days before the Gulf war began, Stothard recorded: '[Campbell] is the man to whom Tony Blair still speaks the most. It is when the two are alone together that the Prime Minister's face is most the face of a friend at a party, an actor offstage, a person who is not Prime Minister. [Campbell] is the one who dares speak most fiercely and directly to Tony Blair. He speaks directly too about himself, more than he has before; more about his mental and physical preparation for the marathon, more about his past mental and physical collapse.'[81] Campbell had endured considerably less stress than Blair since 1994, but he also had allowed himself fewer breaks. He became extremely scratchy in his last few months, and questions were increasingly asked about whether he had lost his touch, as over Blair's New Year message for 2003, criticised by some senior ministers for its overly pessimistic tone.

The press, which he had brought into line so skilfully for 1997, and held more or less on side for some time afterwards, became increasingly difficult to manage. The *Daily Mail* reverted to being the traditional enemy, with the Ecclestone affair and Blair's 'forces of conservatism' speech in September 1999 key turning points,[82] even more worryingly, they moved closer to Brown.[83] The *Mirror* supported Labour in 2001 but it had become increasingly resentful of being taken for granted, and the special favours it saw being showered on its tabloid rival, the *Sun*, notably the story of the apology by the Japanese Emperor over treatment of prisoners of war in the Second World War, and the General Election being postponed because of foot and mouth.[84] After 2001, the *Mirror* became very anti-Blair, though not anti-Labour, especially over the wars in Afghanistan and Iraq, when editor Piers Morgan developed a particular animus towards him, fully vented also by Brown's biographer and supporter, Paul Routledge, its high-profile columnist. The *Guardian*, guided by free spirits like Alan Rusbridger, Hugo Young (until his death in 2003) and Michael White, remained more 'critical' than 'friend', and resented the attitude within Number 10 that somehow it had a 'duty' to be supportive of a Labour government.

Not every paper abandoned Blair. The two main papers Campbell could still rely on were the principal News International titles, *The Times*, which remained supportive after Robert Thomson succeeded Stothard as editor in 2002, and the *Sun*, where the quite extraordinarily pro-Blair David Yelland succeeded the more sceptical Higgins, a line that looked likely to remain in place when Rebekah Wade succeeded Yelland in 2003. Campbell lost much of his relish, though, for the flattery that went with this facet of the job. What little respect he had for the professionalism of his old trade declined even more in Blair's second government, and he grew tired, even though removed from the fray of the lobby, of press stories about him. Increasingly, it was claimed that he showed favour to selected journalists like Roy Greenslade (*Guardian*) and Philip Webster and Tom Baldwin (both of *The Times*) and broadcasters Andrew Marr (BBC), Nick Robinson (ITV), Elinor Goodman (Channel 4) and Adam Boulton (Sky). Campbell's defenders assert that he had little choice. The rest of the media were 'absolutely appalling' said one Campbell ally. 'They would just make up so many things that we had to treat them as if they were bastards.'[85] Despite Campbell's removal from daily briefings with the press, the stories about spin and manipulation still did not let up. 'He became utterly sick of the daily diet of lies from the media,' one close aide said.[86]

Nothing did more damage to the image Campbell had tried to create of a less spun, more open Labour government than Jo Moore, special adviser at the DTI, saying 9/11 was a 'good day to bury bad news'. The inept handling of the episode, which struck middle England as grossly offensive, served to perpetuate 'the image of spin as a constantly corrosive story'. 'Nothing has done the public character of the government and its leader more harm,' wrote Andrew Rawnsley. 'The collapse of public trust bleeds across to everything else.'[87] By 2001, Roy Jenkins was arguing that Campbell had become an 'overmighty and highly dangerous figure, whom it was essential for Blair to dispense with'.[88]

While Campbell was finding the job less rewarding after 2001, Fiona Millar too was becoming disenchanted. She only reluctantly agreed to continue after 2001 because of Cherie's pleas to her not to go. For her, the episode that became known as 'Cheriegate' was the final straw. Both Campbell and Millar were furious with Cherie over her handling of her purchase of two flats in Bristol, and her close association with Carole Caplin, someone whom both distrusted. Campbell made a stab at leaving after his summer in Provence in August 2002, but Blair yet again asked him to stay on, at least until the likely war with Iraq was over.[89] Campbell running the London Marathon on 13 April 2003, an event that generated considerable press coverage, was a way of preparing himself for life outside, a figure in his own right.

Both Campbell and Millar had had enough. Campbell told (not asked) Blair in April 2003 while they were waiting for George Bush to arrive for the summit in Belfast, that with the Iraq war almost over, he was going to leave at the end of the Parliamentary Session in July. Blair accepted the news stoically, realising any further pleas for him to stay on would be futile. Mentally he had had two years to prepare and adjust to losing his closest aide. Campbell even drafted the press release about his departure. Finally, everything seemed in place for him to make a rather overdue exit. At the end of May, however, these plans were torn to shreds by the untimely intervention of BBC reporter Andrew Gilligan.

Campbell had become inordinately angry at the BBC's coverage of the war in March and April 2003, and during his appearance before the Foreign Affairs Select Committee in June, he attacked the BBC for 'having an agenda' and for its 'disproportionate focus' on opposition to the government's position.[90] More cynical leader-writers claimed that this was an attempt to distract attention away from the real issue, the failure of coalition forces to find any evidence of weapons of mass destruction (WMD) in Iraq.[91] This misunderstands the almost obsessive desperation to expose what he considered the dishonesty of Gilligan's story: Blair too became swept up in Campbell's near-manic crusade. The suicide of Dr David Kelly, the government scientist fingered as the source for Gilligan's story, forced the government to hold an independent inquiry, chaired by Lord Hutton. To the original charge that Campbell had 'sexed up' the dossier was added a new allegation that he had been part of a government conspiracy to reveal Kelly publicly as the source, believing that this would (as he wrote in his diary) 'fuck Gilligan'[92] as Kelly now disputed many of the charges against the government in the original BBC report. After several months of careful investigation, Hutton completely exonerated Campbell. He agreed that Campbell 'recognised that nothing should be included in the dossier with which the intelligence community were not entirely happy' and that there was 'no dishonourable, or underhand, or duplicitous strategy to leak Dr Kelly's name to the media'.[93]

On the facts of the case, Campbell was vindicated, yet he must bear his share of the responsibility for allowing the situation to escalate to the extent that it did. By taking such an uncompromising stance against the BBC, he raised the stakes and made it much harder for the BBC to back down, or to agree a compromise: 'I wanted a clear win,' Campbell wrote in his diary, 'not a messy draw.'[94] Even Lord Hutton conceded that the 'exceptionally strong terms' in which Campbell pushed his complaints 'raised very considerably the temperature of the dispute between the government and the BBC'.[95] Once Hutton's report was published, Campbell seemed determined to keep the heat on the BBC, lambasting the failure of the BBC at every level to tell the truth and branding their actions 'unforgivable'.[96] This undignified reaction served only to reinforce the view that for Campbell, no longer even working for Blair, this had been a very personal affair. His victory over the BBC had been won only at tremendous cost, not least in the incredible time and energy the affair soaked up in Number 10, when Blair had been desperate to refocus the agenda domestically. With a little tact and willingness to compromise, the dispute could have been settled far earlier: tact and compromise, however, were never Campbell's strong suit.

After his departure in September 2003, Campbell's relationship with Blair did not end. By January 2004, he had settled into making twice-weekly phone calls to Blair,[97] who is not as close to his steadier if less inspired successor, David Hill. Campbell found it more difficult to adjust to life outside than he had anticipated, and misses being at Number 10.[98] As his primary motivation has always been to see Labour win elections and the Tories smashed, the sense of being away from the heart of the action is likely to grow as the next election approaches.

The Impact of Alastair Campbell

Campbell's most creative and successful period was during 1994–97, in grooming Blair, taming the press and revamping Labour's media strategy. After 1997, he had a major impact in galvanising the government's whole approach to communications and getting Blair's message across. Andrew Rawnsley even suggests that Campbell's consummate presentation skills generated the impression that Blair was 'a leader more decisive and more in control of events than he often was'.[99] The high point of his influence came during the Kosovo crisis in the spring of 1999, when he advised Nato on how to make its case more effectively. He was revered internationally as the master of communication. After 1999/2000, his creative work declined. If he had retired then or in 2000/2001, history would say that, though he had been at times brutal, his contribution was of first-rank importance for Blair, for the Labour Party and the government.

Campbell's impact on policy has been much exaggerated. It was always assumed that he *must* have had a major role, because he saw so much of Blair. But Campbell failed to influence Blair in those areas where he had his strongest convictions. He was opposed to proportional representation and to talks with the Liberal Democrats: the former was introduced for non-Westminster elections, and the fact the latter did not fully flower was not due to his opposition. He supported full and immediate disclosure over the Ecclestone affair in November 1997, to no avail.[100] He opposed selective and independent schools, yet the former flourished, while the latter saw Labour's tough words turned into gentle affirmation. Campbell was Eurosceptic, but was not a major player in Blair's failure to take Britain into the Euro – though the Brown camp say Campbell was decisive in

October 1997 in persuading Blair that Brown had to give an interview ruling out joining. When Campbell protested, 'I am not interested in policy, and I don't have any power independent of the Prime Minister. Full stop,'[101] he was telling the truth in the sense that the policies were Blair's, not his. No clearer demonstration of this can be given than Iraq. Campbell did not see his job as to change Blair's mind. His job was to make his boss's case stand up.

The real significance of Campbell's policy role is less that he changed Blair's thinking on key decisions, but rather that with Blair spending so much of his finite time with Campbell, less time could be devoted to his policy staff. Campbell affirmed Blair in his instincts to think short-term and to prefer short, snappy answers. Blair did not give his Chief of Staff, Jonathan Powell, as much time and regard. 'He always had great respect for everything that Alastair said, whereas he could be casually dismissive of Jonathan.'[102] If Blair had given Miliband, his first chief of policy, the same time from 1994 to 2001, then his premiership would have been very different. He would have been induced to think out his own ambitions for his premiership from his first core principles upwards, which he was never fully to do. Instead of thinking bottom-up, he thought top- (i.e., headlines) down, with predictable results on long-term consistency. Only after 2001/02 did he begin to think through the domestic policy agenda from first principles.

It is ironic that a Prime Minister who believed so strongly in God, in his own fundamental integrity and in his ability to communicate directly to the electorate, should have aligned himself so closely with someone so mistrustful of the media and the world at large and who was an avowed atheist. If Blair bears the blame for Campbell steering his premiership so decisively towards the media, Blair must also take the blame for relying so much on a regime which did so much ultimately to erode trust. Blair was never able to shake off the perception that his government was obsessed with spin, nor was he able, until too late, to wean himself off Campbell, and he misses his presence greatly. Insiders talked about there being much less laughter and Number 10 being a much gloomier place after Campbell's departure. Campbell's exuberant personality was the most powerful force in Number 10 from 1997 to 2003.

Campbell was a brilliant obsessive. His much-trumpeted loyalty to his football club, Burnley, is matched by his loyalty to his mentors. He punched for Maxwell, he defended Kinnock furiously when his fellow journalists had belittled his trip to see President Reagan in November 1986, and he lashed out for Blair repeatedly, as in the *Daily Mirror* when Ken Follett attacked him in 2000.[103] Campbell also deflected much of the criticism that would otherwise have been aimed directly at his boss. He was, in his own words, 'part of Tony's shield'.[104] Yet for Campbell, attack was the best form of defence. His final attack was to defend himself, when he had become a big figure in his own right, against the BBC. He received the vindication he wanted, but the price he forced the government to pay was far too high.

Kinnock had warned him exactly nine years before in Provence that the job would 'ruin' him. Kinnock would have been completely wrong had Campbell left after six or seven years, which is when he wanted to go. By staying on as long as he did, Campbell ensured that Kinnock's prediction became partly fulfilled; he significantly damaged not just his own reputation, but also that of his closest friend, Blair.

Blair came to Number 10 wanting to transform Britain's relationship with the EU, and had convinced many he wanted to take Britain into the Euro. The photograph shows an ambivalent Blair at an EU Council meeting.

23

The Euro Decision, October 1997

'If you seize this moment, then you can shape events and not have events shape you,' Roy Jenkins told Blair in October 1997. 'I will be very blunt on this. You have to choose between leading in Europe or having Murdoch on your side. You can have one but not both.'[1] The period in late September and October 1997 is the key turning-point of Blair's first term, because of what it revealed about Blair's thinking on the core European issue of the day, the Euro, and for what it says about Blair's planning and priorities as well as his relationship with Gordon Brown. Blair said Britain's entry into the single currency was the most important issue of the day, and building an enduringly closer relationship with the EU was one of the primary objectives of his premiership. What happened in these weeks, however, effectively sealed the fate of these ambitions.

Blair's Thinking About Europe, 1975–97

Blair says that his first vote in a national election was cast in favour of Britain remaining in the European Economic Community. He stood at Beaconsfield on an anti-EEC party ticket, but went out of his way to make pro-EEC remarks at his selection meeting at Sedgefield in 1983, where he was struck by hearing positive comments about Europe on the doorsteps from Labour supporters.[2] Once in Parliament after 1983, European and foreign policy were not a particular interest. The staunchly anti-European Bryan Gould said, 'I saw no evidence under Kinnock that Tony Blair took a strong view one way or the other on

Europe. It is quite likely that he did not know what his view was, and therefore chose not to *say* what his view was.' The equally staunchly pro-European Mandelson, by contrast, asserts that Blair's pro-Europeanism was key to his political make-up from the moment they started talking in the mid-1980s.[3]

Gould faded from politics after 1992, about the time that Blair started to declare a keen interest in Europe. Blair had already found the Social Chapter a useful sledgehammer with which to batter open the closed shop. He had always enjoyed holidaying in Italy and France, and had kept up his speaking of French after he finished studying it at 'A' level, spending three months working in a bar in Paris in the summer of 1976. The latent sympathy was there, and when he began to cast around in 1991–92 for ideas to form his wider platform, Europe was an obviously attractive policy to adopt, a popular cause in centre and left thinking circles at the time. 'I've no doubt at all that Britain's future lies in Europe,' he duly wrote in *Renewal* in 1993.[4] When he became leader in 1994, he made much of his eagerness for Britain to participate fully in the European Union. 'It's one of those issues on which you have to mark your line, then stick to it through thick and thin,' he told Paddy Ashdown earnestly that September,[5] and the commitment to 'co-operating in European institutions' was spelled out in the new Clause IV adopted in 1995.[6] In private, he said he was in favour of the Euro,[7] but he was cautious in public: 'In principle it could have benefits,' he said, 'but it cannot be forced upon economies that are not marching in step with one another and where there is not proper political consent.'[8] Blair's thinking about the EU thus lacked the long pedigree of visceral commitment of the true Europhile. His position was pragmatic and opportunistic – as was much of his thinking.

As the General Election approached, Blair began to give serious thought to what his policy would be on Europe, and it formed a major part of the discussions he held in late 1996 and early 1997 with a group of former diplomats convened by David Gillmore and Robin Renwick to broaden his knowledge of international affairs. His 'tutors' were divided on the Euro, but there was a general consensus that there should be a referendum, and that the issue should be decided on economic rather than political grounds. Blair gave them the impression of believing that Britain should not join in the 'first wave' in January 1999, that the Bank of England should take control of interest rates first (though he was careful not to spell out such confidential plans) and Britain should represent itself in European capital cities as being sympathetic to joining the Euro at some point. He struck the former diplomats as being positive but hard-headed in his thinking towards the EU, strong on refusing to abolish frontier controls, against tax harmonisation and against plans for a European defence capability (over which he subsequently changed his mind).[9] John Kerr, later Permanent Under-Secretary at the FCO, talked to the three main Labour shadow ministers when they visited Washington during Kerr's time as ambassador. Brown, he thought, was the most enthusiastic at that time about the Euro; Cook was the most sceptical, for the traditional Labour reasons that he saw the Euro pre-empting Keynesian expansion if Britain fell into a recession; and Blair, though positive, thought that in economic terms it was 'no big deal either way'.[10] At the same time though, Blair was determined to be a major player in the EU, and realised that the only way of doing that fully was by Britain joining the Euro.[11] So at the time of the election one can say he was convinced of the political argument for joining, but agnostic (and willing to defer to Brown) on the economic arguments.

Labour's manifesto in 1997 managed to combine being both pro-European and 'patriotic'. It promised a referendum on joining the single currency, which had been official policy since late 1996, when it was agreed that Britain would only join the single currency subject to a 'triple lock' agreement by Cabinet, Parliament and the electorate in a referendum. During the campaign itself, concerned not to upset a press that he had worked so hard to win over, Blair sounded deliberately sceptical towards the EU. In the *Sun* on 17 April he said, 'I do understand how passionate people are about the pound. And that is why I would let the people have the final say in a referendum if I, as Prime Minister, ever decided to join a single currency.'[12] On St George's Day, 23 April, he wrote in jingoistic vein, 'Let me make my position on Europe absolutely clear. I will have no truck with a European superstate. If there are moves to create that dragon, I will slay it.'[13] Most people accepted that this was posturing designed to mute the carping of the Eurosceptic press.

From within his own circles, Blair was being pressed hard to make more pro-European noises by Peter Mandelson, Jonathan Powell and Roger Liddle, but he largely resisted their calls. Further, and significantly, he refused to assent to Mandelson's wish to be 'Minister for Europe'. He did, however, appoint David Simon, chairman of British Petroleum, as a minister with specific responsibility for the single market, a post based jointly in the Treasury and DTI.[14] Indicative of a certain lack of forethought, Blair only phoned Simon on the night of the election with a brief to 'get Britain close to Europe and prepare for entry to the Euro'.[15] Simon's appointment was important because many in the business community were pressing for entry: now one of their most respected figures was at the heart of preparations. Once in power, Britain immediately signed up to the European Social Chapter (a political act rather than one of conviction, and a decision which caused Blair and Brown anxiety about exactly what they were letting themselves in for).[16] Blair then despatched Margaret Beckett, the new Trade and Industry Secretary, to Tokyo to reassure Japanese companies of Britain's intentions to join and insisted that Cabinet ministers adopt a consciously pro-EU tone in their departments.[17]

Blair's uncertainty on the Euro was compounded by the conflict in Number 10 between two advisers: Liddle, who was passionately in favour of the single currency, and Derek Scott, who was equally fervently against. According to Andrew Rawnsley, 'when Liddle and Scott compared notes on their discussions with Blair, on one thing they agreed. Neither of them could be sure whose side he was really on.'[18] The balance of opinion in Number 10 initially was weighed down more on the sceptical side. Campbell was opposed and put the case forcibly that the damage done to the government's profile with the Eurosceptic press, predominantly the *Sun*, *The Times* and the *Daily Mail*, would be serious, untold indeed, if Britain went in. Tim Allan, Campbell's deputy, was also opposed to joining.[19] Philip Gould's focus groups showed considerable hostility to Britain joining.[20]

When Brown arrived at the Treasury on Friday, 2 May, he found it deeply sceptical about the Euro. Terry Burns, the Permanent Secretary, and almost all the senior figures including Alan Budd, Chief Economic Adviser, and Robert Culpin, Director of Public Spending, were opposed in varying degrees to Britain joining.[21] The only real supporter in senior circles was Nigel Wicks, Second Permanent Secretary and the senior official responsible for Britain's policy on the Euro, who had established many close links with his opposite numbers in Europe. Burns thought there was 'not a cat in hell's chance of Britain joining in the first wave'.[22] The Treasury thought Brown reasonably neutral when he first arrived: his main concern at that time was to keep all the options open. He eagerly fired questions at his new officials: what was the timetable? How long could the options be kept open? What did Britain's EU partners think?[23]

Just after the election Blair agreed in private with Brown that there was no serious prospect of Britain joining in the first wave, not least because the British and European economic cycles were misaligned. Brown repeated the stated position in public that 'it is highly unlikely that we will join the EMU at the first date in 1999'. Brown then commissioned the Treasury to conduct a major study exploring all the options for the government, from joining in 1999–2001 to joining in the second Parliament to putting it off indefinitely. They also asked David Currie, then Professor of Economics at the London Business School, to publish a pamphlet examining the options. In the end he produced two: 'The Pros and Cons of EMU' (1997) and 'Will the Euro Work?' (1998).[24] Exploring ways of buying more time, Blair and Brown even hatched an idea to persuade Britain's EU partners to postpone the launch date beyond January 1999. More seasoned diplomatic hands deemed this absurd and it was soon squashed by Michael Jay and Christopher Meyer, Britain's ambassadors in Paris and Bonn, as well as by Nigel Wicks.[25] Blair and Brown then hoped that technical difficulties with European currencies might still delay the start date, but they overestimated the problems France and Germany were having over the fiscal rules for the single currency, and made too much of Italy's struggle to meet the criteria. They reluctantly had to accept that the deadline of January 1999 would be met.

Blair therefore looked to other areas where he could give leadership in the EU in his first few months, and set out to establish personal relationships with Helmut Kohl and Jacques Chirac in particular. The fact that the former was tired and was shortly to leave the stage and the latter wounded by the defeat of his government in parliamentary elections created an added opportunity for Blair to demonstrate dynamic leadership. His first European Summit at Noordwijk in Holland on 23 May saw him talk enthusiastically about the 'third way' (Chirac asked later whether he was sufficiently right-wing to be 'an honorary member of New Labour')[26] and at Malmö in Sweden on 6 June he gave an ill-judged lecture to European socialists on how they could follow New Labour's lead on modernisation.

Blair's first major test was the Inter-Governmental Conference in Amsterdam on 16 June 1997, which aimed to update and deepen the Maastricht Treaty of 1991. Disagreement over Maastricht had ripped apart John Major's government and Blair prepared himself thoroughly for what was potentially a very difficult conference: the Tories and the right-wing press were portraying it as a final step before Britain became swallowed up in a European superstate, while Blair's EU partners were keen to see whether Labour's much vaunted change of stance towards Europe was anything more than rhetoric. Blair was helped by the fact that the tide towards a federal Europe, reaching a high point at Maastricht, was now receding, if only in the short term. As Philip Stephens wrote, 'The appetite to add political union to economic union had all but gone.'[27] Blair concentrated on just a few objectives, which he pursued tenaciously and skilfully.[28] His modest concession to greater integration by agreeing some increase in co-operation over defence and foreign policy and some strengthening of 'majority voting' on certain issues showed his credentials as a willing European, and did enough to satisfy EU leaders and Europhiles at home. However, he avoided giving away significant powers, such as over taxation or borders. He also captivated European leaders with his style and charm. British officials were also impressed: 'John Major had left him little room for manoeuvre,' said one. 'Tony Blair, like a barrister, quietly absorbed all the details, made the most of his position, and let European leaders think this was a man they could negotiate with, while he reserved the positions that were important to us.'[29] His success, diplomatically and personally, was a significant boost: 'Blair enjoyed Amsterdam. He found he was good at European negotiations, and had a real flair for them. He saw how he could make advances in Europe. The conference was a turning point for him,' said John Kerr.[30] Amsterdam opened Blair's mind to the possibilities that leadership in Europe need not necessarily be through the Euro.[31] But for the time being, he still saw the Euro as the principal motor to fulfil his aspiration of British leadership in the EU.

Buoyed by this success, he aired his European zeal in July during a long talk in the garden at Number 10 with one top official. Blair said, 'The Germans lost the war and have got over it. The French were humiliated by the war and have got over it. The British won the war and have never got over it. My generation do not have the same hang-ups about Europe as older generations. My job is to establish a lasting relationship, and to lead Britain in Europe.'[32] Blair was clear that central to this vision was his desire for Britain to join the Euro, and he was concerned that the timing and the referendum would produce the right result. Around the same time, Blair confided to a close adviser: 'We have to have leadership in Europe. We cannot do that unless we are in the Euro.'[33] Blair talked to Andy Grice in his end-of-summer-holiday interview on 31 August about the huge excitement surrounding his arrival in Europe, and how he was already being tipped as Kohl's successor as 'the main man in Europe'. Grice thought that Blair was convinced the Euro would start on schedule but that 'Britain is unlikely to join until a few years later'. But he thought Britain could still play a big role as long as it was not 'ruling it out for good'.[34]

The October Débâcle

When Brown returned to London after his summer break, his mind was focused even more sharply on the pressing question of the government's response to the Euro. In mid-September, Ed Balls and selected Treasury officials began intensifying the work the Chancellor had set in train in May on Britain's position. This work confirmed all that Brown had been hearing from the Treasury since the election, that Britain's entry in January 1999 was neither feasible, on technical and economic grounds, nor desirable, on political grounds, nor indeed would conditions make entry viable before the next election. It followed that it would be impractical to hold a referendum before the General Election, because the poll would need to be as close as possible to the moment of entry, i.e., without a General Election taking place in the interim. Brown and his advisers were thinking in terms of a possible referendum soon after the next General Election, if the Euro was judged to be a success elsewhere in the Eurozone, with a lightning 'Yes' campaign backed by the government in time for Britain to join in 2002, the formal launch date of Euro notes and coins. Brown decided that he would unveil this thinking when he addressed the CBI and Parliament in early November, with Blair reiterating the message at a dinner the same night in the City of London.[35]

This elaborate plan was smashed irrevocably by a prominent article that appeared in the *Financial Times* on Friday, 26 September 1997, written by Robert Peston. 'The government is on the point of accepting a much more positive approach to European economic and monetary union,' the article opened, 'with a statement shortly that sterling is likely to join at an early opportunity after the 1999 launch.'[36] Peston was a respected journalist in the City with a reputation for knowing what Number 10 was thinking. The City interpreted it as a plant from the highest levels of government. The pound plummeted with dealers anticipating an early devaluation of sterling to bring it into line with other European currencies, while share prices saw a record 180-point rise in anticipation of a low EU interest rate. Peston had been contemplating writing this article on the Euro for about ten days, and had spoken to a number of contacts in Number 10, the Treasury and the FCO, several of whom later disassociated themselves from the story. 'What is so interesting,' Peston said, 'is that Blair's people thought Brown's people had placed it, and Brown's people thought it came from Number 10.'[37] Brown's team believed Mandelson in particular was responsible. Blair's camp meanwhile knew that Peston had recently had lunch with Treasury minister Geoffrey Robinson, which meant Brown and his team were also felt to be the principal source,[38] which they were not. However, this showed that the popular perception of Brown as pro-Euro remained intact. Indeed, journalist William Keegan reports a conversation with a minister close to Brown on 29 July, who told him: 'There is no future for us outside [the Euro]. Gordon Brown wants to enter at the first opportunity.'[39] At this stage, Brown's doubts about the Euro, which had been growing since May, remained largely private.

The erroneous perception that Brown was trying to manoeuvre a reluctant Number 10 into joining the Euro early was given added force by articles in the *Daily Mail* on 13 October, recounting how Britain was poised to join the Euro soon after the 1999 launch and that this represented 'a victory for Gordon Brown who had put enormous pressure on the Prime Minister',[40] and in the *Independent* on 14 October, which agreed that 'the Treasury is trying to bounce Tony Blair into a decision which could lead to the early death of the pound'.[41] Blair had already said that the decision would be the most difficult his government would have to take. Events were getting out of hand, and Brown was increasingly concerned about the destabilising effects on the markets. Over the course of the week beginning Monday, 13 October, he pushed Blair repeatedly for a definitive statement that would indicate that the government had no immediate plans to go into the Euro. Blair, mindful of how such a message would be read by Britain's EU partners, by British business and by his own Euro-enthusiasts like Mandelson, was unconvinced. He had yet to be persuaded by Brown that more damage would be done by letting the speculation continue.[42]

On the evening of Thursday, 16 October, Brown called Blair in the Downing Street flat and once again stressed the need for an immediate statement to calm the markets. Blair, who was in the middle of a difficult meeting with Clare Short, finally buckled and instructed Brown to agree a form of words with Campbell. The line Brown agreed with Campbell was to rule out joining the Euro in the first wave, but back off from explicitly ruling out entry in the current Parliament, while implying that this would be the case by saying that a 'period of stability' was needed after 1999 before Britain would decide.[43] On the face of it, this compromise would calm the markets but avoid sounding overly negative. It was agreed that the vehicle for this announcement would be an interview with Phil Webster of *The Times*, a figure trusted by both the Blair and Brown camps. Webster had been pressing Brown hard for an interview ever since Balls had told him over a dinner at the Labour Party conference in Brighton a few weeks before that Brown was 'cooling' towards the Euro.[44] Balls had already phoned Webster early on the Thursday, telling him that he would be likely to have an exclusive interview with the Chancellor that Saturday, 18 October, but that 'Gordon has first to clear it with Tony'. Webster immediately contacted Peter Stothard, the editor of *The Times*, and asked him to 'clear the front page' for that day, just in case. Webster went to bed that night uncertain whether or not he would receive a phone call the next day from Brown, who was up in Dunfermline.[45]

Campbell and (critically) Balls 'prepared the ground' with calls to Webster on Friday morning, and Brown duly phoned Webster from Scotland in the afternoon. Webster knew what the story was before he spoke to Brown – he had already been faxed an outline of the key points. He asked Brown just a few questions before immediately writing it up. The article began 'Gordon Brown is on the verge of ruling out British membership of a European single currency before the next election'. It then said that the decision came at the end of a five-month internal Treasury inquiry, and that Brown would make the announcement formally to Parliament after it reconvened. The headline, written by John Bryant, the deputy editor and heavily pushed by Webster, stated across all eight columns at the top of the paper 'BROWN RULES OUT SINGLE CURRENCY FOR LIFETIME OF THIS PARLIAMENT'.[46] 'The headline was certainly stronger than the story,' Webster said, 'but I still felt it stood up. I knew I had the scoop of the Parliament and I wanted to make everything of it I could.'[47]

The eruption that followed, when news of *The Times'* story was spread to the BBC and Press Association by Brown's staff, has come to be symbolised by Charlie Whelan's legendary mobile phone calls that evening to Blair and others from Westminster's Red Lion pub. This has become one of the most recycled of all stories about Labour's first term, and the most enduring emblem of all that was wrong with the government's obsession with spin, with a louche political appointee apparently telling the world what the government's policy was on the major economic issue of the day. The roots of the damage, however, can be found in the tardiness of the Prime Minister and the Chancellor to agree and announce government policy on such a major issue. Then, when the press rushed in to fill the vacuum, they panicked, and ineptly thought the best way of releasing news with far-reaching economic and international implications was through a newspaper interview. Worse, the form of words agreed by Number 10 was supplemented by a 'nudge and a wink' from Brown's staff, notably Balls, who was a good friend of Webster.[48] Webster thus felt entitled to 'strengthen the story' in the headline, leaving out the critical phrase 'on the verge of' that had been agreed with Campbell, and declaring that the government would not join the Euro in Blair's first term. 'I did what I did,' Webster later admitted, 'knowing that this was precisely what was going to happen. Brown and the Treasury had no argument with the story.'[49] The issue had not been discussed in Cabinet, which had met that very Thursday morning, nor had the Cabinet big beasts Prescott, Cook and Beckett been told, nor had the Government Information Service (GIS) across Whitehall been briefed about the change of policy. The duty press officer at the Treasury on Friday evening, in direct contradiction to Whelan, thus denied that the Euro had been ruled out, and insisted that options were 'still open' before the next election. Those in the know sought clarification from Nigel Wicks at the Treasury, the official responsible for the policy, who kept trying forlornly to keep everyone focused on the words of the article itself, which he thought was the government's true position, rather than the headline, which he thought was not.[50] Balls, by contrast, who wanted the door to the Euro firmly closed,[51] was saying 'look at the headlines', which, of course, he had engineered. The media enjoys nothing more than a government in total confusion. And this government's confusion was total.

Blair was at Chequers when he received an agitated phone call from Mandelson that Friday night. To Mandelson's dismay about the story, which cut across everything for which he had been fighting, was added the indignity of him reading in the article that 'Treasury sources' had said that the recent press speculation (i.e., in the *Financial Times*) about Britain joining had been placed by 'pro-European ministers said to be out of the decision-making loop'.[52] He took it personally. Blair was shocked when Mandelson read to him the headline of Webster's piece.[53] Blair thought that the spin operation had clearly gone far beyond the careful line agreed with Campbell to restore market stability. Blair tried to speak to Brown but was told he was 'out of phone contact' in his constituency. Campbell, very unusually, proved unreachable. Finally, the Number 10 switchboard connected Blair directly to Charlie Whelan, the press officer he had tried to have sacked, on his mobile on the streets outside the Red Lion: 'What is this about us not going into the Euro in our first term?' Blair demanded. 'Well, I've agreed it with Alastair and Gordon,' replied a nonchalant Whelan. 'What's the problem?'[54]

The media over the weekend was livid with stories about the utter confusion within the government, and with the Tories demanding a recall of Parliament. Fears grew that when the markets reopened on the Monday, 20 October, the uncertainty would precipitate a slump, a spectre heightened by it being the tenth anniversary of the stock market crash on Black Monday in 1987. Could this be the economic crisis that had always crippled Labour governments throughout history some time after they came to power? A broadcast interview with Brown was hastily arranged that weekend from his Westminster flat, but this did little to calm the atmosphere of crisis. Number 10 held its breath. But Monday passed without a dire slump, though the markets were still jittery when on Tuesday Blair called a meeting at Number 10 with Brown, Balls, Campbell, Powell and other senior staff. 'This must never happen again,' Blair said emphatically.[55] They decided that a definitive statement had to be given to the House of Commons as soon as it returned the following Monday, 27 October. But who should give it? Blair, as Prime Minister, in view of the historic importance of the statement? Brown was not happy and wanted to make it himself, another argument that he won, as he did when it was suggested by Number 10 that he apologise for the market turbulence and for not announcing the policy first to Parliament. Brown thought any apology could play into the Tories' hands, and he wanted to be on 'the high ground'.[56] Over the next six days, frantic work took place on the statement within the Treasury and Number 10. Blair wanted Irvine, still his safety blanket, to be brought in to look at the text. Blair flew up to Edinburgh on the Thursday for the biannual Commonwealth Heads of Government meeting and was kept in close touch by John Holmes in the Number 10 Private Office. Blair worked on the statement in Scotland and his aides faxed a redrafted version down to Brown. 'Brown, Balls and Whelan were utterly contemptuous of Blair's drafting,' said one official – 'as only the Treasury can be when someone tries to do drafting for them'.[57]

The lights burned in the Treasury from midnight until dawn on that Saturday and Sunday. For all their agonising, however, there was little fresh substance to their discussions. Their real dialogue, said another official, was not about complex economic or political discussions. It 'was about how to make it look as if Gordon Brown's statement was part of a planned, properly thought-out process rather than the reality, which is that we were jumped, and had to act in a panic to sort out exactly what our position was'.[58] The only two positions Brown could conceivably announce on the Monday were: first, that there was a very faint possibility of entering in the first Parliament (the position of the text in *The Times* article), or, second, that there was no chance of anything happening in the first Parliament (the headline in *The Times*).[59] Blair, strongly supported by Mandelson, pushed Brown towards the former. He remained deeply concerned about the impact too negative a statement would have on the pro-Europeans in business and also, he added, in the trade union movement (many of whom were keen). He also realised that his own personal credibility as Prime Minister was on the line: was he really willing to yield his policy-making prerogative to the press and the Chancellor's aides?

The answer was that he had the power to dictate to Brown, but he chose not to exercise it. Brown began his statement on Monday, 27 October, by saying the decision on the single currency was 'the most important question the country is likely to face in our generation'. What he then went on to say brought some consolation to both Europhiles and Eurosceptics. The former were pleased to hear him reject the constitutional argument that would have ruled out Britain ever joining, thus committing the government to the single currency *in principle*. Brown then announced: 'If, in the end, the single currency is successful and the economic case is clear and unambiguous, the government believes that Britain should be part of it.' A committee would be established to oversee preparation for the Euro, which reassured supporters that it was simply a question of time. More significantly, with the 'five tests', the sceptics were reassured that the judgement would be made on sound economic criteria and that it would be Brown, not Blair, judging whether they had been met. And, as Keegan points out, through referring to a 'successful' single currency once it began elsewhere, Brown had in effect added a sixth test.[60] This would, perhaps even more than the other five, be open to rival interpretations. In an apparent concession to Blair (and Mandelson), Brown added the meaningless rider that, 'barring unforeseen changes in economic circumstances' Britain would not be joining in this Parliament. It was a masterly statement. It quelled the unrest in the markets and the media, it wrong-footed the Opposition, it gave something to those on both sides of the Euro argument and it restored confidence in the government, which had been demonstrably lost. It put the potentially explosive Euro issue to bed for the life of the Parliament, and it allowed the government to go ahead openly making preparations for entry, but without attracting the ire of the Eurosceptic press. It is a moot point whether Brown could have achieved all this had there been no Webster interview.

There were downsides, however. Whelan was allowed to take the blame for the press (the *Daily Telegraph*'s main leader was headlined 'Charlie Whelan, Chancellor') but it was Ed Balls who was more involved in the key briefing. Campbell certainly had no qualms about the plan of using the media to announce the major change in policy. As Tim Allan put it: 'Charlie got it in the neck, but it was mainly Alastair's doing. We didn't realise then that you don't make big announcements in *The Times*, but in Parliament.'[61] For all the *mea culpas* there was to be no sea-change in the way Number 10 used the media; but there was to be a sea-change in Britain's position on the Euro.

'I don't think any of us realised at the time,' said one senior official, 'that October would be such a profound turning-point in the whole Euro story.'[62] Looking back at the history of Blair's premiership, one can see the events of the early autumn as his best chance of taking Britain into the single currency. One Blairite saw it thus: 'This was, effectively, a coup, which Blair had no alternative but to legitimise.'[63] Although the five tests, worked up in final form under Alan Budd, were expressly designed only to rule out joining in the immediate future, and were deliberate about not ruling out the Euro indefinitely,[64] the Treasury was given the final say on whether they had been met. 'The Treasury liked the tests because they always wanted to make things technical: it was their way of keeping control,' said David Simon.[65] At the time, however, Blair interpreted the five tests as to his advantage: and he did not, in October 1997, foresee how deep Brown's hostility to the Euro would become. Blair believed that committing to the tests would take speculation about the Euro out of the headlines. After the next election, he expected the tests would have been met and a referendum would follow. Yet, as Rawnsley points out, although the tests were originally thought to be 'conveniently elastic', they ended up becoming 'serious hurdles'.[66] Blair imagined that Gus O'Donnell, the Treasury official placed in charge of evaluating Britain's readiness for the Euro, would provide the 'right results' when the government was ready for them. Only from early in his second term did the realisation that O'Donnell might not produce the results he was looking for begin to dawn.[67]

So the mists clear. Blair, despite what he said to many different people and different groups, never saw joining the single currency as the defining objective of his first term. Indeed it is extraordinary how many very serious people he did convince about his intent. 'No one close to Blair,' wrote James Naughtie, doubted his objective 'to take Britain into the single currency'.[68] Blair came to Number 10 with neither game-plan on timing nor iron will to drive Britain into the Euro at the earliest possible opportunity, and was content to let all the planning from May be undertaken by the group within the Treasury. Blair's mind was elsewhere. When the turbulence and speculation began in earnest after the summer, which could easily have been foreseen, he was willing to accept Brown's conclusion that a referendum prior to joining could not take place until after the following General Election. What rankled Blair most about the October 1997 débâcle in fact was the developing perception that the Chancellor's spin-doctors, rather than him, were shaping government policy on entry into the single currency. In May 1997, Blair and Brown thought similarly about the Euro: over the next few months, Blair's view did not change, but Brown's did. He absorbed the arguments from the Treasury about the undesirability and impossibility of immediate entry against the backdrop of Balls' longstanding opposition, and became convinced that Britain should not join in the immediate and even medium term. Entry to the single currency, he accepted, would mean not only a significant loss of control for the Treasury; it would also jeopardise his growing reputation as steward of the economy. Delayed entry also meant shafting Mandelson and an increasingly keen Cook – added attractions.

At its bluntest, winning a second General Election landslide mattered much more to Blair than fighting to take Britain into the single currency, with all the memories of the divisions entry into the ERM had caused Mrs Thatcher in her final years. He believed he could win over those who were upset at the delay by talking up the Euro and the EU in general over the following years, preparing the ground for a referendum probably in early 2002. In his mind, entry would become a major objective in his second term. Treasury officials (with the principal exception of Wicks) were cock-a-hoop with the October statement. 'That's ruled it out for ten years,' said one mandarin gleefully. Balls agreed. Brown, for whom the whole issue was inextricably intertwined with his power politics with Blair, rapidly came round to the same realisation. Being able to eclipse Blair on such a major domestic issue confirmed the impression to all that, in line with the 1994 'deal', Brown was the undisputed master of the government's economic realm.

Blair and Europe, 1997–2001

Blair remained throughout his premiership utterly sincere about his intention to make Britain a leading nation in the European Union and at the heart of the debate about its future. Realising that there would of course be no 'unforeseen circumstances', and that the referendum would not happen in the first Parliament, he took his European cause forward on four fronts: defence, economic reform, constitutional reform and preparing the ground for the Euro referendum in the second term. He also realised that he had to use the resources within Number 10 and the Cabinet Office far better than he had from May to October 1997. But he grew increasingly frustrated in 1998 and 1999 with the quality of his policy advice on Europe, and he thus strengthened his capacity to lead discussions within Whitehall and Europe by bringing in a senior figure in the summer of 2000, Stephen Wall, with permanent secretary status to head the European Secretariat in the Cabinet Office. It was felt in Number 10 to be an overdue move, which chimed with Blair's favoured *modus operandi* of having one specialist collating advice on each main area.

Blair proposed the defence initiative at the Anglo-French summit at St Malo in December 1998. Over the year that followed, with his promotion of the European Security and Defence Initiative (ESDI), he did as much as any European leader to make something of the EU's aspiration to build a common foreign and defence policy. He was motivated by a number of factors: desire to show he was giving a lead in Europe certainly, but also a belief that in some areas it was in Britain's interest to promote rather than constrain collective action, and a desire, following the experience of Kosovo in 1999, to provide Europe with its own independent military capability. His work bore fruit in November 2000 with the EU pledging a force of 60,000 troops to be kept in the field for a year. It was not a universally popular cause, and he had to display real leadership, overcoming inertia in the EU and scepticism from the Foreign Office. His initial intention had been to resist plans for greater European defence co-operation, and some in the Foreign Office were dismissive of his change of heart: 'He ran the European defence policy out of Number 10, not the Foreign Office. It was typical Blair, dazzled by the bright lights but short on detail, on planning ahead and on substance,' said one senior diplomat.[69] The Ministry of Defence and the military were sceptical, worrying that it could damage influence with the United States, which, unlike Nato, would not be part of the new European force. The Americans were indeed cool, fearing loss of influence and control. It also created problems with Nato; Blair argued for an EU force as part of Nato, as the United States favoured, while France wanted an entirely independent force. The Eurosceptic press were opposed to ESDI, albeit not with the same venom reserved for the Euro. Despite the objections, ESDI began to be seen by his second government as an alternative membership card to entry to the 'inner' core of EU members. 'Some have conjectured,' said Philip Stephens, 'that defence was Blair's substitute for participating in the Euro. Either way, it has been good politics.'[70]

Secondly, Blair offered leadership in pressing for the EU to adopt a liberal market model rather than the statist ('socialist', Thatcher said) agenda of Jacques Delors. Blair heralded his thinking at the Cardiff EU Council meeting in June 1998, which ended the British Presidency. The thinking flowered at the Lisbon summit in March 2000, and emphasised a dynamic market model rather than *dirigisme* as the way forward for the EU. The Eurosceptic press pricked up their ears: this was the kind of talk they liked to hear. Blair hailed it as representing 'a sea-change in EU economic thinking', and managed to gain credit in Europe and at home for his work driving this agenda forward. The irony was that the greatest agent driving economic liberalism in the EU was the Euro itself.[71]

Blair also exercised a lead in discussions on constitutional reform. At the Nice summit in December 2000, he spoke in the debate about the enlarged EU, the possibility of a second chamber drawn from national legislatures for the European Parliament and for a clearer division between member countries and the EU itself. He also argued for a full-time President of the European Council to reinforce the power of national governments over other EU institutions. As he said in Warsaw, he favoured the EU being a 'superpower' not a 'superstate'.

Finally, he continued to seek leadership in the EU through making positive noises about Britain's entry to the single currency. But his 'prepare and decide' policy, like Major's 'wait and see', was to become a formula for inertia and procrastination. A number of factors explain why his hopes to drive the campaign forward to prepare the country for the Euro, above all via the 'Britain in Europe' campaign, eventually launched in October 1999, ran into the sands. Blair, and fellow pro-Europeans, had taken insufficient account of the Eurosceptic press, which returned to the full force of its attack after a brief lull following the fall of the Tories in May 1997. 'We thought Euroscepticism as a force was over,' said one senior diplomat. 'What we failed to realise at the time was that the static policy on the Euro we announced in October 1997 would allow the virus to recover and grow back with a vengeance.'[72]

Blair did not invest the Euro argument with the personal capital and time it would have taken to win over sceptics in and outside the party. Among his senior ministers, doubters included the heavyweights, Brown, Prescott, Straw, Blunkett and Beckett. Although a slight majority favoured pressing ahead, and holding a referendum in his second Parliament, they contained – apart from Cook – only middleweight ministers, notably Hewitt, Reid, Hain, Byers, Clarke and Milburn, with Mandelson, the greatest enthusiast of them all, lobbying hard from the sidelines. The debate was not just about the merits of the Euro: underneath it lay a darker rivalry between supporters of Brown and Blair. This knowledge constrained some pro-European ministers in Cabinet like Patricia Hewitt from speaking out more because they did not want to upset the Chancellor.[73] Blair gave a series of positive speeches about Europe, to the French National Assembly in March 1998, in Aachen in May 1999, Ghent in February 2000 and Warsaw in October 2000. But only after the 2001 election did he give a major pro-EU speech in Britain. This came in Birmingham in November 2001, in which he said, leaning heavily on the arguments of Hugo Young's book, *This Blessed Plot*, that at every fresh stage in the European Union's development, Britain had been left behind.[74]

The decisive factor tipping Blair against the Euro was Brown's continuing opposition. When John Kerr arrived back at the Foreign Office as Permanent Secretary in November 1997, he found a major change in the thinking of the big three about the Euro. Blair, he thought, was warming; Cook had become much more favourable; but Brown was becoming increasingly negative.[75] The Foreign Office tried from early 1998 to initiate a dialogue within Whitehall, but the Treasury made it clear they were the sole determinants of the five tests and the decision on entry, and closed down discussions.[76] The more positive Cook became, the more negative did Brown, such was their intense personal rivalry – which in one sense suited Blair. Brown became increasingly concerned, as time wore on, not to jeopardise his conspicuous success running the economy, and he was pleased by the way that the Monetary Policy Committee, which had taken over setting interest rates, was functioning. With the pound doing better than the Euro, and with the new mechanism for determining interest rates a conspicuous success, why jeopardise it, he reasoned, for an unknown future in which control would be sacrificed?

Brown and Blair maintained their regular meetings throughout the first term but, to the intense frustration of officials, 'none of us knew what they were saying to each other, which did nothing to help clarify thinking'.[77] When Simon Buckby joined as the head of the 'Britain in Europe' campaign in the early summer of 1999, he was sent by Blair to talk over the campaign with Brown, saying he was too preoccupied to do it himself: 'In other words, Tony voluntarily deferred the strategic direction to Gordon.'[78] The truth is that Blair simply did not want to take Brown on. 'He was never going to win the arguments against Brown,' said a senior Treasury official; 'one, because he was hopelessly understaffed in Number 10; two, Brown worked eighteen hours a day and, unlike Blair, was on top of the arguments; three, the Treasury didn't want it, period.'[79]

Blair was caught in a vice. He did not want to upset the press, nor

Brown, by urging for Britain to join. Equally, he wanted to keep faith with his pro-European colleagues, and the business interests who were lobbying hard for an early commitment on the Euro and whose funds Labour so badly needed. European heads of government also made it known that they wanted him to be more decisive. He therefore continued to give out mixed messages, telling the House of Commons in February 1999 that Brown's October statement meant that 'in principle, the government was in favour of Britain joining a successful single currency'[80] and coming down firmly on the side of Cook and Byers at a confidential meeting with Brown at Number 10 in January 2000 after they had become irate at the inaction on the Euro. Brown reassured Blair he was not trying to undermine the commitment to eventual membership, and the pro-European ministers all left thinking they had a firm ally for their cause in Blair.[81] But Blair did little to help the 'Britain in Europe' campaign: he was on the stage with Brown, Kenneth Clarke, Michael Heseltine and Charles Kennedy for the launch at the IMAX cinema in Waterloo, London, but then worked hard to keep the Euro and Europe off the political agenda in the run-up to the 2001 General Election. The Euro came back on to the radar screen again in Blair's second term. But as he came to realise, the best chance he had had in his premiership to make this his mark on history was in the autumn of 1997. And he missed it.

Jonathan Powell served Blair with intense loyalty for ten years. He once said that he had 'grown like' Blair during their time together. But did he become too like him?

24

Jonathan Powell

Within Number 10, one of Tony Blair's staunchest pro-European allies was Jonathan Powell. 'I don't think anybody knows better what Tony is thinking on any particular issue,' Charles Falconer once said of him. His is 'the authentic voice of Blair'.[1] After Blair was elected leader in 1994, one area in which he was very conscious of ignorance was practical experience of government, as he had never served as even a junior minister. Neither had he run any organisation: barristers do not run or manage anything, and neither do shadow ministers beyond their small teams. Blair placed his faith in Powell to be his *entré* to the Whitehall Establishment. The younger brother of Charles, Mrs Thatcher's most trusted civil servant when she was Prime Minister, Jonathan was to become the longest-serving of Blair's court. After Anji Hunter, Alastair Campbell and Peter Mandelson had all fallen away, Powell remained. 'If Jonathan says "the Prime Minister wants this done",' said Charles Falconer, 'then everyone accepts it because they know it is true. His role is basically being close to Tony. Tony trusts Jonathan and Jonathan is confident enough to say exactly what he thinks.'[2] But what does 'being close to Tony' and being his authentic voice mean? What exactly *does* Powell think, and what effect has that thinking had on Blair, on his policy and on his appointments?

Jonathan Powell, the Man

Powell was born in Lincolnshire in August 1956, the youngest of four sons of Air Vice-Marshal John Powell and Ysolda Moylan, whose father had been a distinguished civil servant. They produced formidably talented and fiercely competitive sons, and have been called 'the most powerful political family in Britain'. Charles was the eldest, and was the most conspicuously successful because of his celebrated relationship with Mrs Thatcher and the dominance he established in Whitehall from the mid-1980s until the early 1990s (he ended his Civil Service career under John Major, of whom he has remained a loyal supporter). Charles married the flamboyant and talented Carla, an Italian socialite, who counts Peter Mandelson among her close friends. Chris, the second oldest, has spent his career in advertising, was a key figure in the Shadow Communications Agency, and is chairman of the advertising agency Boase Massimi Pollitt DDB, which handled Labour's account in 1997 and has seconded staff to work for the party since 1985. He is also chairman of the IPPR think-tank. Roderick, the third son, is the least known but is in many ways the brightest, and is a successful businessman in the United States, where he is senior vice-president of Invensys, a multinational technology firm.[3]

Jonathan is very much the Benjamin of the family (there is a fifteen-year gap between him and Charles). His father's peripatetic career meant that by the age of nine he had attended eleven schools. He was unhappy and from his early teens felt himself at odds with his public school, King's School in Canterbury, much like Blair at Fettes. Powell's headmaster accused him of being an 'armchair cynic sniping from the sidelines', and they clashed regularly, such as when Powell tried to have the school rebellion film *If . . .* screened. 'Since his teens he's been against the Establishment,' says brother Chris. 'He was always questioning and contrary.'[4] Again one hears the echo of Blair.

Jonathan was particularly influenced by Chris, a devotee of Marxism in his youth,[5] who had once organised a Rolling Stones concert. Admiration for Chris was 'one of the reasons I went left rather than right', said Jonathan. In the 1970s he canvassed for Chris when he stood as Labour candidate for Harrow East. Jonathan had thought of becoming a Labour MP himself after reading history at University College, Oxford. But whereas he admired Chris, he most wanted to emulate and outperform Charles. So after taking an MA at the University of Pennsylvania, he spent a year training with the BBC and then working at Granada Television before opting to follow the career path of brother Charles at the Foreign Office, saying he only applied to keep his parents happy.[6] A formative experience had been staying with Charles when he was First Secretary at the Washington Embassy during the Watergate scandal, which, together with his year at Pennsylvania, implanted a lifelong love of the US.

His career was proceeding apace in the Foreign Office, where he served in Lisbon, Stockholm and Vienna, as well as contributing to the negotiations over Hong Kong in 1983–84 and German reunification in 1989–90. His record was solid but, as a fellow diplomat put it, although 'he was pretty good he was not going to go right to the top'.[7] Only after he arrived in Washington as First Secretary in 1991, aged thirty-five, did his career take off. Powell has always been intensely ambitious, and felt himself at the time to be the least successful of all his brothers.[8] He was a young man with a lot to prove. The job of First Secretary, held by Foreign Office luminaries before like Stephen Wall, Nigel Sheinwald, Sherard Cowper-Coles and, during the Second World War, Isaiah Berlin, involved monitoring political developments and keeping the Embassy and London informed, particularly on Northern Ireland.[9]

Powell was fortunate to be in the post at a time not only of the flowering of interest in the United States by Blair and Brown, but also of the presidential election in 1992. Powell, having concluded in the summer of 1991 that President George H.W. Bush could be defeated, monitored the Democrats particularly closely, and tipped Clinton early on as the winner. He forged strong personal links with Clinton's team at Little Rock, Arkansas, and on the campaign trail. 'He really soaked up the whole campaign,' said Elaine Kamarck. 'I saw him on the trail reading *Boys on the Bus*, an American classic. He understood American politics better than any foreigner I'd ever met. At the time, I didn't know if he was just being very conscientious or whether he had other priorities.'[10] Powell's insatiable appetite and curiosity aroused widespread comment. 'He was enormously useful to talk to,' said another of Clinton's team, 'because he was following the Republicans too, and he always knew more about what they were up to than we did.'[11] Other figures from Clinton's team Powell met at this time were George Stephanopoulos and Paul Begala. At the Washington Embassy, and with the encouragement of Ambassador Renwick, Powell instituted regular 'pundits' breakfasts' where leading commentators would come and 'sing for their cornflakes', fostering the impression of the British Embassy being at the centre of debate, while all the time allowing Powell to amass helpful information.[12]

Blair and Brown were impressed by this eager young diplomat who was prepared to cross conventional Civil Service lines to help them. Their January 1993 visit sealed their friendship.[13] Both men were in awe of Powell's grasp of the Democratic election techniques, far beyond what they expected from a diplomat. Blair's favourable impression was confirmed on his visit that November to look at the US attitude towards juvenile offenders.[14] Brown eyed Powell as someone he would like to run his office, but Blair got in first. When the Clinton administration took power in January 1993, one of his regular points of contact at the White House was Elaine Kamarck. At their last meeting in December 1994, before he left for his new post in London, he asked her for advice for his new boss; she told him to avoid reverting to the old left agenda, as Clinton fatally did in his first two years, upsetting many of the 'New' Democrats.[15]

Powell's Relationship With Blair

Powell had not been Blair's first choice. Ideally, he wanted a senior figure from the Home Civil Service or Foreign Office, which proved difficult. The first approach was to Julian Priestley, an experienced administrator who was Secretary-General of the Socialist Group in the European Parliament. Irvine was called on to interview him, and gave him the thumbs-up, but Priestley declined for personal reasons and went off to head the Private Office of the President of the European Parliament.[16] Powell's was one of the next names they looked at. The connection with Charles was significant, and even though Jonathan was a more junior civil servant than they ideally wanted, his obvious relish for New Labour, the rapport Blair had already established with him, and his contacts with the Clinton administration all tipped the balance. Anji Hunter invited him over for an interview, and he readily convinced Blair's team and Irvine that he was 'of our persuasion'. The title 'Chief of Staff' was Powell's own, modelled on the White House post. The Foreign Office were horrified when they learned what was being proposed, and deemed it most irregular.[17] But Blair never worried about Civil Service niceties, while Powell now had everything he wanted in life: the precise job, with the leader he most admired, in the right party, and in the optimal electoral position on the verge of a long period of power.

Powell took up his post with Blair in January 1995 as the Clause IV roadshow was being launched. He had a bumpy start, as he was resented by Labour's old guard as a usurper and not, they considered, really Labour. A story, in fact apocryphal, of a gaffe at a dinner when he asked Dan Duffy, chairman of the TGWU, 'Who are you?' was given wide currency,[18] as was Charles' remark, on being cold-called by a journalist about his brother's declared lifelong support of Labour, 'Well, it's news to me.'[19] A whispering campaign began about Powell from the unions and left who attacked him as proxy for Blair. Jonathan never acquired Charles' polished, easy manner with people, nor did he socialise or network effortlessly like his older brother, which might have helped him become accepted more readily.

Powell played very much the civil servant role in 1995–97. He immediately began instituting proper procedures in the office such as taking minutes of important meetings and conversations. He liaised with Robin Butler over shadow Cabinet ministers meeting officials, and he also oversaw the seminars, where retired officials instructed shadow ministers on the operation of Whitehall. What he could not alter was the contempt that some of the new cadre of politicians had for officials, one mindset of 'old' Labour politicians which was carried on, to its loss, by New Labour. One area where Powell's antennae failed him, which produced his most awkward moment in Opposition, was his involvement in the notorious 'blind trust' that funded Blair's office, although he denies that he knew who gave money to the trust: 'I think we would have been hammered whatever we had done,' he said. 'We could have done without the bad publicity we've had about it ever since.'[20] This episode was a harbinger of the problems Blair had in power with raising money, which was always seized on by a media keen to scrutinise a government which claimed it would be 'whiter than white'.

As the election approached, Powell held fortnightly meetings with Butler and separately with Major's Principal Private Secretary (PPS), Alex Allan. They discussed the transition and Butler assisted Powell in planning out the first thirty days in power. Without apparently sharing his intentions with Powell,[21] Blair decided he wanted to appoint Powell his PPS in Number 10, the key official in Downing Street who is the Prime Minister's senior adviser and who links him with the rest of Whitehall and the outside world. But, as Blair suspected, Robin Butler would not have it. Blair consulted Robin Renwick among others about how he should tackle Butler, and the advice was, 'Just tell him you are going to do it.'[22] A difficult meeting took place a week before polling day when Butler visited Blair (later joined also by Powell) at his Islington home. Blair argued the case for Powell as Principal Private Secretary, but Butler was adamant: the job needed to go to someone from the Home Civil Service, as it traditionally did. It would go down very badly in Whitehall, Butler told the future Prime Minister, if a special adviser, which was Powell's status, was appointed in this key position.[23] Butler had himself served Mrs Thatcher in this capacity from 1982 to 1985, and he still had vivid memories of Charles contributing to Mrs Thatcher's downfall by isolating her, and doing significant damage to the ethos and morale of the Civil Service by his high profile and irregular role. He was not going to let it happen again with another Powell.[24] Butler argued further that a political appointee would find it hard to deal with some facets of the job, which required strict neutrality, such as liaising with the Leader of the Opposition, overseeing the honours system, receiving intelligence briefings and dealing with Buckingham Palace.

Blair accepted the force of these arguments and did not want a major showdown with the country's most senior civil servant just as he was about to take over.[25] So he acquiesced in Butler's suggestion that the incumbent Alex Allan, who had served Major since 1992, be allowed to stay on for the first few months, and they would leave open the question of what would happen when Allan stood down. Campbell in particular was angry: to him Butler, Old Harrovian, patrician, upper-class, symbolised everything he despised about the Establishment. Campbell took revenge against him two days before the election, when he took exception to comments Butler had made in the press about the mechanics of the change at Number 10, and how it would be impractical for a Prime Minister to live in Islington. Campbell swiftly had the story removed from the *Evening Standard* and made some testy comments to Butler, for which he later apologised.[26]

Powell arrived at Number 10 retaining for the time being his Opposition title of 'Chief of Staff' and buttressed by the Order of the Council allowing him (and Campbell) to give instructions to civil servants, a move strongly disapproved of by many senior mandarins.[27] Powell sat in the small Private Secretary's room at the end of the Cabinet Room with John Holmes (then Private Secretary for Foreign Affairs) and Alex Allan, who was eager to make the new arrangements work.[28] Allan, somewhat to their surprise, quickly earned the trust of the new administration, who found that he was not the John Major apologist they had anticipated. They were sorry to see him leave that summer.[29] As Butler had predicted there was considerable concern about Powell's position across Whitehall, and among some Number 10 officials, who found his working style not their own: 'He would be all over the place. He would fire off instructions, and it was all very irritating, but we got there in the end,' said one.[30] 'He was an utter workaholic, totally loyal, completely dedicated,' said another. 'But he was absolutely frenetic, and we had to spend a good deal of time mopping up after him.'[31]

By June the issue of Powell's future title had still not been resolved and Butler had to send Blair a strongly worded memo setting out his arguments yet again against him being Principal Private Secretary; Butler even made a rare public admission that he was 'seriously unrelaxed' about Blair's plans.[32]

Interestingly, any plans to make Powell PPS are completely denied by Powell, and it is possible that Butler thought that it was Powell who lay behind the briefing to the press that he should be given the job. The issue of what to do after Allan left was soon resolved. The Blair team, during all the intensive foreign business and overseas trips in the first three months, came to form a deep regard and liking for John Holmes. Holmes, an official of the highest calibre and discretion, was duly appointed Principal Private Secretary in the summer of 1997. Some in the Blair team were not sorry to see Robin Butler go, but his successor, Richard Wilson, proved no happier with a political appointee at the heart of Number 10. Wilson was never comfortable with the special powers that Powell had been granted in 1997 and continued to try to restore the status quo.[33] When Holmes departed in February 1999, Wilson was happy to see Jeremy Heywood, a career Treasury official already in Number 10, succeed him as Principal Private Secretary and an air of normality return to the heart of government.

According to one observer, 'In his first year at Number 10, Tony Blair was genuinely unsure what Powell's job was.'[34] Although his advice on how Whitehall worked had been invaluable before 1997, Powell came to be upstaged by the more seasoned Holmes, who could negotiate his way around the government machine far more effectively. Powell's job thus began to change during the second half of 1997 and 1998, but it still had not settled down by early 1999, when Powell went through a difficult period, professionally and personally, with talk of him leaving Number 10. His stock was not high, and he still had to find his niche. Holmes was self-evidently filling the job of PPS while remaining Blair's main adviser on foreign affairs better than Powell would have done. Old hands like Campbell, Hunter and Morgan meanwhile had established their own patches in the turf wars around Blair much more clearly. The difficult period for Powell lasted a few months, but by about May or June 1999, Blair decided he wanted to have someone focusing clearly on the same issues that he was, and he decided that he wanted Powell to stay. Decisive factors were Holmes' departure that spring and Mandelson's departure from the government the previous December.[35] From that moment on, Powell truly became Blair's right-hand man.

Powell became the person Blair saw first thing in the morning and with whom he could talk about work regularly throughout the day. He liaised closely with Kate Garvey, the diary secretary, and became the figure who decided which people and what paperwork Blair saw, monitoring closely the flow of information through his Prime Minister's boxes. Whitehall quickly learned that if they wanted Blair to see someone, or something, they should first contact Powell. His own principal policy interests remained Northern Ireland and foreign policy, specifically that which concerned the United States. In the former, he played second string to Holmes while he was there, but after his departure, Powell emerged as the key figure, capable of representing the Unionist case when Mowlam was Northern Ireland Secretary, and the Nationalist case after Mandelson took over. As Blair's attention was drawn elsewhere, he came to rely on Powell very heavily for matters concerning Northern Ireland. Powell also played a key role in encouraging Blair to establish a relationship with Vladimir Putin in 2000 even before he won his first election, advice which ran contrary to that of more experienced Foreign Office diplomats.[36] Blair's 'special relationship' with Putin held particular attraction for George W. Bush, who was very eager to discuss this with Blair during their first meeting at Camp David in February 2001. The relationship with the US assumed growing importance throughout Blair's premiership, and was monitored and facilitated for him at every twist and turn by Powell. John Kerr and the Foreign Office took great care to brief Powell fully on any US issue before taking it to Blair, because they knew Blair would follow Powell's advice, as he would over diplomatic appointments, or access by foreign visitors, or Blair's own travel programme.[37]

Reshuffles and government appointments became another area of particular focus. 'Jonathan was always far more interested in politics than policy,' said one member of Blair's entourage.[38] Blair listened carefully to Powell's evaluation of who should be promoted or sacked: he knew much more about ministers below Cabinet level than Blair, whose knowledge was often weak. Hunter played a significant role on appointments too, as did Sally Morgan. Powell would manage the politics for Blair, including difficult relations with ministers, a role that grew after Mandelson left the Cabinet Office to run his own department in July 1998. If there was a difficult message to deliver, Powell would often be the messenger, which did nothing to add to his popularity.[39] The 'Downing Street poisoner' was how Julia Langdon, Mo Mowlam's biographer, described him after alleging that he had stabbed the Northern Ireland Secretary in the back.[40] He denied he had anything to do with Mowlam's sacking, but admits that he relished tough decisions and the heat; 'One of the things I like most about the job is moving from crisis to crisis.'[41] 'Jonathan liked fixing things above all. He liked making deals, being at the centre, in the know, the person who sorted things out, and would like to make quick, sometimes too quick, decisions,' said one official.[42]

Almost imperceptibly throughout 1999 and 2000, Powell was picking up many of the duties performed in the past by the Principal Private Secretary, although issues of domestic policy remained largely in Jeremy Heywood's hands. When, in 2000–01, Number 10's and the Cabinet Office's foreign policy advice was restructured, with Stephen Wall becoming Blair's adviser on European affairs and David Manning his adviser on non-European affairs, Powell's thoughts on foreign policy had become ingrained to Blair and he continued to offer them, adding the political dimension that was not a prime concern of Wall or Manning.[43] Powell mirrored Blair in another key way too: he was much more interested in – and better at – politics than management. He therefore proved far less successful in his attempts to oversee the office and lead the team around Blair than in other facets of his job: 'He didn't inspire people,' said one.[44] It was a singular failure of Blair that he never found someone to take control of and master Number 10, and its relations with other departments. As a result, Number 10 and the Cabinet Office had seen years of almost Maoist 'permanent revolution', with a bewildering number of changes of design, to little effect. They might well have done better to have left the Number 10 architecture substantially unchanged, or to have found a figure like Julian Priestley who could have knocked it into shape at the outset. A strong administrator compensating for Blair's deficiencies in that regard would also have ensured that Number 10 communicated better with Whitehall departments. These management skills, however, turned out to be a particular aptitude of Heywood, and until his departure in January 2004 he became the closest Number 10 had to a Chief of Staff, helping oversee its smooth running. This let Powell settle into a role that bore far more resemblance to that of a Principal Private Secretary, Blair's key personal adviser, than an American-style chief of staff, overseeing his entire office. Even though their respective titles had become something of a misnomer, Blair felt comfortable with the co-existence of Heywood and Powell, being able to draw on their complementary strengths, at the apex of his office.[45] Powell proved his worth in his handling the detail during the domestic crises of the fuel protests in 2000 and foot and mouth in 2001, and gained further in gravitas as a result.

Powell was also the figure closest to Blair in Number 10 responsible for liaising with the party's fundraisers, a role that he carried over from Opposition. The spotlight fell on him when it was alleged that he had set up the infamous meeting at Number 10 on 16 October 1997 with Bernie Ecclestone, head of Formula 1, who had already donated £1 million to Labour. Powell had made the initial move to establish contact with Ecclestone in 1996, when Labour was still in Opposition.[46] After Blair became Prime Minister, Powell attended the October meeting at Number 10 when Ecclestone and other motorsport chiefs argued against Britain backing a European directive banning tobacco sponsorship in sport. Powell then let the government go ahead and announce it was seeking an exemption for Formula 1 from the directive, leaving Blair vulnerable to allegations of bribery and sleaze.[47] Powell also managed Blair's contact with the very rich Hinduja brothers: after the Hindujas met Blair and

Powell at Number 10 in June 1998, they wrote to Powell to thank him for 'going out of his way' to set things up.[48] Powell's name was also linked to the row over donations from Lakshmi Mittal, the millionaire steel magnate whose company was praised by Blair, and which resulted in Powell becoming the subject of embarrassing headlines.[49] The need for raising money was not in doubt, but questions were asked about whether, in his pursuit of rich benefactors, Powell's judgement had always been wise. When news of Powell's role with Ecclestone became public in April 2002, *The Times* said, 'The disclosure will add to pressure from the top of the Civil Service and politicians on Mr Blair to stop the politicisation of Downing Street.'[50]

These fears of politicisation only increased when, following the General Election of 2001, Powell's role was expanded. He became Head of Policy, one of the three divisions of Number 10, all headed by party figures rather than civil servants: Campbell was placed in charge of Strategy and Communications, and Hunter (then Morgan) took on Political and Governmental Relations. In his new capacity, Powell was not able to make Blair work out his policy priorities for his second term any more than Andrew Adonis, Miliband's successor as policy chief. But Powell nevertheless became a considerably more powerful presence in the second term, the more so as time wore on, and Hunter, Campbell and Heywood left. Although he believed that his job was one 'best done in the shadows', he realised he had been a rather opaque, mysterious figure in the first term. Just after the election, therefore, he agreed to give an interview to Rachel Sylvester of the *Daily Telegraph*, declaring that he hated 'the picture painted of him in the press, and in the Labour Party even more'.[51] Interviewed at his south London home with his partner Sarah Helm and two daughters in the background, Powell did indeed come across as a more human figure. He also spoke openly about his position in Number 10: 'The White House Chief of Staff makes the machine work,' he told Sylvester. 'I like to try and do a bit more than that.' Powell revealed that when Blair went abroad it was him, not Heywood, who acted as the channel between Blair and the rest of the government. Powell's centrality to Blair was seen in his role in the Afghan and Iraq wars, which he supported strongly, and during which he was a member of Blair's War Cabinets, as he had been earlier for Kosovo. Some of the most striking documents supplied to the Hutton Inquiry were Powell's, which show him relentlessly ensuring that his master was basing his decisions on the strongest possible evidence, and making his case in the best possible way.

The Impact of Jonathan Powell

Rachel Sylvester thought Powell was more influential than Campbell or Anji Hunter.[52] Because Blair put his closest team into boxes, and their roles are therefore not strictly comparable, it is an unhelpful comparison. Powell was certainly a quieter presence than Campbell. Later in his premiership, Peter Stothard noted that Powell did not seem as dominant as Campbell.[53] An obvious contrast between both is that whereas Campbell's impact was strongest earlier on, Powell's grew, especially after 1999 when he found his feet at Number 10. But what did Powell's 'influence' amount to? He was always a keen Atlanticist while also a pro-European, and a key generator of the idea that Britain's role should be the bridge between the two: 'The more you can do that with the Americans, the stronger you are with the Europeans,' he said.[54] His solid affirmation of and practical support for Blair's policy of siding with the US over Iraq helped reinforce Blair's instincts. His position, however, denied Blair a coldly objective analysis of the benefits to Britain of total support for Clinton and then Bush, which a less committed Atlanticist would have offered.

Powell was keen on links with the Liberal Democrats: 'Jonathan let slip that he had been in favour of going for a coalition straight after the election,' Ashdown recorded in his diary,[55] and also wrote that he 'was very enthusiastic for the project'.[56] This enthusiasm helps explain why neither the trade unions, nor the Labour Party, developed any affection for him. 'He's not even vaguely "in the party"', said one senior Cabinet minister. 'He's a clever bastard, but he doesn't have an ounce of political commitment.'[57] His dislike of the left was as strong as his distaste for people who are excessively 'political' – but this perfectly reflected Blair's own thinking.

Powell's commitment was to New Labour, which embodied the virtues of the New Democrats in the US; to power, which he loved; and to Blair, to whom he was devoted. His value to Blair stemmed from his lack of any personal or political agenda combined with his ferocious intellect and work rate. 'I've grown like him,' Powell said of Blair. 'I noticed that my brother began to look more and more like Mrs Thatcher when he worked for her . . . It's like dogs begin to look like their owners [sic].'[58] Powell's ability to merge himself into Blair's persona is indeed striking. 'You know when you are dealing with him that he's inside the mind of Blair,' said one Whitehall insider. 'When he speaks, it is Blair's voice you are hearing.'[59] Oddly perhaps, Powell and Blair – though friendly – were never close friends. Their similar life experiences, devotion to family, their outlook on politics and liking for rock music, might have suggested they would become close. But, unlike Blair and Campbell, he and Blair were never real 'buddies'. Powell moved in the opposite direction to his brother Charles, who began at Number 10 as a reasonably conventional official and left as a highly partisan adviser. Jonathan entered as a political adviser and by the end he had become much more of a conventional civil servant, keeping his political master on the rails. Powell is in the mould of Jock Colville with Churchill (1951–55) or Robert Armstrong with Heath (1970–74), both prodigiously able officials. Powell became an outstanding servant to Blair. What he did was make Blair more effective and better able to do his job as Prime Minister. What he did not do was challenge Blair, or force him to think again, about the seminal issues of his premiership, including Iraq and the way he positioned himself diplomatically with President Bush. On many of the great questions of the day, Powell and Blair thought similarly. He was thus neither Blair's puppet-master, nor his *éminence grise*: he was his voice; and his echo.

Gerry Adams (right) and Martin McGuinness outside Number 10 in December 1997. Blair realised he had to speak to all parties if peace was to be achieved in Northern Ireland. He believed progress could similarly be made by talking to the PLO in the Middle East.

25

Good Friday Agreement, April 1998

One of Jonathan Powell's most significant contributions to Blair was the help he gave him in Northern Ireland. The priority that John Major had given to the province as Prime Minister meant that Powell became far more actively involved in Washington with the issues and key players than previous incumbents of his First Secretary post at the Embassy.[1] Powell was thus ideally placed to stimulate Blair's initial interest in Northern Ireland and then to guide him through the Good Friday Agreement. Blair realised that he had the prospect of securing what no previous Prime Minister had achieved: bringing peace and hope to a part of the United Kingdom that had been terrorised for over thirty-five years at a cost of over 3,000 lives. Major had taken negotiations a long way, but had been stalled in 1996 by the loss of his parliamentary majority and opposition from right-wingers in his party and in the press. Now Blair could finish the task.

Major's concentration on Northern Ireland had one unintended legacy for Blair. By making it such a very high personal priority, in contrast to his predecessors as Prime Minister since 1969 when 'the troubles' had re-erupted, it meant that no British Prime Minister for the foreseeable future could afford not to make it one of their principal priorities too. Blair, like Major, came to power with no prior experience or preconceptions about Ireland. He made much of having an Irish-born (and Protestant-raised) mother,[2] his childhood holidays in Donegal and his Catholic wife, but this was window-dressing. As with Major, it was to become one of the most important achievements of his premiership, where his qualities of charm, ability to inspire trust across divides and sheer bloody-mindedness yielded significant results. Indicatively, it was an area of policy on which Brown never intruded – though he tried to 'recruit' Mo Mowlam in her first week in office by phoning her and offering her support (and, by implication, extra money for the Northern Ireland Office), which was interpreted as a bid to win her as an ally.[3] Nor was it an area of wide interest to Cabinet ministers. It suited Blair ideally. He could take his own decisions from Number 10, largely ignore the rest of Whitehall and Parliament, and engage in personal diplomacy with other leaders, above all Clinton.[4]

Northern Ireland was also to be the first of the overtly 'moral' episodes of Blair's premiership, where he saw a clear right and wrong. There was to be little domestic payback for the hours he spent on Northern Ireland; neither the electorate, nor his party, were going to thank Blair for any progress, any more than they did Major. Blair's motivation for investing so much capital in Northern Ireland as Prime Minister was, according to Lord Williams of Mostyn, the former Labour leader in the Lords, because 'he is a man of moral conscience and religion. He has an ordered life. He wanted to give this to the people of Ireland.'[5]

Preparing the Way, July 1994–March 1998

'Even before the General Election I had taken a very keen interest in what was happening in Northern Ireland,' Blair later said. 'I hadn't done or said anything particularly dramatic other than shifting my own party's position away from one of pushing for a united Ireland. That was really because I had a sense that, if I was going to play a part in the negotiations, I should come to it with relatively clean hands.'[6] 'Shifting Labour's position' meant that one of his earliest acts as leader was ditching Labour's opposition to the Prevention of Terrorism Act, and replacing Kevin McNamara as shadow Northern Ireland Secretary in October 1994 (who was deemed too sympathetic to the Nationalists) with his leadership campaign manager, Mo Mowlam. Blair's instructions to her were to 'do the best job [she] could: there was nothing more specific than that'.[7] He was keen for her to build relationships and trust on both sides of the divide, at which she was very skilled. Less delicately, he told her that their policy was to be 'so far up Major's arse that he can never accuse us of not being behind him'.[8]

Blair indeed ensured that at every twist and turn of policy from October 1994 to 1 May 1997, Labour never deviated from loyally supporting Major. The declared reason for the consensus policy was to move the party forwards to strict neutrality between the Nationalists (John Hume's SDLP and the Republicans, Sinn Féin, led by Gerry Adams), and the Unionists (consisting of the UUP, led by David Trimble, and the DUP, led by Ian Paisley). This change of policy moved Labour to a position of 'equi-distance' between the 'green' and 'orange' sides. The latter, the Unionists, now found it much easier to engage in dialogue than before, when Labour were seen for many years as far closer to the Nationalist or Republican side. The change in stance did indeed give Blair the 'clean hands' for future talks, as he himself said. A more important motive for Labour's public change of policy, however, when successful peace talks were still a very distant prospect, was to insulate Labour from attacks from the right-wing press, specifically *The Times*, *Telegraph*, and *Mail* newspapers. These papers were locked into support for the Unionists and had regarded Labour's Irish policy under Kinnock and Smith as too pro-Nationalist and weak on terrorism. They were often the same papers and commentators who were the most ardent Eurosceptics. Labour's policy on Northern Ireland, as on every other policy area from 1994 to 1997, was also subordinate to the governing imperative of winning the General Election. Being seen to be offering no favours to the Nationalists, and being tough on terrorism, were exactly the messages Blair, Campbell and Powell wanted to convey. As Blair said in November 1995, when refusing to give in to pressure to attack Major's policy on Ireland, 'I can't think there is anything in this for New Labour.'[9]

Behind the scenes, however, fresh thinking was going on. Powell had held regular discussions with Nancy Soderberg, whom Clinton had brought in to the White House with particular responsibility for Northern Ireland. 'We certainly had an interest in making sure that New Labour were up to speed on Northern Ireland,' she said.[10] Soderberg also forged a close relationship with Mowlam. The administration admired Mowlam's forthright style – 'engaged, sensible, direct and knowledgeable', said Tony Lake, National Security Advisor[11] – and saw her as an important ally in achieving a lasting settlement in Northern Ireland, an important objective for the President. When Blair met Clinton in Belfast in November 1995 they discussed Northern Ireland in some detail, albeit with less personal enthusiasm on both sides than in their heated discussions about the 'third way'. When they met again at the White House in April 1996, the President stressed that Blair had a real opportunity to make progress in Northern Ireland and that he should seize it with both hands.[12]

Blair began to think creatively about Northern Ireland from about the time of his November 1995 meeting with Clinton. On a trip to Northern Ireland with Paddy Ashdown, the official who briefed them said, 'Ashdown thought he knew it all. In contrast, Blair was like a magnet, he picked up on all the nuances, was quick, empathetic and perspicacious. I've never experienced anything quite like it in a politician.'[13] From late 1996, Blair became even more focused. 'It was absolutely clear to me that Tony Blair was determined to take Northern Ireland very seriously and that he would make it a top priority,' said one observer.[14] By this time, Whitehall's collective wisdom was that Labour would form the next government: peace talks were formally suspended in Belfast on 12 March 1997, but from long before then all parties to the discussions, and Sinn Féin on the outside, had been positioning themselves for Labour's coming to power. Major authorised Robin Butler to keep Blair's office and Mowlam fully informed of developments. Patrick Mayhew, Major's Northern Ireland Secretary, briefed Mowlam, and she and Blair were given sight of key documents, including the confidential history of the 1991–92 talks.[15] John Chilcot, the Permanent Secretary at the Northern Ireland Office (NIO), arranged a dinner at the Travellers' Club in Pall Mall in early 1997, to which he invited Blair, Powell, Mowlam and Quentin Thomas, his deputy, the official most directly involved in the peace discussions under Major. Blair again impressed his interlocutors by his determination. At one point Blair said to Chilcot that the difference between his position and Major's was that 'Major's enemies on Northern Ireland are the same as his European enemies, whereas it won't be like that for me'.[16]

Blair and his advisers studied Major's approach carefully, and learned from what they saw as his mistakes. In particular, they felt Major had been in error not to have pushed the Unionists harder, and that he could have taken a more flexible position on 'parallel talks' and decommissioning, which the Mitchell Commission had proposed in January 1996.[17] The stalemate between the British and Irish governments over Major's call for elections before all-party talks commenced, and the ensuing fallout on the Nationalist and Republican side, culminating in the end of the ceasefire in February with the fatal bomb in London's Canary Wharf, had threatened to derail the peace process. In the aftermath of the bomb, the two governments agreed to the principle of elections before talks and set a date for them to begin (albeit without Sinn Féin) in June 1996. Campbell, who became very caught up in Northern Ireland, was far more dismissive of Major than Blair, who was privately in awe of Major's commitment and tenacity. Campbell, in contrast, thought Major's stubbornness was irresponsible and that he had foolishly destroyed the opportunities for peace.[18] The Labour press machine put it around that Major had been perverse: on this, as in other areas, the idea was to create an impression of incompetence and venality while not compromising Labour's public stance of support. The Clinton administration took a more subtle and generous view, and believed Major was constrained by his own right wing. Tony Lake blamed the 'straitjacket of his domestic political situation, which left him with little leverage against the Unionists',[19] while George Mitchell, the former US Senator who was chair of the all-party talks, said, 'Major did a good job in very difficult circumstances,' and blames the stalled progress on his 'dwindling majority'.[20] What was beyond doubt was that the peace process, which had looked so promising earlier in the 1990s, was crying out for a fresh beginning.

By the time of polling day in May 1997, Blair was convinced that there was major work to be done by him in Northern Ireland. He told Clinton just after the election that Northern Ireland would be one of the most important priorities of his premiership, news that Clinton received warmly.[21] Labour's landslide victory, though no surprise, was the cause of great optimism to those who wanted to see all-party talks. Blair gave a powerful signal of his priority with his seminal trip to Northern Ireland on 16 May, his first visit outside mainland Britain and his first major speech outside London since becoming Prime Minister. He had already told Mowlam to do her best to bring Sinn Féin back into the talks; Sinn Féin were keen to end their isolation, and she was able to report back promising news to Blair before his visit. He offered Sinn Féin the opportunity to meet British ministers: 'The settlement train is leaving. I want you to be on that train,' he told them,[22] but violence would have to end and the ceasefire recommence, or the talks would go ahead without them.[23] Keeping the Unionists on board was a key objective of his speech, and he worked very hard to reassure them that they had 'nothing to fear' from a Labour government under him, and that the Union with London was utterly secure. The 16 May trip and its message proved strikingly successful, but in going so far to reassure the Unionists he managed to unsettle Sinn Féin, who had to be calmed down for several days afterwards and told 'that there was something in it for them', i.e., inclusion in talks if they accepted a new ceasefire.[24] The speech had set the ball rolling again. Not even the Clinton administration, Soderberg says, 'had expected him to move so quickly and decisively'.[25]

Blair became steadily more interested in working on Northern Ireland as the months wore on.[26] 'I know I'm insanely optimistic,' he would tell his staff at Number 10, who were impressed by his obvious self-belief that he could make a difference.[27] He was buoyed greatly by the presence, within Number 10's Private Office, of John Holmes, who had a very deep understanding of the issues and problems gleaned over his previous year in the job. 'Holmes very quickly made Blair's thinking much more sophisticated,' remarked one aide. 'He was the character whose advice Blair quickly came to trust the most deeply.'[28] One of Holmes' first tasks was helping draft the 16 May speech. Blair needed to draw on all Holmes' wisdom and reserves again when exactly one month later the IRA killed two RUC officers in Lurgan, County Armagh, which was eagerly portrayed by some as a huge rebuff to him for his boldness. It was Blair's first major reverse since he had become Prime Minister six weeks before. The intelligence reports were not clear whether the murders were a signal from the IRA that they were not serious about co-operation, or whether it was a rogue unit acting on its own. Blair gave an emotional interview in which he asked, 'What is going on?' For a few days it seemed that sectarian violence might return. But he held his nerve and the province steadied. Then, on 25 June, the government clarified its criteria for Sinn Féin to join the talks, while simultaneously publishing proposals for handling decommissioning of arms, which were designed to reassure Unionists. On 16 July Gerry Adams announced that he had asked the IRA for a new ceasefire, which began a few days later. In September Sinn Féin accepted the principles laid down by Mitchell for non-violence and entered the talks, and David Trimble led his UUP, the more moderate of the two Unionist parties, back into talks. Although Paisley's DUP remained outside, the Northern Ireland Office rightly regarded the UUP's return as a seminal moment.[29]

At the Labour Party conference in October 1997, Blair spoke with real emotion of the possibility of bringing peace to Northern Ireland. The pace of his overseas engagements had eased in the autumn, and he had more time to devote to the province, encouraged by the consensus among senior officials that a 'power-sharing' agreement involving the Unionists and Nationalists might indeed be attainable.[30] Blair now had to bring Sinn Féin more squarely behind the peace process, and he decided to take the bold step (which Major wanted to do but never felt politically able) of meeting Adams and Martin McGuinness, the IRA's former chief of staff, face to face. This symbolically important move occurred first at Stormont in October and then Blair invited them both to Number 10 in December. It was a high-risk strategy, with the right-wing press just waiting to say he had let himself be duped and was giving in to terrorism. Blair was thus not talking lightly when he said to Adams and McGuinness that he would do anything to reach a peaceful solution, 'but if you ever do a Canary Wharf on me, I will never talk to you again'.[31] Blair had to work doubly hard now to reassure Trimble and Paisley, the latter remaining a lost cause. Great emotional energy would be poured by Blair into each meeting and each phone call: all the time he would be asking himself, 'Do I believe these people? Do I trust them?'[32]

As Blair became increasingly involved from the autumn onwards, he found himself and Number 10 becoming the principal conduits for discussions rather than Mo Mowlam and the NIO. For the first six months after the election, the Blair–Mowlam axis had worked well. Blair had given Mowlam his trust, she did what Number 10 wanted, and she was at the height of her powers and physical strength. Her great skill was handling people, and though never good at detail, she delegated very effectively to her junior minister (later Secretary of State), Paul Murphy, who chaired lengthy negotiations in the province. US politicians continued to think highly of her: 'She knew exactly how to handle the Americans. She was damn good on Capitol Hill and with figures in the administration and the Americans liked her. In the truest sense of the word, she spoke American,' said Christopher Meyer, Kerr's successor as Ambassador to the US.[33]

But by October, if not before, Mowlam's relationship with the Unionists was breaking down: 'It took six months for the Unionists to get pissed off with me,' she said, adding, 'They get pissed off with everyone from the British government eventually.'[34] The DUP and the UUP began to feel she was too 'green', reinforcing the long-held Unionist suspicion that the NIO was 'irredeemably "green"', regardless of which party was in power in Westminster.[35] They were also offended by her unconventional manners and her profane language; she dared to tell Paisley to 'fuck off', a word he found offensive, especially from a lady, and she was deemed a 'sinner'.[36] For a while Mowlam would be the figure that Sinn Féin and the SDLP would speak to, because they admired and liked her very unconventionality (preferring it to the patrician style of her predecessor, Mayhew), while Unionists, who always preferred dealing with Downing Street, would speak to Holmes or Powell in Number 10.[37] By Christmas, Number 10 had taken over talking to the Nationalists and Republicans also, a move which produced tensions between NIO officials, who saw themselves as losing out, and Downing Street. One of Mowlam's last major acts was to help get talks going again after a particularly difficult post-Christmas period: in January 1998, she went personally into Northern Ireland's Maze prison to calm Loyalist paramilitaries and reduce tension. David McKittrick, the veteran Northern Ireland journalist, said of this period, 'The talks would have ended. A lot of people thought they were losing face. Mo Mowlam was the person who helped keep everyone's hopes alive.'[38]

From the New Year, Mowlam began to fade. 'It was extraordinary how quickly Blair's attitude to her changed. When he became Prime Minister, she was his ideal Secretary of State. Six months later she was a liability,' said one Number 10 official.[39] Her real contribution had been in the three years after her appointment in October 1994, above all in gaining trust on all sides to pave the way for talks, and making all parties believe a settlement was possible. It is ironic that her role was undermined initially by the Unionists, and then the Nationalists and Republicans, bypassing her and dealing with Number 10 direct themselves.[40] Despite this, she continued to serve as a valuable channel to the Republicans up to and including the Good Friday Agreement. 'She remained able to give Adams and McGuiness very tough messages, in her own forthright way.'[41]

The talks, which had recommenced in June 1997 again under the chairmanship of George Mitchell, were making slow progress and were threatening to grind to a halt. The early weeks of the New Year of 1998 passed without any breakthrough, so Mitchell took the bold step on 25 March of announcing that there had to be an agreement by midnight on Maundy Thursday, 9 April. It was a make-or-break strategy. 'Holy Week' was symbolic not just because of its Christian promise of new beginnings; it was also a resonant date in Irish history since the Easter Rising against the British in Dublin in 1916. Of crucial importance, though, was the fact that the two-year mandate for talks would come to an end in May 1998 and any referendum and assembly election would have to be held before the province's notorious marching season began in July. These approaching dates help explain why Mitchell's tight deadline was not viewed as 'bouncing' the parties into talks; rather it captured their imagination and concentrated minds.

The talks themselves were in three parts, or 'strands': Strand One concerned the internal government of Northern Ireland, and was negotiated by the Northern Ireland parties themselves, typically with the SDLP making proposals and the UUP accepting or rejecting them; Strand Two was between the Northern Ireland parties and the governments in London and Dublin, and concerned the relationship that would exist north and south of the border in Ireland; and Strand Three was between the governments in London and Dublin, and concerned constitutional and other peace and confidence-building measures, with a group reporting back to the parties in Northern Ireland.

Blair was in regular touch in early 1998 with Clinton and with Bertie Ahern, the Irish Taoiseach, and held meetings with each of the Northern Ireland political parties. Holmes and Powell oversaw the detailed monitoring of the discussions at Stormont Castle in Belfast, which were relayed by a secure feed directly into Number 10, allowing it to receive papers and reports in real time and to make suggestions and phone calls to help keep the process moving forward. Given that Paisley's DUP were on the outside, a vital task for the British was to persuade Trimble and his UUP to reach an agreement, or it would all fall apart. Trimble was perceived by London as an enigmatic and prickly man, who had sworn that he would not commit the mistake of his predecessor, James Molyneaux, of being seduced by cosy chats at Number 10 into giving away too much ground to the Nationalists and Republicans. Trimble initially tried to ensure that he had someone with him when he saw Blair (though as their relationship strengthened and trust was built, he began to see the Prime Minister on his own). He took the UUP's Jeffrey Donaldson with him to Chequers to see Blair on 29 March, Blair's eighteenth wedding anniversary, for which he had arranged a special dinner with Cherie. Blair repeatedly reassured his two sceptical discussants that the principle of 'consent' ensured that Britain would not abandon Northern Ireland and the Union would thus remain as long as the majority wanted it.[42] In countless similar discussions, Blair ground down Trimble, and much of his party, and made them realise the Union's future was safe if they reached agreement.[43] Bertie Ahern from Dublin was performing a similar role with Sinn Féin, keeping them focused on reaching agreement, which meant for them the huge sacrifice of abandoning the goal of a united Ireland (without the consent of the majority in Northern Ireland).

The Easter Week discussions at Stormont, skilfully crafted by the Number 10 press machine, have entered folklore: Blair's riding to the rescue in the nick of time with just two days to go to the deadline Mitchell set, his banging of heads together, the lack of sleep and all-night meetings which alone produced the final result. Agreement was close on all three Strands when on Wednesday, 1 April, Ahern went to London for a summit with Blair. The Taoiseach had become fired up at the eleventh hour with the belief that the Irish government was not getting a good deal on Strand Two (which dealt with north–south bodies). Blair assured Ahern that the bodies would be a serious part of any agreement, but warned him of Unionist sensitivities in this area if he pushed too far.[44] Irish and British officials in London were left to work out the detail on Strand Two on the Thursday and Friday, 2–3 April, with – as it appears – both Prime Ministers, George Mitchell and the negotiating parties in Belfast left out of the loop.[45] Number 10 was aghast when it saw the redrafted Strand Two, which contained a long appendix of issues in which north–south co-operation could occur, while Mitchell was apoplectic, and thought the redraft could derail the entire talks.[46] Discussions carried on over the weekend. By the Monday evening, with seventy-two hours to the deadline, Trimble made it clear that he would never be able to accept the new proposals on Strand Two; the UUP's John Taylor said, 'I would not touch it with a forty-foot barge pole.' On the Tuesday morning, Mitchell announced that unless Strand Two proposals were renegotiated, 'these talks were over'.[47] At this point in the story, the accounts from Number 10 on one side and the NIO on the other (backed up to some extent by Mitchell's testimony), diverge. Number 10's record has Blair, Holmes and Powell persuading Ahern he would have to give way and accept the Unionists would never buy his rewrite.[48] The NIO version blames Blair for 'weakly conceding' to Ahern's wish to make the redraft. An NIO official said: 'Number 10's problem was that they were too distant from the discussions in Stormont. Blair should have known the Unionists would never accept the Strand Two proposals: the Irish government had overplayed its hand and Number 10 had gone along with it.'[49] Turf wars lay behind this difference, with the NIO clearly resenting the Number 10 big boys muscling in on their patch after months of their detailed slog just as the prize looked within reach. 'The redrafted Strand Two is what made me most frustrated and angry in the whole negotiations,' Mitchell said, upset that he was being asked to make out that the revised proposals were his own.[50]

Holy Week moved on into Tuesday with no sign of the deadlock being broken. Blair decided he would cancel all other engagements and go to Northern Ireland himself immediately: 'It was pretty obvious if we were to have a chance of rescuing the thing then I had to go there and try to do it. I would have gone in any event but [it] made it sensible to go sooner rather than later.'[51] He duly arrived that Tuesday evening, 7 April, announcing that 'I feel the hand of history upon our shoulders'. The fate of the talks now rested with Ahern. Would he be willing to co-operate and relent on Strand Two? Ahern flew to Belfast on the Wednesday, 8 April, for a 7 a.m. breakfast meeting with Blair and Mitchell, having decided, against advice from his officials in Dublin, to agree to the renegotiation to keep the Unionists on board. Mitchell believed this switch saved the talks. Ahern then flew back to Dublin for his mother's funeral at 12 noon before flying back again to Belfast.[52] At

7.15 that evening, Blair and Ahern met Trimble and his UUP colleagues and assured them yet again that the principle of consent was the absolute guarantee that there would be no unification without it being the will of the majority.[53]

Blair and his staff took over a suite of offices on the top floor of Stormont, while Ahern set up the Irish government's offices on the floor below. Over the next forty-eight hours both men, working within Mitchell's rigid deadline, helped orchestrate the negotiations. Keeping the Nationalists and Republicans on board with the renegotiated, more 'pro-orange', Strand Two was one of their greatest achievements. At one point Blair made to block a door and said, in effect, 'You are not leaving until we have an agreement.' When Sinn Féin threatened to walk out, Blair, knowing the early release of their prisoners was a primary aim, agreed to reduce the timetable for release below the stipulated three years. Late in the evening of Thursday, 9 April, Ian Paisley led a few hundred of his rejectionist supporters into the grounds of Stormont, waving British flags and shouting that Trimble was a traitor. An agreement was hastily reached for his supporters to disband if he was allowed a press conference, broadcast live on television, in which he intoned his negative rants.

Talks continued throughout that Thursday night, after the midnight deadline passed. Strand One became the final obstacle. Clinton made several calls to help smooth progress, beginning at 10 p.m. Washington time. He spoke to Mitchell and Blair, and then phoned first Trimble, then Adams and after that Hume to coax them along, saying in effect, 'This is a rare historic opportunity, for God's sake don't let it pass.' Clinton's greatest impact was with Sinn Fein, reassuring them that there was something in it for them when the Unionists stood to gain so much, including being the majority voice in the Assembly. This was why the concession on the release of prisoners was so important to Sinn Féin: it was something positive they could show to their supporters that had come out of the negotiations. The final draft of the agreement was circulated on the Friday morning. For a while it looked as if everything was resolved. Blair phoned Cherie, who had already flown to Spain with the children for the Easter Bank Holiday weekend, and said he'd be with them that evening.[54] But now the Unionists raised fresh objections about the release of prisoners and whether Sinn Féin would still serve in the new power-sharing executive in Northern Ireland if the IRA had not yet decommissioned their weapons. Suddenly, the situation once again looked grave. 'They were absolutely on the point of rejecting the agreement, and Jeffrey Donaldson was definitely about to walk out,' recalled one Number 10 aide.[55] Mid-morning, Trimble and some of his UUP colleagues met Blair to talk it over. The outcome now was on a knife edge: Blair pushed up all his charm and persuasion skills and told the Unionists that, while it was too late to change the actual agreement, he would give them the reassurance they required in a 'side letter'. The emissary dispatched to deliver the letter to the Unionists initially could not gain access as the door was barred, and no one heard his banging. Minutes were lost before he was able to deliver his missive. At 4.45 p.m., having absorbed Blair's letter and consulted again with his colleagues, Trimble phoned Mitchell to say 'we're ready to do the business'. 'It was a last-minute rush of political courage from Trimble which helped turn the tide,' said a close Blair aide. 'At one stage we were all convinced it was lost.'[56]

At 5 p.m. all parties to the talks, dazed and exhausted, went for a plenary meeting, where Mitchell went around the table asking each party if they agreed to the final draft of the agreement. Sinn Féin reserved their position, but under the rules of 'sufficient consensus', their positive support was not necessary. Trimble was the last to be asked, and uttered one word: 'yes'. It was an electrifying moment, broadcast live on television. 'I'm pleased to announce that the two governments and the political parties of Northern Ireland have reached agreement,' an emotional Mitchell declared. The main facets of the agreement were a Northern Ireland Assembly, which restored devolution in Northern Ireland; a North/South Council (i.e. Strand Two) to improve cross-border co-operation; agreement by Dublin to amend its constitutional claim to the province; a range of policies on decommissioning of arms; release of prisoners and measures on equality and policing. It was a historic agreement. Unionists agreed to share power with Nationalists and to work with the Irish government on a range of cross-border issues, and the Nationalists recognised the legitimacy of Northern Ireland by accepting the principle of consent. It established a permanent link between Dublin and London, provided by a new broadly based British–Irish Agreement which replaced the Anglo-Irish Agreement of 1985, and it told Sinn Féin that they had their own rightful place in Northern Ireland.

Sinn Féin had yet to ratify the agreement formally, and referendums in the north and south were also required to approve the agreement. Yet all the participants on that Good Friday sensed they had taken part in the most hopeful and constructive moment for peace since the troubles began. The final agreement was written in such a way that both sides could proclaim it as a victory to their own supporters. Trimble thus announced that the agreement made the Union stronger, while Adams said it was 'a phase in our struggle' towards a united Ireland. Blair meanwhile was as untriumphalist as he had been eleven months before on election night: 'Today is only the beginning. It is not the end. Today we have just the sense of the prize before us. The work to win that prize goes on.'

In his statement, Mitchell singled out Blair and Ahern for their leadership, commitment and negotiating skills day and night. It was the most gruelling conference of Blair's premiership and also the most nerve-wracking, because so much was at stake, for him personally and for Britain. His arrival in Stormont was ultimately decisive. It was also controversial on the British side. Some NIO officials believed his presence resulted in concessions being made unnecessarily because he had insufficient command of the detail. 'Strategically, it was a mistake to let your number-one figure become so involved in front-line discussions so long before the deadline.'[57] These officials believed they could have reached all-party agreement that prison releases would not take place without decommissioning; but he conceded this position himself.[58] Their other principal concern was the side letter which Blair gave Trimble on that Friday afternoon on decommissioning, and without the Irish government's, Sinn Féin's or the SDLP's knowledge. The letter was deemed absolutely necessary in bringing the UUP back on side, but resulted in future problems and disagreements over arms decommissioning.[59] Number 10's line is that Blair and his aides were the ones who stopped unnecessary concessions being made. They stress the acute dangers of Sinn Féin walking out of the talks, which they were on the verge of doing several times, and their frustration and concern that the real guarantees were being offered to the Unionists, not themselves.

Unsurprisingly, given its traditionally pro-Nationalist leanings, the White House thought that 'Tony Blair on occasion was too willing to accommodate the Unionists'. James Steinberg added, though, that 'these were judgement calls and the White House left him to make his own judgements'.[60] Clinton himself was grateful that Blair invested so much of his time and authority into negotiations. 'Blair cared about it as much as Clinton cared about it,' said a Clinton aide, 'which was a great deal.'[61] Some in Number 10 did not hold the same rose-tinted view of Clinton's White House: 'They never understood for a second our worries about the Republicans as terrorists, or the need for decommissioning, which they never at that stage took seriously.'[62]

Clinton's importance in securing the Good Friday Agreement is one aspect of the story that is controversial. Clinton's role was important, notably his phone calls early on Good Friday itself, which had an effect particularly on Adams, and for his rich lauding of Blair, which made it harder for the Nationalists and Republicans to attack what he was doing. Clinton, however, while keen to see a resolution, was not at all keen to give ground to the Unionists, any more than his own staff, Nancy Soderberg and James Steinberg. 'The idea that they were in any sense objective is a joke,' complained one Blair aide.[63] When Blair most wanted Clinton's support, after the Good Friday Agreement, to help secure a 'yes' vote on the referendums whose positive result he never regarded as pre-ordained,[64] some of the British side believe Clinton was the most reticent in offering it. Clinton's former aides, unsurprisingly, contest this view, and assert that he made a profound difference. Right until the end, they argue, Clinton was in 'constant touch'. What is clear, however, is that he could have played a much greater role still, and might well have done so if his second term had not been so disrupted by the Lewinsky affair.

Although the media's attention faded after the agreement was reached, there was considerable work for Blair still to do. Indeed, in the period up to the General Election in 2001, his private office estimated that Northern Ireland took more of his time than any other 'overseas' issue except Kosovo.[65] Once the referendum in Northern Ireland was successfully won, with a 71 per cent 'yes' vote (the south voted 94 per cent in favour), he devoted countless hours to decommissioning, establishing the north–south dialogue, and the power-sharing executive, and dealing with outbreaks of violence. If the IRA was to return to violence, he realised he would be vulnerable to the charge that he had made too many concessions and would have blood on his hands.[66] The Omagh bomb, which killed 29 people and injured 200 just four months after the Good Friday Agreement, was a horrific setback, although it was the work not of the IRA itself but of the 'Real IRA', who wanted to reverse the agreement and continue the armed struggle. Outrage over this atrocity, which was the bloodiest to ever hit the province, stunned leaders across the political divide, with Gerry Adams one of those to condemn the act.[67] When Blair and Clinton met the bereaved a fortnight later and voiced their resolve, the urgency and need for pursuing the peace process could not have been more pressing.[68]

Blair continued to work very closely throughout with Ahern, in a remarkable partnership unusual for the fact that, unlike many relation- ships between heads of government, they were much closer personally than their staffs.[69] Their friendship sustained them in the gruelling demands of resolving difficulties – decommissioning proved the most intractable – long after the glamour of Holy Week had faded.

Even though Blair's goal of establishing a settled all-party devolved government and assembly for Northern Ireland proved elusive, his commitment to encouraging both sides of the sectarian divide to work together never dimmed. His achievement was to help bring relative peace, stability, economic prospects and optimism to Northern Ireland: whether long-lasting or temporary, only time will tell. The Good Friday Agreement, although severely battered, had proved strong enough to survive the Omagh bomb and other acts of violence, the seemingly endless prevarication over decommissioning of arms, and the ambivalence among the Unionists about whether they were committed to the agreement or not. Whatever happens in the future, it will remain a major milestone in Irish and British history.

The Good Friday Agreement was important to Blair personally because he wanted to show the world that he could achieve objectives where others had failed, and that he had a clear moral vision. His interest and early statements on Northern Ireland before May 1997 were dictated by expediency. By the time he became engaged, he ceased to care what the right-wing press and commentators would say. It was the first occasion he took decisions on an issue that involved terrorism, where human life was directly at stake. Making a success of it, in an area without input from Gordon Brown, boosted his self-confidence immeasurably. The experience schooled him to rely not on the official Whitehall team but on a close cadre of officials within Number 10 and on his personal diplomacy with leaders abroad: it was a pattern he was to return to later. Had agreement not been reached, it is unlikely he would have felt emboldened to go on and take tough decisions over wars abroad in the future. It also boosted his standing internationally. Progress on the talks during Holy Week was an international story and the successful outcome bathed him in personal glory. The Good Friday discussions were the first time he imposed himself on a major problem, took over from the Secretary of State and made history. He was exploring his own ability to take a deep-seated problem and deal with it. It was a life-changing experience for him.

Blair with President Clinton at a press conference in the garden of Number 10.
The nature of the relationship between the two men is palpable.

26

Bill Clinton

Despite Blair's frustration with Clinton in the aftermath of the Good Friday Agreement, and the greater frustration he was to feel the following year over Kosovo, no foreign leader made as big an impression on Blair, nor was as close to him personally, as Clinton. Both men challenged the prevailing orthodoxies within their parties, were non-ideologues captivated by the promise of finding a 'third way' in politics, and they were both natural extroverts who wanted to reach out across conventional frontiers to win new converts to their cause. As with many of his relationships discussed in this book, Blair began very much as the junior partner: full of admiration – indeed, awe – but from afar. Then for a while they were soulmates. But then, after 1999, despite Blair's public protestations to the contrary, a degree of disillusion set in. On close examination, the relationship, for all its undoubted importance particularly early on, turns out to have amounted to less than is widely believed.

Bill Clinton, the Man

Clinton was born on 19 August 1946 in Hope, Arkansas. He was named William after his father, a mechanic, who was killed in a car accident three months before he was born. When Bill was just two, his mother left him with her parents while she went off to study to become a nurse. She remarried Roger Clinton, a car salesman, whose surname he adopted. Ferociously determined, Bill earned a place at the prestigious Georgetown University in Washington DC to study international affairs.

After graduating in 1968, he won a Rhodes Scholarship to study politics at Oxford, before going on to law school at Yale.

Clinton's career moved with extraordinary speed. He graduated from Yale in 1973, and went on to teach law at Arkansas University. The following year, aged twenty-eight, he ran unsuccessfully for Congress as a Democrat, helped by Hillary Rodham, whom he had met at Yale. They married the following year, and in 1976 he was elected Arkansas Attorney General before becoming, in 1978, aged thirty-two, Governor of Arkansas, the youngest Governor in the US. Political impetuosity led to his defeat two years later at the same time as the Republican Ronald Reagan was swept to power in the White House. Clinton modified his political stance and was re-elected in 1982, becoming by 1992 the longest-serving Governor when, at the age of forty-five, he was elected President.

Clinton and Blair

Blair was influenced by Clinton long before they met. The early links via Philip Gould and Jonathan Powell have already been discussed, as has the influence of Blair's visits to the US in 1991–93, on the development of his, and Labour's, thinking and on the creation of Millbank. However, by the time Blair became leader in July 1994, Clinton's presidency was beset by difficulties, culminating in the failure of his landmark healthcare reform bill, which finally crashed that August, and the persistent 'Whitewater' scandal concerning a property investment the Clintons had made in Arkansas in the 1970s. Blair was happy to adopt the name 'New Labour' from the autumn of 1994 in imitation of the 'New Democrats'. But at the same time, he began to distance himself from the 'flip-flop' president, who seemed destined to be just a one-term incumbent after the Congressional mid-term elections that November, when the Democrats lost control of the House of Representatives for the first time in forty-two years. Gould would whisper, 'Clinton could still win a second term,' but many discounted the possibility.[1] 'Two years ago there was much talk about the "Clintonisation of the Labour Party". We will be hearing no more of that,' wrote Rawnsley in late 1994.[2]

By the time of their first meeting, in the US Ambassador's residence in London when Clinton was en route to Ireland in November 1995, his prospects for re-election looked much more promising. Clinton now became the third senior politician, alongside Roy Jenkins and Margaret Thatcher, to whom Blair looked for inspiration about where he might lead Labour in its post-Clause IV age. The common ground between Clinton's

Democratic party and Blair's Labour Party was the main theme of their first encounter. Blair would have recognised many of the weaknesses of the old Democratic party. Branded by opponents as the party of 'tax and spend', it was also seen as soft on welfare, crime and defence. In brief, it had many of the liabilities of 'old' Labour. Like Blair, Clinton saw the progressive left as possessing the key ideas for the 1990s (as the 'new right' had in the 1980s), and the key to moving away from the past and winning and retaining power. Wim Kok of Holland and Fernando Henrique Cardoso of Brazil had been among the earliest leaders to articulate this thinking, and both Clinton and Blair were excited about its international dimension. At their meeting in London, Blair specifically wanted to know more about how Clinton had moved the Democrats into the centre ground and how Clinton went on to win the election in 1992.[3] Blair presented the President with a sheet of paper itemising the problems which he thought centre-left parties had to solve, including how to change perceptions that they were in favour of big government and high taxes, and the opportunities they had to portray the right as sectarian, selfish and opposed to the concept of 'one nation'.[4] Clinton was clearly charmed by the eager young Labour leader, and the pleasure in their discussion was mutual.[5] That evening Blair attended John Major's official Downing Street dinner in honour of Clinton, Blair's first visit to Number 10.

The encounter went so well that Blair and his team decided he should visit Washington before the General Election. Pictures of Blair with Clinton would add to his gravitas, and the trip would demonstrate at home and abroad how much higher Labour's standing now was in Washington than in the past.[6] In John Kerr, the British Ambassador (1995–97), they had someone who took to the task of making the trip work with enthusiasm. On 11 April 1996, over a hundred guests were duly invited to a dinner at Edwin Lutyens' grand ambassador's residence, including journalists, commentators and all the most influential figures from Congress and the administration Kerr could muster. 'There's no doubt that Blair had the scent of victory about him, and he was already the big draw in Washington,' he said.[7] Blair's aura of success was heightened still further by the dramatic news coming through in mid-dinner that Labour had won the Staffordshire South-East by-election, reducing the Conservatives' majority in the Commons to just one.[8] After the dinner, Blair spoke for a few minutes off the cuff, about his plans and hopes for the future, about Northern Ireland and about trade. The American guests were struck not only by his charm and confidence, but also by his modesty. He praised Major's achievement in Northern Ireland and said that, if he were to be elected, he would be very proud of himself if he could do as well.[9] On

economics, he more than reassured his audience that the Labour Party had
indeed changed from its socialist, protectionist past and now backed free
trade: 'I was very pleased and a bit surprised by the speech,' commented
Larry Summers, then deputy Secretary at the US Treasury.[10]

The next day Blair went with Campbell, Powell and Hunter,
accompanied by Kerr, to see Clinton, who 'welcomed Blair to the White
House with the kind of exuberance (and the attendant flood of words)
that he seldom lavished on overseas guests', according to the *New York
Times*.[11] The meeting lasted just over an hour, a long time for Clinton to
grant an overseas leader, especially one who was still only a leader of the
opposition.[12] The Oval Office conversation ranged over problems of
financing welfare reform without raising taxes, the state of play in
Northern Ireland, and the relationship between the prosperous West and
the developing world. 'What struck me most was how well they
immediately got on,' said Kerr.[13] Despite this being only their second
meeting, a close personal understanding was firmly cemented. 'Seeing the
President in the White House and having him treat Tony as a very serious
player meant a huge amount to us,' recalled a close Blair aide.[14] Clinton had
to be very cautious in what he said publicly so as not to offend Major, but
he left his new friend in no doubt that he looked forward to working with
him in the future.[15]

The same sense of novelty and excitement infused the whole three-day
trip. Campbell did his work beforehand to ensure that the Kinnock débâcle
nine years before would not be repeated. The *Washington Post* and *New York
Times* ran substantial and laudatory articles heralding the visit, which was
in itself a feat considering the number of heads of state and government
who constantly pass through the US. Blair made several television
appearances, gave a news conference at the National Press Club, had
meetings with Secretary-General Boutros Boutros-Ghali of the UN and
Alan Greenspan, Chairman of the Federal Reserve. He had a long talk
with Hillary Clinton (who 'instantly felt a connection'[16]) at the
Washington home of Sidney Blumenthal,[17] who had tipped Blair in the
New Yorker as the 'next Prime Minister', and Blair spoke at a breakfast
meeting in New York hosted by Henry Kissinger,[18] where he received 'rave
reviews' from financier George Soros.[19] While in New York he also spoke
to the Chamber of Commerce and reassured his audience that, for all his
pro-Europeanism, he regarded the US highly and would always work to
ensure that the US and Europe were in step.[20] Everywhere he went, Blair
won friends. The more astute in Clinton's team noticed, however, that it
was talk about elections and campaigning rather than detailed policy that
principally captivated him.[21] The coming General Election was obviously

very much on his mind throughout his trip, and he was delighted to have won over so many powerful American friends. No British opposition leader, since Churchill gave his 'iron curtain' speech in 1946, and no Labour leader ever, had been so fêted in the US. One can understand why those in Blair's inner circle rated it as the most exciting experience they had had in opposition after the Hayman Island visit.[22] Much was also made by Blair's camp of the poor relationship between Clinton and Major – too much, in the eyes of many, including Clinton's National Security Advisor Tony Lake: 'Clinton and Major got on extremely well. It was a myth, put around by political consultants and the media, that they didn't.'[23] But, even though the impression was flawed, it stuck, to Blair's gain and Major's chagrin.

Clinton and Blair did not meet again for another year. Clinton was busy fighting for his re-election in November 1996, a contest Blair was most anxious for him to win – defeat would have given the Tories the chance to claim that a modernising, centre-left leader had nothing lasting to offer in the contemporary world.[24] Clinton's defeat of Bob Dole thus came as a huge boost to the Blair camp, and a corresponding blow to Major's. Blair's and Clinton's offices kept in close contact over the next few months until Blair's own victory, which was assisted by liberal borrowing from Democrat experience, including the presence at Millbank of Stan Greenberg, Clinton's former pollster. Clinton's enthusiastic phone call to Blair early in the morning on 2 May was followed by his message to the press: 'I'm looking forward to serving with Prime Minister Blair. He's a very exciting man, a very able man. I like him very much.'[25] 'At last the President has a little brother,' wrote Sidney Blumenthal, who claimed to be prime instigator of the relationship: 'Blair is the younger brother Clinton has been yearning for.'[26]

With Clinton re-elected and Blair now elected, the amiable talk and backslapping had a chance to be turned into something concrete. What substance would emerge from their own and their aides' close fellowship? The answer, from their first meeting in London on 29 May, just four weeks after the election when the Clintons called in en route to Europe, was inconclusive. Clinton addressed the Cabinet, a hugely symbolic event, and he attended a joint press conference in the garden of Number 10. Clinton was full of praise for Blair: 'I cannot keep up with him. I used to be like him,' Peter Riddell reported one of his aides saying.[27] During the day, Clinton expressed his hopes for a fresh start in Northern Ireland, and they both spoke about the 'Anglo-American model' as the face of the twenty-first century in contrast to the *dirigiste* continental and free-market models that had dominated the twentieth century. The principal importance of the meeting was not substance but symbolism. 'For people working in the White House, Tony Blair's election gave us great heart and validated what we were doing. Clinton was intrigued by what Blair was thinking and saying.'[28] Under fire for his relationship with Paula Jones, Clinton also believed that association with his young and transparently clean friend would rebound favourably on him. Blair was indeed just what Clinton needed. 'Clinton was very close to Kohl, and also to Yeltsin; but there was no other foreign leader with whom he was closer than Tony Blair,' said Sandy Berger, Lake's powerful successor as National Security Advisor.[29]

A striking feature was that the wives also struck up a close personal friendship, and that the four bonded as a unit. The fact that all of them were lawyers strengthened the ties. They discussed education and welfare that day, and their shared concerns about 'the pervasive influence of the media', Hillary recalled, which was appropriate in view of the feverish media interest in the visit and the dinner.[30] Cherie listened intently while Hillary spoke to her about the challenges of her new role, about which she was learning fast. Dinner at Terence Conran's Le Pont de la Tour restaurant by Tower Bridge went on so long that many of Clinton's enormous entourage were kept waiting on board Air Force One: 'The delay went on longer and longer, and we just kept saying "they're clearly getting along because we're still sitting here on the tarmac".'[31]

Little substance was added to the glitter at their next meeting at Denver for the G8 summit in June. Personal relationships were again high on the agenda and Number 10 and the White House were faced with the task of arranging a dinner for both couples at the last minute.[32] Nor had the precise substance of a Clinton–Blair agenda been fleshed out by the time Christopher Meyer was appointed to succeed Kerr as British Ambassador in the autumn of 1997. The Foreign Office, which Downing Street marginalised in the handling of the US, as it had under Major, had no guidance to offer Meyer. 'We'll make sure they know you're Tony's choice,' were Jonathan Powell's only instructions for the new ambassador. 'Your job is to get up the arse of the White House and stay there.'[33] Meyer arrived in Washington DC only two weeks after leaving his brief sojourn at the Bonn Embassy. He and his glamorous new wife were very much the 'New Labour' standard-bearers in the US. Invitations from the British Embassy had always been highly prized in Washington's social circles, but Christopher and Catherine Meyer boosted further the social cachet of the Embassy. The more nostalgic (and elderly) drew comparisons with the glamour of Lord Harlech's time as ambassador, when Kennedy had been in the White House. Meyer had ample time for entertaining for a number of reasons. When he arrived in the US at the end of October, he was told by old Washington hands, 'You've come at a quiet time.'[34] So, for a time, it was. Much of the most important 'traffic' between Blair and Clinton also went direct, with the Embassy merely being kept informed. In Meyer's first few months, Northern Ireland was the main issue under discussion.[35]

Much of both leaders' time together in 1997 and 1998 was also spent not on solving pressing world problems but on abstract debate. One of the fruits that emerged from discussions during the Clintons' May 1997 visit was a conference held at Chequers that November to discuss how 'third way' thinking might be developed. The third way, which set out to provide fresh answers to the conventional responses of left and right, had been in circulation for some years. But it was seized on tightly by Blair and Clinton as providing an intellectual cover and coherence for their brand of progressive centre politics. The third way purported to offer, in a way that was never made entirely clear, fresh government responses in the light of the modern challenges of globalisation, technological change and the enhanced position of women.[36] Hillary was the principal mover behind the Chequers conference.[37] She wanted to share the experiences of the Democrats, who had faced major challenges with their progressive policies in their first four years in power, with New Labour, whom she believed would now face similar experiences in office.[38] The foreign policy establishment in Washington, principally the National Security Council, however, was not keen on the conference. They considered it a distraction from hard diplomatic issues, and were worried about offending other US allies by appearing too close to Britain. From a traditional foreign policy perspective, Steinberg felt that there was a lot to lose and very little to gain from an American President pursuing this avenue.[39] Concerns were allayed in part by an agreement that Clinton himself would not attend, and by an agreement that participants would not discuss foreign policy.[40] Hillary duly arrived at Chequers on 31 October, the evening before the conference, and 'stayed up late into the night sitting in front of the large stone fireplace in the Great Hall', talking with the Blairs about welfare policy, sharing their irritation at France for its 'perfidy' over Iraq and Iran, as well as discussing personal concerns, including what Blair called the 'cellular fatigue' that came with their jobs, and the connection of their Christian faith to their political beliefs.[41] Religious faith was another bond that united Blair and the Clintons.

The following day, 1 November, the participants arrived at Chequers, including Brown, Mandelson and Miliband, as well as Professor Anthony Giddens, Director of the LSE and Britain's leading authority on third-way thinking. From the US came a high-powered group including Al From,

Joseph Nye, Blumenthal and several leading figures from the administration. Blair opened the meeting by saying that 'there is a danger that we will, having won power, fail to win the battle for ideas', and he spoke about the role of an 'enabling government' in helping individuals to succeed. Self-interest was best served, he said, when we act for others, not ourselves (a thought which owed more to Peter Thomson than the third way).[42] There was much talk about how global changes in the 1980s and 1990s had affected the task and expectations of government, and the implications for welfare policy.

The reaction to the discussions were mixed. Professor Joseph Nye of the Kennedy School of Government at Harvard felt that 'the seminar was very high quality. Most interesting to me was how ready Tony Blair was to participate in something semi-academic. He would jump in and hold his own.'[43] Another American, who was less impressed by Blair's command of detail, said he was confused about whether 'I should be pleased to be with the First Lady of the United States and the Prime Minister of Great Britain discussing topics they regarded as momentous, or whether there was really a lot of bullshit going on in the room'.[44] The three 'mantras' of the New Democrat zealots − 'opportunity, responsibility and community' − were offered for British consideration, and were taken very seriously, notably, Giddens thought, by Brown.[45] There was no doubting the earnestness of the British contingent to learn: the concern was whether the third-way ideas could be applied to anything more substantial than rhetoric and electioneering.

Hillary was hugely excited by the discussions and persuaded her husband to host a follow-up meeting at the White House, which was timed to coincide with the Blairs' state visit in early February 1998. By this time, the relationship between Clinton and Blair was approaching that of equals: 'Blair was no longer in awe of Clinton,' said one British official.[46] Talk of Clinton being the 'older brother' was no longer heard, not least because Blair was clearly coming to Clinton's aid in his hour of need after another sexual relationship had come to light, this time with a young intern, Monica Lewinsky. The scandal exploded on the Washington scene shortly before the state visit. Many of Washington's senior figures and political observers told Meyer that Clinton was finished, 'he would be gone within a week, three weeks max. There was no way he could survive this.'[47] Meyer reported all this back to London, where his views were carefully scrutinised in Number 10, along with other intelligence, and some concern built over whether the President could indeed survive.[48] Blair told Ashdown he thought Clinton had only a 60 per cent chance of weathering the storm.[49] Serious consideration was given to cancelling or postponing the trip. Anguished conversations took place across the Atlantic. Blair, however, wanted the trip to go ahead (as, naturally, did Clinton). The President's position began to stabilise day by day, and the worry of how a cancellation would be interpreted also contributed to the decision that the trip should go ahead.[50]

Blair was determined to stand by Clinton both for political reasons (Clinton's fall would give heart to the right and diminish the chance of a Democrat successor as President in 2000) and for personal reasons (he genuinely liked and admired him). Aides deny that Blair the moralist and family man disapproved in private of Clinton's sexual encounters with Lewinsky, most of the details of which he had still to absorb, but he had to dodge some difficult press questions in London before he left.[51] One in the large British party recalled that 'honestly, most of the conversation on the flight over was about Lewinsky'.[52] The scandal dominated Blair's and Clinton's joint press conference, when ten of the sixteen questions addressed the matter. Blair had debated his line fully with Campbell and Powell, and they decided that if he were to display a 'scintilla' of reservation about Clinton it would be seized upon by the press. They knocked about his various responses and let Clinton know beforehand what he was going to say. When the inevitable question came whether he feared his support for Clinton might backfire, Blair, visibly ill at ease, gave his response: 'I have found him . . . someone I am proud to call, not just a colleague, but a friend.' Clinton should be judged, he said, on his record, which is 'pretty impressive'.[53] At the state dinner that evening, Clinton more than matched his compliments. 'Tony has acted with lightning speed to bring renewed vigour to the political institutions of his country,' Clinton declared in a toast dedicated to his 'much valued friends and colleagues, Tony and Cherie'.[54] Blair responded with an emotional and personal toast, which brought a tear to several eyes. He quoted biblical remarks by Harry Hopkins, Roosevelt's Special Assistant, to Churchill, in the midst of the Second World War: 'Whither thou goest, I will go, and whither thou will lodgest, I will lodge. Thy people shall be my people, and thy God, my God.'[55] Blair then continued, 'And Hopkins paused and then he said "Even to the end", and Churchill wept.' Some considered the remarks embarrassingly sentimental, but it was just what most in the audience that night at the White House, especially Clinton's team, wanted to hear. But was it measured?

Previously classified US government documents, released for this book under the US Freedom of Information Act, reveal the wide range of foreign policy issues that the State Department was eager for Clinton and Blair to discuss during their meeting. These included Chinese relations, with Robin Cook's trip to China in January and Blair's own plans for a visit later in the year carefully noted. 'The UK will be deeply involved in Chinese diplomacy this year,' Clinton was told; he should use his time with Blair to stress the need to 'continue to draw China into the international economic community'.[56] One briefing paper classified 'secret' reviewed the growing opposition from many in the international community to sanctions against Libya, which the UK and the US were determined to maintain until Gaddafi agreed to surrender the suspects for the Lockerbie bombing; another paper outlined the status of the Northern Ireland peace process, stressing to Clinton the importance of US support in 'reinforcing the credibility and momentum of the peace process'.[57] (This was just weeks before Holy Week.)

Given such careful preparation, how far did the visit advance the foreign policy agendas of the two countries? The most important discussions were on Iraq, where Blair and Clinton agreed that they would be ready to use force if Iraq failed to comply with the will of UN. Blair also encouraged Clinton to nudge Sinn Féin towards reaching a final agreement in the spring. However, little else of great import was resolved during the visit.

Substance overall took second place during the February trip to glamour, style and continuing third-way 'wonkery', as it was known. 'When we arrived at Andrews Air Force base there was this huge line of black stretch limos on the tarmac: it was like a Hollywood movie,' said one of the party who was new to the experience.[58] The formal centrepiece of the visit was the state dinner on 5 February, followed by 'entertainment' in a tent on the West Terrace provided, in Anglo-American spirit, by Elton John and Stevie Wonder, whose songs included 'My Cherie Amour', in tribute to the lady guest of honour. Guests for the evening included Harrison Ford, Tom Hanks, Steven Spielberg and Barbara Streisand. Clinton was determined to do everything in his power to celebrate and thank Blair for his support. 'It was the most coveted state dinner in the eight years of the Clinton administration,' said one White House aide. 'Both sides felt that they were part of the same undertaking. There was genuine, real camaraderie.'[59]

The 'wonkery' aspect of the trip came with a three-hour policy seminar in the White House on the third way, dubbed 'Chequers Two'. Chief among the British wonks were Miliband, Mulgan and Giddens and, among the politicians who flew over for the seminar, Straw, Milburn and Helen Liddell, who Blair boasted were among his finest.[60] Blair argued that the centre-left was redefining patriotism, with Labour's appropriation of the 'one nation' tag from the Tories and the Democrat's talk of 'One America'. Both he and Clinton agreed on the right's advantage with its superior access to media power – about which Clinton spoke with particular feeling as almost hourly media reports came in revealing some new development in the Lewinsky saga.[61] It was not the ideal backdrop for a serious seminar. The consensus was that the seminar did not match 'Chequers One', in part because 'the sequel is never as good as the movie',[62] as one participant put it, and in part because Clinton was tired and distracted. He kept coming in and out of the meeting, making sharp and relevant interjections but then wandering off, leaving participants feeling that, whatever they said, he had already thought of it. Everyone knew what was troubling him: 'Whenever we had a break, the American politicians would huddle in the corner to discuss the latest twist in the Lewinsky scandal,' said Joseph Nye.[63]

Despite the meeting being relatively disappointing, the determination to continue with the third-way dialogue remained strong. The initial drive by the Clintons and Blairs was now taken over with enthusiasm by their aides, many of whom had formed close personal friendships. Blair himself saw a new angle: as he told Ashdown a month later, the third-way discussions were having 'international repercussions'.[64] He was referring to his wish to extend the invitation to left-of-centre European leaders, with he himself acting as bridge between the Democrats in the US and EU social democrat parties who were pursuing common policies. With his hopes for the Euro squashed the previous autumn, this, he hoped, might be another way of him providing leadership in Europe.[65] Clinton too wanted to remain involved, and to bring Brazil into the process.[66] Romano Prodi, the Italian Prime Minister and Goran Persson, the Swedish PM, were invited to the next 'third way' meeting at New York University in September, and Schröder of Germany and Cardoso of Brazil to one in Florence in November 1999. The meetings broadened out still further after the 2001 General Election, with multinational meetings in Britain in the summer of 2002 and 2003.

Blair did not suffer the political damage at home or abroad that some predicted from the February trip. What it did was powerfully bond both men and their teams. As the two leaders walked away from the press conference, Clinton confided in Blair, 'I'm going to make sure you're proud of what you did in there.' Steinberg also came up to Meyer after it was over and said, 'We owe you big time for this.'[67] Meyer reported his comments back to London and suggested they give serious thought to what they wanted the 'payback' to be. His own view was that it should be to support Blair in the coming Northern Ireland crunch talks.[68] Frustration in the Embassy and in London mounted when it was believed that Blair was not demanding enough from the 'gratitude dividend'. Some claim that 'the relationship went on to a higher plain after this visit', but it is difficult to see much evidence of a new level of US willingness to support Britain as a result. Clinton made some contributions to Northern Ireland, but, as already seen, he did not help nearly as much as the British hoped, nor was the American contribution as important as later trumpeted.[69]

As a result of the trip, the link between Cherie and Hillary became exceptionally strong.[70] The backdrop of the Lewinsky revelations made the visit particularly painful for Hillary. Sensing this, Cherie felt stirred to support a fellow high profile woman in need at a luncheon held in her honour in the White House, to which a wide range of successful women had been invited. She gave a lengthy, moving toast to Hillary and everything she represented. 'It was absolutely beautiful,' recalled one member of Hillary's staff. 'Everybody talked about it afterwards.'[71] Neither Hillary nor Cherie was to have a relationship of anything approaching a similar intensity with another wife of a national leader; their friendship continued throughout Bill Clinton's time in the White House and beyond. In 2000, when Blair was in New York City for the United Nations millennium summit, Cherie arranged to catch up with Hillary so that she could introduce baby Leo, an encounter that was important to both women. By this stage, Hillary was engrossed in her election campaign for the US Senate but, to the annoyance of her campaign staff, she willingly took time out to see her old friend again.[72]

For all the bonhomie, Washington was a hard-nosed and also a plural community, and it was not going to prejudice its judgement of American interests to thank a close ally who had ridden to the rescue in the President's hour of need. Number 10 could be equally unsentimental too: 'Blair wasn't starry-eyed about Clinton,' said one top official.[73] But was Blair sufficiently clear-eyed about what he might expect back from Clinton? For the remainder of 1998, the advice Number 10 was receiving from the Washington Embassy was that Clinton was a damaged President. The Embassy did not now believe, barring some damning new evidence, that he would fall, but his political capital was thought to be in terminal decline.

Accordingly, the pace of Blair and Clinton talks was slower for the remainder of the year, the decision about air strikes against Saddam being the principal point of discussion. They met when Clinton visited Northern Ireland in early September and again at the 'third way' seminars at New York University later the same month. This event came at a stage when Clinton was particularly badly mired in the Lewinsky scandal, with new video evidence producing some lurid sexual details. Most of Clinton's team had come up to New York for a UN session in the morning followed by the seminar. As the day wore on, and the latest revelation on the tapes appeared less threatening than they had feared, they visibly relaxed. By the end of the third-way session Clinton's aides were described as 'cock a hoop'. The Clintons and Blairs disappeared into an alcove alone for forty-five minutes, and went over the day's events intently together, with the Blairs offering solace and support. Before he had come to New York, Blair had to throw off criticism of his unwavering support for Clinton. The Labour chair of the Commons Foreign Affairs Committee said, 'It would be absurd to be the last of the Mohicans, clutching the President when all his entourage are deserting him.'[74] But, again, Blair escaped without damage from standing by Clinton, and, overall, 1998 was judged to be a good year in Anglo-American relations. The British Embassy in Washington reported back to London on a 'flowering of British–US relations' with the February visit 'reminiscent of the glory days of Thatcher and Reagan'.[75]

Blair and Clinton had no face-to-face contact again until they met in April 1999, at the height of the Kosovo crisis. Until this point, Britain had been one of several leading countries that were important to the US; after Kosovo, and the increased authority Blair's stance gave Britain, the relationship became more central to the US, and there was less nervousness from Washington about being seen to have such a close and exclusive relationship with Britain. This enhanced status ironically came at the very moment when Blair and Clinton lost some of their mutual respect over the way each conducted themselves during this crisis. As we will see in the next chapter, the relationship became quite ugly at one point, notably over a telephone conversation in May, and both men, each under severe pressure, saw a side to the other that had not been revealed in their previous warm encounters.

Their personal relationship, though it remained strong, never recovered the extraordinary euphoria and mutual adulation of 1996–98. For Blair, Clinton's vacillation on Kosovo and his sexual behaviour took the shine off their rapport. Like Harold Macmillan before him, who was thrown by hearing about Kennedy's sexual exploits, Blair found it hard to comprehend Clinton's proclivities. 'It was all rather embarrassing,' said the unfortunate official who had to brief Blair. 'I had to tell him what Clinton was supposed to have done and when sex was sex and when it wasn't. He couldn't believe it. I thought to myself "he doesn't understand the details of these things".'[76] When the details were revealed of Clinton's philandering and deceit, Blair's intense admiration for an 'older brother' with whom he had spoken about God, and to whose rescue he had defiantly come, turned to disillusion. For his part, Clinton looked across the Atlantic wistfully, and realised that the future was Blair's, while he had become just a shadow of what he had once promised.

The dialogue between the White House and Number 10 still chuntered on in Clinton's twilight. Much time went into thinking about a state visit, an honour to be afforded instead to President Bush in 2003. But with the distraction of impeachment (official reason) and Blair's concern about how such a state visit would be seen (unofficial reason), the idea 'ran out of time'.[77] Clinton's marginalisation from the London–Washington dialogue was becoming obvious to all in the second half of 1999, as the focus shifted to what the State Department and Pentagon thought, and who would be the next President. By the end of 1999, Meyer felt that the year had been more argumentative for GB/US relations, due in part to the Clinton–Blair differences over Kosovo but also because of suspicion from other parts of the administration to the post-St Malo European Defence Initiative, which Blair was pushing heavily.[78] Number 10 had also come to the view that Washington was not being sufficiently firm on Saddam following their joint air attacks at the end of 1998,[79] although White House officials deny this was ever brought up in discussions with the British.[80]

Clinton was a lame duck in his final year in office in 2000. Blair had little further political need of him, and Number 10's focus during 2000 was very much on the next incumbent of the White House. They looked to Gore, but felt nowhere near as comfortable with the prospect as they had with Clinton when the relationship was at its height. There was none of the ready camaraderie with Gore, nor the same political affinity – Gore was not excited by the third-way agenda that had so fired Clinton and Blair.[81] So Number 10's hopes for a Gore victory in 2000, with Cherie one of the more prominent voices, was not born out of great love or admiration, but out of a desire to see a Democrat win and the Clinton legacy secured. Nevertheless, cooler heads around Blair took the point, often repeated by Meyer and Kerr, who had become Permanent Under-Secretary at the FCO, that it was important to avoid repeating the Conservatives' 1992 mistake of openly favouring the new President's beaten rival.[82]

'Don't screw up your election like Al did' was indeed one of the messages that Clinton gave Blair when he stayed overnight at Chequers on 13 December 2000, just after the news had come through that the Supreme Court had finally decided, six weeks after the presidential election, that the victor was Bush, not Gore.[83] Gore's mistake, said Clinton, was 'to move away from the centre', which seems partly a euphemism for Clinton's well-documented feelings of frustration at being excluded from Gore's campaign.[84] His other advice was 'get as close to George Bush as you have been to me', and 'don't underestimate George W. He's a shrewd, tough politician and absolutely ruthless.'[85] Melanne Verveer, then Hillary's chief of staff, and a very popular figure with the British,[86] described the meeting as reminiscent of their intense encounter in Britain in late May 1997, when everything in the world seemed possible; 'They could have kept on talking: it was hard to say goodbye.'[87]

Clinton's farewell trip undoubtedly recaptured some of the earlier intimacy, but it also highlighted the fact that the potential of those early contacts had not been realised. Clinton's own regrets were broader than his under-fulfilled relationship with Blair: thanks largely to the Lewinsky scandal, he had squandered much of his second term, an acute source of frustration for Hillary.[88] In December 2000 Meyer had reached the view that the year had been one of 'safety first'. There were no significant differences between Blair and Clinton, in part because Number 10 was asked that big international issues, like Iraq, the Middle East in general and India/Pakistan relations, should not be raised with Clinton. Washington was 'relieved' that the Australians and the British had resolved a problem in East Timor themselves without needing US help, and that Milošević fell. The British were grateful that Washington dropped missile defence, albeit not for long. In general, the sense in the Washington Embassy was that the testing times would all lie in the future.[89] On this, they were quite extraordinarily prescient.

The Impact of Bill Clinton

Clinton made much more difference to Labour in opposition than in government, and he had more impact on Brown's thinking than Blair's. The importance of Clinton and the New Democrats to Labour's planning for the 1992 General Election, and preparing for power between 1994 and 1997, is beyond doubt. Once in office, the perceived closeness between Clinton and Blair caused resentment in some EU capitals, particularly in the first half of 1998 when Britain held the EU Presidency.[90] Despite this closeness, British disappointment over key areas of US policy was palpable. Kosovo stands out, as does Clinton's reluctance to do more to help in the implementation of the Good Friday Agreement. There were no great Anglo-American peace initiatives, in the Middle East or elsewhere; no new globalisation or environment initiatives; no common stand on Europe or on trade. There was nothing to compare with the historical sweep of Thatcher's and Reagan's work together on the Soviet Union and the ending of communism, nor even Attlee and Truman, which, for all the strains, had seen the formation of Nato; still less Churchill's wartime relationship with Roosevelt, alluded to by Blair at the White House dinner in 1998. This said, the two leaders deserve recognition for their efforts to shape the framework in which foreign policy was conducted. With the Cold War over, pressure was growing in the US for a more isolationist approach to world politics. Clinton, strongly supported by Blair, resisted this impulse. In his final years, Clinton even devoted considerable time to promoting aid for Africa, and to finding peace in the Middle East, initiatives which Blair whole-heartedly supported.

But what of domestic policy? How did the extraordinary 'third way' fervour translate into policy? Thatcher and Reagan had not held a series of 'new right' symposia for their followers, yet the cross-fertilisation across the Atlantic was considerable. What flowered from this unparalleled personal commitment of Clinton and Blair? Their enthusiasm in looking for practical applications for third-way thinking was undoubtedly deep and genuine. They wanted to show that it was more than a political tactic to gain power and that it was a serious and valid response to meet the challenges of globalisation.[91] Both leaders hugely enjoyed the seminars, and the intellectual excitement of bringing together very bright people from different countries. The enthusiasm of the leaders was not reciprocated by many of their followers, however: in the White House, the conferences came to be seen as 'junkets', and were only tolerated in so far as Clinton was committed to the idea: 'When the phrase "the third way" was mentioned in the White House, many foreign policy staffers would roll their eyes,' said one White House aide.[92] In Britain, 'third way' thinking remained very much the vogue in Number 10 and among many special advisers. But the Civil Service did not take to it, some of whom considered it the worst kind of academe, shot through by meaningless jargon. At a seminar for permanent secretaries at the British Academy, Giddens was received sceptically: 'They were like a group of leopards dissecting what he said pretty mercilessly. It was quite brutal,' said one of them.[93] 'He's the best on it we've got,' one Number 10 aide told a mandarin with a shrug.[94]

This experience highlights the deficiencies of the whole third-way agenda. As Peter Riddell has written, the third way 'overreached itself by exaggerating its novelty and coherence' and was dominated far too much by 'grand, but often vague theories'.[95] The permanent secretaries thus had little time for Giddens' abstract ideas, as they were more concerned with the specifics of policy implementation. This is not to say that the third way was without value, but that it was best understood as an intellectual quest, rather than anything approaching a political ideology.

Blair had initially jumped into this quest, believing that it might offer a new paradigm for public policy that could shape his agenda. Yet, by 1999, he began to lose faith in the third way as a source of policy solutions. The New York seminar was a turning point. After listening to the keynote speech, a prominent British diplomat said: 'It was either utterly brilliant, or it was one of the most vacuous pieces of exposition ever heard in New York. Most people, frankly, thought it was crap.'[96]

Blair's perseverance with the associated conferences, albeit with considerably less fanfare than before, can be explained by his desire to foster international relations and build bridges across the Atlantic, and his desire not to disappoint its more committed supporters, like Mandelson. He thus spoke at the third-way seminar at Hartwell House in June 2002, and offered encouragement for the 'progressive governance' conference in the UK a year later. The third way was yet another of those ideas that he picked up, trumpeted enthusiastically for a time, only later to drop.

Brown, in contrast, derived real benefit in government from New Democrat and third-way thinking, partly because Balls and Mulgan were also avid US-watchers. Brown's three most important first-term policies were all US-influenced. American influence on his decision on the independence of the Bank of England has already been discussed. The Working Family's Tax Credit was based directly from the earned income tax credit in the US. Finally, the 'New Deal', borrowing its name from Roosevelt's great campaign of public works in the 1930s, was lifted from schemes operating in several US states, notably Wisconsin, which the Embassy in Washington had examined very closely in 1995–96.[97] Brown also looked to the US for inspiration in other reforms, including 'back to work', a similar concept to the US 'workfare', and childcare assistance to persuade single mothers to return to employment. Giddens thought Brown was the most interested of all British politicians in third-way thinking (followed by Hewitt, Milburn and Miliband).[98] But it is debatable how far those policies owed to the third way, rather than to Brown's great openness to US thinking and experience in general. One powerful strategy Blair absorbed from Clinton which exasperated Brown and his camp was 'triangulation', the defining of a way forward by identifying a policy against the Labour and Tory parties' positions. To Brown, this approach needlessly antagonised the party and was not a policy but a substitute for one.

Despite the periodic difficulties between Downing Street and the White House, the personal friendship between Blair and Clinton continued after the latter had left office. According to Philip Stephens, Blair still regularly sought Clinton's advice once Bush had taken over in the White House and Clinton became an infrequent visitor to Number 10 and Chequers.[99] Clinton's visit to the 2002 Labour conference was a major boost for Blair: light on substance but high on seduction, Clinton's appeal to Labour to back Blair on Iraq won many converts: 'I've just been for a fag,' said a senior minister afterwards. 'I always like a smoke after being made love to.'[100]

What then has been Clinton's overall influence on Blair himself? Blair's Number 10 was modelled to some extent on the White House, but it was as much Powell's and Campbell's work as Blair's. Blair has sought to make himself presidential, but his model here is more Thatcher than Clinton. In personal terms, no relationship Blair had with another foreign leader compared to the excitement and promise of those early encounters with Clinton. Indeed, few Prime Minister–US President relationships throughout history ever appeared to promise more. Despite the continuing intensity of their personal friendship, much of the shared vision over foreign and domestic policy began to be lost after Blair's first year in power. The reality thus contrasts starkly with the myth. The enduring impact of Clinton was that his presidency helped school Blair into thinking he could help shape US policy and its relationship with Britain and the rest of the world, a realisation that was to flower fully with Blair's far more historically important relationship with Clinton's successor, George W. Bush.

Blair on a visit to talk to British troops in Kosovo. His tough stance on Kosovo pushed him to the limits, and this photograph reveals the stress. He is overseen by General Sir Charles Guthrie.

27

Kosovo, 1999

Kosovo was the watershed not only in Blair's relationship with Clinton; it was also a watershed for Blair himself. Three successive events in Blair's first two years as Prime Minister – Northern Ireland, Iraq, Kosovo – were like steps on a ladder: on each step up, he became stronger and more assured of his own judgement. This chapter discusses Iraq in 1998 and then Kosovo; of all the wars in which Blair was involved, Kosovo saw him most in the lead in pressing for military action.

Blair's First War: Iraq, 1998

Labour had travelled a long way under Kinnock from its position at the 1983 General Election, where it was characterised as defeatist or defensive. Kinnock, although no militarist, oversaw the abandonment of the unilateral nuclear defence policy and the adoption of a more credible position on defence that could no longer be ridiculed by the Tories or the right-wing press. The *volte face* by Blair in opposition over Northern Ireland has already been discussed. After 1994, Blair, Campbell and Powell ensured likewise that they sounded stronger on defence than Labour had done at any point since the Attlee government built the British atomic bomb and took the country into the Korean War on the back of a massive rearmament programme. The Labour front bench thus offered supportive comments about Major's backing for troops on the ground in the Balkans, despite private reservations. Apprehension, nevertheless, remained in many quarters of the British Establishment. After so many years of being 'weak' on defence, had Labour really changed? None of Labour's front bench had any military experience, nor did they know much about the armed services. Blair had mocked the Combined Cadet Force at school and displayed no real interest in military matters before becoming party leader in 1994. Nor did Brown have any form. Labour's most senior figure with any record on defence was shadow Foreign Secretary Cook, but he had been known as a unilateralist in the 1970s and 1980s.[1] 'I think everybody in the Ministry of Defence was worried about what New Labour's attitude would be to defence,' said Charles Guthrie, Chief of the Defence Staff.[2] To seek reassurance, when it seemed almost certain that Labour would win the election, Guthrie asked to see Blair.

Robin Renwick, who had helped to set up the seminars for Blair on foreign policy, was mindful that Labour would face an imminent defence review, and was happy to arrange for Guthrie and the outgoing Chief of the Defence Staff, Peter Inge, to meet Blair at Claridge's Hotel in London.[3] The Chiefs of Staff had grown restless with the Tories' indecisiveness on defence, and the cuts forced on them by Tory Chancellor, Ken Clarke. But would Labour be any better? The two top brass cast their eye over Blair. In the end, they decided he passed muster. They were pleased by his assurance that he was genuinely committed to the nation's defence.[4] They were able to convey to their subordinates that the realm's defence might indeed be safe under a Labour government.[5]

Once in power, four early episodes showed the military that Blair's words were not empty. He appointed George Robertson, a party heavyweight and known to be 'sound' on defence, as Defence Secretary. In the Strategic Defence Review of 1997–98, Blair supported the armed services – albeit not as firmly as they would have liked – against Brown, who wanted to find real savings. 'I felt, in my naïveté,' said one of the senior officers, 'that a Prime Minister would just tell the Chancellor to get on with it and give us the money.'[6] At an early Defence and Overseas Policy Cabinet committee on nuclear matters, involving complex and secret issues on deterrence and the loading of missiles and warheads, the military thought Blair's chairmanship was 'impressive and helpful'.[7] Finally, when SAS forces were fired on in Bosnia and an indicted war criminal was killed, 'Blair was extremely robust, much more so than the Conservatives were, in actually arresting war criminals. He held his nerve.'[8] Blair's early outings in charge of the nation's conventional and nuclear forces, marking the first time his actions were scrutinised by men in uniform since Fettes nearly thirty years before, had gone down well.

Sterner tests, however, were to come in 1998. Iraq was to provide the first occasion when Blair became involved in a serious military issue. Saddam Hussein had been creating difficulties for the UN weapons inspectors since the end of Operation Desert Storm in 1991, when the allies retook Kuwait but fell short of advancing into Iraq. The inspectors, Saddam argued, along with many sympathisers in the international community, were not objective in their search for weapons of mass destruction (WMD), but were stooges of the US. The inspectors, however, complained that they were unable to fulfil their obligations under the ceasefire of 1991 because Saddam was claiming that certain places, such as his palaces, were 'off-limits'. The French and the Russian governments were keen to find a peaceful way forward that would allow the inspectors to do their work, but were also pressing for sanctions against Iraq to be lifted.[9] As Christopher Meyer observed, 'All the outlines of the great fissure of the 2003 Iraq War were already there in 1998.'[10] The Clinton administration were saying in private that as long as Saddam remained the Iraqi leader, the longer the arguments would rattle on; they had lost faith in their ability to negotiate with him, and they would never lift sanctions as long as he remained in power.[11] Britain's position was that there must be the hope for the Iraqi people of seeing sanctions lifted, but Saddam had to comply with the weapons inspectors.

From very early on in his premiership, Blair took the threat of WMD – i.e., nuclear, chemical and biological weapons – very seriously. He confided to Ashdown in November 1997 that he had been looking at the intelligence on Saddam's WMD: 'I have now seen some of the stuff on this. It really is pretty scary. He is very close to some appalling weapons of mass destruction. I don't understand why the French and others don't understand this. We cannot let him get away with it.' Blair's aim was to have the evidence published, for all the world to see, as Kennedy had done with the Soviet missiles in Cuba in 1962, and he pressed Clinton to do just this.[12] Even then, his instincts told him that the information on what he was doing should be put into the public domain. In November 1997, after Saddam expelled the weapons inspectors, he said in public: 'It is absolutely essential that [Saddam] backs down on this . . . If he does not, we will simply face this problem, perhaps in a different and far worse form, in a few years' time.'[13] Further reasons for Blair being tough on Iraq were his desire to show domestic doubters that he would not flinch from combat in a just cause and his conviction that he had to support a Democratic President internationally.

By the beginning of 1998, Washington was losing patience with Saddam's prevarications: 'He had been messing around with the inspectors for too long, and had now put lack of co-operation up to a new level,' said Sandy Berger, Clinton's National Security Advisor. 'So we decided we had to take action.'[14] Accordingly, plans were drawn up for a barrage of air strikes, codenamed 'Desert Thunder'.[15] The administration wanted to act in consort with Britain and France, 'though, even then, we were never absolutely confident about Chirac'.[16] Blair, however, was stalwart, and agreed that Saddam's obstruction of the UN could not go unanswered, and took the view that this was just the episode he needed to display his unswerving support to the Americans and to Clinton in particular.[17] According to a January 1998 memo seen by Cook, Blair pledged support for Clinton in action against Iraq even if a further UN resolution was 'unachievable'.[18] However, as the likelihood of air strikes increased, Kofi Annan, Secretary-General of the UN, intervened, flew to Baghdad and met with Saddam. On 23 February he brokered a settlement which allowed some inspections of the contentious presidential palaces. Annan praised Saddam's 'courage, wisdom [and] flexibility', and said he was a man 'I can do business with'.[19] The words stuck in the gullet of many in the Clinton and Blair camps.

To the intense irritation of the Americans, who remained sceptical of Saddam's assurances of greater access, inspections resumed in Iraq. 'We didn't like it, but we had to live with it,' said one administration official.[20] Blair told the House of Commons that only the threat of force had persuaded Saddam to back down, and that he would have supported the US if military action had proved necessary. 'It is important,' he said, 'that we have an American administration and an American people who are not isolationist but will take on responsibilities . . . Thank heavens that the Americans are there and willing to stand up and be counted.'[21] Although air strikes were put on the back-burner, as a Number 10 official put it, 'there was a sense of inevitability that it would come to force in the end'.[22]

The inevitable happened in October, after Saddam again withdrew co-operation from the inspectors. To prepare the British public and the Labour Party for action, Blair acted on his earlier proposal of laying the facts before the people. In November, a document entitled 'Iraq's Weapons of Mass Destruction' was presented to MPs, outlining Iraq's known use of chemical weapons. Hopes of undertaking the attack jointly with the French, however, failed. As they suspected, Chirac would not support any military action, so Clinton and Blair were on their own. For legal justification, in the absence of a new Security Council resolution endorsing an air attack, they fell back on Resolution 678, passed before the Gulf War in 1991. This authorised the allies to use 'all necessary means' against Iraq and remained valid, certainly in the view of the UK and the US, so long as Iraq remained a threat to peace in the region.[23] A combined Cruise and Tomahawk missile and plane attack was to be launched against some 250 suspected WMD and 'command and control' targets. But once again Kofi Annan intervened. On Saturday 14 November, Saddam Hussein informed Annan that he was ready to resume co-operation with the inspectors. Annan's public announcement that he was satisfied with this apparent climb-down led Clinton to call off the attack, even though some B-52 planes were already airborne and heading to their targets. The planes returned to base.[24] Initially, Blair and Robertson felt that the strikes should have proceeded in spite of Saddam's offer, which they felt was just another ploy to buy time.[25] Sure enough, once the Americans dissected the offer, they very quickly declared it 'unacceptable' and 'riddled with more holes than Swiss cheese'.[26]

The administration were deeply divided over what to do next, but Clinton came under pressure to reschedule the air strikes for the next day.[27] But now it was Blair who believed that the attack would have to be postponed. After discussing it with his close advisers, Holmes and Powell, he made a crucial phone call to the President, arguing that it would look very bad to go ahead with the strikes less than twenty-four hours after apparently agreeing to give diplomacy once last chance.[28] Clinton agreed. Once again, Saddam had won a reprieve.

This time, however, it was to last only a month. As Berger put it, 'The Clinton administration realised that containment was not workable over the long term with a man like Saddam. The longer he acted with impunity, the more sanctions were evaded by him, and the more money he got. Delay was just making everything more difficult for us.'[29] Clinton and his advisers – Madeleine Albright, Secretary of State; William Cohen, Secretary of Defense; Vice-President Al Gore and Berger, who was emerging as Clinton's key foreign policy adviser – decided the week after the aborted 13 November attack that there were to be no more last-minute reversals. They had run out of patience. Unless Saddam complied unconditionally with every last 'dot and comma' of the UN demands, Iraq would be attacked from the air in December during the week between Clinton's visit to the Middle East and the Muslim holy month of Ramadan.[30]

Accordingly, while in mid-flight to the Middle East on Air Force One, Clinton phoned Blair on 11 December. Blair was at the EU Heads of Government summit in Austria and a secure line had to be installed at the Vienna Plaza Hotel to take the call.[31] The two leaders concurred that Saddam once again was obstructing the inspectors, and that the attack should now proceed. On 12 December, Clinton spoke from Jerusalem to Cohen by video link and told him to 'prepare to execute' the four-day attack. The inspectors were whisked out of Iraq over the next two days, and on his flight back home to the US on 15 December, Clinton agreed final battle arrangements for the following day. The difficulty they faced was that the other permanent members of the UN Security Council, Russia, France and China, were of Annan's view that Saddam had to be given more time, and that the sanctions against Iraq should progressively be lifted to allow Iraq to get back on its feet. The US and Britain would be acting on their own.

Blair called a meeting of the Cabinet's Defence and Overseas Policy committee on the afternoon of 15 December to secure British agreement for the attacks. Those present were struck by Blair's calm resolution: when it came to giving his authorisation, he said simply, 'Okay, that's it.'[32] Communications were also discussed: he was clear, once the decision was taken, that they had to be robust in managing the public reaction. It was agreed that Cook should go on the BBC's *Today* programme the following morning to prepare the British public for the attacks, and Blair should do *News at Ten* that evening to make the official announcement. The stage management paid off but did not extend to events in the US. While the British media on Wednesday, 16 December, was full of stories of Iraq's non-compliance and the likely attack that day, the US media focused on Clinton's imminent impeachment for evasions over the continuing Lewinsky affair. Inevitably, the attack came to be known as 'Monica's War', with the charge that Clinton had contrived it to deflect attention away from his domestic troubles, an accusation the White House fervently denied. At 7 a.m. that Wednesday morning, after an hour-long meeting in the Oval Office, Clinton gave the order to commence what became known as 'Operation Desert Fox'.[33]

The Blairs were due to go to the theatre with Barry Cox and his wife on the evening of Wednesday, 16 December. Cox received a call from Number 10 to say the play was off in favour of a supper in Downing Street. In contrast to his calm manner earlier in the day, Blair was clearly nervous that evening up in the flat: with the first British Tornadoes going in just before 10 p.m., the possible loss of British servicemen weighed heaviest on his mind. He was also troubled by his isolation from world opinion, with EU leaders – apart from Schröder, who gave qualified support – mostly opposed. Searching questions were again being asked, not least in Britain, about why he was going so far out on a limb to

support a damaged and morally compromised American President. At 10
p.m., Blair duly appeared on television, and then went over to the
Commons to make a statement.[34] Campbell and Holmes would come up
to the flat with regular updates. Only when Blair was told that the first
British pilots were all home safely did he begin to let go of his pent-up
anxiety. Compared to the full-scale assault on Iraq just over four years
later, this was small beer. But his nerves had yet to be ratcheted upwards,
and this episode was a new and slightly overwhelming experience for
him.

Blair slowly relaxed over the four days of the air attack, especially
when it became clear that none of his dire fears had materialised.
Holmes, Powell and Campbell were his main supports. The last proved
his worth in winning the communications battle, putting the Clinton
communications team to shame. The smaller Downing Street team
could often react quicker than the more bureaucratic White House, and
by capitalising on the different time zones, Campbell ensured that Blair
always put his statements out first. 'Employing Blair's oratory and
Campbell's golden pen,' said one awed Number 10 official, 'we were also
able to explain in a very clear way what the British and Americans were
doing and what they hoped to achieve and why.'[35] Blair was careful
throughout to stress to Parliament and the British public that the quarrel
was not with the Iraqi people but with Saddam Hussein and 'the evil
regime he represents'. Military action was regrettable, he said, but the
only course open in view of Saddam's refusal to co-operate. Clinton's
broadcasts usually followed Blair's an hour or more later, by which time,
certainly in the UK, they had lost much of their impact. It gave the
impression that London was playing a more important part in the action
than it was: in fact, it was only playing the part of chief supporter. There
was only one principal in this drama, and it was Washington.

Clinton and Blair called off the attacks on 20 December, after some
650 sorties on 250 targets had been launched. They were pleased with
the action, and that they had more or less escaped adverse world opinion.
The White House estimate was that they had caused Saddam 'a year or
two's delay in his weapons programme'. World opinion was not yet ready,
however, for them to attempt to take a more full-blooded path, such as
assassinate the Iraqi leader: 'Only after 9/11 did Bush have public
support for action against Saddam,' Berger said, adding, 'even though
Saddam was not connected with that tragedy.'[36] Blair had achieved all his
objectives: supporting the Americans, limiting the scope of the
inevitable air strike, and successfully managing the public reaction in
Britain. There were no marches or demonstrations, and precious few

angry outbursts. He went into his Christmas break in 1998 a relieved and happier man than for some weeks.

One more lasting effect of the attacks on Blair was to entrench his preferred method, first seen over the Good Friday talks, for conducting crises and wars: 'It was clear early on that he didn't want to operate through Cabinet but through a small, tight-knit group,' said Guthrie, approvingly.[37] Blair was to adopt this same *ad hoc* structure for future wars. The biggest impact on Blair of Desert Fox, however, concerned his self-confidence. He had been bold and decisive in the face of world opinion, had stuck by what he believed to be morally right, and he had carried the day.

Kosovo, 1999

Blair became involved relatively late in the tragic Kosovo story. Once he did engage, however, he took a central role, and showed considerable courage and force of will to achieve his objectives. Before the 1997 General Election Blair had wanted to know why Britain had not been more decisive over humanitarian abuses in the tragedy of the former Yugoslavia, which had dominated the headlines in the early and mid-1990s. What had stopped Britain doing more? In particular, why had Britain and the UN done nothing about the massacre at Srebrenica in July 1995?[38] He thought that Major had been too reticent, and that an opportunity to exercise moral leadership in Bosnia had been wasted. Once in Downing Street he was content in the first year to leave these issues to Cook, who had a deep commitment to the region, as well as to Robertson, the Defence Secretary.[39] Cook had been a leading player in reformulating Labour policy from 1995 to an acceptance that military force might be necessary, particularly to prevent the horror of ethnic cleansing.[40] Kosovo was to be the issue that saw him at the height of his effectiveness as Foreign Secretary, and also saw the Cook–Blair relationship work at its best. Human rights abuses were being committed under Yugoslav President Slobodan Milošević, whose Serbian forces were turning on the Muslim majority in Kosovo, initially in response to violence by the Kosovo Liberation Army (KLA). Blair's personal involvement came after the successful conclusion of the Good Friday Agreement in April 1998. He came to realise that resolving the conflict in Kosovo would require not only the threat but also the reality of force.[41] Blair considered Milošević, like Saddam, to be a bully and a deeply evil man.

Britain's allies also noticed that Blair's government, initially with Cook in the driving seat, was changing towards a more active policy. 'The British no longer had to be dragged along to confront the Serbs,' said one US State Department official. 'We saw a completely different attitude.'[42] Britain played a leading role in the 'International Contact Group' on Kosovo, alongside the US, Russia, Germany, France and Italy. In October 1998, the Contact Group helped secure UN Security Council Resolution 1203, warning of an 'imminent human catastrophe' in Kosovo, and insisting that the Kosovo refugees, who had been driven from their homes, be allowed to return. Following negotiations between US envoy Richard Holbrooke and Milošević, a ceasefire was agreed, which would be monitored by unarmed civilians, backed by a small Nato force in neighbouring Macedonia. The violence, however, continued. In the wake of the Serbian massacre of forty-five Kosovo Albanians in Racak in January 1999, Britain and France chaired talks between the Serbs and Kosovars at Rambouillet in February. In return for the disarmament of the KLA, the proposed framework required Milošević to withdraw his forces from Kosovo, accept its autonomy and also agree to the introduction of a Nato peacekeeping force, which in the end he rejected. Madeleine Albright was the real driving force at Rambouillet, pushing the Kosovars hard to accept their side of the deal and leave Milošević isolated.[43] She also was pleased at how resolute Blair's government was becoming in finding a solution.[44] Rambouillet was to prove a last attempt to put concerted diplomatic pressure on Milošević and avoid war. A watershed for Clinton himself had come on 12 February 1999, when the Senate voted against removing him from office, which eased considerably his difficulties over the Lewinsky scandal. While Clinton's aides insist that the scandal had no impact on his foreign policy,[45] the perception from the British side (and in most foreign capitals) was that it had 'clouded thinking' in the White House.[46] With the spectre of impeachment no longer haunting him, Clinton now had more time and authority to expend on his administration's foreign policy agenda.

In mid-March 1999, and despite Rambouillet, the refugee position in Kosovo deteriorated significantly, and public pressure for stronger action rose as television pictures showed 25,000 inhabitants of Kosovo being forced from their homes. Diplomatic efforts now made way for preparations for a Nato military response. Nato itself was coming up to a major anniversary: it had been in existence for fifty years since 1949. But it had been a defensive, not an offensive, alliance. Could it now adapt? Of the nineteen Nato countries, Greece and Italy in particular were opposed to military action, so intensive lobbying had to take place before they were won over.[47] Yet Milošević did not appear worried at this huge coalition ranged against him. His apparent indifference stemmed from the fact that he never believed Nato would remain united against him, nor did he believe any air attacks would prove successful. He also believed that if he fell into difficulties, his ultimate saviour, Boris Yeltsin, would come to his rescue. The Russian threat of a veto at the UN Security Council already meant there would be no UN endorsement for an air war, but Blair was determined that this should not prevent them going ahead.[48] He had become utterly convinced that this was an issue that needed to be seized, and that his own leadership was vital if the right outcome was to be achieved.

Air attacks duly began on 24 March at 8 p.m. local time. Speaking with tangible conviction and passion, Blair had told the House of Commons the day before that 'to walk away now would not merely destroy Nato's credibility; more importantly it would be a breach of faith with thousands of innocent civilians whose only desire is to live in peace, and who took us at our word'.[49] The original plan was for intense aerial bombardment to last seventy-two hours, striking at Milošević's key military and communications sites, with the hope that he would rapidly capitulate and be prepared to negotiate for his troops to leave Kosovo. But this neat outcome did not transpire: the bombing had several results, none positive. On the first night the RAF Tornadoes failed to hit any of their targets, and with the Pentagon's insistence that US planes keep above clouds for safety, even their sophisticated weapons failed to dent Milošević's military power.[50]

Milošević's forces proved far more wily at concealing themselves and their weapons than the military planners had foreseen. What the bombing was doing, however, was rallying his supporters and others behind him, having the opposite effect to the one they ultimately intended. When, as inevitably was bound to happen, innocent civilians were killed, Milošević's stock rose still further. The bombing was also used by Milošević's Serb forces as a cover to accelerate the ethnic cleansing in Kosovo.[51] Hundreds of thousands of refugees were uprooted, far more than the allies had envisaged in their worst scenario. Yet the allies at this stage had no alternative to aerial bombardment, and kept going with more of the same. By doing so, they were beginning to lose not only the propaganda but also the military war.

Blair was becoming seriously unsettled about the lack of progress. In the first days of the air war, he would want to agree the targets for that night's sorties, and would ask the military planners searching questions. He would then want to know each day whether the pilots were back safely.[52] The Cabinet was behind the action, but for how much longer, he worried, if the bombing continued to be so counterproductive? Blair was in Berlin on Thursday, 25 March, so Prescott chaired Cabinet in his absence. In contradiction to the recollection of one Cabinet minister, who told John Kampfner that Cabinet never discussed the principles nor conduct of foreign affairs in Blair's first term,[53] unpublished diary evidence suggests that almost the whole of this Cabinet meeting was given over to it. Robertson warned that this would 'not be a casualty-free conflict' on either side, and said the aim was to prevent a humanitarian catastrophe, not to bomb Milošević back to the negotiating table, and that 'if he stopped his violence towards the Kosovo Albanians, we will stop the action against him'. Irvine wanted to lock the Tories into supporting the action by putting down a motion for debate, but Margaret Beckett and Ann Taylor worried it could expose doubts on Labour's side. Frank Dobson said the question most were having difficulty with was, 'How is it any country can take military action against a sovereign state and fellow members of the UN without the approval of the Security Council?' But such sceptical comments were rare. Prescott summed up at the end by saying that the Cabinet supported the action and congratulated 'our armed forces'.[54]

Blair reached a nadir over the Easter weekend, Friday 2 April to Monday 6 April 1999, in contrast to the euphoria of exactly one year before. The continuing failure of the bombing, and the mounting refugee problem, made it one of the bleakest moments so far in his premiership.[55] He confided to one aide, 'This could be the end of me.'[56] He feared that the bombing action he personally had done so much to precipitate had led to 'a nightmare, creating human misery and death rather than saving life', one Number 10 aide recalled him saying, describing it as the worst few days Blair had ever experienced in his career.[57] The media began to raise questions, as they were to again over Iraq in 2003, whether Blair's personal commitment on Kosovo put him in a similar position to Anthony Eden over the Suez crisis in 1956, when Eden's foolhardiness precipitated the end of his career and did untold damage to Britain's standing in the Muslim world. The BBC were particular targets of Blair and Campbell, and they were enraged especially by John Humphrys and John Simpson, who they felt were giving succour to supporters of Milošević by their critical questioning and reporting.[58] Blair's physical isolation at Chequers that Easter was heightened by Campbell being on holiday in France as well as by Holmes, Blair's foreign policy stalwart, having recently departed: his successor, John Sawers, had yet to prove his worth, and build the same deep trust. At 7.15 a.m. on Good Friday, Blair phoned Sawers at his home for the latest news, which was not good.[59] Cloud cover had again meant that the bombers had failed to hit their targets. Easter weekend saw the first use of Cruise missiles, a source of great excitement at the Ministry of Defence: but again with conspicuous lack of success.

This was the moment when Blair decided that he had to take personal charge, and could no longer rely even on the US to get it right. 'It was one of those rare occasions in his premiership when he focused single-mindedly on just one issue,' said one senior official.[60] Blair felt that he, and he alone, could find the way forward. He summoned his trusted military chief, Guthrie, up to Chequers twice in the week following Easter. As he would often do, he reverted to his barrister's training and got down to first principles, quizzing his well-disposed, no-nonsense general: what were we hoping to achieve? Why were we not having more success? How could British objectives be better accomplished? During their discussions, Blair realised that unless ground troops could be threatened in a way Milošević would find credible, then defeat and humiliation could result.[61] Nothing else would make him sit up and listen. Guthrie concurred, but pointed out the huge difficulties: the Americans were adamantly against the use of ground troops, and Blair himself had suggested in the Commons that this option was not on the table: 'We do not plan to use ground troops in order to fight our way into Kosovo,' he had declared, pointing out that it would require at least 100,000 troops to do the job properly.[62] There was also the risk of the war escalating out of control, the Vietnam scenario, and an even larger failure and humiliation at the end of it. Guthrie's role in all this was pivotal: he coaxed his young and still comparatively inexperienced Prime Minister through all the options and was forthright with him about the severe problems and dangers. Blair concluded coolly that there was no alternative to the threat of deploying ground troops. On 16 April he wrote a long letter to Clinton setting out the arguments.[63] The Ministry of Defence was wheeled into action and told Blair that the latest possible date for a ground offensive before the winter was 17 September. To allow time for the necessary planning, a decision had to take place by 6 June at the latest, just seven weeks away.[64] The clock was ticking.

Blair at last had some concrete plans to address the crisis, in contrast to the pre-Easter torpor. He now raced ahead on a number of fronts. He authorised Robertson and Guthrie to tell their staff in secret to prepare for a ground war. To ease the refugee crisis he leaned on a very engaged and on-side International Development Secretary, Clare Short, who, helped by her Permanent Secretary John Vereker, managed to take a grip on the problem and give an international lead, which has been an undervalued aspect of Britain's contribution to easing the conflict.[65]

Blair also realised that he had to win hearts and minds. Everyone at Number 10 had been struck by how, during Operation Desert Fox, 'all the key participants on both sides were following the war by watching CNN'.[66] Blair later said that one of the earliest facts to strike him about Kosovo was that 'Milošević had charge of the media agenda . . . When you fight actions like this in our modern media world, you're fighting it on television.'[67] Blair thus intensified the propaganda war in Britain to ensure the humanitarian case was being made. This tack, he hoped, would counter the rainbow selection of opponents of the bombing, ranging from armchair generals like Sir Peter de la Billière and Sir Michael Rose, to Tory grandees like Lord Carrington, to the hard left, like Tony Benn. On 16 April Blair sent Campbell to Brussels to teach the Nato media machine how to put over its case more effectively; in a strange reversal of the Eurosceptics' fear of the Brussels model being imposed on Britain, the Millbank model of media management was imposed wholesale on Nato's running of the war, with significant effect.[68] Robertson drew on Desert Fox as a useful 'dress rehearsal' for Kosovo because it showed the value of high-quality press conferences and setting the news agenda rather than reacting to it.[69] By 18 April Blair was feeling much more confident. Lance Price, deputing for the absent Campbell, spent an hour after Sunday lunch talking about Kosovo with him in the Chequers garden; Blair said 'stalemate or reversal couldn't be allowed to happen'.[70] On 20 April, Blair himself went over to Nato Headquarters: afterwards he told Clinton, 'We can win this, but not unless we run it the way you and I run election campaigns.'[71] Here was language Clinton understood.

Blair further told Clinton that the Nato decision-making machinery, in trying to keep all Nato allies happy, was too cumbersome, and that the effectiveness of the air campaign was being significantly stymied as a result.[72] Blair had met General Wesley Clark, the Nato Supreme Commander and the senior US general in Europe, who had become convinced of the need to threaten Milošević with the use of ground troops. Clark did not need to convince Blair, though some thought he was responsible for Blair's conversion; but he did see in Blair an ally who might help persuade a reticent Washington to change their minds and become less squeamish about ground forces.[73] Blair resolved that he would use his forthcoming US trip as a major opportunity to lobby the administration, from Clinton downwards, to commit to ground troops.

On 21 April, to stake out his position before he left, he told MPs that ground troops were an option. Campbell had also been orchestrating a media campaign for some days, briefing the press that preparing for a ground war was the best way of achieving their humanitarian objectives.

Blair decided he would use the peg of a major speech on 22 April to the Chicago Economic Club to articulate thoughts that had been forming in his mind over the previous year on the justifications for military action. He had never in his life before seriously addressed himself to the philosophy of foreign and defence policy, in contrast to his frequent musings on domestic policy, and his thoughts were inchoate. With all the turmoil over Kosovo since Easter, he had had no time to write the speech, so Jonathan Powell approached his old friend, Lawrence Freedman, the doyen professor of defence studies, whom he had known since they had worked together on the planning staff at the Foreign Office. Freedman's task was to draft Blair's credo on foreign affairs, providing clear guidelines for when the international community could legitimately intervene in the internal affairs of a sovereign state, as had happened in Iraq and was now happening in Kosovo.[74] Freedman proved himself the right person for the hour, as he had been puzzling out these issues himself, so his own intellectual thought processes collided with Blair's at precisely the right time for maximum effect. 'Jonathan phoned me up in early April and asked for a few ideas for a speech. I had no idea that they would be used so heavily; I decided to remain schtum about it for some time after.'[75] Five 'criteria' for intervention were crafted by Freedman, mixing academic arguments with what he dubbed 'common sense'. He had been researching the Cuban Missile Crisis, which informed his first criterion, 'Are we sure of our case?', which was the question that had taxed Kennedy and his advisers in 1962. The other criteria were: have all diplomatic options been exhausted? Can the military operation be prudently undertaken? Is there a will to hold out for the long term if required? Finally, are there national interests involved?[76] The drafts were only finalised in mid-flight over the Atlantic. Blair often left speeches to the last minute, and liked to knock ideas around with those he trusted, fuelled by the adrenalin of the imminent deadline. On this occasion there were strong feelings expressed about his need to acquire better speechwriters. The key phrase in the talk, 'The Doctrine of the International Community', only came to him late on in the flight.[77]

Blair opened the most important foreign policy speech of his premiership to date by lamenting the fact that he was the first serving British Prime Minister to have visited Chicago. Pleasantries over, he moved on swiftly to Kosovo, which was witnessing 'awful crimes that we never thought we would see again – ethnic cleansing, systematic rape, mass murder . . . This is a just war, based not on territorial ambition but on values.' He then set the struggle in a wider global context where traditional notions of national sovereignty had to be re-examined for the fast-approaching twenty-first century; he then outlined his five criteria for principled intervention, which became known as the 'Blair doctrine'. He was delighted with the speech. The Foreign Office lawyers most definitely were not: they had received no prior notice of the content and were highly concerned about where it left international law and the position of the United Nations.[78] Washington too was not pleased. Some like Berger and Steinberg were unhappy with the notion of producing a humanitarian rationale to legitimise intervention, believing that the strongest argument for intervention in Kosovo rested on the security implications of Milošević's actions.[79] The administration disapproved even more strongly of the implicit endorsement Blair gave to the threat to use ground troops in Kosovo. The message, which he repeated at full blast on the US media, was clear: the time had come to get tough. If the American President was not going to take that lead, he would. 'Britain yesterday emerged as Nato's most hawkish country on the issue of introducing ground troops,' declared the *Financial Times*, which remarked pointedly, as did other press outlets, that this was 'an option resisted by most other members'.[80]

Blair was troubled by the rift with the Clinton administration. He had been so close to Clinton on so many issues, he had never anticipated finding himself so firmly in the opposite camp. He had a disagreement with Campbell on the flight up to Chicago from Washington, which had been their first port of call on the trip, arguing over how far he should go in pressing for ground troops at the risk of annoying Clinton. He was still very uptight when he aired his concerns to Christopher Meyer in the car on the way from the airport to deliver the Chicago speech. 'I am out on a limb here,' he said in exasperation. 'Clinton is firmly opposed to ground troops: how are we going to pull all of this together?'[81]

Blair had expected to convince Clinton at a crucial meeting at the White House on 21 April the night before the Chicago speech. Clinton knew what was coming and steeled himself against Blair's full-frontal attack, which mixed charm with strong-arm persuasion. It was to be one of their tensest meetings. On the British side were Blair, Campbell, Sawers and Meyer, and with Clinton sat Albright, Berger and Steinberg.[82] Blair insisted that the sooner they developed plans for the deployment of ground troops, the better. Only this threat would

convince Milošević to back down. The Americans remained
unconvinced. According to Steinberg, the disagreement was largely a
tactical one: everyone on the American side was open to the benefits of
ground troops, but they felt it was crucial not to destabilise the Nato
alliance, many of whom were strongly opposed to deploying troops.
Introducing the debate at the imminent Nato summit would fracture the
alliance and destroy their credibility in the eyes of Milošević.[83] Another
member of Clinton's team stressed a deeper concern: 'We had a rather
jaundiced view of Blair's position on ground troops as it would not be
British but predominantly US troops that would go in.'[84] Conscious of
this concern, Blair pushed for troops to be deployed only in a 'semi-
permissive environment', i.e., where the Serb forces were so 'degraded'
they would not put up much of a fight.[85] This argument, he hoped,
would allay American fears of 'body bags' being flown home. But the
line cut little ice. Berger stressed that even *talk* of ground troops would
create great difficulties for them politically in Congress and with the
American public. The US was already providing over three-quarters of
the air power and they felt that they were already doing more than their
fair share.

Clinton, visibly uncomfortable, sat almost silent throughout, apart
from interjecting, with an extinct cigar hanging idly in his mouth, that
Moscow would take talks of troops badly.[86] According to Albright, the
impasse was only broken after Blair and Clinton disappeared together on
the pretext of finding the White House toilet.[87] Another participant in
the meeting confirmed that when the two returned, after a considerable
period of time, it was evident that a further discussion had taken place.[88]
The deal the two had settled on was that in return for Blair not bringing
up the issue of ground troops at the Nato summit, Clinton would agree
to do 'whatever was necessary' to ensure victory. This was taken as a
signal of the US willingness 'to go down the ground-troop road without
actually using the "G" word'.[89] Blair and Clinton then divided up their
fellow Nato leaders to lobby each one personally in favour of this
formulation. They also agreed that once the summit was over, Anglo-
American forces should begin secret planning for the ground war.[90]

Blair left for Chicago to give his speech, to which he was committed,
aware of the gulf between him and Clinton. Hence his anxiety about his
decision to be so gung-ho on the use of ground troops in the speech and
with the media afterwards. The stance did not damage the Nato summit,
which he travelled on to directly after the speech, and the summit
achieved the harmony the Clinton administration feared it might lose.
All nineteen members also agreed that the Serbs had to be removed

from Kosovo, and the refugees brought back as soon as possible –
although there was no discussion of exactly how they were to achieve
this end other than by continuing with the air war.

After a private dinner with the Clintons late on Saturday evening,
Blair and his party flew back to Britain relieved that they appeared to
have found a way forward with the administration. They remained
worried, however, about how enduring their concessions would prove,
and whether their strong-arm tactics would backfire if Clinton felt
bounced.[91] Blair spoke to Nato colleagues as planned, trying to win them
over to the possibility of ground troops. Many, notably Schröder, were
unreceptive. The worsening refugee situation heightened Blair's own
sense of the need for dramatic action. On 3 May he journeyed with
Cherie to Stankovic in Macedonia to see things for himself. Trains full
of refugees from Pristina, the Kosovo capital, were resulting in up to a
quarter of a million refugees living in tents, with insufficient water. 'This
is not a battle for Nato, this is not a battle for territory, this is a battle for
humanity. It is a just cause,' he said. It was Blair's first experience of a
refugee camp, and marked, according to Kampfner, a turning point in his
commitment to intervention.[92] 'Blair was touched, immensely so, by the
reaction to him in the camp,' said a senior aide. 'It helped convince him
of the rightness of his course of action and the need to intervene
appropriately in other countries.'[93]

The historical reference point Blair chose to make sense of the
potential human catastrophe, perhaps inevitably, was the Nazi
treatment of the Jews in the Second World War. He made much of this
analogy when he flew to Bucharest to address the Romanian Parliament
two weeks later. His looming fear, with the approach of winter, was the
refugees still being out in the open with no resolution in sight. His
excessively moral language, 'good against evil', 'civilisation and
barbarity' were, as Peter Riddell wrote, arousing concern about his
judgement.[94] In mid-May, in a moment of hubris, he compared himself
to Gladstone, the high moralist of late Victorian politics, about whom he
knew little. At other times he seemed to see himself as a latter-day Raoul
Wallenberg, the Swedish diplomat who saved hundreds of Jews from the
Holocaust. Pressure built on Blair from early May, with Nato air attacks
killing at least seventeen at Pec on 3 May, and a misdirected bomb
hitting the Chinese Embassy in Belgrade on 7 May: Blair immediately
dictated an apology from Chequers to the British Ambassador in Beijing
to pass on to the Chinese Premier. The same day, sixty were killed by
an allied bomb in a market in Nis.

Blair's worries about the loss of innocent life were exacerbated by the fear that he was losing the propaganda war in the court of world opinion. He spent a deeply worrying first half of May. So identified had he become in Britain and Europe, as well as in the US, as the principal figure driving the war forward, that he worried that if it failed, it could well end his premiership. For the second time in the crisis, Blair confided to his closest aides: 'This could be the end of me.'[95] Blair's anger and disillusion continued to be projected on to the media for what he and Campbell saw as blatantly hostile reporting. Increasingly it was the Clinton administration that he saw as thwarting progress. 'After we came back to London in late April there was an ominous silence from Washington,' Guthrie recalled. 'It was maddening because they would tell us "oh yeah, we quite agree, we must go in on the ground", but then their people used to wimp out, quite honestly.'[96] Not so, insists one Clinton official, who notes that bilateral military planning began in April.[97] The problem for the British was that such planning remained secret and deniable: they were growing increasingly concerned that something more concrete and open was required.[98] Blair saw that the 6 June deadline for deploying ground troops was rapidly approaching: he believed it was inevitable they would have to go in, even if they were to be met by hostile forces.[99] To Blair's concern about whether the Nato alliance would hold together was added a new fear that Clinton would cut loose from him and do a separate deal with Milošević, thereby 'selling him down the river'. Lance Price's diary for 7 May records him saying, very angrily, 'If he does that, that's it. I'm finished with him.'[100] Blair dispatched Cook to Washington to find out what was going on. It was a bleak time.[101]

The battle to make the US administration change its mind now shifted to the territory Campbell knew best. Criticism of Clinton for his passivity on committing ground troops began to appear in the press. A widely read leading article in the *Financial Times* on 17 May said, 'Mr Clinton's prevarication about offering the US troops that are vital to a successful outcome has left time on Mr Milošević's side.'[102] The leader was picked up by the *New York Times*, which cited a range of British voices suggesting that Clinton should start giving some leadership, and overcome the reservations in Congress and among the American public. Clinton was incensed, and had his most difficult conversation with Blair that evening. Blair spoke on the secure line in 'the den' at the end of the Cabinet Room. He knew it would be an awkward call because Berger had spoken to his private office earlier in the day and accused Campbell of being the informant for the *New York Times* piece. The conversation began reasonably, with Clinton saying that it was not helpful for Britain to air its views on ground troops in public: differences should be kept private. Then the article was mentioned. Clinton exploded, 'I am sure it gives you and your people a lot of pleasure to see me done down.' Blair denied Campbell had spoken to the papers, and spent a long time calming Clinton down, later joking to friends it had been no worse than dealing with difficult colleagues.[103] 'I suspect if it had been Alastair who had spoken to the *New York Times* as a way of putting leverage on Clinton,' said one insider, 'he wouldn't have told the PM about it so he could deny knowledge convincingly.'[104] Number 10's disillusionment with the White House was fully reciprocated. They were tired of the briefing against them, they were tired of London's grandstanding, which they thought was designed to show up Blair personally against Clinton for his own political advantage, and they thought the incessant pressure for ground troops was risking the gains already achieved against Milošević.[105]

Diplomatic moves and further civilian deaths went on for the next two weeks. Blair managed to nudge the US and Nato allies some way in the direction of his *idée fixe*. On 27 May, Robertson stunned his US counterpart, Bill Cohen, by telling him that the UK was ready to contribute 50,000 troops to a Kosovo campaign, which would stretch the UK's military capacity almost to breaking point.[106] The seriousness of British intent was beyond doubt. 'Blair's pressure did help steel some of us in the administration,' admitted one Clinton aide, 'but ultimately his input was merely to speed up what would have happened anyway.'[107] Finally, the British came to believe that Clinton was on the verge of telling his Joint Chiefs of Staff to 'press the button' on ground troops.[108]

Robertson says, 'Milošević and his generals only capitulated when they became convinced that the allies would use ground troops.'[109] This indeed is the British line. But such pressure was to be only one factor in the resolution of the conflict. The former Cold War superpowers, the US and Russia, not Britain, were in the end the ones who finally persuaded Milošević to back down. On 14 April, Yeltsin appointed his pro-Western former Prime Minister and fixer, Viktor Chernomyrdin, as his special envoy to the Balkans. He worked closely with Strobe Talbott, US Deputy Secretary of State, and Martti Ahtisaari, the Finnish President. On 25 April, Yeltsin phoned Clinton as the Nato summit was closing to discuss their joint thinking on Kosovo, and on 3 May Chernomyrdin met Clinton in Washington. Blair was not involved directly in these talks, although he was kept fully informed at every stage.[110] The US aim was to complement the military pressure on Milošević by persuading the

Russians to cut their support for the Serbs and to make it clear beyond all doubt that they would not intervene if Nato launched a ground invasion. What few realised at the time was the intense pressure that the US put on the Russians to fall in line with this strategy.[111]

Throughout May, Chernomyrdin, Talbott and Ahtisaari held discussions in Moscow, Helsinki and Bonn. On 1 June they began their final round of talks, which were concluded by a phone call from Yeltsin to Chernomyrdin two days later confirming his agreement to a tougher line towards Milošević. Chernomyrdin and Ahtisaari flew to Belgrade to tell Milošević that if he failed to withdraw from Kosovo, Nato military action would continue indefinitely.[112] Implicit in this was the message that Clinton was on the verge of authorising the deployment of troops in preparation for a ground war, which the Russians would do nothing to oppose.

Blair was at the EU Heads of Government summit in Cologne on 3–4 June as reports came through about this breakthrough. A lasting settlement could still take months, it was feared, yet the final deadline for the decision on the use of ground troops was just hours away, and Nato allies were still deeply divided as to the desirability of this option. It made for a tense summit as Blair and other leaders picked up scraps of news about the far more important discussions taking place on the other side of Europe. As the EU leaders stepped down from their formal photograph at lunchtime on Thursday, 3 June, Blair was intercepted by Campbell; he had just picked up news via Reuters that the Serbian Parliament that morning appeared to have accepted the demands for their troops to withdraw. But there were still questions. Was Milošević sincere? Was he positioning himself to drive a wedge between the Nato alliance, whose cohesion he had always thought paper-thin? The Ahtisaari talks did indeed break up briefly when Milošević's commanders insisted on keeping some troops in Kosovo, and bombing continued for a further two days. But on 9 June, the Serbs finally gave reassurances about withdrawal, and the next day Nato Secretary-General Javier Solana suspended the bombing. Discussions had at the same time been taking place between leaders at the G8 talks, which met in Cologne a week after the EU summit and which paved the way for UN Security Council Resolution 1244, authorising the deployment of Nato troops in Kosovo to oversee the return of the refugees. The conflict was effectively at an end.

As with Desert Fox, what was sold as a clear-cut victory was anything but. Downing Street told a story about Blair's single-minded drive for ground troops finally breaking Milošević, resulting in the avoidance of a humanitarian catastrophe in the Balkans. As we have seen, however, Blair's continued pressure for ground troops may have been courageous but it was only one contributing factor in Milošević's climb-down. The air attacks were less significant: they did have some impact on Serb forces, but on their own would never have forced a withdrawal. Nato's continuing unity was important in facing down Milošević, but in the end the crucial factor was diplomacy between the US and Russia, which left Milošević isolated.

In withdrawing his troops from Kosovo, Milošević believed the Russians would establish their own position in the north of the territory, which would allow him continued leverage. Evidence of Russian designs on Kosovo appeared to be unfolding two days later when Russian forces sped out from Bosnia and occupied Kosovo's Pristina airport. As Berger said, the unilateral and unheralded advance by the Russians caused great anxiety about what their motive was, and 'whether they wanted to stake out their own area, which would have made it very difficult to have a unified Kosovo'.[113] To the British, a major international crisis was in the offing as Wesley Clark ordered the Russians to be removed by force. Only the restraint of General Mike Jackson, the British commander, who refused to obey the order, defused the tension. The Americans, by contrast, were furious with Jackson, whom they believed had left the Russians thinking they could get away with this underhand action. Either way, the moment passed, and the Russians became legitimate participants in the peacekeeping force in Kosovo. When Milošević did fall, a year later, it was at the hands not of Nato but his own Serbian people. Eight months after they toppled him, he was sent to The Hague to face the Yugoslav war crimes tribunal.[114]

Nor was the crisis the unqualified humanitarian triumph it has been portrayed. The air war, and Milošević's reaction to it, exacerbated the refugee crisis. By early May there were 200,000 refugees within Kosovo itself, and 850,000 who had fled beyond its borders. The human cost and distress of all this dislocation is untold. As one of Blair's closest colleagues told John Kampfner, 'Our whole policy was saved by the refugees. Milošević provided evidence to prove the case for bombing,' i.e., the outrage against Milošević provided the public support to allow the air campaign to continue. Since 1999, some 200,000 refugees have left Kosovo, some Serbian Kosovars have left of their own volition, but others have been driven out by the very people the humanitarian action in 1999 was designed to protect. Ethnic cleansing goes on, and the Kosovo and Balkan story is far from over. Much good has undoubtedly flowed from the campaign that would not have happened if Milošević had been allowed to go unchecked in Kosovo. But the humanitarian picture is not as shiny or as singular as the government has sought to portray it.

The Impact of Kosovo on Blair

The war had several consequences. It changed the fortunes of many in Blair's team. The war bolstered George Robertson's profile abroad, a contributing factor in his appointment as Nato Secretary-General later in 1999. Clare Short's and her department's stock rose for their crucial humanitarian work. Cook, who put in more work than any minister except Blair, received least, and Kosovo failed to pave the way to a closer relationship with Blair. Campbell, who had ridden to the rescue of Nato and only fell foul when he turned his spinning guile on the most powerful man in the world, saw his power reach its apex. Blair's very high regard for Guthrie, the closest relationship he had yet had with a military figure, was one factor explaining the significant rise in the defence budget in the 2000 spending review.

The frustration over the use of troops in Kosovo convinced Blair of the wisdom of pressing ahead with the controversial European Security and Defence Initiative for a Rapid Reaction Force, as unveiled at St Malo in 1998. Blair thought it was 'rather pathetic for a rich and populous group of European nations'[115] with substantial armies not to provide forces for operation in support of its common will on foreign policy. Schröder's and Chirac's pleasure at Blair's championship of a European defence force (in the face of US reservations) made them more willing than they might otherwise have been to go along with him on air attacks on Kosovo.

Blair's Chicago speech proved a seminal text. In contrast to the mishmash of aims for his foreign policy that he had previously offered, such as to the party conference in October 1997, he now had given a very clear statement for when humanitarian intervention was justified in the internal affairs of another country. It provided him with an intellectual rationale for not intervening in support of Chechnya following its brutal treatment from the Russians (a course of action never even remotely considered in Number 10),[116] and it provided him with the justification for intervention in East Timor, where Britain played a minor part in the Australian-led UN operation, and in Sierra Leone in mid-2000, when British troops initially intended to evacuate British nationals ended up helping to restore stability.[117] It paved the way for intervention in Iraq in 2003. Robertson said the Chicago speech was the foreign policy equivalent of Clause IV: 'It was one of those occasions when Tony Blair set out a bold line which changed the whole geography.'[118]

Kosovo ingrained in Blair that he was the bridge between the United States and Europe, and that he uniquely could explain the one to the other. Clinton's equivocations gave him a mistrust of the ability of the US to reach the right conclusions without him. After Kosovo, Blair saw the Atlantic relationship as *the* fundamental axis for the preservation of a liberal world order. Clause IV propelled Blair on to the national stage; Kosovo propelled him on to the international stage. After it, Blair's profile and standing reached heights abroad from which it rarely fell back. He liked the prominence, and relished the opportunities it gave him in the future for decisive action on clear issues of moral principles.

Finally, Kosovo had the profoundest effect on Blair himself. He was isolated in the Western Alliance, and largely isolated in the government. It took him to the very brink of his self-belief and his ability to endure stress. He had never before felt so much weight on his shoulders. The stakes were very high, and if it had gone wrong the consequences for him, and for the refugees, were almost beyond contemplation. But he trusted his instincts, and he came through. Very few had shared his sense of certainty: it further increased his reliance on and trust in the small circle around him and increased his suspicions of the Whitehall Establishment. It was to this tight-knit group that he would turn again in future foreign crises. No previous single episode had so challenged him and no other test provided the same powerful boost to his self-belief as Kosovo. It was the key overseas episode of the first term.

Blair leaving a meeting in Number 10 in October 1999 followed by John Prescott. Blair appears uncertain exactly where he is going, but Prescott is adamant he is following him wherever that might be.

28

John Prescott

One of John Prescott's most humiliating moments under Blair came in April 1999 when, standing in for Blair and to the jeers of the House, he badly mispronounced 'Milošević'.[1] Often targeted for his creative use of the English language, Prescott's persona sometimes belied his importance to Blair, and of all Blair's relationships described in this book, the one with Prescott is perhaps the most surprising.

No serious observer would have predicted in the early 1990s that Prescott, the working-class, 'old' Labour traditionalist, would serve as Blair's loyal deputy for ten years at the very apex of New Labour, and keep the modernising project afloat through some very difficult periods. The odd coupling provides one of the keys to Blair's success as party leader and as Prime Minister. With Brown consistent in his unreliability, and with Blair's attachment to the Labour Party so rootless, it has been Prescott who has provided the ballast to allow Blair to prosper largely untroubled (at least until 2003) by the party turbulence that bedevilled his predecessors Gaitskell, Wilson, Callaghan, Foot, Kinnock and Smith.

Prescott, the Man

Prescott was born in the north Wales town of Prestatyn in May 1938, the son of Bert, a railwayman and lifelong union and Labour activist, and Phyllis, a former maid from a mining family, who was also active in the Labour Party.[2] Unlike his brother and his sister, who went on to grammar schools, John failed his eleven-plus, a scarring experience. At fifteen, he left school without any 'O' levels to work in hotels and in 1955, aged seventeen, he joined the merchant navy as a steward with Cunard.[3] He rapidly immersed himself in union activity, becoming a key organiser of the unofficial seamen's strike of 1960. While at sea he discovered a love of learning he had never possessed at school, and from 1963 to 1965 he attended Ruskin College, Oxford, to study economics and politics. 'It taught me I had no need to feel inferior to anybody,' Prescott said.[4] Raphael Samuel, one of his tutors, found him 'the very incarnation of Jude the Obscure, with a tremendous appetite for learning, fiercely independent opinions and a determination, like the tragic hero of Hardy's novel, to crack the secret of knowledge'.[5] The academic bug had bitten, and he went on to study for a degree in economics at Hull University. While there, he became a Labour candidate and fought the 1966 General Election in the safe Tory seat of Southport. He also wrote a pamphlet defending the seamen in the major 1966 strike, whose leaders were denounced by Harold Wilson for being a 'tightly knit group of politically-motivated men'.[6] Some of Prescott's friends and colleagues were Communists, but he favoured parliamentary action.

Prescott was elected to Parliament in the 1970 General Election aged thirty-three, as the National Union of Seamen-sponsored MP for Hull East. At this time, Blair had not even sat his 'A' levels. Once in the House, Prescott established himself as a left-wing, pro-union outsider, and a staunch opponent of the European Economic Community. His anti-Europeanism partly explains why Peter Shore appointed him his Parliamentary Private Secretary after Wilson was returned to power in March 1974, campaigning with Shore for a 'no' vote on Britain's remaining in the EEC in the 1975 referendum. Prescott backed Tony Benn for the party leadership in 1976, but came to identify more with the pragmatic rather than the hard left in the party. When Callaghan was defeated in 1979, he was appointed a junior shadow transport spokesman to Albert Booth, where he met Peter Mandelson, Booth's researcher. Prescott rated Mandelson's mind and commitment, and they worked together to produce a policy statement on transport, one of the more constructive policy pronouncements to have emerged under Foot's leadership from 1980 to 1983. Prescott's interest in the regions developed when Foot appointed him shadow regional affairs spokesperson in 1982, a new post designed to find an acceptable policy for the English regions in the event of Scottish and Welsh devolution succeeding in the future. He argued for devolving more power to the regions while also raising the standards and performance of local government, two areas he was to preside over twenty years later.

After the 1983 defeat Prescott was elected to the shadow Cabinet, and was appointed shadow Transport Secretary by Kinnock, who promoted him again to shadow Employment Secretary the following year. While there, Prescott shifted party policy some way towards an acceptance of the market, while keeping the unions on side, and had progressive ideas about party organisation. He might, with encouragement, have flowered into a moderniser. But he and Kinnock never gelled, and they fell out over economic policy, resulting in his being demoted in 1987 to shadow Energy. Kinnock's anger at Prescott challenging Hattersley for the deputy leadership in 1988, in tandem with Benn's challenge to him, resulted in his further demotion that year to shadow Transport Secretary. Another reason for the change was to clear space for someone who Kinnock thought would represent the party's case far better in the fight with Cecil Parkinson over electricity privatisation – Tony Blair.

Prescott and Blair

The relationship between Prescott and Blair moved from suspicion tinged with some mutual admiration in 1987–94 to a realpolitik acceptance of each other's values in 1994–99, to a relationship of genuine appreciation and even affection from 1999 to 2004. Prescott had challenged Hattersley in 1988 partly because he thought him an elitist, but also because he thought he could do a much better and a more active job.[7] He had even more reason to dislike Blair, whose social background, political views and ambitions for the party were so very different from his own, and who was now being promoted by the leader over him.

The first time Prescott encountered Blair seriously was in the mid-1980s when he visited Sedgefield for a 'Jobs in Industry' rally. Blair's easy and warm relationship with his local party made a real impression on Prescott, though he still thought him a 'posh boy'.[8] In 1987, when Kinnock set up a group of up-and-coming junior shadow ministers to work on job plans for their departments, Prescott dubbed Brown, Blair and Straw 'Kinnock's Colonels', and he found Blair's manner and contribution particularly irritating. In the later 1980s, he proved irrepressible. If Kinnock had wanted to subdue or sideline Prescott at Transport, he failed, and by the summer of 1989, he had established, despite Mandelson's efforts, a higher media profile than any other Labour front-bencher apart from Kinnock, Smith and Brown. That October, for the first time, he won a seat on the NEC, replacing the more left-wing Ken Livingstone, which pleased Kinnock, and led to a short-term improvement in their relationship.

Prescott indeed was far more open to the whole modernising agenda than his popular perception at times suggested. At Transport, he produced innovative plans of marrying private with public investment in the railways, and he became interested in what Blair was trying to achieve as shadow Employment Spokesman from 1989 to 1992. He had himself backed the move away from the militant trade unionism that he had endorsed in the 1960s and 1970s, and had worked hard for the party to support unions balloting their members before strikes, and abandoning support for secondary picketing. He thought Blair was right on the closed shop, but was irritated that he had not got the unions fully behind him before announcing the change. He thus saw the turbulence Blair encountered as poetic justice.[9] Prescott's attitude to Blair in 1987–92 can best be described as 'guarded approval': he thought Blair and Brown were two sides of the same coin, with Brown at the time possessing the stronger personality.[10]

While Blair was busy blaming the 1992 General Election defeat on insufficient modernisation, and some near Smith were blaming it on too much, Prescott was arguing that it was the fault of the unelected advisers around Kinnock: 'I call them the "beautiful people" – who have in fact won the elections the last two times and we've still lost.'[11] Clarke, Hewitt, Philip Gould and Mandelson (wrongly, as he had nothing to do with 1992) were those he had in mind. He blamed them for keeping him and the great majority of the shadow Cabinet away from election strategy and the television cameras. Prescott stood again for the deputy leadership in 1992 on a platform of change to the party's organisation ('I like organisation,' he said) and a return to Labour's core values – full employment, redistribution and strong public services. Blair and Brown backed the victorious Beckett against him; he had not expected their support so was not unduly upset at their decision. But the young contenders rated Prescott sufficiently highly to go and see him in his room for forty-five minutes after the 1992 leadership election was over to try to build better relations with him in the new Smith regime.[12]

Prescott moved towards Blair over the next two years, and began to see him as a stronger figure than Brown. Prescott had fought for one member, one vote in trade unions, but disliked what he considered Blair's excessive and self-serving drive for OMOV. But at least he felt he could have an argument with Blair. In contrast, he found Brown would not argue with him openly: instead Prescott would often find himself briefed against behind his back.[13] Prescott was flattered that Smith turned to him in the autumn of 1993 to give the party conference speech to encourage the party to back OMOV. The vote was probably already won before his speech, but he earned great credit with Smith, and with Blair. He was thus promoted back to the position he had held nine years before, shadow Employment Secretary. Smith was a Labour right-winger whom Prescott liked and respected. Unlike Kinnock, Smith gave Prescott the space to be himself, and Prescott was shattered by his death.

Prescott decided, for the third time, to stand as deputy leader, and he also ran for the leadership. Five days after Smith's death, Blair phoned him to establish an understanding. Prescott had already been told that Blair would be standing: having seen Blair on 13 May, one of Prescott's most trusted aides reported back: 'I have never been in the presence of a man so sure of his destiny.'[14] During this time Blair and Prescott maintained regular contact through two of Prescott's allies, Dick Caborn and Ian McCartney, who were sympathetic to Blair. A 'non-aggression pact' was thus established where both sides agreed not to run the other down: this held throughout the campaign. The moment of greatest potential danger was when Brown announced that he was nominating Beckett for deputy. Blair's immediate response was to allow Mo Mowlam to go on television to say that she would be nominating Prescott, thus retaining their understanding. Blair's concern was that Brown's unilateral action would create a split in the party, which he had fought so hard to avoid, and which would also make leading it once the contest was over much more problematic. Brown's relationship with Prescott was exceptionally poor at this time and in some ways became even worse in 1994–97.[15]

Prescott realised he had no chance of winning the leadership over Blair. His decision to stand in the hope of boosting his chances in the deputy leadership election was seen as self-indulgent and unnecessary by some senior colleagues, who felt it harmed the chances of other potential candidates on the left of the party.[16] But his tactics paid off and he was almost childishly thrilled to be elected deputy leader at long last. He was further buoyed by the satisfaction of beating Beckett, who had triumphed over him two years before. His aim now was to be supportive of Blair, and he felt almost protective towards his much younger boss. But Prescott also carried a huge chip on his shoulder. He suspected that Mandelson, whom he heartily disliked, was behind every move Blair made. He remained at odds with Kinnock's court, who found their way back into the leader's confidence with Smith gone. He also remained at war with Brown, which made life even more difficult. Campbell's appointment eased matters, as Prescott 'knew where Campbell was coming from' and liked him. Not even Campbell's presence, however, prevented Prescott from being excluded from the Chewton Glen seminar in early September 1994. When Prescott was told about it by Rosie Winterton, who ran his office, he said simply,

'I can't believe that's happening,' because he trusted Blair to be open with
him. He phoned Campbell to find out what was going on. 'Don't ask me,'
was the gruff reply.[17] When he realised he had been left out, and the
whole seminar had been held behind his back, his goodwill turned to fury.
He confronted Blair: 'What's all that crap you sold me about Old and
New Labour working together?'[18] This was the nadir of their personal
relationship, and it was significant that it came at its outset. Blair would
never again so betray Prescott's trust. The two men had a frank discussion
after the fracas. Prescott told Blair of his wish to be made 'Deputy Prime
Minister' after the General Election. Blair demurred. Blair asked him if he
would back New Labour. 'I can't do it unless you agree.' Prescott was
unhappy but bowed to the inevitable, on the argument that the new name
would help persuade lost voters that the party had indeed changed. Blair
said he would 'give consideration' to Prescott's request for the title.[19] But
he was not completely certain how far he could trust him.

The formative experience for their new leader–deputy leader relationship was thus not Chewton Glen but the party conference the following
month, when Prescott agreed (albeit reluctantly) to support Blair's line on
Clause IV on two conditions: that Blair had to carry the party with him,
and not bounce them, and that he had a veto over the new version of
Clause IV. If Blair did this, Prescott said he would campaign for the
change.[20] Blair never forgot Prescott's pivotal role in his first defining test
as party leader. Tensions remained in 1994–97 and there were regular
explosions, but they were containable. Prescott was not going to sacrifice
a Labour victory at the General Election by having a public bust-up: Tom
Sawyer, Labour's new General Secretary, said, 'It was grim for a long time
with Prescott – life would have been much easier with Beckett. But things
got better as the election approached.'[21] Prescott's gradual warming towards
some of Blair's agenda was also evident publicly. Although Prescott had
been highly critical of Blair's praise for Clinton in January 1993, by August
1996, during a most significant visit to the US, he was happy to declare
that 'there is a lot in the Clinton administration to admire'.[22] Prescott was
more willing to embrace change than many Old Labourites. But he had to
be handled well, and Blair was still learning.

The European Union, links with the Liberal Democrats and trade
unions were all areas, however, that saw clear and significant policy
differences between the men. Prescott also believed that the deputy leader
should have responsibility for managing campaigns. However, given
Prescott's views on the 1992 campaign, and his Old Labour, union-
friendly image, Blair wanted him nowhere near the spotlight given the type
of campaign they were planning. Consequently, Prescott saw the job he

craved being given to Brown and Mandelson, which made it doubly galling, while he had to content himself with overseeing party organisation and boosting party membership, at which Blair judged his qualities could be used to best effect, and which were jobs to which he was committed and had a proven track record. Prescott managed to achieve from Blair what he wanted, however, with the promise after the election of the title 'Deputy Prime Minister': Brown feared greatly this position would give Prescott *carte blanche* to interfere across domestic policy, especially as he would not only be chairing Cabinet in Blair's absence, but Blair had also said he would chair all Cabinet committees. Brown fought to resist this idea, and won back the concession of chairing the Cabinet's economic committee. Prescott also lobbied Blair hard to secure his ideal government post. He spoke to many, from ambassadors to fellow politicians, about whether he should go into Number 10 working alongside Blair or gain experience first running a department (he had never served as a minister). The advice was almost universally that he should do the latter. He then picked up the idea from fellow MP and friend Dick Caborn that having a big department with a massive budget would give him great power in Whitehall, so he asked Blair for, and he received, a massive department with a big budget, with responsibility for the environment, transport and the regions (the specially created DETR).[23] These were not topics that interested Blair, and they proved unwieldy, initially requiring much of Prescott's time forging them into one unit. He sought advice from Michael Heseltine, who had experience running large departments, and was impressed by what he said: 'You listen to the advice of your civil servants then you make your judgements.' Prescott told Blair he would agree to run the DETR for one Parliament but then he wanted to come into Number 10 and operate from there as Deputy Prime Minister. 'That was *my* deal with Tony,' he would say.[24]

After the 1997 election, Prescott threw himself into the DETR with a vengeance. But his relationship with Blair in the first two years was not always easy, and he threatened to resign if Blair let Liberal Democrats join the government, which created bad blood.[25] 'Tony's fear that John would be threatening to resign every twelve months was a big early anxiety of his,' said one aide.[26] But he chaired the early Cabinet meeting in Blair's absence when the decision to proceed with the Millennium Dome was taken: Prescott thought people would want to celebrate the anniversary and was quite happy to support the new building's construction. In the first few months Blair would meet each week in his office with the 'Big Three', Brown, Prescott and Cook, who had all jockeyed so much for power in opposition. The chemistry proved no better in power than it had before, however, with Brown in particular making it evident that he resented having to attend and behaving in an awkward way.[27] Before long the meetings were quietly phased out and Blair kept up with all three through his favoured forum of bilaterals instead.[28]

Blair's weekly meetings with Prescott on Thursday mornings concentrated on four main areas. On his department's work, Prescott felt squeezed between Brown and Blair. Number 10 became concerned about Prescott's agenda, and was especially worried about the perception that it was anti-car, with damaging electoral consequences: Prescott, by contrast, thought it quite wrong to pretend one could keep building new roads for ever, and believed a stand had to be made. Blair was not abreast of, nor particularly interested in, many of the details of the issues Prescott raised, whether on Kyoto and climate change or congestion charging. He feigned an interest but worried Prescott was becoming an 'unguided missile' in his huge department. Prescott thought his achievements, such as securing finance for the Channel Tunnel link, bringing EU partners together on climate change at Kyoto and putting the legislation in place for the congestion charge, were downplayed, and he suspected that Number 10 was behind negative briefings about his ministerial work. Rather than challenging Blair directly he turned his fire on Geoffrey Norris, the Policy Unit aide responsible for overseeing the DETR, who had no respect for Prescott. This feeling was reciprocated and Prescott had Norris in mind when he spoke about Number 10's 'teeny boppers'.[29]

Blair brought a succession of junior ministers into the DETR to keep an eye on Prescott – John Reid, Helen Liddell briefly, and then Gus MacDonald in July 1999, who forged the best relationship with him – and relations with Number 10 accordingly improved. Transport remained, however, one of the main areas in which the government failed to deliver in its first term – albeit on the impossible timescale that it had led the public to expect to see change. Prescott's attempts at achieving an integrated transport system in Britain, while paving the way for increased public transport usage, achieved little in the time Blair required change to be shown. Progress on the railways, meanwhile, was called in to question by the train crashes at Paddington in 1999 and Hatfield in 2000, which shot a relative backwater to the top of his political agenda. Number 10 said that he should have had his plans for legislation and improvements in place before these disasters struck. Prescott's defence was that insufficient allowance had been made of years of rail underinvestment, and that the management structure he inherited was not amenable to the kind of rapid change Number 10 demanded. The perception that the government was at sea on its rail policy crowded out the real policy successes Prescott achieved elsewhere, including climate change and reforms in regional and local government.

Prescott and Blair also discussed general government business together. Prescott proved himself a tenacious chairman of Cabinet committees, and was at his best solving problems and resolving disputes. 'Banging heads together, that's what I like,' he would say of this work. Blair realised early on it was much better to keep Prescott informed of what was going on and share with him his concerns: 'John would get very scratchy if Blair ever left him out of the loop,' one aide said.[30] Brown's anxieties about how Prescott would interpret his 'Deputy Prime Minister' role led to early tension, but they were allayed when it became clear that Prescott had neither the will nor the interest to impose himself on Brown's own economic sphere, and an improved relationship resulted. On his side, Prescott's own deep mistrust of the Treasury and the damage it could inflict on a Labour government lessened once in power.

Prescott and Blair's discussions also ranged over wider party issues. By 1997 Prescott had been in Parliament for twenty-seven years, and there was little about the Labour Party he did not know. He would speak up for the views of Old Labour and the trade unions in a way that Blair realised he needed to hear, even if he did not much relish doing so. Blair 'keeps floating off with these airy-fairy ideas', Prescott told Paddy Ashdown in 1998, 'but I am here to keep his feet anchored firmly to the ground'.[31] Prescott remained very suspicious of 'New Labour'; he hated the term, its associations and its more triumphalist exponents among special advisers and in government. When cajoled by Number 10 into standing in at the last minute for Blair at a sixth-form conference in January 1998, and asked by the chair beforehand whether he would be reading Blair's speech, he replied, 'I'm not going to read out that fucking New Labour crap.'[32] Prescott was never comfortable with most in Blair's court (except Campbell), nor with middle-class Labour intellectuals like Patricia Hewitt or arch-Blairites like Byers and Milburn, nor above all with Mandelson, though he rated Philip Gould.[33] His strongest disapproval was reserved for those he judged were rocking the boat. He had made great sacrifices and compromises to keep the Blair premiership afloat and electorally successful, and he would not tolerate anyone jeopardising that for their own ends. Not that he forgot his roots. One Old Labour issue Prescott fought Blair over was the level of the minimum wage, which he pressed hard in their bilaterals to be set at a higher level.[34]

Personal matters constituted the final topic of discussion between Blair and Prescott, centring largely on how the latter was feeling. He was very conscious of his humble origins, and would talk to Blair about how odd it felt to have come from such a background and now to be finding himself representing his country at the highest international level. He was intensely proud of his position, but wracked with doubt, which he would share quite openly with Blair, who was touched and engaged by his honesty and trust. Being mocked was one of his greatest dislikes, as when Tories in the Commons would ask him for a drink (referring back to his time as a waiter at sea). He worked ferociously hard to ensure he was very well-briefed and not humiliated when he stood in for Blair at Prime Minister's Questions. His bleakest moment came in April 1999, when he made a series of errors including the one referred to at the beginning of the chapter, described by Steve Richards as 'the most damaging and confidence-shattering half-hour of his political career'.[35] Blair sensed Prescott's vulnerability and he bolstered his confidence. One of Blair's greatest personal gifts is his ability to let go of hurts, and he encouraged Prescott to adopt the same approach. Prescott would also listen to Blair's own political (more than personal) concerns, and would help him out too with some of the ceremonial aspects of the job he found tedious.[36]

Some tensions remained, and occasionally erupted into the open, as when Prescott publicly rebuked Blair for his 1999 'scars on my back' speech, which Prescott interpreted as an attack on public sector workers. Although usually loyal, this was one step too far for Prescott. Blair's frustration with his failure departmentally, above all with transport, remained a running sore. The early summer of 1999 was particularly tense, as the July reshuffle approached. Gordon Brown reportedly cautioned him: 'They went for my people last year. This time they will go for yours.'[37] Prescott even feared for his own survival.[38] But after 1999, the relationship became increasingly productive, even affectionate. Prescott's reward for his loyalty was an assurance that he would remain *in situ* after the General Election: colleagues noticed how much more calmer and confident he seemed after he received this reassurance.[39]

In the most recent phase of their relationship, from 2001 to 2004, it was at its strongest and most productive. Prescott had his 'deal' honoured after the 2001 election, 'he got into Number 10 to be with Tony', which meant being based in the Cabinet Office and overseeing even more of his beloved Cabinet committees. But he did not find his Camelot provided the fulfilment he had hoped for. Blair wanted him to streamline the committee structure in 2001 as part of a galvanised centre, a task that proved difficult to achieve. He found himself at odds with the policy staff ('Mekons', he dubbed them, harking back to Dan Dare's enemy in the *Eagle* comic of his childhood).[40] He was also ground down by the constant politicking at the centre and found himself at odds with Blair's style of taking decisions not collectively but in bilaterals, and then often at the last moment.[41] 'My God, I tried,' he said of his efforts to make it work. When Byers' departure from government in May 2002 led to a reshuffle, he seized the opportunity to get back into a department overseeing regional and local government, insisting that he did it from his own DPM's office. With Blair so heavily engaged on overseas matters, even more fell on Prescott to manage in his absence. Prescott's relationship with Brown improved markedly in the second term, and he emerged as the pivotal broker between Brown and Blair, when their relationship hit new lows at the 2003 party conference.[42] 'Prescott was just hugely chuffed to play this role,' said one observer.[43] Brown realised that he needed Prescott's support if he were to succeed Blair as leader and that he should back off Blair: but Brown also realised that Prescott was going to back him, and that their long-standing differences were largely over.[44] Prescott mellowed after his sixty-fifth birthday in May 2003: he realised he was not going to go any further himself and much of the fight and restlessness went out of him. More than at any time in his career he relaxed back into a position he clearly filled with success. He had learned what he could and could not do, and he knew his worth. 'Mr Prescott has probably never been more indispensable to Mr Blair than now,' Don Macintyre wrote in the build-up to the Gulf War. 'He can still reach parts in Labour few other Cabinet ministers can.'[45] In the row over 'top-up' fees in early 2004 Prescott worked ferociously to deliver the party for Blair in the knife-edge vote and he also proved hugely significant to Blair in the row in April 2004 over the referendum on the EU constitution.

The Impact of John Prescott

Prescott offered the ideal 'dream ticket' for Blair. He proved fertile in his ideas as a minister, but did not come up with policies that Blair felt particularly fitted in with his agenda; he did not help him on presentation, where Blair already had too many helpers; he was not a star departmental minister, though Blair needed more such stars. What Prescott did was to coax a reluctant Blair to take the Labour Party in and outside Parliament more seriously than he would instinctively have done. Earlier on, Prescott was important in making an even more resistant Blair take the unions seriously too, but Prescott's standing with, and his enthusiasm for, the unions dwindled after Labour came to office. Indeed, his impatience with the Fire Brigades Union in 2002–03, over their strike action, demonstrated how much his relations with the union movement, especially with those on the hard left, had changed. Prescott may not have liked many aspects of

Blair's politics, but he admires Blair's strengths, and the electoral success he brought the Labour Party. He also likes Blair's personal loyalty to him, and particularly in keeping Prescott in his post, which gave him a status, experiences and standard of living he had never in his life known before. Prescott and Blair were often said to personify the old and the new Labour Party. It was Prescott's importance to Blair, and to history, that in 1993, in 1994 and in 1997–2004 he helped keep a modernising Labour Party on the road. His importance cannot be overestimated. He created nothing of New Labour, but he had it in his power to destroy it. He was not the architect of New Labour; he was the man who helped secure its foundations and who stopped ill winds from blowing it away.

In popular culture, however, Prescott will probably be best remembered not for helping to achieve Labour's electoral success under Blair, but for an episode in the 2001 General Election when his always volatile temper got the better of him. After being hit by an egg while campaigning, Prescott instinctively lashed out and punched the protestor responsible firmly on the jaw. The Tories hoped it would derail Labour's campaign. Blair and his team were initially worried too. But as we shall see, Labour's hold over the electorate was far too strong to be dislodged by a stray punch from the man from Prestatyn.

Blair at a primary school in west London in March 1999, four months before his 'scars on my back' speech. Education, he promised, would be his government's highest priority. But enduring improvements, as with the public services at large, would be harder to achieve than he imagined.

29

'Scars on My Back', 1997–2001

One of the facets of Prescott Blair found difficult, in addition to the infrequent outbursts, was his failure, as Blair saw it, to produce the results he had hoped for from his 'giant' department. Blair had somehow expected Prescott to 'deliver' much more in the first term, above all on transport. On coming to office, New Labour quickly enacted the specific proposals that had been worked out in opposition. It soon became clear, however, that Blair had failed to work through his own thinking for implementing reform elsewhere, and had placed too much blind faith in others. With his efforts focused so heavily on winning the election, too little time had been given to the challenges of government. In 1998, the recognition of growing chaos at the Department of Social Security forced Blair to reassess his priorities for government and exactly how to achieve them. By 1999, Blair was coming to the conclusion that he would need to focus far more attention on improving public services than he had initially intended. Yet as the government's self-styled 'year of delivery' in 1999 failed to produce the results he hoped for, his anxieties turned into real frustration: 'You try getting change in the public sector and public services,' he told an audience of entrepreneurs that July. 'I bear the scars on my back after two years of government.' By the time he uttered these words, failure to make progress on the delivery of public services had become a major criticism of his government from outside and a source of tension within, between the Civil Service and their New Labour masters. This chapter examines the key question of what went wrong with Blair's domestic agenda in the first term and why progress proved so difficult.

Age of Innocence, 1997–98

Blair had performed a *coup d'état* on the Labour Party when he became its leader in 1994, and he performed a similar *coup d'état* on British government in 1997. The Millbank model of tight control, the use of special advisers as 'shock troops', and the primacy of communications, were all imposed wholesale on the ancient system of Whitehall. And it worked; or rather it appeared to them that it did early on.

The first year in government was hailed as a glowing success. 'Blair has established himself as the most powerful Prime Minister since Churchill's wartime premiership,' wrote Steve Richards in a first-year survey on 1 May 1998.[1] The polls continued to give Labour an unprecedented lead, the press was still on side, and the Tories under William Hague were nowhere, politically or electorally. The big tent was still billowing up, with Chris Patten appointed to review policy in Northern Ireland, Michael Heseltine involved with the Millennium Dome, John Gummer invited to participate in the Earth Summit, the Liberal Democrats sitting on Cabinet committees and Roy Jenkins chairing his Commission on Electoral Reform. With the appointment of Richard Wilson to succeed Robin Butler as Head of the Home Civil Service and Cabinet Secretary, Number 10 had high hopes that they would be able to harness the Civil Service to produce the results they wanted. Blair's inner circle saw Wilson as far more 'one of us' than Butler had been and were pleased by his initial responsiveness to their requests. At his first meeting with Blair, Wilson picked up on the Prime Minister's desire for a stronger Cabinet Office, allowing Blair more effective control over the government, and produced proposals accordingly; the final draft reached Blair in April. After consultation with his trusted advisers, he agreed to its implementation, creating a new 'Performance and Innovation Unit' at its heart to 'complement the Treasury's role in monitoring departmental progress', and other changes to improve policy initiation, co-ordination from the centre and the delivery of policy.[2] Only with the passage of time did Wilson understand that Blair not only sought more effective control – he wanted more personal control over Whitehall too.

All looked rosy for policy too. The economy was strong, despite some tense discussions about the need to reduce the PSBR and rein in public spending. The 'New Deal' was successfully launched with relatively little hostility from the large companies that had to pay the Windfall Tax and the Working Families Tax Credit was introduced in Brown's second Budget in March 1998. Education was an area where the government was particularly active: numeracy and literacy strategies were swiftly introduced for primary education. Constitutional reform, specifically devolution and human rights legislation, was also proceeding smoothly. Government departments were sending Number 10 glowing reports of what they had achieved in their first year. It was the perfect honeymoon, and it showed no sign of ending. Number 10 thought it could achieve anything it wanted to: all it had to do was give orders and everything would fall into place. 'For the first year we all thought, "God, we can do a lot!"' said a Policy Unit member.[3] Early harbingers like the Euro in October 1997, the Ecclestone affair in November, the revolt on lone-parent benefits in December and the clash between Blair and Brown in January 1998 were all sailed through with no apparent damage or impact on the government's standing. This was 'Teflon Tony' at his non-stick height.

Reality Dawns, 1998–99

The first serious indication of cracks in the winning formula came with the dysfunctional relationship of Frank Field and Harriet Harman at the Department for Social Security. Up to that point, the belief had been that all Blair had to do was to appoint people of good will and high ability, and everything would work out. In May 1997, Blair had coupled Harman, a loyalist, as Social Security Secretary, with Field, one of the party's most original thinkers on welfare, as Minister of State. The synergy, it was hoped, would 'magic up' bold and imaginative welfare policies and result in the 'Beveridge report for the twenty-first century'. Instead they proved an utter disaster together, with their regular rows a matter of public knowledge. Campbell was forced to send them an identical fax in February 1998: 'I see from today's papers that no matter how much we urge silence, congenital briefing goes on.'[4] Campbell completely lost patience with both, as he made clear to Blair. The Number 10 Policy Unit and the Treasury had also lost confidence in Field's ideas; they thought he was a loose cannon whose plans were over-ambitious, incoherent and simply unworkable. His Green Paper on Welfare Reform, intended to be a major statement of the government's innovative thinking on social policy, had to be heavily edited by Number 10 officials before being restructured by David Miliband in the Policy Unit and his brother Ed in the Treasury, emasculating what Field was trying to say in the process.

Blair became concerned by the failure of departments to achieve more of substance. Voices within Number 10 began to be raised that he was too remote from domestic policy (apart from one-off areas like education) and that he was leaving too much to Brown.[5] From early 1998, the Chancellor had begun pressing for the government to take immediate action to improve public services rather than waiting until the end of the Parliament, by which time the electorate might have become so disillusioned they would discount such improvements and turn away from Labour. Gould's polling evidence also pointed to the case for the government being seen to deliver more.[6] Number 10, in contrast, argued that there had to be a period of pain before voters would be convinced that improvements had been made.[7] The battle between the opposing points of view was eventually won by Brown, who announced in the comprehensive spending review in July 1998 generous plans from the end of the two-year public spending freeze at the end of April 1999. These included £40 billion of extra cash over the following three years, with the chief beneficiaries being health and education. The clear losers were transport and law and order, neither of which was considered to be a priority, in part because Number 10 did not yet appreciate how bad the position was becoming on either.[8] However, Brown's promise of £40 billion turned out to be one of the most 'spun' announcements of Blair's first term. The triple counting of figures, and the grossly inflated expectations the figures aroused, was to rebound badly against the government, and take away much of the credit for the extra cash. Furthermore, the money would not be available until April 1999 at the earliest, causing great frustration among those who felt they needed the funds immediately.[9] The innovation in July 1998 of the government's first 'annual report', designed to celebrate what had been achieved so far, also fell flat and shone the media spotlight on how few concrete improvements had been made.

So in the summer of 1998 Blair began to realise that he had to become more involved in the domestic scene, having spent considerable time over the previous six months on Northern Ireland, the British Presidency of the EU and other overseas matters. Blair's first tactic to re-energise himself and the government was also his most personal. In July, he made his first Cabinet reshuffle, designed to achieve two aims: to increase the effectiveness of departmental ministers, and to enhance his authority over Brown and the Treasury. The centrepiece of the reshuffle was his decision to sack Harman and move Field. The latter, however, resigned in protest, claiming that when first appointed he had been promised a rapid promotion to Cabinet.[10] Their departure led to speculation that the government's welfare reform programme was in disarray, which was largely true. For Blair it was a major personal blow: he had had very high hopes of Field, a fellow Christian Socialist, and looked to him to produce a 're-moralising' agenda which enshrined his own beliefs in community and moral responsibility. It was also a blow because the person who had done most to hamper Field's work was Brown, who made it clear that he regarded welfare reform as his territory and that he would not tolerate the costs involved with Field's proposals.[11]

David Clark, Gavin Strang and Ivor Richard, whom Blair considered deadwood, were also asked to leave the government, while Mandelson was promoted to the DTI and the experienced Jack Cunningham, whom Campbell rated very highly, took on the role of Cabinet Office 'enforcer'. Gordon Brown was angry about both these promotions, as he was by the demotion of his great ally, Nick Brown, from Chief Whip to the comparative backwater of the Ministry of Agriculture.[12] Other Brown stalwarts also suffered. Tom Clarke and Nigel Griffiths were dismissed, and Douglas Henderson was moved from his job as Europe Minister. On top of these changes, the ultra-Blairite Stephen Byers was moved into the Chief Secretary job at the Treasury, one below Brown himself, and Patricia Hewitt was moved into the Economic Secretary post.[13] It was Blair's boldest move yet against Brown, who swallowed it all, but fought successfully against the sacking of the Paymaster-General, Geoffrey Robinson, a very close ally. Brown signalled his immediate anger by refusing to take part in a photo call with Mandelson and Byers.[14]

It was Blair's first reshuffle, and he was distinctly uneasy about it.[15] For moral support, and to signal the enhanced role of the Cabinet Office in his premiership, he asked the newly appointed Cabinet Secretary Wilson to sit in the corner of his office in the House of Commons while he saw each minister. By the end, Blair appeared 'utterly drained'.[16] Shortly afterwards an aide noticed that he had almost lost his voice.[17] For all Blair's agonising, the results were to be disappointing. Cunningham's role as Cabinet Office enforcer failed to galvanise delivery from the centre, as such appointments generally did, while his departmental appointments did not lift their performance. More alarmingly, though Brown's wings may have been temporarily clipped, his authority over domestic policy was not. He became more, not less determined to run affairs himself, while social security was brought even more tightly within the orbit of the Treasury with the appointment of Alistair Darling, a Brown loyalist, as the new Social Security Secretary.

Continued disappointment with many of his ministers led Blair to look around for another mechanism to boost departmental performance, and his gaze settled on the Civil Service. Many of the problems that Blair encountered as Prime Minister were because, like Thatcher before him, he either did not understand or accept the way that Whitehall operates. Changing its culture to make it more responsive to their wishes was a bigger challenge than either Prime Minister realised. The reforms designed by Richard Wilson in April 1998 to strengthen the Cabinet Office were enacted, but discontent continued to be expressed by Blair about Number 10's lack of grip over the departments. The reforms may have brought more coherence to policy implementation across the government, but still they did not provide the massive boost he sought for the Prime Minister's authority. Blair yearned for the power actively to direct policy across government as he had done over the party when in opposition. To help him achieve this, Blair aimed to use Wilson in his capacity as Head of the Civil Service as 'our chief whip in Whitehall',[18] an idea that produced a wry smile and a shake of the head when put to Wilson himself by political scientist Dennis Kavanagh.[19] Blair found it hard to accept that the primary loyalty of the top civil servant in each department is to his or her Secretary of State, not to the Prime Minister or the Cabinet Secretary. The British system of government would allow neither Blair nor indeed Wilson to dictate actions to the departmental bureaucracy. Neither could Blair impress day-to-day policies upon departmental ministers. Blair had arrived at Number 10 not realising the very real limits on his executive power: under Britain's constitution, it is the departmental ministers who have the task of executing policies. 'You are a chairman, not the chief executive,' he had to be told. 'So who is chief executive then if I am not?' he asked.[20] To make matters worse, reports had begun to circulate in the press, which Balls was thought to be behind, that the 'real' chief executive in the government was Gordon Brown, and Blair was merely the non-executive chairman,[21] a line that hurt greatly, in part because Blair knew it contained some truth.

By 1999, Blair hit on a new approach to improve the government's output as, at the suggestion of Gordon Brown, he agreed to brand 1999 the 'year of delivery'. This, it was hoped, would focus minds and give the electorate a clear impression of how much was happening. Blair returned to London in January from a New Year holiday spent in the Seychelles with the family and announced a 'mini-relaunch', as Patrick Wintour dubbed it,[22] the first of many. In this 'year of delivery', Blair said, the government should be judged on bread-and-butter domestic issues and not by cheap political gossip. Shrewd voices advised that such talk would only raise expectations still further, ahead of any noticeable improvements in public services, which would take a long time. Sure enough, when the next 'stock-take' of progress took place in July 1999,

Number 10 realised that little had changed and that the phrase 'year of delivery' had created a rod for their backs.

Number 10 then began to look for reasons *why* the public services were proving so hard to improve. They were not short of explanations. Progress was hampered by the paper-thin policies on which Labour came to office, with detailed plans only in very limited areas. Too much government time, albeit not a great deal from Blair or Brown, had been spent in the first fifteen months on constitutional reform: Smith's unfinished business rather than a Blair project. Individual ministers were another target. Blunkett was felt to be doing well at Education, and Straw at the Home Office. But Prescott was blamed for failing to improve roads, Dobson for failing to get to grips with the NHS, while Brown was criticised for his insistence on sticking to the Tories' spending limits for the first two years, which meant the money was not available. Everyone sought to shift the blame. The Tories said the government was squandering their economic inheritance, while the Tories were blamed for running down the public services so much by 1997, especially transport, higher education and the NHS. Ministers in turn blamed Number 10 for meddling in their work and slowing them down: 'The strong centre was meant to drive the agenda forward, but in fact it held everything up,' said one Cabinet minister.[23] Number 10's obsession with jargon words like 'connectivity' and 'liveability' were singled out as being irrelevant distractions: 'If you weren't excited by the buzz words, you wouldn't get far in Number 10,' said one unexcited official.[24] Number 10 was blamed for 'target-itis', the setting of goals for everything, even though the bulk of the targets were Treasury-imposed, an idea first picked up from the education team.[25] 'Number 10 meanwhile believed that if they gave everybody in the departments a bloody good kick and set them enough targets, the right outcomes would result,' said another insider.[26]

When Blair read Philip Gould's confidential memo, 'Half-Way There: Mid-Term Assessment', it brought cold comfort, not least because it reminded him that 1 May 1999 was the likely half-way mark between General Elections. In contrast to the party's own published annual reports, here was an audit that had real insight. 'Time after time,' Gould wrote, 'in internal meetings the same frustrations about delivery, implementation and follow-through are vented.'[27] The strengths of the government to date, Gould said, were its remaining popular for longer than any modern government, taking from the Tories the reputation for being the party of 'economic competence', and some policy successes, notably Northern Ireland. The 'vulnerabilities' were extensive, however, and included an erosion of trust, principally due to sleaze and the reputation for spin and broken promises. On public services, Gould wrote, 'people simply do not see evidence of improvement' while the government's devolution policy risked 'national fragmentation'. Europe was high risk, he said, as opposition to the Euro from the media and social classes C2/Ds and Es 'gives the opportunity for the Conservatives to reinvent themselves'. The media was hostile and likely to become even worse, and Blair failed to provide the clear sense of 'crusade, mission and values' which he had led the electorate to expect from him. All these vulnerabilities meant running the risk that at the coming General Election, and even the one after, Blair might have 'left little behind by way of legacy'.[28]

Gould's solutions to the problems he identified were for Blair to take a higher profile and to articulate with more conviction his vision on community, rights and responsibilities and, above all, education. Spin must be killed, he wrote, in favour of genuine substance. Number 10 itself needed remodelling to provide and communicate a clearer strategy and ensure that the departments delivered. Blair also needed to identify three or four major achievements, including Euro entry, that he could 'leave behind' after two terms. Officials inside Number 10 considered this to be yet another example of Gould's fondness for the apocalyptic and certainly not the consensus view on the progress and prognosis for Blair's government.[29] Even when judged at the end of his second term, many close to Blair in Number 10 thought these warnings otiose. It was an astonishing lack of perspective. Blair appeared to agree with them, and mostly ignored Gould's recommendations. Had he acted more fully on the memo, however, his premiership and his legacy would have been very different. Gould had identified, with admirable clarity, a number of reasons for the relative lack of progress and the government's difficulties. Blair chose to highlight one.

In his 'scars on my back' speech to the British Venture Capital Association Blair pointed the finger of blame towards the public sector and implicitly the Civil Service. They are 'more rooted in the concept that if "it's always been done this way, it must always be done this way" than any group I have ever come across'.[30] It is revealing that after two and a quarter years on a steep learning curve, Blair chose to draw this conclusion. New Labour's lack of confidence in the Civil Service is one of the biggest stories of 1997–2004. But it was not inevitable. Almost the entire senior Civil Service welcomed the arrival of Labour in May 1997. They had grown tired of the lack of decisiveness of the Major government, they welcomed the excitement of a change after eighteen years, and they were very eager to show the incoming government that they would serve them loyally.[31] 'They had marked up our manifesto with yellow Post-it labels, and made a big show of saying that they had thought through all the implications. They could not have been more willing to be supportive of the new government,' acknowledged one Policy Unit member.[32]

'What happened in May 1997 was that two ships [Number 10 and the Civil Service] passed in the night and barely noticed each other,' said one senior official.[33] Many explanations have been offered about why this relationship went wrong, including the inexperience of many in Labour's top ranks of government. The core factor, though, was that Labour came into office in 1997 with a belief in the efficacy of a model of tight-knit groups, working with special advisers focused on presentation. They came up against an organisation whose resources and morale had been depleted since the 1980s and which did not, or could not, act in the way incoming ministers expected of it. 'Having spent three years since 1994 running circles around Tory ministers and their civil servants, the habit of contempt was difficult to throw off,' said one.[34] Special advisers, many of whom were jockeying with each other for position, were imported wholesale into Whitehall, and by 1998 numbered seventy-four, with a threefold rise in Number 10 from eight to twenty-five.[35] Too many of these advisers were stuck in 'opposition mode' and when they found it difficult to make the progress they sought they blamed the civil servants for being obstructionist.[36] Some, like Mandelson, chose to run their departments (in his case the DTI and the NIO) conventionally, and were admired by their officials. Many others, like Alan Milburn and Stephen Byers, chose to run their departments not using the traditional Civil Service hierarchy but through their special advisers and selected civil servants they trusted. The most conspicuous example of this trait was Brown, who quickly side-lined many officials at the Treasury in favour of his advisers Balls, Ed Miliband and Sue Nye, and a small number of officials they deemed 'sound'.

Blair was never as dismissive of the Civil Service as some of his ministers, and unlike some of them, he never bullied or belittled his officials. But he was nevertheless deeply disappointed and frustrated that it did not produce immediate responses: 'You ask it for something and they give you five reasons why they can't do it,' he was wont to say.[37] 'Oh, for God's sake, you guys go away and sort it out,' he would complain to end meetings when tired.[38] His initial preference for the familiar inclined him to rely on Powell and Campbell to run Number 10, rather than civil servants, but he became enamoured by individual officials who served him in Number 10, notably Holmes, Heywood and Manning. He never developed the same trust for the Civil Service machine as a whole. Established mechanisms like Cabinet committees were not used to the full by him. 'He had no time for Cabinet committees,' said one top adviser. 'They just went around and around in circles and did nothing.'[39] Others, notably Brown, Prescott and, for a time, Irvine, used them to good effect. New Labour had declared that it wanted to have 'joined-up government' (the meaning of which was never totally clear) yet it shunned some of the very mechanisms that had been ensuring joined-up government for a hundred years.[40] 'Talk to virtually any former permanent secretary,' wrote Riddell in mid-2004, 'and you will hear a torrent of criticism of Mr Blair's style of governing.'[41] Had Blair made more effective use of the tried and tested resources of the Civil Service, and retained the goodwill of mandarins more, he might possibly even have achieved more.

Taking Personal Control, 1999–2001

When Blair lost trust in others to reach the outcomes he desired, his resort was always to take personal charge himself. He now did this from mid-1999 until the election in 2001 in two main ways. First, he decided to re-order his priorities to allow him more time on domestic policies. Campbell and Hunter were of one mind: 'They were absolutely determined that he was going to have a domestic autumn in 1999, and the foreign affairs people were not going to distract him.'[42] Blair spent more time having bilateral meetings with the Secretaries of State for education, health, social security and transport, the key delivery departments, along with the Home Office. He spoke to Straw regularly about reducing crime and with Brown about economic and social policy. The problem was that he still did not really know how he could improve delivery and performance in these areas. 'A lot of this time was spent going round in circles,' said one insider.[43]

Where departments were doing well, conspicuously Education and the Home Office, his personal input was an important factor. Critical also was the carefully costed planning put together while still in opposition, a clear sense of mission and a stable team of dedicated individuals driving through the policy, namely Blunkett, Barber, Conor Ryan and Bichard, the Permanent Secretary. At the Home Office, Straw had worked out with his adviser Norman Warner much of what they wanted to do in power, for example with 'anti-social behaviour orders'. Education was the major success story among the public services in the first term, above all with the literacy and numeracy strategy.[44] Blair's personal input was felt through regular meetings with the education team every other month; giving his clear backing for Blunkett's agenda, which he shared, including a tough line on standards, school failure and a deep scepticism about the role of local education authorities; holding receptions at Number 10 and giving honours to figures from the education world; making 'helpful' speeches on education and going on high-profile school visits; and finally by promoting the 'Excellence in Cities' initiative, designed to raise standards, and which mixed Blunkett's concern for the disadvantaged with Blair's striving for success.[45] They initially managed to keep on side Chris Woodhead, the controversial Chief Inspector of Education, whose relentless drive for standards and school improvement had upset unions greatly (a result which did not greatly perturb New Labour). Also important in education's success was having two powerful and knowledgeable Policy Unit members backing the agenda – Miliband, the head, and Andrew Adonis, his successor. Miliband's support was signalled at the very beginning of the premiership, when he asked Barber to prepare a paper on literacy and numeracy for Blair to read on the plane to Denver for the G8 summit in June 1997.[46] Blair was constantly asking about education, typically, 'Why can't we free up secondary schools?' 'Isn't it all about getting the right heads into schools?' and (a constant mantra), 'What's happening with exam results; are they improving?'[47] Despite Blair's commitment and notable drive, the success of education policy in the first term was not as wide-ranging as many had hoped. The 'standards not structures' formula, while useful in opposition, proved hollow in government, and the expansion of 'specialist' schools and the introduction of new 'city academies', while valuable for pointing the way, was timid, with much work deferred for a second term.

Another window into the soul of the government was provided by Philip Gould's memo 'Recovery and Reconnection' (2000), which reviewed progress one year on from his 'Half-Way There' memo of mid-1999. Gould found that Blair was still not being seen to be doing enough to connect with voters. Education and the economy he listed as the only two successes, but it was not enough. Gould said that in all the areas he had identified as the government's and Blair's personal vulnerabilities in 1999, 'things have not got better but have got worse'. His two main policy worries were crime, which had 'erupted as an issue and we are back on the defensive', and the NHS: 'We must use the NHS as the principal vehicle for reconnecting the government and TB . . . **it absolutely has to happen,**' he wrote in bold type. Other concerns Gould highlighted were asylum, which was to become a major

preoccupation of Blair's second term, and Europe, which Blair wanted
to become a preoccupation of the second term, and on which Gould's
findings showed great concern that Labour was seen as not sufficiently
patriotic nor protective of interference from Brussels. Again Gould
replayed his theme that Blair had failed sufficiently to articulate his core
beliefs on responsibilities, crime, family and aspiration, and that, as a
result, the government lacked a clear sense of 'mission, passion and
conviction'.[48]

Blair again did not enjoy reading Gould's words, in part because they
reminded him how far he had departed from his own core principles, to
whose development he had never given sufficient attention. He did
immediately seize on one piece of advice, however – identifying himself
personally with improvements in the NHS. The lack of progress had
come to national attention in January 2000, when the media made much
of the case of a patient whose operation for throat cancer had been
postponed four times. Lord Winston, the fertility doctor elevated to the
peerage by Labour, said that the government had been 'deceitful' over
the NHS, and that the quality of care was deteriorating.[49] Blair was
deeply troubled by the furore and called in a number of specialists and
commentators for advice. One who had written critically recounted how
he 'went to see Blair in the den and I found him in an absolute state. I
had never seen him like that. The moment he saw me he leapt up and
for about ten minutes waved his arms around acting in a manic way. "So
you think I'm doing everything wrong?" he said. When he calmed down
we spoke about the problems in the NHS. He said he wanted to
decentralise it but I don't think he knew what decentralisation meant.'[50]
Blair's den visitor was right in his hunch. The lack of any significant
planning for NHS reform was a major omission in New Labour's first-
term programme: 'It was too big for us to handle,' admitted a senior aide,
'so we left it alone for the first term.'[51]

Blair, heavily influenced by Simon Stevens, who became his health
adviser for the 2001 election, decided he would resort to the old Labour
recourse of pumping in public money, but doing so in a way which would
establish himself clearly in the public's mind as 'doing something about
the NHS'.[52] Accordingly, he went on the *Breakfast With Frost* television
programme on 16 January 2000, and announced that if the economy
permitted, within five years, increased spending by his government on
the NHS would mean that it would equal 'the average of the European
Union'.[53] The Cabinet and more importantly his Chancellor were
presented with a *fait accompli*, as Blair's unexpected initiative seized the
headlines and boosted the public's expectations.[54] Brown was furious, in

part because he considered the promise reckless and the arithmetic primitive, but critically because he was not consulted before Blair's TV announcement. The usual dance of briefing and counter-briefing between Number 10 and the Treasury ensued, but Blair refused to back down, and Brown was forced to bring forward his plans for health spending, announcing the increase in his March Budget, rather than as planned in the July spending review. Blair kept up his personal involvement and pressure. In March, his decision to chair a new Cabinet committee to monitor NHS standards was announced, while he was 'deeply involved', said aides, in the 'NHS Plan', published in July, achieving exactly the personal identification with the NHS Gould had suggested.[55]

But Blair realised that he could not personally commit himself to every area without losing overall focus, which explained his resort to his second strategy during 1999–2001, promoting 'modernising' ministers to do the work for him. After all the traumas of the July 1998 reshuffle, he decided to make the July 1999 reshuffle a minor affair, with only one Cabinet change: Paul Murphy becoming Welsh Secretary in place of Alun Michael, who went off to become First Secretary in the new Welsh Assembly. The major reshuffle was delayed until October, partly because of prevarication over Labour's challenge to Ken Livingstone as Mayor of London and the appointment of the new Secretary-General for Nato: Frank Dobson eventually bowed to pressure to contest the former, and George Robertson was selected for the latter. Blair thus had the opportunity for major remodelling of his government to bring in more Blairites, in a similar way to Thatcher in her autumn 1981 reshuffle when she also promoted her allies after holding office for almost two and a half years. In what was to be his last major reshuffle before the General Election, Blairite ministers were given major jobs – Milburn (Health), Mandelson (Northern Ireland) and Hoon (Defence) – and those who were thought to have outlived their usefulness were moved on, Mowlam to the Duchy of Lancaster, and Cunningham into retirement, having enforced little and diminished spin even less. Dobson, who had to work within rigid spending limits for two years, had managed to avoid NHS scare stories, but was deemed neither effective enough nor sufficiently committed to Blair's policy agenda. Speculation had been rife about Prescott's and Beckett's futures, though both survived. Neither was going to advance Blair's agenda significantly, but both had other values to him.

Blair's Cabinet from 1999 to 2001 was composed substantially of two categories: big hitters he was stuck with and with whom he established a *modus vivendi*, including Brown, Cook and Prescott; and loyalists like Blunkett, Straw, Mandelson, Reid, Hoon and Milburn. On this latter group he pinned his trust and hopes. When appointing Milburn to Health, he told him expressly to 'get a grip' on his department and produce results.[56] Blair was frustrated by the limited pool of talent he had to draw upon, and became convinced that many of the best brains and leaders in Britain had careers outside politics. He would have liked to appoint more businessmen, like David Simon, to head departments, but had to be told by a senior official 'you must be joking. They have jobs to do, and giving up their salaries to come in to government and drink a poisoned chalice is not on their radar screen.'[57] Blair continued to be disappointed by the lack of ideas and drive from the Whitehall departments, especially the permanent secretaries at their heads. Should there be a wholesale purge to freshen up departments with young blood? The tactics had some advocates, but it was decided not to repeat the widespread removal of heads of information which had occurred in his first two years. Instead, senior officials judged to be 'dead wood' were by-passed, and departmental ministers ran their empires in their own styles, using special advisers extensively and middle-ranking officials, who were felt often to be of higher quality than the top levels.[58] When the disinherited later protested from the safety of retirement, Number 10 was full of scorn.

It was only towards the end of the first term that Blair began to accept that real, unspun change to the delivery of public services would take many years, and that Labour had been in error before and immediately after 1997 to imply they would bring instant improvement. So departments were asked to produce ten-year plans. Blair accepted that his initial palliative of strong central control – lambasted by senior mandarins as an attempt to 'sweat' more out of public services for the same funds[59] – was not the answer. Instead, a change in culture, backed by a new approach to management, was needed. This realisation eventually led to the establishment of the Delivery Unit, in July 2001, as the key innovation for ensuring more effective delivery. Chapter 39 plots the course of this new flagship institution and other innovations through the choppier waters of the second term.

The Impact on Blair

In the 2001 General Election campaign, Labour had as one of its core messages: 'A lot done. A lot still to do.' Number 10 began to brief that the aim of the first term had merely been 'laying the foundations' for the second term, and establishing a reputation for economic competence and sound government as the necessary prerequisites.[60] This is a rewriting of history and it greatly overstates the coherence and forethought that had gone into the programme for the first term. Blair, on later reflection, realised he had not made the most of the extraordinary opportunities he was afforded by the size of the majority in 1997, and rued the fact that he had not done more when his political capital was so high.[61]

What explains the relatively modest record of his first term on the public services, with little achieved on crime, transport, the NHS or welfare reform, and only primary education seeing significant improvement? In his 'scars on my back' speech, Blair chose to point the finger of blame at the Civil Service, who were at most only partly responsible, and eschewed opportunities to think more deeply about other reasons. A core explanation of the problems lay in New Labour thinking that it could run government like it had run the Labour Party in opposition. The mistrust extended not only to the Civil Service, but also to many of its own ministers and back-bench MPs. Before the 1997 election, Jonathan Powell had famously warned senior civil servants to expect 'a change from a feudal system of barons to a more Napoleonic system'.[62] He kept his word. In fact, once in office, Blair's aversion to collective decision-making led Cabinet Secretaries Butler and Wilson to ask Blair repeatedly to make greater use of the Cabinet.[63] But to little effect. 'There was never any intention of having collective Cabinet government,' said one insider. 'He was going to run a centralised government, with a commanding Policy Unit which was solidly New Labour.'[64] Although the Policy Unit threw up some interesting initiatives, most of the key figures in Number 10, as well as in the departments, were intensely focused more on presentation than policy, as the demands of opposition had required before 1997. 'They were always so concerned about the media,' said one official inherited from the Major government. 'Jonathan Powell's regular refrain was "what will the headline in the *Evening Standard* be?"'[65] 'They just couldn't shake off their opposition mindset,' said another observer. 'Alastair took charge very capably and quickly, but it was all about "what are we going to say in the Sunday papers and what will be the follow up on the Monday?"'[66]

The focus on presentation and the short term not only led to the debilitating charge of spin, which the government could never shake off, but it also, with Campbell's dominance in Number 10, squeezed out time for thinking about the medium and long term. Policy had been largely ignored by Blair in opposition on the grounds that everything had to be subordinated yet again to winning the General Election; the radicalism, he promised, would come later. Once in power, however, policy was subordinated because he did not have the time to give to it. He also lacked a figure as powerful as Campbell to help him. The post of Head of the Policy Unit was left vacant in May 1997, which is highly revealing in itself. Attempts were made to bring in a powerful figure from outside like Clive Hollick, or a civil servant like Rachel Lomax, the Permanent Secretary at the Welsh Office. A sympathetic business figure like Hollick would have brought practical know-how on how to make bureaucracies work, as John Hoskyns had done when Head of the Policy Unit for 1979–82, and a senior mandarin would have explained to them how government operated and how to get the most from the Civil Service, which would have compensated for it being the most inexperienced Labour government since 1924. Terry Burns, the Permanent Secretary at the Treasury, was sounded out to see if he would take the helm. However, increasingly concerned by Brown's style as Chancellor, Burns doubted that the unit would be able to play a useful role and so declined the offer.[67] Some influential advisers, including Philip Gould, would have liked to have seen Patricia Hewitt appointed to head the Policy Unit: 'She would have brought a much more politically astute approach,' said one aide.[68] However, her election to Parliament made such an appointment almost impossible.

David Miliband had to bide his time before being appointed the head officially. The delay did not help his standing in Whitehall and he was further handicapped by knowing little about how government worked, as well as by Blair's own policy gap. As Miliband observed himself, 'Early on, we were consumed by making announcements, by setting up task forces and by legislation, which gave the illusion we were changing things whereas deep down, we weren't.'[69] Another problem that dogged clarity of thought on the domestic policy agenda was Gordon Brown. 'It was just a constant problem, which can easily be underestimated. So much time had to be given to squaring matters with Gordon. Serious bottlenecks were created. One of the reasons he found it hard to push ahead on public services was this constant struggle with Gordon,'[70] said a very senior official. Part of Blair's frustration was that he could never speak openly about how debilitating he found Brown's character and style of conducting himself, and he found himself regularly having to play down the extent of any differences. For all Brown's prodigious competence, and for all their undoubted achievements together, neither he nor Blair had fallen upon any effective answer for improving public services beyond throwing more money at them, having spent the first two years in power starving them of cash. This spending policy raised two further problems: how would the money be found if Labour committed itself, as it did in the 2001 election, not to raise income tax? And what would happen if the extra cash did not improve education, the NHS and transport? As one commentator neatly put it, 'There is no Plan B.'[71]

'They were obsessed from day one about winning a second term,' said one official. 'It was government by perpetual election preparation.'[72] What it meant was that rather than giving primary energy and focus to what its mission and agenda actually was, Number 10 put its energy and focus too much instead into worrying what the media might say. It made for a government which underperformed because it was too often reactive rather than proactive. The real test, Blair increasingly came to realise, would lie in the future. Ultimately, more had not been achieved in the first term because Blair had not worked out fully what he wanted to achieve, nor had he worked out in detail how to achieve the goals he *did* articulate. It is as simple as that.

Blair at the Remembrance Day service at the Cenotaph, November 2002. The photograph focuses on the figure looking over his right shoulder, Lady Thatcher, who had more influence on his thinking than any politician bar Gordon Brown, who is partially obscured behind her.

30

Margaret Thatcher

One area where Blair believed he could outshine Mrs Thatcher, one of the iconic figures in his life, was on improvements to public services – education, health, transport – to which she had latched on too late in her premiership to make much of an impact. When he found problems delivering on public services in his first term he comforted himself by arguing (ahistorically) that after her first four years she had built the foundations but had yet to put in place many of her enduring achievements. He was also transfixed by her performance in foreign policy.

Blair's frequent comparisons during the Kosovo crisis to the dilemmas of Mrs Thatcher during the Falklands War showed the significance of the status she had acquired in his life. He discussed progress on Kosovo with her, about which she had predictably firm views, and his strong leadership during the crisis was inspired in part by her own strength of purpose. The Falklands was to have been Thatcher's only war: in this respect, if in no other, Blair was easily to eclipse Thatcher, the politician who had the most impact on him.

Mrs Thatcher had become Conservative leader when Blair was just twenty-one, and Prime Minister when he was still only twenty-five. His interest in politics began only after she entered Downing Street: earlier Tory leaders like Macmillan and Heath hardly registered with him. Blair's whole understanding of politics was thus forged under her shadow. He was mesmerised by her use of language, her emphatic leadership style and intolerance of dissent, and her authority on the world stage. As Blair gazed at the Labour Party he saw no comparable figure and certainly none within his direct experience, though he often praised Labour's great reformer Clement Attlee. He admired and liked Kinnock, but had little time for

Wilson, Callaghan or Foot. Blair absorbed her influence consciously and unconsciously all the way through to her fall in November 1990. For a period afterwards, Thatcher thought Blair could be of use to her. Within the Conservative Party she saw no potential leader who could take her crusade for the country forwards. Conferring her favours on Blair exorcised some of the fury she felt at her own party, and the contempt she felt for its leadership under Major. Blair too saw great advantage from a relationship with her.

Their mutual admiration society worried some of her more conventional supporters. It also worried some of his. It was a part of their characters that both enjoyed the dismay their relationship caused. For a long time they represented only ideals to each other. It was a platonic relationship based on ideas; once they started to meet, and the ideas materialised into human form, their 'affair' began to change, and by the end it was based not only on admiration but also on mutual sympathy and warmth.

The Learning Curve, 1975–94

Thatcher was a figure of hate to Labour in Blair's early political years. The year he joined the Labour Party, in 1975, she was elected Conservative leader. She remained a shadowy figure to him for her first four years as party leader, and it was only after she defeated Callaghan in May 1979 that she began to make a real mark. She established her identity as a right-wing leader committed to cutting back trade union power and putting the economy back on its feet, even at the cost of high unemployment. She made her first direct impression on Blair by leading Britain into war to recapture the Falkland Islands from the Argentinians, at the same time as he was fighting the Beaconsfield by-election. Later, she was to stand out for her close relationship with the American President, Ronald Reagan, for promoting Britain's position on the world stage as a force mediating between the United States and the USSR, and at home by privatising nationalised industries. Late in her premiership, too late for effective action, she began to reform the welfare state. Blair was ambivalent about or opposed to all these positions at the time. Later, he was to adopt them all.

His first serious encounter with her, in October 1984, left a sting. He asked her at Prime Minister's Questions whether she really understood the full employment implications of the 1944 Employment White Paper, which she had recently endorsed at the Tories' party conference at

Brighton. Indeed, she did: 'I have a copy of it in my handbag,' she said. 'In a thrice she had whipped it out and was waving it about,' wrote David McKie of the *Guardian*, 'quoting selected excerpts designed to show not so much that she was Keynes reborn as that Keynes was the Margaret Thatcher of the Glenn Miller era.'[1] Blair sat down 'to huge gales of laughter', according to one colleague. 'He was absolutely shafted.'[2] Much later, according to Charles Powell, he recounted the story at a dinner at which she was present, adding that what made it doubly humiliating for him was when a Tory MP came up to him afterwards and said in disbelief: 'We always thought you were one of us.'[3]

Blair regretted his slur on Thatcher during the 1987 General Election for possessing 'an unchecked and unbalanced mind',[4] which was itself the product of an unchecked and inexperienced tongue. His comment also ran counter to the way he had begun to think about her. According to James Naughtie, Blair, Brown and Mandelson started to talk about her in an admiring way from shortly before the 1987 election. 'Blair would talk wide-eyed of Thatcher's success in reworking the geometry of politics. "She's changed it all," he would say.'[5] He would also talk about how Norman Tebbit, chief architect of the Tories' 1987 election victory, often spoke about aspiration: both Tebbit and Thatcher personified how those from ordinary backgrounds could, through hard work, achieve much for themselves and their families. Tebbit's autobiography was something of a bible for many Millbank apparatchiks: despite their distaste for some of his views, Tebbit had proved a master in appealing to the working class, something New Labour knew was vital.[6] In fact, Tebbit was the kind of Tory Blair liked; he reserved his contempt for patrician Tories like Douglas Hurd, who came up through Eton. This might seem paradoxical, given that Tebbit was on the right wing of the Tory party and Hurd on the centre-left, but Blair admired those who came up the hard way, just like his father.[7] The importance of both Thatcher's and Blair's fathers in their lives was indeed exaggerated, not least by themselves, to the eclipse of their mothers.

One of Tebbit's great achievements had been helping bring the trade unions within a legal framework. Blair later admitted that 'Labour was too slow to recognise the importance of trade union reform'.[8] One of Blair's main achievements in Opposition was to reconcile Labour to retaining the trade union legislation of the Thatcher governments.[9] When in 1990–92, with the closed-shop scalp behind him, Blair began to cast around for broader philosophical ideas to shape his political credo, and to make Labour again a credible electoral force, he alighted on the Thatcherite 'hegemony'. This notion was popular with *Marxism Today*, whose analysis

of how Thatcher had established and maintained her dominance over
Britain, allowing her to win an almost talismanic three General Elections
in a row, powerfully shaped his thinking. Blair noticed how she built a close
relationship with the most powerful financial, commercial and media forces
in the land, and also how she used language that articulated popular
values – of morality, aspiration and rights of ownership – which struck
a deep chord with the electorate.[10]

Martin Jacques, who mediated Blair's agenda-setting article in *Marxism
Today* published in October 1991,[11] noted at the time how 'Blair's constant
point of reference is Margaret Thatcher. He admires her radicalism, her
sheer courage and determination, and much of what she did. Blair was the
first leader to recognise that many of the changes of the 1980s,
globalisation, privatisation, the redefinition of the state, the growth of
individualism, were both invaluable and desirable.'[12] Philip Gould's research
endorsed the strategy of stripping from Thatcher anything that could be
of value to Labour. The public, Gould found, 'want politicians who are
tough, honest and courageous, and who govern with principle. That is why
they respected Margaret Thatcher.'[13] Gould's influence, here as in so many
other areas, was profound in opening Blair's eyes to Thatcher's relevance
to him. From as early as the mid-1980s, Gould's opinion polling had
thrown up the concept of 'Thatcher's children', those voters who had
started to think about politics during her term as Prime Minister.
'Thatcherism, we discovered, was the political norm for those people.'
What he found was that the aspirational working classes, part of Labour's
natural voting block, saw little in what Labour had offered them in the
1970s and early 1980s. These voters saw value in self-reliance – they were
the people who wanted tax cuts and wanted to own their own council
houses and so they turned to Thatcher's Conservative Party.[14]

Thatcher's strong *moral* lead was also consistently found by Gould's
research to be widely admired, and it is no surprise that Blair articulated
an uncompromising moral agenda against the grain of Labour's traditional
stance when shadow Home Secretary in 1992–94. His and Thatcher's
shared admiration of the United States was another link, and it was during
these same two years that the US experience began to make a deep
impression on him. The New Democrats' appeal to the aspirational
working and middle classes chimed with much of the message he had
imbibed from Thatcher. During the leadership election in 1994, Blair cited
Thatcher to justify his lack of a detailed policy agenda: 'Look at Thatcher,'
he told journalist, Simon Walters. 'Before the 1979 election she didn't put
out 2,000-page documents. What she said was what she believed in, and
that's what I will do.'[15] The Thatcher analogy, of an outsider who came

in with a 'project' to reform their party, was given widespread currency in the press during the leadership election, encouraged by his supporters. 'He does not share her ideological rigidity,' said Matthew Symonds in the *Independent*, 'but he does have her certainty and her toughness.'[16] Warming to the theme, Blair told Riddell and Webster of *The Times* that what he admired about Thatcher was 'the clear sense of an identifiable project she provided for her party'.[17]

Controversial Role Model, 1994–97

Once elected party leader Blair continued to look to Thatcher for inspiration. He told Andrew Rawnsley in October that Labour had the opportunity to do what Attlee did after 1945 or Thatcher after 1979, to create a sea-change in British politics.[18] That autumn, Campbell organised a lunch for Blair at the Savoy Hotel's River Room with Richard Stott, then editor of *Today*. Campbell was keen for his old boss to meet his new boss, and also hoped to sound out Stott on the likelihood of securing Murdoch's support. As they discussed New Labour's priorities, Blair stressed that he wanted to be a leader in the same radical mould as Thatcher.[19] Blair was rapidly realising, now he was leader, that praising Thatcher brought new benefits. It reassured the business community; it pleased the press, especially *The Times*, *Telegraph* and *Mail* newspapers, whose admiration for her remained boundless; and his drawing attention to her strength created divisions within the Tory party, by highlighting unfavourable comparisons with the performance of John Major. The rhetorical zenith of this thinking was when Blair snubbed Major at Prime Minister's Questions on 25 April 1995: 'I lead my party. He follows his.' As a piece of rhetoric, Major judged this 'brilliantly effective . . . the best one-liner he ever used against me'.[20]

It suited Blair that influential commentators like Paul Johnson saw Major only as 'an uninteresting interlude between Thatcher and Blair'.[21] Some of her closest friends in journalism, including Simon Heffer and Matthew d'Ancona, began to write approvingly of his leadership in contrast to Major. The vaunting of Thatcher as the standard by which Prime Ministers should be judged was enthusiastically championed by Major-haters everywhere. John Rentoul goes so far as to argue that Blair 'kept her alive' at a time when she 'was dying politically'.[22] Blair did not hate Major personally: he merely resolved to make his own premiership as unlike his as possible. Campbell in contrast did despise Major, and did everything he could to humiliate him personally, creating difficulties for him politically, and belittling his record, whether in Northern Ireland, Europe or his relationship with Clinton. Major's contempt for Campbell is as strong as that for any figure, but he did not dislike Blair. The one episode that he regarded as a breach of their trust came over the Dunblane tragedy in March 1996, when schoolchildren and teachers were mown down by a crazed gunman. Major thought that they had reached a clear agreement that they would visit the school together and neither party would make political capital over it. To his surprise and disappointment, he thought Labour did, attributing the lapse to the influence of someone in Number 10.[23] Blair's aides respond that the row was the fault of Major, who tried to stop Blair going to Dunblane, a contested assertion.

Thatcher's deep-seated resentment of Major gave her the motive to display the most disloyal behaviour of any Tory leader to their successor in the party's recent history — a criticism Thatcher's camp have always denied, saying she never treated Major anywhere near as badly as her predecessor Heath treated her. Her resentment of Major stemmed from her perception that he had taken her job, abolished her flagship policy (the poll tax), and promoted her prime enemy, Michael Heseltine, who joined the Cabinet. Initially, her personal relationship with Major, as opposed to their political relationship, remained friendly.[24] However, her corrosive comments about him, initially in private but increasingly in public, took their toll. Egged on by her acolytes, and by alcohol, she would periodically lapse into indiscretion, and became consumed by the notion that she had been treated treacherously, and that everything she had done as premier was good, and anything Major did was weak and hopeless.[25] 'Undoubtedly a degree of bitterness may have lain behind her courting of Tony Blair,' admitted one of her closest aides.[26]

Thatcher's vanity and curiosity in Blair was played on brilliantly by him and by his court. She had singled him out as early as 1989 as formidable and potentially dangerous to the Conservative Party. She did not rate Kinnock, and thought Smith a clever windbag and 'just another Edinburgh lawyer'.[27] After Blair became party leader, she would study him on television fascinated, and according to one aide 'would listen very intently and carefully to what he was saying'.[28] Thatcher's private sympathy for Blair when he was attacked in 1994 for being like 'Bambi' turned into public approval the following May in the Sunday Times. Responding to his praise of her achievements the month before,[29] she described him as probably the most formidable Labour leader since Hugh Gaitskell. She also described him as a 'thoroughly determined person', and praised what he had done to the Labour Party, comments that circulated extensively in the British media.[30] In his Hayman Island speech that July, Blair committed himself to free enterprise, had warm words for the Thatcher–Reagan relationship, and developed the theme that 'Mrs Thatcher was a radical, not a Tory'.[31] The radical idea linked in to his discussions with Roy Jenkins about wanting to make the twenty-first century the 'progressive' and 'radical' century, in contrast to the 'Conservative century' drawing to a close.[32]

Blair was eager to go a step further than just conversing in print. He wanted to meet her. Just before he left to see Clinton in April 1996, he told the *New York Times* that a Labour government would fail if it were seen to be 'dismantling Thatcherism'.[33] The growing warmth of Blair's comments had not gone unnoticed in the Thatcher camp and soon after Blair's return from the US, Julian Seymour, one of Thatcher's closest aides, phoned Jonathan Powell and they agreed to open a special line of communication.[34] The fact that Jonathan was Charles' brother helped immeasurably to build trust across enemy lines. Jonathan was Blair's right-hand man, and Charles one of the two figures (along with Bernard Ingham) who Thatcher leaned on most in Number 10, and remained exceptionally diligent towards her in retirement. The value of this fraternal link was proved that September, when Conservative Central Office planted a story that Thatcher thought Blair was 'creepy'. The Powells went immediately to work and extracted a rebuttal that she thought he had 'many admirable qualities'.[35] The role of the Powells in each of their lives highlights another common trait, their impatience with conventional Civil Service advice and with Cabinet government, and their preference for dealing with business in a personalised way, relying on the advice of just a few key aides.

Jonathan Powell was invited to lunch by Seymour before the 1997 General Election, and pressed for a meeting, offering earnest assurances that it would be kept strictly confidential and that they would not exploit it for political gain.[36] Thatcher carefully considered the proposition with her advisers, but came to the conclusion that it would be too risky, given the already widely circulating criticism of her disloyalty to Major.[37] Blair had to content himself for the time being with a series of chance meetings at ceremonies and other public events. 'He was extraordinarily solicitous of her,' said Charles Powell. 'He had the same kind of charm with her as David Owen. She admired Tony Blair's strength of leadership. She was also seduced by his courtesy and fantastically good manners.'[38]

The need for extreme caution on Thatcher's part was highlighted by her praise of Blair to Peter Stothard, editor of *The Times*, during a private dinner in January 1997 at a Pall Mall club. Several weeks later, Stothard wrote a diary piece in which he attributed her precise words – 'He won't let Britain down' – to a 'very senior Tory', saying each word 'falls singly with a thud and repeats like whispered thunder'.[39] The source of the quotation, Thatcher, was discovered by Charles Reiss, who wrote it up in the *Evening Standard*.[40] The effect was explosive, giving succour to Labour and further damaging a demoralised Tory leadership. Stothard denied he was trying to cause mischief: 'I could have splashed with it in *The Times*,' he responded, not unreasonably.[41] Thatcher was deeply upset by the row it caused. 'She has no recollection of saying [it],' wrote her friend Woodrow Wyatt in his diary, adding, 'Maybe she did it when a bit tiddly.'[42]

Blair Turns to the Lady, 1997–99

Thatcher wrote to congratulate Blair on his election victory. Ever a stickler for detail, she began the letter 'Dear Prime Minister'. Her office had made it clear that she would be very happy to meet him after the General Election was won, to talk about running Number 10, Nato, or any other subject he might find helpful.[43] An invitation for her to visit duly arrived at her Mayfair office, and she saw him for an hour on 22 May. They discussed the United States, Russia, Europe and Hong Kong, and she urged him to maintain Britain's strong defences and to 'avoid the single currency at all costs'.[44] ('She relished being asked for her views,' said one aide.)[45] Many in the party were appalled by his invitation but he was unapologetic.[46] The Number 10 media machine milked the visit, indifferent to criticism from the party. 'For seven years Margaret Thatcher was almost a non-person in Downing Street,' one 'senior civil servant' was reported as saying: 'It is fascinating that a Labour government calls her in after three weeks in office.'[47] Thatcher's influence continued to have a powerful pull on Blair: when he faced the first major parliamentary challenge of his premiership, the back-bench rebellion in December 1997 over reduced benefits for single parents, he invoked Thatcher's name in Number 10 and said he would sooner be seen as 'unbending like her than vacillating like Major'.[48]

Thatcher and Blair kept in touch after their meeting, with Jonathan Powell the principal intermediary. If any issue arouse concerning the Falkland Islands in particular, a pet interest, Number 10 would be meticulous about sending someone to give her a briefing. She returned to Downing Street on several occasions, although she always made a discreet entrance to Number 10 through the Cabinet Office, rather than using the famous front door in the full glare of the media.[49] They had a long conversation about the expansion of Nato, on which he valued her experience,[50] and about Kosovo, where she said he should lead the Americans.[51] They discussed relations with the White House. Her success in building a very close relationship with the US President was an approach he emulated. On the purpose of the 'special relationship' however, they differed. While Blair's aim has been to act as a bridge between the US and Europe, Thatcher was far less accommodating to the latter. As one aide put it, her view was that 'if the UK and the US were together, Europe would have little option but to follow'.[52] On a personal level, Blair always made a great fuss of Thatcher whenever they met on public occasions. 'She is very vulnerable to charm and courtesy in handsome men,' said one intermediary. 'He flattered her by always treating her with great courtesy and by keeping her in touch and making her feel still important.'[53]

It always seemed improbable that the volatile chemistry that made their relationship work would endure in the long term. Thatcher's aides say that a little over two years after Blair's election, disillusion had started to settle in. She began to say that she had always believed he was an 'empty vessel who would say anything to get votes'. Some in her court insist 'she never believed he was guided by a firm set of principles'.[54] Given that he had not taken Britain into the Euro in 1997 or gone soft on the unions, had done what she wanted in Kosovo and Sierra Leone, and did not undo any of her legacy, the relationship might perhaps have flourished a little longer. But Major had gone, Hague needed her support, and she disliked what Brown was doing with 'stealth' taxes. An issue also arose which damaged her opinion of him irrevocably: his treatment of General Pinochet, the former leader of Chile, whose serial abuse of human rights had made him the *bête noire* of the left. According to one aide, 'She was *livid* with him over Pinochet. She felt he had been utterly weak in not overruling Straw,' who did nothing to prevent Pinochet's arrest,[55] although the General was later sent back to Chile on health grounds. As Charles Powell put it, 'The Falklands War was the defining moment of her premiership. Pinochet had been loyal to Great Britain in that war, which was a huge factor for her, and she also believed he had saved Chile from communism.'[56] The 2001 election damaged the mutual admiration, when Blair deliberately set out to distance himself from her, and she attacked him during the campaign. But, to the surprise of many, they then embarked on a second honeymoon as he became a more beleaguered figure.[57] Blair fought off his critics at the 2003 party conference with the phrase: 'I've not got a reverse gear,' a conscious throwback to Thatcher's language. Just as Blair echoed Thatcher's 'the lady's not for turning', back in 1980, so Bush echoed Reagan in his 2002 reference to an 'axis of evil', implicitly recalling Reagan's 1983 branding of Soviet Russia as an 'evil Empire'.

Thatcher continued to be fascinated by him.[58] On his side, his attention
was still caught immediately by mention of the words 'Mrs Thatcher', said
a senior official.[59] Aides say 'the love affair goes on'. It was now based
increasingly on their sharing a bond of sympathy that can, but rarely does,
exist between those who have faced the challenge of the highest office.
Cherie slipped unobtrusively into the back of the church for her husband
Denis' memorial service in 2003. There were many acts of kindness from
Blair towards her, which touched her. She was also warmed by much of his
second-term agenda, with his advocacy at home of tough policies on crime
and asylum, 'top up' fees for higher education and of foundation hospitals,
and abroad in his uncompromising stand on terrorism, his support for the
US on Afghanistan and Iraq, and his announcement in April 2004 of a
referendum on the European Constitution. In these, Blair echoed – indeed,
often went beyond – her own policies.

She believed that, late in the day – underpinned, her supporters would
say, by her own intellectual positions – he was discovering some of the very
principles she felt he so singly lacked. Blair's most senior official advising
him on domestic affairs, Jeremy Heywood, who had worked in the
Treasury in the 1980s on privatisation, was indicatively labelled a
'Thatcherite' by Labour traditionalists. Indeed, it was only when Blair
began fully to embrace Thatcherite ideas of choice and diversity in his
second term that he found the answers to his policy 'gap' that had long
eluded him.

The Impact of Margaret Thatcher

It is quite wrong to see Blair's admiration of Thatcher as cynical. Urged
on by his lieutenants, he did exploit her remorselessly in the 1994–97
period for political purposes. Favourable remarks from Thatcher, the
scourge of the old left, were tremendously helpful in demonstrating how
far New Labour had travelled.[60] But for Blair, the relationship went much
deeper. It differs from all other relationships in this book because for much
of the time it was an influence based on example, not on a personal
relationship, which was never more than guarded and strictly formal. Yet
the influence has been profound, and existed on several levels.

On policy, she helped shape three of his five core strands: social
moralism, direct democracy (for example through her reforms to the
unions) and the commitment to the free market. She had no impact on his
other two principles, community ('dangerously socialist', she would have
said) and Europe (until he 'came good' on the referendum). On elections,

she influenced both his determination to win at all costs, and the method of achieving it, by winning back the working- and middle-class voters who had become alienated from Labour because they thought it not aspirational, and by finding the language to connect with voters. Her third election victory was for him the ultimate achievement to emulate. On leadership style, she influenced him to be bold. Just as many traditional Tories despised Thatcher, so many traditional Labour voices poured scorn on Tony Blair: they were both outsiders in their own parties and their changes to their parties' ideologies were tolerated for only as long as they kept winning elections. Thatcher's example showed Blair how to ride over Cabinet and Parliament, and not to worry about being an isolated voice at home or abroad. He was influenced by her impatience with the Home Civil Service, and the Foreign Office, preferring like her to rely more on measurable business techniques than traditional Whitehall managerialism, and a cadre of loyalists within Number 10, with the Powell brothers the purest emblem of symmetry. On management of his party, he was impressed by the way she sought not to include but to take on her internal critics – most famously in her case, 'the wets'; in his case, the hard left and those who resisted modernisation. Hugo Young's biography of her was titled *One of Us*, a phrase which summed up her approach to politics: it could equally be applied to him. On communications, he and Campbell looked to the trenchant manner of Bernard Ingham and their courting of the popular media, as opposed to the correct and unconfrontational styles of Ingham's predecessors, and successors under Major. Finally, on history, Blair was struck that they were both late developers.[61] She did not emerge as a real leader until 1974, when she fell under Keith Joseph's influence, and he only emerged when he spoke out against the closed shop in 1989. She then provided him with a role model of dominance on the domestic and world stage, which he sought to emulate. He wanted to be in her league, along with Gladstone, Disraeli, Lloyd George, Churchill and Attlee. No other role model, he thought, was worth as much. She even eclipsed Roy Jenkins in his mind. Though nothing like as close to him personally, she was the stronger influence. In Blair too, rather than in any of the Tory leaders who succeeded her, she found her truest heir.

Blair's trait of focusing on a single issue and immersing himself in it completely was seen during the foot and mouth outbreak in spring 2001. Here he is visiting a burial pit in Scotland. His preoccupation with the crisis deflected him from thinking in detail about policy after that summer's General Election.

31

General Election, 2001

The reforming Liberal government had come to power on a landslide victory in 1906. Labour won power under Attlee in 1945, also on the back of a great landslide. Yet both governments, despite their considerable achievements, went on to see their large majorities extinguished at the General Elections that followed. Blair's obsession from 2 May 1997 was to improve on their examples by not only winning the next election, but wining it handsomely: this was dubbed the 'historic' aim. Only then would he feel entirely safe and free to follow his instincts. Because the prospect of the next General Election constrained so much of what he and the government did in the four years after 1997, and because key decisions taken in 2001, or not taken, conditioned so much of what followed up to 2005, the 2001 General Election is as important a turning point in Blair's development as the 1997 election. The crucial questions are: what did Blair do to ensure a large majority in 2001, what was his role in the election itself, and what preparations did he undertake for a second term in office?

Manifesto Preparation and the Fuel Crisis, September 2000–March 2001

The dominant feeling in the Labour Party as the 2001 election approached was that the manifesto in 1997 had been too cautious and lacking in detail. The party generally understood and accepted the need for 'safety first' then. But Stephen Byers articulated the expectations of many when he spoke in early 2001 about his hopes for the coming

General Election: 'It provides us with a once-in-a-generation opportunity to change our country fundamentally. We need to ensure that the manifesto is modernising and radical. It is a golden opportunity.'[1] The fact, though, is that the chance to develop radical plans was not grasped in the run-up to the election, or in the 2001 manifesto. One explanation, favoured by the Blairites, lies in the failure of the intellectual left and associated think-tanks to produce the ideas that could have given a second Blair government a radical edge.[2] Indeed, think-tanks provided only one main idea that was eventually incorporated in the manifesto, the child trust fund, and ownership of this was quarrelled over by the Fabians, the SMF and the IPPR.[3] But, while a certain policy vacuum among the intellectual left, and among third-way thinkers, provided an important backdrop, the main reasons for the paucity of Labour's radicalism in 2001 lie elsewhere.

According to one member of the Policy Unit: 'Winning the second term, but not planning for the second term – note the important distinction – was an obsession from the 1997 General Election.'[4] A key reason for the cautious approach to the 2001 election was Gordon Brown's absolute determination to win a second victory. He refused to take any risks that might jeopardise this prize, thinking in part of his own succession. His particular fear after 1997 had been the risk of a recession in the second and third year of the government, knocking it off course as had happened to Labour governments in 1931, 1947, 1967 and 1976, with the worry that, as Chancellor, he would be blamed, and his political fortunes might never recover.[5] Demonstrating that Labour could manage the country competently thus became an end in itself. From Brown's successful stewardship of the Treasury sprang the argument, as 2001 approached, that Labour had proved it was capable of managing the economy and had thus laid the foundations for largesse in the second term. Why not base the appeal in the General Election around this? The second Comprehensive Spending Review in July 2000 was heavily influenced by the coming election, with military spending boosted in part to neutralise criticism that Labour had gone soft on defence, and the arts given priority, again partly for electoral reasons.[6]

Blair must take even more responsibility than Brown for the cautious approach in the run-up to the 2001 election. In part, this resulted from the responsibilities over domestic policy yielded to Brown, yet more significantly, as one insider put it, 'Blair simply was not engaged in driving the agenda forward in a consistent way in the first term.'[7] With no strong lead in favour of radicalism, those in Number 10 who favoured consolidation gained the upper hand.[8] Blair's biggest commitment to policy formulation was to the third way, yet as we saw in Chapter 26, his hopes of translating these ideas into practical policy were fading by 1999. The most significant ideas that Blair latched on to were those thrown up during the battle from 1999 onwards to improve delivery of public services. Undreamt of in 1997, these included specialist schools and city academies in education, primary-care trusts in the NHS, and planning for a portmanteau 'delivery unit', all in their infancy but ripe for a bigger stage. Blair pinned his faith on these methods, and on ideas for extending market disciplines in the welfare state.

During the preparation of the manifesto in 2000–01, the search for a 'big idea' (or even a series of smaller ideas) that would shape the agenda for the Labour's second term intensified. In 2000, Andrew Adonis had generated some thoughts on how governments renew themselves,[9] but it is surprising that, with so many intellectually brilliant special advisers in the Number 10 Policy Unit and in the departments, more was not achieved. Requests went out 'to ministers, think-tanks and anyone else with a fertile idea in their political mind that this time Mr Blair seeks a sweeping programme of far-reaching reform to put to voters'.[10] Ed Richards was appointed specifically to prepare ideas for the 2001 manifesto and succeeded in bringing new energy to the process. In discussions with a range of think-tanks and other creative groups, Richards began to generate a number of promising ideas, including enthusiasm for a strong push on social mobility and opportunity. Yet many of these ideas were smothered by Blair's and Brown's preference for caution, while others fell foul of their political preferences.[11] In the end few made it into the manifesto.[12] Senior aides, including David Miliband and Geoff Mulgan, expressly warned Blair that this safety-first approach could leave the government short on policy by half-way through the second term.[13] So it is not just with hindsight that one says that 2001 was a missed opportunity. Powerful voices at the heart of Number 10 were saying it at the time. Blair proved unwilling or unable to act on this advice. First, he had no intention of provoking a major clash with Brown, who had very different ideas on both tactics and strategy. Second, he did not know himself exactly what he wanted to do in the second term – ideas aplenty, certainly, but few hard plans. Third, as we have seen, there was no 'climate of opinion' of ideas as there had been for Attlee and Thatcher. Finally, even by late 2000, Blair was not focusing on the manifesto with the attention that the task required. 'We put huge effort into consulting widely for the manifesto,' insisted one member of the Policy Unit, 'but I have to admit that Tony Blair was not really engaged in the exercise.'[14] Instead, the Prime Minister was forced to devote increasing time and energy to entirely unforeseen domestic events that now buffeted his premiership. He knew that one reason Brown's agenda had been more fully enacted in the first term was because he had planned it all out beforehand. Yet he let this chance go by. It was one of the most serious domestic errors of his premiership.

Blair's first serious domestic crisis came out of nowhere that September. Transport hauliers and the farming business were angry that the government had levied such high fuel taxes. Blair had acknowledged that the price of fuel was high, but insisted that it was the job of government to take such tough decisions. At the end of August 2000, French lorry drivers and farmers blockaded oil refineries, protesting at their own high fuel costs, a problem the French government resolved by giving in to their demands. Not for the only time in his premiership was Blair exasperated by the Elysée Palace. Inspired by the French example, irate truck drivers in Britain began to blockade refineries, hoping for a similar capitulation. When oil companies at first asked the government for police protection for their tanker drivers, the government dismissed their plea. Early on Monday, 11 September, Number 10 denied there was a crisis, branding fuel shortages 'isolated problems'. The last thing it wanted to do in the run-up to the election was to revive memories of Old Labour bowing to industrial pressure. But by midday, Number 10 learned that two-thirds of London's petrol stations would be dry by that evening. Blair decided to proceed with a regional tour to convey the impression of calm, and it was only when Number 10 contacted him with this latest information that he realised the extent of the crisis. He immediately assented to Richard Wilson's request to set up a meeting of the task force that met in Cabinet Office Briefing Room A, known as 'Cobra', and for the Cabinet Office to co-ordinate the government's response. He also asked for very regular updates.

Cobra is a windowless basement room beneath Downing Street, brimming with high-tech equipment.[15] It is activated in national emergencies and has pre-prepared plans to deal with a wide variety of crises, including terrorist attacks, epidemics and natural catastrophes. But it had no up-to-date plans for a government response to the country running out of oil and petrol. Blair had been due that Monday evening to have dinner at a Chinese restaurant in Hull to celebrate Prescott's thirtieth year in politics: greeted by protestors, they cancelled the dinner, and Blair was driven to the Hilton Hotel at Sheffield, ready for the next leg of his tour. On arrival, he read the faxed conclusions of the Cobra meeting earlier that day, chaired in his absence by Straw, which spoke of a position out of control. He decided to cancel the rest of the tour and to leave the next morning for London.[16] As in other episodes when Blair sensed there was an emergency, his immediate response was, 'I'm going to sort this out.'[17]

Blair's first impulse was to ensure the oil refineries were kept open so the tanker lorries could flow in and out. As soon as he returned to Downing Street, he gave instructions by phone for senior colleagues in London to speak to the heads of oil companies to reassure them that their tanker drivers would have proper police escorts, and to speak to police Chief Constables to ensure that all the requisite police protection was in place. That afternoon, Blair and his staff at Number 10 saw the television news and learned to their disgust that the tankers were still not moving. Blair began to suspect that the oil companies, who themselves had an interest in seeing fuel tax reduced, were not encouraging their drivers to move. While covert instructions were sent out by Millbank to compliant MPs to get out on the media and blame the oil companies, Blair sat in the den with his shirt sleeves rolled up, 'working the phones' and telling the oil companies himself to ensure that their drivers did their work. Others with better relations with unions spoke to their bosses to ask them to tell their members 'to stop colluding with a bunch of militant farmers and poujardiste small businessmen and get driving'.[18] Blair was so pleased with the way it had gone that he said on television that Tuesday evening that 'we hope within the next twenty-four hours to have the situation on the way back to normal'. It was rare for him to be overconfident in a crisis.[19]

Twenty-four hours later a trickle of tankers were leaving the refineries, but the overall position had deteriorated, and Blair had to admit that there was now a national crisis. Number 10 battled to get ministers to appear on the airwaves to defend the government. Most refused, or were conveniently out of contact. 'Brown had been in denial all week, ultimately refusing to discuss it and saying it shouldn't be allowed to become a tax issue,' one diarist recorded.[20] Brown had in fact been working behind the scenes, including attending a secret meeting in Leeds to attempt to win over around twenty key hauliers.[21] But on Wednesday he was eventually persuaded out into the open to give an interview, as were Byers, who was felt by Number 10 to be very poor, and John Reid, who 'showed himself to be the only one with the necessary balls'.[22] Blair remained utterly determined and calm: 'He was very frustrated at his inability to pull the necessary levers, but he didn't lose his temper. He hardly ever does,' said one official.[23] Disillusioned with his lack of success on the telephone, he now summoned the most senior UK representatives of oil companies to Number 10 in person, and told them very directly what power he had under emergency provisions, and that this time they would do exactly what he wanted and get their oil tankers moving.[24] Milburn was also ordered to go on television to say from a health perspective that the fuel blockade was putting people's lives at risk. By Thursday the protestors had had enough and called off the protests without the government making any concessions.

The fuel protest was a nasty jolt, reminding government how vulnerable it was. Sharply adverse polls on the back of the crisis came as a profound shock to Labour, showing how suddenly the country could turn from it. The episode was thus another powerful reminder of the need for caution. Philip Gould, playing his not infrequent role of Jeremiah, warned Blair that he was now out of touch with the electorate and had to 'reconnect'.[25] Blair was particularly disturbed that he had not picked up warning signs of the crisis before it materialised,[26] and was worried that government had been slow to act and recognise the public's anger, which Hague and the Tories had understood and articulated much more readily.[27] After the crisis was over, Blair said privately in mid-September that the coming General Election result would be at risk less 'because of issues raised by our opponents', than from 'events *constructed* by our opponents', with asylum, health scares and other tales of failures of the public services, real worries in his mind.[28] But given that Labour's lead in the polls soon recovered, and the Tories were floundering in the mud under Hague, was the cautious stance justified?

Foot and Mouth, and Election Timing, March–May 2001

One lesson Blair drew from the fuel crisis was that he could not wholly rely on the government machine, or even his Cabinet colleagues, to take the right action in a domestic crisis. In the middle of the drama he had even wanted the Cobra operation closed down so that he could direct affairs exclusively from his own office in Number 10. Officials remonstrated with him, and adaptations were made, including setting up a base within Cobra for the fuel industry representatives and the police to work together.[29] Cobra thus survived, to be activated again by the Cabinet Office on his instructions on 23 March 2001, to deal with the next domestic crisis to hit the country, foot and mouth (FMD).

This was the first major outbreak of the animal disease in Britain since 1967–68, when Harold Wilson was Prime Minister. Whereas the earlier episode had come in the government's mid-term, this outbreak occurred in the politically volatile time of the run-up to a General

Election.[30] The first sign of the problem came on 21 February with the first veterinary confirmation that pigs in an Essex abattoir had FMD, which was followed rapidly by the realisation that the disease had already spread throughout the country. This left Britain with a potential national disaster on its hands, as other countries swiftly imposed bans on British beef exports and thousands of farmers watched helplessly as their cattle became worthless. The Ministry of Agriculture, Fisheries and Food (MAFF) was in charge, but the strict measures it introduced to control the spread of the disease were inadequately executed. MAFF was in danger of being overwhelmed. Sensing the scale of the crisis, Blair assumed personal control on 23 March, instituting centralised decision-making through Cobra. Learning from his reaction to the fuel crisis, which had given rise to a perception that he was out of touch, Blair made a point of visiting disaster-ridden areas himself and listening to those who had been affected.[31] A new phase began with the introduction of armed forces and the institution of Draconian pre-emptive culling programmes to 'get ahead' of the epidemic and prevent further trans-mission. A reaction against the zealous culling campaign began in early April, along with concern that the tourism trade was suffering. A peak in the disease was reached in the second week of April with over 1,200 farms affected. After that, the number of new cases began to fall, and the government decided to relax the culling policy. Blair announced on 3 May that the government was on the 'home straight'.[32] Sweeping up lasted until January 2002, when the country was officially declared 'disease-free'. Over 4 million animals were culled over the ten-month period, ten times the number during the 1967–68 outbreak. Questions were inevitably raised whether the government, for electoral reasons, had over-reacted and had killed many more animals than required. It was just the kind of distraction that Blair could have done without.

The FMD crisis was a defining moment for Blair when compared to the other episodes described in this book. But it is important to understanding him. Once he had become drawn in, his own credibility was at stake and he could not be seen to fail. For six weeks it took him over. During that time his mind focused on the one issue. He was constantly frustrated by his inability to solve the crisis: 'every time he thought he had got the problem cracked, it went wrong again', said one official.[33] He was impressed by the performance of the military, and liked their ability to respond immediately to instructions, as they had done so convincingly in the various overseas campaigns in his first term. He was correspondingly disillusioned with their civilian equivalents, especially with MAFF but also, less fairly, with the Civil Service overall.[34] His experience of listening to aggrieved parties and visiting disaster-ridden areas confirmed his belief that he should not shrink from difficulties and should go out and try to convince those who disagreed with what the government was doing.[35]

The crisis had two specific effects on the General Election. Blair typically left decisions to the last minute, and had intended on putting aside time in the run-up to the election to plan for the future. But FMD took away six weeks of his attention, and his energy, at a crucial time.[36] Even after the intense crisis was over in early May, it continued to require his attention. It is of course quite possible that, even without the crisis, he would not have devoted sufficient time to thinking deeply about the second term. What is beyond doubt is that he did not put enough serious long-term thinking into what he wanted to achieve after the very significant victory he was intent on achieving.[37]

The crisis also had an impact on election timing. The general assumption, in the media and in government, was that the election would be held on 3 May, the same day as the local elections. Even after the FMD crisis broke out, most in Number 10 wanted to hold on to that date. They worried that a delay, which would receive worldwide publicity, would further damage tourism, with visitors thinking that it was too dangerous to visit the British countryside, and give the impression that the government was not in control of events. Blair was under intense strain to make a decision in the week beginning Monday, 19 March: he was 'very twitchy' about what to do, and angry when he learned that money for a poster campaign in April had already been committed without his approval.[38] An hour-long meeting under Brown at the Treasury on 21 March was inconclusive: Brown was himself worried and in two minds, and the mood was tense. With the party far ahead in the polls, the advice from Labour Party figures in Number 10 was to hold to 3 May, a position also urged by Prescott, Straw and Blunkett. Their case was bolstered later in that week by concerns about the US economy wobbling and having a progressively bad effect on Britain.[39] Blair's dilemma became public knowledge when, at an EU summit in Stockholm on Friday, 23 March, his response of 'ten days' to Romano Prodi's question of how long before he had to decide on the date was picked up by an ITN microphone.[40] On the plane, he asked his officials for their opinions, and they advised on delay.[41]

Mandelson spoke to Blair every day that week and observed the change in his thinking. Sunday, 25 March, was the day he recognised finally that delay was inevitable. Mandelson, who was himself in favour of delay until June, admitted that Sunday that '"the umbilical cord" between us and May 3rd has snapped'.[42] Campbell, who had already given the *Sun* an exclusive on the election date, was furious. He was visibly angry at the morning meeting at Number 10 early the following week, when the postponement decision was formally taken, banging his fists and shouting at the head of communications at MAFF, the department he blamed for the delay. As he walked out of the meeting, he muttered, 'Bloody stupid day, bloody stupid decision.'[43] Blair was uncomfortable that Campbell was so opposed to the decision, especially as his views were dramatically opposed to Hunter's.[44] On 2 April he duly announced that the local elections would be rescheduled to 7 June, signalling a clear, if as yet unstated, message that the General Election would also be held on that day. He was adamant, however, that he would not under any circumstances delay until the autumn: 'Even if the lead is down to 6 per cent in June, I am still going then,' he told colleagues in private.[45] The decision to delay 'was in defiance of most of the press gang', Rawnsley wrote.[46] They changed their minds, however, after the decision was taken: 'The media have generally supported [the delay],' noted Lance Price in his diary, 'with everyone, except the *Mirror*, suddenly discovering they were in favour all along.'[47]

What convinced him to delay? The polls showed 44 per cent were strongly against a May election.[48] But he did not opt for June for this reason. Brown saw the risks of both May and June, but left the final decision to Blair: Brown then said Blair had got it wrong once he had decided to delay.[49] Election timing is one of a Prime Minister's most lonely decisions: the core reason Blair opted for the later date was because he did not think he could persuade the country that the government was yet on top of the FMD crisis, and he thought, even if it meant less votes, that it would be wrong to hold an election in May while the crisis was still so severe.[50] It was still a risk because the FMD crisis might have been no better in June, and it might even have been worse. Delay was a brave personal decision by Blair, and it showed he had a better feel for the national mood than many of his colleagues.

Election Campaign, May–June 2001

Blair compared the 2001 election to getting into the boxing ring and then finding there was no opponent.[51] Brown's old friend, the US Democratic consultant Bob Shrum, who was observing the election from Millbank, commented more graphically that it was like 'machine-gunning a corpse'.[52] Blair had none of the nervousness or anxiety about the result that he had in the 1997 campaign: he thought the electorate was on his side and that the lead was growing.[53] 'What struck me most was how relaxed he was during it,' said one Number 10 official.[54] His confidence, FMD notwithstanding, was understandable: in mid-March, Labour's lead stood at 18 per cent. The Tories under Hague, who performed weakly during the campaign, and the Liberal Democrats under Charles Kennedy, who tried to outflank Labour on the left, never proved a serious threat.

Comfort did not, however, spell harmony. Millbank, which one might have expected to exude confidence and good humour, was not a happy operation. The principal cause was the difference in outlook between Blair and Brown, and their rival camps still more. Brown managed the campaign and took the daily press conferences. He wanted to fight narrowly, focusing on the strength of the economy, the improvement in living standards, and tax remaining low. Blair wanted the campaign to be broader, looking for the affirmation of a mandate.[55] Brown's private comments on an early draft of 'the grid', the road map Labour used to guide them through the campaign, show him arguing forcefully that the first week had to be used to destroy the Tories. The campaign would then move to the economy, before focusing on public services and then returning to the economy once again at the end.[56] The campaign followed his wishes closely, but so long was spent initially talking about the economy and the tax question that it did not need to be returned to as planned. Brown was at his most defensive during the election. 'The problem with Gordon during the campaign was he did not want to share decisions or the limelight with anyone,' said one neutral observer.[57] The froideur, down-played by their aides, was obvious for all to see. Robert Harris wrote: 'The Brown body language during the campaign whenever Blair was speaking (yawning, consulting his watch, discovering hitherto unsuspected fluff on his jacket) was as obvious as semaphore.'[58] Their teams found it hard to find common ground, with Blairites alienated by the 'cliquey' way Brown was thought to be running the campaign. The two main bridge-builders in Brown's camp were Sue Nye, who maintained her open line with Hunter, and Ed Miliband, found to be more urbane and collegiate than the singular Mr Balls. Douglas Alexander in Brown's camp did not have an easy working relationship with the Blairite Margaret McDonagh. This time there was no Mandelson to scapegoat, as there had been in 1997; nor were there ideological differences to blame. It was difficult to conceal the truth that there was one cause for the turbulence: mistrust. Mandelson spoke regularly in private to Blair, and followed the election from a distance, but he was still badly wounded by his dismissal that January and had little influence in the campaign or even on Blair's own thinking.[59]

Labour's manifesto failed to ignite much interest, for all its promise of being 'radical', a word widely regarded as debased by New Labour's repetitive use. Part of the reason for its lack of rigour lay in the budgetary discipline introduced by New Labour as part of the three-year comprehensive spending review regime. As one of the manifesto's contributors acknowledged, 'as the substantial spending commitments for the three years, 2001–04, had all been announced in the 2000 spending review, it left us with the problem of having little genuinely new to say'.[60] Hugo Young thought the Labour programme 'sounds exceedingly boring. There's not a trace of glamour about it.'[61] To defend themselves against such criticism, Labour battled, with some success, to spin the line that the manifesto never sought to be novel, but merely proficient, and that what it needed was a full second term to 'get the job done'.[62]

Some in the manifesto team were apparently unconcerned by the lack of radicalism. 'A lot of the thinking we did on policy was only partially set out in the manifesto,' one aide insisted, suggesting that further ideas were deliberately withheld.[63] Radical manifestos, defenders insist, have been a rarity in post-war British political history. Why therefore should Labour's in 2001 have been any different? The answer is simple. After a relatively tame first term, and facing no obvious electoral threat, this was the moment when Blair could have spelled out the radicalism he had promised since before the 1997 election. If the detailed planning had been done, and the policies were ready, including them in the manifesto would have made them the subject of debate during the campaign, firing up supporters with new solutions to the country's problems and ultimately allowing Blair to win the clear mandate he sought for their implementation. More valid historical parallels would be with Thatcher's manifestos in 1983 or 1987, in which she outlined her plans to extend privatisation. Her substantial election victories then left her with a mandate to implement these specific policies, which she duly did, supported by Conservative MPs who felt bound to vote for the policies on which they had been elected. Blair, by contrast, may have won the 2001 election, but there was little in the party manifesto that gave him a mandate for radicalism, or indeed anything else. This weakness, the ultimate consequence of Blair's reluctance to think out and drive forward his own policy agenda, and Brown's obsession with caution, would have serious repercussions throughout Blair's second term.

As the election loomed, these shortcomings began to become apparent at Number 10. Blair resolved to seize the initiative. On 21

April, he circulated a highly confidential minute to ten key aides, including Campbell, Powell, Hunter, Morgan, Heywood and Sawers, but not Gordon Brown. Fifteen pages in length and written wholly by him, it contained his personal manifesto for the second term. An examination of his core beliefs, and the continuing relevance of 'New Labour', it constitutes one of the clearest statements he made of his objectives as Prime Minister. He wrote that he planned to flesh out these thoughts in 'five or six speeches' during the campaign, which he wanted to deliver to give him his own personal mandate.[64] He wrote about a wish to break away from Thatcherism and old-style social democracy, and about how he looked forward to a 'post-Thatcherite political system'. Abroad, he wanted Britain to play a major role in the world, and to be positive about Europe. He wrote of his intentions to concentrate on the social services and to make 'radical' reforms. He had much to say about the importance of community, and his rejection of individualism. But it amounted to little more than chapter headings. The intention to be emphatic about his agenda was there, but the substance would have to wait for the speeches.

Blair gave six keynote speeches during the campaign. He wrote much of the material himself, assisted by Campbell, Hyman, and the Policy Unit member whose field it was.[65] He opened the campaign at St Saviour's and St Olave's Comprehensive School in Southwark on 8 May, the day he formally called the election for 7 June. Like his other speeches in the campaign, it was a blend of the themes articulated in the campaign 'grid' (e.g. 'there is a lot done: there is a lot more to do') with the themes outlined in his 21 April memo, speaking, for example, about 'seeking a mandate' to improve schools and hospitals, extend opportunities, and to make Britain stronger.[66] Five days later, delivering his first keynote speech in his own heartland of the Trimdon Labour Club, he launched his assault on Thatcherism. 'More than once I took flak from inside the party for saying that not everything Mrs Thatcher did was wrong,' in particular, he said, for supporting her economic reforms. But he now attacked what he picked out as her 'four great failings': economic recession, under-investment in public services, a belief in selfish individualism and a 'destructive' rejection of Europe. The speech was classic Blair: 'I stand as New Labour,' he told his audience, pledging to lead a 'modern, liberal, social democratic party', occupying a centre ground between 'crypto-Thatcherites' and 'old-style socialists'.[67] This was where his party stood, which he said allowed every citizen the chance 'to aspire' to reach their full potential. As an aide remarked, 'In 1997 we were accommodating Thatcherism. We had to reassure the middle class that they were not threatened. In 2001, Tony wanted to put a full stop to Thatcherism.'[68] Indeed, so confident was Blair of the middle-class vote that the final week of the campaign was given over to assuring the working classes, hence the decision to keep on with the public services theme rather than to revert to economic policy.[69]

Public services were the theme of Blair's speech launching the manifesto in Birmingham on 16 May. Increases in public service funding linked to a readiness to reform lay at the heart of what he said. For each of the three years to come, he announced, spending was to rise in real terms on education by 5 per cent, on health by 6 per cent and on transport by 20 per cent, all made possible, he stressed, by the strong and successful economy.[70] Despite these pledges on public services, many voters were unimpressed. Indeed, one of the most memorable images of the campaign came when Blair was accosted outside a hospital by Sharon Storer, a member of the public whose partner was undergoing treatment for cancer. As Storer harangued Blair for the inadequate treatment she believed her partner was receiving, Blair stood by, apparently lost for words.[71] Initially seen as a disaster for Blair, his entourage came to see it as a positive for Labour's campaign, showing that Blair was meeting and listening to real voters.[72]

On 21 May, Blair delivered a major speech on public services in Gravesend. He candidly admitted that, despite all the endeavour of his first term, British schools, hospitals and railways were 'sub-standard' and fell a long way behind the best in Europe. 'World-class' public services were his aim in the second term, and he announced three principles to shape government policy in the future: decentralisation of decision-making, high standards nationwide, and flexible services tailored to the consumer. A fourth principle, 'choice', was added after the General Election.

Blair focused on the European theme when he spoke in Edinburgh on Sunday, 25 May. This was the one speech of the six where he disagreed strongly with Brown, who was very unhappy about Europe being made an issue.[73] Labour's own polls showed working-class Labour voters were hostile to the Euro, and the party feared Hague might gain real capital out of the issue. Blair pressed ahead regardless, in part because he doubted Hague's ability to inflict much damage as he had become so discredited, in part because he wanted Europe to figure larger in the second term and he was damned if he was going to let Brown stop him.[74] Blair set out to stress that 'patriotism' and 'internationalism' were not enemies, that engagement abroad was Britain's only serious option, and that the European Union was inescapably the best and most immediate forum for Britain's international involvement. On the Euro, he said nothing significantly new and stressed his general belief that it would be in Britain's interest to join the single currency, though without saying why. He nevertheless conveyed the clear impression that the speech was the beginning of a two-year campaign for Britain to hold a referendum before joining, and that he was seeking a clear mandate in the General Election as a first step to that end. As a *Guardian* leader said, the speech 'started the process . . . which could lead either to Mr Blair's own apotheosis or nemesis'.[75] William Rees-Mogg wrote, 'Mr Blair has decided to stir up the referendum campaign for the Euro . . . [he] has now thrown down the challenge.'[76]

Blair's fifth major speech, in Newport, Shropshire on 30 May, was built around a commitment to the three R's – 'rights, responsibilites and reform' – which he proclaimed would guide efforts to build a strong civic society. He also stressed his commitment to education and pledged harsher sentences for those who assault public service workers. Blair rounded off his keynote speech series in Yardley, West Midlands on 5 June with a plea against voter apathy, which had become an increasing worry during the campaign. In an effort to stir up the passions of traditional Labour voters, Blair painted the election as an opportunity for Britain to put the Thatcher years behind it. The vote would mark a 'real and historic turning point', he declared – somewhat audaciously given that his new principles for public service reform had a distinctly Thatcherite hue.

Blair got into his stride fully only in the final days of the campaign. Dennis Kavanagh noted, as he had earlier done about Thatcher, that it is hard for serving Prime Ministers to adjust to campaigning mode, and it takes time for them to switch from running the country to fighting a General Election.[77] Blair had found none of the euphoria or nervous excitement of 1997. He even let slip to two interviewers during the election that he was not 'happy' being Prime Minister.[78] His dysfunctional relationship with Brown constantly gnawed away at him. His downbeat demeanour was most evident on election night, 7 June. The eventual results, a majority of 167 in contrast to 179 four years before, and 413 Labour MPs compared to 419 in 1997, did not inspire joy because this time he had expected it, or even something better. The turnout, despite his last-minute efforts, had disappointed him severely as he had set great store by his premiership leading to 'democratic renewal': down 12 per cent, it was only 59 per cent,[79] considerably below his target of 65 per cent.[80] Yet that day, with its 'historic' second landslide in a row for Labour, marked indisputably his greatest achievement as Prime Minister up to that point.

The atmosphere at the Newton Aycliffe Leisure Centre for the count and at Trimdon Labour Club for the coronation was far more subdued than in 1997. So was the flight south from Teesside Airport with Campbell, Hunter and Powell.[81] Back in London he called in at Labour's celebratory party at Millbank, but gave the impression that he could not wait to get away. Observers noticed that he and Brown could barely bring themselves to shake hands and exchange a sentence in public.[82] Once back in Downing Street he delivered a downbeat message on the steps outside Number 10: 'It is a mandate for reform and for investment in the future and it is also very clearly an instruction to deliver.'[83] Only in the morning did the tension and fatigue make way for a more cheerful humour. Up in the flat, his closest officials and political team had breakfast ('copious sausages and fried eggs'[84]) while Blair met with Richard Wilson in the den to talk about what he had to do for the rest of the day.[85] Said one official: 'He was now very relaxed, very calm and very happy.'[86]

The Impact of the 2001 General Election

Blair had achieved, if not the popular mandate he sought, at least the majority in the Commons he required to deliver the government's programme. He had been able to set out, in his 21 April memo and in his speeches over the campaign, what he wanted to achieve – undercooked, certainly, but as full an exposition of his core beliefs as he had achieved at any point since he became Prime Minister. But the gaps in the detail were telling.

On international affairs, his wish to talk up the European Union and the single currency were clear, though there was little said about the relationship with the US, Britain's role as 'bridge' across the Atlantic or the doctrine of the international community and 'humanitarian intervention', which were so to dominate the second term. On domestic policy he eschewed the breezy rhetoric and millennial promises of a 'New Britain' in 1997 in favour of downbeat pledges on delivery, and statements of principles – 'community not individualism', 'aspiration' for each person to fulfil their potential, a 'post-Thatcherite political system', and 'radical reforms to the social services' – again without being clear exactly what he meant, or what policies would flow from the principles and values. No mention was made of plans for future constitutional reform, including the abolition of the position of Lord Chancellor that finally took place in 2003, mainly, according to one aide, because Blair 'never got round to thinking seriously about it'.[87] Of the biggest domestic battles of his second term, foundation hospitals were not

mentioned by name, although there were more oblique mentions of a
role for the private sector in the NHS. A reference to 'top-up fees' for
university was included, but only to say that such fees were ruled out.
The inescapable conclusion is that the hard thinking had simply not
taken place. Blair was thus vulnerable to the criticism of one of his
former ministers that 'we went into the 2001 election with no idea what
we were fighting about. There was no ambition at all about why we
wanted a second term.'[88]

Blair pinned his hopes on structural reforms at the centre backed by
large injections of public funding to ensure that domestic policies would
be implemented more effectively in the second term than in the first.
Number 10 was reorganised with Campbell, Powell and Hunter taking
enhanced positions, and with a wholesale reform of his foreign policy
advice under two senior advisers. With Miliband now an MP, Blair turned
to the member of his team who he found the most creative and
sympathetic, Adonis, as his senior policy adviser. These moves were all
safe consolidations rather than bold departures. But he chose to be more
radical in his Cabinet appointments. His biggest decision, and the only
one that effectively mattered, was to make no move against Gordon
Brown. While the nuclear option, moving him to the Foreign Office, was
judged unrealistic, ideas were developed for clipping Brown's wings by
hiving off parts of the Treasury and handing control of them to a separate
Chief Secretary in charge of his own department reporting directly to
Blair.[89] Brown, however, was implacably imposed and Blair did not want
to take him on. Even Blair's critics marvelled at his power after the
election results: 'He commanded the political landscape in a way that
Margaret Thatcher never quite managed, even at the peak of her power,'
wrote Peter Oborne in the *Daily Telegraph*. 'The Tories pose no threat. The
Liberal Democrats hardly count. The economy is benign. The press is
astonishingly well-disposed, as the past four weeks have demonstrated.'[90]
He had even proved Brown wrong over election timing: delay to June was
seen as the wise choice. Once this moment of great personal authority
passed, the last time it was to stand as high, he never again had the power
to move against Brown. This ensured that the greatest governmental
obstacle to the single currency remained, and that he would also have a
Chancellor who would fail to back whole- or even half-heartedly much of
what he wanted to achieve in domestic policy in his second term.

Blair played his Cabinet selection cards exceptionally close to his
chest. He had made up his mind some while before that he wanted to
move Cook out of the FCO. Fears that the move, if trailed early, would
result in campaigning for him to stay and unwelcome press stories meant

that Cabinet and most aides in Number 10 were not informed. Yet Blair was determined. Cook had not, he judged, been the successful or loyalist Foreign Secretary he had hoped for, and he also badly wanted to move his own key supporters into the major posts, especially given that Brown was not moving. Straw was one such figure, and to his surprise, Blair asked him to become Foreign Secretary. Straw had expected to be going to the DETR in succession to Prescott, who had his wish fulfilled of going to his job at the centre, based in the Cabinet Office. Not even Prescott knew of the changes, even though he had spoken to Blair in Sedgefield at length on election day. Suddenly, on the day after the General Election, everything was up in the air. A very unhappy Cook agreed to become Leader of the House. In his place came Straw, who Blair believed could be brought round to embrace a more positive attitude towards Europe and might well prove a more effective advocate of the Euro in the country than Cook, not least in countering the Eurosceptic press.[91] This move neatly created a vacancy at the Home Office for another strong Blair loyalist and disciplinarian, Blunkett, charged with tackling the most sensitive subject of the rise in crime. The ultra-loyalist Byers was promoted to produce the tangible improvements Blair demanded to see at Transport, boosted by significant cash increases. The other key delivery responsibilities were entrusted to Estelle Morris, who succeeded Blunkett at Education, while another Blairite, Milburn, was retained at Health where he was deemed to be doing a very good job. The other delivery department, Social Security, was left in the hands of Alistair Darling. Former 'Kinnockites' were rewarded, with Clarke becoming Party Chairman, Hewitt Trade and Industry Secretary, while Reid remained at Northern Ireland. Margaret Beckett had her wish granted for a bigger department and became Secretary of State for Environment, Food and Rural Affairs, a reward for her loyalty in the first term.[92]

Thus was the script for the second term written. Dynamic, loyalist ministers were to take the place of those who had disappointed in the first term, manageable and regularly monitored targets would replace general expressions of good intent, while substantial injections of public spending would take the place of parsimony. Blair was confident that, at last, he had affairs more or less as he wanted them. He remained concerned about Brown's ambitions, and felt that further reforms were needed at the centre. But these issues aside, all it needed, Blair felt, was for his big 'delivery' ministers to stay in place, as he assured them they would until the next election, and for no further external shocks like FMD to strike – and all, he believed, would be well.

*Anji Hunter, extreme left, watches proudly as Blair greets Clinton on his first
visit to the White House in 1996. Her eyes are fixed on Blair, as they were for
much of his political career.*

32

Anji Hunter

No one was more single-minded than Anji Hunter in encouraging Blair to delay the 2001 election. By so doing she encountered the wrath of many in the Labour Party, and in Number 10, including Campbell. Yet her instincts told her it would go down badly if the General Election went ahead in May while the foot and mouth epidemic still raged. Hunter's instinct for the sensibilities of middle England, and her representation of their views to Blair, was one reason for her remaining in his inner circle for so long. Other reasons were that she was such an effective fixer and organiser of his life, and because he felt immediately reassured to have her looking after him, knowing also that – unlike Campbell – she would never publish diaries or a memoir about the experience.[1] Her role frequently reinvented itself. Yet, however the role changed, she always had the ability to adapt and to make herself essential to his life.

Anji Hunter, the Woman

Anji was born in Malaya in 1955 of Scottish parents, Arthur ('Mac') and Joy Hunter. Mac had fought valiantly in the Far East during the Second World War, escaping from the advancing Japanese army before joining the Special Operations Executive in Burma. After the war, he remained in the Far East, becoming a successful rubber planter in Malaya, while Joy ran a school for local children. By 1965, Mac Hunter had secured his financial future, and retired to settle down in his large house near Brechin in Scotland where he himself had been brought up.[2] Anji and her brother Johnnie were sent south to attend prep schools in the Home Counties,

with the plan that she would go on to senior school at Benenden and John
to Rugby.[3] Her world changed utterly when, the year after their return to
Britain, her mother died following a car accident. This loss, while Anji was
still only a child, drew her much closer to her father, whom she adored. 'He
was an incredible man. He was strong, voluble, opinionated – a hunter, a
fisherman, an adventurer and a great *bon viveur*. After he died, he carried on
being an incredible presence in Anji's life,' recalled a family friend.[4]

The children went back up to Scotland to be nearer their father, and
Anji was sent to the prestigious St Leonards, a traditional independent
girls' school in St Andrews, while Johnnie was sent to Glenalmond, a
public school similar to Fettes. She hated the restrictions at St Leonards
and was asked to leave at the age of sixteen for 'being against the
Establishment'. Her father realised that his fiercely independent daughter
would not adjust to the confines of another conventional boarding school,
so in September 1971 he allowed her to go off to study for her 'A' levels
at St Clare's sixth-form college in Oxford, where she enjoyed much greater
freedom, and loved the social life of a city heavily populated by students.
Afterwards, she chose to study at the University of East Anglia because it
'was rebellious and the fashionable place to be'.[5] But she could not settle,
and left after six months with the intention of changing to law and
beginning the following year at one of the polytechnics in London. In
April 1979, a few days before her father's beloved Mrs Thatcher entered
Downing Street, and on the day they returned from one of their holidays
together, her father suffered a massive heart attack and died in front of
Anji's eyes. Three days later she entered the polling booth in Angus and,
for the first and only time in her life, she says, she voted Conservative in
memory of her father.[6]

Back in England in the late 1970s, Hunter worked as a practice manager
for a group of solicitors when she became engaged to Nick Cornwall, a
landscape gardener who managed Richmond Park. They married in
December 1980 at Wandsworth Register Office, and settled first in
Ireland and then in Sussex. She gave birth to two children, Finn and Lara,
in the early 1980s. She hankered after the degree she had never completed,
and when the children were both still toddlers she enrolled at nearby
Brighton Polytechnic (now Brighton University) to study History and
Politics, having received an unhelpful response when she had tried for an
undergraduate place at nearby Sussex University. She found Brighton
extraordinarily welcoming and in particular fell under the spell of the
Politics teacher and author, Bill Coxall, and a Marxist historian, Roger
Wells.[7] It meant a great deal to her that she graduated with a first-class
degree in 1987.[8]

Hunter and Blair

Hunter met Blair in 1970 at a party through a mutual friend, Chris Catto of Forfar, when she was fifteen and Blair was seventeen. They struck up an immediate friendship. 'She became his companion and always has been since. They were like brother and sister,' said a mutual school friend.[9] She insists they were never sexually involved, nor indeed attracted to each other, but were always 'just good friends'. They kept in touch after she went to Oxford in 1971 and for two years, 1972–74, when he became an undergraduate, their two worlds coincided again. They introduced each other to their respective circles, with Anji becoming friends with Peter Thomson and Geoff Gallop. They clearly enjoyed each other's company, and she was a significant help and support to him when his mother, Hazel, died in July 1975, when she drew on her own sorrow of losing her own mother at an early age. They kept in touch but saw little of each other over the next ten years, though Anji attended the Blairs' wedding in Oxford before moving to Ireland with her husband. She noticed when he was selected for Beaconsfield and then elected at Sedgefield, thinking to herself, 'How incredible to have a friend who's an MP!'[10]

Hunter started to connect with his new world when, at Brighton, she wrote a dissertation entitled 'Whither Labour?' She had the opportunity in 1986 of writing an 'independent learning assignment' on Parliament entitled 'The Summer Session, an Inside View'. To gain first-hand experience, she asked Blair if she could help out in his office for two days a week unpaid. Delighted when he agreed, they re-established their old relationship quickly, and she proved herself so invaluable that he asked her to join his office permanently as soon as her degree was completed in the summer of 1987. When she joined, Blair's instructions were that he wanted her to 'drive him on', which she did with missionary zeal, making careful note of figures like Charles Clarke in Kinnock's office, whom she thought might be helpful. She very early on established herself as a much more dynamic and independent figure than most MPs' research assistants. Although clearly from an upper middle-class background, and not a conventional Labour supporter, during her four years working for Blair she had won friends across the party with her intelligence, capability and charm. She fought for his interests like a lioness, helping him make contacts in the media, in business and academe. She organised and focused him, and with her irreverent sense of humour brought fun and laughter to his job. Most important of all, and least understood, she gave him self-belief. It is no coincidence that her arrival in his office from 1987 onwards coincided with his rapid advance through the party.

Domestic tensions, however, proved a constant weight on her mind. She felt a tug from home, aware that the long hours she worked meant that she saw little of her children during the week. So in 1991, she decided to pack up the job, handing over to Roz Preston, and to look for work nearer home. She spent some time following her mother Joy's career working in the local primary school in her village, Newick, near Haywards Heath. Before she had a chance to become bored, she received a phone call from Charles Clarke asking her to join the 'advance team' for Kinnock's campaign for the 1992 election. She was delighted to be back at the centre. During the fraught weekend after the defeat, Anji received calls from senior party figures, including Blair himself, requesting her help in running Margaret Beckett's campaign for deputy leader.[11] She worked out of Blair's office on Beckett's campaign and it soon became clear that she would return to work for Blair permanently after the leadership election, although this was never properly discussed.[12] His subsequent promotion to shadow Home Secretary, and his ambitions to rise to the very top (seen in his toying with the idea of standing for deputy leader in 1992), promised even more exciting prospects for her than before. She sensed he could go all the way, and she would remain by his side without a break for the next ten and a half years.

From 1992 to 1994 she ran Blair's office and built his team, making friendships and alliances that were useful to him inside and outside Parliament. She also groomed him, telling him which clothes looked good, how to style his hair, when he was good in meetings, speeches and on the media, and when he was not. With Hunter behind him, egging him on and paving his way, he rose above Brown during these two most critical years. After Smith died, she came fully into her own. Her utter certainty that Blair had to stand, and her dynamism in putting his campaign together, sealed her centre-stage position in his political life. Once he became leader, she displayed her hard side by telling various people that they had to go. She did not make policy or help write his speeches, though she was kept in the loop and suggested the odd phrase, and she was not afraid of making her views known (particularly on education).[13] What she did was show that she had the acumen and skills to shift her conventional roles of organiser, networker and personal adviser on to a much higher level still. At times Hunter and Blair felt it hard to believe that he had risen so quickly and that he was now Prime Minister in waiting. When Powell arrived in January 1995 he took on much of her organisational and administrative role, leaving her to focus more fully on Blair. As he drove himself forward to ever greater challenges, he relied on her for emotional and psychological support. It was this role in particular that brought her into friction with Cherie, who resented, not just the time that Hunter spent with her husband, but also the affirmation that anyone in Hunter's role necessarily gives to a high-profile boss. Hunter's upper-class background and assurance and ease with the Establishment also highlighted Cherie's own insecurities at a time when she felt particularly vulnerable, facing the prospect of becoming Britain's 'first lady'.[14] If Blair was conscious of Cherie's jealousy, he did nothing about it. Hunter was too valuable to him.

A new role for Hunter crystallised during the 1994–97 period: representative of middle England. The myth, which had some truth, was that she would come back after the weekend in Sussex having spoken to people at country dinner parties on Saturday and on the train up on Monday morning, and be fearless in telling Blair what they thought. Gould used focus groups: Hunter used the 8.06 from Haywards Heath. Of all those close to Blair, she best represented this swathe of thinking, of huge importance at a time when he was moving Labour into the middle ground. Where Campbell would hold his nose at the big tent strategy, she 'would ensure the flaps remained wide open'.[15] She was central to building relations with News International, as reflected in her accompanying Blair and Campbell on the trip to Hayman Island. Her exceptional vivacity was deployed on businessmen and financiers, and she used her throaty voice and flirtatious charm to telling effect with 'high value' donors.[16] Few disliked her. On long-haul flights she would pay visits to the back of the plane and share a cigarette with journalists. She flattered and charmed, and would listen acutely to their views. She hoovered up the opinions of influential people on who they thought was up or down, logging the information carefully, and later advising Blair. Like Campbell, she would press for the advancement of her favourites, one being Margaret McDonagh, who rose to become General Secretary of the Labour Party.

During the 1997 election campaign she lived in Geoffrey Robinson's penthouse flat in the Grosvenor House Hotel overlooking Hyde Park. Her focus was wholly on the campaign. She was on the road with Blair throughout, orchestrating his every move, noting people's reaction to him and encouraging him on whenever the sapping routine took its toll. She would also tell him home truths, and 'bring him down a peg or two if she thought he was getting too big for his boots'.[17] After remaining up all night with Blair on 1 May 1997, she fell asleep on the train down to Sussex on the Friday, and missed her stop. She spoke later in the day to Blair, already ensconced in Number 10, but his attention was drawn elsewhere.[18]

During the campaign she had not discussed with Blair the detail of any role she might perform after the election and had not been privy to

Powell's discussions with officials about the transition. For a few hours on that Friday it was not clear whether Blair would press her to join Number 10. She had some reservations herself about whether she wanted the total commitment that she knew Number 10 would entail, with the heavy impact on her domestic life. But she was far too engaged to get off the ship as it reached the most exciting stage in the voyage. So she spoke to Blair, who wanted her on board, and she arranged to come in to speak to Powell the following week.[19] The civil servants were wary of the role she was given, that of 'Special Assistant'. No such figure existed under Major, and those with longer memories recalled Marcia Williams, *éminence grise* under Harold Wilson, who was disliked by civil servants and was thought to have possessed far too much power and control over him. Hunter's initial niche, in contrast, however, was quite narrow and defined: to take a strategic view of Blair's diary commitments, on which she worked with Kate Garvey; to plan regional tours, and to assist with summits held in Britain and trips abroad.[20]

Hunter's job at Number 10 was thus a simplification of what it had been in opposition. Whereas just three years before, when Blair was shadow Home Secretary, she managed his whole political life, he now had within Number 10 a large group of civil servants and political aides to look after policy advice, administration, communications and public relations, and who took on many of the roles she had once filled. This meant that she had even more time to focus on him personally, in contrast to Campbell and Powell, who were bowed down with major jobs. She was one of very few — Campbell, Powell, Mandelson and Brown being the principal others — who could look in and see him at any time. She won the respect of officials in Number 10. 'Anji was incredibly close to him,' said one. 'They would conflab for hours on a plane together, and they would have a sandwich together in his study behind closed doors. No one would know what they had talked about.'[21] 'She could read him and anticipate him like no one else,' said another official.[22] Officials would note how, early on in his time as Prime Minister, he would spend the last few minutes before Parliamentary Questions alone with Hunter: 'She was psyching him up,' one said.[23] It was in this new role as a moral supporter rather than policy adviser that she continued to have most influence. Her advice against him making the 'forces of conservatism' speech in 1999 was not heeded,[24] and she became exasperated when ignored over his Women's Institute speech in June 2000. Lance Price's diary records: 'TB is due to make a very important speech tomorrow and everybody's in a total panic about it . . . Hyman is trying to rebuild it with scraps of paper containing stuff TB has agreed to add. Anji is going round saying, "Why is a speech for 10,000 women being written by men?'"[25] She failed to make herself heard in debating how to address an audience she understood better than anyone in Number 10. Against her advice and despite repeated warnings from Campbell, Blair used the speech to deliver a political message. Price recorded the sorry fate: 'Speech turned out to be a total disaster, and was all blamed on the spin doctors.'[26] When Hunter and Campbell were agreed on something, Blair was usually very unwise not to take note.

Anji had an acute eye as well as nose. A skill she honed after she joined Number 10 was spotting photo-opportunities: she would choreograph regional tours and summits in Britain and abroad, such as for his sensitive visit to a refugee camp in Macedonia in May 1999 during the height of the Kosovo crisis, when she flew out ahead of him to select the ideal backdrop for the television cameras.[27] She had a natural instinct for finding the right locations for him to be filmed to his best advantage. She maintained close contact with the media after May 1997, nourishing many of the most high-profile links, including those with proprietors Murdoch and Black and with editors Yelland (*Sun*), Morgan (*Mirror*), Stothard (*The Times*) and Rusbridger (*Guardian*). She consorted with influential journalists across the political spectrum from Paul Routledge on the left to Paul Johnson on the right. Simon Heffer on the latter wing described her as 'a highly intelligent political adviser [with] a brilliant grasp of politics'.[28] She could play 'good cop, bad cop' with Campbell when they briefed against someone who had fallen out of favour or who Hunter felt had let Blair down.[29] When Campbell and Hunter were working harmoniously they were a deadly combination.

Hunter became Blair's most confidential conduit, passing messages from him to senior figures in politics and outside. She was his chief intelligence gatherer in Westminster and Whitehall, spending more face time with him than the heads of MI5 and MI6 combined. Her intelligence role included liaising with Tory defectors. On reshuffles, her opinion could make or break a politician's career, all the more so when Blair's knowledge of junior and middle-ranking ministers was not deep. As troubleshooter, one of her most difficult assignments was returning to Geoffrey Robinson's penthouse flat to persuade him to tone down his memoirs, which followed his bitter dismissal in December 1998. The book, perhaps in consequence, was much less explosive than anticipated.[30] She was also his prime fixer and smoother within Downing Street, possessing an acute ability to read the close and, at times, tense relationships in the inner circle. 'She was bubbly and warm, she knew everyone's partner's names, children, about their illnesses. She was extraordinary at all that,' said one aide.[31] She also proved her worth by instilling a sense of camaraderie and teamwork between officials and political appointees, a skill that did not come naturally to the Chief of Staff, Jonathan Powell.[32] Most importantly she acted as a key conduit with Gordon Brown's office. She was on particularly good terms with her former flatmate Sue Nye, who ran Brown's office, which helped to keep the channels between Number 10 and the Treasury open even at the most highly charged of times.[33]

Hunter was not universally popular, however, and her most difficult relationships were definitely with other women in Downing Street. Although she and Sally Morgan were once described as 'fighting like ferrets in a sack', they had a genuine regard for each other's political skills.[34] Hunter clearly had the closer relationship and better access to Blair, which may have caused some resentment on Morgan's part, and their politics were not close, with Morgan a Labour partisan to her core and Hunter so unsocialist some suspected she was a closet Tory voter.[35] Rumours came and went that Hunter tried to manoeuvre Morgan out.[36] There was certainly no love lost between them. Fiona Millar and Hunter disliked each other even more strongly, and Millar protested adamantly to Blair in early 2001 that she would not remain at Number 10 if Hunter was to be given an enhanced 'political role'.[37] Campbell himself had a love–hate relationship with Hunter. They had shared much together since 1994, but Campbell was assumed to have been influenced by Millar's negative views, to which were added his own doubts about Hunter's politics and her influence. Indeed Campbell did not attend Hunter's farewell party in 2002, to which neither Morgan nor Cherie was invited[38] because he would not have known what to tell Millar.[39] Campbell and Millar were close to Sally Morgan, with whom they shared the same commitment to the Labour Party and its traditional values. They were very different people from Hunter, from very different backgrounds and with very different outlooks. It is unsurprising they did not always get on: each sought to serve Blair in their own way while fighting mostly successfully to keep personal tensions to a minimum and out of the public eye.

Hunter's most difficult relationship by far, however, was with Cherie. This required careful management once they were all in Downing Street, from Blair himself as well as from Campbell. The relationship had never been good, but it seemed to sour considerably after May 1997. One insider sympathetic to both parties put it: 'You have to describe Cherie's and Anji's relationship as a total disaster.'[40] Cherie had come to Number 10 determined to play a much bigger public role than Norma Major had done.[41] She wanted to be a real force and presence in her own right in her husband's premiership, hoping to emulate the role played by her friend Hillary Clinton in the United States, which was one reason for their close affinity. Such a role did not, however, materialise, and Cherie resented seeing Hunter, whom Cherie could never forget had known her husband longer than she had, spending much more time with him than her. Blair never disguised either his fondness or his need for Hunter, which was either commendably honest or lacking in tact, depending on how one looked at it. 'Most women would have found it very hard to have their husband so close to somebody else,' said one insider. 'Wherever he was, Anji would always be turning up. What she took that as saying was that Anji was more important to him than she was.'[42] The tension was compounded by Hunter's belief, shared by others, that Cherie lay behind some of the problems he had encountered in Number 10.

As the year 2000 wore on, Hunter felt increasingly ground down by all these personal pressures on top of eight years' continuous work for Blair, which had left her extremely weary. She had thought for some time that helping to secure a second term would be a fitting legacy for her, and saw the attractions of working in business or industry. Hunter and Campbell had always agreed that they would not leave at the same time and that Campbell would 'get away' before her.[43] So she entered discreet talks with BP about a future communications role there, and, in early 2001, told a reluctant Blair that she would like to leave after the election.[44] This news he relayed to a delighted Cherie.[45] Losing Anji, though, was a prospect Blair soon began to recoil from. 'Tony likes Anji because he likes the people who have made it work for him in the past,' said a close aide. 'She made him feel secure.'[46] As Blair gazed ahead into a second term without Hunter by his side, he resolved to make her change her mind. After discussion, they agreed during the election campaign, in utter confidence, that she would remain at Number 10 with an enhanced title, Head of Government Relations, and an increase in her salary to £120,000.[47]

Incredibly, Blair kept the news of Hunter remaining entirely to himself: one senior Number 10 official who thought he knew everything was surprised to be told by an exhausted Blair on the day after the 2001 election that not only was Cook being replaced by Straw at the FCO, but that Hunter was staying.[48] Blair told Cherie about it in the den that afternoon. Her face as she emerged was described as 'frozen'.[49] One aide said, 'What was so bizarre was that we had six major government changes to process that afternoon, but our time was taken, not on the new people and briefings, but on sorting out the rumpus that followed his announcement that Anji was staying on.'[50] Another complained that 'everyone believed Anji was going and we knew what was happening. Then all these last-minute arrangements were made. It was really bad.'[51] Hunter's remaining at Number 10 meant that it was Morgan who would have to go (after she made it clear to Blair that she would not tolerate Hunter taking on an enhanced role). So it was Morgan who left his side after seven years, which she did with a peerage and a ministerial post at the Cabinet Office, in charge of women's issues, a move that was interpreted as a victory for Hunter.[52]

Blair's last-minute success in persuading Hunter to remain appeared, before too long, to have been a substantial misjudgement. Even with her new title, she did not find post-election life in Number 10 as congenial as she had hoped. Although nominally on the same level as Campbell and Powell, she was disappointed to find that her job turned out in effect to be substantially the same as before, and that sapping rivalries and frictions within Number 10 remained unabated.[53] She began to feel trapped and her enthusiasm waned. The lure of the private sector, and of the BP job in particular, became all the more appealing.[54] Her detractors in Number 10 insist that Blair 'very quickly came to realise that he had put her into the wrong job and she no longer had the same niche'.[55]

Hunter's plan was to leave in September 2001, and had been on the verge of announcing her resignation when the planes hit the Twin Towers. Blair suddenly had a new reason for needing her to help him face the world and he asked her to stay on a while longer.[56] She spent two months flying on 40,000 miles of overseas trips before finally announcing her resignation in early November.[57] Blair bowed to the inevitable. Campbell's continuation at Number 10 after the election, and the decision of Heywood not to proceed with a planned two-year sabbatical after the birth of his baby, returning instead to Number 10 after only a short leave, helped cushion her departure.[58] Blair had also grown in confidence and independence, and no longer needed Hunter by his side as much as he had in the past. Morgan's return to Number 10, taking over Hunter's job, to Morgan's surprise, made the transition straightforward.[59] Many in Number 10 were pleased with the switch, particularly the Labourites who felt that Morgan's knowledge and contacts across the party would prove invaluable.[60] While New Labour loved Anji – indeed, in many ways she was the epitome of it – she was always mistrusted by traditional Labourites.

Hunter's departure left a hole, however, and the press were quick – too quick – to blame every mishap that befell Blair subsequently on her departure. One particular episode, however, that she might well have ameliorated was the storm over 'Black Rod', an unnecessary row with Buckingham Palace in the spring of 2002 over the Queen Mother's funeral. Had Hunter still been at Number 10, her contacts in the Establishment and her common sense might well have avoided the fuss.[61] She might well also have avoided the ramshackle reshuffle of 2003, about which she lambasted Blair; and have discouraged Campbell from taking on the BBC over the Gilligan affair, as she had earlier dissuaded him from going after the *Mail*,[62] a paper he hated and whose editor, Paul Dacre, he described as the 'most poisonous man in British public life'.[63] As with many who leave organisations, their real value is only truly appreciated after they have left.

The Impact of Anji Hunter

Hunter was most important to Blair early on in his political ascent because she had proportionally greater influence. Her boundless belief in him, her bonhomie and her mesmerising ability to capitalise on the flood tide and win over friends to his cause across all kinds of frontiers were most apparent in 1987–94, in the days before Campbell, Powell and the army of advisers who helped him once he became Prime Minister. She worked closely before 1994 with Mandelson, to whom she had always been close, and from whom she learned much, not least about the media. Without the self-belief Hunter gave Blair, it is quite likely he would not have felt sufficiently confident to have considered standing as deputy leader immediately after the 1992 General Election, and to have stared down Brown in 1994. She shaped and affirmed him as party leader in 1994–97, and did as much as anyone to pave his way into becoming a non-tribal Labour leader, which is why some Old Labourites hated her. She was one of the most effective ambassadors for the New Labour project, being able to reach out to parts of the body politic and fourth estate that many others could not or would not do.

She continued to serve Blair well after he became Prime Minister, when her total, unconditional loyalty remained useful to him when he did not always know who to trust. But when he began to rely on officials like Holmes, Heywood and Manning, and with Powell and Campbell providing not just the advice but also the companionship, he became less dependent on her. Unlike Marcia Williams, she knew when to leave after her job was over; unlike Williams, she also avoided miring her boss in scandal. After her departure from Number 10, they remain close and speak regularly on the telephone. In 2004, she took part in talks wth Campbell to plan Blair's 'exit strategy'. Hunter's greatest service to Blair was to help him to grow into the role, first of aspirant leader, then party leader, then Prime Minister. There is no higher service a friend can offer than to help one to become independent.

Blair, two weeks after 9/11, with Muslim community leaders in London. His immediate instinct after the attacks was that links with the Muslim community should be deepened. The struggle, he argued powerfully at the time, was not with Islam.

33

9/11 and Aftermath, 2001–02

Tony Blair worked through lunch in the Fitzherbert Suite at the Grand Hotel in Brighton on Tuesday, 11 September 2001, putting the final touches to a difficult speech he was to deliver to the TUC annual conference early that afternoon. At 1.48 p.m., his focus was interrupted by an aide telling him that there had been a plane crash in New York at the World Trade Center. He absorbed the information but it did not break his concentration. He had a critical speech to deliver and he wanted to ensure it struck the right note. Like most people, he presumed the crash had been a freak accident.

The events that were to unfold over the next few hours and weeks were to change his premiership profoundly. It is impossible to know what he might have achieved domestically had 9/11 not happened: after the faltering progress on delivering improvements to public services in his first term, he knew this would require his unbroken attention in the second. Indeed, public services were to be the subject of his keynote speech that afternoon at the start of autumn's political season. Had 9/11 happened earlier in his premiership, before Northern Ireland and Kosovo, he might have been overawed by it. Instead, what impressed close observers was his self-possession.[1] 'Sometimes things happen in politics, an event that is so cataclysmic that, in a curious way, all the doubt is removed,' said Blair. 'From the outset, I really felt very certain as to what had to be said and done.'[2] What he said and did affected not only his premiership, domestically and internationally, but the course of world history.

Day of Terror

The second plane, United Airlines Flight 175, hit the South Tower at 9.03 a.m. New York time, 2.03 p.m. British Summer Time. When it happened, Blair was the only one of his close team in Brighton not glued to a television screen, his mind still on the intricacies of private sector involvement in the public services. When Godric Smith, an official Number 10 spokesman who was watching *Sky News* intently with Campbell, broke the news to him, he immediately switched on the live coverage and watched in horror and disbelief as events unfolded. Then, at 2.43 p.m. Brighton time, the third plane crashed into the south-west face of the Pentagon. They realised they could be witnessing the beginning of a concerted attack on America. Blair consulted with Campbell in Brighton, and with Powell and Wilson in London, and resolved to cancel his speech. He put in a fleeting appearance at the TUC at 3.10 p.m. where, 'visibly shaken', he told the delegates in the Conference Centre that 'there have been the most terrible, shocking events in the United States of America in the last hours. I am afraid we can only imagine the terror and carnage there and the many, many innocent people who have lost their lives. This mass terrorism is the new evil in our world today.'[3] His words, broadcast across a nation switching on their televisions in their millions, were as skilfully crafted as his words about Diana almost exactly four years before. TUC delegates had been preparing to greet his keynote speech, foreshadowed as one of the most difficult of his premiership, with scepticism. Instead, his words were listened to in shock and bewilderment; when he finished and was leaving the podium, spontaneous applause broke out.[4] He was driven at speed to the station to catch a train to London, deemed the quickest and safest way back to Downing Street.

In Number 10, there was a vacuum. Most heard the news when they returned from lunch just after 2 p.m.: 'We immediately feared we were about to be attacked also,' said one official. 'No one seemed to be in charge or giving orders.'[5] The Ministry of Defence was contacted for instructions on whether to evacuate, 'but the Secretary of State's office were all still at lunch too'. 'There was no one of sufficient authority to brief us,' another official recalled,[6] while yet another described how 'the picture rapidly emerged that there was no precedent for dealing with such extreme risk. There was no plan to tell us who was in charge.'[7] To make matters worse, the newly established Civil Contingencies Unit, whose task it was to deal with such emergencies, and which had absorbed many of the lessons from the fuel and FMD crises, was up in

Yorkshire on a 'bonding seminar'. The key members of the Whitehall body responsible for co-ordinating foreign policy, the Defence and Overseas Policy Secretariat, meanwhile, were on a coach on their way to Herefordshire. David Manning, Blair's senior foreign policy adviser, was caught in New York and out of contact.[8] From his aeroplane window, Manning had looked down on Manhattan and saw the smoke billowing from the North Tower. As soon as he landed at JFK airport, he tried to phone London, but to his frustration all mobile phones and land lines were down, and he had no option but to spend the night in a louche hotel in Queens, a district just outside Manhattan.[9] If al-Qaeda had indeed planned a deadly attack on London, it could not possibly have chosen a better day to strike.

Richard Wilson, the most senior official in the land, took charge in London. His immediate concern was whether sensitive London targets were in immediate danger from hijacked planes. The dearth of information and intelligence made it all the more worrying. Wilson spoke to the intelligence agencies, to Buckingham Palace, to key figures in Parliament and to the police. Concerned about the threat to UK flights, Jonathan Powell contacted the Department of Transport,[10] and an immediate ban on flights over London was agreed and put in place by Transport Secretary Byers.[11] Other government departments worked on further measures to protect London, including extra security for all British airports. City Airport, close to Canary Wharf, was immediately closed down, and two fighter jets were scrambled to enforce a 'no-fly' zone over the capital. Wilson ordered the coach heading to Herefordshire to return immediately to London in time for a Cobra meeting he set for late afternoon.[12]

Blair himself was not immediately concerned by any terrorist attack on Britain. Such extreme risks never ranked high in his mind. 'We had to make him take the immediate threat to London seriously. But he seemed quite immune from the risk,' said one figure. 'The way we made him take it seriously was to say, "Look, it is not just you, it is Cherie, and the children and Leo who are also in danger." Then he took us seriously.'[13] Blair spoke to Stephen Lander, head of MI5, and John Stevens, Commissioner of the Metropolitan Police, en route to London: 'Have you got everything you need?' he asked them in turn. He then trusted them to do their jobs without further interference.[14] Calls were also made to Blunkett, whose job as Home Secretary entailed overseeing the police and security, to Hoon, Defence Secretary, and Straw, Foreign Secretary. Straw's words on seeing the second plane fly into the South Tower were: 'That's it. The world will never be the same again.'[15] One

of his immediate concerns was to get out on television and assure the
nation that 'the institutions of the British state have not collapsed. It's
still there, in control.'[16] The fear was that, with the terrorist acts
dominating the airwaves and the government in the US and Britain
nowhere to be seen, widespread panic could break out.

Once these initial phone calls were made, Blair's mind went
immediately to the foreign policy implications of the attacks, and how
to handle President Bush.[17] He spent part of the fifty-minute train
journey to London deep in thought. 'On the train . . . I could see what
the terrorists would want was not merely to cause carnage by the original
terrorist act, but to set in train a series of events, including setting part
of the Muslim world against America.'[18] While he was in transit between
3.20 and 4.10 p.m., the picture was still very confused and worrying.
Predictions were circulating of 50,000 dead in the Twin Towers, both of
which by now had collapsed. A fourth plane had come down in
Pennsylvania countryside at 3.37 p.m. The White House had been
evacuated, save for Vice-President Cheney, who was ensconced behind
the vault doors of the East Wing bomb shelter, guarded by sub-machine
gun posts hastily erected by the Secret Service outside.[19] Bush
meanwhile was airborne on Air Force One, location unknown. The
United States and Britain were out of communication with each other
and bracing themselves for further attacks. The world held its breath.
Those old enough to remember recalled the Cuban Missile Crisis of
1962: the world had seen no peril like it since. Up to a thousand Britons
were also feared dead when the towers collapsed, as several British
companies and many British nationals had worked in the World Trade
Center. Blair's team were kept informed of developments as his train
sped towards London, but 'he was not interested in what the
government machine was doing. His mind already was on the world
stage.'[20]

They were met at London's Victoria Station by police escort and
whisked straight to Number 10, where Blair convened a quick meeting
in the den with Wilson, Campbell, Powell, Lander, and John Scarlett,
the new head of the Joint Intelligence Committee (JIC), which co-
ordinated findings from MI5, SIS (MI6) and GCHQ. 'This is grim,' were
his opening words. By now it was 4.30 p.m., and nerves were stretched
tight with fears of parallel attacks on British targets still a present anxiety.
Westminster, Whitehall, the City, or sensitive targets outside London
including nuclear power stations were thought to be the principal targets.
The fears were not idle. Credible intelligence reports had come into
Blair in July from the JIC which had spoken of an imminent attack on

the US or Israel and mentioned UK targets as vulnerable to 'collateral damage'.[21] The focus of intelligence chiefs was, naturally, on current risks as well as on the likely perpetrators. Although Scarlett thought there was an outside chance that a far-right militia group could be responsible, he was almost certain that Osama Bin Laden was behind the attacks.[22] The problem was that Bin Laden, al-Qaeda and the Taliban were all virtually unknown to most in the den. Blair had heard of Bin Laden but knew little about him. Powell asked for a book to be obtained on the Taliban by Ahmed Rashid, which was later passed around Number 10. One aide admitted, 'We thought honestly that al-Qaeda was a bit of an American obsession.'[23] Blair's focus was on the future, on the big picture and the need to co-ordinate a response to terrorism and to assess the likely US reaction: direct communication could still not be established with Bush, and Number 10 had no idea what he was thinking. Blair kept asking, 'How is Bush going to react? What will he do?'[24]

The meeting in the den broke up inconclusively at about 5 p.m., with the clear understanding that immediate research was needed on al-Qaeda, its methods and objectives. Blair updated his most senior ministers individually and then chaired the Cobra meeting at 5.30 p.m., which included Brown, Straw, Blunkett, Hoon, Byers and Milburn and their officials. The mood was sombre and hushed: there was a sense that they were all participating in historic events. Blair confirmed that they were still unable to establish contact with Bush, stressing that the US needed 'allies to get through this'.[25] MI5 and SIS gave brief presentations of the information they had to date, which was not advanced. Lander said, 'This is al-Qaeda, almost certainly,' and Blair asked him to brief everyone present on what he knew about the group. Lander filled in some key details; one thought he was 'marvellous' at compensating for the dearth of knowledge of most of those present.[26] Most left the meeting still feeling ignorant and bewildered about what the terrorists were intending and what was really going on. These were Britain's leaders, but they knew little more than the British public. Wilson asked who should give the order to shoot down a plane that breached the 'no-fly' zone over London, and the decision was reached that it should be Admiral Sir Michael Boyce, Guthrie's successor as Chief of the Defence Staff.[27]

The Cobra meeting broke up shortly after 6 p.m. with all ministers charged with undertaking immediate precautionary moves within their departments, while Lander and Wilson stayed behind for a few final words.[28] Public reassurance was now Blair's priority. He stepped outside the door of Number 10, and delivered the statement that had been forming in his mind from within moments of the second plane hitting the South Tower. 'We've offered President Bush and the American people our solidarity, our profound sympathy, and our prayers . . . This is not a battle between the United States of America and terrorism, but between the free and democratic world and terrorism . . . We, like them, will not rest until this evil is driven from our world.'[29] Blair might not have been able to speak to Bush directly, but he was keen to talk to other world leaders, and his staff booked calls with Chirac, Schröder and Putin. He was gratified that the French and German leaders were 'totally on board, right from the outset . . . This was an outrage, a terrible act against humanity, not just against America.' He was even more relieved and pleased with his conversation with Putin, which he said was not 'read from a script of very carefully chosen words in a very deliberate way', as it would have been when a Russian President spoke to a Prime Minister in the past. 'It was straight from the heart. He was outraged by it. He supported America . . . He had no doubt at all that we had to get out there together and stand with America, get the menace and deal with it.'[30] Through backing the West in their 'war on terror', Putin believed he could gain their support, or at least acquiescence, in what he saw as his own fight against terrorism in Chechnya. Having established that the West's major powers were on-side, and that the safety of the realm was as secure as it could be, there was nothing more that Blair could do or say. Until Number 10 knew what was happening in Bush's camp, they were deadlocked.

With each passing hour, the likelihood of an attack on Britain receded. But the fear grew of a disproportionate American reaction. With Bush still stealing around various airbases in the US to ensure his safety, Dick Cheney, the Vice-President, was in charge: Defense Secretary during Operation Desert Storm in 1991, his hawkish tendencies gave rise to considerable apprehension in London. Blair shared his growing fears with his aides: was Bush properly in control of events? Why on earth was he not giving a lead?[31] With Manning still out of communication in the US, John Sawers was summoned back from leave to help out, arriving in jeans at 7 p.m. The evening wore on with still no word from Bush. Speculation in Number 10 grew that he was planning to unleash an immediate attack against some unknown Middle Eastern target.[32] Like the rest of the nation, Blair and his closest aides whiled away the evening watching the television screen recycle the same horrific pictures and those of Middle East terrorist training camps. The ignorance and impotence were palpable. According to one aide, Blair remained 'shocked, deeply shocked, because he was the first one to grasp the full significance of what had happened'.[33] By midnight, most in Downing Street decided to go home. They realised there was nothing they could do but wait on events.

Lights burned long into the night at the headquarters of SIS at Vauxhall Cross and on the second floor of the Cabinet Office in Whitehall, which houses the JIC staff in a secure 'closed area'. One of their overnight tasks was to prepare a briefing paper on al-Qaeda, the Taliban and Afghanistan.[34] Lander and MI5 meanwhile turned their spotlight on possible al-Qaeda and other Middle Eastern terrorist suspects and threats within Britain. No one was under any doubt about the scale of the challenge they faced. Blair remained deep in thought that night. One close aide said, 'He knew what it meant, even then, in terms of a war on terrorism, and in terms of an invasion of Iraq. He knew that evening that this would be the defining issue of his premiership.'[35]

Working With Bush, 12–20 September

Blair, like millions of others, awoke on Wednesday, 12 September, anxious to know whether further disaster or violence had occurred overnight. Relieved that it had passed without incident, his principal task now was to make an impression on Bush. He knew that he had to earn his trust, and do everything he could to influence Bush's actions in what he sensed equally would be the defining issue of his presidency.

At a meeting of Cobra convened for 8.00 a.m., those present noted that Blair's principal concern was 'the Americans, and how we should handle them'.[36] All the designated departments were making progress on the assignments they had been given the afternoon before, but there was little new to report, so the meeting broke up quickly. Blair was fixated on preparing fully for his phone call to Bush, and he wanted to have all the facts at his fingertips. He was now armed with the intelligence briefing prepared overnight by Scarlett and the JIC, 'but it was clear that although he had the briefs, he didn't feel it inside himself, he just wasn't sure of his ground'.[37] A briefing, planned for forty-five minutes but in the end lasting two hours, was thus convened later that morning with Whitehall's best brains from the intelligence services, the FCO and Ministry of Defence. 'He was terrific. He listened and then fired sharp questions at those briefing him. He locked away the information as soon as he was sure of it.'[38]

Blair now felt armed for his all-important phone call with Bush, which finally came through at 12.30 p.m., 7.30 a.m. Washington time. Indicatively, it was Bush's first call to a foreign leader. Officials, listening in on the conversation in Downing Street, noted 'it was clear that Blair had woven everything that he had picked up that morning into his advice to and handling of Bush. Indeed, he had mastered it to the point that he could spiel out information on al-Qaeda as if he was one of the world's great experts.'[39] He found Bush shocked but 'very calm'. He judged the call to perfection.[40] He began by expressing his outrage and shock at what had happened and his relief that Bush himself was safe: all traces of his irritation and frustration at Bush's 'disappearance' were disguised. After commiseration and gestures of friendship and support for America, he moved on to the subject most troubling him, the question of the US response. He said he did not himself share fears expressed by some voices about the US acting precipitously or disproportionately – while making it abundantly clear that he did not favour such a course. Perhaps Blair would have been less optimistic had he witnessed a meeting in the White House the night before, shortly after Bush's return to Washington. 'I don't care what the international lawyers say,' Bush shouted when being told that force could not be used purely for retribution. 'We're going to kick some ass.'[41]

Yet by the time he spoke to Blair, the President was calm and collected: 'We are not interested in simply pounding sand for the sake of demonstrating we are going to do something,' Bush insisted. They then discussed diplomacy, and agreed to move swiftly to build support in Nato and the UN, capitalising on the extraordinary outpouring of sympathy for the US internationally: Jeremy Greenstock, Britain's Ambassador at the UN, had been working overnight on a resolution reaffirming the right of countries to respond to terrorism 'as they saw fit'. Similar moves were afoot in Nato, which later that day invoked Article Five, declaring the attack on the US to be an attack on all members of the Nato alliance. Towards the end of their conversation the two leaders returned to the issue of the US response, and Blair discussed the distinction between 'effective' and 'rapid' action. The former, Blair said, would require preparation and planning. Bush concurred but concluded by relaying to Blair the chilling message that he had broadcast to the American people the evening before, that he would make no distinction between the terrorists who committed these acts and those who harboured them. Bush stressed it would be a long haul: it was a 'mission for a presidency'.[42] Thus did Bush herald the war on terrorism.

The record of the call reports Blair saying that he would send Bush a note of his thoughts.[43] He wanted to ensure that Bush understood unequivocally his anxieties and thoughts about the complex strategic considerations that were now in play. He immediately sat down and drafted a handwritten, closely argued note, in similar style to his impassioned note to Clinton at the height of the Kosovo crisis. When typed it became a five-side memorandum and was faxed to the White House for Bush's personal perusal. The style was typical of Blair, bullet points and staccato sentences, as opposed to the polished, fluent prose produced by mandarins. His core argument was that Bush should prepare for a measured and properly executed response, bolstered by international support, and it should focus on hitting al-Qaeda, whose complicity in the attack should be proved by releasing a dossier of information, the device he had earlier urged over Kosovo. He was at pains to stress that they had 'to prove to the bar of public opinion who is responsible'.[44] The Taliban regime in Afghanistan that was sheltering al-Qaeda should be given an ultimatum: hand over Bin Laden and his senior associates, shut down terrorist training camps and let in international inspectors.[45] Assuming the Taliban did not yield, Blair argued that they had to ensure that countries surrounding Afghanistan would be prepared to back tough action. Pakistan would be the lynchpin, but this would be awkward to pull off owing to the country's close links with the Taliban. Relations with Iran, on Afghanistan's western border, also needed to be improved. Blair further argued that restarting the peace process in the Middle East would help build Arab support for the war on terrorism. Finally, he stressed that the cancer was not confined to Afghanistan, or indeed al-Qaeda, and they had to make plans to act against all who financed, supported or sponsored terrorism, wherever they existed in the world.[46] Composed only twenty-four hours after 9/11, it is a remarkably lucid and sophisticated exposition of his position, from which he deviated little in the weeks and months to follow.

Blair spent the rest of 12 September taking stock, phoning world leaders, and arranging with Cook, in his new capacity as Leader of the Commons, an emergency recall of Parliament for that Friday. Work on his parliamentary speech, assisted by Sawers and others at Number 10, provided the opportunity for him to collect his thoughts still further. He also agreed that the heads of MI5, MI6 and GCHQ should fly over to the US on a military plane to meet with their US counterparts on the evening of Thursday the 13th. After concluding with dinner at the British Embassy, Britain's intelligence chiefs returned, bringing with them a much-needed David Manning as well as John Major, who had also found himself stranded in the US after the attacks.[47]

MPs rushed back from holidays around the world to attend the special parliamentary session that Friday, where Blair told a rapt House that plans under consideration might change the 'present world order'. In a clear warning to countries like Afghanistan, Iraq, Iran and Libya, Blair said that nations who harboured and assisted terrorists would have to choose between them or the West. The risk of nuclear, biological or chemical attacks from terrorist groups, he said, justified extension of war to the rogue states who protected them. (He returned repeatedly over the next eighteen months to these words in the speech to illustrate his long-standing concerns about WMD.[48]) Mindful of the concerns among certain MPs, and in the country at large, he praised the US's restraint earlier in the week. 'They did not lash out. They did not strike first and think afterwards.' Some of the strongest words were left for Straw to deliver. 'To turn the other cheek,' he said, 'would not appease the terrorists, but would lead to a still greater danger,' and drew comparisons with the disastrous attempts to appease Europe's rising dictators during the 1930s.[49] The Foreign Secretary warned of the risk of 'copycat' attacks on Britain, and Blair emphasised the need for concerted international action on extradition, and the proscription of terrorist groups and their funding. Bar a few voices expressing fears about disproportionate American reaction and the dangers of giving Bush unconditional support, the Commons was united behind Blair's and Straw's words.[50]

A second phone call to Bush also took place that Friday. Having staked out his ground in his memo to the President and in Parliament, Blair now wanted to know more of what America was thinking and planning. The President began by thanking Blair for the huge outpouring of support for America in the UK, which he said he found quite overwhelming, and he thanked him for his memo, which he said 'mirrored' his own views. Blair pressed him on the need to win over world opinion by presenting clear evidence linking the 9/11 attacks to al-Qaeda and Bin Laden, whose complicity was being clearly confirmed by the intelligence. He said the immediate focus should be on al-Qaeda bases in Afghanistan, though he believed they would have to pursue the terrorists far beyond the shores of that country. Bush again agreed, and spoke of an analogy of a series of circles emanating from a pebble dropped on water: 'We focus on the first circle,' Bush said, 'then expand to the next circle.' Again Blair stressed the need to give the Taliban an ultimatum, as outlined in his memo. They shared news of their phone calls with world leaders: Bush said he was hopeful of full co-operation from Pakistan. Blair finally offered Bush one piece of advice that he said he had learned from the Kosovo experience: decide clearly what you want to do, then focus very single-mindedly upon it. Bush said he agreed 'one hundred per cent'.[51]

The weekend, 15–16 September, provided another opportunity for Blair to take stock. Britain had come through unharmed from any terrorist attack, and Number 10's concerns that Bush might be overawed, or pressed into knee-jerk military response, had proved unfounded. After Chirac, who had negligible influence with Washington, Blair was the longest-serving leader of all the West's major powers. He was aware of his authority on the world stage, which had been bolstered further during the days after 9/11 when he had come across, in contrast to Bush, as measured and assured. He was also conscious of his role, about which he had often spoken, of being the 'bridge' across the Atlantic alliance, now heightened by there being an inexperienced US President coping with a very serious crisis. Some, including John Kampfner, have seen the days immediately after 9/11 as the high point for Blair's metaphorical bridge.[52] By the weekend Blair's own stance on the whole terrorism question, sketched out in his 12 September memo to Bush, had become settled across the board: sticking by the US and consolidating Britain's position as its closest ally; an unequivocal commitment to defeating al-Qaeda and other similar terrorists, initially in Afghanistan and then beyond; doing so multinationally by building an international coalition of support; the search for a breakthrough in the Middle East peace process, and winning over world opinion through the release of intelligence of al-Qaeda's complicity in the 9/11 attacks. Place this speech and detail of planning alongside his fumblings and gropings towards a plan for his domestic policy, most recently three months before in the General Election, and his achievement here is all the more striking. Manning's return from the US had also stiffened Blair's resolve to stick very closely to the Bush administration and shower it with praise; but Manning was pushing at an open door.

The impact of Blair's work during the first week is, as always, hard to gauge. According to US authors Daalder and Lindsay, Bush found Blair's ideas 'useful and heartening'.[53] Did Bush desist from immediate retaliatory attacks because of Blair's carefully modulated pleas for restraint? This seems highly doubtful: as early as 12 September Bush told Blair that he had no intention of immediate retaliation. Did Blair's several promptings to Bush to concentrate on Afghanistan rather than Iraq have an impact, as many in Whitehall fervently believe?[54] Perhaps, although by the time of his second call on 14 September, Bush was already talking about his 'concentric circles', with Afghanistan in the first circle. As Bob Woodward's 2004 account reveals, in the immediate aftermath of the attacks, Donald Rumsfeld, Secretary of Defense, suggested that there was now 'an opportunity' to attack Iraq, a view strongly reinforced by his hawkish deputy Paul Wolfowitz. However, after exhaustive debate at Camp David on 15 September, Bush's inner circle were united in advising against an attack on Iraq, with the exception of Rumsfeld, who abstained.[55]

Bush knew he had to go after al-Qaeda first. Blair's voice was just one, albeit an important one, in the almost unanimous chorus urging him to take this course. Where Blair's support was important was on the margin: Bush phoned Putin early on at Blair's suggestion, and he also phoned Ariel Sharon in Israel, following Blair's prompting, about restarting the Middle East peace process. British intelligence was made fully available to Washington: 'With Britain's colonial heritage, it had huge insights into Pakistan and India that was very helpful to us with the Taliban. It made a big difference,' said Richard Armitage, Colin Powell's deputy at the State Department.[56] Bush noted carefully Blair's unfailing public support. Like his father, he valued loyalty, and Blair had been very loyal. It was yet to be seen whether Blair would be more successful claiming a payback from Bush for his loyalty than he had earlier been with Clinton.

One cannot detect much British influence in the essentially American planning of the war against Afghanistan. The key question was, should the conflict be a limited one against al-Qaeda, or should it be widened to 'regime change' by removing the Taliban leadership under Mullah Omar? Blair, in discussion with Manning and Powell, would have settled for the former course, but believed that unless the Taliban moved very quickly to isolate al-Qaeda, regime change would become essential.[57] Where Blair might have made a difference was in another debate within the administration. Rumsfeld and the Pentagon wanted to fight the Afghanistan war alone. Colin Powell saw the opportunity to use Blair's support to broaden out the military attack. 'Blair was saying to us, don't rush. Make it a global coalition. It helped Powell win the argument,' said Armitage.[58] This debate within the administration foreshadowed the later one over Iraq between the unilateralists like Cheney, Rumsfeld and Wolfowitz, who favoured the US acting alone, and the multilateralists like Powell and Armitage who did not.

Blair's priority now was to shore up the international coalition he believed essential in support of the coming war, a task made no easier by Bush's pronouncement on 18 September that the US wanted Bin Laden 'dead or alive', lending weight to the stereotypical image of the President as a trigger-happy cowboy.[59] Much of the Monday and

Tuesday, 17 and 18 September, Blair spent on the phone again to world leaders, including President Jiang Zemin of China, talking to intelligence chiefs and his departmental ministers in London about civil contingencies, and making preparations for the British contribution to the war in Afghanistan, just weeks away. It was agreed with Washington early in the week that it would be a predominantly American attack, with Britain and France in support, and with a willing Putin offering intelligence and logistical help. After the experience of Kosovo, and the problems of achieving a concerted Nato response with so many jockeying nations, Washington decided to keep Nato effectively out of the war, a decision that might have made good military sense but was not handled well diplomatically, especially in view of Nato's warm support in the immediate aftermath.

On Wednesday, 19 September, Blair left for Berlin, accompanied by Manning, where he had dinner with Schröder in the new Chancellery building. Schröder was sympathetic, but with limited military forces at his disposal, and the anti-war Green Party in his ruling coalition, he felt he had to restrict his initial contribution to political, not military, support, although German troops did later serve as peacekeepers. Later that evening, Blair flew to Paris to spend the night at the British Embassy. Thursday, 20 September, was to be one of the longest and most emotional days in Blair's premiership. It began with breakfast at the Elysée with Chirac, who had himself just flown back from meeting Bush in Washington, and appeared surprisingly friendly towards the Americans. He and Blair discussed the outline of the military plans. Despite earlier British doubts about French wobbling, Chirac seemed entirely happy with arrangements, telling Blair, 'We're with you all the way.'[60]

Blair was then sped to Charles de Gaulle airport for a 10.30 a.m. flight to Washington. Already in their seats in business class was a party of four men from the Ministry of Defence and SIS, authorities on al-Qaeda. Half an hour into the flight, Blair made a call that had been set up on his own initiative with President Mohamed Khatami of Iran, the first time a British Prime Minister had spoken to the leader of Iran since the Shah's overthrow in 1979. Past differences were laid aside in their new common interest: Iran too disliked the Taliban regime because it had flooded its borders with refugees. In their fifteen-minute conversation, Blair thanked him for his support and stressed his theme that this was not a struggle between Islam and the West, but between civilisation and terror. Blair later said it was one of his most exciting moments in the whole post-9/11 drama, and he was proud to tell the Americans later that day about the breakthrough.[61] After the call, the four military personnel were called forward to join Blair in his screened-off first-class cabin at the front of the plane, and briefed him on their current knowledge of Bin Laden's likely whereabouts, and discussed different strategies for his capture.[62] Again, Blair wanted to ensure he was as well-briefed as possible before he met the Americans.

The plane touched down at New York's JFK airport in early afternoon, local time. The roads into Manhattan were gridlocked, as they often had been since the attacks, and the start of the service at St Thomas's Church in memory of the British victims, the prime purpose of the New York stopover, was delayed. During the service Blair read a passage from the end of Thornton Wilder's *The Bridge of San Luis Rey*, a novel that discusses the cruelty of sudden death and describes love as 'the only survival, the only meaning'. Opinions are divided on the choice, but all agree he struck just the right chord when he spoke some of his own words: 'Nine days on, there is still shock and disbelief. There is anger, there is fear, but there is also, throughout the world, a profound sense of solidarity, there is courage, there is a surging of the human spirit.' Christopher Meyer read out a message from the Queen which contained the words 'grief is the price we pay for love', now engraved into the masonry of the church. Blair, ever courteous, sent a handwritten note of thanks to the church afterwards in which he spoke of a 'wonderful service' which 'sent such a strong message of love and support throughout the world'.[63] The Fifth Avenue church was close to the still smouldering 'ground zero', where the Twin Towers had tumbled to the earth: in the congregation were the families of the British dead, as well as Kofi Annan and Bill Clinton. Blair had scarcely time to talk to them, and plans for him to meet local fire and police chiefs had to be abandoned, in favour of Cherie, accompanied by Meyer's wife, Catherine, visiting a fire station together with Clinton.[64] Brief though his visit to New York was, it made a quite extraordinary impression on New Yorkers, and Americans at large. Blair was very visibly moved by the harrowing meetings he had with relatives, and the scenes of destruction he witnessed. His decision to visit so soon after the tragedy and his expressions of compassion struck a deep chord. The *Washington Post* rated Blair alongside Rudolph Giuliani, the New York Mayor whose response to the events of 9/11 was widely admired, as 'the only other political figure who broke through the world's stunned disbelief'.[65]

Next stop was Washington. After an additional delay while the authorities at New York's JFK airport insisted on searching the entire British party, including a more than usually large group of journalists, their plane touched down late at Andrews Air Force Base at 4.45 p.m. and was met by a convoy of black Lincoln limousines. In 'Sedan 1' were Blair and Manning, in 'Sedan 2' Campbell, Powell and Hunter. Blair and Manning rehearsed yet again what he would say to Bush and discussed what they thought the Americans were planning. On arrival at the White House, they were ushered into the Blue Room for drinks. Bush immediately took Blair to one side to a window overlooking the Washington Memorial, and reassured him that 'the job in hand is al-Qaeda and the Taliban. Iraq we keep for another day.'[66] Blair did not take this to mean Iraq would necessarily be invaded 'another day', but merely that the issue would be addressed. Blair offered no objection. Bush also reported to Blair what he would tell the historic Joint Session of Congress later that evening. It included him saying categorically that governments had to choose: 'Either you are with us or you are with the terrorists.' Blair, aides confirm, was delighted to hear that he was going to give such an unequivocal statement, not that he was being asked for comments: the American press corps had already been told what the President would say.[67]

A pre-dinner meeting had to be scrapped because of their late arrival, so discussion of the coming attack and how to defeat al-Qaeda were held over dinner in the State Dining Room. The Americans filled in the details of their joint CIA–military attack plans. It was more information-giving than debate on strategy and tactics, and Bush talked about the 'full force of the US military with bombers coming from all directions'.[68] The British guests were struck by the remarkable sang-froid Bush displayed throughout the dinner, just hours away from delivering the most important speech of his life: 'We almost began to feel nervous for him,' said one.[69] Bush was determined to make Blair feel special and honoured as a way of showing his appreciation for Britain's unquestioning public support. So he invited him to the White House residence after the dinner. In the lift on the way up, Blair asked him directly if he felt apprehensive about his imminent speech. Bush's reply made a big impression: 'Well, actually I'm not that nervous about it because I know what I want to say, and I know what I am saying is right.'[70] Bush then invited Blair to travel in the President's car with him to Capitol Hill, another special honour. Once in the Congress building he was taken to the 'heroes' gallery to sit next to the First Lady, Laura Bush. Bush's speech was punctuated by thirty-one spontaneous standing ovations, and in it, he officially named Bin Laden and al-Qaeda as responsible for the 9/11 terrorist attacks. 'Our war on terror began with al-Qaeda, but it does not end there,' he said, to tumultuous applause. He then turned to a visibly moved Blair to say, 'I'm so honoured the British Prime Minister has crossed the ocean to show his unity with America . . . Thank you for coming, friend.' Just five and a half years earlier Blair had gingerly paid his first visit to the President like an eager schoolboy; now he was being put on a pedestal on a par with Thatcher and Churchill. With such private and public displays, Bush showed Blair that Britain had become America's closest ally. But what did it all mean in terms of influence?

After the post-speech pleasantries, an exhausted Blair and his party were driven back to the plane, to fly overnight to Brussels for an emergency EU summit, where he briefed his fellow leaders about the President's plans for Afghanistan. Blair was too exhausted to study his briefing notes in detail, and he settled down in his cabin for a few hours' sleep. Thus ended Blair's twenty-two-hour day.

War in Afghanistan, October–December 2001

The US had decided on the date, 7 October, to launch its attack on Afghanistan. The details of the operation, however, had still to be finalised. So had the extent of international support for the attack, which is where Blair played an active role. In the eight weeks after 9/11, he went on thirty-one flights covering 40,000 miles and held fifty-four meetings with foreign leaders.[71] In this marathon he was helped by the wide network of contacts he had built up since taking office: 'He was incredibly good at getting to know foreign leaders and making a positive impression on them,' said one observer.[72] Blair's certainty and force of argument helped bring world leaders round to the war in Afghanistan, though many had other reasons for doing so.

In the weeks that followed 9/11 Blair was a man possessed. 'He found extraordinary long-distance energy for a man who normally had the stamina of a sprinter,' said one aide.[73] Another striking feature about Blair that autumn was his utter conviction about the course of action he was pursuing. At a time when many were dazed and cautious, 'he developed a new certainty about his own role, which was really quite remarkable. He gave out a sense of having truly found himself.'[74] What exactly was Blair so sure about? He was convinced that terrorism, backed up by the threat of WMD, was the major threat the West faced, and that the way to tackle this scourge was not through appeasement but through a tough military response. He believed in his unique persuasive powers in bringing the international community behind US plans, and that he was engaged in a clear-cut moral struggle pitting the forces of good against evil, and with his particular responsibility being to create a better world.

One result of the depth of his conviction was that he did not want to consult beyond a narrow circle of trusted aides and colleagues – principally Manning, Powell, Campbell, Straw and Wilson, and the intelligence chiefs Scarlett, Dearlove and Lander. Cabinet met only once in the three weeks after 9/11, on 26 September, which was largely an information-giving meeting: there was reported to have been 'little discussion'.[75] Once the war began in early October, to counter concerns about his 'presidential' style of leadership, Blair announced the creation of a War Cabinet of seven ministers, as he had for Operation Desert Fox in 1998 and Kosovo in 1999.[76] Campbell and Powell were also in attendance, but real decision-making remained in the hands of the inner circle who congregated for meetings throughout the day in Blair's den.[77]

Blair spent the last few days in September working on his speech for the forthcoming party conference and bolstering domestic support for the coming war. Iain Duncan Smith, the Tory leader elected that month, went to Number 10 for a briefing on 24 September and was reported to be 'completely on-side', while Liberal Democrat leader, Charles Kennedy, was supportive but insisted there were no 'blank cheques'.[78] When Clare Short caused consternation by criticising Blair for saying that Britain was 'at war' with the terrorists, press stories were planted that her Cabinet colleagues were 'furious' with her.[79] Blair and Hilary Armstrong, the Chief Whip, worked hard to win over doubters in the party, such as Peter Kilfoyle, who mistrusted the Republican Bush and who were repulsed by his 'wanted dead or alive' phrase and other macho boasts. Some others, like George Galloway, the staunchly anti-war Labour MP, were regarded as too entrenched to be persuadable.

The party conference opened in Brighton on 1 October and was inevitably overshadowed by the aftermath of 9/11. Blair spoke on the second day, giving a speech described by Michael White as 'almost certainly the most powerful speech of his career . . . the sweep and moral fervour caught friend and foe off guard'.[80] Blair hardly mentioned the General Election victory of just months before, concerned as he was to speak as a world statesman, not a partisan politician. The speech built on and developed the central theme of his Chicago speech of April 1999 about the doctrine of the international community and the justification for liberal intervention in the affairs of other sovereign nation states. Blair, his Number 10 foreign policy advisers and many at the Foreign Office, had always regretted that the full import of that earlier speech had been swallowed up in the contemporary furore over the Kosovo war, and thought an updated restatement would help prepare the ground for what was about to unfold shortly in Afghanistan and possibly beyond.

The speech reads now as extraordinarily hubristic, but it did not in the highly charged atmosphere of the time. Of the American people, he declared 'we were with you at the first. We will stay with you to the last.' Of al-Qaeda, 'There is no compromise possible with such people, no meeting of minds . . . just a choice: defeat it or be defeated by it. And defeat it we must . . . I say to the Taliban: surrender the terrorists or surrender power.' He acknowledged the fears that 9/11 might lead the world into recession, or be followed by terrorist attacks against Britain, real fears in the minds of many. Mindful of the ethical scruples of some about war, and reflecting his own beliefs, he spoke of the moral imperative not to stand aside. Intervention would have stopped the slaughter, he said, in Rwanda, where 1 million had been killed in 1994, and he was glad that he had acted to limit ethnic cleansing in Kosovo in 1999. The same moral need to act, he said, applied to Afghanistan, with over 4 million refugees, ousted by the Taliban, needing food and shelter. Islam itself was not the enemy, and he repeatedly stressed the need to reconcile Islam and the West. Once the terrorist 'cancer' was defeated, he pledged to work for a better world morally and economically, where new hope would reduce the breeding ground of terrorists. In particular, he wanted to help heal Africa, 'a scar on the conscience of the world', and the 'slums of Gaza' by easing the Israeli–Palestinian conflict. 'The starving, the wretched, the dispossessed, the ignorant, they are our causes too,' he said with deep feeling and to rich applause. Global warming was a further wrong to be addressed. His conclusion referred directly to an idea Jonathan Powell had advanced, which was that the post-Cold War, post-9/11 world offered new dangers, but also new opportunities: 'This is a moment to seize. The kaleidoscope had been shaken. The pieces are in flux. Soon they will settle again. Before they do, let us reorder the world around us.'[81] The speech offered a magnificent vision of a better world, with echoes of the Marshall Plan of 1947 and Kennedy's inaugural speech of January 1961.

It was widely admired at home and abroad: 'One of the most eloquent and one of the most significant of our times,' declared one Canadian journalist.[82] There was criticism, however, for the way he moved almost seamlessly across to the issues to which he had planned to devote his whole speech – entry into the single currency, private investment in the London Underground, improvements to public services before tax cuts – where he appeared to imply that the same moral certainties applied. By doing so, Anatole Kaletsky said he risked turning 'his speech into a grotesque caricature'.[83]

On Wednesday, 3 October, the day the truncated conference ended,

Bush asked Blair to confirm his agreement that the US could make use of a number of British military assets, including the base of Diego Garcia in the Indian Ocean. The final plans were now in place. The next day, Blair published a document entitled 'Responsibility for the Terrorist Atrocities in the United States', which was the basis for the government's case in an emergency session of Parliament called for that Thursday. It laid out the evidence proving that al-Qaeda had carried out the 9/11 attacks, that British targets were under threat from terrorists, and that al-Qaeda were helped by the Taliban regime in Afghanistan.[84] In his personal memorandum to Bush of 12 September Blair had argued for the disclosure of such information to win over the media and public opinion: Campbell now jogged him to push for this again in Washington before fighting broke out. Manning was delegated to argue the case with Condoleezza Rice, the National Security Advisor, with whom he had a close relationship. The Americans, however, were reluctant and did not see the need for such disclosure, but were content nevertheless for Number 10 to go ahead.[85] Scarlett and his 'Assessments Staff' in the JIC took several days to produce the document, which contained a mixture of published material and intelligence cleared for publication by SIS. It encountered little dissent in the Commons or from the mainstream press. Some European leaders, however, notably Chirac, felt that the document, in pointing the finger of blame so singly at the Taliban and al-Qaeda, was 'straining a little bit too hard' in doing the Americans' work for them.[86]

Blair flew off later that Thursday for the second of his post-9/11 intercontinental tours. First stop on the forty-eight-hour trip was to see Putin in Russia. The two leaders had enjoyed a strong relationship ever since Putin hosted Blair and Cherie in St Petersburg in January 2000, before he was even elected President. Putin had realised that with the US locked into election year, overtures to Clinton would be pointless and so he singled Blair out as the European leader to court. With Putin's KGB past, widespread criticism of his role in the war in Chechnya, and the election still to take place, it was a risky visit for Blair. But it proved a success, and Blair was thus well placed to broker Russian–American links after Bush's election, when he made a real difference in encouraging the administration to treat the Russians, to whom they were inclined to be standoffish, as serious partners.[87] Blair arrived in Moscow in the evening, and held talks at the Kremlin. Putin then asked Blair, accompanied by David Manning, to have supper with him in his *dacha*, a thirty-minute drive by high-speed motorcade from Red Square. Halfway through the meal they broke off for a three-way telephone conversation with Bush. To Blair's surprise Putin then took him for a midnight walk in the woods, all part of the Russian ritual.[88] A tired Blair arrived back at the ambassador's residence at about 2 a.m., where Powell and Campbell were waiting up for him. Putin had pledged not only to support the action in Afghanistan but to share his intelligence, and to offer former Soviet bases in Central Asia.[89] Blair prided himself on his diplomacy, but it was his earlier work in helping forge links between Bush and Putin that had made the impact.

The next leg of Blair's journey was physically the most dangerous: Islamabad, the Pakistani capital, to see President Musharraf, the last major world leader still to support the Taliban regime in Kabul. As his RAF VC-10 made a steep dive into the capital, conscious of the risks of terrorism in the air and on the ground, Blair became maudlin and, unusually for him, began to talk about death.[90] His path into Pakistan had been paved for him by Charles Guthrie, who had retired in February 2001 as Chief of the Defence Staff. Guthrie had known Musharraf since he had been a student at the Royal College of Defence Studies in London, when he had helped the young Pakistani with his dissertation. Guthrie had been sent out by Blair after Musharraf's military coup in 1999 to express Britain's unease at the way Musharraf had come to power, but also to keep a line of contact open. This strategy proved its worth, as Guthrie described: 'After 9/11, Musharraf was finding it very difficult to make up his mind about what to do. Blair sent me to see him. By this time, I probably knew him better than anyone else from Britain or, indeed, the United States. I was able to talk through with him the advantages and disadvantages of the courses of action he could follow.'[91] With the groundwork laid, Blair could speak plainly to Musharraf on his visit: 'We had everyone out of the room and just talked, the two of us.' Blair explained, before outlining his case, that he was also speaking on behalf of President Bush.[92] He was surprised at how ready Musharraf was to be supportive, agreeing to abandon Pakistan's support for the Taliban, help round up al-Qaeda members, supply intelligence and patrol the border with Afghanistan. In return, Pakistan was to be welcomed back into the international fold from which it had been excluded since the coup, and it gained access to world markets and debt relief, to assist it in 'its return to democracy'.[93] Musharraf took a severe risk in aligning himself so closely with the West, not least because of the unpopularity of such a policy with many in his country, but he had judged the gains worth it. Vastly relieved, Blair praised Musharraf's decision as 'the right choice. The result will be a lasting strengthening of the Western world's relations with Pakistan.'[94]

Blair rounded off the trip with a stop-off in India, where he saw Atal Bihari Vajpayee, the Prime Minister, whom he lobbied on behalf of the war, and on the need not to unsettle Pakistan. Blair flew back from Delhi late on Saturday, 6 October, exhausted but pleased by his responses in the three capitals.[95] On the way from the airport to Downing Street, he received a call in his car from Bush. As had been planned for several days, the first air attacks would begin that night, and they talked over the final plans and Blair's trip. Buckingham Palace and the major party leaders were then told of the imminent attack. US F-18 strike aircraft, and B-1 and B-52 bombers were launched, and the Royal Navy's nuclear submarines, *Triumph* and *Trafalgar*, fired Cruise missiles. Thirty-one al-Qaeda and Taliban targets had been selected for that first wave of attacks, many around Kabul and Kandahar, the powerbase of the Taliban, and al-Qaeda training camps near Jalalabad. Blair was proud that British forces had been involved from the outset. This was a moment of 'the utmost gravity', he said to a press conference on Sunday, 7 October. 'None of the leaders involved in the action wants war. None of our nations want it. We are peaceful people. But we know that sometimes to safeguard peace, we have to fight.' His mood was described as 'tense and sombre'. According to Philip Webster of *The Times*, who knew him well, Blair had 'probably never felt more lonely'.[96]

With the war now under way, Blair's priorities changed to seeing it concluded as swiftly as possible, to maintaining the international coalition and public support at home, and to making progress with the Middle East peace process. Blair was content to delegate operational responsibility to Geoff Hoon and Boyce, who had a strong relationship with his American counterpart, General Myers.[97] This left Blair free to focus on his other objectives. Winning the propaganda war became a priority after his exceptional approval rating began to fall following its highpoint in September and October. Images of innocent Afghan victims, of refugees and anti-war riots in Pakistan supplanted the pictures of the collapsing Twin Towers and the simple moral verities of the early days after the attacks. On 30 October, polls showed a twelve-point drop in support for the war from 74 per cent to 62 per cent. Blair responded with a powerful and highly charged speech to the Welsh Assembly in Cardiff, in an effort to regain the moral high ground: 'It is important that we never forget why we are doing this: never forget how we felt watching the planes fly into the Trade [Center] towers; never forget those answerphone messages; never forget how we felt imagining how mothers told children they were about to die . . . September 11 is no less appalling today than it was on September 11.'[98] The speech was larded with references to new intelligence proving Bin Laden's culpability. As always, Blair wanted to offer 'proof' to justify the line he was taking. Similar speeches were made by other ministers including Straw and Hain, the Europe Minister, who addressed the rising fears of terrorist retaliation against Britain by saying: 'By far the greater danger would be to leave the threat of terrorism unchallenged, and to let it strike over and over again.'[99] The opinion polls, however, failed to respond. Shortly after 9/11, Campbell had instigated the creation of an Islamic Media Unit in the Foreign Office. He now orchestrated with the White House the setting up of the 'Coalition Information Centre' to combat pro-Taliban propaganda with its own stories pumped out twenty-four hours a day. Blair and Campbell rapidly became as jaundiced about the hostility of the British media, especially the BBC, however, as they had been earlier during Kosovo.[100]

Reservations now began to emerge in Whitehall about American war aims. Blair himself had often spoken about widening the war on terrorism, but only on the basis of having evidence of complicity in 9/11. But after just one day of fighting, Bush issued a statement on 8 October saying the war in Afghanistan was merely the 'first phase' of a general war against terrorists. The influence of the 'neo-conservatives', or 'neocons', like Rumsfeld, Wolfowitz and the former Reagan aide, Richard Perle, aroused particular concern in London. These were the unilateralists or hawks (also dubbed the Vulcans) who were as passionate about rooting out terrorism, regardless of consequences, as those of a like mind had been in rooting out communism in an earlier generation. One senior figure at the top of the Foreign Office said: 'People like Wolfowitz and Perle were talking this incredible crap in the latter part of 2001. They were already pushing for going straight on and doing Iraq.'[101] John Kerr, the Permanent Under-Secretary of the Foreign Office, concerned that the legality of the war should be based firmly on the undisputed right of self-defence, ensured that the carefully drafted British war aims specified that the British quarrel was with al-Qaeda and its Taliban protectors, not with the Afghan people and still less with the Iraqis.[102] Many in the Foreign Office were becoming unhappy at the prospect of unbridled American power, and the prospect of Britain being sucked into supporting them.

Blair's constant anxiety to reassure world, particularly Muslim, opinion that the struggle in Afghanistan was not with Islam explained why he set off on 10 October on his first diplomatic tour since fighting began, armed with a copy of the Koran, which it was said he had much studied. His defence of Muslims in Kosovo and his support for the Palestinian cause also gave him some initial credit. 'What we had to do was to get across very strongly,' Blair said, 'that this was not about taking on Islam.'[103] He wanted to discuss with moderate Arab leaders how to 'capture some of the ground from the extremists who said they were talking on behalf of Islam, when no sensible Islamic scholar or cleric could possibly support such an interpretation of Islam permitting something such as the attack in New York'.[104] His journey took him first to Oman, where he visited British troops, and delivered a blunt message for consumption worldwide that 'no country will be attacked unless there is evidence', and aides emphasised that there was no evidence linking Iraq to the 9/11 attacks.[105] Blair's paramount concern was that an invasion of Iraq would shatter moderate Arab opinion. While dining with the Sultan of Oman, Blair received a call from Palestinian leader, Yasser Arafat, about kick-starting the peace process.[106] The next day he flew on to see President Mubarak in Cairo, and discussed Islam and terrorism with him in the Ettehadia Palace, before returning late on 12 October. The brief tour was punctuated by frequent interviews on Arab television stations, and was accompanied by a 'blizzard' of articles in Middle Eastern newspapers.[107]

Blair's hopes for rapid progress in the peace process were to be dashed on his next tour at the end of October, a setback all the crueller because on this trip he was acting on his own initiative, not as America's quasi-emissary. Indeed, he was flying in the face of hawks in Washington who wanted no bridge-building with 'marginal' or 'rogue states' who had sponsored terrorism in the past, nor did they wish to see progress on Israeli–Palestinian talks. Awareness of the British–US divergence in the capitals he visited made his task doubly difficult. Setting off on 30 October, his first stop was in Damascus, where he spent the night before seeing the youthful new leader Bashar al-Assad early the next morning. Number 10 had earlier dispatched Charles Powell to sound out the Syrian leader, and Michael Levy, Blair's personal envoy in the Middle East, had drawn on his own contacts with the Syrian government.[108] Blair was hopeful. Flush with his success in restoring diplomatic links with Iran and Libya, Blair believed he could wean Syria off supporting terrorism and back to the negotiating table with Israel. All went well until their concluding joint press conference, when Assad humiliated Blair by defending terrorism against Israel and attacking the war in Afghanistan. It was perhaps no coincidence that this disastrous press conference occurred on one of the few occasions when Blair was not under Campbell's watchful eye: the Director of Communications had not accompanied Blair to Damascus. Blair achieved limited success in Riyadh also, which had earlier rebuffed a proposed visit, and in Amman:

neither Crown Prince Abdullah of Saudi Arabia nor King Abdullah of Jordan were prepared to endorse the bombing of Afghanistan. On the morning of 1 November Blair flew in to see Ariel Sharon, the Israeli Prime Minister, who was uncompromising in his policy of responding to Palestinian violence with force, and declined to withdraw his troops from disputed territories to help restart peace talks. A helicopter journey to Gaza to meet Arafat yielded nothing new.[109] The whole trip played into the hands of those who said Blair was over-estimating his own capabilities, and that he was 'globe-trotting' at the expense of his domestic agenda. Simon Jenkins summed up a general feeling: 'By all accounts, his voyage to the Middle East was brave, miserable and fruitless.'[110] Israel's shooting dead of two Palestinians during Blair's visit showed the same indifference to his mission as did the US, which tactlessly ordered the beginning of carpet bombing of Afghanistan while he was in Syria.[111] Some in London viewed it as a deliberate affront to undermine him.

Blair saw himself as a peace-maker, as in Ireland, and had invested much in trying to make progress in the Palestinian–Israeli conflict, focusing not on a specific peace plan, but simply on the need for all parties just to re-engage in dialogue. He had a deep feeling for Israel, born in part from his faith, and had visited the country twice before becoming Prime Minister. Early on in his premiership, Blair had been cool towards the right-wing Netanyahu government, and had been as dismayed by its policy when he visited the Gaza Strip in April 1998 as he was moved by visiting the Yad Vashem Holocaust Museum in Jerusalem. But he forged a close relationship with Ehud Barak, the Labour Prime Minister from 1999 to 2001, becoming much more sympathetic to Israel, guided in part by Manning's enthusiasm for generating momentum for the peace process. When Sharon won power in early 2001, Blair worked hard at building a relationship, with some success. But Sharon succeeded in turning the Bush administration against talking to the Palestinians, in stark contrast to Clinton who had laboured hard in 2000 to secure progress. Indeed, the very fact that Clinton had been so closely involved led many in the Bush administration to react instinctively against it. Sharon cleverly went direct to the White House and showed Bush an intelligence intercept, purporting to prove that Yasser Arafat, the Palestinian leader, was a liar.[112] In contrast, Blair responded positively to Arafat, whom he had met thirteen times since becoming Prime Minister. As with Adams and McGuinness in Northern Ireland, he saw some good in Arafat, regarding him as essential to future negotiations. Blair was disappointed that the trip provided no evidence that 9/11 had opened up a new kaleidoscope of opportunity in the Middle East: rather it had entrenched key figures in their own hard-line positions.[113] Deep fatigue and lack of time also played their parts in the lack of success. Blair was indeed over-extending himself.

Mounting criticism of Blair for his self-appointed role as peace-broker and America's fixer was also now heard increasingly in the capitals of the EU. He had been working hard behind the scenes to bind EU leaders into American policy. Some of them, like Louis Michel, the Foreign Minister of Belgium, which held the EU Presidency at the time, believed fighting terrorism was a distraction from the main priorities of the Euro and European enlargement.[114] However, in concert with Chirac and Schröder, Blair brought EU leaders round to offering their full support for American policy in Afghanistan. Chirac was due to meet with Bush on 6 November, the day before Blair's visit, and so he proposed they meet together beforehand to co-ordinate their message. Blair thus invited Chirac to dinner at Number 10 on 4 November. As Schröder had just returned from talks with Putin in Moscow, Blair thought he should also attend.[115] Blair made the mistake of not mentioning and explaining the forthcoming dinner to Berlusconi, whom he called in to see in Genoa (for 'pasta and fish' the press said, which rejoiced in giving such culinary details) on the way back from Israel. Seeing the forthcoming Downing Street dinner as a summit of the *de facto* EU leadership, Berlusconi was hurt and angry not to have been included. He therefore invited himself to the dinner too.[116] Other EU leaders had already been stung by their exclusion from a similar meeting at Ghent on 19 October, organised by Chirac. In this volatile atmosphere, complaints were made that smaller EU countries were being 'treated like candidates [for membership] and being informed after the decisions were taken'. Blair felt compelled to widen the dinner invitations to José María Aznar of Spain, Guy Verhofstadt of Belgium, Wim Kok of Holland and Javier Solana, the EU's foreign policy chief.[117] By all accounts, rarely has a dinner invitation so eagerly sought proved of so little pleasure or value to those in attendance. The guests arrived in poor humour, believing they were being excluded from American plans and resentful of 'them and us' politics. Blair tried to propose a European-wide response to terrorism and to explore ways to reinvigorate the Middle East peace process. But fears of American intentions and the risks of the Afghanistan war dominated the conversation. Chirac delivered a Jeremiah-like warning of civilian casualties – 'a mosque will be bombed during Ramadan' – and the risk of a humanitarian catastrophe, which served to heighten their sense of powerlessness.[118] Blair agreed he would represent their concerns when he saw Bush in Washington the following week. But his role as 'envoy' of the EU to America was itself another factor causing unease and mistrust. Blair did not hold the EU Presidency to justify his role as spokesman, nor was Britain the temporary chair on the UN Security Council. None was angrier with him than Romano Prodi, the EU Commission President, for whom Blair had little respect.[119]

By this time, Blair was growing increasingly anxious over the course of an essentially surrogate war. The deployment of a substantial force of coalition ground troops had been ruled out by Pakistan, whose support extended to allowing the coalition use of Pakistani air space, but no more.[120] The war on the ground was thus fought mainly by existing Afghan resistance groups, principally the Northern Alliance: 'It was all about Special Forces, intelligence and suitcases of money,' said one of Britain's top brass, the last being needed to bribe individual warlords to fight against the Taliban.[121] At one point in early November, his frustration boiling over, Blair fired off a 'testy' note to Geoff Hoon questioning the progress that had been made and asking 'shouldn't it have been sorted out by now?'[122] While officials remained concerned about too rapid an advance on Kabul, which past history suggested could precipitate a bloodbath, Blair wanted the capital taken as a priority. 'Blair's judgement was that we were in a war, and the task in a war is to take the capital,' said Robert Cooper, the government's Special Representative on Afghanistan. 'That's the sort of clear thinking you want from a leader, which puts officials in their place. His instinct throughout Afghanistan was to go for it.'[123] Meanwhile, the Americans continued to make heavy use of 'cluster' and 'daisy cutter' bombs, which were causing widespread civilian casualties and turning public opinion in Britain and abroad further against the war. The lack of apparent American concern about public opinion, or the brewing humanitarian crisis in Afghanistan that had so worried Chirac at the Downing Street dinner, was a growing cause of division between the UK and the US.[124] It was against this backdrop that Blair set off to see Bush on 7 November.

Blair's fleeting six-hour visit to Washington marked a low point in his relations with the President. Blair argued that a settlement of the Arab–Israeli conflict should form the lynchpin to winning Muslim hearts and minds in the war against terrorism: the White House flatly disagreed, and in particular wanted nothing to do with Arafat. To Blair's chagrin, Bush said at the joint press conference that al-Qaeda would be defeated 'peace or no peace in the Middle East'.[125] Bush told the media that the US had 'no better friend in the world' than Britain, and there was 'no better person to talk to than Tony Blair. He brings a lot of wisdom and judgement.' But in private there was little evidence that the Americans wanted to hear either virtue from Blair. Blair briefed Bush about the concerns of EU leaders, and the need to maintain the international coalition behind the campaign in Afghanistan. But the administration, flushed by what they sensed was an imminent breakthrough, and marvelling at their logistical success in the war so far, gave little impression that they cared much whether they had international support or whether they stood alone. As Rumsfeld said publicly, in a clear riposte to Blair's position: 'The [international] coalition must not determine the mission.' There were continuing differences over Iraq. Blair maintained his position that Iraq was utterly off-limits unless solid evidence could be produced linking Saddam to Bin Laden.[126] Blair might have described it as 'a very full, good meeting',[127] but he returned to London more worried by divisions in the alliance than he had been for a long time.[128]

Had the Afghan war continued into the new year, which at one stage looked possible, the differences between Washington and London would have come out into the open. But the fighting ended speedily. Two days after Blair's return from the US, the strategic town of Mazar-i-Sharif fell, followed on 13 November by Kabul itself, and with it the fall of the Taliban. Regime change had indeed been achieved, as the Americans had always intended. Blair, who had become increasingly obsessed by the need for a rapid and relatively blood-free end to the war, was overjoyed at the sudden end, and the minimal loss of life. His and Campbell's venom at the journalists who had been highly critical of the war, and of Britain's role in supporting America, was powerfully released when Number 10 published a journalists' 'roll call of shame'.

With all four Afghan factions signing a deal at the post-war conference in Bonn in early December, the future looked settled and secure. But difficulties with Washington continued to simmer. The Americans rebuffed the offer of British troops to hunt down Bin Laden, who had evaded capture, despite the intense pounding of al-Qaeda caves at Tora Bora. This was the Americans' war. They also wanted it to be their peace. They did not share Britain's enthusiasm for post-war peacekeeping and reconstruction. The Americans 'were immensely allergic to the notion of either "nation-building" or "peace-keeping". We had to come up with another phrase so we weren't mentioning those hideous terms,' said Meyer.[129] Britain was very much in the lead of the seventeen-nation International Security Assistance Force (ISAF), but America fought successfully to keep its role to a minimum.[130]

Blair signalled his commitment to working for post-war nation-building by flying with Cherie to Afghanistan. They visited Bagram just before midnight on 7 January 2002 on a secret and highly risky mission. Fears of a missile attack from Taliban units still at large meant that they travelled in an RAF Hercules plane specially equipped to counter ground-to-air missiles.[131] Once on the ground, Blair met Harmid Karzai, the interim leader, and pledged his support to ensure 'Afghanistan becomes a stable country, part of the international community once more'. Blair also met British troops, shortly to be increased in numbers to help flush out the remnants of al-Qaeda. While Rice continued to talk to Manning about ensuring the post-war stability of Afghanistan,[132] the dominant forces in Washington remained resolutely uninterested. The victory, according to the British Embassy in Washington, had strengthened those in the administration who believed in the essential benevolence of American power.[133] Their attention now moved westwards, to Iraq.

Blair firmly believed that his influence in the aftermath of 9/11 had been extensive, affecting the nature, strategy and timing of the military action that followed.[134] Yet for all his extraordinary efforts, British influence over the largely American plans had been severely constrained. Blair no doubt played a significant role in coalition-building, and in shaping the conflict as a war against terrorism, not as a clash with the Muslim world, a point he felt he had to stress repeatedly to the Americans.[135] Yet in terms of the conduct of the war, one can point to just two areas where he made a difference. British insistence, against American wishes, resulted in ISAF being in Afghanistan, albeit with its role heavily constrained by Washington. In this way, Blair helped imprint the concept of nation-building on a reluctant administration. British airpower, intelligence and special forces (i.e., the Special Air Service and Special Boat Service) also made an impact, backing up the surrogate Afghan warriors on the ground. One senior official said, 'One thing our presence did was to stop the Americans from shooting the prisoners.'[136] This seems overstated but, given the way the American military conducted itself in Iraq, it is very likely that the British acted as a restraining presence on the Americans.

The Impact of 9/11 on Blair

It was commonplace in the golden period after 1997 to say that Blair might be doing very well but his real quality as Prime Minister would not be tested until he had to cope with a crisis. The attacks on 9/11 was a crisis with greater global significance than any a Prime Minister faced since Eden learned of Nasser's nationalisation of the Suez Canal in July 1956. The events of 9/11 changed Blair profoundly, and deepened his sense of the moral futility of being a powerful nation but not acting in the face of grave wrongs. Eighteen months later, as the inevitable Iraq war loomed, he reflected, 'It's all very well being a pacifist . . . but to be a pacifist after September 11, that's something different. It's all new now: terrible threat, terrorist weapons, terrorist states.'[137] Blair responded to 9/11 with some magnificent oratory, with stiff resolution in his commitment to root out terrorists, and with imagination and compassion in his desire to build a better world out of the ashes of Ground Zero. His party conference speech, building on the ideas of his Chicago speech, gave him the philosophical underpinning for humanitarian intervention and showed his utterly sincere desire to use Britain's power as a force for good in the world. It was hubristic and naïve, but the autumn of 2001 saw Blair at the zenith of his self-confidence and his standing in the world.

He experienced something of the limits of his powers of persuasion (in which his belief remained undimmed), above all with his EU colleagues and with his rebuffs in Syria and Israel. His much-vaunted role as a bridge between the US and Europe was tested severely in October and November, although its buckling was to lie in the future. Blair realised after 9/11 that the United States would be prepared to act entirely on its own if it was sufficiently confident of a course of action, and especially if the 'neo-cons' were driving the policy. The all-governing mantra that Blair stuck to with the White House was 'total support in public, total candour in private'. His influence, he believed, was best exercised behind the scenes. 'There is a world of difference,' said one Number 10 aide, 'between influencing the US in private and boasting about it in public.'[138] No doubt, but this strategy relies crucially on a willingness to push the US hard in private. 'The problem,' said another official who was intimately involved, 'was that we didn't push nearly hard enough.'[139] Again, little seems to have been learned about the efficacy of the 'total support' article of faith.

Blair did not appreciate at the time the havoc that 9/11 and its aftermath in Iraq would play on his domestic agenda. As we saw earlier, little detailed planning for the second term policy agenda had been completed before the 2001 election: domestic policy would thus need his personal input and drive if the government was to make progress. But much of his creative energy was given over to foreign affairs, and managing the domestic reaction to it. A referendum on the Euro, public service reform and his relationship with Gordon Brown were all casualties. 'Without 9/11 it would have been an utterly different second term,' admitted a close aide.[140] Whatever Blair might have achieved abroad, there is no doubt that the steady drain of time and political capital to international affairs, which began after 9/11 and greatly increased with the war in Iraq, left his domestic agenda in disarray.

The most significant effect of 9/11 on Blair personally was to build confidence in his own judgement, and his unique place on the earth. He prayed often, and derived answers and inspiration from his prayers. It is to his all-important relationship with God that we now turn.

Blair discusses the Iraq crisis with God's representative on earth, Pope John Paul II, in February 2003. Blair's belief underpinned his entire public and private life: but not even the Pope could make him question the wisdom of his course of action on Iraq.

34

God

Blair's relationship with God is more important than any other described in this book because, uniquely, it has coloured his relationship with all other nineteen figures, and it has affected his response in differing measures to all twenty turning points. Not only has the relationship been all-embracing; it is also peculiarly hard to understand. His religion explains why he became the person he did, why he entered politics, why he holds his beliefs, how he relates to others, and from where he derives much of his inner strength and convictions.

Few Prime Ministers have been so influenced by their faith. Gladstone was a strong believer in the latter nineteenth century, as was Stanley Baldwin in the inter-war years. But none of Blair's predecessors as Labour Prime Ministers was notably religious: MacDonald was not, Attlee admitted publicly that he did not believe and in private was a vehement atheist,[1] while Callaghan lost any belief he once had long before he entered Number 10 in 1976. Wilson (a Congregationalist) is the only previous Labour premier to have made anything of his faith, proclaiming he was a socialist 'because he was a Christian'. He appointed ten practising believers to his Cabinet in 1964, and asked for a service to be organised in the House of Commons chapel after the 1964 General Election to bless the new government.[2] Yet a government that opened with such a celestial fanfare rapidly became mired in worldly concerns, and one heard little subsequently of Wilson's actions being inspired by God. Of Labour leaders who never made it to Number 10, Keir Hardie (a Nonconformist), George Lansbury (an Anglican), Arthur Henderson (a Methodist) and John Smith (a Presbyterian) were believers; Hugh Gaitskell, Michael Foot and Neil Kinnock were not. But no Prime Minister since Gladstone, who

finally left Downing Street in 1894, exactly one hundred years before Blair
became Labour leader, has been so influenced by his religion.

Keeping God Out of the Limelight, 1972–96

Blair's commitment to the Christian faith while at Oxford, and its impact
on the evolution of his political thinking, has been described in earlier
chapters. His was not an evangelical Christianity as it was for many who
were active Christians at university. He never tried to convert anyone to
Christianity, then or since. He was less concerned to save his own soul, still
less those of others, than to make the world a better place.[3] Chief
responsibility for helping Blair to see God as a relevant, practical force in
his world rather than as an abstract concept lies with Peter Thomson.
Matthew d'Ancona, who has written persuasively on the subject of Blair
and religion, sees Blair's religious awakening at Oxford as the defining
moment of his life.[4] It so affected him that he began thinking seriously
about entering the church,[5] to the surprise of his friends from pre-Oxford
days, who had not seen any indication of seriousness about religion at
school.[6] Quite the opposite.

The idea of his Christian duty to engage actively in the world, together
with his excitement over the idea of community, explain his decision to
take politics seriously, which he had never done before Oxford, and to join
the Labour Party. His religion sustained him as he contemplated his
mother's death in 1975 and afterwards, as well as through the hard and
largely solitary graft to become a barrister. Meeting Cherie deepened his
faith. It is no coincidence that she too is a believer: here was someone of
his own age who took religion as seriously as him.

For the eleven years after their marriage in 1980 Blair's faith remained
largely a private matter. He attended Catholic Mass most Sundays, taking
communion with Cherie.[7] The children were all baptised into the Catholic
Church.[8] Throughout the 1980s, he rarely referred to his belief in public
and only his close friends knew about his church-going. Gordon Brown,
the son of a Church of Scotland Minister, was another believer, but their
common Christian bond did not play a major part in their close friendship
in the 1980s. Brown spelled out his thoughts on Christianity and ethics
at a lecture in 1990 in St Stephen's Church in Glasgow, yet it was not until
Blair appeared on the BBC's *Question Time* in 1991 that his Christianity
became a matter of public knowledge when, to the surprise of many, he
professed his belief in front of the cameras.[9] Blair joined the Christian
Socialist Movement (CSM) in June 1992. It attracted little attention,

however, and when he spoke at a CSM meeting shortly afterwards he attracted an audience of just a dozen.[10]

With his faith out in the open, Christianity was to provide a bond with John Smith, the son of a church elder, and a regular attendee at the Church of Scotland. Indeed, it was Smith who had originally invited Blair to join the CSM.[11] Partly in reaction to Kinnock's atheism, Smith's platform as leader was based on his own Christianity. 'I am an active and professing member of the Church of Scotland,' Smith declared when running for the leadership, and in his first party conference speech in October 1992 he deliberately used moral language and Christian references to differentiate his Labour Party from Major's government.[12] Blair was in the vanguard of this quest: 'We are trying to establish in the public mind the coincidence between the values of democratic socialism and those of Christianity,' Blair said boldly during the conference. He continued, 'There's a desire in the Labour Party to rediscover its ethical values: the ethical code that most of us really believe gave birth to the Labour Party.'[13] This was a dangerous ploy, and in stark contrast to Labour's traditional post-war style.

The murder of James Bulger in February 1993 sparked a period of moral reflection by all political parties. Blair's strongly ethical if not overtly Christian message caught the popular mood better than any other politician. He spoke about the moral chaos that results when society does not clearly understand what is right and what is wrong. The press began to label him 'Labour's New Moralist'.[14] A month after the Bulger murder, Blair wrote a foreword to a book of essays on Christianity and socialism, launched on the day that John Smith gave the Tawney Lecture at Bloomsbury Baptist Church in London.[15] Smith's private office had cautioned against him making an overtly religious speech, and so the talk contained only a single direct reference to God.[16] Blair felt no such restraint. In his foreword, he wrote that 'Christianity is a very tough religion . . . It places a duty, an imperative on us to reach our better self and to care about creating a better community to live in . . . It is judgemental. There is right and wrong. There is good and bad . . . we should not hesitate to make such judgements.'[17] Chris Bryant, the CSM Labour MP, said he had to badger Blair hard to produce the piece.[18] But it created a big impression. Patrick Wintour and Michael White wrote an article about Blair's foreword titled, 'Mr Clean Gets His Hands Dirty', noting Blair was obviously not 'embarrassed' by his faith.[19]

Blair kept his faith in his back pocket during the leadership election and his first party conference as leader in 1994. He did not yet sense that the moment had come to talk openly about it. But by his second party conference in 1995 he was wanting to share with his party what his faith was and why it was important to him. His enthusiasm to show them the authentic Tony Blair was not shared by Campbell. They eventually agreed that his speech should be devoid of direct biblical quotations or professions of faith. So he spoke of 'the simple truths: I am worth no more than anyone else. I am my brother's keeper. I will not walk by on the other side. We [are] members of the same family, the same community, the same race. This is my socialism.'[20] It was the most powerful and emotional of his conference speeches as party leader in opposition.

Blair's seminal public profession of faith came six months later when he was interviewed by Matthew d'Ancona for the *Sunday Telegraph*, on Easter Sunday 1996. Hunter was as enthusiastic an exponent of this interview as Campbell was sceptical.[21] 'You must remember, this was very early Blair,' d'Ancona later said. 'The spin machine had not yet closed him down on God. I spoke to Alastair after the interview. He made it clear this kind of thing would never be allowed to happen again.'[22] Campbell's atheism was not the sole reason for his antipathy: Blair as confessing Christian did not fit the image of the normal family that was being carved out for him. For Campbell there was the extra fear of ridicule and satire; when *Private Eye* began its 'Vicar of St Albion' column from May 1997 mocking Blair's religiosity, and Rory Bremner began to imitate Blair's 'preachy' manner, Campbell's fears appeared fully justified.[23] The portrait of Blair is not of an unworldly dreamer, which would be damaging enough, but of a sanctimonious, calculating hypocrite. Campbell did not become more indulgent of Blair with age, hence his emphatic statement in mid-2003 to *Vanity Fair* journalist, David Margolick, 'We don't do God.'[24] Campbell thought Blair on this subject was naïve, indeed irrational. Episodes, such as launching the 2001 campaign before a school's stained-glass window, hymn book in hand, which produced predictable scorn, merely served to convince Campbell of the correctness of his convictions.[25]

As Blair was largely closed down on religion, the *Sunday Telegraph* piece is the key text for understanding what his religion meant to him. D'Ancona interviewed him on tape in his room in the House of Commons for well over an hour, from which he produced a first draft, which was then batted back and forth between their offices until the final version was settled.[26] 'Very unusually for a politician, the text came back stronger. Most politicians make anything they correct more anodyne,' d'Ancona said.[27] So what did Blair say? The piece has four distinct parts: the nature of his faith, his ethical beliefs, the influence of religion on his political beliefs, and finally, the impact of his beliefs on his political actions. In the first, he discussed the nature of his faith and professed the centrality of his Christian beliefs. He then said, 'I find prayer a source of solace and I read the Gospels,' though he finds the Old Testament 'more vivid than the New Testament'. He described himself as an 'ecumenical Christian', who is baffled by the argument between Protestant and Catholic. He proclaimed 'deep respect for other faiths', relishing, not being deterred by, the 'religious pluralism of this country'.

Through reflecting on the Easter message, he looked in an abstract way at how Christianity interacts with politics. Blair found Pontius Pilate an intriguing example for a politician because he was caught in the age-old dilemma between doing 'what is right and what is expedient'. The influence of his history 'teacher', Roy Jenkins, can be seen in the three examples he selected where politicians were caught in such a dilemma: the Great Reform Act of 1832, the Corn Law debate in the 1840s and the Munich agreement and appeasement debate in the late 1930s.

Blair then described how his religious beliefs shaped his political thinking. He drew attention to the Christian stress on community as opposed to the 'narrow view of self-interest' represented by Conservatism, 'particularly in its modern, more right-wing form'. This Christian stress on community, on man's relationship not only with God, but also with his fellow man, 'is the essential reason why I am on the left rather than the right'. The Christian's stress on the individual's free will and responsibility for his own actions 'helped to inspire my rejection of Marxism', where individual behaviour, Marxists believe, is pre-determined. He acknowledged his debt to John Macmurray, though did not mention Peter Thomson. Against the grain of his thinking at this time, he took on Mrs Thatcher, challenging her reference to St Paul in a controversial speech she made in 1988 that 'if a man will not work, he shall not eat': Paul did not mean that we should abandon the helpless and vulnerable, Blair said. Finally, Blair waded deep into the quagmire of sin and morality. He stressed the presence of sin, and the dangers of taking the wrong course in life, which leads to alienation from God.

The interview was a sincere attempt by Blair, in alliance with a serious journalist, to discuss his religious convictions and to explain how they informed his political beliefs. His implication that Tories were too selfish to be good Christians was perhaps his only error of judgement. He had no obvious political motive for expressing these views: indeed, the political advice he received was to shut up. He received little praise for his honesty and candour. As Roy Greenslade described it, the piece resulted in 'party political point-scoring. A notable lack of charity from a handful of church-going Tory MPs. Carping criticism from newspaper leader writers and commentators. Accusations of sanctimony. One charge of annoyance and another of philosophical weakness.' Greenslade's conclusion was that newspapers, which had once scorned those who pronounced themselves atheists, now treated Christians as 'deviants'.

Belief into Action

Blair's relationship with God can be approached thematically around the four themes discussed in d'Ancona's interview. First, the nature of his belief. George Carey, the former Archbishop of Canterbury, described Blair as a 'Robinson Crusoe believer. He is an island who doesn't have Christian believers all around him to nourish him.'[28] It is indeed striking that, apart from Cherie, Blair does not have more Christian soulmates. Campbell's atheism was shared by Powell, Hunter, Heywood, Mandelson and Gould. Blair's religion rarely became a cause of difference, but in the tense build-up to the Iraq war, it was. Blair wanted to conclude a television address with the words to the nation 'God bless you.' Peter Stothard described 'a noisy team revolt in which every player appeared to be complaining at once'.[29] Their will prevailed: he ended with a limp 'thank you'. Bruce Grocott, his Parliamentary Private Secretary in the first term, is a devout Christian, Adonis is an Anglo-Catholic, Peter Hyman a practising Jew and Robert Hill, one time Political Secretary, an evangelical, but they are the exceptions that prove the rule, and none of them was in Blair's inner circle. Among senior ministers, the main Christians are Jack Straw, Gordon Brown, Paul Boateng, Tessa Jowell and Hilary Armstrong, Chief Whip from 2001, who is a Methodist.[30] In his constituency, John Burton is a devout Christian. After getting Blair on to the shortlist for Sedgefield in 1983, Burton headed to the local church in Trimdon to give thanks and ask for strength: unbeknown to him Blair later did the same in Durham Cathedral.[31] But God does not appear to loom large in their conversations. Blair had taken a conscious decision to appoint individuals to posts in Number 10 or in Cabinet not because they were or were not Christians, but because of their merit at the particular job. He was thus unlike Iain Duncan Smith, who deliberately advanced Christians among his team. Blair's approach can be seen in his rebuff to the Church when it lobbied for a senior Church representative to be on the newly formed Social Exclusion Unit in late 1997.[32] He is also quite unlike Bush. When Jeremy Paxman and David Frost asked Blair whether he prayed with Bush, they failed to understand the kind of believer Blair is. Although religion was an important common bond between the two men, such open exhibitions of faith, including saying grace before and after meals, he would find embarrassing and even mawkish.[33]

Wherever he is in the world, his office has to ensure that there is a church nearby, in which he can pray each Sunday.[34] When Cherie is with him, it will be a Catholic church. 'My wife is Catholic, my kids are brought up as Catholics . . . I have gone to Mass with them for years because I believe it's important for a family to worship together.'[35] Blair would indeed be happy to worship in any denomination of church, as long as it was not aggressively fundamentalist.[36] He specifically asked for the ecumenical service at the start of the Labour conference in 1997 to include Communion for the first time, in which representatives of Methodist, Anglican and Roman Catholic churches would take part.[37]

Blair's relationship with Catholicism has aroused particular interest. In Sedgefield, the Blairs have forged a close personal relationship with the local Catholic priest, Father John Caden, who like Peter Thomson has been much inspired by the Church's social mission and 'liberation theology'. Caden baptised the Blairs' children.[38] When the family lived in Islington, Blair regularly took Communion with them at his local Catholic church, St Joan of Arc. A change of priest, and new guidance from the church authorities on who was eligible to receive Catholic Communion, prompted Cardinal Basil Hume, the head of the Catholic Church, to ask Blair to restrict his practice, except when on holiday if there was no Anglican church nearby. Blair wrote back agreeing to desist, but making his disapproval clear: 'I wonder what Jesus would have made of it.'[39] He remained on good terms with Hume, however, and visited him shortly before his death in 1999; but he continued to attend Catholic Mass, albeit usually refraining from Communion. When at Chequers, the family would worship at the Catholic Church of the Immaculate Heart of Mary in nearby Great Missenden, and in London they attended the Catholic cathedral in Victoria.

In March 1998 the Press Association's Sarah Schaefer reported, to Number 10's fury, that Blair had attended Mass alone at Westminster Cathedral, the leading Catholic church in Britain. Michael White, who wrote up the story, believes he might one day convert.[40] The news of his solo visit prompted George Carey to write a concerned letter: 'As you know, I have no difficulty personally with your worshipping regularly with Cherie and the children at Roman Catholic worship.' But, he continued, not all shared his views. 'I know there are many who are deeply troubled by a view being disseminated by the press that you are about to "convert".' Carey's hope to Blair, to allay such fears, was that he would 'be seen, occasionally, at an Anglican or free Church act of worship'.[41] Blair replied the same day to reassure him that he was not about 'to defect': the explanation for his solo visit to Mass, he responded, was entirely prosaic –

he was to have been joined at the Mass by Cherie and the children but they were delayed, hence his attendance alone.[42] The rumours of a conversion, however, refused to die down. Later that year, Mgr Gaetano Bonicelli, Archbishop of Siena, broke confidence and reported a private conversation where Blair had apparently told him during his summer holidays that he felt 'very close to the Catholic Church, and to the world of Catholicism'.[43]

Speculation was reignited by his visit to see Pope John Paul II on 22 February 2003, on the eve of the Iraq war. The audience was intended for Cherie, who had long been seeking to meet the Pontiff, a wish the Vatican granted because of her devout Catholicism. The invitation was then extended to include him also.[44] 'He was very moved to be seeing the Pope, and was deeply proud of the honour for Cherie and their children,' said an aide.[45] To Blair, about to take the most important decision of his life, one on which he had been praying deeply, there was an added dimension to the windfall visit. He had found the accusation that an Iraq war would be immoral difficult to bear, and he hoped it would help to talk it through with the highest Catholic authority on earth.[46] The audience itself took place on the Saturday evening, and was followed by the Pope giving the family an apostolic blessing.[47] The family stayed the night at the Irish College, which trained young men for the priesthood, and at 7.30 the next morning the family attended a private Mass given by the Pope, a very rare honour for the family of a politician, especially non-Italians. Churchill, granted an audience with Pope Pius XII in August 1944 towards the end of the war, was the last British Prime Minister to have been received at the Vatican.[48]

Blair, however, did not receive either the solace or the understanding he sought. The Pope had strongly opposed the first Gulf War in 1991, and, although Number 10 thought it had an agreement that there was to be no disclosure on either side of what was said in the audience,[49] the Vatican immediately released a statement saying the Pope had urged Blair to do everything he could to avert 'the tragedy of a war' in the Middle East, which he feared would create 'new divisions' in the world.[50] Could the Pope have pulled him back and made him think again about the wisdom of the war? The meeting had potentially great importance for Blair personally. But he was totally convinced of his rightness, he shrugged off even the Pope's total opposition. Aides made light of it: 'Tony is a complete pragmatist: he's used to people saying negative things. He wasn't particularly deflated by it.'[51] Indeed, he was used to ignoring the advice of religious figures, however senior, whether George Carey, Basil Hume or now Pope John Paul II, if he did not agree with them. But for all that, it was one of the loneliest times of his life, and, on the eve of his biggest decision, to have been so comprehensively rebuffed must have been a bitter experience.

Speculation about Blair's conversion to Roman Catholicism remained throughout his premiership. While his liberal stance on abortion and homosexuality sit very uneasily with the Catholic Church's unbending opposition, he is drawn to the 'certainties and liturgies of Catholicism', as d'Ancona put it, and he reads Catholic texts exhaustively, including Pope Paul VI's bulls on human reproduction, a well-thumbed copy of which has nestled in the den.[52] Being united fully in worship in the same Church as Cherie and the children is immensely important to him and is the principal attraction of Catholicism. A conversion, if it comes, will only take place after he has left Number 10.

Blair thus remained institutionally a member of the Anglican Church. He was taken very much under the wing of George Carey, the Archbishop of Canterbury, who wrote to him shortly after he became party leader in 1994: 'I made a point of meeting informally but regularly with John Major about every six months for a quiet tête-à-tête. I would find it valuable to adopt this same pattern with you.'[53] They struck up a close relationship, with the Archbishop frequently offering words of encouragement and advice in person or on paper. When the Tories, for example, began their 'demon eyes' campaign against Blair in 1996, Carey wrote, 'I am so sorry you were "demonised" recently by the publicity stunt. It was a most unworthy attack. May I suggest – forgive me for interfering in issues that do not concern me directly – that your party does not follow suit?' In the same letter he offered Blair the opportunity of coming to Communion with him at Lambeth Palace, and hoped he would never fail to draw on him for spiritual support.[54] Just before the 1997 General Election, Carey wrote to wish him 'good luck and God's richest blessing', and to say: 'You have a strong Christian conscience and . . . Christian philosophy which is a marvellous basis upon which to create a vision for our society.'[55] Carey maintained the tempo of his advice throughout his tenure, criticising intemperate behaviour (e.g. Prescott's punch in the 2001 election campaign) and personalised attacks by politicians of all parties, and praising when he thought Blair had done well, as with his speech in November 2000 to the Lord Mayor's banquet, saying he gave 'every sign of becoming a truly great Prime Minister'.[56] The two men would discuss religion and belief: when Carey saw Blair had a book on the synoptic gospels published in the 1920s, which he thought hopelessly out of date, he recommended new books, which Blair duly read.[57] After the 2001 election was won, he praised the 'enthusiasm, commitment and sincerity' he displayed, and the restraint when he was personally the subject of a 'hysterical' attack: 'You took it calmly and listened.'[58]

Carey was a benign figure in Blair's early years as premier, and his gentle advice and watchfulness played a role in underscoring his Christian instincts. Carey prayed regularly for Blair. But Blair did not turn to him, nor indeed to other Anglican figures, at times of crisis. His disagreements with Carey were few. The Archbishop was disappointed Blair did not support the Church of England more openly, not least in his own religious practice. They disagreed early on over filling the vacancy for Bishop of Liverpool, when Blair asked for more names to be put forward by the Church to succeed David Sheppard.[59] Blair's critics seized on this as evidence of his determination to minimise opposition from within the Church,[60] although senior clergy insist the problem related to the ability of the candidates rather than their political views.[61] When a vacancy arose for Bishop of Carlisle, Blair made known his pleasure that it went to Graham Dow, the chaplain at St John's College who had prepared him for confirmation, who had caught the eye of Carey[62] and had always been a frontrunner for the post.[63] Blair's relative interest in senior appointments, influenced in part by the theology of Peter Thomson,[64] contrasted sharply with Major and even with Thatcher; despite concerns about the interference of the latter, she in fact accepted most of the Church's recommended candidates for bishoprics.[65] Blair was often wary of Establishment candidates, preferring 'men of vision' to take the Church forward.

The most widely reported disagreement on an appointment came over Carey's own successor: Carey would have preferred Michael Nazir-Ali, Bishop of Rochester, who had spoken out against Blair's Catholic links. Blair, however, favoured Rowan Williams, a Welshman, an intellectual and poet, who was appointed to Canterbury in 2002. Simon Jenkins called it Blair's 'most exciting act of patronage so far'.[66] Williams had been arrested in the 1980s for breaking into an American nuclear air force base to sing psalms on the runway and had condemned the war in Afghanistan in 2001 as 'morally tainted'. He was an outspoken critic of governments for not doing more to alleviate poverty, and had been critical of the Blair government for its 'obsession with image control' which was 'light years away from the humane, socialist tradition'.[67] It was clear that Williams would not be a pushover. It was an even more daring appointment because Blair knew that, if Williams attacked his policies, he would not disparage him in the way Mrs Thatcher had done with her ecclesiastical detractors as crypto-Marxists or woolly liberals.[68] Thatcher would not have placed such a critic in the Church's key post.

Williams' appointment coincided with the run-up to the Iraq war, to which he was implacably opposed. His most outspoken criticism came in a carefully worded critique, delivered as the Mere Commemoration Sermon in April 2004. While not mentioning Blair explicitly, Williams attacked 'government' for repeatedly not listening, and thus for weakening trust in the political system following the rush to war in Iraq. He reminded Christians that Anglican theologians have never sanctioned compliance with 'unjust law', nor 'uncritical obedience' to government. He went on to note that in extreme cases of governments losing sight of 'truth', mass civil disobedience would be an appropriate response, although his office later insisted that the UK had not yet reached this stage.[69]

Despite their differences, Blair favoured Williams because he wanted someone who would talk about God in 'today's terms'. The transition from Carey to Williams echoed to some extent the changeover in Whitehall from the traditional Butler as Cabinet Secretary to the freethinking, youthful Wilson. Williams, like Blair, accepted homosexuality, abortion, and gender equality. While Carey was an Evangelical, Williams is overtly Anglo-Catholic and thus closer to Blair's distinctly non-evangelical position. Both Blair and Williams are interested in multi-faith dialogue, not from a patronising viewpoint of Christian superiority, but out of a genuine respect for and interest in other equally valid religious traditions. Blair, following Peter Thomson's lead, is more interested in what unites human beings than what divides them. He believes all world religions, correctly followed, lead to the same God and took great pride in supporting a major multi-faith service in Parliament in early 2001 to mark the new millennium. Blair spoke of the need 'to recognise that humanity is one' and that 'religion should remain the bedrock of civilisation'.[70]

He became the first Prime Minister routinely to send goodwill messages to leaders of other faiths during their religious festivals. His interest in Islam long pre-dated 9/11. In a remarkable interview for *Muslim News* in March 2000, he described Islam as 'a deeply reflective, peaceful and very beautiful religious faith and I think it would be hugely helpful if people from other religious faiths knew more about it'.[71] By this time, Blair had already read the Koran three times, most recently on his New Year holiday in Portugal in January 2000. The Muslim community was particularly pleased by Blair appointing the first Muslim life peers, and by the provision of specifically Muslim places of worship in hospitals, both of which happened before the al-Qaeda attacks.[72] Blair took particular pride in Christian Europe coming to the aid of the Muslims in the Kosovo conflict.[73]

Blair's active engagement with other faiths can in part be attributed to the influence of Hans Kung, the radical Swiss Catholic theologian who had fallen out with the Vatican, and whom Blair first met in 1999. Kung's thinking, as well as that of Jonathan Sacks, the Chief Rabbi, on the value of different religious traditions informed an inter-faith speech Blair gave in March 2001 at the launch of the CSM's report 'Faith in Politics'. Blair spoke with feeling about religious unity: 'The concerns of something bigger than the self is at the heart of our religious faith.'[74] Blair was keen for George Carey to attend the launch. Carey responded that, although he was already committed, he hoped Blair would praise the work of vicars, and other religious figures, and the contribution Christianity made to social capital, especially in the face of so much media scorn.[75] Blair took note in the speech, and deliberately singled out the contribution of the clergy and other religious leaders, strongly attacking the culture of cynicism. He also launched a new body to examine government interfaces with faith committees across Britain.

After 9/11 Blair was thus in a uniquely strong position among his fellow Western leaders to speak with authority about Islam. 'Workers of all faiths including Islam were killed in cold blood,' he wrote. 'Nothing in Islam justifies such wholesale slaughter of innocents . . . I know that Islam is a peaceful, tolerant religion.'[76] In his determination to build bridges with the Muslim community, Blair enjoyed probably his most fruitful co-operation with Carey. They had a long phone conversation on Sunday, 30 September 2001, on Christian–Muslim dialogue, when Blair was as surprised to learn about the many networks already in existence as he was by Carey's enthusiasm for genuine exchange with Islam. Together, they convened a meeting for twenty faith leaders on 8 October to discuss common understanding in the light of 9/11. In January 2002, Carey hosted a two-day conference of world religious leaders at Lambeth Palace to try to defuse tensions and build bridges between Christianity and Islam. Blair gave a strong message at the conference about the 'perversion of religious faith' by extremists. To maintain momentum, and to help him keep in touch with faith communities, he appointed Leeds MP John Battle as his 'faith adviser', and in the summer of 2003 he established a working group for representatives of all major faiths to help ensure their different perspectives were considered in future government policies.[77]

So Blair's religious beliefs are ecumenical, multi-faith and anti-fundamentalist but also judgemental. Indeed, it is the very clear division between good and evil that he learned first from Christianity that he sees as the principal uniting force behind all major world faiths. His is an intensely practical faith, not interested in doctrinal disputes, nor in dogma, nor in a world to come, but in this world now.[78] His religious beliefs are closely intertwined with his ethical beliefs, the second of the areas in Blair's d'Ancona interview.

Blair's ethics were given their fullest airing in a lecture he gave in June 2000 to Hans Kung's 'Global Ethics Foundation' at Tubigen University in Germany. Blair had read Kung's two best-known books, *On Being a Christian* and *Does God Exist?*, and responded strongly to Kung's assertion that 'what we need is not just the globalisation of the economy, of technology, and of the media, but also a globalisation of ethics'. The speech was not primarily religious, but rather concerned to set out the ethical thinking behind his government's policies, from globalisation, full employment, world trade, nuclear arms control, good schools, welfare to work, help for businesses and safe streets.[79] These policies, he said, were guided by two pivotal principles: 'belief in community' and belief in 'the equal worth of all'. He acknowledged the clash across the modern world between the traditionalist and modernist outlook, but argued that the resolution could be found in applying the unchanging ethical values of all religious traditions and applying them sensitively to the modern, rapidly changing world. He spent a great deal of time preparing for the speech – far too much for some in Number 10, who viewed it as an indulgent distraction. What he was trying to do was to reconnect, after three years in power, with the principles that had brought him into politics – a quest of which Philip Gould would have approved. He also sought validation. As the Catholic Hugo Young wrote, the speech was also prompted by an even deeper need: 'His personal desire is for the linkage of his life with goals that will pass muster at the last judgement.'[80]

Young saw the speech as 'the gratuitous act of a decently troubled man'. But to others it was a cynical attempt to steal a march off Hague, who had been trying hard to win over the Christian vote. Campbell viewed it with suspicion also. This serious speech, exploring the Prime Minister's thoughts on the ethical underpinning of his government's policies, was thus spun as a call for on-the-spot fines for drunks and louts, to which Blair referred only in one small passage in the middle of the speech.[81] It did the trick. The headlines were all about Blair's tough talk on 'yobs'. The ethics and the agonising were all but ignored in the media.

Blair's ethical beliefs, which cannot fully be separated from his non-doctrinal religious beliefs, can be faulted, not because they are insincere, but because they are fuzzy, and were never fully worked out in policy terms – a leitmotif of his premiership. The speech to the Hans Kung Foundation contains many uplifting thoughts on community at home and internationally, partnership, responsibility, and meeting the challenges of modernisation. But there is a sense of him shoehorning his policies in to fit the principles retrospectively, rather than seeing the former stem seamlessly from the latter. A more fully worked out, ethical-based agenda would have resulted in a more cohesive and coherent Prime Ministership.

The third facet of the interview, the influence of his religion on the evolution of his political thinking, has already been discussed in this chapter and elsewhere in the book, which leads us on to the final topic aired in the d'Ancona interview, the influence of religion on his political actions.

The Influence of God on Blair

Non-believers, i.e., all of Blair's inner team, tend to ascribe little influence to his beliefs. To them, his Christianity is an add-on, an enigma that is neither much discussed nor valued nor comprehended in Number 10. One key aide, with him through all his most difficult decisions, said, 'I simply cannot see any evidence that religion affects what he does. He might rationalise it to himself in those terms, but it doesn't spring from them.'[82] To Graham Dale of the CSM, however, 'His policies are totally influenced by his beliefs. It affects his thinking more than anything.'[83] The contrast in these viewpoints could not be starker. It can be explained in part because those who are irreligious tend to conceptionalise religion-inspired actions in secular terms, while those who *are* religious tend to see its influence as ubiquitous. It can also be explained by the difficulty Blair often encountered in translating his religious impulse into concrete actions.

'He never discusses religion with us,' said a close aide, 'but religion is what gets him through. That and his family.'[84] Where some politicians turn to drink, Blair, who is a light drinker, turns to prayer and religious reading, as well as to his family, who are inextricably bound up in his mind with his faith. As his premiership ground on, these two, family and God, loomed ever larger in his life. A rare glimpse into how his faith and family intertwine came when Euan was arrested drunk in Leicester Square after exams in the summer of 2000. Abandoning his text the next day at a conference for black Church leaders in Brighton, he admitted, in a voice heavy with emotion, how he had derived solace from his faith and from reading Henry Longfellow's poem 'The Village Church' on the night of the arrest. 'It says "For Thine own purpose Thou has sent strife and discouragement". We need the strength when the strife and discouragement is there.'[85] The joy and love he has for his family stems from the same source as the love he tries to project on the world at large.

His religious pronouncements can sometimes sound hopelessly naïve and unworldly, and have been interpreted as cynical, vote-seeking or even unhinged. His two most powerful conference speeches, in 1995 and 2001, both exhibit an almost messianic vision of creating a better world. This is Blair the idealist speaking. 'Let's build a new and young country that can lay aside the old prejudices ... where your child in distress is my child, your parent ill and in pain is my parent, your friend unemployed or homeless is my friend; your neighbour my neighbour.' In the 2001 speech, described in the previous chapter, he extended his impulse beyond Britain to the world at large. He sought good out of the 9/11 experience, whether peace in the Middle East or an active engagement in Africa. His identification with the dispossessed, the wretched and the starving was Blair at his most spiritually inspired. These are not the speeches most politicans would dare, or want, to give.

The 2001 conference speech was widely applauded or mocked, but little understood. Author A. N. Wilson saw it as 'Jennings saves the world', guilty, like Gladstone, of 'the incurable liberal impulse to improve other people'. To military historian John Keegan, he was 'an old-fashioned public schoolboy, ready to do his duty'.[86] Minette Marrin dismissed it as 'irresponsible adolescent waffle' and 'the crudest of neo-imperialist cultural colonialism'.[87] Most cutting of all, Clare Short said, 'He hadn't taken a blind bit of notice in Africa in his first term. But then he made this very powerful speech. He was questing for a legacy. My intuition is that he sits in Chequers, and there's all these books, and there's Gladstone and Disraeli and Churchill and he thinks, "Oh, what about me? What am I going to be known for?"'[88] Self-interest undoubtedly interlaces with Blair's religion. Within moments of John Smith's or David Kelly's death, Blair, while undoubtedly deeply shocked on both occasions, was also calculating how they might affect him.[89] But all successful politicians have strong egotistical centres, and few religious leaders across the world have not been, to some extent, self-interested.

In the end, few radical improvements may have flowed from Blair's subsequent and energetic attempts to improve the lot of Africa, with the New Partnership for Africa's Development (Nepad), launched at the G8 summit in Genoa in July 2001, and other initiatives, including a four-day tour to West Africa in February 2002. Nor may he have made as much impact as he would have liked on bringing peace to the Middle East, nor did his attempts to bring peace to Northern Ireland and Kosovo result in wholly satisfactory solutions. His motive for intervening in these areas was shaped by his religious concern, however inchoate, for human rights and the good of humanity. 'You could always get Blair interested in an African idea if you put it to him in moral terms,' said John Kerr.[90] In Kosovo, he thought it would be 'criminal' to 'allow such genocide to happen right on our doorstep'.[91] On Iraq, he was ready to 'meet his maker' to answer for the decisions he had taken.[92] Blair was not only an idealist, but a pragmatist too, believing that it was better to act, even if the end result was imperfect than not to act at all. One could justifiably criticise Blair's objectives as wrong-headed and unattainable. But one cannot deny he believed profoundly in what he was doing.

Blair has been as much criticised for his religious as his political beliefs. Figures on the right like Ann Widdecombe and Peter Oborne have attacked him for flaunting his faith and failing to stand up for the 'tough' morality they associate with Christianity, an approach completely at odds with Blair's liberal stances on most issues (though not, interestingly, on crime and punishment, where he is authoritarian, not libertarian).[93] Widdecombe, a Catholic convert, was particularly incensed by Blair implying that the values of Christianity and Labour were closely connected.[94] The left meanwhile have attacked him for not doing more to help the poor in Britain and abroad, for not limiting the arms trade and for toadying to the rich and famous. To Geoffrey Wheatcroft, writing in the *Atlantic* in June 2004, the strong morality that Blair evinces 'in principle' sits uneasily with 'a tendency toward notably amoral behaviour in practice ... few Prime Ministers have ever been more sincere in their piety, and few have been capable of greater deviousness or even unscrupulousness'. Frank Field, a devout Christian within the PLP, is one of many Christian Socialists who have been disappointed by Blair's autocratic style of leadership, while his brutal treatment of political opponents including John Major bore little mark of Christian compassion. The reality of power, Blair found, was that one often had to deal with unsavoury people, turn a blind eye and make compromises: to return to the Pontius Pilate analogy Blair made in the 1996 interview, he found he had often to be both principled and expedient.

The clearest riposte to those who see him wholly as shallow, insincere and dictated by focus groups (though at various times all have been in evidence) is to highlight the centrality of religion in his life. In a post-Christian country, there was little incentive for him to espouse his faith. His core political beliefs, notably community and rights and responsibility, are Christian-inspired, while the others, one-member democracy and modernisation, are ethically inspired. His clearest actions came when he was acting from his religious convictions, in Northern Ireland, Kosovo, Afghanistan and Iraq, or from his ethical convictions, as (to some extent) over Clause IV, improving educational opportunities for all children, and his tough stance on crime. His vacillations, over the Euro, realignment of the left and over much of domestic policy, were compounded because he was not being driven by these same convictions. In his 2000 party conference speech, he grappled with the principles that brought him into politics, and which he said led him to seek a second term from the electorate. His 'irreducible core', he told delegates, was his desire to do what was 'morally right'. Journalist Anne Applebaum, who was out of the country from 1997 to 2001, interviewed him on her return and found that he had become more interested over that time in religion and morality, including the notion of 'natural law'.[95]

Blair's religious belief informs his unshakeable confidence that he alone can resolve difficulties, especially in a crisis, even when the highest Christian authorities on earth differ from him. More subtly, he believes that in him alone all differences can be synthesised. When he is decided on a course, contrary arguments, even when strong and clear, are heard but not acted upon. D'Ancona noted in 2001 that, for all the strengths he derived from his religion, he also had 'a grave inability to understand those who disagreed with him'.[96] This tendency was to be most singly felt in late 2002 and early 2003, with vast consequences. He went much further than any national leader would have dared at engaging with his critics, at times in front of cameras. But he was doing it to persuade them he was right, and not to be swayed by them. In this sense at least, his faith narrowed him, and made him less willing to listen, even when palpable good sense was being uttered. His convictions also made it very hard for him to admit that he has ever done anything wrong. In this trait he is similar to Thatcher. But her convictions were intellectually and ideologically rooted, which made her decisive across the waterfront of policy; his convictions were spiritually and emotionally located, and gave him a much more restricted map to the world, strong for foreign but uncertain for domestic choices. Misunderstand his convictions, and one misses the point of Blair completely.

Cherie arrives at the press conference in Westminster to make her 'I am not Superwoman' speech at the height of the 'Cheriegate' crisis in December 2002. Behind her, and apparently walking off in a different direction, is Fiona Millar, her core aide since she entered Number 10, but whose relationship with Cherie was one of the many casualties of the episode.

35

'Cheriegate', 2002

Blair's religion made him peculiarly sensitive to accusations that he, and indeed Cherie, had not told the truth or had acted in less than a fully moral manner. He loathed press intrusiveness, he could not bear it when Cherie in particular was attacked, and he shrank from arguments within Number 10 among those closest to him when these touched on her role or behaviour. In an episode in late 2002, which was of trifling importance compared to the great foreign and domestic issues he was debating at the time, all these *bêtes noires* were rolled into one grim event. Dubbed 'Cheriegate' by the press, it caused him great pain and anguish, and had several unexpected consequences.

Morality and New Labour

Disgust at Tory 'sleaze' in the latter days of John Major united Blair's circle; the media frenzy was encouraged by Millbank's spin machine. The unspoken supposition was that, once in power, New Labour would be different, cleaner, more open, less prey to being corrupted by money or sexual temptation. Blair promised, if elected Prime Minister, to 'restore faith in public life', and, in an echo of his famous 'crime soundbite', to be tough on sleaze and the 'causes of sleaze'. He and Cherie were spotless and devout in their personal lives, Campbell was brutally hard-working and ascetic to a fault, and the integrity of his close team in the Leader of the Opposition's office beyond reproach. With more experience, Blair might have realised that 'issues' would be bound to arise during his premiership, that he could not control the actions of those around him, and that the media, so benign before and for some while after 1997, would turn on him as lividly as it had turned on Major for the last five years of his premiership.

The first time after May 1997 that the public questioned whether Blair's New Labour party was in fact morally superior to the Tories came in the 'Ecclestone Affair' which broke in the autumn of 1997, when the government had been in power just six months. Blair came under suspicion for receiving substantial donations to the Labour Party from Bernie Ecclestone, the Formula 1 entrepreneur, before the election (£1 million in January 1997, followed by the promise of a further donation in the summer and one each year for three years).[1] When Margaret McDonagh, Labour's General Secretary, asked Blair whether to include a general ban on tobacco advertising in the manifesto in October 1996, he insisted that the removal of sponsorship to Formula 1 would jeopardise the continuation of the sport in Britain, at the loss of 50,000 jobs.[2] The manifesto included a general policy to ban advertising, but made an exemption for tobacco sponsorship in sport. A couple of weeks after the election, however, Frank Dobson, the new Health Secretary, announced that the government would shortly legislate to ban 'all forms of tobacco advertising, including sponsorship'.[3] Considering his earlier views, aides expressed surprise that Blair had authorised this announcement.[4] Inevitable confusion now arose over whether Formula 1 would be exempted from a general ban. A furious Ecclestone demanded an audience with the Prime Minister. When Blair met the tycoon in Downing Street on 16 October 1997, he confirmed that motor racing would remain exempt from the overall ban on tobacco advertising and instructed Dobson to make provisions in the proposed legislation.[5]

The possibility of a conflict of interest was first aired in the press in early November 1997. How much money had Ecclestone given? When exactly had Blair met Ecclestone at Number 10? Had Ecclestone 'bought' a change of government policy? The questions could have been smartly dispatched, if Number 10 had responded to them fully once they first began to be asked. But information trickled out over a few days, giving the impression of a cover-up. Martin Bell, the former television journalist who had become the celebrated 'anti-sleaze' MP in the 1997 election, asked pointedly whether Blair agreed that 'the perception of wrong-doing can be as damaging as wrong-doing itself', and 'Have we slain one dragon only to have another take its place with a red rose in its mouth?'[6] Even the loyal *Sun* asked, 'Why did Downing Street deceive us for days?'[7] Number 10 was seen as being in a cold funk. No one in government would respond on the media. *Newsnight* displayed an empty chair in the studio and Jeremy Paxman declared that 'no ministerial bottom' could be found to fit it. The whole episode has been exhaustively written up since, and it is the consequences that interest us here.[8]

Blair found this first reversal of his premiership difficult to handle. He attempted to make good come out of the episode by extending the remit of the Committee on Standards in Public Life under Sir Patrick Neill, originally set up by Major, to include party funding, a field the Tories had resisted being included. But he refused to believe he had done anything wrong, and indeed, apart from the tactical error of not being immediately candid about the donations, he had not. The episode got to him hugely and depressed him; he thought it could even end his premiership, and told one aide 'they'll get me for this'.[9]

To close the issue down, Blair agreed to give his first 'live' interview since the General Election: on Campbell's suggestion, he submitted himself to being cross-examined by John Humphrys on television's *On the Record*, screened on Sunday, 16 November. But he was agitated and did not acquit himself well, even with Humphrys, some thought, not being as forensic as he could be. Blair, on camera, was less than fully frank about the donations and why and when Number 10 had sought advice from Patrick Neill. Number 10 had first tried to deny the story, then obfuscate, and only came out with the truth when the media storm made it impossible for them to do otherwise. Worst of all, Blair failed to comprehend how others saw the events, concentrating instead on his own moral rectitude. He refused to apologise for accepting the original donation, which was returned later, or for the protracted confusion surrounding the whole affair.

His key defence to Humphrys was that he was sure the country realised that he would never do 'anything improper, I never have. I think most people who have dealt with me think I am a pretty straight sort of guy.'[10] In saying this, he was right literally, but wrong overall, because by focusing just on himself, and his own self-image, he was blind to the fact, obvious to most of the rest of the country, that the affair had been an almighty bungle, and that in attempting to conceal the truth, the cover-up became far more serious than any original sin. Blair refused to believe not only that he, but that others close to him, would have behaved dishonestly. Like Harold Macmillan, he showed a touching faith in the integrity of those around him. It was very naïve. Blair's religious belief gave him many strengths: the question was left open after Ecclestone whether his particular religious outlook would grow to encourage a wider picture than whether he thought he had done right or wrong, and to embrace a more subtle understanding of the multi-layered actions of others.

Ecclestone is also important because it showed Number 10, for all its slickness and undoubted high intelligence under New Labour, as dysfunctional when it had conflicting objectives and with heavyweight figures in Blair's inner circle on different sides. Blair had been naïve in raising the expectation that his government would be morally superior to its predecessor: when the first onslaught on its integrity came, he was in a box, as any seasoned counsellor would have forewarned him. Disclose at once, and the media would label him a humbug: try to bluff it out using New Labour's battle-tested rebuttal tactics, and risk an even bigger stink if the truth eventually came out. Blair was already under suspicion from the far left of his own party for his courting of business leaders, such as Gerry Robinson of Granada, as well as those who had previously donated to the Tories, like Alan Sugar. He had earlier distanced himself from Ken Follett because of unfavourable comment. Labour needed to form close links with business to help build a reputation for economic credibility: one of old Labour's greatest failures was its suspicion of business. It also needed its cash. But Blair should have been more cautious not to give any whiff of suspicion that business was buying influence, or receiving special favours from the government. As Frank Dobson put it, 'Number 10 was seduced by the glamour of having these figures to Number 10. If they had thought about it, they would have realised how bad it looked.'[11]

But did Number 10, and Blair in particular, ever fully accept how badly some things played and how differently they looked in the world beyond the gates of Downing Street? The tendency of most political leaders is to become increasingly isolated the more time winds on. Ecclestone was followed by other issues, including 'cronyism' and 'Drapergate', and the Hindujas, discussed elsewhere. The play Blair personally made of his integrity was brave: but it was a ploy full of jeopardy, especially when disillusion grew, and when the press, with the *Daily Mail* in the lead, began its vituperative attack on Blair and Cherie personally.

Had lessons been learned? A test case came up early in the second term. Lakshmi Mittal, an Indian-born businessman, was courted in July 2000 at one of a series of dinner parties, organised by Blair's friend and chief fund-raiser, Michael Levy. In May 2001 Mittal made a donation of £125,000 to Labour funds, and was subsequently invited to a post-election party at Levy's home, at which Blair was also present. This was all routine and above-board schmoozing of a kind that Levy excelled at, and which made him such an effective fund-raiser for Labour: it was indeed the game that political parties had to play to acquire the money that they needed to fight campaigns. Nothing was wrong with any of this. The problem arose, however, when Richard Ralph, Ambassador to Romania, asked Blair to sign a letter to the Romanian Prime Minister supporting Mittal's bid to buy some steelworks in Romania. Although unwise, this was not improper.

Prime Ministers sign large numbers of letters in their name, the drafting and details of which they have to take on trust. When questions were asked, Blair opted for a strong rebuttal which had recently worked well when the government had been accused of being too close to the failed US energy conglomerate, Enron. Number 10 based its defence of Blair's signing the letter on two lines: it was defending British business interests, and it was applying standard procedure which was to accept recommendations for support from British ambassadors. Blair was enraged by these latest assaults on his integrity and was at his most scornful when answering questions in the House on the alleged scandal: 'It was not Watergate, it is Garbagegate. It is the biggest load of garbage since the last load of garbage, which was Enron.' Blair said he 'had not known . . . that Mr Mittal was a party donor'.[12] This was an error. What he should have said was he had not 'remembered' that he had met Mittal (at Levy's party) and that he was a party donor. When the truth came out, Blair was branded a liar. In fact he had been careless checking his facts and over-defensive in his response. He did not deliberately lie.[13] But the label of 'liar' stuck.

Blair blamed the Tories and the media for making much ado about nothing. The row was not going away, however. Andrew Rawnsley thought 'the Mittal affair is worse than the Ecclestone affair'.[14] Matthew d'Ancona, also no knee-jerk Blair critic, agreed that 'the Mittal affair stands as one of the indelible punctuation marks of the Blair years . . . Businessmen like Bernie Ecclestone, the Hinduja brothers and Mr Mittal have run rings round the Prime Minister and made him look ridiculous with embarrassing ease.'[15] It is easy to see what had happened. Blair had just returned from a trip to Africa, a continent he was keen to help more, and his mind was elsewhere. Hearing about this latest attack he had lost his patience with shallow point-scoring, saw red, and in doing so, failed utterly to make allowances for why the affair aroused legitimate public concern or to check his facts first. It revealed two facets of Blair's character: his difficulty in admitting that he has ever done anything wrong himself, in this case hitting out before clarifying his ground; and then trying to bluster his way out rather than accept responsibility. As one official close to him put it, 'The Mittal episode was very, very bad. He will do anything to think that someone else is at fault and not himself. It's too much for him to admit.'[16] It also touched on his awe of money, and those who had made it, which troubled even his closest friends. As he had admitted in an interview disingenuously, he was struck by 'how many friends I was at school and university with [who] ended up so rich'.[17] Neither he nor Cherie were rich, for all their hard work and sacrifices for their country. Both these personality traits were displayed in the episode which exploded later that year.

Cherie in Number 10

Cherie is an unusually able woman, with firm beliefs and principles, who made considerable sacrifices to be the devoted wife and mother she is. She has fulfilled many facets of the hugely complex and undefined role of spouse of the Prime Minister very well. But in the eyes of her detractors, of which there were many, she lost stature as a person and as a lawyer after 1997, compromised her egalitarian principles, and unwisely became involved with a woman of dubious character, culminating in an inevitable dénouement of the unseemly scandal dubbed 'Cheriegate'. That she fell prey to such charges, which contain some truth, says at least as much about the almost inhuman strains of life in Number 10 for any Prime Ministerial partner, especially if they choose not to be docile as Cherie herself. No other Prime Minister's spouse in the twentieth century had built such a high-flying, independent career, which they wanted to continue after entering Number 10, and none had to combine that job with managing a family of three children, still less give birth (at the age of forty-five) to a fourth and then have a miscarriage. And all this while in Downing Street itself, with her husband preoccupied in fighting the biggest and most bitterly contested war that the UK had been involved in since the Suez Crisis. Many have chosen to mock and scorn Cherie: doing so, however, reveals little about her. Most women would have buckled under the conflicting pressures: the fact Cherie fell short at different points, and increasingly so as time wore on, is as much a matter for concern as for condemnation.

Compared to the position of spouse to many leaders of governments abroad, support for the British Prime Minister's spouse has been lamentably lacking. Denis Thatcher's ebullience and maturity (he was one week off sixty-four when he entered Number 10 in May 1979) got him through, but Norma Major was nearly crushed by her lot at first when she followed her husband into Downing Street in November 1990.[18] Cherie, who was aged only forty-two in May 1997, resolved that she would continue with her independent legal career, while not skimping on her role as a mother and wife. To assist her, she employed a paid nanny and also leaned heavily on her ubiquitous mother, Gale, for help with the children. For her own support, she employed Fiona Millar, long-term partner of Campbell, and a reassuringly close friend, as her media and personal adviser. The flat above Number 11 may not have been ideal, but it gave her and the children much more space than the cramped and more institutional perch above Number 10. She looked forward to her new life in Downing Street with some trepidation and no little ignorance, but with huge excitement and expectation.

Cherie made it clear from the outset that she would be a very different figure from Norma Major, who never gave the impression of much enjoying her role. Officials in Number 10 were impressed that Cherie 'was far keener than Mrs Major to take on responsibilities herself, travelling to events and representing the government or the Prime Minister'.[19] She threw herself whole-heartedly into charity work and behind causes in which she believed (as in fact did Norma Major). After her rude wake-up call, when she was snapped by photographers outside their Islington house two days after the 1997 General Election in her nightgown and with untidy hair, she quickly learned how utterly different her new life would be. Fiercely protective of her privacy and her children's, in the early years she worked well with Millar and Campbell to ensure they were shielded from the intrusive media spotlight. It was her decision to keep a low profile with the press: they agreed that Millar would take the blame as the 'hard guy' for insisting that Cherie keep quiet.

Cherie told a fellow barrister that she wanted 'to set a new climate for the spouses of prominent people', and she wanted 'to be a professional in her own right'.[20] For a while after May 1997, she delivered on her promise, and accepted some cases, such as representing the TUC on parental leave, that challenged legislation passed by Blair's government. She was forceful in expressing her own legal opinions too when they conflicted with government policy.[21] She made it very clear to staff in Number 10 that her roles as 'Cherie Booth QC' and the Prime Minister's wife were to be utterly separate, so there could be no conceivable conflict of interest.[22] But after some years, fellow lawyers expressed surprise that she had not fulfilled the pioneering role she set for herself: holding legal consultations within Number 10 aroused unfavourable comment.[23] Her work as a barrister, while boosted by the attraction to some clients of employing the Prime Minister's wife, had not been as regular or committed as some hoped.[24] For a long time, colleagues were prepared to be understanding: her difficulty in functioning as a normal

QC because of security and travel restrictions, and having her cases interrupted by frequent trips abroad, were two of many constraints under which they realised she laboured. But even when allowances were made, some collegues still felt disappointed.[25]

Her lifestyle also produced some bewilderment among even her most fervent supporters. Once the left-wing advocate of equality, and scourge of conspicuous affluence and decadence, Cherie now appeared to become seduced by the glamour of the new world in which she now moved. To find oneself transformed almost overnight into a hugely sought-after person, jetting off first-class to stay with world leaders as their personal guest, and to have celebrities queuing up to meet you, is a huge change to adjust to for anyone. She managed it well earlier on, and was widely praised for the dignified way she managed herself in her role, dubbed by some 'superwoman'.[26]

A transition in Cherie seems to have come about at the time she became pregnant with Leo in the summer of 1999. Now the demands on her built up to almost unbearable proportions and her legal work came under renewed strain. 'After Leo and the miscarriage, she never got back into her stride at Matrix. She lost her clerk and it was never the same again.'[27] Leo's birth in May 2000 brought her great joy, but her new baby also severely constrained her freedom.[28] She was breast-feeding him, and it took a lot of her energy. To help recuperate after Leo's birth, she went to stay in July in the Portuguese home of Cliff Richard: it was while she was there that Euan was arrested in Leicester Square for being drunk, leaving Blair to cope alone with his son.[29] It also raised questions about her willingness to accept hospitality from wealthy benefactors. A new baby always unsettles relationships within even the most normal of families. How much more so when the family was living in the Downing Street goldfish bowl, and the three elder children were all teenagers with their own special needs and demands. Blair's pleasure in Leo's birth was unalloyed. But it also inevitably meant, despite his best efforts, that he gave less attention to his other three children.

Cherie's anxiety about money, which originated in her financially insecure and anxious childhood with her wayward father often away, began to be far more evident once she had ceased to work full-time at the Bar herself. An old friend who had lunch with her in 2000 was taken aback to see how obsessed by her appearance and image she had become, and how her conversation revolved around designer labels, money and photographs of herself in the press.[30] A colleague was equally surprised by a conversation with Cherie, when all she seemed to want to discuss was money and clothes.[31]

The fascination with money seems quite irrational. As Prime Minister, her husband received a good salary (£175,400 p.a. in 2004) with immense earning potential after leaving office, not the least from his memoirs, which would be conservatively worth at least £1 million. She had not been earning as much at the Bar as she had while at Number 10, but she could easily revert to earning a quarter of a million pounds a year and much more when she returned seriously to her work. Their living expenses meanwhile were not excessive at Number 10; they had no high mortgage repayments or school fees to pay, unlike many middle-class couples. The money from the sale of their Islington home was invested in a trust fund, which yielded some interest. Cherie clashed frequently with the Civil Service, who oversaw Number 10, about which expenses should be picked up by the government and which by them. Being Prime Minister's consort, she argued, involved her in many extra costs, not least the substantial outlay on clothing, with a hypocritical press eager to jump on her if she wore outfits of which they did not approve. She was particularly angry when officials said that they should pay for their own holidays rather than accept hospitality from friends, as they were wont to do especially early on.[32] Her husband's job made holidays notoriously difficult, especially with the needs of privacy and, after 9/11, heightened security. Not unreasonably, she did not see why they had to foot the whole bill.

Cherie's conspicuous consumption was never more in evidence than in her ill-starred visit with the children to Australia in April 2003, where she spoke at the Commonwealth Lawyers' Association Conference in Melbourne. Cherie unwisely accepted an invitation from a shopping chain, Globe International, to take free purchases for herself and the children: as the Melbourne *Herald Sun* reported: 'The shopping frenzy saw her walk away with sixty-eight trendy designer clothing items. The free haul is believed to be worth about $5,000.'[33] The British press swooped on her, and Downing Street had to announce she would be paying for the goods herself because of UK rules regarding gifts.

Cherie's difficulties and anxieties were heightened by an increasingly poor relationship with the press. As Philip Stephens noted, once the initial honeymoon was over, 'the Conservative-leaning tabloid press saw criticism of Cherie as a way to undermine her husband . . . Cherie became a frequent target of their invective.'[34] An insider of the *Daily Mail* admitted, 'If you want to have a go at him, having a go at her is a good way of doing it.'[35] Cherie certainly epitomised the kind of person the *Mail* disliked: a working mother, feminist, politically correct and left-wing. Stephen Glover was as venomous in the *Mail* as Richard Littlejohn in the *Sun*, who called her the 'wicked witch'. The ire of the *Mail* intensified in 2000–01 when the paper turned its gaze on to her domestic life, asking whether or not baby Leo had received the controversial MMR vaccine; then they found out she visited beauty parlours.[36] But poor relations with the left-leaning *Mirror* were not so expected. The relationship soured after Piers Morgan, the editor, told Number 10 that he knew Cherie was pregnant with Leo (via the publicist Max Clifford, Number 10 learned)[37] which resulted in Downing Street releasing the story after a rash of calls were made to the Press Office.[38] The *Mirror* believed Cherie never forgave Morgan.[39] Relations sank to a new low after 2000, and Morgan claimed in an interview in July 2002 that 'every time she sits next to one of my bosses, she tries to get me fired'. Morgan accused her of being hypersensitive, manipulative, and helping poison the *Mirror*'s attitude towards the government as a whole.[40]

Cherie blamed the media for the poor relationship she developed with journalists. She thought many in the media were loathsome and purely out to get her, particularly the *Mail*. The media responded by blaming Cherie and the Number 10 press machine for 'wrapping her in cotton wool' and not letting them engage with her, and for then using the media to her advantage when she felt like it. Brick by brick, as so often happened with this government, a wall was built: one side 'angry and bitter', as Falconer put it, at the treatment they received; the other, fired up by being shut out, though often at fault for making up mendacious or half-true stories in their battle for readers, or responding angrily on seeing competitors receiving 'juicy' stories ahead of them. She decided to decline any press requests for interviews altogether, realising that her words could easily be manipulated if she accepted them.[41] When a newspaper tried to publish part of a book by the nanny, Ros Mark, an injunction stopped them dead. The media speculated. Was the blackout of information because Cherie was too left-wing and outspoken? Were there dark secrets?[42] In fact, Mark had signed a confidentiality agreement and the Blairs believed, not unreasonably, that it should be upheld.

There were no dark secrets in Cherie's life. But her relationship with Carole Caplin, and the inept handling of it, made it look as if there were. The relationship – of a brilliant, serious-minded woman with a 'New Age' stylist – has caused widespread puzzlement among the country at large. It need not. Cherie's assured exterior concealed an insecure woman, especially about her appearance and her status. Cherie's success academically and then as a barrister in a man's world had given her a confidence and position she had never known before in life. Then, almost overnight, she ceased to be an independent person. She became the wife of Tony Blair. As she herself had earlier said in an interview (with Fiona Millar), she had begun life as the daughter of someone, was now the wife of someone and would probably end up as the mother of someone.

Cherie needed a new role, and she found it in being a political presence in her own right. Some in Number 10 speculated whether, unconsciously, the death of Diana inspired her to fill a role for a campaigning, charity-minded public woman.[43] In the first term, she became increasingly involved in policy issues that interested her, such as race and gender equality, health and the law, and she would discuss such issues with Cabinet ministers. She sat in on Number 10 seminars and played a leading role on 'third way' discussions in association with her close friend, Hillary Clinton. 'Bit by bit, as the first term wore on, she became increasingly involved not just in representation but in policy work,' said one Number 10 aide, an assertion others dismiss.[44] As the 2001 election approached, she was asked to make her own visits to highlight the government's achievements. In the second term, she continued to run seminars in Downing Street, on topics including culture and transport.[45] Cherie became increasingly outspoken in private, such as her frequent hostile comments about Gordon Brown, whom she described at one lunch as 'the rot at the heart of the government',[46] or to Bush in June 2001 at a private dinner when she condemned US policy on the death penalty.[47] She also became increasingly outspoken in public, saying in June 2002 that young Palestinians 'feel they have got no hope but to blow themselves up'; she attacked John Howard, Prime Minister of Australia, on Australian immigration rules, and declared at the inaugural Longford Lecture in July 2002 that British jails contain many inmates who should not be there.[48] Her fearless views won her detractors but also friends. Mary Riddell asked in the *Observer*, 'Why on earth should not Ms Booth offer her views like any other citizen and justify them?'[49]

Cherie had found her voice. She had also begun to find her body. Cherie had never felt comfortable with her physical appearance: armchair psychologists speculated that the absence of an affirming, loving father for long periods in her formative years played its part. Neither did she, or Blair, have a natural sense of style, as visitors to their various homes have commented. Unlike some husbands, he was happy for her to wear comfortable, unflattering clothes. A close friend said that until she was in her late thirties she never wore make-up. All that had to change. From the moment Blair emerged as a national politician in the early 1990s, scornful and hurtful remarks were made about her frumpy clothes, awkward appearance and inelegant hair.[50] Carole Caplin, whom she had met at an exercise class in a Marylebone gym in 1990, filled a gaping hole in Cherie's life. One of the first successes of her advice was Cherie's appearance at the 1994 party conference – her first as leader's wife.[51] Caplin showed her what to wear, how to carry herself, what to eat and how to exercise.

Under her expert tutelage Cherie blossomed. Much of the transformation of Cherie from the defensive, unsure woman – encountered, for example, in Barbara Amiel's 1992 interview – into a woman of composure, serenity even, was down to Caplin. '[She] transformed Cherie from a rather plain blue-stocking with no sense of style into a strikingly beautiful and fashionably dressed prime ministerial consort,' said one friend.[52] Hitherto, Cherie had relied heavily on her mother, Gale, but Caplin gave her much that was utterly beyond her mother's experience. For a while after the 1997 election Millar tolerated Caplin's presence, recognising the positive effect she was having on Cherie; but others in Number 10 warned about Caplin's past, her attention-seeking, her controlling manner, as well as her high fees.[53] 'For a long time she was happy to be left in the background. But then at some point [Carole] decided she was going to go for it. It could just as easily have been Posh Spice as Cherie Blair. She was going to use someone as her route to fame,' remarked one insider.[54] Observers noted how Cherie began to be influenced by Caplin's conversation, not just about clothes and money, but also encouraging her to be assertive about not having to pay for all her clothes herself. The royal household, she said, had proper dress allowances.[55] The departure of Anji Hunter in late 2001 was another factor making Cherie feel she could at last 'cut loose' and do more what she wanted.[56] Number 10 began to worry about Caplin trying to mould Cherie into becoming a different kind of person: 'It's all about dependency and control with her,' said one. Alarm bells began to ring loudly in Downing Street when Caplin was allowed to invite her personal friends to Chequers for a private party to mark her fortieth birthday in January 2002. Could she be trusted? But the suspicions of Caplin within Downing Street, with Millar now a chief sceptic, perversely only heightened Cherie's bond with her, which deepened in mid-2002 after Cherie miscarried what would have been the Blairs' fifth child. To Caplin's role as adviser was added a solace role, needed all the more with her husband so busy for much of the time abroad following 9/11.[57] Caplin was Cherie's friend, independent of the cocoon with which she was surrounded in Number 10. In the second term, she was either visiting Cherie in Downing Street every day or speaking to her on the phone.[58] The disapproval from the Number 10 machine gave their relationship an added piquancy and meaning.

Cheriegate, December 2002

The stage was set for the Blairs' nastiest episode together in Downing Street. To the Blairs and their supporters, 'Cheriegate' was a set-up operation by a vindictive press, led by the *Mail* titles; to critics in the press, it was conclusive evidence of the Blairs' hypocrisy, mendacity, and unworthiness for their roles. The crisis had three main ingredients: Cherie's fondness and need for Caplin, Blair's love and total indulgence of Cherie, and Cherie's irrational but very deep financial anxiety. The Blairs had wanted to keep their Richmond Terrace house in Islington after May 1997 as a bolt hole for weekends and holidays: neither Cherie nor the children, especially when they became teenagers with their busy social lives, enjoyed their trips to Myrobella in Sedgefield, and Chequers was fairly formal and intimidating for the family. But Special Branch, charged with the Blairs' security, advised that as Richmond Terrace had open spaces behind it, it would be very difficult to make secure without closing off that space and part of the street, making life very difficult for their neighbours.[59] The alternative, renting it out, was rejected because of the fear of it being occupied by some unsuitable tenant: great embarrassment had been caused to Tory Chancellor, Norman Lamont, in the early 1990s when his house had been rented by a 'sex therapist'.[60] The Blairs thus sold Richmond Terrace in July 1997 for £650,000, just before the house-price boom of the late 1990s, which pained Cherie in particular. Myrobella was worth at most £250,000 and they had no other assets in property.

Blair let Cherie live her own life, partly out of respect for her independence and unwillingness to change her into anything she did not want to be; partly because of his workload. Cherie's own life was often chaotic: she ran late and was disorganised, so she was very relieved when Caplin agreed on her behalf in the autumn of 2002 to view two flats in Bristol, where Euan had started at university that term. One flat would be for him over his three years at university, the other Cherie saw purely as an investment for their future. All of this was completely above board and indeed sensible, although Blair himself was under the impression they were only buying one flat.[61] The problem originated when the purchase of the two flats was assisted by Caplin's maverick lover, Peter

Foster, a convicted con man and fraudster whose colourful life had been splashed over the tabloids in the summer of 2002, after Caplin became pregnant by him. A disaster was in the making.

On 1 December 2002, the *Mail on Sunday* broke the story of Foster allegedly 'boasting' to a business contact that Cherie had asked him to negotiate the purchase of the two flats and was in effect her 'financial adviser'. Neither Powell nor Heywood were around that weekend, and Campbell was away from the office with gastric flu. Number 10 were immediately suspicious of the story when they heard about it on the Saturday, given the *Daily Mail* and its Sunday sister title's track record, and the police also warned them that attempts had been made to 'set up' Cherie in a photograph with Foster. Campbell himself knew nothing of the flat purchases. On the Saturday he phoned Blair, who was with Cherie at Chequers, to find out what was going on. After talking with Cherie, Blair rang Campbell back informing him about the flat purchases, adding that Foster had not become her financial adviser, nor had he been involved in the flat purchases.[62] Campbell and the Number 10 Press Office duly constructed a rebuttal to the *Mail on Sunday* story, but fatally, as one senior Number 10 figure later put it, did not 'test their line to destruction'.[63] Most of the press accepted the denial of the *Mail on Sunday* story in good faith, which was amplified when Godric Smith, one of the two official spokesmen in Number 10, said any negotiations on the flats had been carried out purely by Mrs Blair and her lawyer. It looked as if the story would die away. But the *Daily Mail* had procured some e-mail correspondence between Cherie and Foster which purported to show that he had indeed been closely involved in the purchase of the flats, and had managed to lever the price down by some £20,000. At 7 p.m. on 4 December, David Hughes, the *Daily Mail*'s Political Editor, phoned Campbell, who refused to take the call but referred him to Godric Smith. 'I spoke to Godric and said, "Look, I have got some e-mails," and quoted some sentences at him. There was then one of those epic moments of silence and he said, "We'll get back to you." But he didn't get back to me.'[64]

Campbell was now not only very angry; he was utterly fed up with Cherie. He had been struggling to establish a more open and honest relationship with journalists since the 2001 General Election, but following incomplete information from Cherie, his press officers had ended up giving misleading statements to the media. He and Millar's anger at what they saw as Caplin's malign influence on Cherie, and the way she had 'wormed' her way into the organisation, was about to explode into the open.[65] Caplin's presence had already damaged Millar's relationship with Cherie, by taking over her own role as counsellor.[66] A final straw for Millar was when she heard almost certainly apocryphal reports that Cherie had been praying with Caplin's mother, Sylvia, in an attempt to contact the 'spiritual world' and had been engaging in New Age rituals. To Millar and Campbell, ultra-rationalists and atheists both, this was not only drivel but verging on the dangerously unhinged. Sympathetic voices tried to put a positive construction on these practices. To Mary Ann Sieghart, for example, Cherie's interest in these holistic therapies stemmed in part from her Catholic upbringing, which had many similar rituals.[67] Increasingly large numbers were indeed turning in Britain to such practices. But to Number 10, it was beyond comprehension. Caplin, whom Campbell, unlike Millar, had always loathed, was just the kind of disaster-waiting-to-happen from whom they had fought for five years to preserve Cherie. 'What is that bloody woman doing here?' Campbell was frequently heard to utter of Caplin in Number 10.[68] Millar had already decided that she would cease to work for Cherie as her personal press adviser, to concentrate on organising events and visits at Number 10. 'Carole saw a gap because Fiona was no longer with Cherie so much. She rushed in, grabbed the opportunity and squeezed Fiona out,' said one aide.[69]

That Wednesday evening, 4 December, Cherie and Blair had taken the evening off to see the latest David Hare play in the West End. When they returned at 11 p.m. to Downing Street, they were greeted with the news of the alleged e-mails in the hands of the *Mail*. These included one Cherie had sent to Foster, telling him, 'You are a star', and thanking him for helping her negotiate the purchases for £260,000 and £265,000.[70] Blair was horrified and rang Campbell immediately, who advised from his bedside that Cherie log on to her account and look for the e-mails in question. The Blairs retired to their flat where, some time after midnight, they both spoke to Caplin, and Cherie reassured her she would always be her friend.[71] Early the next morning, Campbell and Sally Morgan went through the e-mails with Cherie to confirm that she had indeed sent them to Foster, and the *Mail* story was correct.[72] The realisation suddenly dawned that Cherie had kept the details of the flat purchases entirely from Millar and Campbell: they felt she had treated them as though they were in the same category as the *Daily Mail*.[73] A very tense meeting took place that morning as the truth hit home that Downing Street, on Cherie's word, had misled the press and the public. After the *Daily Mail* splashed the e-mails, Cherie issued an official statement confirming that she had indeed involved Foster in the purchase of both flats, but had paid him no fee, nor did she know anything of his past, and he had never met Blair.[74] This let Godric Smith off the hook, whose integrity had come into question. But the media was incensed that Cherie had been responsible for the Number 10 Press Office lying to them over Foster. Campbell was incensed too. A report appeared in *The Times* on Saturday, 7 December, that 'the trouble is that Cherie does not listen to Alastair or Fiona's advice on media relations at the moment. She is more likely to say "I'd better ask Carole about that".'[75] The Sunday papers were full of similar stories reporting Cherie in a poor light, for misleading everyone in Number 10 over the purchases and the involvement of Foster, and discussing her 'lack of judgement'.

Cherie believed correctly that Campbell had been behind the press briefings, which had distanced him, Millar and the Number 10 Press Office from her and her actions.[76] This was indeed the worst occasion in the premiership of the inner court turning in on itself, and its tensions then being exposed to the public gaze. 'The office collapsed during Cheriegate and Alastair was in the forefront of the collapse,' said an insider.[77] Now it was Cherie's turn to be livid at the briefing against her, turning her fire in particular on Fiona Millar, who strenuously denied talking to the press.[78] Millar believed that Caplin and Foster, aided by their publicist Ian Monk, lay behind a drip-feed of stories which aimed to fracture the relationship between the Blairs and their closest advisers in Downing Street.[79] Blair himself became deeply troubled over the weekend, 7/8 December, when it appeared he might lose Campbell as well as Millar over it.[80] He now turned to Mandelson, who had been out of the country when the story broke and had just flown into Heathrow from New York. After a brief phone conversation early on Sunday morning, he went straight to Downing Street to talk with Blair about the ensuing crisis.[81] He spent much of Sunday and Monday in Number 10 and in the flat trying to offer counsel to Blair and Cherie in an atmosphere that had now become highly tense and emotional.[82] 'Tony was tearing his hair out,' recalled one insider. 'It was a bleak moment in their relationship together.' It went to the heart of their partnership and his confidence in her. Mandelson was the person they chose to open their hearts to, and who in their hour of need helped restore calm. 'That's my job,' he said. 'It's called "Being Peter".'[83]

Matters took an even uglier turn when press reports appeared accusing Cherie of using her position to influence a case pending on Foster's deportation from Britain, an allegation hotly contested by Blair on the Monday: 'At no point did Mrs Blair intervene in the immigration case proceedings. Nor would she.'[84] This latest allegation paradoxically helped bring the warring parties within Number 10 back together again:

on the Tuesday, Downing Street accused the media of a 'deliberate campaign of character assassination' against Cherie.[85]

It was decided that Cherie must make a full statement of apology to try to end the affair once and for all, to put all the facts into the public domain, and for Cherie to be contrite. While Cherie spent that Tuesday afternoon hosting one of her monthly children's tea parties, Campbell, assisted by inputs from Mandelson, Falconer, Millar and Morgan, composed a statement for Cherie to deliver live on television that evening in the Atrium at No. 4 Millbank, where she was scheduled to present child care awards.[86] She barely had time to look at the speech before she delivered it. In a direct reference to how she was described, in her honeymoon days at Number 10, she memorably declared, 'I am not Superwoman.' She admitted to two errors in particular: not being open with the Number 10 Press Office (Campbell insisted on this) which she explained by her desire to protect her son's privacy (her voiced cracked when she mentioned Euan being away from home at Bristol for his first term); she also confessed to an error of judgement in allowing Foster, 'someone I barely knew', to become involved in her family's affairs. The speech put her predicament down to the difficulty of 'juggling a lot of balls in the air' – wife, mother, Prime Ministerial consort, charity worker and barrister (the affair was judged to have had a damaging impact on her client work at the Bar).[87] She left without taking any questions from the assembled crowd of journalists.

'Cheriegate' had become the nation's number one pre-Christmas talking point. Reactions to her speech inevitably varied widely, from those who thought it admirable and honest, to those who thought it nauseating and insincere. Sarah Sands, in the *Daily Telegraph*, reported that 'most people were impressed by her performance, but few thought she was telling the truth about the specific allegations'. Sands thought the only other woman who had possessed the ability to 'overpower argument with emotion' was Diana, 'another mother, another martyr'.[88] It looked for a while as if it had succeeded in its primary objective of putting out the flames. But then another tranche of allegations appeared two days later, initially in the *Scotsman*, alleging that Cherie had asked for and received the defence case against Foster's deportation, which had been faxed to Downing Street.[89] This charge was initially denied, then partly admitted. Blair, at an EU summit in Copenhagen, at the end of a second dreadful week dominated by the episode, urged people to 'move on', saying that everyone had had 'their pound of flesh'.[90] Not all felt they had, however: the saga was eked out by the Tories and by the two *Mail* titles and others into the New Year. Even heavyweight commentators entered the fray. William Rees-Mogg argued in *The Times* that there had been three separate lies ('fibs') over 'Cheriegate'.[91] But, for all the continuing attempts by the press to keep it alive, the steam had effectively gone out of the story until March 2004, when Foster made particularly sordid claims about the relationship between Caplin and the Blairs. In an interview with an Australian newspaper, he alleged that Blair himself relied heavily on Caplin for advice and support.[92] Seen as a desperate attempt to publicise his autobiography, the claims were denied by Caplin and Downing Street as 'pure fantasy'.[93]

The Importance of 'Cheriegate'

'Cheriegate' can be seen as the latest link in a chain of events including Ecclestone and Mittal where the Blairs were caught out by the media and responded by obfuscation until, under the force of media scrutiny, the truth mostly came out. Their stance, while understandable in the face of an invasive press, had the effect of steadily eroding public trust in them. On Cheriegate, some blame certainly rests with Cherie for her failure to read Foster correctly and to be open about her contacts with him over the whole flat purchases affair. Blair too cannot escape blame-free from Ecclestone or Mittal. Both Blair and Cherie can be criticised also for letting theatricality when defending themselves get the better of their judgement.

But these were not hanging offences. To reply to the question their critics in the press posed, 'Are Blair and Cherie corrupt, dishonest and unworthy to be occupants of Number 10?', the answer obviously is 'No'. They are both intelligent and thoughtful people, and as honest as most professional people. The episodes discussed in this chapter are far less important for what they may or may not reveal about moral turpitude in high places, than for other matters.[94] 'Cheriegate' raised questions about the media and ethics, in particular about the *Daily Mail*, self-professed champions of morality and decency. Cherie is a vulnerable woman, unable properly to defend herself, despite the seeming great power of her position. The hounding of Cherie for her appearance, her views and her foibles, caused her considerable pain and did much to explain why she felt the need to seek guidance and reassurance on her appearance from someone who oozed confidence like Caplin. The *Mail*'s obsessive attack included accusing Cherie of publicising her 2002 miscarriage to compete in the sympathy stakes with Gordon Brown, whose own baby daughter Jennifer had recently died. The vendetta made Cherie often miserable and defensive, as presumably they intended.[95] Philip Stephens was one of surprisingly few journalists to ask at the time whether the media's necessary task of questioning the country's leadership had 'become infected with a lethal cocktail of personal venom, laziness and sheer mindlessness'.[96]

The episode made Blair angrier than he had ever been before in his premiership, his aides said, with the press and the way it was treating his wife.[97] 'He lost his cool, raging around Downing Street and acting irrationally in a way that staff had never seen before.'[98] 'The sight of his wife being pilloried for weeks in the press caused miserable stress to Tony Blair,' said Stothard, who believes the experience significantly hardened him to develop the grit required to lead Britain into war against Iraq.[99] The distraction from his heavy overseas and domestic worries in the lead-up to Christmas 2002 was not the least of Blair's reasons for his fury with the whole episode.

Number 10's mistrustful attitude towards most sections of the media had grown steadily since 1997. Such a response was understandable given the way that the media treated them, which was not dissimilar to the way the royals were treated, often with more reason. But the Blairs and their inner team had been to some extent the authors of their treatment. The key figures in New Labour had used and managed the media remorselessly since the mid-1980s. Far too many enemies had been created, who showed no mercy when errors were made, which they magnified beyond all reasonable proportion.

'Cheriegate' reveals very clearly the almost intolerable burden of living and raising a family in Downing Street. True, the Blairs, with Cherie every bit as firm as him, knowingly wanted the party leadership in 1994. They were concerned about the effect on their children and their family life, but any anxieties were very hazy, and were trumped utterly by the prospect of the prize within their reach. Their naïve questions during 1994–97 about what domestic life would be like in Downing Street, and their ignorance of how security would constrain them, showed how little they had thought about how their lives would have to change. The children's lives have been enhanced in some ways by their father being first Labour leader, then Prime Minister, but the constraints and negatives of their lives have been much more real and significant.[100] The Blairs have fought fiercely to put their children's interests first, seen initially in their controversial decision to choose the London Oratory school. All the children – Leo less so – will have been affected profoundly for the rest of their lives by the experience of being brought up in Downing Street. Despite all that their parents have tried to do, it is hard to see that the experience will have enhanced their chances of happiness later in their lives. The record of children of Prime Ministers is not an encouraging precedent – and most were fortunate enough to have already fled the nest before the premiership began.

Blair found it easier to adjust to Number 10 life than Cherie, though he has had some very bleak moments since 1997. Cherie's insecurities have been displayed for all to see. Unfortunately for her, perhaps, her vulnerability is not of the kind that immediately draws people in to her. Her loyalty to Caplin was affirmed partly by the guilt she felt about Caplin's own miscarriage, which occurred after the episode.[101] 'She knew how dreadful it felt. She blamed herself for Caplin's lost baby; and that guilt also made her more determined not to drop Caplin,' said one friend.[102] This fact helps explain why she refused to drop her after 'Cheriegate', as Campbell, Millar and many others advised, not the least after she accepted a lucrative contract as a columnist on the *Mail on Sunday*, the very paper that had caused the hares to run. She refused to drop her after a BBC television film *The Conman, His Lover and the Prime Minister's Wife*, in which some in Number 10 thought Caplin (and Foster) had taken advantage of Cherie.[103] She would not stop seeing her after Caplin sold her story to *Hello!* magazine, with full-page photographs of her talking about her life as Cherie's 'lifestyle guru'. Her obstinacy and fidelity to this 'problem woman' left many in Number 10 shaking their heads in disbelief, and many members of the public completely confused. Most baffling of all to many, in the summer of 2003, Cherie did not stop a photographer from *Marie Claire* magazine, against Millar's advice, taking a photograph of her defiantly having lipstick applied to her lips by Caplin sitting on the very bed she shares in Downing Street with her husband.[104] Cherie would not stop because she continued to need Caplin, and was not prepared to give up her close relationship and guidance from her – regardless of who told her it was unwise, undignified and dangerous. The only person who could have persuaded her to part with Caplin was her husband. And he refused to do so.

Blair also refused to listen to Campbell when he suggested that Cherie, following the Foster allegations, should keep a low public profile, so Blair could be 'protected' from further problems that might arise.[105] Millar eventually left Number 10 in 2003; a move she had long planned for personal reasons, having battled for too many years to protect Cherie from the media, and unable and unwilling any longer to control Cherie.[106] Campbell also made his long delayed departure the same year for personal reasons: although the Cherie–Caplin relationship was not a factor in his departure, it had certainly soured his final months in Number 10. The two couples had been very close for many years, and especially since Campbell joined Blair in 1994. Stothard said of them in March 2003 that 'the four are like friends who have been on holiday together too long'.[107] Although the men recovered their friendship, the women yet have not. Campbell was not alone in regretting the irreparable damage 'Cheriegate' did to their 'family' relationship.[108]

The wonder of 'Cheriegate' was not how much damage, but how little damage, was done. A known con man had been allowed to get quite extraordinarily close to the Blairs, and at a time when they both had their guard down: Blair preoccupied with the build-up to war, Cherie vulnerable because of her miscarriage. With the media prepared to pump Foster for all possible titbits, havoc could have resulted if the story had not broken when it did, and he had been allowed to worm his way deeper.

What the episode revealed most fully was Blair's utter devotion to Cherie. 'His total instinct during it was to protect her. He realised during it how totally devoted he was to her,' said one close aide.[109] It occurred to him how much he had neglected her during the fifteen months since 9/11, and how self-absorbed he had let himself become.[110] The episode, and Cherie's helplessness at the hands of the media, reawakened his profoundest protective instincts. He was also reminded how much he needed her, and how much she gave him. When they are together, they still touch and look at each other constantly. One close friend said 'they are as much in love, and their relationship is as fresh, as the day they met'.[111] If it took 'Cheriegate' to remind him of their love, then the excoriating experiences for them both served their purpose, because Blair was going to need to draw on his relationship with his wife as never before in the hard year shortly to begin.

Charles Falconer, Blair's lifelong friend and soulmate, who offered himself up as lightning conductor for Blair over the Millennium Dome, one of the most hubristic manifestations of New Labour.

36

Charles Falconer

One of the people Blair and Cherie instinctively turned to at the height of the Cheriegate trauma to help draft her tortured 'confession' address was Charlie Falconer, Blair's longest-lasting male friend in politics, and close family friend of Cherie. Unlike many around them, he and Blair have both travelled 'lightly' through life. They are both very ambitious, which they disguised; less self-confident than they appeared, and did not weigh themselves down with hurts and animosities. Their status as 'outsiders' has helped bind them together: like Blair, Falconer was never entirely absorbed by his life either at the Bar or in politics. Neither were tribal Labour supporters, or indeed ideological people at all. It is not difficult to understand why it was Falconer to whom Blair turned in 2003 to fill the shoes of Derry Irvine.

Falconer and Blair, 1976–97

Falconer was born in November 1951 into a comfortable middle-class family. One of four children, his father was a Scottish lawyer, like Blair's, and like Leo Blair also, a Conservative. He attended Glenalmond, a Scottish boarding school not dissimilar to Fettes. Like Blair, he was not party political at school, but was impressed by John Smith, who lived two doors away from the family home in Edinburgh. Falconer was shown around the Commons by Smith in 1970, shortly after his election to the House.[1]

Falconer first met Blair in the same year, when they tussled over the affections of Amanda Mackenzie-Stuart, a contest won by Falconer, apparently amicably. Falconer went to Queen's College, Cambridge to read history and law, and kept periodically in touch with Blair at Oxford. Their choice of the Bar led them both to Crown Office Row in the Inner Temple, albeit to different chambers, where they renewed their acquaintance after bumping into each other on a staircase in 1976. Blair, deep into establishing himself in his new profession, was delighted to make contact again with this most convivial of friends.

In September 1979, Falconer invited Blair to become a tenant in the house he had bought in Wandsworth in south London. Blair enjoyed his new housemates' company, and their common interest in the Labour Party.[2] Another shared passion was rock music: Falconer himself can still recall the names of the B-sides of almost every hit single in the 1960s and early 1970s. Blair, at the time, was the more serious of the two, often up at dawn to work on his legal briefs.[3]

Their careers diverged after Blair moved out to live in north London and then married Cherie in 1980. While Blair became preoccupied with finding a career in Parliament, Falconer began to focus seriously on the Bar, building an impressive career first as an employment lawyer (an interest he shared with Blair) then as a commercial lawyer, becoming a QC in 1991. He became renowned for his sharp legal mind, and if not quite in the same class as Irvine, he compensated by his genial and persuasive manner in court. Unlike Irvine, however, he was on the same level as Blair, more like a brother than a dominating father-figure.

In 1985, Falconer married Marianna Hildyard, a diplomat's daughter, described as a 'pre-Raphaelite beauty'.[4] Also a barrister, she formed a close bond with Cherie, and the four regularly went on holiday together to Spain and elsewhere. Nicky was born at the same time as the Falconers' first child, and Kathryn at the same time as the Falconers' second. With the Falconers also living in Islington, they were frequently in and out of each other's homes, talking about politics, the law, and children. Typically, Blair would go up to Sedgefield alone on Friday evening and return by train on Saturday afternoon to join Cherie and the children. They would then spend the rest of the afternoon and evening as families together. Sunday lunches were often also spent in each other's homes.[5] The two families were the ideal match for each other.

Blair was keen for Falconer to follow his path and become an MP as well – he represented just the kind of independent-minded professional he thought the party needed. Falconer had done occasional pieces of work for the Labour Party, but after Wandsworth had not been active in Labour politics in the 1980s and early 1990s, nor notably sympathetic to it. Quite the opposite: he had taken on several cases which were considered hostile to the left, including acting for the National Coal Board against Scargill's National Union of Mineworkers. This encouraged rather than deterred Blair. The Falconers' Islington home became a venue for campaign meetings during Blair's leadership bid in mid-1994, and Falconer himself raised £40,000 for the party by hosting an auction at the River Café in west London shortly before the election.[6] He offered Blair periodic advice during his period as Leader of the Opposition, including 'killer arguments' for use against the Tory government on the publication of the Scott Inquiry into arms for Iraq.[7]

Blair's election as leader considerably heightened his desire to have Falconer in the House, not least to fill one of the posts of government law officer. Falconer's annual salary of some £500,000 would be drastically cut, but he nevertheless became increasingly attracted by the prospect. 'Charlie is far more ambitious than people give him credit for. He always wanted to become an MP and enter the Cabinet,' said one insider.[8] Shortly before the 1997 election, the veteran Labour MP, John Gilbert, was persuaded to stand down from his seat in Dudley West and take a peerage. The way seemed paved for Falconer's smooth passage into Parliament. First he had to go before the NEC panel that screened election candidates. Ian McCartney, the future party chairman, asked him if he would be willing to move his children out of private education when the expected improvements were made to state education and whether he would move to the constituency.[9] Falconer said, with commendable honesty, that he could not guarantee doing so. The panel were impressed by his candour but by little else. He failed to get on the shortlist.[10] 'I completely mucked it up,' he later said.[11] 'Plain arrogance on his part,' was another verdict.[12] Though he accepted he would have been of much greater use to Blair in the Commons, he nevertheless accepted a peerage in May 1997 to enter the government via the House of Lords as Lord Falconer of Thoroton, becoming Solicitor General, the junior of the two law officers. Some speculated that Blair had promised Falconer the prospect of becoming Irvine's eventual successor as Lord Chancellor: fellow lawyers cannot imagine why else Falconer would have been prepared to give up his legal career at the very moment his earning potential was reaching a high point.[13]

Life as a Minister, 1997–2003

Falconer had to tread carefully at first when he entered the government because some Labour back-benchers regarded him as a wealthy 'public-school educated barrister with a taste for the high life'.[14] 'Isn't he a Tory?'

some asked. Accusations were also made that he had secured his ministerial job not on merit but because he was a 'crony'. In the light of this predictable reaction, Solicitor General was thus a prudent first post, because it was relatively out of the limelight, yet it gave him the chance to impress sceptics with his quick mind and ability to get jobs done. From there his ascent was rapid. In his first reshuffle in July 1998, Blair moved him to the job that the promoted Mandelson vacated at the Cabinet Office, Minister Without Portfolio – one close friend and ally replacing another. Falconer was nominally deputy to an old Labour hand, Jack Cunningham, the Cabinet 'enforcer', but he rapidly proved himself a far more adept operator. 'Falconer resolves the policy problems, devours the paperwork, picks holes in arguments, synthesises conflicts,' wrote Michael White in the *Guardian*.[15] As well as attending the Monday morning planning meeting in Number 10, and being placed on fourteen Cabinet committees, he in effect took on the role of being Blair's 'eyes and ears' in Whitehall, which Mandelson had undertaken in 1997–98.[16]

His jovial, self-disparaging manner and shambolic appearance endeared him rapidly across the board. 'He is great at shrugging things off. He would come out of a meeting and say to a colleague, "Well, that was bloody awful, wasn't it? Anyway, let's have a drink." His ability to laugh things off and to move on despite setbacks is one of the things that Blair likes about Charlie,' said one aide.[17] It was a positive strength too to Blair that he belonged to no faction or wing of the party.

When Mandelson came under scrutiny in December 1998 for not declaring his loan from Geoffrey Robinson, Blair asked Falconer, who already knew about it, to be one of his chief inquisitors in his quest for the truth.[18] He then gave Falconer the poisoned chalice of overseeing the Millennium Dome in Greenwich. The project was largely doomed by the time Falconer took it over, with just twelve months until Millennium night itself. 'I didn't make it any better,' he said, continuing less plausibly, 'but it did allow me to experience pain, which put me more on level terms with colleagues who had spent eighteen years of pain in Opposition.'[19] Falconer might not have made the Dome a commercial and public relations success, but the stoical way he bore himself throughout the inevitable witch-hunt when the Dome failed won him admirers. Given that his experience as a barrister had no more equipped him to run anything than it had Blair, one could question the wisdom of the appointment. Falconer openly admitted to Andrew Rawnsley that his only experience of the entertainment industry had been twenty-five years before, as a member of the Cambridge College summer ball committee.[20] The media and the Opposition gave him a hard time, and many bayed for his head, rising to a crescendo in late

2000. The Dome was indelibly associated with Blair's (and Mandelson's) name, and became to many a symbol of New Labour's hubris and lack of substance, which ended up costing the taxpayer millions of pounds. Falconer became the lightning conductor for Blair: had he resigned, Blair might himself have become vulnerable.[21] Falconer stayed put and toughed it out. Blair's estimation of his old friend went up several notches further.[22]

During the 2001 General Election, Falconer's role as a trusted inner-circle adviser continued, counselling Blair, for example, on the legal status of Prescott's famed punch.[23] Silent as the night, without anyone noticing, he was taking over from Irvine as Blair's favoured oracle when he wanted a legal judgement. In the post-election reshuffle in June 2001, Falconer was moved to Housing and Planning Minister, although he retained responsibility for the Dome until its sale in 2002. Trumpeted by many as a demotion after the Dome fiasco, the move was in fact a carefully crafted tactic by Blair to give Falconer shelter to recover ground before moving him on to higher office. He also wanted the politically sensitive issue of the housing shortage in one of the government's safest pairs of hands.[24] Falconer was phlegmatic: 'It was my first proper job where I was purely a politician rather than lawyer,' he said.[25] 'Tony always wanted to promote him, but was biding his time after the Dome débâcle,' confirmed one insider.[26]

The expected preferment came in June 2002, when he was appointed Minister for Criminal Justice, a post under Blunkett in the Home Office. He was Blair's choice but Blunkett was only too happy to accept him. This was a major job in a mainstream department, and Blair needed someone more adept than the former whip Falconer replaced. The brief he was given from Number 10 was to smooth fraught relations between the Home Secretary and the legal profession, which were being ruffled by the government's major shake-up of the criminal justice system, and which was threatening to derail the whole process.[27] After years of rising statistics, and high-profile cases such as the murder in November 2000 of the child Damilola Taylor on a south London housing estate, Blair and Blunkett were determined to be tough on crime and criminals, and gentler on victims and witnesses. 'Number 10 felt that Falconer had the kudos within the profession to provide reassurance as well as an understanding of what had to be done,' said one aide.[28] The Criminal Justice Bill was their main task together, which was described when enacted in 2003 as the 'flagship' of Blair's second term. 'Falconer and Blunkett complemented each other on this work: they are both players; they are both operators,' said one official.[29]

Falconer busied himself on a wide variety of initiatives in his year in the job, including measures to deal with 'neighbours from hell', parents of persistent young offenders, gun crime, abusers of spray paint and anti-social behaviour in general. When Blunkett fell out with the judiciary over tougher sentencing, Falconer defended him against his former profession: 'It is right that Parliament should set the framework', he said.[30] Figures from the British Crime Survey began to show many indicators of crime were declining, but *fear* of crime was not falling commensurately. Blair was continuing to hear from his own constituents in Sedgefield, and across the country, that the electorate still did not think enough was being done to reduce crime. The judiciary loomed in Blair's mind as increasing the obstacles: it was too resistant to change, too lulled into traditional ways of thinking and too much on the side of the rights of the criminal suspect, and indeed judges. Blair was being pushed to take on the judiciary by Adonis and Heywood from within Number 10. 'There were massive battles between Blunkett and Falconer on the one side and Irvine and Peter Goldsmith, the Attorney General, on the other,' remarked one insider. Issues in contention included disclosure of previous convictions in trials and changing the rule on double jeopardy.[31] 'Irvine and Blunkett would fight it out for a week in letters and phone calls and then go to Number 10 to get it sorted out. It was really grinding Tony down.'[32]

Something had to give in the clash between two very different visions. Blair's growing disenchantment with Irvine is chronicled in Chapter 16. A particular irritation was the reaction to Blair's plan to move the administrative courts to the Home Office. A judicial revolt ensued, whipped up by Irvine, with top judges like Lords Woolf and Bingham arguing that the judiciary would be outraged if the plan went ahead.[33] Blair pulled back, but was not impressed by Irvine's lobbying of fellow judges to obstruct his wishes. Before long, Blair's exasperation eventually reached the point where he decided Irvine had to go.

A Messy Reshuffle, June 2003

Who should replace him? Lord Williams of Mostyn was considered a strong possibility. Late in the day, Peter Goldsmith, the Attorney General, loomed up as a stray candidate, whose skills in handling the Charter on Human Rights in Brussels earned him admirers in Number 10 and outside. But Goldsmith's claims were trumped by Falconer, whose debating, diplomatic and political skills, and sworn loyalty, were judged more valuable by Blair. At one blow Blair would replace an increasingly awkward and obstructive colleague by one loyal and supportive. It suddenly seemed a blindingly obvious course.[34] 'Blair thought that Falconer was capable of moving at a much quicker pace than Irvine, and he knew that Charlie was on the same wavelength when it came to legal and constitutional reform,' said one aide succinctly.[35]

The delicacy of these proposed changes meant that Blair kept information about it to a very tight circle in Number 10. But, encouraged by aides in Number 10, notably Adonis and Heywood, Blair also envisaged a whole raft of constitutional changes being announced in a major mid-term reshuffle. Cabinet was not involved, nor was a Cabinet committee or other mechanism established to work out the full ramifications of the ground-breaking changes at the heart of the government that Blair proposed. The decision to keep the changes 'in house', and the lack of prior consultation and discussion, were just two reasons which explain why the reshuffle on Thursday, 12 June, was the most muddled not just of Blair's premiership, but arguably for many years. A bewildering kaleidoscope of pressures and half-worked-out plans converged in one week on a Prime Minister whose energy and long-term planning had been another casualty of the Iraq war.[36] Consideration had been given to creating a Minister of Europe in the Cabinet, which was abandoned in the face of opposition from Straw, and creating a 'Ministry of Justice', hiving off responsibility for criminal justice from the Home Office.

Views within Number 10 had been expressed for several years about the desirability of abolishing the posts of Secretaries of State for Scotland and Wales in the light of devolution since 1997. A solution to this issue was to have been part of the reshuffle, but the detailed consideration of the loss of these traditional posts had not taken place; nor had all the details of the plan to abolish the post of Lord Chancellor and redistribute some of his functions. The reshuffle had further been earmarked as Blair's opportunity to clean out middle-ranking ministers and bring in fresh blood to show the government had fresh energy and purpose. A finely poised reshuffle was finally blown to pieces when, just days before it, Blair learned that Alan Milburn wanted to resign as Health Secretary for family reasons: having already lost two Blairites, Byers and Estelle Morris, since the General Election, this was a bitter blow. Blair tried to persuade him to stay on, but failed, which left him having to find a Health Secretary, a key post in the government's delivery priorities, with no notice. John Reid seemed the most suitable candidate, but his appointment raised the question, hotly debated in Number 10, about whether a Scotsman could take over as English Health Secretary. The issue was left unresolved until the day of the reshuffle.[37]

As the reshuffle approached intense frustration simmered below the surface in Number 10, much of it focusing on Blair's characteristic reluctance to make up his mind until the last moment. He was not helped by his schedule for the five days before the reshuffle being unusually full. Blair flew back from seeing Chirac in Paris on the morning of Thursday, 12 June, to chair Cabinet, which discussed Iraq and the EU, with Irvine and Milburn attending their last meeting, but with key decisions about their successors still not finalised.[38]

Blair held Irvine back after the meeting and told him he would be leaving the government. One observer described this as 'one of the hardest things he ever had to do', and his resolve had to be stiffened at the eleventh hour by Number 10 aides to thwart a rearguard plan to allow Irvine to stay on.[39] Milburn's resignation was announced by Number 10 at the same time on Thursday morning to a stunned Whitehall and media.[40] Number 10 officials saw their long-mooted constitutional changes imploding before their eyes. 'Milburn's resignation became the story, rather than just a part of an imaginative, all-encompassing reshuffle. For six hours, until the announcement at 5.45 p.m., the media speculated about why a leading Blairite had resigned. The initiative and opportunity to explain was totally lost.'[41] While serious commentators saw the underlying wisdom and necessity for the changes, they were drowned out by those who saw the holes in the new constitutional proposals, and by those obsessed by the personality issues in the reshuffle. So what had gone wrong? This was an occasion when the government badly needed to 'spin' but it was unable to do so. Instead of being able to concentrate after Cabinet on the reshuffle and confirming Milburn's successor, Blair lost two valuable hours having to host a long-standing lunch for BBC executives in Number 10. His absence would have been judged bad manners, and likely to convey the impression of a government even more out of control than it was. Only at 2.30 p.m. could he call in Reid to persuade him to accept the job of Health Secretary: Reid, who had only been Leader of the Commons for ten weeks since Cook's resignation, and who had held three separate jobs within the last year, reluctantly agreed at 3.00 p.m.[42] 'It was amazing that they hadn't learned the lessons of 2001, which was a disaster when one minister dug his heels in at the last minute,' said one aide. 'It took just one person in 2003, Milburn, to make it all go wrong again: it really should have been foreseen.'[43]

Campbell, Powell, Heywood, Morgan and Chief Whip Hilary Armstrong discussed the reshuffle intently that afternoon under a June sun on the terrace at Number 10.[44] They already knew they were losing control, and that they had neither the time, nor even the full information to brief the press properly at 5.45 p.m. in time for the six o'clock television news. They hoped to build their case on the argument that because legislation would be required to institute many of the changes, consultation and discussions would follow rather than precede the announcements.[45] But the future responsibility for Scotland and Wales was left unclear, as was the precise future of the Lord Chancellor. The official announcement suggested the post would be abolished; but legislation would be required before this could occur. Gordon Brown was not pleased that his ally Nick Brown was dismissed, and Yvette Cooper, wife of Ed Balls, still did not receive her expected promotion.[46] The Chancellor was indeed left out of the loop on all these major changes, which never augured well for the way Number 10's announcements were received. As the changes intimately affected Scotland, his patch, the oversight was a particularly acute tactical error. The pleasure in the Chancellor's camp at the way the Euro issue had been settled finally earlier in the week, and at the departure of Milburn, who had taken over from Blunkett as the principal anti-Brown candidate in Cabinet, was swallowed by their anger and suspicion at Blair's covert decision-making.

Rarely can any Cabinet career have been born in such turmoil. It was announced Falconer would become Secretary of State for Constitutional Affairs, and would have 'responsibility' for Scotland and Wales. But then Downing Street said later that evening that there would still be Secretaries of State for Scotland and Wales, and they would be 'attached' to two different Cabinet ministers. The next day, Falconer, in the full glare of publicity, was summoned to the House of Lords to enable it to sit. The media were in clover, portraying the reshuffle as the 'biggest cock-up in history', and the Tories, sensing they had the government on the run, enjoyed one of their rare days in the sun: Lord Onslow, a Tory peer, accused the government of playing 'Pooh sticks' with the British constitution.[47]

It was a mark of Falconer's skill that out of the confusion he restored equilibrium, helping the new Department for Constitutional Affairs to find its feet after an unpromising start. He piloted the Constitutional Reform Bill through Parliament in 2004, but faced with considerable opposition from the legal establishment (including a withering attack from Lord Woolf, the Lord Chief Justice, who described Falconer as a 'cheerful chappie') as well as from Opposition peers, the Bill was obstructed and delayed.[48] Plans to remove the remaining ninety-two hereditary peers from the Lords were also shelved, partly because of criticism that Blair would fail to honour his agreement with Lord Cranborne in 1999.[49] As room for manoeuvre in the parliamentary timetable began to slip, and despite Falconer's best efforts to steer his master's constitutional programme out of troubled waters, reform would have to wait until after a General Election.

The Impact of Charles Falconer

Apart from stabilising a very unsteady ship of state, one of Falconer's earliest services to Blair in his new capacity was to suggest Lord Hutton to chair the judicial inquiry into the death of Dr David Kelly, the arms expert, in July.[50] Falconer maintained a steadying and calming presence by Blair's side in the difficult months during and after the Hutton Inquiry. To Blair he was a beacon of common sense and rationality.

The relationship between Falconer and Blair may not have been as formative or intense as many described in this book. But their relationship was never about intensity. Falconer did not forge his method of working, like Irvine or Campbell, nor influence his thinking, like Thomson or Gould. Blair had more than enough of such advice. What he needed, more so as time went on, was some utterly reliable presence, who did not throw tantrums or get into scrapes, and whom he could trust continually and implicitly. Blair's continuing loyalty to old friends from school, like Ryden, or university, like Palley, despite his powerful station in life, is one of his most striking human qualities, and it was amply reciprocated by those friends. As with the Clintons, and other friends like Campbell and Millar, Haworth and Rae and Cox and Kay, it was significant that the relationship was a foursome, involving Cherie and Marianna Falconer also. Blair had 'friends' in Cabinet, like Brown (on and off), Prescott, Blunkett and Straw, but they were nowhere near as constant nor as close personally as Falconer.

Blair would have been virtually the same person if he had never met Falconer. The ultimate importance of Falconer to understanding Blair is that he offers a mirror image of him. That is why they are so comfortable together. Falconer is more like Blair than any other figure highlighted in this book. The differences — Blair is more driven, Falconer intellectually sharper — are slight. Understanding Falconer takes us a long way towards understanding Blair.

Tony Blair giving one of the speeches of his life in the House of Commons on 18 March 2003, arguing that Britain should commit itself to war in Iraq. To his left, Clare Short makes clear her displeasure.

37

Iraq, 2003

The single issue that will most affect judgements about Tony Blair and his premiership is the war against Iraq in early 2003. It will not dominate it totally, as the Suez episode did the brief premiership of Anthony Eden (1955–57), because there is so much more to the Blair premiership, but it will be judged a far more defining episode than the Falklands War in 1982 was for Mrs Thatcher. Why did Blair take Britain to war? Why did he follow the Americans so completely, rather than standing back as many of Britain's European partners did? What difference did he make to the pre-war diplomacy, to the prosecution of the war and to post-war policy? Many books will be written on these events, which will go into every detail: the challenge for this chapter, however, is to explain Blair's decisions within the context of his life.

Regime Change in Iraq from Clinton to Bush

Regime change in Iraq had been official US policy since the Clinton administration. This was laid out explicitly in a White House statement of December 1999 that committed the US government to maintaining 'vigilance against Iraq and working to bring about a change in regime'.[1] Operation Desert Fox in 1998 showed American military intent. It will always be a matter for speculation how far Clinton would have pressed regime change in Iraq, and actions against al-Qaeda, had it not been for the distraction of the Lewinsky scandal. Blair rued the limitations that had been imposed on Clinton's second term and regarded it as a cautionary tale for the distraction and torpor he had to avoid in his.[2]

George W. Bush's arrival at the White House in January 2001 brought new resolve to the decade-old struggle with Saddam Hussein. During the 2000 campaign, Bush was surrounded by a group of Pentagon-trained, pro-military, foreign policy advisers, many of whom went straight into high-ranking positions in the new administration.[3] They included Vice-President Dick Cheney, Defense Secretary Donald Rumsfeld, his deputy Paul Wolfowitz, Secretary of State Colin Powell, his deputy Rich Armitage and the National Security Advisor, Condoleezza Rice. The 'Vulcans' were drawn together by their core conviction that 'American power and ideals are, on the whole, a force for good in the world'.[4] From this assumption, they helped Bush to foster a 'revolution' in American thinking about its world role.[5] Two conclusions were central: American security demanded that it act unilaterally, shedding traditional constraints imposed by allies or international bodies; and American power should be used actively to seek out its enemies before they could attack the US. Given the evolution of this doctrine, a tough American stance against Iraq was inevitable from the moment Bush was declared President.[6] Many of the Vulcans had served in George Bush Senior's presidential team during the first Gulf War in 1991, and had supported his decision not to pursue Saddam inside Iraq's borders. Since then, however, an important subset within the Vulcans had come to believe that a grave error had been made in not 'finishing Saddam off' when they had the chance. Bush may have begun his presidential quest an innocent in foreign affairs, but he quickly learned and absorbed many ideas propagated by the Vulcans: the decisions taken before and during the Iraq War were fundamentally his own.[7]

Paul O'Neill, Bush's first Treasury Secretary, has claimed that from the outset Bush was seeking a way of replacing Saddam.[8] However, before 9/11, there is no evidence that the administration sought to develop a plan for an all-out invasion of Iraq. Outdated attack proposals certainly existed deep in the Pentagon, but only alongside sixty-seven other longstanding plans for wars or contingencies across the globe. There had been some low-level rumblings about what Colin Powell called the 'suppose-we-ever-have-to-do-this' option, not least from Iraqi exiles, but no plan was ever discussed at meetings of Bush's top officials, let alone with the President himself.[9] That said, Bush had asked for the Department of Defense to develop a 'more robust option' that would 'put some serious weapons on Iraq', in the event of a US pilot being shot down during the routine enforcement of the no-fly zones.[10] In August 2001, Rice confirmed publicly that the administration was growing increasingly frustrated with 'tit-for-tat' responses to Iraqi attacks on US and UK planes and hinted that a more forceful response was under consideration: 'Saddam Hussein is on the radar screen for this administration,' she declared.[11] At this stage Britain's dialogue with Washington never mentioned the possibility of an invasion. Instead, according to British Ambassador Christopher Meyer, 'The focus was on how to tighten a crumbling sanctions regime and make the "oil for food" programme work better.'[12]

Whether or not America would have invaded Iraq without the events of 9/11 remains an open question. What is clear is that 9/11 greatly accelerated the administration's thinking. As early as 12 September, Rumsfeld suggested to his White House colleagues that 9/11 could present an 'opportunity' to attack Iraq.[13] According to the counter-terrorism expert Richard Clarke, Rumsfeld argued that as there were no decent targets in Afghanistan, serious consideration should be given to attacking Iraq, because it had better targets.[14] Clarke has also recounted an exchange with the President that evening in which he was asked to look again at the possibility that Iraq was involved in the 9/11 attacks: 'He never said "make it up", but the entire conversation left me in no doubt that George Bush wanted me to come back with a report that said Iraq did this.'[15] Wolfowitz, the most relentless voice for action against Iraq, argued forcefully that there had to be a link.[16] He was also the strongest advocate of the view that the US had missed a trick in not taking out Saddam in 1991. Yet, despite early talk of attacking Iraq, cooler heads prevailed. On 15 September, after a lengthy meeting with his top five advisers, Bush resolved to focus his response to 9/11 on Afghanistan. Cheney, Powell, Rice and Tenet (the Director of the CIA) had voted against attacking Iraq at this stage, while Rumsfeld abstained.[17] Given the near unanimity of advice Bush received, the role Blair played in this decision was minimal.

Iraq was off the agenda for the time being, but for how long? An account in *Vanity Fair* (May 2004) has claimed that Bush told Blair over dinner on 20 September 2001 that he was 'determined to topple Saddam', leading Blair to acquiesce in a decision to go to war with Iraq less than ten days after 9/11.[18] However, Christopher Meyer, the magazine's principal source for this account, has since made clear that this claim is untrue.[19] Nevertheless, Blair knew that Saddam would return to Bush's radar screen at some point. What remained unclear was when and how the President would seek to address the issue. In fact, unbeknownst to Blair, Bush secretly asked Rumsfeld to develop updated invasion plans for Iraq as early as 21 November 2001.[20] Bush's 'State of the Union' address in January 2002, in which he spoke of an 'axis of evil', listing Iraq, Iran and North Korea as rogue states intent on developing

WMD, caught Number 10 on the hop but the thrust of the comments came as no surprise.[21] Shortly after the speech, building on his earlier request to Rumsfeld, Bush instructed the Pentagon and the CIA to develop contingency plans for a second Gulf War.[22]

Poodle or Bulldog? Blair's Thinking on Iraq and WMD, 1997–2002

As we saw in Chapter 27, Blair's concern about WMD and terrorist attacks dates back to the early days of his premiership.[23] Dirty bombs, where conventional explosive is used to disperse radioactive material, were a particular fear of Blair's, owing to the relative ease of constructing such a device and the difficulties of prevention.[24] Blair had been influenced, among many others, by Robert Cooper, then head of the Cabinet's Defence and Overseas Secretariat, who had argued that the greatest threat to international security in the twenty-first century would come from WMD proliferation combining with international terrorism.[25] Cooper wrote up his thoughts in a book, which he said started out as a memo to Blair.[26] But Cooper's influence was far less than some other advisers: he was too cerebral and not sufficiently 'operational' for Blair. Far more important were Powell and Manning. His advisers and his own intuitions led him to treat the threat from WMD with the utmost gravity. 'Tony Blair believed very strongly from quite early on that if we did not deal with the weapons now, we would have to deal with them in ten years' time when proliferation would have made the problem intractable, and international checks and systems would be overwhelmed,' said one Number 10 official.[27] Straw concurred that Blair 'was on to the issue of WMD long before 9/11: he has greater facility for seeing beyond the horizon than anyone else I've met in politics'.[28] In April 2002, Blair said, 'To allow WMD to be developed by a state like Iraq . . . would be grossly to ignore the lesson of September 11 and we will not do it.'[29]

Blair's deep-seated concern over WMD is one riposte to the claim that he was passively following Bush's line. Another rejoinder is that Blair urged the Clinton administration to tackle Saddam in 1998 in the lead up to Operation Desert Fox. 'Tony Blair was thinking hard about military force and the responsibilities of the international community long before 9/11,' said one insider.[30] In early 2001, Blair defended the joint US–British air strikes in response to Iraqi attacks on their planes, and spoke out against EU leaders for being critical of the action. Blair described Saddam as a 'serial sinner when it comes to weapons of mass destruction and a threat to the external world'.[31] He believed that the repeated violation by Saddam of UN resolutions was offensive not just to the integrity of that body, but also to the international rule of law.[32] As early as November 1997, Blair said at the Lord Mayor's Banquet: 'Saddam Hussein is once more defying the clearly expressed will of the United Nations . . . the current determination to stand firm against a still dangerous dictator is unshakeable.'[33] He thought that the cat-and-mouse charade of the preceding six years had to end, and that if the West failed to confront Saddam, then concerted international pressure would be shrugged off by other rogue states, who would defy the UN with impunity. To Blair, Iraq provided the test case between a new world order and global chaos.[34]

The third key strand of Blair's thinking was his personal moral revulsion with Saddam Hussein. 'He saw Saddam as the Pol Pot of the Middle East,' said one Number 10 aide. 'With hindsight,' he said, 'we should have made much more of the whole humanitarian argument.'[35] As Blair wrote to George Carey in March 2002, 'Getting rid of Saddam would be highly desirable, not least for the Iraqi people.'[36] Blair would tell visitors in private at Number 10, 'I can't understand why people on the left oppose it. Hasn't the left always been committed to fighting injustice in the world?'[37] His revulsion at the brutality of dictators was a common theme. 'They ask me why we don't get rid of Mugabe,' he said in March 2003. 'Why not the Burmese lot? . . . I don't because I can't, but when you can, you should.'[38]

Blair's moral disgust with Saddam provided the strongest motive for his wish to confront him, and the most powerful rebuttal to the argument that he was Bush's 'poodle' blindly leading Britain into an American war against Iraq. The problem for Blair was that he was never able to make as much of this as he wished, because the government's lawyers would never let 'regime change' become an explicit goal of British policy as it was for the US.[39] Nevertheless, Blair did what he could to get the humanitarian arguments across. A clear philosophical thread can be drawn from his November 1997 Lord Mayor's speech, through the Chicago doctrine of April 1999, via Kosovo and Sierra Leone, his post-9/11 pronouncements (notably the catch-all party conference speech in October 2001) and a key statement in April 2002 to his Sedgefield speech in March 2004 justifying military intervention in another country for moral reasons. The speech in April 2002 was given at the George Bush (senior) Presidential Library in Texas: 'I have been involved as British Prime Minister in three conflicts involving regime change,' Blair said. 'Milošević. The Taliban. And Sierra Leone.'[40] In the speech, he tried to mould two principal motives for action in international affairs, the utilitarian (i.e., self-interest) and the utopian (i.e., building a better world) into a new approach for the twenty-first century, where enlightened self-interest demanded on occasion intervention in the sovereign affairs of other nations.[41] Hugo Young thought the speech made him sound 'like the man in charge of Western policy'.[42]

So Blair was far more bulldog than poodle to Bush, at least up to March 2002. He had his own clear philosophy for confronting the problem of Iraq. At the end of that month, he summarised his thinking about Iraq in a letter to a trusted confidant: 'My objectives must be to pull the Americans towards a strategy that is sensible in Iraq, contemplate military action only in the right circumstances; and broaden strategy so that it is about the wider world, including the Middle East peace process, Africa, staying and seeing it through in Afghanistan.'[43] These were fine ideals. What happened to them over the following months?

From Crawford to Camp David: April–September 2002

Critical to the whole story was the way the US administration chose to interpret Blair's words immediately after 9/11, such as when he said, 'We . . . here in Britain stand shoulder to shoulder with our American friends . . . and we, like them, will not rest until this evil is driven from our world.'[44] His sentiments at this time helped cement in a large section of the administration the belief that 'the Brits will be with us through Afghanistan into Iraq, come what may'.[45] As Meyer put it, 'The administration had a working hypothesis from September 2001 onwards that we had committed ourselves fully to whatever they were going to do, whether we in London thought we had or not. It was in their bloodstream.'[46]

A turning point in world sympathy for the US came after Bush's 'axis of evil' speech in January 2002. Up until that point, EU leaders including Chirac were supportive of America. After the fall of the Taliban and Bush's new and uncompromising rhetoric, they pulled back. Was Bush serious in fighting an effective 'war on terrorism', or would the post-9/11 environment provide cover for a return to Iraq to finish off what the 1991 Gulf War had left unfinished? Blair could have joined the sceptics, and made UN backing not a desirable end but a precondition for British military support. He did not do this. Instead, the idea that he had to keep close to the Americans at all costs, exercising influence in private but avoiding public criticism, became imbedded.[47] Why did he make this choice?

By the final years of the Clinton administration, Blair was becoming concerned by the risk of US isolationism, especially after Bush's victory on the Vulcans' unilateralist foreign policy platform.[48] The US was the most powerful nation on earth, and, in general Blair believed, a force for good. In his view, the only way to influence American foreign policy was to establish a constructive relationship with its policy-makers, hence the store he set by his personal relationship with Bush. 'Bluntly, I am the one Western leader the US will really listen to,' he confided in a friend in March 2002.[49] If his aims of seeing progress on peace in the Middle East and in bringing greater prosperity to Africa were to be realised, US support and enthusiasm were essential.[50] 'Blair always thought it would be disastrous for Europe and Britain to leave the US alone at the time it faced its greatest external challenges in recent history, and when unilateralist voices were at their height,' said one official.[51] Blair began to face his first serious opposition from within the Labour Party that month. On 7 March seventy Labour MPs signed a Commons motion declaring that an Iraq war would be unwise,[52] which came shortly after a difficult Cabinet discussion on Iraq. Cook wrote in his diary: 'For the first time I can recall in five years, Tony was out on a limb . . . The balance of the discussion pointed strongly in the reverse direction of his intentions.'[53] Cook and Clare Short were the most sceptical, though David Blunkett also expressed concern at the way events were heading. Blair summed up by saying, 'I tell you that we must stand close to America. If we don't, we will lose our influence to shape what they do.'[54]

Blair's next opportunity to influence Bush came when they met at the President's ranch at Crawford, Texas, in early April 2002. The administration had clearly resolved that the talking had to stop: 'Fuck Saddam. We're taking him out,' Bush had told Rice the month before.[55] But there were divisions within the administration and even within the Vulcans. 'Hawks' like Cheney, Rumsfeld and Wolfowitz thought beating Iraq would be an easy contest; Powell and Tenet and other 'doves' saw an invasion as full of hazard, and highly unpredictable.[56] In response, the hawks argued, despite the lack of evidence, that Saddam had links to al-Qaeda, and that regime change in Baghdad would have beneficial effects throughout the Middle East, leading to a lasting peace between Israel and the Palestinians – though exactly how was never made clear.[57] At Crawford, the administration discussed with Blair the possibility of an invasion of Iraq in the spring of 2003, with the autumn of 2003 another potential date. Some see Crawford as the 'turning point' for Blair when he committed Britain irrevocably to a war in Iraq that was now 'all but inevitable'.[58] However, the reality is that no formal agreement was made as to whether or not to attack Iraq, still less when.[59]

Blair did make it clear that he would support the US policy on Iraq, but he was determined to influence the shape of that policy.[60] Throughout the discussions, Blair repeatedly stressed three points on which he felt very strongly: he wanted any planning for war to be in concert with progress on the Middle East peace process (MEPP), efforts to assemble the largest possible coalition against Saddam, and a commitment to working through the UN.[61] Blair argued passionately against the hawks that it was much better for any invasion to be seen as part of a commitment to democratic nation-building by the international community than as a naked demonstration of America's military superiority.[62] Blair said these things, and implied that his support was to some extent conditional on them happening, but what the Americans *heard* Blair say at Crawford was that he was with them.[63] Blair's crucial error was his failure to lay out explicitly the status of his conditions. With hindsight, it was here that Blair lost leverage. As Richard Armitage, Colin Powell's deputy, later put it to one British official: 'The problem with your "yes, but" is that it is too easy to hear the "yes" and forget the "but".' What happened subsequently was that the 'but' faded away in US thinking, exposing Blair's stark bottom line: 'Come what may, we'll be with you.'[64]

Blair was taken aback, but perhaps he should not have been, by Bush's bluntness at the joint news conference on 6 April at the end of the Crawford summit. 'I explained to the Prime Minister that the policy of my government is the removal of Saddam . . . we support regime change.' Blair's own statement concentrated on the risk of Saddam's WMD programme and his defiance of UN resolutions.[65] Blair knew that the hawks were intent on war at the earliest possible opportunity. But he believed his unique persuasive powers, in conjunction with the advocacy of Powell, would be able to prevent the Americans acting precipitously.

Blair reported on the visit in full to Cabinet on 11 April, saying, 'I do believe in this country's relations with the US.' His colleagues were not so sure, and some, like Patricia Hewitt, spoke up about the importance of securing UN approval. Blair responded that 'we should not tie ourselves down to doing nothing' without such approval.[66] Elsewhere, support for Blair's line was beginning to haemorrhage as the post-9/11 chorus of approval started to dissipate. EU partners were not pleased by what they saw as a 'council of war' in Crawford; the Labour Party were increasingly concerned and critical; the Foreign Office and many officials across Whitehall were sceptical; the media and public opinion were turning hostile;[67] even Number 10 was divided, with Jonathan Powell strongly advocating closeness to the administration, and Sally Morgan in particular pressing single-mindedly for the need to go down the UN route.[68] Yet Blair drove on.

John Kampfner, chief among the sceptics to have written on the war, says that from Crawford onwards, Blair's talk that war was not 'inevitable' was just a 'front', and that he concealed the truth from the Cabinet, Foreign Office and others: in fact, he argues, Blair had committed Britain to war with Iraq as the price worth paying for US friendship.[69] As evidence, Kampfner cites Blair's instructions to Brown on his return from Texas: rework your April Budget to take account of expenditure on an Iraq war, which would cost an initial £1 billion.[70] Senior officials, however, deny Kampfner's interpretation, suggesting that he confuses military preparations, which had to be made for war to be a credible threat, with decisions taken to wage an inevitable war. Diplomacy with Saddam worked better with the threat of force, as even Kofi Annan admitted back in 1998.[71] One senior UK military figure, intimately involved in the mobilisation, explained: 'I had the impression that Tony Blair wanted to make it sound very real to Saddam, but that he continued to hold out hopes for a peaceful outcome in the end.'[72] It is hard to say at which point British involvement in military conflict became inevitable, but it was certainly not at Crawford. It became more likely all the time, especially from the autumn of 2002. By March 2003, with British troops massed in the Gulf and Blair's unwavering support for the US, British participation in any war seemed all but inevitable. However, even then Blair claimed that conflict could be avoided, hoping for a last-minute collapse from Saddam.[73]

From April to August 2002, Blair worked hard on convincing the Americans on his three priorities: progress on MEPP, which is discussed later; attempting to build international support for confronting Saddam; and working through the UN. Blair spoke regularly to Bush on the telephone – 'More often,' said one official, 'than the conversations between Churchill and Roosevelt during the Second World War.'[74] Even more regular a conduit was between Manning, who had been with Blair in Crawford, and who was a trusted interlocutor in Washington, and Rice: often the two would speak more than once a day by telephone.[75] A key difference was that whereas Manning spoke totally for the British government, Rice was often unable to speak for the Bush administration. She acted as Bush's confidante, but could not impose her will on the powerful figures in the administration, who constantly pulled Bush in different directions. Manning made regular visits to Washington to talk face to face with Rice, Tenet and sometimes Armitage.[76] The message he reported back to Blair echoed Meyer: the drums of war were sounding.

At the end of July, Manning made an important trip to the White House, following up a personal letter from Blair. 'I'm with you,' Blair insisted in the letter, but he went on to stress the crucial importance of building UN support, particularly given Blair's difficult position at home. Lord Goldsmith, the Attorney General, had also advised Blair that without a UN resolution an invasion might break international law.[77] The UN had a third importance: as Meyer put it, 'If you needed UN backing if at all possible for fighting a war, you sure as hell needed the UN for the period afterwards when you would be hoping to stabilise and help democracy take root.'[78] Manning also put the case directly to Bush, when the President happened to walk in on Manning's meeting with Rice. Bush listened intently, but did not commit himself.[79]

The divisions within the US administration between the hawks and the doves had deepened since Crawford in the spring. Cheney had become deeply suspicious of Blair's influence over Bush, and disapproved strongly of Colin Powell, whom he saw as 'Britain's Ambassador', and of Manning's relationship with Rice.[80] These fault-lines became increasingly open and were heavily reported in the media. The administration's top figures debated the issue hotly all July and August, in a series of meetings that appeared in their private schedules as 'Regional Strategies Meetings' to conceal their true import.[81] Powell and Cheney came to represent the two polar views. Powell, the dove, who had worked so hard to assemble the multinational coalition after 9/11, wanted to go via the UN and use force only as a last resort. Cheney, the hawk, feared that the UN route would be exploited by Saddam to delay war indefinitely, lose valuable time and let opposition to war grow still further. Cheney continued to argue the case that multilateral support was unnecessary, and that America should exert leadership alone – the rest of the world would see the wisdom and brilliance of its actions once the deed was done. Bush had spoken powerfully in favour of solo pre-emptive military action against America's enemies in a speech at West Point in June, but was now beginning to have doubts about whether unilateral action was right. Domestic opinion in the US, so solidly behind him after 9/11, was turning. In Congress, the powerful Senate Foreign Relations Committee, and key Republicans in the House of Representatives, were expressing reservations about the war – with and without allies. Closer to Bush's heart, with his filial piety, were the key figures in his father's administration who made it clear they did not share Cheney's militaristic intent. James Baker, his father's Secretary of State, and Brent Scowcroft, his National Security Advisor, both counselled caution privately and in public.[82]

Over the summer, the doves gained ground. If prudence suggested America ought to take a partner, then Britain would be the most suitable ally; and, if the price for British partnership was to be going down the UN route, it was a price worth paying.[83] An important video conference took place in August, in which Powell prevailed over Cheney and convinced Bush, holidaying in Crawford, to take the issue to the UN – though quite what role Bush envisaged for the UN, and – critically – whether he would ask for a new resolution, remained undecided.[84]

Cheney was furious, and in late August resolved to deliver his own verdict on the UN. In a bellicose speech in Tennessee not cleared with anyone in the administration,[85] Cheney raised the spectre of Saddam gaining nuclear weapons and poured scorn on the UN inspection process: 'A return of inspectors would provide no assurance whatsoever of his compliance with UN resolutions,' Cheney declared. 'On the contrary, there is a great danger that it would provide false comfort that Saddam was somehow "back in his box".'[86] Three days later, in an address to the Korean War Veterans in Texas, his language was slightly more measured than in Tennessee, but the damage had been done. Cheney's words, high on emotion, low on evidence, were widely reported in Europe, and widely reviled. This stiffened Schröder's and Chirac's opposition to war, and made Blair's task of holding the EU together much more difficult. It is not surprising that Number 10 blamed Cheney (far more than Rumsfeld, Wolfowitz, Perle or all the other hawks) as the villain of the pre-war period, as reflected in Philip Stephens' well-sourced account.[87]

The stage was set for a difficult Camp David summit between Blair and Bush on 7 September, ahead of a key speech Bush was due to deliver to the UN five days later. On the plane on the way over, Blair read briefs detailing Saddam's failure to comply with UN resolutions on weapons inspectors, and on the concerns about Iraq's WMD.[88] It chimed with his deepest apprehensions. On arrival, the British were surprised, and less than delighted, to find Cheney waiting with Bush: 'He just sat there throughout like a lump,' one British official recalled.[89] The central discussion, however, focused on the UN. Blair pushed his argument hard: if Bush chose to work for a UN resolution, Blair would find it much easier to 'deliver the Europeans' as well as his own party. In summary, he offered a deal: 'We must go through the United Nations. If it works, fine. If they won't disarm through the UN, Britain will back you in a war with Iraq.'[90] 'Blair was passionate to ensure that all possible non-violent means of dealing with Saddam and WMD were explored before any war occurred,' said one close aide,[91] but he made it clear to Bush that if it came to war, he would commit British troops to battle. Bush would not be alone. This was the promise the President had been seeking and he accepted the deal with open arms. 'Your man has got *cojones*,' he told Campbell afterwards.[92] Was this the moment when Blair lost the opportunity to be far more emphatic about his other two 'conditions' for British support?

Blair flew home, stopping off at Balmoral for a truncated audience with the Queen, much relieved by the outcome. Cook later wrote: 'Blair deserves credit for persuading President Bush that he must take Iraq to the United Nations for multilateral agreement. It is the only point in the whole saga where it is possible to pinpoint a clear instance where British influence made any difference to US policy on Iraq.'[93] Number 10 believes that 'Bush would never even have tried to use the UN without Blair'.[94] But is this view right? According to one senior State Department official: 'Bush's mind was pretty much made up before the Camp David September summit.'[95] Bush's decision to fly in the face of his own hawks had more to do with the powerful US voices urging caution than Blair's advocacy. Blair's role was not insignificant, but it affirmed the way Bush's mind had been moving. Blair was also relentless, as one Number 10 adviser put it, in 'banging away at Bush to achieve a breakthrough in the Middle East peace process'.[96] Bush made some encouraging noises, but remained reluctant to engage with the commitment and energy that Blair wanted. 'What the White House heard was that Blair was going to be with America, come what may, peace process or not, UN resolution or not – and Downing Street did not exactly disabuse them of that notion.'[97]

Advice Blair received from diplomats that autumn was that Britain could be the swing vote on whether or not the US would go to war in Iraq.[98] The guarantee of British participation in a military campaign was Blair's trump card. With hindsight, in September at Camp David he played this card too early, which may have reinforced Bush's view that he had to go to the UN, but left Blair with too few other concessions tied down. From then on the Americans tended to take him for granted. If the administration had been united in its sincere determination to make multilateralism work, or to search for peace in the Middle East, his faith in Bush might have been justified. But many influential voices around Bush sneered at Blair's idealism: 'Scooter' Libby, the powerful aide in Cheney's office, would jibe, 'Oh dear, we'd better not do that or we might upset the Prime Minister.'[99]

Rumsfeld had already pencilled in 15 February 2003 as the date the war was to begin, even though the Pentagon had real anxieties after

Afghanistan about whether it would have enough Cruise missiles and other weapons ready in time.[100] The UN route would fail, most in the administration believed, or hoped, and the British would go with them into battle. With Camp David over, Bush's immediate task was his speech to the UN General Assembly on 12 September, which was the subject of violent pressure within the administration, and which went through a couple of dozen drafts and more. Cheney and the hawks lobbied hard for Bush not to call for a new UN Resolution, but simply state that the UN Security Council should 'meet its responsibilities' under existing resolutions. Uncertainty as to what Bush would say remained up until the last minute. Even the State Department, which lobbied under Powell for a resolution, was not sure.[101] 'Despite what was said at Camp David, it wasn't clear to us until the last couple of days that he would agree to the UN route, and it was not until the morning of the speech that we were made aware of the wording,' said Jeremy Greenstock, Britain's representative at the UN. Bush resolved to ask specifically for a UN resolution, a decision the President later suggested that 'Blair had a lot to do with'.[102] However, 'confusion was reawakened when Bush was on the podium in front of the General Assembly, as only then did he realise he had been handed the penultimate draft of his speech, containing no request for a resolution. From memory, Bush reinserted the phrase: "We will work with the UN Security Council for the necessary resolutions." The problem was he misremembered it, saying resolutions in the plural even though the final draft referred to only one resolution. That caused further speculation later on.'[103] Blair and his team stood helpless in front of a screen in Number 10 watching anxiously as the American President ad-libbed the lines on which so much hinged.[104]

Blair now had something concrete – Bush's public agreement to seek UN support against Saddam – even if Cheney and other administration unilateralists kept trying to undermine the attempt. The President's words allayed some fears in Europe about US intentions, but not for long. Blair and his aides kept hoping all the way through to March that war would be avoided if Saddam agreed to co-operate. Steel oratory and the mass deployment of men and munitions were now the chosen way to make Saddam know the threat was credible. But Blair the realist accepted war might well be difficult to avoid, whether under UN auspices, or just as an American–British operation. Was he anxious about the likely British casualties, the danger of the war being long-lasting or spiralling out of control, or acts of terrorism against Britain for its bellicose stance? If he was, he did not show it. Indeed, during these

months, colleagues speak of his absolute calm and his conviction in his
own rectitude. His certainty was not a shared experience. As Sally
Morgan had long warned, the Labour Party were becoming increasingly
restless at the prospect of war in league with a Republican President.[105]
Bush's reassurance that he would seek a UN resolution helped limit the
scale of Labour's back-bench rebellion in the emergency Commons
debate on 24 September to fifty-six MPs, but this was a worryingly large
margin by historic standards. No one in Cabinet shared Blair's
confidence in the need to prepare for war, and offer Bush total support.
Few felt as strongly as Cook and Short, but many others held profound
reservations. According to one senior diplomat, in the summer and
autumn of 2002, 'An awful lot of people in the FCO felt that policy on
Iraq was a huge mistake.'[106] Straw himself shared some of their concerns
and spoke regularly to Colin Powell, his opposite number in Washington,
who had his own reservations. But Straw's experience in foreign policy
was limited in comparison with Blair, and he kept his reservations mostly
to himself.[107] Brown's views were opaque, and it was unclear to his
colleagues whether his lack of obvious support or enthusiasm, as before
in Kosovo and Afghanistan also, stemmed from philosophical objections
or from the fact that Iraq was transparently 'Blair's show'.[108]

Blair's support came mostly from his closest advisers. In theory, key
decisions over policy on Iraq would be resolved not by full Cabinet,
which was too unwieldy, but by the committee on Overseas Policy and
Defence (OPD or the 'War Cabinet'), which met on Thursday mornings
just before the full Cabinet. Yet Blair found OPD 'too formal' and
'insignificantly focused' and so he secretly established a smaller informal
meeting before each OPD. Held in the den, this involved Blair, Scarlett,
Dearlove, Boyce, Manning, Powell, Campbell and Morgan, who would
subsequently take a circuitous route through Number 10 to join the
OPD meetings to avoid other OPD members growing wise to the earlier
gathering.[109] It was this group that was the real decision-making body.

The September Dossier

Trying to secure UN backing for action against Iraq locked Blair into
stressing the threat from WMD. The principal charge against Saddam
was his repeated refusal to comply with UN resolutions requiring him to
disarm verifiably. This argument chimed well with Blair's own long-
standing concerns, obsessions almost, of the dangers posed by WMD.
On the plane on the way back from Camp David, Blair had shared his

fear of Iraq's WMD with journalists: 'I am not saying it will happen next month, or even next year, but at some point the danger will explode. This is not an American preoccupation. It is our preoccupation. It must be the preoccupation of the entire world.'[110]

Blair was preparing the ground for his pitch that Iraq had to be confronted because of its WMD, and if Saddam did not comply with UN resolutions and inspectors this one final time, war would result. Blair had always been keen on putting the facts before the public, so it could see for itself why the government was acting as it was. In the wake of 9/11, he had, in the face of American reluctance, insisted on publishing a 'dossier' showing the complicity of Bin Laden and al-Qaeda in the attacks.[111] A dossier had been due to be published in March 2002 based on SIS intelligence examining Iraq's WMD capabilities, but had been held back for fear it was insufficiently convincing.[112] Blair wanted it published now. Manning and Meyer were not in favour, because they thought it shifted the burden from Saddam to prove his *innocence* to Britain and America having to prove his *guilt*.[113] Others argued that a dossier was irrelevant: Saddam had broken UN resolutions, which was sufficient justification for going to war. Blair saw the point, but with anti-war pressure building at home, and America forcing the pace abroad, he thought publication was for the best, and duly secured Bush's agreement at Camp David on 7 September.[114] Bush said the Americans would provide a dossier too, but subsequent opposition from the CIA and Pentagon prevented it being published. On one crucial point, all key players – Blair, Manning, Powell, Campbell in London, Meyer in Washington and Greenstock at the UN in New York – were in agreement: Saddam had been working on WMD in breach of UN resolutions throughout the 1990s and had been 'cocking a snook' at the UN. Greenstock was more sceptical about WMD than most, but he was still under no doubt that Saddam had worked to acquire them.[115] 'If we did not believe there had been WMD, we would not have been on board with the strategy,' said one of Blair's close team.[116]

At his first domestic political challenge of the autumn, the TUC conference on 10 September, Blair stressed the threat from Iraq and WMD. 'I for one do not want it on my conscience that we knew of the threat, saw it coming and did nothing.'[117] Number 10 had feared walkouts, but he escaped with a sullen silence, and a standing ovation of less than a minute. Critically, Blair failed to give delegates a guarantee that military action would go ahead only with the express approval of the UN, saying only: 'If the will of the UN is ignored, action will follow.'[118] Cook spoke to him the day after, and found him attaching 'great

importance to the forthcoming dossier' to win back support at home, and
'he was also hopeful that he could turn around international opinion'.[119]

Frantic work took place in the intelligence community in September
strengthening and updating the March dossier. Scarlett, chairman of the
Joint Intelligence Committee (JIC), presented the fruit to Number 10
on the morning of 17 September. Powell sent Scarlett an e-mail that
evening, arguing that the dossier, as it stood, did not do enough to
demonstrate an imminent threat from Saddam.[120] To Campbell and
Manning, Powell said, 'we need to make it clear Saddam would not
attack us <u>at the moment</u> [his underlining]. The thesis is he would be a
threat to the UK in the future if we do not check him.'[121] It was left to
Campbell to give Scarlett Blair's reaction, which was that it was
'convincing' – though, as Campbell pointed out to Blair, he did not
exactly come to the dossier 'as a "don't know" on the issue'. Blair
thought that the dossier did not focus 'enough on human rights', but in
general he thought it would do the job.[122]

Blair published the re-worked fifty-page dossier, 'Iraq's Weapons of
Mass Destruction – The Assessment of the British Government' with a
massive public relations fanfare on 24 September, the day of the
parliamentary recall. The only sound legal justification for war was non-
compliance with UN resolutions and this was reflected in Blair's speech
to the Commons: 'Our purpose is disarmament . . . Disarmament of all
WMD is the demand. One way or another it must be acceded to.'[123] The
dossier then highlighted the risk from Iraq's WMD. The foreword to the
dossier, signed by Blair, said 'documents show that some of Iraq's WMD
could be ready for use within forty-five minutes'. 'Saddam's WMD
programme is active, detailed and growing,' Blair told MPs. '[It] is not
shut down. It is up and running.' The reaction to the dossier was mixed
in the House, and beyond. 'Chilling reading,' said an editorial in the
Jerusalem Post.[124] 'No compelling evidence that immediate military
action is needed,' said a leader in the *Financial Times*.[125] Critically, EU
leaders were unimpressed by the September dossier. They thought it
made war no more justifiable.

The principal question the dossier did not answer was, 'Why now?',
which Powell himself acknowledged was a weakness. It was one being
increasingly voiced, not least by Blair's colleagues. At the long-awaited
Cabinet meeting attended by Blair's recalled ministers, Cook asked the
question. Hoon attempted a response, which in essence was because
9/11 had happened. 'The problem with this,' Cook noted wryly, 'is that
no one has a shred of evidence that Saddam was involved in September
11th.' Blair did not respond to the 'why now' question when he summed

up the two-hour meeting: 'To carry on being engaged with the US is vital. The voices on both left and right who want to pull Europe and the US apart would have a disastrous consequence if they succeeded.'[126]

The best response to the 'why now' question that Number 10 could muster was that Saddam's ignoring of the UN was bringing the body into disrepute and would embolden other rogue states and international terrorists to think they could ignore it too. A related point was that the longer Saddam was left untackled, the greater his stockpile of WMD would grow. Blair was exercised by an intelligence intercept that recorded Saddam saying he wanted to get hold of nuclear weapons 'to pose a threat to the West'.[127] But the intelligence, distilled from GCHQ, SIS and MI5 and collated by Scarlett's Joint Intelligence Committee, was far from clear-cut, as Number 10 knew. Every last drop was squeezed from the raw material to make the dossier, and hence the justification for war, as strong as possible. Evidence of any nuclear weapons programme was very inconclusive, although it was much firmer on chemical and biological weapons.[128] Some on the inside felt at the time that 'the intelligence community were telling the government exactly what it wanted to hear', yet this is hotly contested by others.[129] One military figure, who did not bother to read the dossier but went straight to the raw intelligence instead, was totally convinced that Saddam had WMD: 'It was not simply that the intelligence people were telling Blair what he wanted to hear,' this official insisted.[130] Most of Blair's most senior advisers in his tight-knit group who met in the den thought similarly: Saddam had WMD.

Many in the intelligence community had reservations about their material being used in a public way to justify going to war, and they remained concerned about how reliable some of the material in the dossier was. According to Cook, by March 2003, 'it was clear' that Blair himself did not believe all the claims in the dossier,[131] a stark contrast with his public pronouncements that the intelligence was impeccable.

It is easy to see why Blair allowed himself to become so committed to the September dossier. Disclosure of evidence was a laudable objective. With hindsight, however, it can be seen to have been a failure as a document of persuasion, flawed in its evidence, and deeply injurious to Blair's own credibility and to his case for the war. 'Blair should have been more critical of intelligence,' insists Hans Blix. 'He was creating a virtual reality.'[132] By any standards, this is a damning indictment. The dossier became a *cause célèbre* after BBC journalist Andrew Gilligan alleged on air in late May 2003 that the government had 'sexed up' the material by including the claim that Iraq could deploy WMD in forty-five minutes, which precipitated the suicide of Dr David Kelly and the whole protracted saga of the Hutton Inquiry.[133]

It transpired that the forty-five-minute claim for Iraq's deployment of WMD came from a single, uncorroborated source, and that it referred only to battlefield biological or chemical weapons, which posed no serious threat to other nations. Another sensational claim in the dossier, that Baghdad had sought uranium from Africa for use in its nuclear weapons, was admitted later by senior intelligence figures to be flawed.[134] Nevertheless, Hutton found Number 10 not guilty of manipulating the evidence, and the dossier's defenders insist the document was a 'good piece of work' which fell victim to the 'shoddy journalism of the BBC'.[135] Either way, the dossier's flaws ran far deeper than presentation. 'We were almost all wrong,' declared David Kay, former top US weapons inspector in January 2004: Saddam had no WMD stockpiles after all.[136] SIS, the CIA, the intelligence agencies in many EU countries and Israel, and the weapons inspectors, had all reached the wrong conclusions and Number 10 and the White House had taken major decisions on the back of erroneous intelligence.

Many factors could explain the comprehensive failure of Western intelligence, including Saddam being duped by his own scientists and aides into believing he had WMD, defective satellite intelligence, and reliance on Iraqi defectors, who were desperate to see a Western invasion and who exaggerated to build the case against Saddam. At the heart too was a clash of cultures between the secretive intelligence world and a hyper-media-conscious government. They did not sit easily together.[137] So great was Number 10's need for results, so short the time available, and so few the decision-takers involved, that customary checks were omitted. The conclusion many of Blair's fellow citizens reached was that he knew that Saddam did not possess WMD, but he lied about it to take the country into the war. As shown, Blair did believe Saddam still had WMD, or he would never have spoken and acted as he did. Had the September dossier appeared in 1997, almost all would have believed it. Five years later, few did.

Blair's Efforts at the UN, September 2002–March 2003

The first UN resolution took eight weeks of hard slog to achieve, rather than the fortnight expected. 'We all went in knowing the UN route would be agony, and it was real agony,' said one Number 10 aide.[138] Blair was nevertheless buoyant as he set about the challenge of convincing

Security Council members to support a resolution. At this stage, there was little talk of unanimity; the target was to carry the resolution with only a few abstentions.[139] Blair had boundless optimism that his persuasive skills would win through.

Blair's stance was clear to everyone: he was going to deal with Iraq and the threat of WMD. If he could do it multilaterally with UN support, that was much preferred, for domestic reasons, and because it was clear that his fellow EU leaders as well as Russia were deeply apprehensive about American unilateralism. He was convinced the inspectors would find WMD hidden in Iraq: if their work was made impossible, the recourse to war would be much more palatable to the international community with UN backing. The UN, he knew, would also be invaluable after the war.

Blair now embarked fully on his self-appointed role as the 'bridge' between Europe and the United States, with considerable determination, just as he had done in the build-up to the war in Afghanistan. The difference was that, this time around, his role as bridge was even less appreciated in Europe, especially by Schröder and Chirac, than it had been before. Nor was the bridge role valued by the hawks in Washington, who cared little for what Europeans thought, and one of whom, Perle, spoke of the UN disparagingly as a 'looming chatterbox on the River Hudson'.[140] Number 10 believed Bush to be utterly sincere himself in trying one last time for a peaceful resolution; but they were concerned that 'the neo-cons and unilateralists wanted to go all-out for war'.[141] This separation of Bush 'the head', who was willing to see diplomacy through, and Bush 'the gut', who sided with the hawks, now became a leitmotif in the British camp. Blair thus regularly reminded Bush that 'we are going to have to take "yes" from the UN for an answer', hoping to bolster 'the head' over 'the gut'.[142] So negative were the hawks about the UN route, however, that they set about sabotaging the process from the start. 'Scooter' Libby admitted to one British official that they were desperate to avoid a new inspection process as they were all but 'locked on' to the spring 2003 window for a military attack.[143] The hawks tried to make the wording of the resolution as unsympathetic as they could in the hope that it would prove unacceptable to the other members of the Security Council. A hard-line version of the text was leaked to the *New York Times* in early October. The timing could not have been worse for Blair, coming in the middle of the Labour Party conference just as Blair was squaring up to an increasingly sceptical party. He was forced to secrete himself away with Straw in an airless 'secure room' at the Imperial Hotel at Blackpool as they made long phone calls dealing with the fall-out.[144]

The minutiae of the negotiations on the UN resolution over those eight weeks were handled for Britain by Greenstock at the UN and by Straw in London. Blair and Bush were kept regularly informed, but were not involved in the detailed discussions in New York.[145] Blair's principal task, the persuasion of fellow world leaders, was made still more difficult for him when Congress gave Bush a green light to use armed force against Iraq as he deemed 'necessary and appropriate'. This victory for the hawks gave them even more ammunition for asserting American independence from international restraints. On 20 September, their labours were further rewarded in a new statement of national security strategy, which asserted the right for the US to overthrow other governments by force if it suspected they were acquiring WMD, or harbouring terrorists. Cheney confidently suggested that no fewer than sixty countries fell within this bracket, a statement that sent a chill wind blowing across the Western world.[146] During this period, the Pentagon took the final decision to prepare for the war in the spring rather than the autumn of 2003. This window was dictated largely by the desire to avoid the summer heat and the fear that leaving troops in position inactive for too long would stifle their motivation.[147] Outside the Pentagon, there were also concerns that the American economy could suffer badly if the uncertainty was protracted for another six months.[148]

The focus now switched back to New York. On 8 November, after prolonged lobbying and disagreement over the precise words, the UN Security Council eventually passed Resolution 1441. Blair and Bush were both delighted that agreement had been reached, and that it was unanimous.[149] They were also pleased by the wording of the resolution, declaring Saddam in 'material breach' of his responsibilities under previous UN resolutions, and giving him one final opportunity to comply or face 'serious consequences'. Putin, who dismissed the September dossier as 'propaganda', had been particularly difficult to win over and had been lobbied by the US and by Blair in mid-October in Moscow.[150] Blair's persuasion played some part in all the fifteen permanent and non-permanent members of the Security Council signing up. He had thus achieved his goal of securing international backing for a UN resolution, acting not only as bridge but also as explainer of the US to the rest of the world. He also proved to those who had doubted Blair's influence in Washington that he was indeed listened to by Bush,[151] and that the unilateralists were not the sole drivers in their hell-bent lust for war. As one senior State Department official said, 'If Saddam was generally perceived to have met the requirements of Resolution 1441, Bush would have faced tremendous pressure to have called off the invasion, both from within the administration, and from Tony Blair.'[152] Blair downplayed his own role, but in his heart he felt more relieved when Resolution 1441 was passed than he had done for many weeks.[153]

But, as so often happened in the Iraq story, a moment of apparent triumph for Blair proved short-lived. Agreement on the resolution rested on several fudges. One concerned the exact nature of what would constitute a 'material breach' of the resolution,[154] while the second concerned the response to such a breach. The Americans wanted force to follow automatically, while the French and Russians wanted an explicit commitment to seek a second resolution authorising force. The end compromise was that the Security Council would meet, but it remained unclear if this would be a consultation meeting prior to war (the American view) or the forum to debate a second resolution (the French view). Herein lay the seed of the future battle about whether the war had or had not been legitimate.[155] Britain, however, was for the moment too relieved to have achieved the unanimous resolution after weeks of hard slog to register that work should have begun immediately on lobbying for a second resolution. As Greenstock admitted: 'We sat on our laurels longer than we should have. With hindsight, we should have started negotiating straight after that first resolution.'[156] Meyer described why the fudge was doomed. 'As we moved from celebrating 1441 to analysing what it actually meant in practice, the camouflage was stripped away. The conventional wisdom was that, when you get into a dispute with the French over an issue like that, it would take a lot of diplomacy to get round it, but, in the end, the French would come round.' As Meyer concluded, this 'episode' rewrote the textbooks. 'At some stage in January, the penny began to drop: maybe we were going to have to write a new conventional wisdom for French foreign policy.'[157]

Had Saddam caved in and complied fully with 1441, Bush would indeed have had to take 'yes' for an answer, however bitter his hawks might have been. Had Saddam rebuffed 1441 completely, the world, or most of it, would have seen it as a clear act of defiance justifying resort to military action. So Saddam did what any averagely clever figure would have done when faced with such a dilemma: he complied partially, thereby splitting the allies straight down the middle.[158] Saddam let the inspectors back into Iraq, yet failed to provide the 'full' declaration of Iraqi weapons programmes that the resolution demanded. The Iraqi response of 7 December 2002, despite being 12,000 pages long, seemed to the US like a 'warmed-up rehash' of what Saddam had said on WMD years before.[159] Blair told his staff this was 'the defining moment. This was his big opportunity. He's blown it.'[160] Even as late as November,

doves in the White House had been telling Meyer that the best outcome
for the administration would be if Iraq imploded, resulting in Saddam
falling rather than an invasion.[161] Now, however, the wind blew very
strongly in the war party's sails. Cheney urged Bush to declare Saddam's
response a material breach and thus grounds for war.[162] Although no one,
including Bush, agreed that diplomacy could be abandoned there and
then, gears began to shift in Washington from diplomacy to military
build-up. On 18 December, Bush told the Spanish leader Aznar privately
that he considered the Iraqi declaration 'a joke'. Saddam is a 'liar and
he's no intention of disarming'.[163] The next day, Colin Powell declared
Iraq to be in 'material breach'. By the end of December, Number 10 had
reached the conclusion 'that the administration had decided Iraq was not
serious about wanting to comply'.[164] Yet still Blair did not give up hope
on the UN route. He could not. Without UN endorsement, he knew he
would be in big trouble.

British military preparations were also accelerated in December, with
plans made for troops to be deployed to the Gulf. Blair stressed in public
that the build-up was to make the threat against Saddam seem credible,
but by Christmas 2002, most world leaders had decided that talk of a
peaceful solution was merely playing for time. If the United States had
crossed the Rubicon to war in December, or certainly by mid-January,[165]
Blair kept believing for another three months that a non-military solution
was at least possible. Many voices in Number 10 warned him that without
a second UN resolution, specifically authorising the use of force, he would
not be able to carry his party or country. 'Blair had convinced himself that
1441 had authorised the use of force, but he knew he had to do more than
that to convince the British public and Parliament,' said one official.[166]

Less noticed was a second reason for Blair's wanting to stick with the
UN. He wanted to keep the Security Council together and explore every
last avenue in order to prevent a condemnatory resolution being put
down by the Security Council as soon as any military action against Iraq
opened – as the Russians had instigated over Kosovo in 1999. 'This time
it would have been even more embarrassing for us,' said a British official.
'It would probably have been carried, and then we'd have had to veto
it.'[167] Greenstock thus slaved away at the UN until 17 March 2003, even
after it became clear that support for a second resolution was leaching
away. Was it worth the effort? Greenstock believed it was. 'Even though
our pure objective, a second resolution, proved elusive, the fact we tried
so hard to find a peaceful way to avert war achieved the secondary
objective that no hostile resolution was tabled and we were not
condemned for going to war.'[168]

In the opening weeks of the New Year, Manning in Number 10 would speak to Rice at least daily, and Blair to Bush almost weekly.[169] The two main themes of their conversations were Number 10's wish to have American active support, not just a nod of the head, for a second resolution, and the plea for more time to use diplomacy to solve the crisis. 'All the time we probed to find out what preparations they had for actually initiating "armed force" – we didn't call it war.'[170] Yet the problem was that, as one British official put it, 'power swirled around the Vice-President and the Department of Defense',[171] not around Rice and the National Security Council. But the British had no corresponding close link to the key players in the Vice-President's office and the Pentagon. Manning would repeatedly ask Rice to agree something, but she would be 'outmanoeuvred by Rumsfeld time and again'.[172] Where, one might ask, was the President in all this?

It was a frantic race against time, and against the juggernaut of war-planning in the Pentagon that had developed its own logic. Blair realised in early 2003 that control of events was slipping away from him. Aides in Number 10 picked up the mood: Morgan warned of drift while Campbell urged them to 'get a grip'. Cabinet was also jittery about where Blair's policy was going. 'Trust me. I know my way through this,' he told Cabinet colleagues who were not wholly convinced.[173] The jibbing and the growing anti-Americanism in Britain made Blair even more determined to find a diplomatic solution. 'He saw the downside of armed force with greater apprehension than the Americans,' said one Number 10 adviser, 'because we are far smaller players globally, Britain needs relations across the Arabic and Islamic world, not to mention the EU, and we can't do without those relationships for an extended period in the way a superpower can.'[174] During January and February 2003, British diplomacy thus operated at full stretch trying to prepare the Security Council vote for a second resolution, providing for the use of force, if Saddam continued to be obstructive.[175]

While the bridge support was crumbling on the far side of the Atlantic, the always insecure base on the European side was simultaneously disintegrating. On 20 January, Dominique de Villepin, the French Foreign Minister, ambushed a furious Colin Powell at the UN with a bitter attack on American preparations for war. At a Franco-German summit in Paris two days later to celebrate the fortieth anniversary of the Elysée Treaty, Schröder and Chirac's hostility to American policy was made clear. 'War is always an admission of defeat,' declared the latter, with the German leader seemingly in agreement by his side.[176]

'The timing of that remark was a real disaster for us,' declared one Number 10 aide, who thought that Iraqi hawks noted this division among Security Council members and decided to ease up on co-operation, believing that any concerted will against them by the international community was already in the past.[177] The divisions within Europe were deepened by a high-risk article in the *Wall Street Journal* supporting the US stance, signed by some European leaders, which had been designed to show that the Paris–Berlin axis was not representative of all of European opinion.[178] Yet, in the face of all the evidence, Blair still believed he could bring Chirac round eventually, while it was agreed that the Americans would target Putin, who proved unexpectedly resistant to their persuasion.[179]

Blair was like a man trying to prop up a weak bridge with flood waters raging beneath it, dashing madly from one end to the other to secure their connections on dry land, while all the time surging waters were undermining the foundations. Following Bush's belligerent State of the Union address on 29 January, Blair rushed over to the American end of the bridge two days later. His trip to Washington was not looked forward to eagerly by many in the administration. The night before he arrived Blair received a telegram from the Washington Embassy warning him that neither of his two main hopes for the visit, namely more time for negotiation and US support for a second resolution, had yet been accepted by the administration.[180] There was a great deal of work to be done.

In a very worrying development, Blair found Bush, Cheney and Powell united around opposition to a second resolution. In the end, however, according to Bob Woodward, Blair won the President over by stressing that a second resolution was absolutely necessary for him domestically: Blair was asking for it as 'a favour'. 'If that's what you need,' Woodward recounts the President saying, 'we will go flat out to try to help you get it.'[181] Yet the reality is somewhat less heroic than this American-sourced (and pro-Powell) account suggests. Although Blair and Bush made real progress in their bilateral, agreeing a strong formulation in support of a second resolution and the time to negotiate it, the President backed away from announcing this publicly after his Press Secretary, Ari Fleischer, warned that he had never gone so far before. 'True, but some of us have,' chipped in Rice. 'But the President hasn't,' insisted Fleischer, stressing that it would be 'a big story'. Blair at this pivotal moment said nothing; Bush sided with Fleischer.[182] 'I was amazed that Blair did not interject and point out that Bush was being made to deviate from what they had agreed,' said one observer to the scene.[183] At the joint press conference that followed, Bush said merely that if the UN chose to pass a second resolution, it would be 'welcome'. There was little evidence of Bush 'going flat out' to help Blair here.

Blair's political difficulties now stepped up a notch. On Saturday, 15 February, a 'Stop the War' rally, the biggest demonstration in British history, marched through London. The next day Andrew Rawnsley stated the conventional wisdom with blinding clarity: 'Without a second resolution, much of Blair's party will revolt, many of his MPs will mutiny, and some of his ministers will resign.'[184] Blair was thus much relieved when, on 24 February, after further intense lobbying about Blair's domestic difficulties, the President finally agreed to the introduction of a formal second resolution. But, mindful of his military, he insisted that a vote on it had to be concluded by mid-March at the latest. Blair fought hard 'for the Americans "to give us until the end of April" but all he could get out of them was another couple of weeks till mid-March'.[185] Blair, albeit late in the day, had used every last drop of capital he held with the administration to extract this concession: but his gain was a perishable good, and the rapid expiry of its shelf-life robbed it of any real value.[186]

The Sands Run Out, March 2003

With US support for a second resolution in the bag, Blair was confident of achieving UN backing. He had the support of Spain and Bulgaria guaranteed on the Security Council, on top of the US and UK vote. He thus needed the support of only five other non-permanent members to secure the nine votes necessary to pass a second resolution, assuming no permanent member dared veto it. At the rejectionist end of the spectrum stood the five states – France, Germany, Russia, Syria and China – who he believed would now never vote in favour of a new resolution. In the first two weeks of March, Blair made a show of a desperate 'last gasp' effort to build consensus and exert pressure on Saddam to make him comply. The six 'middle ground' members of the Security Council – Angola, Cameroon, Chile, Guinea, Mexico and Pakistan – tried and failed to put their own proposition forward, and then they asked Greenstock to try on their behalf.[187] Blair was hyperactive, and he spent a week from 7 March working feverishly, rarely off the phone, but was time and again frustrated by an increasingly apathetic approach in Washington.

The Bush administration had its own political and military reasons not to want his efforts to succeed and have any further delay, and they worried that it would only lead to further postponements. American pressure behind the scenes might have made all the difference. But Washington did little to woo France or Russia, or put serious pressure on Chile or Mexico, or any other player.[188] When Blair needed Bush most, his support was half-hearted at best.

The American premonitions about the risks of delay were well grounded. The balance of opinion in the Security Council was not moving in a warlike direction. Quite the opposite. Blix's first report of 27 January had been quite critical of Iraq. However, as inspections proceeded, no WMD were found. Furthermore, Blix discovered, unsurprisingly, that Iraqi co-operation gradually increased. Baghdad was reading the international mood correctly. Blix's report on 14 February was far more equivocal than the first, while his third report (7 March) clearly suggested an accelerated pace of Iraqi co-operation. It seemed to many members that the US wanted to junk the UN route at the very moment it was beginning to work. Straw and Greenstock nevertheless continued their efforts in New York and beyond, knowing there would be little further chance to avert war. Their plan was for Saddam to have to agree to meet tough and very precise 'benchmarks' (first suggested by Chile, one of the middle-ground Security Council members) or else face war. The benchmarks were an imaginative initiative, into which the British put a great deal of effort. Bush accepted Blair's request to try to sell them to the Security Council, and Manning was dispatched to see President Fox of Mexico and President Lagos of Chile to try to win them round.[189]

On the evening of Monday, 10 March, however, Chirac made the startling announcement that France would veto a second resolution, 'whatever the circumstances'. Since December 2002, the Americans had regarded the French as enemies of the UN process, prepared to do anything to undermine attempts to gain a second resolution. Now that belief appeared to be confirmed: 'After Chirac made that pronouncement, we knew the game was up. Why should middle-ground members like Chile and Mexico take huge risks with their own public opinions at home when any resolution would be vetoed anyway?'[190] Blair could not at first believe that Chirac had said this, and told an old friend that he felt that he felt bitterly betrayed.[191] The uncompromising French position, coupled with the negative stance of Germany and Russia, did as much as American over-hastiness to undermine the frenetic attempts to build a fragile coalition in the Security Council: 'All the middle-ground members came on board at different times, but never together. It was very, very close.'[192] On 11 March, Greenstock reported to Downing Street that the second resolution attempt was losing ground. 'I'm not sure we are going to get it through,' Blair told his aides in Number 10, Manning, Powell, Campbell and Morgan. 'Hell, we are stuck then!' one of them said as they began to ask themselves quite how they ended up in this position.[193] Some in Number 10 were clearly shocked to find themselves in a box with no escape plan. On the evening of Wednesday, 12 March, Bush and Blair had two sombre phone calls. At Blair's direct request, Bush called the Presidents of Chile and Mexico to discuss their position on a second resolution, but the calls sounded more like a request for information than an attempt at serious presidential persuasion. Neither would pledge their support. Bush later called Blair back and delivered the news: 'It's over.'[194] Hoon phoned Rumsfeld to warn him that without a second resolution, Blair might not be able to win the necessary support to commit British troops. However, this only prompted Rumsfeld to declare publicly that the US would be willing, if necessary, to go it alone, requiring another call from Blair to Bush to smooth things over.[195] On 14 March, Greenstock confirmed to Blair that the second resolution attempt had, as he fatally put it, 'lost traction'. It was formally withdrawn on 17 March.

American apathy underpinned the failure of the second resolution, but Blair, at the time, chose rather to place the blame squarely on Chirac. To Kampfner, blaming Chirac's wrecking tactics was a convenient pretext by Blair, allowing him to return to a course, war, on which he believed he had set himself a year before.[196] But is this a fair reading? Blair was genuinely shocked by Chirac's pronouncement, chastising it as 'such a foolish thing to do at this moment in world history'.[197] It is true that Chirac's statement provided the pretext for Blair to go to war without further UN authorisation, because he could claim that French action had made UN diplomacy redundant. But, useful though this face-saver might have been, it was not where Blair had wanted or even perhaps expected to be. Blair's much-vaunted persuasive skills had failed spectacularly and not only with Chirac. 'Tony rightly had great belief in his powers of persuasion,' said one senior Cabinet ally, 'but on this occasion he had persuaded himself he could win over those who were never going to respond.'[198]

These were bleak days for the Prime Minister. He had a persistent chest cold, was often exhausted and depressed.[199] His audience with the Pope on 22 February had failed to give him the lift and strength he sought. It was the most anxious period of his premiership so far. Chirac's stance, Number 10 thought, was a blend of principle and self-interest.

The French President, a veteran of the Algerian conflict, genuinely believed war against Iraq would irreparably damage Muslim relations with the West. He also mistrusted American assertion of its power, and disliked those countries that went along with it. Equally, Blair thought Chirac was motivated by expediency: elected President on an insecure base, he seized on the role of being 'champion of the streets' and leading rejectionist in the Gaullist tradition to rally support behind him. He also came to believe, on the basis of intelligence intercepts, that Chirac's hostility was personal: he resented Blair's usurping of his own position as unofficial 'leader' of the EU, and he saw his own stance on Iraq as a chance to bloody and even perhaps destroy his rival. Blair went as far as to tell a colleague that Chirac was 'out to get him'.[200] Blair was, and still is, reluctant to criticise Washington, but his quarrel with the Americans at the time was principally their failure to work harder to build support at the UN, which might have stopped Chirac before he realised his mission as standard-bearer for the rejectionists in December.[201]

Blair now faced one of his biggest and loneliest decisions as Prime Minister. He had failed to secure a second resolution. He had no fall-back position except war, and he had no strength left, nor time, to develop another strategy short of war. He need never have found himself in this position. But there he was. Cook recorded in his diary that he appeared 'mystified as to how he got into such a hole'.[202] 'It was all much scarier than taking big decisions during a General Election campaign,' said one of his inner team.[203] 'It was only in the last four days before military action was taken, 16 to 20 March, that we finally saw it as inevitable, not before,' said Straw, who despite his own reservations had emerged as one of Blair's staunchest Cabinet colleagues.[204] Could Blair have backed down at this stage? Although it would have been extraordinarily difficult, not least with the British troops deployed in the region, it would have been technically impossible. Indeed, earlier in March, fearing that Blair's government might fall, Bush had offered Blair the chance to drop out of the military coalition with British troops coming in only after the conflict as peacekeepers. Blair had steadfastly refused this offer.[205] One reason lay in the strong opposition from the British military, who felt that their failure to participate would have created animosity in their US counterparts. They also feared being tainted by a heavy-handed US approach. As one very senior officer put it, 'we had no desire to go and clear up after the US had trashed the joint'.[206] But 'Tony Blair didn't back down at this point because he didn't want to back out,' said Nigel Sheinwald, Manning's successor in Number 10. 'Even if he had known all the consequences that have happened since, I suspect he would still have gone for it.'[207] Although he regretted bitterly not having secured UN support, this omission fell within the parameters of what he was prepared to stomach to stick with his convictions.[208] 'Tony Blair took Britain to war because he was convinced that the multilateral option was finally exhausted after twelve years, and he believed Iraq under Saddam posed a serious threat that now had to be confronted. It was as simple as that,' said one close aide.[209] It was left to Straw to articulate the other main motive for supporting Bush: he told MPs in early March, 'We will reap a whirlwind if we push the Americans into a unilateral position.' Blair believed, wisely or not, that at all costs he had to stay by Bush's side.

Although absolutely clear in his mind he was doing the right thing, Blair knew he now had an almighty domestic battle to fight. 'Once the decision was taken there was no point in worrying about it,' said one Number 10 aide. 'We just had to get out there and deal with it.'[210] Blair shored up support with Brown and Prescott, who had not been part of the inner-loop discussions, at dinner on 11 March. Neither objected to Blair's views on Iraq, but both were alarmed that he presented no option other than all-out support for America. These were the two key figures if Blair was to carry the Cabinet and party, and he realised he needed them bound tightly to him.[211] Vocal dissent within Cabinet was confined to Clare Short, who had publicly lambasted his handling of the crisis as 'reckless . . . reckless . . . reckless', and Cook, who announced just before Cabinet on Thursday, 13 March, his intention to resign if the UN process was abandoned – which it was, and he did, four days later. Persuading Parliament was going to be even tougher. A close aide described Blair's 'second biggest decision' of the crisis as 'the decision to face a parliamentary vote, and to do so in a very open way'.[212] Several voices believed a vote was unnecessary, and dangerous, as it would expose and inflame divisions.[213] A formal vote by Parliament before going to war is not required in Britain, but Straw, who saw even bigger risks of now having the mandate behind them, insisted that Parliament had to have its say. The whips, backed up by Blair, Brown and Prescott, worked furiously over the weekend of 15/16 March ahead of the key vote on Tuesday, 18 March. An announcement of progress in the Middle East 'road map', on which Blair had been pushing very hard in Washington for many weeks and with great persistence, helped bring some back into the fold. On Sunday, 16 March, Blair flew to the Azores where, joined by Bush and Aznar of Spain, final military plans were discussed, and where Blair also tried, with middling success, to persuade Bush that victory should be followed by a concerted drive for peace in the Middle East. The summit overall was a non-event. Blair returned to

Downing Street at midnight, knowing he faced the most historic and challenging week of his premiership. To Peter Stothard, this Sunday was the day when Blair was at his most grave throughout the whole crisis.[214]

On Monday, 17 March, when UN talks were declared officially over, Goldsmith declared the war against Iraq was 'legal' on the basis of existing UN resolutions. This was a reassurance that Michael Boyce, the Chief of the Defence Staff, had sought before committing any troops to action,[215] but later became controversial after the resignation of the Foreign Secretary's deputy legal adviser, Elizabeth Wilmshurst, who contested the legality of the war.[216] On the Monday and Tuesday before the debate, government virtually ground to a halt as Cabinet ministers were enlisted in last-minute lobbying of Labour MPs. 'I think I can win,' Blair told Bush around lunchtime on Monday, '[but] I'm concerned about the margin of victory. I don't want to depend on Tory votes.'[217] 'We did not know whether we would win a majority of our own MPs,' confirmed one Number 10 insider. 'It kept going one way then the other.'[218] The stakes were very high: 'Everyone believed in the run-up to that vote that Tony had put his premiership on the line, and those who are very close to him would go down with him,' said Blunkett.[219] Andrew Turnbull, the oddly low-profile Cabinet Secretary, dusted off plans for the procedure for a Prime Ministerial resignation, while the Ministry of Defence warned the US military that they might have to 'disconnect' British forces from military action.

A variety of arguments were used to win the dissenters round, from Saddam's humanitarian abuses to the unity of the Labour Party and the authority of the Prime Minister. The US Embassy in London was in regular touch, and also ensured that Duncan Smith's Tories would not change their mind and vote against the war: had the Americans been as assiduous in lobbying in the UN, a multilateral path might have been achieved. Blair gave two speeches that Tuesday, the first to Labour MPs in private, and judged the more impressive, while his second, in the House, was still estimated to have been one of the most accomplished of his premiership. It was also one of his most thoroughly prepared. It was passionate and stirring, for all the laboured calculations that went into it. His assurances about the dangers of the Iraqi WMD threat, which he told the House was real and growing, and his willingness to stake his career on the issue of Saddam's repeatedly ignoring the UN, won him admirers if only a few extra votes from MPs who had mostly made up their minds before he rose to speak. The back-bench rebellion, a larger than expected 139, was not, however, large enough to deny him a majority among Labour MPs, and Campbell immediately sold it to the media as a great victory, a line they mostly bought. 'Had we not got a reasonable majority among Labour MPs,' said Straw, 'we wouldn't have gone to war. It would have been like Chamberlain in 1940 who won the vote, but lost office: it was that serious.'[220] 'If he had lost, he would have resigned,' confirmed John Burton, Blair's Sedgefield mentor.[221] Blair returned to Number 10 that night relieved but without any sense of triumph.[222] As always at moments of high strain, he just wanted to be alone with his family, where he felt most at peace. At the same moment, three thousand miles away along the borders of Iraq, British soldiers were readying themselves for battle.

Blair slept well that night.[223] Now that much of the uncertainty was over, he felt more energised and confident. He had even decided to give up his modest intake of alcohol for the duration of the war, and to adopt a deliberately healthy lifestyle. Soon after hostilities began, in the early hours of Thursday, 20 March, with the failed 'decapitation' attempt on Saddam, Blair shared with Bush his belief that 'the decisions taken in the next few weeks will determine the rest of the world for years to come'.[224] There is no doubt that he was fully aware of the major historical significance of the events he was shaping. From the start of hostilities, Blair monitored developments very closely from Number 10, beginning with an early morning meeting when his core team were briefed by Scarlett on the state of Saddam's regime, and Straw on the overnight 'diplomatic traffic', and then Boyce on how British servicemen were faring. The early days of the campaign were blighted by incidents of friendly fire and unexpected pockets of resistance. Every British death struck him a hammer blow. He spoke of being ready 'to meet my Maker' and answer for 'those who have died or have been horribly maimed as a result of my decisions'.[225] Similarly, Bush did not rely on his colleagues for strength during the conflict, nor even his father, George Bush Snr: 'There is a higher father that I appeal to,' he told Woodward.

The first two weeks of the war did not provide the sudden collapse Blair, in his heart, had hoped would happen.[226] He became increasingly drawn in, and, in unconscious imitation of Churchill, whose Cabinet War Rooms still lurked in the bowels of Whitehall nearby, he wanted big maps on the wall of the den so he could follow the progress of the troops. 'We wouldn't let him. It would have looked awful,' said Morgan, adding mockingly, 'He really would have liked a sandpit with tanks.'[227] War might not have been the three-day dash into Baghdad with soldiers garlanded along the way by cheering Iraqis that hawks in the Bush administration absurdly imagined, but achieving victory in just a month greatly exceeded secret British military forecasts that it might take two to three times as long.[228] British troops seized most of Basra by 7 April and American forces stormed the centre of Baghdad on 9 April, with the symbolic felling of the Saddam statues. Fighting continued for a few more days, but the outcome, to Blair's intense relief, was clear.

British participation was of great importance to the Americans, so it was unsurprising, having taken Blair's support for granted for a year and more, that they worried at the end whether the vote in Parliament would be carried. British military sources insist that their contribution to the invasion was vital. The original war plan had provided for one US infantry division to attack from the north through Turkey. The latter's refusal to co-operate meant that this division had to be redeployed in the south, but would not be operational until mid-April. Without both this division and the British contribution, an invasion would have been extremely hazardous for the Americans. In addition, the planned air assault drew upon British missiles and planes, which were carefully integrated into the attack, while the British were also due to lead the amphibious assault on the al-Faw peninsula. Non-participation by the British would not have stopped the war, British military chiefs said, but it would have set it back by a good few weeks.[229] Even more important was that British involvement in hostilities encouraged other nations who had been initially reluctant to support the war to do so – such as Australia, Poland and the Netherlands. The sense in the US State Department was that 'without the British, we would have been fighting unilaterally. Other countries would have been much less likely to join us had the British not been on board.'[230] This point was not lost on Bush, who placed great value on being able to tell his domestic audience that the US was not standing alone. Whether Britain received its just reward for all its loyalty is a matter examined below. For the time being, Blair, while impressively anxious to avoid any public display of triumphalism was intensely relieved the fighting was over after just twenty days and without greater loss of British life.[231] He began to give interviews to the press, in which he spoke of his anguish and of how he had been prepared to resign if he had not carried his party with him.

Blair had taken the most quite extraordinary risks over Iraq, greater than any British Prime Minister since the end of the Second World War. Now, with the fall of Baghdad, he thought he was vindicated. The talk in Westminster was of the 'Baghdad bounce',[232] a surge in Blair's ratings and strength, and rumours originating in Number 10 that Brown would be moved to the Foreign Office. Reports circulated that Blair now felt 'more on top of the job' and more ready to take risks than ever before.[233]

The Impact of the Iraq War on Blair

Tony Blair believes that the war in Iraq is the most important event for a generation and that in twenty years' time it will make his reputation in history.[234] He is certainly right that many years will have to pass before his actions can be finally adjudicated. The al-Qaeda bombing in Madrid in March 2004, widely perceived as a response to Spanish support for the war, was just one reminder that the consequences of Blair's decisions could be in their infancy. But some questions can be answered now. This final section will examine why Blair took Britain to war, the influence of the US, and the effect of the war on Blair.

Amid the millions of words spilled over the Iraq war, and all the obfuscation, it can be easy to lose sight of the simplicity of Blair's decision. He believed WMD were a menace to the future security of the free world, that taking on Iraq for defying the UN on seventeen resolutions over twelve years was necessary, and he believed WMD would be found in Iraq. He thought the war would be over very quickly, and that Saddam was evil, abused human rights and had sacrificed any right to continue his rule. His dictatorship should therefore be replaced by a democratic regime, which would bring greater security to the Gulf region. He believed that if the US were allowed to go it alone it would be more dangerous for world peace, and that he had a duty to monitor and restrain them.[235] The strong moral conviction he held was underpinned by his religious faith. The Pope may not have been helpful, but his own prayers told him he was taking the right course. He would have preferred to have had a second UN resolution, but he believed he was acting lawfully based on past resolutions. Geoffrey Wheatcroft has written that Iraq marked the culmination of Blair's 'Antinomian tendencies toward self-deception, misrepresentation, and "constructive ambiguity" . . . all of which drove him to mislead his country for what he believed was the greater good'. Yet Blair did not lie about why he took the country to war. His irrepressible self-belief in the rightness of his decision indeed fired him to go before public audiences absolutely sure that he could convince them. The worst that can be said about him is that his very certainty militated against him seeing other truths and perspectives.

Blair was bolstered in his convictions by those around him. While many in Cabinet had profound reservations, it is quite untrue, as Short maintained, that they lacked the opportunity to discuss Iraq. According to the Cabinet Secretary, Andrew Turnbull, it was discussed at virtually every Cabinet meeting he attended since taking on the job in

September 2002.[236] Blair received warm affirmation from some like Tessa Jowell, who reassured him that standing up for what he believed would secure his place in history.[237] Prescott fell in solidly behind the action, while Brown, once he saw that British involvement was inevitable, supported Blair fully in public. Many senior diplomats in the Foreign Office were deeply concerned but failed to speak out (though some took the unprecedented step in April 2004 of signing an open letter criticising the government's Middle East policy). According to one inside observer, the strength of Blair's personality and his autocratic style of leadership entrenched an 'oppressive sense of conformity and political correctness' among some at the top of the FCO: 'Few dared question or criticise him.'[238] Within his closest team in Number 10, Campbell and Morgan had private reservations while Manning was often uneasy, but accepted Blair's commitment to the US and worked to try to make it compatible with action through the UN, something Blair himself strongly favoured.[239] Jonathan Powell, whose Atlanticist sympathies were beyond doubt, echoed this view. Boyce, the senior military adviser, was convinced that Saddam possessed WMD, and agreed that the time had come to take action against Iraq, providing it remained lawful.[240] The intelligence chiefs Scarlett, Lander and Dearlove were not counselling caution. None of Blair's advisers were bad or reckless people. The very worst that can be said of some of them is that they told Blair what they thought he wanted to hear, and that Blair was too ready to listen to the people whose advice chimed with his own instincts.

Where do the Americans stand in this? We have seen earlier how, when Clinton was President, British influence was not as extensive as some in London believed, any more than it had been during the Afghanistan war. The Clinton and Bush administrations were very grateful for British support, but essentially were going to do what they wanted to do regardless. Unilateralism did not begin in January 2001 when the Bush team rode into town. It has been a common error in London, as with Macmillan during the Cuban Missile Crisis, to exaggerate the degree of influence exerted by the British. The intensely divided nature of the administration meant that any agreement Blair thought he had reached with Bush risked being undermined later on by the hawks. With hindsight, Blair placed too much trust in the Americans, who themselves made a series of misjudgements.

Washington exaggerated the fragility of support for Saddam and the readiness of opposition to him within Iraq. The intelligence team favoured by Cheney, the 'Office of Special Plans' based in the Pentagon, fatally relied too much on the Iraqi National Congress and on defectors, who in their eagerness to see the hated dictator deposed either invented or exaggerated information. Cheney's office seemed determined to push what could be extracted from the intelligence beyond the comfort zone of others in the administration. At one point, 'Scooter' Libby drew his colleagues' attention to a transcript of two Iraqis allegedly discussing experiments with the poison ricin, despite the fact that the CIA's Deputy Director had previously judged this 'evidence' as unreliable. According to one author, Cheney himself was fixated with providing a link between Iraq and al-Qaeda: 'Powell thought that Cheney took intelligence and converted uncertainty and ambiguity into fact.'[241] British officials certainly detected no unmanly doubt in the hawkish Vice-President. In January 2003, he assured one official that there was no need to worry about attacking Iraq: 'All the difficulties and questions will be forgotten once we pull it off,' he declared. 'Just hold your nerve.'[242]

The administration's obsession with Iraq from Bush's election, and especially after 9/11, skewed the rationality of the West's thinking. Far too many in the administration were less intent on fighting a 'war on terror' and more interested in rounding off unfinished business from 1991. Blair himself wanted to be tough with Iraq for evading the UN, as he had been in 1998. He hated Saddam and everything he stood for. But he had no burning, preconceived fervour to invade Iraq. This was the Bush administration's obsession, and Blair allowed himself to be swept up in it.

Blair believed the administration was more serious about reaching an agreement within the UN than it ultimately proved to be. He let his support, through his early pledges after 9/11 and at Crawford in March 2002, be taken for granted. It was too easy for the unilateralists to win the argument in the face of a hesitant UN, and with time ticking away, by saying they could rely on the British in any event. So certain were the hawks of a swift and definitive victory, and a grateful, democracy-loving and stable Iraq following the war, that they never gave Blair's pleas for the multilateral route the serious consideration they deserved.

Simplistic administration belief in the ability of the Saddam opposition to form a government after his overthrow contributed to the baleful – indeed negligent – lack of planning for the peace. Greenstock, who went on from the UN job to become Blair's senior envoy in Iraq, admitted publicly that the administration's thinking about Iraq post-war was hopelessly inadequate, and that some in the administration realised this error but thought it politic to keep quiet.[243] The Pentagon, charged with post-war planning by Bush, carried out these duties in absolute secrecy, refusing even to share their strategy with the State Department, let alone the British government.[244] Having bought the INC line that the invading forces would be welcomed and new Iraqi leaders could simply take over in Baghdad, their efforts were largely misdirected. US forces thus entered Iraq with a plethora of detailed plans for dealing with displaced populations, controlling disease and putting out fires at sabotaged oil wells, most of which proved redundant, but very few plans for restoring viable governance to Iraq. Blair was himself too distracted by other concerns, including the Hutton Inquiry, to give the post-war reconstruction of Iraq the undivided attention it needed,[245] but the Bush administration must squarely bear the brunt of the blame. Cooler heads and wiser planning would have meant the path to constitutional government in Iraq would have been quicker and more foolproof. Post-war Iraq was a model of American policy at its worst. Britain was badly let down by its closest ally.

Finally, the Americans, despite the plan for Israeli withdrawal of Gaza announced in April 2004, failed to make the serious and lasting commitment to achieving a just peace in the Middle East many expected, despite Blair raising the issue with Bush at almost every opportunity over eighteen months since 9/11. Blair's battle with the Americans over this issue will be discussed in the next chapter.

The impact of the war in Iraq on Blair has been immense. It has been not only the defining issue of his second term, but of his entire premiership. 'Forget your contribution to public services,' advised one of Blair's closest intimates, 'what you'll be remembered for is winning two fucking great election victories and four wars.'[246] Maybe, but the Iraqi 'victory' came at the heaviest price. Whether or not the original decision to go to war was correct, attempts to stabilise the post-war situation have proved ineffective, with the problems exacerbated by the heavy-handedness of US troops. The 'special relationship' has been severely tested. Blair may have established himself as Bush's First Ally, but the costs of doing so have led many to question the value to Britain of maintaining the 'special relationship'. His relationship with EU leaders has been seriously damaged, and his hope (if such it was) of taking Britain into the Euro has been finally dashed. At home, the war profoundly damaged his relationship with the Labour Party and the media, further sullied his reputation with the electorate as someone who could be trusted, and tarnished Labour's electoral prospects. The whole Iraq experience drained his energy, his political capital and his reputation.

On a personal level, however, the war strengthened Tony Blair, at least in the short term. 'He's become much more confident because during the war he had to stand up to the most senior military and security figures in the land. It made him grow up very quickly,' said one insider.[247] It also bonded him with his team. 'We all felt very alone in the world,' said another. 'It made us a close family.'[248] But of 'the team', only Morgan and Powell remained one year after hostilities had ceased.

If Iraq settles quickly into a peaceful democratic nation, if the world becomes a safer place, if no terrorist bombs in Britain follow the 3/11 attack in Madrid, if WMD proliferation slows, then the view of the war and of Blair's judgement will change. He knows this. He is the eternal optimist, believing everything will work out in the end. By mid-2004, however, he accepted that it would not provide the clean victory that the Falklands did for Thatcher, and Kosovo did for him (at least until the problems resurfaced in early 2004). Blair is still understandably in self-justification mode, as Eden remained over Suez. One day, however, he will ask himself why he sacrificed so much – indeed, many thought his premiership – out of trust for George W. Bush. To answer that question, we must take a deeper look at Bush, and his surprising relationship with Tony Blair.

Marching in step: Blair with President Bush at the White House in July 2003.
Bush glances to his right; Blair marches boldly on, as if by clockwork.

38

George W. Bush

All Blair's most influential relationships were with figures he met before he became Prime Minister, except one, whom he did not encounter until he had been in the job for nearly four years. The oddity of the bond between an insular-minded Texas conservative, most of whose advisers were on the hard right, and a modernising left-wing leader who was a sworn internationalist cannot be exaggerated. This was to be Blair's most significant relationship with any overseas leader, and it changed the whole course and tenor of his premiership. It was with George W. Bush, forty-third President of the United States.

George W. Bush, the Man

Bush was born on 6 July 1946 in New Haven, Connecticut, where his father, who had recently returned from the war, was studying at Yale University. His mother, Barbara, gave birth to five more children, one of whom, a sister, died of leukaemia in 1953. After Yale, the family settled in Texas, where Bush Sr. set out successfully making his fortune in the oil business. Bush Jr. was sent to elite schools back in the east, studying at Yale, and then Harvard Business School, where he acquired an MBA in 1975. He married Laura, a librarian, in 1977, and in 1981 she gave birth to their twin daughters.

While his father's career blossomed, serving as Director of the CIA in the 1970s and then as Ronald Reagan's Vice-President in the 1980s, Bush Jr.'s own career did not. He failed to acquire a seat as a Republican in the House of Representatives in 1978, and his attempt to emulate his father's success in the oil business flopped. He began to drink heavily, reaching a crisis before giving it up on his fortieth birthday in July 1986. A reawakened Christian faith played its role in this renunciation, and religion thereafter became central to his life. A revitalised figure, he worked for his father on his successful presidential campaign in 1988, and then entered a new field, baseball, becoming managing partner of the Texas Rangers. His newfound profile and confidence, and family backing, helped him win the Texas governorship in 1994. He served the four-year term and was a popular candidate for re-election in 1998, winning nearly 70 per cent of the vote.

It proved the ideal launch pad for his assault on the presidency, in a quest to become the first son of a President to win the White House since John Quincy Adams in 1824. Bush was able to raise more money than Vice-President Al Gore, and fought as a 'compassionate conservative' who would unify rather than divide the country, while Gore stressed his competence and experience in government, but implicitly distanced himself from Clinton. The election in November 2000 was one of the closest in American history. Although Gore won half a million more votes than Bush, after five weeks of controversy about the count in Florida and a divisive and divided Supreme Court decision, the American voting system delivered 271 Electoral College votes for Bush against 266 for Gore. Bush was duly inaugurated on 20 January 2001.

Blair and Bush: First Contact to 9/11

Number 10 had been extremely nervous about the outcome of the 2000 presidential election. While Blair would have preferred Gore, but remained philosophical, many around him were ardent Gore supporters. They saw in a Gore presidency the chance to complete the Clinton agenda, put on hold by his crippled second term. Number 10 was, however, conscious of the ill-will generated within the Clinton White House by the Conservatives' support for the defeated Bush Sr. in the presidential election campaign of 1992. The British Ambassador, Robin Renwick, had cool relations with the Clintons at first as a result, and the in-coming Ambassador in 1995, John Kerr, was determined that he would avoid a similar mistake in the future. He thus made a point of getting to know Governor Bush, travelling to Austin, Texas to establish a good personal relationship with the family.[1] Kerr's last dispatch to London in 1997 before returning home said that while he thought Gore would become the Democrat candidate when Clinton stood down, he thought he would lose to any 'half-decent' Republican.[2] The next Ambassador, Christopher Meyer, continued where Kerr left off and visited Bush in Texas in 1998 and 1999. He reported back to London that while Bush admitted his ignorance in foreign policy, he was savvy, masterful at 'working a room', and he admired loyalty.[3] Meyer was concerned that the mythology of the intense Clinton–Blair relationship might prejudice the formation of a good relationship with the Bush team if he won. Accordingly he raised this fear with two of Bush's closest associates, Condoleezza Rice and Karl Rove, later in 2000. They reassured Meyer that the Blair/Clinton relationship would not prove a problem. In fact, he was told the loyalty Blair had shown to Clinton was something Bush admired. As far as Bush was concerned, Blair would start with a clean slate.

Blair, throughout the 2000 election, adopted a studiously impartial line between Gore and Bush. The advice he was receiving on the likely victor swung from side to side, understandably so given the closeness of the final result. Jonathan Powell and David Miliband returned from a visit to the US convinced that Gore would win.[4] At the British Embassy, however, Ambassador Meyer and Political Officer Matthew Rycroft were far from convinced: 'Don't underestimate Bush,' was their constant refrain. 'He may be an appalling public speaker and not a good debater, but he can take Gore.'[5] Powell, who remembered Gore from the 1992 campaign trail, recalled him as a very good electioneer: Bush, in contrast, he thought, was a 'hick'.[6] Some of the partisans in Number 10, particularly those close to Cherie, could not bear the thought of a Bush victory. Indeed, the carefully hedged line from the Embassy and Meyer's growing relations with the Bush entourage led to problems with Number 10, who accused the Embassy of being biased towards Bush.[7]

Meyer and John Sawers, the Number 10 Foreign Affairs Private Secretary, had pressed for an invitation for George Bush Sr. to visit Number 10 while on a private visit to Britain. The meeting, and George W.'s success in securing the Republican nomination, gave Blair the pretext to fire off a letter in May to Bush Jr. saying how he had enjoyed meeting his father, and that he very much hoped to meet the governor himself later in the year. Bush was pleased by the letter and sent back a reply, which was anodyne, but established a friendly tone.[8] The ice was broken. Hopes rose of a Bush visit to Europe before the November election, with London the first stop. But plans were shelved owing to the very negative press coverage Bush was receiving in Europe and fears among his advisers that he would be universally ridiculed.[9] The exchange of letters was to remain their only personal contact until after the election had been finally decided.

Number 10's anxiety about the result reached fever point ('They became demented,' said one witness) during the Florida recount in late 2000.[10] The Embassy submitted regular, elaborate reports about what was happening, suggesting the best- and worst-case scenarios. While some at Number 10 were spitting blood at the Supreme Court's final verdict, Blair immediately sent Bush a message saying, in summary, 'Warmest congratulations. I know that together we will strengthen the special relationship. I look forward to working with you.'[11] A new anxiety now gripped Number 10: that the Conservatives would claim that Labour could not work with a Republican in the White House.[12] With a General Election looming, such a line ran the risk of becoming just the kind of scare story that Labour had tried so hard to neutralise in 1997. So Blair followed up his message with a hastily arranged phone call to Texas on 14 December, made while on a visit to Warwick University.[13] Blair poured all his charm down the phone line. The official with him recalled, 'It was a very promising first talk. They immediately struck up a friendly, open relationship.'[14] Even though there had been no real substance to the call, Blair returned to his official tour relieved that he had established a personal rapport with Bush, and that Bush had given no indication of being put out by Blair's close relationship with Clinton.[15] As Blair and his advisers discussed the call later that day, they admitted they had as yet little if any idea exactly what a Bush presidency would mean for Britain's relationship with the US, or indeed the world.[16]

Blair's chief concern was to establish a close relationship with the incoming administration as speedily as possible. With reports coming in to Number 10 that the Bush team would consciously react against the policy positions of the out-going Democrats, including fears that Bush would abandon Clinton's qualified internationalism and search out other close, possibly non-European allies, Blair's anxiety was understandable. The Tories were continuing to sniff out the possibilities the Bush victory might afford them, and it required heavy lobbying and nimble footwork from Downing Street to counter overtures from Tory HQ. In the end, the White House agreed to turn down the Tories' request that Iain Duncan Smith, still then their Defence Spokesman, be seen by Bush's people before Hoon, the Defence Secretary.[17] Some in the Bush camp, notably the hawks, certainly had little taste for a Clinton-loving, Labour government in London. This attitude was mostly kept hidden, but could be detected in the restrained reception Foreign Secretary Cook received from Cheney when he made the first official British government visit to welcome the new administration in January 2001.[18] Cook struck up a much better rapport with Colin Powell, whom he had met in London before the election.[19]

The Gore-lovers and Bush-sceptics in Whitehall were told firmly to shut up while all energy went into building a solid relationship with the new administration ahead of the British election planned for that spring. No deep stock-take had been made of what the vast British investment in Clinton had delivered for Britain, nor had any thorough evaluation taken place in Number 10 of the gains they might hope to achieve from the Bush presidency, and what their own bargaining strengths were. It was Blair's gut instinct that everything hinged on establishing a quick and exclusive relationship with the new incumbent. That was the governing imperative. Everything else was secondary.

Chief responsibility for establishing close relations when an administration changes falls on the Ambassador on the spot: and with the long hiatus between a twilight Clinton and a delayed Bush administration, even more fell on the incumbent Ambassador. Meyer had already established three 'indispensable' contacts in the Bush camp: once Bush was elected, Karl Rove continued as chief political strategist; Condoleezza Rice was appointed National Security Advisor; and Paul Wolfowitz became Deputy Secretary of Defense. Rice had worked in Bush Senior's administration in the National Security Council and had gone on to become the first female, first non-white head of Stanford University. She had articulated firm unilateralist views in a 2000 article for the journal *Foreign Affairs*, which was studied closely in London.[20] Rice's position in the administration made her Meyer's most significant contact: he was thus relieved when she told him 'our most important bilateral relationship has always been with Britain. We must ensure it gets off to a good start.'[21] Rice and Rove continued to reassure Meyer that although the Blair–Clinton bond was not a problem for them, everything depended upon how the personal relationship worked out between Blair and Bush.

The first face-to-face meeting was thus going to be crucial. Dismay was caused temporarily in London that the first European leader to meet Bush was not Blair but Chirac, though reassurances were given to Number 10 not to worry: Chirac was in town for a 'routine' EU/US summit and his meeting with Bush was not substantive. The visit was to play to Blair's advantage, however, because Chirac made it clear France envisaged Europe as a counterweight to US power. In contrast, Bush's team were realising that Blair's vision saw Britain as an intimate partner with the US, ready to make sacrifices for a place at the top table.[22] Whether Blair, then at the height of his power on the world stage, needed to adopt this position as his opening gambit with the incoming administration is a moot point. The Embassy in Washington advised that Downing Street had a rare opportunity, but also a risk, in the new relationship. The opportunity was to shape American foreign policy while it was still in embryo; the risk was to be seen as just America's 'bag-carrier', a story the American press was already airing.[23] Such advice, however, was rare, and, in the blistering race to establish credentials with the new tenants of the White House, all too easily lost.

Meyer pressed tirelessly on Rice to agree a date for the summit. She was friendly but adamant. Bush had to see Vicente Fox of Mexico first – 'That's the way it's done' – and no space was available in his diary before March at the earliest.[24] But the ground began to move, not least when it became clear that Schröder and other European leaders were no more enthusiastic about a cosy relationship with the US than Chirac.[25] 'When we looked out at Europe we soon drew the very obvious conclusion that Britain was going to be the most sympathetic nation,' as one senior insider put it.[26] Much is made in the literature of the role of Bill Gammell, a mutual friend of Blair and Bush, in brokering the new friendship: in fact, his work as intermediary amounted to little. It was cold calculation that drove the Americans towards the British.[27] After weeks of negotiation, Rice phoned Meyer. 'We can do 23 February,' she said.[28]

Feverish planning now took place in London. Number 10 was in the driving seat: the Foreign Office barely got a look-in.[29] Because Bush's team were so largely unknown to Blair and his advisers, it had been decided to send Jonathan Powell and Sawers over on an unpublicised fact-finding mission the week before Bush's inauguration. They saw almost all the senior figures except Bush, including Cheney, Powell, Rice and Rove. 'The lack of face-to-face acquaintance had been very worrying. The meetings helped build relationships and establish the groundwork,' said one aide.[30] The talks ranged over areas such as Iraq and the Balkans, where there were no major differences, US plans for a national missile defence system and European defence, which were contentious and required urgent diplomatic attention. Powell and Sawers were conscious of unilateralist currents, notably on America's missile defence plans, about which they learned Bush was 'hot, hot, hot', and which threatened to tear up the long-standing Anti-Ballistic Missile (ABM) Treaty.[31] But they did not detect any seismic shifts in policy nor a new belligerence, not even on Iraq. Indeed, for all the new rhetoric and the determination of the incoming administration to play up the differences with their predecessors, the changes in policy can all too easily be exaggerated. After all, Clinton had not been immune from unilateralism, as seen for example in his scepticism towards the International Criminal Court.

For all the warm words, Blair was still apprehensive on the flight over to the US in late February. Number 10 laid out its stall before they left, saying that the trip would underline Britain's role as America's closest ally, uniquely placed to bridge Europe and the US. A joint US–UK air attack on Iraqi installations outside Baghdad just before the visit was tangible proof of intent.[32] The party on the plane went over yet again how to play the meeting, and who exactly the Prime Minister would be dealing with. Blair felt that the stakes could hardly have been higher. For all the affirmation now emanating out of the White House, he knew the relationship, and the meeting, mattered much more to him than to Bush, who, if need be, could operate perfectly adequately without Britain. Personal chemistry, he knew, would be crucial, as Rice had warned them, as it always had been when the relationship worked best, as with Churchill and Roosevelt, or Thatcher and Reagan. Blair had decided back in the autumn of 2000 that if Bush were to come out above Gore, he would aim to become his 'best friend',[33] the very words Clinton recommended when they met just before Christmas.[34] This task was made easier because, like Blair, Bush was not a tribal politician, they both had outgoing personalities, and they were practising Christians. A greeting in Washington from Vice-President Cheney, whom the British never found easy or sympathetic, did not ease the tension. As Blair surveyed the issues with Cheney – European defence, the Middle East, Russia – he feared that if the Vice-President was indeed representative of Bush's thinking and his new team, the going would be much heavier than he had hoped.[35]

The contrast with Bush's warm greeting, after Blair's helicopter touched down the next morning at Camp David, could not have been starker. Bush, wearing chinos and visibly relaxed, made Blair and the British team – Campbell, Powell, Sawers and Meyer – immediately comfortable. He deftly slipped into the conversation early on how pleased he was that Blair was his first overseas visitor to the President's retreat.[36] The Blair team were struck immediately by the quality of the Bush team compared to the depleted quality of Clinton's – 'It was obvious to us that, with people like Powell, Rice and Rumsfeld, this was a much more impressive group,' said one, who described them as 'stellar'.[37] Bush too struck Blair as a much more serious and knowledgeable President than he had anticipated: "The real revelation was Bush's decisiveness and grasp,' said one aide.[38] Whatever the forty-third President might prove to be, he certainly was not the bumbling Texas buffoon of popular caricature.

Proceedings began with a working lunch. Blair had been briefed by the Embassy on how best to handle the new President. 'Be informal, practical, get to the point, no pomposity, no high-falutin' stuff, just get stuck straight in. Informality is everything.'[39] Accordingly, as an observer described it, 'They sat down for lunch, looked at each other across the table and they sort of grinned. And the President said, "Welcome, Tony. Looking forward to having you here for twenty-four hours." And that was it. Off they went. No more small talk.'[40] In the 'agenda' faxed to Number 10 a few days before the meeting, Iraq was to be a lead item for discussion: the focus, however, was on tightening sanctions against Saddam. There was no talk of invasion. Indicatively, Bush handed over to Powell, his leading dove, to outline the new administration's thinking on Iraq before he left early on a tour to the Middle East. Bush then summarised Powell's thoughts in a way that struck the British by its 'lucidity and grasp'.[41] The British team also noted how Bush constantly flattered Blair over his knowledge of international affairs, above all about the Russians. He was intrigued to learn more about Putin, and regarded Blair as an authority on the Russian leader.[42] Blair talked enthusiastically about Putin and his hopes for progress in the Middle East peace process, on which the Americans listened patiently.

After lunch, Bush and Blair, in jeans too tight for his advancing years, went off for a much-photographed walk in the woods, during which they sealed the exclusive relationship, which was to become so important in the year that followed. After their return, a long informal meeting took place over drinks in the large lodge, 'shooting the breeze' and allowing the two teams to bond. The party then split, with the Bushes and Blairs going off for a dinner on their own. This was difficult for Cherie. She had been on her best behaviour since her arrival at Camp David, but was finding it difficult: the foursome dinner contrasted starkly with the heady, euphoric meals and get-togethers with the Clintons, a highpoint of her early days at Number 10. She did not feel comfortable amid Republicans, and had made no secret of her desire for a Gore victory, and her liking for his wife, Tipper. After dinner, Bush decided he wanted all his guests to see a film, *Meet the Parents* with Robert de Niro, in the small Camp David cinema, which was unusual because he normally favoured going to bed early.[43]

The next morning George Tenet, head of the CIA, joined the party for an intelligence briefing. For the final press conference, officials on both teams had been 'slightly Soviet' and drafted a conference statement some days before, which was signed off by Rice and Sawers once they were at Camp David. In a straight trade-off or 'deal', which glossed over many contentious points, the British secured American support in principle for the European Defence Initiative which Blair and Chirac had launched at St Malo, 'as long as it was not in conflict with Nato', the Americans insisted. In return, Blair made the major concession of agreeing to the new administration's plans for national missile defence, as long as other countries, principally Russia, were consulted. This was a key sacrifice from Blair, as many of Britain's allies had serious concerns about America's plans, fearing it would unpick many years of work on arms control. Blair even agreed to let the US upgrade its early warning stations on British soil. The left were strongly opposed to this, but Blair was sympathetic to America's hopes of developing a defensive shield to protect itself against the risk of nuclear attack from a 'rogue state'. By concluding this deal in advance, 'during those vital twenty-four hours together at Camp David, we were free to meet and get to know each other without being weighed down by substantive and possibly awkward issues,' as one official put it.[44] For all the prior groundwork, the press conference was the one awkward part of the visit. Blair in his open-neck shirt and Bush in his bomber jacket looked ill at ease together, and the President's gauche quip in response to a question about what they had in common, that they shared the same taste in toothpaste, led to the press dubbing it the 'Colgate summit'. For all that, the summit exceeded Blair's hopes. He and Bush had looked into each other's eyes and sized each other up. The chemistry had worked. Both administrations had also agreed in outline on a broad range of policy positions. After months of worry, and with the British General Election just weeks away, Blair had the President exactly where he wanted him to be. The Tories were nowhere to be seen, and Britain was acknowledged as the US's closest ally. But to what end?

Blair realised that Bush was a serious politician and that he presided over a team that was not just hugely able but also, as he was beginning to appreciate more, highly polarised. But even after Camp David, Blair and his advisers were no closer to working out where exactly Bush himself stood. Blair made much of his delight in finding that Bush was very 'straight' in his talking at Camp David. Blair regularly praised Bush's 'straight' manner in the following months. But 'straight' about what? Was he instinctively an internationalist, like Powell and Armitage, or more of a unilateralist like Cheney and Rumsfeld? Was he a dove, who would often err, like Clinton, on the side of caution, or a hawk, like many of the Vulcans, who would not baulk at using force in pursuit of American national interests? An enduring problem for Downing Street, certainly prior to 9/11, was that it never pinned down where Bush stood. Even after 9/11, there remained a division between 'Bush the head', willing to work multilaterally and explore diplomatic avenues, and 'Bush the gut', whose instincts chimed more readily with the hawks. Was too much reliance placed on 'Bush the head' being 'straight' with Blair while 'Bush the gut' kept quiet, only to emerge once Blair was safely out of earshot? The failure to nail Bush, due in part to his own gyrations around his disputatious and divided advisers, and in part to Blair's own miscalculations, lay behind some of the difficulties Britain's foreign policy encountered over the next three years.

Bush's two main preoccupations between the Camp David summit in February and the 11 September attacks were national missile defence, which was a passion he brought with him to the White House, and his search for a new relationship with Russia, which became a growing, almost messianic, personal quest. At Camp David in February, Bush had secured Britain's acquiescence on the former. Now he sought to milk Blair of his understanding on the latter, especially his relationship with Vladimir Putin, the Russian leader, which had built up since their first meeting in March 2000. 'What Bush got out of us in those first few months was some very pointed and expert advice on Putin,' said one British insider.[45] Blair's most significant contribution was to convince Bush that, with Putin in power, they faced a historic opportunity to bring Russia into the orbit of the West. Blair also had to pacify Putin, who was incensed that Bush's missile defence plan meant abrogating the ABM Treaty. When Bush in March announced the expulsion of fifty Russian diplomats from America who were, allegedly, FSB spies, it was again Blair who stepped in as peacemaker. As a result, Putin gave a measured, not a proportional response, and expelled only a handful of American diplomats from Russia.[46]

Bush was thus in a positive frame of mind when he met Putin in Ljubljana, the capital of Slovenia, in 2001 for their first and seminal summit. The two-hour meeting went well. Religion proved a key ingredient. Putin showed Bush a crucifix that his mother had given him: 'I sensed that we had the cross in common,' Bush later said, adding, 'I looked the man in his eye. I found him to be very straightforward and trustworthy. We had a very good dialogue. I was able to get a sense of his soul.' Russia, almost seamlessly, became a 'partner and ally' and could in time become 'a strong partner and friend'.[47] The Bush administration had come to power in January 2001 with a distinctly standoffish attitude to Russia, wanting to cut it down to size: 'We'll see them, certainly, but they must wait their turn. Where is Russia in the GDP league table anyway?'[48] Blair had been a catalyst in changing American thinking and making Bush realise he had more to gain from engagement than proving points. Steve Hadley, Rice's deputy, spoke almost euphorically of the hope that America would develop a relationship with Russia in the future as close as its relationship with Britain in the past.[49] Blair had succeeded brilliantly in being the John the Baptist figure to this messianic new vision of America's foreign policy. But what again did he receive in return from his ally in the White House?

Bush's embrace of the Russian bear was even more intense following the EU–US summit at Gothenburg in June, when he was thoroughly disgruntled by Chirac and Schröder's sceptical reception, and their hostility to US rejection of the Kyoto protocol of 1997 on climate change and global warming. Blair was working overtime on his role as bridge-builder. But Schröder spoke for many when he said that the problem with Blair's bridge was that the traffic seemed to be going in only one direction.[50] The summit at Gothenburg confirmed Bush in his earlier judgement that Britain was the only dependable European state and thus his decision to give preferential treatment to the British, and he was conspicuously friendly when he went to Chequers for an overnight visit on 19 July. His meeting with Blair was a *tour d'horizon* of all the principal issues, missile defence, Russia and the ABM Treaty, Iraq, the Balkans, and the Middle East. On Russia, Bush was particularly buoyant, and hoped to clinch a missile defence deal, he said, 'by the end of the year'.[51] An identity of outlook was manifest across the waterfront, US rejection of the Kyoto agreement on global warming being a rare disagreement, on which Blair pressed Bush for at least a positive gesture. Bush's increasing regard for Blair was signalled by his willingness to refer to the 'special relationship' in public.[52] Cherie's continuing pique at the Bush victory was revealed in her undiplomatic challenge to the President at dinner that evening over his tolerance of the death penalty.[53] Of far greater import was that the Chequers visit heralded the first meeting between Rice and David Manning, who had recently succeeded Sawers as Blair's foreign policy adviser. The Manning–Rice relationship ('a marriage made in heaven'[54]) was set to become a core channel.

Bush had been looking forward greatly to his London visit, which included lunch with the Queen at Buckingham Palace. Bush had his sentimental and traditional side, and he enjoyed the pomp and occasion vastly more than the drudgery of the 'G7/8' summit at Genoa, on to which both he and Blair travelled on 20 July. 'The idea of being locked into meetings for eleven hours listening to "bullshit", to the sounds outside of tens of thousands of shouting protestors was not his idea of fun,' said one Bush aide.[55] Genoa proved indeed to be every bit as unproductive as Bush had anticipated, the main solace being provided by Putin: 'There was a definite feeling among the leaders that it was good to have a Russian leader who doesn't get drunk and who can add up,' an observer noted.[56] Bush and Blair kept in touch over the summer holiday, anticipating an autumn of close co-operation on a series of issues that were moving towards resolution. To prepare for a busy diplomatic autumn, Manning flew to America on 10 September, and had dinner on the terrace of the British Embassy with Rice and Meyer, enjoying a late summer evening, dipping in and out of substantive issues, with peacekeeping in the Balkans the most pressing item.[57] As they sat together basking in the warmth of an early autumn evening, al-Qaeda operatives were putting in place their final plans for the following morning, and savouring their final night on earth. Terrorism, however, did not once enter the discussions on the Embassy terrace.

Blair Loses His Touch, 9/11 to 2004

The events of 9/11 did not create a new relationship between Blair and Bush: they deepened a bond that had already been forged.[58] The attack transformed an identity of interest on a range of international issues over the preceding eight months into one shared passion: to tackle international terrorism and rogue states who harboured it. There were no shades of grey here: Osama Bin Laden, Saddam Hussein and his fellow travellers were evil people. Blair's and Bush's shared Christian outlook fortified them in their belief that they were engaged in a moral crusade, in which justice had to prevail, and in which there were good people and evil.

In launching this struggle, Blair believed that his guidance and restraint were vital if America were not to revert to the unilateralism favoured by the hawks. He took pride in helping tutor the transition of Bush from the Texan governor who had little knowledge of or interest in the world beyond America's shores to an internationalist, keen to work with allies where he could, and determined to build democracies in the place of dictatorships. He played a similar role to the one Roy Jenkins had with him. But would he make more impact on Bush than Jenkins had on him? While building a relationship with Bush, Blair kept up his links with Clinton, who, at Blair's request, addressed the Labour Party conference in October 2002, to remind a sceptical party that Blair was the only figure in the world who could be trusted to moderate America.[59] Blair shared his fear of American unilateralism with Peter Stothard when he told him that, if he was not there side-by-side with Bush on Iraq, he feared America would just rush in, topple Saddam, then rush out, careless of the stability of the country it might leave behind.[60] The whole thesis of Stothard's diary, *Thirty Days*, when he followed Blair closely before, during and just after the Iraq war, was that Blair's primary motivation was to keep in close contact with Bush at all costs.[61] Blair was fortified in the necessity of this mission by reports coming out of Washington that, post-9/11, the country was even less keen on international co-operation than before.[62]

Blair's relationship with Bush went through several phases after 9/11. In the immediate aftermath of the attacks, when America was still in shock, the relationship was at its closest. Bush's lavish praise in his address to the joint session of Congress on 20 September and the warmth of the reception from its members brought tears to Blair's eyes and helped cement his belief in the supremacy of the relationship. It was the kind of unqualified public adoration he used to receive in Britain in his earlier days as a shadow minister and party leader, but heard little of any more. During the Afghan war Blair and Bush discussed progress closely,[63] but as we saw in Chapter 33, differences began to emerge, particularly over the Middle East peace process. Concerns over plans for US tariffs on UK steel also caused difficulties. As soon as the Afghan war was deemed over, reports from the British Embassy suggested that US thinking was moving swiftly to tackling Iraq.[64] Blair's response was to try to bind himself even closer to the US administration.

As Iraq returned to the radar screen, a new phase in Blair's relations with Bush began. This lasted from around the time of their Crawford meeting in April 2002 until the end of the war almost exactly a year later. Much was made of their intimacy during this time. Colin Powell even suggested 'they're essentially inside each other's thinking. They complete each other's thoughts.'[65] Yet during the immediate build-up to war, the two leaders conducted themselves not like brothers or close friends but like businessmen, 'like two CEOs who were clinching a major deal together'.[66] They each articulated high praise for the other's stalwart support. 'I like George's directness. I like the way he has understood my political problems,' said Blair.[67] 'Americans admire character and courage. And Tony Blair has true character and courage,' said Bush.[68] Records of their many phone calls were studied carefully by aides on both sides of the Atlantic, and much store was set in London if not always in Washington by Blair's regular handwritten notes, fired off periodically to the President outlining his latest thoughts.[69] Some in London considered them of similar status to Churchill's jottings to Roosevelt in the Second World War. Churchill was certainly a hero of Bush's, and he had a bust of the great man in his office, thoughtfully loaned to him for the duration of his presidency at the instigation of Meyer. But what did the meeting of minds, the phone calls and the notes amount to?

Less than was made out, is the answer. One crucial area in which Bush and Blair co-operated highly effectively was in easing the tensions between India and Pakistan, who at one point in 2002 appeared close to nuclear confrontation. On this issue the two men worked closely and successfully together to prevent military conflict. Elsewhere, the end result was less convincing. In Chapter 37 we considered Blair's difficulties in shaping Bush's Iraq policy during this period. In the aftermath of 9/11, Blair's tactical error was to allow the Americans to believe that the British would be with them come what may. At Crawford and more formally at Camp David in September, Blair consolidated the administration's belief that his support could be taken for granted. Blair's 'trump card', the guarantee of British military support in any war in Iraq, was played too early at Camp David. In return, Blair received from Bush only the promise to work through the UN, at least initially, a decision that had been largely taken before Blair arrived. As we saw in the preceding chapter, with the Americans believing from the start that ultimately the British would be with them, Blair's 'conditions', principally exhausting the UN process, building an international coalition and making progress in the Middle East peace process, were seen as a 'wish list' rather than cast-iron requirements for British support. As it became clear that 'exhausting the UN process' actually meant very different things in Washington and London, the limits on Blair's ability to impose his interpretation became all too obvious. Without the UN, building an international coalition was also difficult. But how did Blair fare in influencing Bush on his third principal objective: support for the peace process in the Middle East?

Blair's line with Bush was consistent: if we do have to go to war, we will improve the reception considerably if we are seen to be making efforts in good faith to stem the cycle of violence between Israel and the Palestinians. It was Blair's great hope to show that, out of the horror of 9/11, a more just world would result, with the principal cause of Muslim hostility to the West, the denial of a sustainable state for Palestinians, lanced. Blair's need to find a post-war outcome to appease his left wing at home was a further motive, but not the principal driver behind his desire to push the agenda forward. Only with the Americans on board, he reasoned, would there be any hope of persuading Ariel Sharon and his Likud party to make the necessary concessions.

By April 2002, Blair believed he was making progress. Bush's statement of 4 April, in which he urged Sharon to withdraw from Palestinian cities recently occupied and halt further incursions into Palestinian-controlled areas, proved the highpoint of Bush's toughness with the Israeli Prime Minister. Blair's visit to Bush at Crawford came two days later and was 'heavily focused' on the Middle East. Shortly afterwards, Bush dispatched Powell to the region to put over the President's new resolve in person. Yet, while Blair applauded this approach, many in the Foreign Office remained suspicious: 'Hell is likely to freeze over before Bush is ready to treat Sharon with a big stick,' one official warned.[70] And so it proved. Powell's trip was constantly undermined by the hawks back in Washington, who assured their Israeli counterparts that Bush's tough words would fade. At the

Pentagon and in the Vice-President's office, there was little enthusiasm for engaging with the peace process on the lines Blair envisaged. Sort out Iraq first, they confidently predicted, and the rest of the Middle East, including Palestine, would soon come to heel.[71] They never quite explained how this transformation would come about, but they were confident that MEPP should follow, not proceed in tandem with, removing Saddam. A key problem for Blair and the doves, as the British Embassy in Washington learned, was that Sharon had a 'direct line' to the Vice-President's office and a determining influence on policy with an administration fearful of alienating the pro-Israel lobby.[72]

After successfully thwarting Powell's mission, Sharon played on his ready supporters within the administration and called Bush's bluff. Their constant refrain with the President was that there was no difference between Arafat and Bin Laden: could Bush really afford to give out mixed messages by fighting a 'war on terrorism' internationally, but appearing to reward Palestinian terrorism against Israel?[73] Bush's statement of 24 June 2002, in which he called for the Palestinians to elect new leaders 'not compromised by terror'[74] was a victory for the Sharon vision and a significant set-back for Blair's. The talk from the administration now focused on 'Palestinian reform' and the need to work with a 'democratic Palestinian authority', i.e., not Yasser Arafat. This was 'all rather cynical' according to one British source, given how unrealistic this goal was under the circumstances.[75]

Supporters of MEPP on the British side started to become frustrated that Blair was not being emphatic enough with the administration. If the peace process was one disappointment, another came in the more prosaic area of US attempts to limit EU steel imports. Initially Blair failed to press British opposition home with the imperious Cheney when he passed through London in March 2002, and after Bush imposed hefty tariffs, Blair was left impotently criticising America's policy as 'unjustified and wrong'.[76] Prior to the most important of his frequent phone calls to Bush, in the run-up to the Iraq war and on other issues, pointed briefing notes would be prepared for Blair, urging him to tackle the President directly: 'We'd then read the record of the conversation and see that Blair had gone off at a tangent,' said one insider. 'He just seemed oddly reluctant to confront Bush head-on.'[77] Reports began to circulate round Whitehall that Blair did not read his briefs, and that his character shied away from tough one-on-one encounters.[78] These criticisms extended beyond his relationship with Bush. Conversations with Chirac and Sharon would often be 'embarrassingly one-sided, with him hardly getting a word in edgeways, and then only a few platitudes or the odd question', according to one insider.[79]

In July 2002, Blair received direct advice that he should tell Bush that the US was damaging its reputation irreparably in Europe and the Middle East, and that the time had come for Britain to spend some of the considerable capital of goodwill that it had banked in the US. Meyer went as far as to share with Manning his fears that Britain was being taken for granted by Washington, and it was getting little in return for its public support.[80] These apprehensions were echoed in press articles on both sides of the Atlantic backed up by cartoons which, to Blair's immense irritation, portrayed him as 'Bush's poodle'.[81] Unfavourable comparisons began to be made of how Thatcher, despite her strong personal relationship with President Reagan, and her ardent pro-Americanism, would still stamp her feet and protest when she did not like what his administration did, and would ensure the British voice was heard, as over the invasion of Grenada, or the Siberian pipeline.[82] Blair's defence was always the mantra of support for the administration in public, influence in private. But how effective was this influence in private? Some insiders at the time – not with hindsight, but at the time – thought the answer was 'not sufficiently effective'.

By the beginning of 2003, Blair redoubled his efforts to shift Bush on the Middle East peace process. On 23 January he dispatched Michael Levy, his Middle East envoy, to see Arafat and press him to agree to appoint a new Palestinian Prime Minister with real powers, an American pre-condition for proceeding with the peace process. Levy duly returned with the written guarantee from Arafat that Blair had been looking for. Intense lobbying of Washington followed, particularly during Blair's visit at the end of January. Downing Street argued that publication of a Middle East 'road map' was essential if Blair were to acquire the support of a parliamentary majority at home in support of military action in Iraq. These efforts finally paid off when, on 14 March, Bush announced that the road map would be published as soon as Abu Mazen, the new Palestinian Prime Minister, was installed.[83] Palestinian independence by 2005, to which Bush secured Sharon's agreement, was the goal. None of these proposals would have been finalised, least of all so quickly, without Blair's pressing;[84] yet it remained to be seen how far Bush would push for the road map's implementation.

A new phase of the Blair–Bush relationship began with the end of the Iraq war, and was characterised by high hopes of British influence on Washington, soon followed by disappointment. By mid-2004, many around Blair had begun to become disillusioned by Bush's failure to deliver on what he said. The period opened with Blair telling Bush frankly that, following 9/11, and the wars in Afghanistan and Iraq, America had to become more engaged with the rest of the world.[85] Specifically, Blair pressed for a US commitment to a significant role for the UN in post-war Iraq, as well as a serious re-engagement in the stalled Middle East peace process. He pressed both issues with Bush when he visited Camp David on 27 March 2003, and when they met again at Hillsborough Castle in Belfast on 8 April. The former trip saw Blair believing he had made a real impression on Bush's thinking, while the press conference after the latter was described as 'closer to a wedding than a media event'.[86] Blair had indeed secured a real breakthrough at Hillsborough when, after heavy British lobbying, the President promised no less than eight times at the press conference a 'vital' role for the UN. Stothard recorded that the British team were 'delighted with what Bush had said' but 'Rice does not look so happy ... "Vital role. Fine. But did he need to say it eight times?"' Rice, whose position had shifted steadily towards the Cheney–Rumsfeld side over the months, began to suggest to her boss that some of their colleagues back in Washington might not be best pleased.[87] Typically, once Bush was safely back home cocooned with these same colleagues, notably Rumsfeld and Cheney, his resolve began to crumble, and the UN was clattered out of the major role Blair had envisaged. To Richard Haass, 'The cold fact is that this was an area which demonstrated the limits of British influence.'[88]

Hillsborough also saw progress on the Middle East peace process, with Bush declaring that he was now ready to engage seriously in the region. At the end of April 2003, the 'road map' to a Palestinian–Israeli peace was duly published, and Bush travelled to Jordan in June for a summit with Abu Mazen, now ensconced as Palestinian Prime Minister, and with Sharon. Blair was delighted that after months of false starts and frustration, real progress seemed to be being made. But, as violence increased, hopes began to fade. Mazen resigned after difficulties with Arafat, and Sharon successfully reawakened the rejectionism of America's Israeli and Christian right lobby. On 14 April 2004 Bush endorsed Sharon's own plan for a Middle East settlement, which provided for an Israeli withdrawal from the Gaza strip, but made major Israeli settlements on the West Bank permanent and ruled out any return to Israel for Palestinian refugees displaced by previous wars. While the first concession was welcomed, the second two conditions were greeted with fury in the Arab world. Blair's supporters admitted that this deal was a 'significant' setback for their hopes, as it appeared to signal a decision to abandon the road map.[89] However, during a visit to Washington two days later, Blair embraced the President's decision, and later told one Cabinet colleague that, far from abandoning the road map, this could be the first step to its implementation.[90] Yet when he repeated this line in public, many dismissed it. The open letter in April 2004 to Blair by fifty-two former diplomats, questioning his influence with Bush and criticising him for supporting a peace plan that was 'doomed to failure', could perhaps too readily be dismissed as special pleading by mostly Arabist 'has-beens'. But it remained to be seen how far any developments would match the proposals and hopes Blair articulated so enthusiastically after 9/11. As if in acknowledgement that the high hopes of a better world emerging from 9/11, about which he spoke so eloquently in the 2001 party conference, was not coming to fruition as he hoped, he threw himself in April and May 2004 into initiatives again to heel Africa's 'scars'.[91]

Some of the gloss had already begun to peel off the Blair–Bush relationship, even as the two highest-profile events of their celebrated bond unfolded. On 18 July 2003, Blair was afforded the rare honour of addressing a joint session of both Houses of Congress, before receiving the Congressional Gold Medal. Under greater pressures at home than at any point in his premiership, because of the difficulties in post-war Iraq, the failure to find WMD and the muddle over pre-war intelligence, he saw the speech as the chance to vindicate his policy of closeness to Bush and re-emphasise Britain's role as bridge between America and Europe.[92] Blair told his audience, 'America must listen as well as lead,' and warned against the dangers of isolationism. Yet he underplayed a unique opportunity to remind America of its wider obligations, and to talk as a candid friend about its diminished standing in world opinion. Having made some enormous sacrifices for America throughout the entire Bush administration, such an occasion was his best opportunity to press home some truths that America needed to hear diplomatically but firmly in language incapable of being misinterpreted. Later that day, while on a plane flying to the Far East, Blair learned of the death of the weapons expert, Dr David Kelly. This tragic event rather than his speech to Congress took the media headlines, and it was to plunge the government into turmoil.

Anti-war feeling overshadowed the second grand event of their union, Bush's state visit to Britain in November 2003, an honour that Blair had initially been keen to extend to Clinton. Again, a potentially major event was severely overshadowed. Fear of widespread demonstrations cast a pall and the schedule was curtailed, while the suicide attack on the British Consul in Istanbul led to questions being asked about how effectively al-Qaeda had been suppressed, and whether the Iraq war had in fact made the West safer from terrorism. The state visit was a significant favour to Bush, affording him powerful media coverage in the company of America's favourite overseas leader at the very portal of his re-election year. Again,

Blair failed to seek a full *quid pro quo*. He was certainly pleased that Bush was willing to spend forty-five minutes during the visit discussing aid to Africa,[93] but what gain, even his close supporters now began to ask, did the state visit bring the British Prime Minister?[94]

Both countries had been diverging anyway before the state visit. Blair's wish to mend bridges with EU leaders, damaged so badly over Iraq, led to his decision to join in a separate EU warning to Iran on its nuclear programme, and to collaboration on EU defence, which 'wasn't winning him any friends in the White House'.[95] Bush, from late 2003, was firmly fixated on his hopes of re-election, accompanied by a shift in his platform not to the centre but to the right, while Blair was embroiled in his own domestic concerns. Bush's domestic need to clarify the record on pre-war intelligence led to him setting up its own inquiry into why intelligence had failed on Iraq so spectacularly: Blair effectively had little option but to do the same under Robin Butler, just when he had hoped the dust had settled after the Hutton report was finally published. Britain and America were still conjoined in their attempt to bring a peaceful solution to Iraq, and on a range of other projects. During his Washington visit of 16 April 2004 Blair managed to persuade Bush to agree that the UN would guide the make-up of the new Iraqi administration.[96] But as Bush turned his attention to his re-election, no longer the foregone conclusion it had been in the immediate aftermath of the war, the logic behind rebuilding bridges with the Democrats became more compelling. Blair, however, continued to put great store by his special relationship with Bush, inflaming the Labour Party and Cabinet in mid-May 2004 by his limited efforts to distance himself from an increasingly discredited American policy in Iraq.

The Impact of George W. Bush

Clinton's effect on Blair as Prime Minister, rich in rhetoric and promise, had not fulfilled itself as it might have on policy, and was characterised by false starts and disappointed hopes. Bush, in contrast, affected Blair's premiership very profoundly. While Blair and Clinton were the more compatible personalities, and shared a much closer view of the role of government and domestic politics, Blair and Bush had a greater identity of interest overseas, and shared a similar moral and religious view of the world that would have been alien to Clinton (even though Bush and Blair, despite popular belief, never 'prayed together'). Blair had spoken in Chicago in April 1999 about his new vision of the 'international community'. Bush, with the might of America behind him, gave Blair the chance to turn his breezy philosophising into concrete action – hunting down international terrorists, confronting states holding WMD, removing dictators suppressing human rights, bringing peace in the age-old struggle between Israel and the Palestinians. This was the promise Bush offered Blair. What did he deliver?

'I can think of no period in history when the special relationship has been closer, or our impact on the US more substantive,' declared one Number 10 aide without a flicker of doubt.[97] Bush's supporters insist that the President delivered on all Blair's 'conditions' for British support over Saddam. 'He fulfilled every promise to Blair. He went to the UN over Iraq; he did everything he could to win international support for the war; he pushed the road map between Israel and the Palestinians; and he will not cut and run in Iraq,' said a Bush sympathiser.[98] Yet does such a 'tick list' gloss over the truth? Blair was influential in persuading the Americans to obtain UN Resolution 1441, and dragging them reluctantly back to the UN in search of the elusive second resolution, a quest which, as we have seen, did as much harm as good. But, as officials pointed out at the time, the administration put a very different construction on what 'exhausting the UN process' meant. Had it believed deeply in achieving UN backing, it would have put more time and higher-level support to achieve it. By implication, then, the administration did not do everything in its power to achieve international support for the war. Neither was Bush willing to push the road map in the face of the implacable opposition of the hawks and the pro-Israeli lobby in Congress and in the country. It is to be seen whether America will 'cut and run' in Iraq, but its inconsistent and inept leadership of the post-war reconstruction, epitomised by its extraordinary decision to disband rather than reform the Iraqi police and army, which created a security vacuum that has yet to be filled, is not auspicious. The conclusion one must draw, as over Afghanistan and Blair's alleged restraint on the administration in the immediate aftermath of 9/11, is that the Americans only listened to him when his suit matched what they wanted to wear anyway.

In a host of other matters, including tariffs on British steel imports, treatment of Britain nationals in Guantanamo Bay and the failure to acquire a new air services agreement, British influence amounted to less than trumpeted. Did Bush deliberately mislead Blair? No. There are many reasons why Britain did not punch its weight with the Bush administration. A problem was that Rice, by whom Manning and London set great store, proved a far less powerful voice in the administration than they at first thought she would be. She and her National Security Council office carried considerably less authority in Washington than her Clinton predecessor Berger, while Cheney, who was consistently unsympathetic to the British, proved a far more powerful Vice-President than many, including his immediate predecessor, Gore. Powell and his deputy Armitage were both Anglophiles and instinctively in favour of many of the lines Blair pushed. But they lost out in the power struggle within the administration to the hawks. Ultimately Bush, bobbing around like a buoy in a choppy sea, tugged by his heart and then by his head, had to make a choice. And power and electoral politics in Washington meant that the wishes of Blair, for all his deep personal regard for him, did not rank as high as other imperatives. 'Straight talking', about which so much was made with Bush, was only of value when the interlocutor is consistent and can deliver on his 'straight' exposition. Often Bush could or did not. By failing to insist that Bush follow up his encouraging words with cast-iron guarantees *before* pledging British support, Blair made it too easy for the Americans to take him for granted. To many, he committed the greatest error in diplomacy: declaring his hand too early. Whether a little less eager trust and a little more Thatcherite rigidity would have given Blair more ability to shape the world will be one of the enduring historical questions of the age.

Blair, visibly aged at the Labour conference in Bournemouth in September 2003, broods over his response to Gordon Brown's speech, which had openly challenged his leadership.

39

The 'Wobble', 2004

Tony Blair's ambitions for the second term, in as far as he had formed them by June 2001, focused on two main areas: delivering public service reform and improving relations with Europe with a view to Britain joining the Euro before the next election. Proving he could work closely with a Republican administration in Washington was a third aim. He remained unconvinced, however, despite some institutional changes in his first term, whether the machinery of government was as yet sufficiently geared to the delivery of policy. The 'revolution at the centre' would have to continue, aided by the appointment of loyalists to the key departments. He knew also that he would face mounting opposition from Gordon Brown. The two men had grown apart, not just personally, but increasingly over policy. Brown was content as long as Blair's domestic policy remained inchoate and containable. But Brown disagreed strongly with Blair's 'choice and diversity' agenda gradually emerging from Number 10. While Blair aimed to limit Brown's authority over domestic policy, Brown fought to increase it. Brown was determined to dominate the second term, which, he confidently believed, would pave the way for his own premiership.

With no agreement between Blair and Brown on key objectives, or an agreed *modus operandi*, division and confusion were inevitable in the second term. If one then takes account of the 'unforeseens' which all governments encounter – asylum at home and terrorism and the Iraq war abroad – and which so drained Blair's political capital, it is unsurprising that so little was achieved during these years. Blair's principal obstacle was not the official Opposition, which proved no more effective under Duncan Smith and Howard than it had under Hague, but his own Chancellor. In

November 2003, the deteriorating relationship between Blair and Brown led Prescott to intervene and broker a truce. Blair gave strong indications that he would quit in the autumn of 2004 to make way for Brown. During the spring of 2004, domestic setbacks and continuing difficulties in Iraq further sapped Blair's morale. He pulled back from quitting after the 'mid-term' elections in June 2004 showed him he could win with a three figure landslide. Blair realised that his legacy was far from secure, that he could not quit with Iraq still in a quagmire, and he no longer trusted Brown to entrench his legacy (quite the opposite). Brown's failure to provide the loyal backing he had promised to give Blair in November 2003 became the pretext for Blair's decision to battle on. His announcement that he would fight the 2005 General Election and, if elected, serve until 2008, thus marked the final turning point of the second term.

Objective 1: Public Service Reform

Neither the 2001 election campaign nor the manifesto had produced a clear blueprint for the second term, due in part to lack of agreement between Blair and Brown and their supporters on what should go in it, and in part because Blair did not provide a clear sense of direction. Number 10 in particular had not worked out a strategy for how progress would be made on the Euro, or what exact role the private sector should play in the provision of public services. Insiders acknowledge that launching the 2001 campaign by proposing a role for the private sector 'far beyond anything that was likely to happen' aroused suspicions and resentment quite unnecessarily.[1] Blair had articulated his 'principles' for public service reform: uniform national standards, decentralisation and flexibility during the election campaign, and a fourth, 'choice', had been added at the strong urging of Jeremy Heywood. But as we shall see, it took another year for Blair to work out what choice was to mean in the public services. Nor did the manifesto include much detail on a 'second tranche' of constitutional reforms, including the Lord Chancellor's department, because, as one aide put it, 'Blair hadn't got round to thinking it through yet.'[2] It promised a more 'representative and democratic' House of Lords but with no strategy on how to achieve it. Blair had very high aspirations for his second term. It would be a government concerned with long-lasting and enduring improvements, he announced outside Number 10 on the day after the election: short-termism and the culture of spin were over. He loathed the repeated 'spin' accusations. Substance, not style, would define his second term.

A lesson Blair had absorbed from the first term was the need to appoint the right ministers to run key departments and to set up the right structures at the centre, in Number 10 and the Cabinet Office, to drive his agenda forward. This approach rested on his growing, if misplaced, belief that if the centre were not involved, the right outcomes would not result, and that he personally had to drive the centre forward.

This determination to show leadership masked Blair's continued failure to grasp the importance of management: 'Your problem,' said the Cabinet Secretary, Richard Wilson, a few months after the 2001 election, 'is that neither you nor anyone in Number 10 has ever managed anything.' Blair looked shocked, not least because there were others in the room. 'I've managed the Labour Party,' he replied. 'You never managed them, you merely led them. There's a big difference,' Wilson was heard to retort.[3] Wilson went on to explain that overseeing the delivery of a complex public service was very different from barking out instructions to party officials or standing up at a conference and announcing a major change of policy, as Blair had done with Clause IV. Blair 'wasn't interested in management', confirmed one of his Cabinet Ministers: 'He had the "Blair garden look" where his eyes glazed over and he looked out at the Number 10 garden whenever the word "management" was used.'[4] 'His experience as a barrister simply didn't prepare him for managing people and institutions to deliver results,' said one disillusioned mandarin. 'Worse for him,' he continued rather unfairly, 'Gordon Brown had no more idea. Gordon hadn't the faintest clue how to get himself out of a paper bag.'[5]

Blair knew he had only one last chance to get it right: the excuses used for the disappointing progress in 1997–2001 on health, transport, crime and, to a lesser extent, education could not be used again. He had learned the lesson that having unsuitable ministers in these key positions, not making it sufficiently clear to all that they were his flagship departments, or moving ministers around between elections, would not produce the real, sustainable improvements he sought. Shortly after the 2001 General Election he thus told Milburn (Health), Byers (Transport), Blunkett (Home Office) and Estelle Morris (Education), over dinner, that he considered them the heads of the four key departments delivering public service reform in his second term: 'I want you to stay in your posts until the next General Election.'[6] Morris told her ministerial team at Education after the election, 'There are Blair departments and there are Brown departments. We are the former and we will be dealing with Downing Street.' Clinton's words – 'Don't waste your second term like I did' – echoed in Blair's ears.[7]

Blair's main control mechanism to ensure that the improvements happened as promised in the second term was the Delivery Unit, an idea originating with Jeremy Heywood and Richard Wilson, and strongly supported by Jonathan Powell.[8] Set up after the 2001 election, its big idea was to broaden out the approach of targets and monitoring used successfully in the first term at Education. Indicatively, Michael Barber, on the back of his success with the literacy and numeracy strategies, was chosen to run the new Unit. Within the four key departments, only a relatively narrow range of objectives and targets were concentrated upon, derived from the spending reviews of 2000 and 2002, and from Blair's own preferences – Education (with the focus on secondary schools but not higher education), Health (e.g., hospital waiting times), Home Office (e.g., crime, drugs and asylum) and Transport (e.g., road congestion). The Unit convened regular (often bi-monthly) 'stock-takes' and presentations with the four Secretaries of State and Blair to review progress made in each area towards meeting the targets.[9] This system had two main benefits: it meant that, however distracted Blair might be by other events, domestic and international, the work of monitoring his targets went on regardless ('The Unit never sleeps,' Blair was told).[10] Second, it established beyond all doubt Blair's priorities in key domestic policy areas and in a notionally 'Brown-proof' manner. From 2002, the Unit was placed physically within the remodelled Treasury building to encourage close co-operation with Brown's team, though this did not prevent battles raging and Brown disparaging its work.[11] Heywood's plan for a Cabinet minister to oversee the Unit's work (a 'Chief Secretary to the Cabinet') failed, however, because Prescott, the minister Blair selected, would not carry out the task.

The Delivery Unit nevertheless proved the most successful of the several post-2001 election innovations. Always a monitoring rather than a policy-making body, it derived much of its effectiveness from the knowledge within Whitehall that it carried the Prime Minister's imprimatur in all it did.[12] Within Number 10, the Policy Unit was merged with the Private Office to create the 'Policy Directorate', to work on short- and medium-term policy. This change was another fruit of Heywood's thinking, in particular to fit in with Blair's preferred way of working, which was to have just one 'expert' advising him on each subject, thus ending the duplication where the Private Office or Policy Unit both had specialists on all the main topics. Heywood also believed the traditional model of the Prime Minister's Private Office, concerned primarily with administrative routine, was no longer appropriate, and was incapable of driving forward the Prime Minister's agenda across Whitehall.[13] The development aroused concern within Number 10, particularly from Campbell and Morgan: not only was it being overseen by the career civil servant Heywood, but with Adonis as his deputy heading up the policy side, it was seen as more social democrat than Labour.[14] Some insiders indeed rued the Directorate's lack of political experience and feel for the Labour Party that had infused the Policy Unit under David Miliband.[15] The Policy Directorate made Number 10 into more of a policy-making powerhouse for the Prime Minister, but concerns emerged that it was detracting from, emasculating even, some of the Whitehall departments' 'creative' role, while also overburdening an already fully stretched Number 10. In consequence, some second-term initiatives were insufficiently thought through, notably the new tranche of constitutional reform and the broader implications of the 'choice' agenda.[16]

The revolution in Number 10 went further still. Blair believed that the Performance and Innovation Unit (PIU) set up in his first term could not provide the strategic thinking needed in the second term. John Birt, the former Director-General of the BBC, who had stressed to Blair the importance of strategic thinking, was closely involved in the changes introduced in 2001.[17] Blair wanted a new body more under Number 10's control, with a clearer focus on working up policy from first principles ('blue skies thinking'). The Forward Strategy Unit was the solution (renamed 'Strategy Unit' when merged with the PIU in late 2002) and was run by Geoff Mulgan, though it never found a settled niche. A final innovation was the Office of Public Service Reform (OPSR), headed by Wendy Thomson, which sought to strengthen the institutions of central and local government, allowing them to deliver public services better.[18] Its creation came as a surprise to Wilson, Head of the Home Civil Service, who learned about its inception the day before it was made public.[19] 'Clearly somebody at Number 10 believed that the Civil Service needed shaking up and needed to get a grip,' was the jaded view of one of the growing numbers of mandarins who felt alienated by Labour's interface with the Civil Service since 1997.[20] Of all the new offices, the OPSR made the least impact. Alongside all these changes, the Strategic Communication Unit was strengthened. The reforms were underpinned by the reorganisation of Number 10 itself into three 'directorates' under Blair's three 'biggest hitters': Government and Policy (Powell), Communications and Strategy (Campbell) and Government Relations (Hunter, then Morgan). These innovations had been the product of much creative thinking about the machinery of government before the election. The Cabinet Office too was remodelled under four new divisions, and David Manning and Stephen Wall became Heads of

Secretariat and Number 10 advisers on Europe and defence/foreign policy respectively. Many government departments were radically reorganised and the Departments for Work and Pensions (DWP) and Environment, Food and Rural Affairs (DEFRA) were created, following the dismantling of Prescott's DETR empire.

Blair was indeed deadly serious about ensuring his second term ran to plan. These changes amounted to the biggest restructuring and upgrading of the Prime Minister's resources in the history of the office.[21] The combined 'strategy' team (PIU and Forward Strategy Unit) rose from 30 in 2000 to 130 in 2002. Even Number 12 Downing Street was commandeered from the Whip's Office to house some of the newly appointed staff. Contrasts were drawn with the French and United States presidential models, while press briefings stressed that the changes were designed to counter the overemphasis on communications in the first term, by the huge upgrading in policy advice.[22] Tony Wright, Chairman of the Public Accounts Committee, said Blair now had 'a Prime Minister's Department in all but name', and a 'growing capacity to drive policy from the centre'.[23] But was all this elaborate new machinery of government an improvement on what had gone before, and did it deliver what Blair needed?

More attention was certainly devoted to targets in education, health, transport and crime, and improved co-ordination of departments also began to make a difference.[24] The initial results from the wholesale reorganisation of the centre seemed promising, and confidence grew in 2001–02 that the right formulae had been found at last. But disappointment began to be expressed from mid-2002, and by the summer of 2003, Blair felt compelled to commission yet further work to examine ways of driving through his agenda from the centre. In fact, deep beneath the surface, real improvements *were* beginning to be made, but at nothing like the pace many expected. One explanation given at the time was that the new ministerial team, for all the thought put into their selection, and Blair's heavily signalled personal support, did not begin with anything like the verve that ministers had in the euphoric first three months after the 1997 election. Commentators from across the political spectrum noted the torpor with surprise: one wrote, 'This government appears to be losing the initiative and running out of momentum when its new mandate is less than a month old.'[25]

External factors impinged to distract Blair: early on, hostility from union leaders to private sector involvement in public sector reform, and the latest impasse in Northern Ireland, ranked high. Then came the far more significant distraction of 9/11 and the Afghan war. Neither international event sapped his political capital in the party as the Iraq war was later to do so badly, but the tangential affair of Jo Moore, Byers' political aide, who insisted 9/11 was a 'good day to bury bad news', did. Her refusal to resign immediately, and the government's refusal to apologise, re-awoke all the chants of media spin and cynicism that Blair prayed had been safely buried with the first term.[26] In its perhaps understandable reluctance to sacrifice a loyal aide to the media storm, the government scored a spectacular own goal.

Blair's response to the distractions of the war on terrorism was to delegate even more responsibility to favoured (and non-Brownite) ministers, especially Blunkett, Byers, Clarke, Milburn and Morris. But the failure to think through his policy platform fully in time for the 2001 manifesto now began to make itself felt. Muddle was the result. In the section of his October 2001 conference speech not devoted to foreign affairs, he failed to provide any overall strategic sense of direction for the public services. Then Brown, in his November pre-Budget statement, slipped in that taxes would have to rise to make good the huge under-investment in health identified by the report he had commissioned from the banker, Derek Wanless. Here was the first admission since 1994 that Labour would have to increase tax revenue to pay for its much vaunted 'world class' public services.[27] Blair recognised the need to increase NHS spending, but Milburn and the artful Number 10 health strategist, Simon Stevens, were coming up with radically different ways to improve healthcare. Rather than just pump in extra money, they wanted to free up all hospitals from interference by the Secretary of State and devolve power totally to them (i.e., foundation hospitals), as well as allowing a range of alternative providers (from the private sector) to take over failing hospitals.[28] Several Treasury officials were keen. Brown and Balls were not. To them it smacked of privatisation, and a divisive distraction from what they wanted the NHS story to be about – greater public funds than ever before going into improvements. They lost the argument.[29] On transport, however, government policy was moving in an anti-private direction with Byers, supported by the Treasury, replacing Railtrack with Network Rail, thus stripping away much of the freedom of private management to invest in the railways and compensating for it by increasing public subsidies. At the Home Office, meanwhile, Blunkett placated the party's liberal wing by easing cannabis laws but then outraged them by announcing fierce anti-terrorist legislation in the wake of 9/11.

Blair collected his thoughts before Christmas 2001, aided by a paper by Peter Hyman, which said the next six months until the summer of

2002 would be crucial, because by then 'the pattern for the Parliament will be set. The legislation that will have time to be felt this Parliament will be passed.' He itemised four objectives for Blair over the next seven months: 'successful exit from the war' and building TB's 'enhanced reputation abroad' (no mention of Iraq); 'real momentum on public services'; win the 'tax and spend argument' by greater 'public willingness to pay' and, finally, 'crank up the temperature on Europe'.[30] Blair had his plan, but the first half of 2002 did not provide either the clarity, the momentum or the evidence of success Number 10 sought. The perception of an inchoate and, increasingly, of an underperforming government began to grow. Matthew Taylor, then at the IPPR think-tank, voiced the views of many when he said that at the heart of the government's problem was 'the lack of clarity about where it is going'.[31]

Blair took stock over his summer holidays in 2002 about why the second term had failed to make the start he had hoped for. He returned at the end of August with a series of handwritten notes, which became a twenty-four-page typed secret memo sent to close aides on 30 August.[32] In this seminal document, Blair articulated the agenda he had been groping towards at least since he became party leader eight years earlier, if not before. 'There will be a year of struggle and challenge, but also a tremendous opportunity,' he opened by saying. The coming twelve months, Blair wrote, would be 'make or break' for the government, and would be dominated by three domestic issues – public service reform, the Euro and law and order – and abroad by the war on terror and Iraq. The challenge for the coming year 'will be to keep the centre ground; to force the Tories out to the right; and to persuade ourselves that radical reform is the answer, not the problem'. He noted that 'we have built New Labour around the idea of traditional values – solidarity, social justice, opportunity for all – applied entirely afresh to the modern world', but now a new formulation was required to take the party beyond the 'Big Stage' prescription of the 1945 Labour government. He called for a fresh debate in the party around values of 'greater interdependence plus greater individuality'.

At the heart of Blair's key paper was public service reform. He wrote that in the future he wanted 'to rebuild the service around the consumer'. This meant 'diversity of supply, choice . . . an end to old practices'. For health, this required 'ridding ourselves of the monolithic NHS . . . can we make foundation hospitals a reality?' He was pleased with Milburn's work, who 'was certainly pushing [change] radically'. In education, his other chief priority, he was less convinced they had the right momentum. He thought 'the notion of a specialist school system replacing the comprehensive system, just about gets there' and noted that Adonis 'had dreams of a radical agenda'. But he worried whether the DfES was 'equipped to push it through', the concern being that 'there was a real timidity in taking big policy changes on board'. Overall, it constituted one of the clearest philosophical statements of policy Blair would ever make. A legitimate question, however, is why he had to wait until August 2002 to reach these conclusions. To sceptics like Clare Short, Blair's new stance, which included a commitment to search for progress in Africa, was dictated by his desire to find his 'place in history'. This is overly cynical. What had happened was that Blair, who had never found that the graft of policy formulation came to him naturally, had suddenly realised that his time remaining as Prime Minister was finite.

The issue that had shot up Blair's agenda in 2001–02 was law and order. With statistics on street crime in London and elsewhere providing worrying reading for the government in mid-2002, Blair convened a number of Cobra sessions pulling together all the relevant agencies and departments.[33] The sessions set the ball rolling on a more active approach for tackling crime, but this was soon to be taken over by asylum as the new issue at the top of his domestic agenda. It had become, he wrote, 'the toughest immediate issue', with 'the capacity to explode at any moment'.[34] Asylum numbers began to take off in the summer of 2001, as repeated attempts by refugees to escape to Britain from the Sangat camp in Calais achieved widespread media coverage. Philip Gould's research during the first term had repeatedly warned that asylum and illegal immigration was a major issue for voters, but it had lost its salience as the General Election approached. A tough line would have played well with the *Daily Mail*, but, as Sally Morgan regularly reminded Blair, they needed to avoid upsetting Labour supporters with an illiberal response on this sensitive issue.[35]

Blair had long been interested in asylum, and gripped the issue firmly. 'In terms of time,' a Number 10 aide believed, 'it was his number-one domestic priority from the summer of 2001.'[36] He worked on it closely with Blunkett, who gave a strong speech at the 2001 conference and whose work in the first half of 2002 resulted in the closing of the Sangat camp. Blair felt very frustrated by the existing asylum regime, which he considered perverse and dysfunctional: his political antennae told him that people did not respect the system and felt it was being exploited.[37] He demanded asylum figures be sent to him each week, and declared he wanted to have the numbers cut by 50 per cent.[38] Even in the turbulent first few months of 2003, he retained a focus on the issue, despite the war in Iraq. Asylum continued to pose difficulties throughout the year, with new arrivals from Iraq and Zimbabwe in particular, and in 2004 from Eastern Europe. In April 2004, in the wake of the resignation of Home Office minister Beverley Hughes after controversy over waived immigration checks for Bulgarians and Romanians, Blair convened an all-day summit in Number 10 to refocus his efforts on asylum once again. Restrictions on immigration were promised: tougher than any Labour government had previously dared to pass. But what did Blair gain for all the time he spent on the issue? He no doubt softened some of the negative headlines in the right-wing press. But in terms of fulfilling his agenda and credo for the second term, it was an issue that took much but added little.

Blair's speech at the annual party conference in October 2002 was intended to display he was firmly in command and had a clear mission. Looking abroad, he defended his tough line on Iraq, but the main focus was domestic. Declaring 'we're at our best when at our boldest', Blair drew heavily on his August memo and laid out the ideas for public service reform that were at last becoming clear in his mind. He called for a move to a 'post-comprehensive era' of education, a more 'personalised' NHS, thus paving the way for foundation hospitals and declared his support for the private finance initiative (PFI): 'Come on,' he challenged the party, 'this isn't the betrayal of public services. It's their renewal.' This was 'the latest phase in [Blair's] New Labour revolution,' said the *Scotsman*, which, it added, 'his audience seemed reluctant to embrace'.[39] This 'modernising' agenda was shaped powerfully by Heywood and Adonis, and by Blairites elsewhere in government. Owing more to the philosophy of Thatcherism than socialism, it sent a deep shiver through the party, especially as Brown had not been won over to its merits.

Blair knew he had a struggle on his hands to convince the doubters, yet very soon he was hampered in his effort by two new domestic factors. One was Cheriegate in the late autumn, already discussed; the other was the fire-fighters' dispute, the most difficult trade union struggle Blair was to face. It was not a battle Blair could afford to lose, even though the fire-fighters had widespread public support. It emphasised again to Number 10 their irritation that some unions, unlike the Labour Party, remained fundamentally unreconstructed even after eight years of his leadership. After equivocating for too long, losing support from the right-wing press in the process, Blair ordered troops in to man the fire engines. The fire-fighters' union eventually caved in, but at the price, Brown noted, of Blair making deeper enemies in the movement.

Meanwhile, there were few signs that Blair was succeeding in winning over his critics on public service reform. Foundation hospitals, the private finance initiative and Blair's growing support for 'top-up' fees, whereby universities would be able to charge students more for tuition, were coming under fierce attack. Some fire came from the left but, far more worrying for Blair, criticism also came directly from Brown's office. Blair's response was that his own new agenda showed clearly that just increasing spending was insufficient unless there was greater 'diversity and choice' in the public services, coupled with structural reform. To many Labour traditionalists, this thinking undermined the very principles of the universal welfare state and threatened to entrench a two-tier service. These differences came out in a 'political' Cabinet to discuss strategy on 8 November, when Brown voiced the concern that Balls had raised a few days earlier, that 'if you go down the marketising route, you run grave risks with [the] ethics of public service'.[40] When Brown let slip to journalists that he thought tuition fees would be a 'disaster', Balls had to intervene and persuade the editor not to publish the story.[41] Blair now realised that even with his major reform of Number 10, coupled with a coherent 'modernising' agenda which had taken shape by the autumn of 2002, his most intractable problem – Brown's jibbing – would remain. Worse for Blair, as the second term progressed, this distraction to his agenda only grew. Nowhere was this more evident than in the struggle over the Euro.

Objective 2: The Euro

Blair would sometimes say his biggest regret of his first term was missing the opportunity to take Britain into the Euro in the autumn of 1997. By 2001, only two other members of the EU apart from Britain, Denmark and Sweden, had not joined the Eurozone, and Blair believed Britain's future lay with the twelve who were part of it. He regularly signalled to his inner circle that he wanted to join in his second term and that, this time, he was utterly determined to prevail: the more Europhile the person, the warmer his enthusiasm. In October 2001, he told the first party conference of the second term that joining was Britain's 'destiny'. Brown, however, remained opposed. His repeated public refrain was that Britain would only join when the conditions were 'right', while his aides were believed to be secretly telling journalists and trusted figures in the City that a referendum would be in the third, not second, term.[42] Every time Blair tried to raise the matter with Brown, 'he met with a complete blank wall. He never got anywhere.'[43] Blair believed he had Brown's agreement to review the matter again in the second term, and was nonplussed by his refusal even to discuss it. To the same economic reservations Brown had held in 1997 were added, with greater piquancy than before, a desire to thwart Blair, and a real concern that if he let a referendum go ahead and it was lost, as many feared it would be, it would damage him personally, and Labour electorally. In short, being positive had nothing to commend it. Balls too remained implacably opposed, and had highlighted in his Cairncross lecture, organised in December 2002 by the Institute of Contemporary British History, the disasters that had occurred when governments in recent history had let political factors override economic ones. Blair was known to favour the Euro for political reasons. The message was clear.[44]

In 2002, there was still hope in Number 10 that a referendum might be held in the autumn of 2003 or early 2004.[45] Some aides even imagined that, when the British went for their holidays that summer, they would become so enamoured of using the single currency notes and coins, introduced at the start of the year, that they would return convinced supporters of the Euro.[46] 'Number 10 was in a process of denial [over the timing of Euro entry],' said one insider.[47] Most of Blair's aides were in favour, Powell, Mandelson, Stephen Wall and Hyman; even Campbell was not opposed.[48] Bolstered by the positive enthusiasm of his staff, Blair was determined to press ahead.

Heywood was thus dispatched to the Treasury to see Balls and Gus O'Donnell, who had succeeded Turnbull as Permanent Secretary, and persuaded them that discussions had to take place, as a decision on whether to call a referendum had been promised by Blair within two years of the General Election, i.e. by 9 June 2003. Brown still refused to budge: his view was that in the 1994 'deal', and again in the autumn of 1997, Blair had ceded economic decisions to him, and thus he believed that, in trying to pre-empt the Treasury's economic judgement on the Euro, Blair was breaking his promise.[49] Brown also deeply resented suggestions that he should yield on the issue as the price for Blair giving him a retirement date.[50] Despairing officials came up with the idea of holding joint seminars at Number 10, beginning in January 2003, to debate the issues (some six of which were eventually held). Blair could not understand why the seminars were necessary, but agreed to go along with them. The early sessions indicated that the time for joining was not right, and that the balance of the assessment of the five tests on which the Treasury had been labouring was likely to be negative. So the damning final judgement came as little surprise.[51] Brown wanted mention of the negative verdict to be made in his April Budget speech, but Blair flatly refused. A complete impasse was reached between Number 10 and the

Chancellor's office. Powell and Wall thought the extensive assessment that the Treasury had produced did not justify the judgement, and argued that the overall message should be 'Yes, but not yet'.[52] Blair and Brown then met alone several times. 'No one was debriefed on either side. It was very hard to know what they were saying.'[53] There followed another round of meetings with both teams – Blair, Powell, Heywood and Wall from Number 10 and Brown, Balls, O'Donnell and John Cunliffe from the Treasury. Blair was determined to keep the door open, above all to show pro-Europeans, at home and abroad, that in principle he was still keen on joining the single currency; Brown was equally determined to stress the economic perils of joining in the near future, and the damage that would be caused by continual uncertainty.

Cabinet began to discuss the issue in May. Initially, Brown had wanted to deliver the verdict without any discussion by ministers, but Blair would not allow it. Brown then said he wanted to see all Cabinet ministers individually to talk it over with them, but Blair would not allow that either.[54] Brown yielded, judging that in any case the balance in Cabinet was against a referendum this Parliament. The main enthusiasts were Clarke, Hain, Hewitt and Ian McCartney, the party Chairman. Prescott was neutral, and Straw, in the key post of Foreign Secretary, was against.[55] Blair and the few enthusiasts in Cabinet did manage to shift Brown some way, and the statement on the Euro he delivered to the House on 9 June 2003 was more positive in tone than the tenor of his recent pronouncements. The statement, supported by a 246-page report, 'UK Membership in the Single Currency – An Assessment of the Five Economic Tests', was accompanied by nineteen technical documents, amounting to the biggest economic exercise the Treasury had ever undertaken. The analysis showed that in some ways Britain was closer on convergence than countries that had joined the Euro, but critically, the Treasury alone drafted the conclusions. They could be simply summarised – the five economic tests had not been met. As a concession to Blair and Euro-enthusiasts, the statement said there would be a review at the next Budget on whether to conduct another assessment in the light of fresh circumstances. An Enabling Bill introducing a Euro referendum was to be published in the autumn, but that meant little. Another concession was the staging of a new 'roadshow campaign' publicising the case for the Euro, due to begin in the autumn of 2003, but the idea fizzled out. All of this was window-dressing to allow Euro supporters to claim there had been a 'fundamental shift' in Brown's thinking.[56] There was no commitment to legislation, nor any indication as to how the current blocks to meeting the five tests could be overcome by the spring 2004

Budget. The Treasury's 'trump card' was its belief that, if interest rates were to be reduced to European levels during the Parliament, politically unacceptable raises in taxes or cuts in spending would be required to compensate.[57] After it, no one seriously thought that there was any chance of a referendum until the third term. All remaining hopes for the Euro in Blair's premiership were effectively at an end.

The most ardent Euro-enthusiasts believed that Blair had been deliberately strung along by Brown, and that the Prime Minister was deceived as the Chancellor and the Treasury were implacably opposed from the outset.[58] But there was no conspiracy. After passions cooled, Blair was not unhappy with the settlement announced by Brown on 9 June. His fear that it would be seen as a climb-down prompted his powerful pro-Euro speech in Tokyo in July 2003, giving the impression his ardour was undiminished. He also spent a long time on the phone to EU leaders and others he wanted to assure that it was only the circumstances that militated against Britain joining now.[59] He would indeed have liked to take Britain into the Euro if it had popular, political and media support.[60] But it transparently had not. Enthusiasts told him this was because 'we have not been able to make the case yet in a referendum campaign'. And indeed, part of Blair suspected that all he would have to do was stand up on a platform with captains of industry, and a cross-section of heavyweight politicians like Ken Clarke, and he would persuade the whole country.[61]

Widespread speculation, encouraged by Mandelson, emerged that Blair might drive flat-out for the Euro in the wake of a successful conclusion to the Iraq war. But in the event the 'Baghdad bounce' subsided quickly. Blair had moved on, and by the late spring of 2003 his focus had returned to health, education, asylum and crime. He worried he had already been far too neglectful of these subjects, and, given his belief that his own personal attention was vital to ensure success, they now demanded his undivided concentration.[62] A Euro referendum would have been deeply divisive, and profoundly alienated the cooling, if not already hostile, Eurosceptic press. Brown had supported him on Iraq: he had yielded to Brown on the Euro, and he did not want to create another deep rift by reopening the issue.[63] He was being warned by Sally Morgan in particular that one of the Euro-enthusiasts' prime motives was to needle Brown, and they knew the best way to make him very angry was to press the Euro button hard.[64] Blair was keen to avoid being boxed in as part of that whole game. Lurking at the back of his mind was the realisation that he had so exhausted his political capital on Iraq that he would not have enough left in the bank to win on this highly contentious issue. He was beginning to realise at last that his seemingly bottomless belief in his ability to persuade people of his favoured courses had its limits. He had failed to persuade Brown. He accepted that he would fail to persuade the nation also. In his heart of hearts he did not mind that much.

A Difficult Autumn

By July 2003, Blair considered that the parliamentary year just ending, while not 'breaking' the government, had clearly not 'made' it either. He was not happy. The bungled reshuffle, in which Irvine finally departed, as did Milburn, the most radical Blairite in the Cabinet, brought the parliamentary year to an untriumphant end. Indeed, following Byers' and Morris' departure, it meant that two years in, Blair had only one of his big four (Blunkett) still *in situ*. He analysed other reasons why the 2002–03 parliamentary year had not brought his desired 'lift-off'. Institutional inadequacies, lack of detailed policy planning, increasingly unsympathetic interests, above all the media, trade unions and the professions, and the intervention of unforeseen 'events', most recently the Iraq war and its disappointingly flat aftermath, followed by the Kelly death, had all played their part. Defeat in the Euro debate in the early summer had led to great despondency and indeed anger among Blair's pro-Euro supporters. It mocked Blair's October 2002 boast of being 'bold', as did other policy shifts or 'climb-downs', as they came increasingly to be called. Foundation hospital plans were much watered down, 'top-up fee' plans were already being modified after it became clear they had been launched with too little consultation, and the main area where Blair had been 'bold', Iraq, was the very area his party most wanted him to show restraint.

The July press was the most critical Blair had yet received as Prime Minister. In one of his final columns before his premature death, Hugo Young argued that Blair had run out of steam: 'His unique contribution to political renewal is already made . . . all Blair's passion spent, someone else deserves a turn.'[65] Few commentators had more ability to stir centre-left opinion than Young: his article was logged deep in the party's consciousness. Others followed in similar vein. Steve Richards wrote: 'The second year in a government's term should be the most creative and daring . . . The Prime Minister has managed to lose an entire year.'[66] Peter Riddell, another journalist who was prepared to view Blair sympathetically, characterised the months since the end of the Gulf War as 'a time of drift, stumbles and wobbles'.[67] While the Iraq war damaged relations with the party, the Kelly affair had caused more problems with the electorate, especially over 'trust', the attribute for which Blair had wished above all others to be praised by the electorate.

Number 10 now came into the firing line from party and media for failing to give a strong lead, despite its major overhaul of just two years before. Several of the innovations, notably the Office of Public Service Reform, were felt to have been disappointing, and the Number 10 Cabinet Office nexus overall was thought to have become unwieldy and inefficient, with too much overlap of responsibility and inadequate internal communication.[68] One response was defensiveness and passing the buck. An aide who joined in 2001 said, 'There was a real bunker mentality. The dominant ethos was that the media and the world out there were all against us.'[69]

Blair spent another summer recess pondering how to re-energise and refocus the government. His arrival at the landmark of the longest continuously serving Labour Prime Minister on 2 August 2003, passing Attlee's record, cast an unwelcome spotlight on his achievements to date, a record he felt convinced in his bones was far from complete.[70] He received much advice, not least from Geoff Mulgan, who had carried out a study of renewal by long-serving governments abroad. He came up with four themes that he put to Blair as the way forward: fresh blood, new ideas, a clearer narrative to explain where the government was going, and new methods of communication.[71] To provide the first of these, Blair asked Mandelson, John Birt and Heywood to carry out a major overhaul of Number 10's operations, with Campbell's imminent departure in September a catalyst, and a chance for yet another attempt to announce the 'death of spin'.[72] Their advice was seen in a number of changes. David Hill, the long-serving media aide who had been rebuffed by Blair as recently as 1997, came in as the new Director of Communications. But he never forged a close relationship with Blair. Mulgan himself took over for a short period as Policy Chief from Adonis. Blair had found Adonis a more creative and sympathetic thinker than Miliband in the first term, but he lacked Miliband's political skills and never carried the same weight in Whitehall. His lack of Labour credentials made his advice more appealing to Blair but it did not endear him to the party. 'If anyone knew Andrew was behind a policy, it immediately made people suspicious,' said one aide.[73] Matthew Taylor, the Labour intellectual, came in to help oversee the next manifesto, while Pat McFadden, one of the most respected figures in Number 10 among the PLP, became Director of Political Operations to help rebuild the battered relationship with the party.

These changes came on top of Andrew Turnbull's succeeding Wilson in September 2002, who was felt would be more in the 'can do' mould of civil servant desired by New Labour. Blair's personal relationship with Wilson remained amicable until the end,[74] but several insiders recounted a feeling of disappointment in Number 10 that he had not done more to facilitate delivery.[75] His supporters say he was made a scapegoat. Number 10 aides had wanted his successor to come from outside the Civil Service, but Wilson was utterly opposed to yet another onslaught on convention by not promoting a senior official to the top job, and they relented. The post was stripped of various roles, such as honours and intelligence, to allow the new incumbent to concentrate on what Blair most desired, ensuring the Civil Service delivered on the government's policies.[76] Mandelson stayed on at Number 10 after these new appointments, charged with chairing a weekly strategy meeting on Monday of key Number 10 personnel, while Birt continued to work on detailed plans for transport and drugs policy, some of which were adopted in 2004. Birt was praised by some in Number 10, not least for producing high quality internal reports. Detractors say they were barely read, and that his significance was slight, partly because so many mandarins were hostile towards him.[77]

'Fresh ideas', Mulgan's second requirement for renewal, provided much debate among Blair's aides, and was discussed at a 'summit' at Chequers at the end of August 2003. Many wanted Blair to offer policies and ideas that connected far better with the Labour Party faithful. Blair, who was in a minority, argued that they would be much better to stick in the centre ground, keep pushing ahead with the radical ideas that he had produced since 2002 for reforming the public services, and that would be sufficient to meet the aspirations of the electorate.[78] Others wanted far more time put into working up new ideas before they were announced, and for them to be placed in an ideological framework that the government had as yet failed to provide.

A new 'narrative' was given in Blair's party conference speech in October. Blair spoke about how, in the past, Labour's history had been characterised by long periods of opposition punctuated by brief periods of government, which were foreshortened by internal division and charges of 'betrayal' against the leadership, preventing the achievement of the party's ends. But the unity of the 'narrative' was far from clear. At the conference, the tag 'New Labour' was subtly downplayed, while the prefix 'New' was dropped altogether from party member cards. Blair still commanded enthusiastic support from the wider party, but it begged the question of whether there was any one narrative any longer to which all major sections of the Labour Party could sign up. A new method of communication, Mulgan's fourth prerequisite for renewal, was offered by the suggestion in his speech of the biggest consultation exercise in the party's history, called the 'big conversation'.[79] This last device, launched formally in November, had a precedent instigated by one of New Labour's most derided figures, John Major, who in order to renew himself in 1995 launched 'the biggest consultative exercise in the party's history'.[80] Some in Number 10 even feared the inconceivable, that Blair's government would, if not careful, begin to be labelled with the same charges of aimlessness that had bedevilled Britain's last Prime Minister for five whole years following 'Black Wednesday' in 1992.[81]

Nevertheless, there was still cause for optimism in Number 10 in the autumn of 2003. The economy was performing well, and poll numbers seemed relatively strong for mid-term. Widespread scepticism over lasting improvements in public services remained, but Blair believed that nine months of headlines about Iraq and terrorism had distracted attention away from the real progress that was being made.[82] 'Green shoots' were now beginning to emerge in the NHS, with indications that the new investment was beginning to bite. Blair's aides began to speak of health with the same reverence accorded to education in the first term, with a similar combination of highly effective figures working together on the issue, namely the Secretary of State (Reid, Milburn's successor), an aide in Number 10 (Simon Stevens) and Paul Corrigan, special adviser to both Milburn and Reid. Number 10 planned a 'bold' Queen's Speech for November 2003, to introduce the last full parliamentary session before the General Election. Most controversial was the Higher Education Bill, introducing top-up fees, but there were other major bills on asylum, immigration and House of Lords reform. Blair's aides were banking on the Hutton Report into David Kelly's death exonerating Blair when published in late November and producing a major cathartic moment for the government.[83] Just one stumbling block remained, denting their optimism. Gordon Brown.

Dinner with Prescott, November 2003

Beneath the heat of the divisions over the Euro and public service reform lay a much deeper schism in the Blair–Brown relationship. Brown's conference speech in October was an open challenge to the Prime Minister and his policy direction. With Blairites Mandelson, Byers and Milburn thought to be stirring on one side and Balls and Nick Brown fermenting discontent on the back benches on the other, commentators and Labour MPs speculated publicly about the damage being inflicted. Matters deteriorated further when Blair twice rejected Brown's request for a position on the NEC, a snub that soon became public. Sensing danger, Prescott was moved to action: 'We have the potential here to split the Labour Party,' he confided in a friend. 'Blair and Brown have to realise that it is in their interests to harmonise.'[84] Over a series of private meetings with each, Prescott made his case forcefully, emphasising that their differences were not insurmountable. 'John was extremely influential. He was the broker; no question about it,' said one Blair aide.[85] When the three men met for dinner on 6 November, in Admiralty Arch, Prescott was blunt: 'If you carry on as you are, you will destroy the Labour Party. And I won't let you do that.'[86]

The underlying sore was the succession and it was the principal issue at dinner. Still without a fixed date for the handover, Brown felt deeply angry and betrayed. Blair, however, maintained that he had never committed himself, back in 1994, to stepping down within a set time frame and had himself grown increasingly angry at Brown's positioning. In as far as Blair had formulated any precise plans for his departure, he had worked on the assumption that he would leave towards the end of his second term. A heart flutter that had required a brief hospital visit in October was far more significant than was admitted at the time. Concern about his condition, and the prolonged strain of Iraq, had exacted a heavy toll. Blair's old guard, including Alastair Campbell and Anji Hunter, now out of Number 10, were doing nothing to dissuade their old friend from following suit. Leaving Downing Street before the next General Election remained a very real possibility in Blair's mind. But did he give Brown a precise date? The Brown camp are certain that he did, and believed that Blair would announce his plans to step down in the autumn of 2004, naming Brown as his preferred successor. 'Nonsense,' say Blair's camp: 'Tony said that I am not going to go on indefinitely and you are obviously my favoured successor. But you have to work with me.'[87] They state categorically that no precise date was given. So which side was telling the truth?

Blair was a troubled man in late 2003. The Hutton inquiry, whose report was delayed until January, continued to gather evidence and, for all Blair's confidence that he would be vindicated, the fall-out for his government was difficult to predict. More seriously, Blair's personal popularity and trust ratings had been severely depressed by the continuing uncertainty over Iraq. He had often said that he would not remain as leader if he became a liability to his party: maybe that time had now come? On the very day that Blair had dinner with Prescott and Brown, Michael Howard formally assumed the leadership of the Conservative Party, generating a growing belief that the Tories at last had a worthy leader. Blair had feared Howard's intellect since they sparred together in the Commons ten years before. While no one expected Howard to transform Tory fortunes overnight, there were clear signs of a renewed sense of purpose and confidence within the party. It was sufficient to reawaken the possibility of a Tory revival in Blair's mind, a fear that had haunted him regularly throughout his career. His heart trouble bothered him too: he did not feel at all himself and was worried that he might suddenly have to stand down, leaving the country and his family in the lurch. One aide confirmed: 'He had been under par for a long time, and it was dragging him down.'[88] If Brown was willing to work with him, Blair might yet be able to leave office on a high point before the coming election, with real achievements to his name. To pull it off though, as Mandelson told Blair, Brown would have to be '120 per cent loyal'.[89]

Such were the thoughts in Blair's mind as the three men talked that evening in Admiralty Arch. Blair, urged on by Prescott, was thinking aloud. Brown admitted that their feud had been allowed to get out of control: 'Gordon realised he had gone over the top,' said one Brown aide. 'That more than anything made him realise he had to listen to Blair when he said, "work with me".'[90] Brown accepted that Blair's support was the *sine qua non* if there was to be a smooth and uncontested succession, and the last thing he wanted was to inherit a party that had gone through a divisive leadership contest. Yet, as in mid-1994 after John Smith's death, the two men left the meeting with different understandings of what had been agreed: Brown believed that Blair had promised to be gone before the next election. Blair insisted that, while certainly not ruling out leaving office in 2004, he had given no precise pledge. The discrepancy is partly down to Blair's incorrigible lack of precision and his desire to pacify a potentially dangerous Brown by telling him what he wanted to hear, and is partly down to Brown taking away what he wanted to hear rather than the more nuanced account that Blair had uttered. But it is beyond doubt that Blair did mention the autumn of 2004 as a departure date, subject to Brown's support in entrenching his political legacy over the year ahead. Blair's camp are disingenuous to claim that departure in 2004 was not mentioned by Blair at the dinner.

January 2004 should have given Blair a positive start to what he thought might well be his last year in office. But the delayed publication date for the Hutton Report had engendered further uncertainty. The media and the nation at large had been transfixed by the outpouring of emails and evidence unearthed during the inquiry: it was courtroom drama at its height, with even the Prime Minister summoned as star witness. The media had relished the prospect of more revelations from the Hutton 'serial' as much as Number 10 dreaded it. When the report was finally published in January, however, it failed to provide the 'lift-off' Blair had hoped for. 'We'd planned to give a number of interviews and that would be it. Chapter closed,' said one Number 10 insider.[91] But rather than merely blaming the BBC and exonerating the government, as the Blairites wanted, the Hutton Report plunged the Corporation into crisis, prompting the resignations of Chairman Gavyn Davies and Director General Greg Dyke, thereby shifting public sympathy firmly to the BBC and against Number 10. Blair gave a commanding performance in the Commons, eclipsing a surprisingly lame Michael Howard. But Blair's aides were angry that Alastair Campbell jumped on to the airwaves and, against advice, came across as vindictive in contrast to Blair who had been statesmanlike. 'The result was that Tony had no "post-Hutton moment". No catharsis,' one aide said.[92] The report was widely perceived to have been a whitewash. It caused further damage by shining a piercing light on Blair's 'denocracy', the group of aides who met informally in his den and who decided great issues of state without properly minuted discussions or prior paperwork. Although other Prime Ministers have operated in a similar way, none, not even Thatcher, had gone quite so far in usurping the traditional practices of government, and least of all on such grave issues as war, international diplomacy and claims of weapons of mass destruction.

Neither did the Hutton Report close the chapter on intelligence and WMD in the run-up to the Iraq war, as Blair and his entourage had hoped. Quite the opposite. It sharpened the demand to know whether Blair had taken Britain to war on a false prospectus, and eventually forced his hand over establishing another inquiry, under Lord Butler, to investigate the quality of British intelligence in the run-up to war. Blair seemed unable to free himself from either the causes or the consequences of the war in Iraq. He began to worry increasingly that, if he left in the autumn with Iraq unresolved, he would be accused of 'cutting and running'.

In early January 2004, over 160 Labour backbenchers signed an 'early day motion' opposing the introduction of top-up fees. Intensive lobbying went on over the next few weeks, but with Gordon Brown's staunch ally Nick Brown and other Blair critics leading the protest, Blair's ability to carry the vote was in doubt. In the forty-eight hours before it took place on 27 January, Charles Clarke made further concessions, undermining, some felt, the whole logic of the government's proposal. More crucial though was Nick Brown's decision, at Gordon Brown's prompting, to switch sides on the day of the vote.

It was just enough. After the largest backbench rebellion for fifty years, the government majority was just five. As in the Iraq and foundation hospital votes in 2003, the government had won only because of the 'payroll' vote, i.e. the almost-assured vote of ministers on the government's payroll. That a government with a 161-seat majority was almost defeated on a much watered-down bill, which was merely requiring university graduates to repay a part of the cost of their education when they could afford to do so, showed how far out of step Blair had become from his party. The PLP was still deeply angry about the Iraq war and the failure to achieve closure; about foundation hospitals; and about the feeling they were being taken for granted. They wanted to teach Blair a lesson. And they did.

Opposition to Blair over tuition fees emanated from a coalition of disgruntled ex-ministers and increasingly vociferous left-wingers in the PLP, but also contained a sizeable rump of Brownites. Blair was infuriated that Brown had held his counsel until so late in the day, and was particularly contemptuous of his riposte that he had 'no power to influence Nick Brown and his acolytes.'[93] By delaying his support until the last minute, Brown delivered only a handful of votes and thus ensured that the government came within a hair's breadth of defeat. Brown's silence had spoken volumes within the Parliamentary Party: 'Gordon was merely playing to the gallery on the left,' said one Blair confidant.[94] Observers, like Anatole Kaletsky, drew their own conclusions: 'The Chancellor has shown that he is the only man who can save the Prime Minister in his hour of need,' while backbenchers loyal to Brown have shown 'they can undermine the government at any moment on almost any issue.'[95] This point was not lost on those in Number 10: Brown was seeking to build up his support on the centre and left of the party for the coming leadership election. At the time, Blair did not see this as a reason for not going in the autumn: but, later on, it would prove most useful as a justification for refusing to budge.

From Early Jitters to Rampant Wobble

The spring went no better for Blair. His morale and concerns about his health continued to dog him. Iraq remained critical to his thinking. Senior figures such as Dr Brian Jones, formerly head of the Ministry of

Defence's intelligence branch, continued to cast doubt on Hutton's findings. Then at the end of February, Clare Short alleged that British intelligence agents routinely bugged the offices of Kofi Annan, the UN Secretary General. Blair refused to confirm or deny the claim, but it was embarrassing. In Iraq, meanwhile, the death toll continued to rise, and the insurgency showed little sign of abating.

Opinion polls in February and March revealed Labour stuck on level pegging with the Tories, while Blair's personal satisfaction rating remained obstinately negative. Over twice as many people declared themselves dissatisfied with Blair as Prime Minister than claimed to be satisfied. [96] Blair's morale sunk so low that in March he floated the idea past Gordon Brown of pre-announcing his intention to leave office in the autumn. According to Robert Peston, Brown rejected the plan. 'Don't do that. It would be crazy,' he told Blair, 'you'll make yourself a lame duck. You'll send the Labour Party into turmoil.' [97] Brown calculated that Blair's plan would have spread advance knowledge of the timing of the leadership election, giving other candidates at least six months to gather support.

By early April, Brown's aides were certain that Blair's days in office were numbered. One leading Brownite told this author that Blair, now a 'shrunken and weakened Prime Minister', might be gone as early as July, or 'by the autumn at the latest.'[98] Yet according to the Brownite account fed to Peston, by now Blair was 'already well on the way to reneging once again' on his supposed deal with Brown.[99] Persuaded by his closest allies, Peston argues, Blair was resolving to fight on as Prime Minister but chose not to apprise Brown of his intention. Brown's associates believe that the cynically minded Blair played Brown for a fool, pretending he would quit before the election only to mute opposition from his old rival. But Blair did not advise Brown in April that he had decided to remain as Prime Minister for the simple reason that he had not yet made any such decision. April was to prove one of the most difficult months he faced as Prime Minister. It was at this time that his jitters became a fully-fledged wobble.

April was to be Blair's cruellest month. Europe saw his first humiliation. The issue this time was not Euro entry, still locked away in Treasury behind Brown's five tests, but the calls for a referendum on the proposed constitution for the EU. Back in June 2003, a draft of this constitution had emerged from the year-long convention chaired by former French President, Valéry Giscard d'Estaing. Talks between EU leaders on whether to endorse the constitution had broken up without agreement in December, but after the election of a new socialist government in Spain in March 2004, the leaders agreed to meet again in June and thrash out the final wording of the constitution. Each EU country would then have to ratify the document, either through its national parliament, or through a referendum.

The Eurosceptic press and the Conservative Party seized on news of this summit to press for Britain to hold a referendum. Blair consistently opposed the idea, claiming it was a matter for Parliament, which he believed would be much more likely to provide the 'yes' vote he wished for. While Howard and the Eurosceptic press stepped up their attack, Cabinet colleagues and advisers warned Blair that his position would become untenable. An unlikely alliance of Brown and Straw proved the most potent lobbyists, while Prescott insisted 'you can't maintain your position going into the European, local and General Elections with Europe dominating everything because of the treaty going through Parliament'.[100]

Blair bowed to the inevitable. 'I know when Blair is about to change his mind on something because he starts to make rather pompous statements like "I never make any U-turns". That's when you know he's about to make one,' one close associate unkindly remarked.[101] Although the logic now pointed ineluctably towards a referendum, Blair resented being forced into the decision. Initially, the only ministers to hear of Blair's rethink were Straw and Prescott. Blair then consulted John Reid and Brown inside the Cabinet, but few others. Plans were developed for a carefully managed public announcement. But not everyone proved willing to wait, fearing that Blair might change his mind once again. On 16 April, while Blair was at a summit with President Bush in Washington, press reports appeared claiming that 'leading members of the Cabinet' were pushing Blair towards a referendum. These claims were later borne out by a leak to the *Sun*, confirming Blair's U-turn. His allies speculated that either Straw (or someone close to him), having urged Blair for months to soften his line on a referendum, had finally lost patience and used a leak to force Blair to make his commitment public.[102]

Some Cabinet ministers, like Charles Clarke, were said to have 'hit the roof' when they read the stories, not the least because they had not been properly consulted.[103] Other Europhiles, like Mandelson, expressed their dismay, warning that Blair could not hold two referenda (on the Constitution and the Euro) in the same Parliament. Amid the fallout, Blair and his aides set to work on a statement. Ever the optimist, he wanted to present the referendum as an historic opportunity for the British people to vote for a bold, new, confident Europe as opposed to a 'no' vote which could see Britain being forced out to the margins of Europe. 'Let the issue be put and let the battle be joined' were the final words of a bravura performance in the Commons.[104] Yet in private Blair was dispirited. Not only had he been forced to yield, but his climbdown had been exposed publicly. He had been humiliated and his authority as leader was lower than it had ever been.

At the same time that Blair was struggling to regain the initiative over the EU referendum, ongoing difficulties in his family life became significantly more intense. These were the source of much speculation at the time, notably on the internet, after it was made clear that discussion of the issue was 'off limits' for the British media. Close aides say the Blairs now wonder if they were right to insist on the news blackout, which only heightened speculation over its seriousness and Blair's intentions. To the dismay of the Blairs, Lord Bragg, a close family friend, later alluded to these problems and suggested that Blair had seriously considered quitting around this time.[105] Brown's camp, meanwhile, noted knowingly that these problems could provide Blair with 'an honourable exit strategy that would win public sympathy.'[106]

A further blow came on 28 April, when the first pictures showing the abuse of detainees by US soldiers at the Abu Ghraib prison in Iraq appeared on American television. Shortly afterwards similar photographs allegedly depicting abuse by British troops were splashed across the front page of the *Mirror*. These were later exposed as fakes and the *Mirror*'s editor, Piers Morgan, was forced to resign. No one, however, doubted the genuinely horrific nature of the abuse at Abu Ghraib. Blair had argued, particularly after the failure to find WMD in Iraq, that the war could be justified on moral grounds, with the US and the UK bringing justice and liberty to the oppressed people of Iraq. Until news of the abuse broke it was, in the words of the *Independent*, 'possible to believe in the fairy story'.[107] Afterwards, it was not. Blair's moral case for Britain's involvement in Iraq now lay in tatters.

As the furore over Abu Ghraib continued into May, Blair's morale reached its low point. His heart condition, though never life-threatening, remained a worry gnawing at the back of his mind, particularly when the symptoms, a racing heartbeat and a feeling of dizziness, again flared up. Aides confirm that he felt worse at this time than he let on. It seemed for a while that relinquishing the premiership would be a welcome relief. Within the party, speculation grew regarding Blair's intentions, further damaging his authority. Senior ministers debated transferring their loyalty to Brown. On 15 May, Prescott admitted that Cabinet ministers were now talking about life after Blair: 'When the plates appear to be moving,' he declared, 'everyone positions themselves.'[108] Alarm spread rapidly, fuelled by the press speculation and by Blair's inability, in his depressed state of mind, to reassert his authority. Some feared meltdown, with years of jockeying for power between the Blairites and Brownites breaking out into the open. Blair's ultra loyalists, who had nowhere else to go, feared a Brown takeover, and with it the end of their political ambitions.

The fight back begins

At this point, Blair began to re-examine his imminent departure plan. In late May, friends and close allies rallied to his side. Cabinet allies like Tessa Jowell and Charlie Falconer offered words of encouragement, but far more powerful voices came from John Reid and Charles Clarke, both figures with clout in the party and with leadership ambitions of their own, and from Alan Milburn, the ultra loyalist. They anticipated a Brown premiership with horror. But Blair's recovery from his wobble was down to far more than the pleas of self-interested colleagues. He was beginning to realise that still, by mid-2004, he had failed to entrench his reform agenda: Blairism had barely left the drawing board. Meanwhile, the situation in Iraq remained bleak. Blair believed that if only he could stay the course, everything would come right in the end. If he were to step down now, he would put all this at risk. His hope had always been to leave on a high point, yet he had found himself facing his lowest period in office since becoming Prime Minister. Also critical in emboldening him to stay on was Cherie, in part because of her loathing for Brown, and the ever loyal Mandelson.

The decisive event that changed Blair's mind came in June. The results of the local and European elections were hardly good news for Labour: yet neither were they the triumph for Howard's Conservatives that Blair had once feared. The party's much-heralded resurgence was failing to materialise. Philip Gould came to see Blair just after the results came in: 'this means you can win a three figure majority at the next general election.'[109] Blair became increasingly optimistic that he could lead the Labour Party to a record third successive election victory. Another cloud evaporated in July with the publication of the Butler report. While Butler had harsh words for Blair's style of government, he stressed, to the surprise of many impartial figures, that he believed Blair had always acted in good faith. The next day, Labour lost its seat in a by-election in Leicester South to the Liberal Democrats, but narrowly held on in Birmingham Hodge Hill. With pundits predicting that Labour could lose both seats, the results seemed almost encouraging, particularly given the performance of the Tories, who came a distant third in both.

Had Blair the confidence that his job would have passed to a true believer, who would entrench his ideas and safeguard his legacy, he might have come to a different conclusion. But Brown's ambivalent stance since the November 2003 dinner, over tuition fees in January, and more recently over the EU constitution, now came to be seen as providing legitimacy for his change of mind. Treasury objections to a series of five-year plans designed to implement Blairite reform in health, education, home affairs and transport provided further ammunition. He believed Brown had been far more concerned to bolster his support among trade unions and constituency Labour parties for the forthcoming leadership election than to support him. Brown's camp was also seen as developing an alternative platform to that offered by Number 10. If he stood down now, instead of entrenching his legacy, Blair believed Brown would dismantle it. 'Suspicion that Brown would rubbish his legacy was what finally sealed it,' admitted one very close to Blair.[110]

On 18 July, Blair, Brown and Prescott met again over dinner. Brown had become anxious. His aides were planning intently for the takeover: Ed Miliband had even drawn up lists of who would serve in Brown's new government.[111] Orders had gone out to key Brown figures to cancel their summer plans to prepare for an imminent takeover. Brown, however, was suspicious that another 'betrayal' might be visited upon him, so he pushed Blair hard over the date of his departure. Blair, to Brown's horror, told him that he needed more time and would take the summer to reflect on his options. It was during August, spent partly at Cliff Richard's villa in Barbados, that he finalised his fight-back strategy. There would be two principal strands. First, there would be a reshuffle in September. The critical change would be the return of his close and purist Blairite ally, Alan Milburn. Originally Blair wanted Milburn to replace Ian McCartney as Party Chairman but Prescott, who was close to McCartney, objected. Blair could not overrule his powerful deputy, least of all at such a perilous time, and instead set his sights on Douglas Alexander, the Brownite minister in the cabinet office who was also serving as Labour's election coordinator. Blair told aides that Alexander, although a rising star in the party, was far too close to Brown to be trusted with running the campaign.[112] In the reshuffle of 9 September, Alexander was demoted to Minister for Trade while Milburn returned to the Cabinet as Chancellor of the Duchy of Lancaster, with special responsibility for election coordination.

Milburn had reservations about returning to the frontline of politics and knew his position would depend on Brown not becoming Prime Minister. Reassurances had to be given that Blair would stay in office at least until the General Election. This led on to the second strand of Blair's plan, his 'September Surprise'. Blair had continued to suffer from periodic heart flutters and, if he were to continue in power, he would need urgently to undergo an operation to restore his heart's rhythm to normal. Unbeknownst to the public, the Blairs were also close to completing the purchase of a new house in London's West End for their post-Downing Street life. Both announcements would be sure to re-ignite raging fires of speculation as to Blair's future intentions. He resolved therefore to take the novel step of a single announcement: his heart operation, the news of his new home and his determination to fight the next election as Prime Minister and serve a full third term. This last move would give time for Milburn, or another Blairite, to establish their credentials as a challenger to Brown for the leadership. In consultation with Milburn, Blair decided to make the announcement at the very end of the party conference, late on 30 September. Brown, it was agreed, would not be told in advance.

The 2004 Party Conference was a mixed affair for Blair. Brown, still reeling from Blair's reshuffle earlier that month, delivered a thinly veiled attack on Blair's 'choice and diversity' agenda. 'There are values far beyond those of contracts, markets and exchange,' he proclaimed to the applause of delegates.[113] Blair meanwhile used his speech to present ten pledges for action on the domestic front in the run-up to the election campaign and beyond. Iraq yet again overshadowed his appeal. Shortly before Blair's speech there was increasing speculation that he would use the occasion to apologise for the Iraq war, but it was not to be. 'The problem,' he told delegates, 'is I can apologise for the information that turned out to be wrong, but I can't, sincerely at least, apologise for removing Saddam.'[114] This statement, rather than Blair's domestic pledges, made the headlines.

Late in the evening the next day, exactly as planned, Blair unleashed his bombshell. Brown, conveniently, was out of the country at the time. On a flight to Washington for an IMF meeting, he only heard the news once he arrived. Blair's actions, one Brownite complained, were reminiscent of an 'African coup'.[115] It was Blair at his most brutal. There would never again be any semblance of trust between the two men. Brown could do little in the short term other than send off an immediate telegram wishing Blair well on his heart operation. But he was determined to exact vengeance.

Many expected Brown to use his pre-budget statement in early December to present his personal manifesto as an implicit challenge to the policies Blair wanted to pursue. Yet the statement remained largely on message. Later on that month Brown gave a speech in New York,

which infuriated Number 10 after it was spun to the Murdoch press as
backing Bush's foreign policy and to the non-Murdoch contingent as
against the US line. Far more damaging was the publication, whose timing
many in the Brown camp deplored, of the Brownite book by Robert
Peston, *Brown's Britain*, which appeared in January 2005. Grabbing headlines by reporting that Brown told Blair, 'there is nothing that you could
ever say to me now that I could ever believe,'[116] Brown's camp were
adamant they did not want to rock the boat ahead of the General Election:
the showdown would come later. So they distanced themselves from it. As
one Blair adviser put it, 'it was typical of the Brown camp to cooperate on
the book and then dismiss its contents as tittle-tattle.'[117]

The Impact of the 'Wobble'

Blair's decision to fight a third General Election says everything about
his continued quest for a legacy and about his deep mistrust of Gordon
Brown. In the short term, Blair's decision to pull back from quitting in
2004 outflanked the Brown camp. In the longer term, however, it remains
unclear how wise Blair's decision will prove. Having pledged not to
fight a fourth election, Blair may find his political capital diminishes
swiftly during his third term. To counter this, his first priority will be
to neutralise Brown's power base in government and prevent him from
again creating the havoc with his personal agenda that he has caused
ever since 1997. In the spring of 2005, with so much going Blair's way,
he believed that his decision to stay on was one of his best as Prime
Minister. Aides confirm that he felt invigorated after his heart operation.
But if the General Election is not won by a large margin, if Blair's diversity
and choice agenda flounders, if the referendum on the EU is defeated
(and Brown can distance himself from it), and if the situation in Iraq
again deteriorates, then Brown will be well placed to offer the alternative
agenda which he has developed throughout his political career. Whatever
the final consequences of this decision may be, its immediate effect
was to terminate any hope of resurrecting a personal partnership with
Brown based on anything more than a transitory overlap of self-interest.
Blair's relationship with Brown, a factor more important than any other
in explaining the shape of the Blair premiership, is the subject of our
final chapter.

The perfect Blair–Brown photograph: joined at the hip and shoulder, yet looking in utterly different directions. Blair gazes resolutely to his right while Brown looks imperiously to his left.

40

Gordon Brown

Gordon Brown spent the first nine years of his relationship with Tony Blair helping him build himself up, and the next thirteen years wishing he had not. When Blair became leader in 1994, Brown believed that the crown had been unjustly seized from him, and that he was far better qualified for the job. Without Brown, Blair might never have acquired the ideas, the edge and the weight to become party leader. Without Brown, he would have been a very different, a less frustrated but ultimately less successful Prime Minister. One cannot understand Blair's place in history without Brown, nor indeed Brown's without Blair. It was the most important yet tempestuous relationship in politics of their age. One has to go back to Churchill's relationship with his heir apparent, Anthony Eden, from 1940 to 1955 to find anything approaching its significance, passion and bitterness. As it was Brown who more than anyone shaped the beginning, the middle and the end of Tony Blair's political career, it is appropriate that this chapter is the last in his biography.

Gordon Brown, the Man

Gordon Brown's background is the best-known of all the personalities described in this book, so need not detain us long. He was born on 20 February 1951 in Glasgow, to John, a church minister, and Elizabeth Brown, who had married four years before. He was one of three brothers. The family moved to Kirkcaldy in Fife in 1954. Two influences shaped the young Gordon Brown. One was the accelerated education system then run by Fife, which channelled him through the academically selective Kirkcaldy

High School from the age of ten. He took 'O' levels at fourteen and Highers at fifteen, in which he achieved five straight A grades, before starting at Edinburgh University one year later. A serious rugby injury before he went up left him sightless in one eye, delaying his start by one term, yet neither disadvantage prevented him winning a first-class degree in history. His successful negotiation of the demanding education regime honed not just his outstanding intellectual ability but also his extraordinary drive and ambition. But his injury, which severely impaired his ability to play sport, which he loved, and his resentment at being fast-tracked through school, led to an enduring sense of unfairness at how life had treated him. Some have speculated that this has contributed to his difficulty in accepting reversals.[1] The second influence was Brown's home background, which was unquestioningly socialist and unquestioningly Christian, and imbued in him a profound certainty of his convictions and a belief in his duty to serve the less fortunate in society. In stark contrast, Blair received no ingrained 'world view', nor politics from his home background, and his schooling was not an unsettling experience. Blair's early life taught him to be trusting, not suspicious, and his politics were bolt-on, not innate. Therein lie the seeds of much of what has happened between the two men.

At university Brown spread his wings, becoming involved in under-graduate newspapers, student and Labour politics. He first came to national attention in Scotland when elected student Rector in 1973 and won a place on Labour's Scottish Executive. In 1976, aged twenty-five, he was selected as Labour candidate for the Tory-held constituency of Edinburgh South. He took the challenge very seriously, while writing and speaking widely, notably on the merits of devolution. After his defeat in the May 1979 General Election he switched to television journalism, but his heart remained in politics and in writing. After ten years of intermittent work, he completed his doctoral thesis on the Scottish Labour Party in the 1920s, and continued work on a biography of James Maxton, founder of the Independent Labour Party, which was eventually published in 1986. His history tutor at Edinburgh, Paul Addison, has noted how much Brown learned from his study of Labour history, not least the party's ability to self-destruct in economic or political crises.[2]

The search was on for a safe seat: like Blair at Sedgefield, he benefited from boundary changes, and he was selected for the newly created seat of Dunfermline East, which he duly won at the General Election of 1983.[3]

Perfect Union, 1983–90

Gordon Brown was clearly the star of the 1983 intake of Labour MPs. It was inevitable that he would soon strike up a close friendship with the other figure soon identified as a high-flier, Tony Blair. Blair was flattered by the attention of the older and celebrated Brown, and was 'chuffed' when he moved offices to share with him. Paul Routledge, an early Brown biographer, captured the atmosphere: 'The two shared a tiny, windowless office, facing each other across desks jammed tightly together by the wall. There was little space left for filing cabinets or shelves, and Brown's moving paper mountain often encroached on Blair's desk.'[4] Brown was unstinting in his help and support of his young protégé. He educated Blair in the ways of Parliament, the Labour Party and politics, finding his companion bright and eager, but surprisingly naïve and innocent for a new MP.[5] Brown also rejoiced to find in Blair a politician far more free-thinking and open than his coterie of Scottish friends, who included Doug Henderson, Martin O'Neill and, of course, John Smith.[6] So the traffic, even in the early days, was not all one way. Together they despaired of the old, unreconstructed Labour Party and debated how best to modernise and to reconnect with the electorate in the changed world of Thatcher's Britain. They were described variously as 'joined at the hip' or 'the brothers'. One longstanding Blair aide recalled, 'Tony and Gordon were an extraordinary duo. I used to watch them. It was indescribable. It was thrilling listening to them. It was exceptional the regard they had for each other, the love, the human warmth.'[7] The 2003 television drama, *The Deal*, failed utterly to convey the joy, laughter and indeed love in their relationship in the 1983–90 period.

As they worked their way up the party hierarchy, Brown began to school Blair in the national media: 'He taught me the essence of how to put my arguments across,' Blair has said.[8] Some of what Brown passed on to Blair he learned from Mandelson, who had started work as the party's Director of Campaigns and Communications in 1985. Although Brown was demonstrably the senior and Mandelson the junior, from 1986/87, as we have seen, the three men were constantly in each other's company, with the shared crusade of modernisation always the focus of their conversations. 'Their relationship ran deeper than any I have ever seen,' said Gavyn Davies. 'It was rare to find three men so locked in to just one mission – and that was to save the Labour Party.'[9] The 1987 General Election defeat gave them another powerful spur. All three agreed that the party had to distance itself from the trade unions, warm up relations with business and the right-of-centre press, and appeal beyond Labour's traditional heartlands. Brown was primarily responsible too for integrating a new element into their thinking, the American experience, to become a rich vein of ideas and inspiration in the transformation of Labour. Throughout the late 1980s, there were no enduring differences between Blair, Brown and Mandelson. Brown remained indisputably the senior figure, underlined by his acclaimed handling of the shadow Chancellorship during Smith's illness, and his success in shadow Cabinet contests.[10] Brown was also unquestionably the clearest thinker and strategist. This was an article of faith for all three men.

Seven-Year Itch, 1990–92

From 1990 to 1992 the Blair–Brown relationship shifted almost imperceptibly. Brown still clearly had more support in the party, topping the poll for elections to the shadow Cabinet in 1992 shortly after Smith was elected leader. Smith saw him as ahead of Blair at this time, although after he became leader he began to play Brown and Blair off against other.[11] Kinnock also recognised Brown's lead, although he did say 'half jokingly' that 'if Brown was able to fall in love more quickly and marry, it would help him a lot'.[12] But there was a sense that Blair, with the closed shop scalp under his belt, was sniffing the air in 1990–92. Gerald Kaufman was one of the party's elder statesmen who encouraged Blair to raise his ambition at this time: 'Tony, you have got to stop thinking of yourself as the junior partner of Brown-and-Blair.'[13] Jack Cunningham and Roy Hattersley reputedly also had Blair ahead of Brown in 1991–92.[14] Some in Brown's camp believed that Mandelson had identified Blair by 1991 as a better prospect for leader, a contention Mandelson hotly denies.[15] Brown himself remained unaware of any heightened ambitions Blair might have acquired in these two years: Geoff Mulgan recalls how, in late 1991, when Blair was under attack for being lightweight, Brown sprang to his defence: 'I think Blair could well one day be leader of the party after me.'[16]

The first serious difficulty their relationship encountered came when, after the 1992 General Election defeat, Kinnock and Hattersley stood down as leader and deputy. Blair moved so quickly to put himself forward as a possible deputy leadership candidate that it appeared to some that he had planned the move for several months. He first pressed Brown to stand against Smith for leader, and when he declined, he announced he wanted to stand himself as deputy leader. 'Gordon was immensely suspicious. He didn't think it appropriate for either of them to stand, and he was very surprised that Tony had even thought of it,' said a Brown ally. 'He hadn't realised how ambitious Tony had become.'[17] Brown's condemnation of the proposal was decisive in Blair abandoning the quest. Cherie never forgave Brown. Brown never fully forgave Blair, nor trusted him so totally again. Blair realised that if he wanted the crown after Smith, he would have to fight his old friend tooth and nail. Blair's supporters deny the bid to stand for the deputy leadership was long pre-meditated: 'Did he know Labour would lose? Did he know Hattersley would stand down? The thought might have been brewing somewhere at the back of his mind, but he never discussed it until after the defeat.'[18]

Living Apart, 1992–94

Brown now saw himself as next in line for the leadership, but realised that he needed to build up a loyal personal team around him, and Blair was not part of it. Symbolically, after nine years of living side by side, Brown moved his office to 7 Millbank, while Blair retained his office at 1 Parliament Street. Both camps think the physical separation after so long together was very significant. Some impute to it a sinister reason, a wish to build up separate power bases. This theory is not entirely supported by the facts. What is clear, however, is that, after the 1992 election, they were both men who were increasingly going their separate ways.

Brown realised he had a serious job of work to do as shadow Chancellor. The election had been lost in 1992, he believed, because of Labour's image as a tax-and-spend party. 'He saw this as the great issue that he had to address,' said one associate. 'His task was made much harder because some colleagues took advantage of the difficulties he encountered. It was further compounded because he did not have the full support of John Smith, hardly surprising as he was the architect of the very tax-and-spend policies Gordon was now trying to jettison.'[19] Brown, who had embarked upon his new portfolio in good spirits, began to change humour three or four months after the election. 'Gordon became very gloomy,' said one aide who worked in his office. 'It was painful for us to watch: even though we weren't the person suffering, we all suffered along with him.'[20] Brown's predicament was to be compounded by other factors. The exchange rate débâcle in September 1992, when Britain was forcibly ejected from the ERM, caught him on the hop. He had been a supporter of the ERM, and was determined to avoid being thought a devaluationist. So he became tarred by the Black Wednesday 'brush', and lost some standing in the party and country as a result.[21] Brown further found himself having to take tough decisions on the shadow Cabinet's spending promises, which he exacerbated by insensitive handling of his colleagues. Some, he thought, did not understand, or accept, the need for the tight fiscal regime. Others, like Cook, did, but saw it as an opportunity to make life difficult for him.[22] Brown was angry at his predicament. He was becoming the lightning conductor for the PLP, taking the blame for something his strategic mind told him the party had to do, but without being afforded the full protective cover of the leader.[23] He continued to lose ground among both front- and back-benchers, reflected, to his disquiet, in shadow Cabinet and NEC voting, when he fell behind Blair. 'Labour's back-benchers became frightened by Gordon. He was so focused on what he was trying to do, that he neglected the parliamentary party – not a mistake he has made since,' said one supporter.[24]

Sharpening Brown's anguish, though in no sense its primary cause, was the sight of his protégé basking in the sunlight of public acclaim, while he was unable to push aside the dark clouds. 'Gordon saw that Tony was engaged as shadow Home Secretary in a stunning piece of politics and theatre that was changing the party's thinking on law and order,' said a Brown associate, 'and it hurt. It really hurt.'[25] 'The first time I was aware of a change in the balance of power between Tony and Gordon,' said one mutual friend, 'was over the Jamie Bulger episode.'[26] Brown found it deeply galling that he was being submerged under a constant deluge of bad press while Blair could do no wrong.[27] The steady flow of press articles, such as the *Sunday Times'* 'leader in waiting' article placing Blair above Brown, gnawed away deep inside him, with each new article intensifying his irritation.

Brown realised that he needed to boost the firepower of his office. After the General Election, Geoff Mulgan wanted to move on, leaving his team numbering just Ed Richards and Sue Nye. The former focused on policy, while the latter, who had been Kinnock's diary secretary, performed a similar role to Anji Hunter in Blair's office, albeit with less licence. 'Everyone who knows Gordon knows he punishes himself by working incredibly long hours, and he expected others to do the same too,' said one associate.[28] Brown told Mulgan he had to stay on until he had recruited a successor: he soon identified Ed Balls, a leader writer at the *Financial Times*, aged twenty-five, and a brilliant intellect. Balls willingly accepted the offer and was joined in 1993 by Charlie Whelan, after Mandelson suggested Brown needed an additional figure focused solely on handling the media. The arrival of Balls and Whelan utterly transformed the power of Brown's office. It also changed Brown's outlook. Neither Balls nor Whelan had been party to his intense and longstanding friendship with Blair. They shared none of his preconceptions nor any of his loyalties. Brown was their man. He was all they cared about. Their ambitions rested on his success. Balls wanted a career in politics; Whelan set his sights on becoming the Number 10 Press Secretary.[29] Balls and Whelan both arrived with a scepticism about Blair. In Whelan's case this soon developed into thinly veiled contempt, although Balls remained for a time more circumspect.[30] They viewed Blair as devious and profoundly ambitious: they were soon telling Brown that his old friend and his acolytes were politicking, currying favour with the party and with journalists to position himself above Brown. Luridly, some of Brown's more ardent supporters believed Blair's friends were asking questions about why Brown was not married, to contrast him with Blair's wholesomeness and appeal as a family man.[31]

The Blair–Brown bond remained strong though, even after Balls' and Whelan's arrival, and was underpinned by the ubiquitous presence of Mandelson. Blair and Brown still took a sympathetic interest in each other's work: Blair applauded Brown's achievement in repositioning Labour economically, and Brown supported Blair's commitment to repositioning the party socially.[32] These two thrusts were the opposite sides of the modernising coin. They shared the same frustration with Smith's lack of urgency as leader, but they would no longer spend so much time together, and friends noticed they had lost their easy spontaneity. To third parties, however, they were still the closest of allies, and they still hunted as a pair: at shadow Cabinet meetings, 'they sat together, often at the corner of the table, would mutter to each other out of the corner of their mouths, pass each other notes and projected an air of disdain for much of the discussion', said one attendee.[33] 'I was conscious during 1992–94 of a cave with three people in it,' said Cook, 'Brown, Blair and Mandelson. They plotted and briefed endlessly.'[34]

Marriage of Convenience, 1994–97

If the tight bond between Blair and Brown was loosened between 1992 and 1994, it was to be shattered by the events following John Smith's death on 12 May 1994. Brown came to believe that Blair was triply guilty. First, of scheming for the succession from the moment the death was announced, while he and his own supporters observed a dignified period of restraint. Their rapid response, Brown believed, allowed the Blair bandwagon to roll to a speed where it was unstoppable by the time he and his entourage girded up their own chariot.[35] Blair's supporters deny this, and believe that Brown's team was moving stealthily behind the scenes soon after news of the death.[36] More seriously, Brown believed Blair was guilty

of reneging on their prior agreement that he would support him in any
leadership contest.[37] Blair's followers, while accepting that Blair had readily
seen Brown as the senior partner, deny any such formal agreement was ever
made. Finally, Brown thought Blair had given him a clear understanding
('the deal') that not only would he cede control over domestic policy to
him, which he mostly fulfilled (at least until 2001), but that he would also
stand down during the second term.[38] When it became clear to Brown that
Blair had no intention of handing over in this timeframe, he came to
believe that Blair had lied to him. If Brown had not received these
assurances, it is said, he never would have agreed to make way in the
leadership election for his younger colleague. Blair's camp deny any such
definite understandings were given, in particular over a precise date for any
handover. They also say that short of any noble 'falling on his sword', as
the *Guardian* put it, Brown only decided to abandon his own candidature
when it was clear Blair would humiliate him in a straight fight.

For Brown, Blair's standing was the worst blow of his political life. Some
suggest this sense of betrayal flowed from a belief that hard work would
be rewarded, hence his deep resentment at seeing someone whom he
thought had worked much less hard taking the crown.[39] That he felt
cheated and betrayed by his old friend, and withdrew himself emotionally,
is beyond doubt. What is in question is whether he was right to feel
cheated. The rage and bitterness, which should have been directed at, if
anyone, Blair, was instead projected mostly on to Mandelson, whom Brown
never again trusted, nor liked, and whom he treated for much of the time
as a sworn enemy.[40]

Brown signalled his mistrust of the new regime and a change in his way
of conducting business by insisting, to Blair's amazement, that his 'advisers'
attend the Chewton Glen summit in September 1994; it was here that he
unveiled his plans for domestic policy, which he now firmly believed was
his domain. Superficially, Blair and Brown remained on friendly terms;
below the surface, on Brown's side, there was hurt and bewilderment which
turned to coldness. For Blair, there was initially embarrassment, and some
guilt at Brown's demonstrable feelings of injustice, but as Brown became
increasingly inscrutable and withdrawn, his guilt began to dissipate,
although it returned periodically.[41] The deep gratitude and affection he
felt for Brown meant he refused in this period to hear a bad word said
about him.[42] The aides of both men played a significant and growing part
in stoking up their bosses' suspicion and indignation with each other, but
the relationship was manageable during 1994–97. Blair praised Brown
repeatedly in public, at his most flamboyant comparing himself to Asquith
and saying of Brown, 'He is my Lloyd George', a reference to the

formidable Liberal Chancellor of the Exchequer credited with establishing an embryonic welfare state just before the First World War. (Had Blair known more history, he might have hesitated before making this analogy: Lloyd George seized control from Asquith, and the party was split in two.)

Blair and Brown had every reason to work closely together. There was a General Election to be won, and much modernisation of the party and its policies still to be worked through. When differences arose between 1994 and 1997, they were all resolved, at least on the surface. Chewton Glen showed Blair that he was going to have to work hard to win Brown back. The following month they differed again over Clause IV. Brown was happy enough for Blair to take it on, but thought it meaningless and token leadership: 'It was what someone would do to respond to advice that he had to show himself to be tough,' said one close Brown associate. 'Gordon's thoughts were, "Was it really worth it? Did it matter in the long run? Was it worth the six months it took?"'[43] Critically, in this, Blair's first big test as leader, Brown was absent from his side and he learned to rely on others, notably Campbell.

The press became an enduring concern for Brown in this period: a key reason he had failed to win the leadership in 1994, he believed, was because of his indifferent public image at the moment when Smith died. So Brown told Whelan that he expected media coverage every bit as good as the other big beasts in the shadow Cabinet, principally Prescott and Cook: ideally, his coverage should rival Blair's. He was impressed by Whelan's work, although he remained frustrated that, as shadow Chancellor, it was difficult to achieve the level of media attention given to the party leader.[44] Whelan used every device to further Brown's profile, and in doing so became deeply mistrusted in the Blair camp. Blair and Campbell thought him divisive, and resolved that he had to go at the earliest opportunity after the election.[45]

Brown challenged Blair on any initiative which he viewed as giving Blair or his followers an advantage over him. Brown thus viewed with suspicion Blair's clearout of party staff. He failed to have his own candidate, Michael Wills, installed in a senior position, but Blair, overcome with remorse as he always was when he rebuffed Brown, then tried to compensate by working overtime to help Wills secure a parliamentary seat.[46] Brown fought successfully to have Joy Johnson appointed as the party's media director, to give him an ally to help advance his own profile. She was appointed in February 1995, but it was not an easy ride. Her departure in January 1996, after Mandelson as well as Prescott were said to have made her life impossible, engendered much bitterness: Blair's camp believed she leaked one of Gould's hard-hitting memos in the run-up to the election, an assertion denied by the Brownites.[47] Brown now had no choice but to accept Blair loyalists like Margaret McDonagh being promoted up the party hierarchy.[48]

Blair's relative lack of interest in policy was both a source of irritation but also relief to Brown. The desire not to trespass on what Brown declared was his domain in economic and social policy provided one, but only one, reason why Blair did not plan more policies in Opposition. Had Blair tried to produce more concrete plans, policy differences with Brown would have come to the fore earlier. 'New Labour' to Brown was vital as a label to help win the coming General Election. Once in office, Brown and Blair agreed that the priority would be to stabilise the economy and establish Labour's reputation for economic competence. After that, Blair's ambitions remained indistinct. Brown, on the other hand, looked forward to the time when he could reassert Labour's core values, under Blair for a time, but then in his own right as Prime Minister. Brown, like Balls, had a profound commitment to reducing poverty: but he complained to aides that 'when I talk to Tony about these things, his eyes glaze over'.[49] Behind closed doors, Brown and his team pressed ahead, intently planning their own economic and social policy proposals. This meant serious staff time and work, put in by Balls and a burgeoning group of aides, financed in part by Geoffrey Robinson.[50] In contrast, Brown considered Blair's activities at this time to be self-indulgent or dangerous and, in the case of the flirtation with Ashdown on a putative pact with the Liberal Democrats, both. Brown did not want to co-operate with the Liberals: he wanted to destroy them and take their supporters. He thought that Blair's efforts in this area, typically, lacked strategic clarity.[51]

The Euro was an issue simmering under the surface: 'I'm a pragmatist on Europe,' he said in 1996. 'Tony is emotional.'[52] Brown was, however, more pro-Euro pre-1997 than is generally believed, though his view changed rapidly after the election. He did not welcome Blair's occasional forays into economics, a subject he thought Blair little understood. The one crucial economic policy detail on which Brown and Blair fought was the proposed tax rate for higher earners. Both before and after the election, Brown battled hard for it to be set at 50p in the pound, but this was a rare argument he lost.[53] Jockeying for power with Prescott and Cook was a further source of difference: Brown would have preferred it if Blair had been more emphatic about him being his *de facto* second-in-command, especially after Blair said Prescott would be Deputy Prime Minister. He also wanted to have a special say on patronage. Blair rather liked an element of 'divide and rule'. But a reshuffle of shadow portfolios in July 1996 assuaged Brown's sensibilities and provided the reassurance that he, not

Prescott, would be Blair's prime confidant on appointments.[54] This role was very important to him.

Remaining differences were put firmly behind both men during the General Election campaign. Victory was the goal of fourteen years of tireless endeavour. Nothing would prejudice it. Brown accepted the 1997 result as in large part Blair's personal victory, and believed his popularity and leadership was worth 'up to fifty seats for the party'.[55] As soon as the election was over, Brown moved rapidly to implement his plans for the Bank of England and a freeze on public spending: 'Everything that the Brown team did was strategic and had been carefully thought through. Balls gave me a blow-by-blow account of everything that was going to happen in those first four years. They had it all mapped out,' said one commentator.[56]

Cold War, 1997–2001

Blair's relations with Brown came under intense strain during 1997–2001, but remained manageable. Too much was made of their fall-outs by the media at the time, which overlooked how closely they worked in many areas. Critically, as one close official observed, 'In these years they had very few policy disagreements.'[57] They were united around the determination to make a success of Labour's first term and on much of what they needed to achieve. In Blair's mind, success would build his legacy; in Brown's it would set the stage for his own time as Prime Minister, which he confidently expected would come soon after Labour's second election victory. Blair rated Brown and his work extremely highly at the Treasury and was content to leave the Chancellor to his job. He had absorbed from Roy Jenkins a profound lesson, that if the Prime Minister and the Chancellor were to fall out, a government would be doomed.[58] Blair still had great affection for Brown, and refused to believe for some time after 1997 that he and his aides had their own agenda: 'It took a year or two before the scales dropped from his eyes,' said one Blairite minister.[59] What came to divide the two men was less a struggle over *policy* than a struggle for *power*. Against this backdrop, the few policy differences that did exist were magnified by increasingly bitter exchanges between the Brown and Blair camps. During the first term the principals stayed out of these clashes, at least in public, but beneath the surface their relationship deteriorated. Blair realised that he had no alternative but to manage Brown to the best of his ability, limiting the damage he could inflict. Having established his dominance, Brown was willing to bide his time. Nothing was to be gained by taking Blair on. Containment was the order of the day.[60]

Following the 1997 victory, Brown was overcome by his delight at the sheer fact of becoming Chancellor of the Exchequer after so long in the wilderness.[61] His quick and widely applauded move on Bank of England independence, although absurdly claimed by some in Blair's camp as their idea,[62] was seen as his own personal triumph, and gave him just the media spotlight and boost to his authority for which he had long craved.[63] He was now undisputed master of economic policy: to Michael White, 'it showed Blair had effectively ceded sovereignty to Brown in the economics sphere'.[64] The move helped to free Brown from the Chancellor's traditional focus on interest rates and inflation targets, although he still discussed these issues with the Governor of the Bank of England monthly. He could now set about making the Treasury the policy department that he intended it to be,[65] intervening in any area of the domestic sphere that interested him.[66]

Officials were struck by the careful plans for the Bank's independence that Brown's team brought with them when they arrived. They had done it their own way and it worked well. But a group of senior Treasury officials soon became critical of Brown's insistence on maintaining his own *modus operandi*. 'Proper papers, discussion and minuted records were not favoured by Brown's team,' said one official. 'They had neither the interest nor the understanding to know how government properly operated.'[67] Although Brown's team deny this, pointing to the Chancellor's effective use of Cabinet committees,[68] tensions quickly arose between Number 10 over the conduct of business. 'Very soon after the election, key figures in Number 10 were complaining they were being frozen out.'[69] Within the Treasury, all power was centralised in the Chancellor's office, which effectively meant Brown, Balls and Whelan. Some officials, who had worked in the Treasury all their lives, found themselves out in the cold.[70] Above all Terry Burns, the Permanent Secretary and most senior civil servant in the department, found himself excluded from Brown's inner thoughts.

Brown's staff were unrepentant. They arrived in power with similar suspicions of the Treasury as Labour figures did in 1964 and 1974. 'Look,' said one, 'these officials had been running the country for eighteen years and had taken us into two recessions and the ERM fiasco. Why on earth should we have given them automatic respect?'[71] They found Burns too focused on organisational reform at the expense of policy and this difficult relationship deteriorated further following their decision to cancel Burns' plans for the renovation of the Treasury, which they found too grandiose.[72] While some officials found Brown inflexible, suspicious and prickly, others managed to establish strong working relationships with their new political masters. Steve Robson was respected for his work on the private finance initiative and Nigel Wicks for his knowledge of overseas finance, while Alan Budd and Gus O'Donnell were seen as shrewd sources of advice.[73] Others fared less well. Charlie Whelan made life extremely difficult for Jill Rutter, the Treasury's director of communications, who was driven to resignation. Brown urged Whelan to cool it: 'Remember,' he said, 'these people have their own lives too.'[74]

The Treasury's new masters also made it clear that they had no time for Derek Scott at Number 10, nor did the Economics Private Secretary, Moira Wallace, fare much better, and found herself shut out from key meetings between Blair and Brown.[75] Brown's camp felt she was instinctively hostile to the new regime and so kept her out of the loop.[76] A painful search began for a new interlocutor who would be acceptable both to Brown's office and to Number 10. 'It was all terribly political and went on for a long time,' said one aide. 'A series of names was produced, but one after another wasn't acceptable to one side or the other.'[77] Jeremy Heywood's name then emerged, a high-flying Treasury official who had been a brilliant Principal Private Secretary to Tory Chancellor Norman Lamont, and the Brown team accepted him.[78] 'Brown told Heywood that he would have to get along with Ed Balls – it was always "Ed Balls", never just "Ed" – and on that condition it would work.'[79]

Heywood managed to establish a working relationship with the Chancellor's office, and became a crucial policy link between Number 10 and Brown's team. Heywood and Balls would meet weekly in the Churchill Café in Whitehall opposite the gates of Downing Street, or in the Treasury: 'Balls wasn't comfortable meeting in Number 10 and it wasn't worth an argument,' said one aide.[80] Often David Miliband, who got on well with Balls and thought similarly, would join them. Miliband was another important figure relied on by Number 10 to liaise with the Treasury over the details of policy, working both with Balls and with his own brother, Ed, another Brown aide.[81] Where Brown and Blair agreed on the fundamentals, these links were useful in hammering out the details. However, some on Brown's side were suspicious, particularly of Heywood: the minutes he took 'bore no relation whatsoever to what had gone on at the meeting', said one Brownite.[82] His record of the discussions over Post Office reform in late 1998 caused particular ire in the Treasury, who considered it very one-sided.[83]

In addition to being the policy wonk, Balls remained, as he had been in 1993–97, a trenchant lieutenant and political activist for Brown. The two men grew very close: 'They lived together every day, every evening and every weekend; they were constantly in touch,' said a mutual friend.[84] Number 10 held Balls (as well as Whelan) responsible for much of the negativity that they felt was emerging from the Treasury. In fact, the die was cast from the outset of their coming to power. In the last week of the 1997 election campaign, Balls told a colleague, 'You know, this will be a government fought on tomorrow's headlines.'[85] Blair's team thought him exceptionally arrogant and high-handed: 'All you can say is that he treated the Prime Minister every bit as badly as he treated everyone else,' said one neutral observer.[86] Balls had a very strong 'one of us' outlook on life. Those he considered not purist enough in their support would be locked out. Politicians and journalists would complain that he could be boorish and unpleasant if he felt slighted: like his boss, he found criticism difficult. Through intense hard work, single-mindedness and intellectual grit Balls established a dominant presence at the Treasury: 'Balls and Brown *were* the Treasury,' said one close observer.[87] This overstates the case, but what is true is that all the most significant Treasury business would emanate from them or pass through them. For such a senior and powerful figure as Balls to be so disdainful of the Prime Minister, and for him to believe Blair was so lacking in any commitment to traditional Labour values, made for constant political difficulties.

More poisonous early on, however, was the relationship between Number 10, especially Campbell, and Whelan, described as 'vicious on both sides'.[88] Whelan dates the problems from the day of the 1997 election victory. 'Tony phoned Gordon at 5 p.m. on the first of May and spent an hour trying to persuade him to sack me. Then back in London he tried again with Gordon in the garden of Number 10. Gordon came back furious because Tony Blair wasn't interested in the Bank of England becoming independent. He just spent ages telling the new Chancellor I should be sacked. How pathetic can you get?'[89] Even Brown's camp dismiss this Whelan anecdote as largely apocryphal, but it gives one an insight into Whelan. What is true is that Blair did not want Brown to carry on Whelan's appointment after the election, and that much of the Blair–Brown tension in the first eighteen months centred around Whelan. 'It was clear to everyone at Number 10 that Brown was letting Whelan, with his knowledge or otherwise, run a pro-Brown and anti-Blair campaign in the press,' said one Blair aide. 'Everyone in Number 10 wanted it stopped and for Blair to bring down the big stick. It was really intolerable.'[90] Yet Brown's camp insist that Whelan's actions were essential not only to ensure Brown's profile stayed above his Cabinet colleagues but also to compete with what they saw as an overly powerful Number 10 media operation.[91] Much irritation was caused in Number 10 by a 'fly on the wall' documentary made by Scottish television heavily featuring Balls and Whelan. Brown's team deliberately orchestrated its screening just after the General Election to ensure that the spotlight would focus on Brown, and show Number 10 the powerful media attention it could command in its own right.[92] In the end, even Brown was not delighted by the final product (any more than Number 10 was by the Michael Cockerell documentary *News from Number 10* in 2000). Whelan, ever the natural extrovert, became the star, upstaging Brown in the process.[93] Such distractions made a mockery of Number 10's boast that it had managed to keep everyone 'on message'.

The low point in relations with Whelan came over the Euro in the autumn of 1997, one of the few genuine major policy differences to emerge between Blair and Brown at this stage. Though Balls was the principal protagonist behind the press stories, and even more the thinking that came to rule the Euro out for the lifetime of the first term, Blair's ire fell principally on Whelan. His antics outside the Red Lion and his manipulation of the press caused rage in Number 10.[94] But Blair, to the disappointment of many in Downing Street, refused to insist that Whelan be dismissed. Critically, Campbell had not called for Whelan's head. Campbell had played an intimate role in the disclosure of information to *The Times*, and thought he was every bit as culpable for the story 'spinning out of control' as Whelan, and thus argued he should not go. Yet many in Number 10 saw weakness in Blair's decision. 'People mocked Blair over not sacking Whelan that autumn,' recalled one aide. 'Blair just did not seem willing to over-rule Brown over it.'[95]

The Euro aside, broad co-operation on policy continued, but personal squabbling was becoming vicious. In January 1998, Brown's team launched a new offensive in the media, briefing that Brown was the government's chief executive, and Blair merely its 'chairman'.[96] Number 10 were furious, and blamed Balls and Whelan: the former for devising the quotation, the latter for telling the press.[97] Blair found it demeaning and offensive. A new book was now commandeered as a weapon in the growing struggle between the Brown and Blair camps. Paul Routledge's publication in January 1998 of his sympathetic insider Brown biography, raking over all the old sores, infuriated Number 10. A way was sought to strike back. 'I have a terrible feeling that I may have played a part in coining the fatal phrase,' said one senior official, 'because Alastair asked me early on what I thought of Gordon and I said I thought he was brilliant, formidable, but perhaps with psychological flaws. Alastair clearly logged the phrase.'[98] The words 'psychologically flawed' duly emanated from Downing Street to describe

Brown's character. 'It was Number 10's response to put Brown back in his box.'[99] Campbell denies he was the source: many thought otherwise, or at least that he had fed the phrase to an intermediary who then briefed accordingly.[100] Brown's camp were '99.9 per cent' certain that Campbell was responsible. It was now the Chancellor's turn to be 'deeply offended and outraged'.[101] Blair was angry at the temperature being further raised by his subordinates and apologised to Brown. Whelan and Brown never fully forgave Campbell.

Brown refused to be put in a box of any kind, and in the first half of 1998 his way of working was to cause even greater concern in Number 10. A Treasury mandarin described him mid-year as 'overly suspicious and jealous', noting that he believed 'Number 10 had too many people'.[102] Concerns reached Blair over the irregular way in which some thought Brown was running the Treasury. In the discussions over the coming public spending round, for example, Brown was said to be holding bilateral meetings without officials or the Treasury submitting papers. Blair 'seemed surprised', said one official, but seemed to think that this had always been the case.[103] Intelligence also filtered back to Blair in mid-1998 that Whelan, Balls and Geoffrey Robinson were 'doing the things that Brown cannot do', but were 'acting with his full support'.[104]

Mandelson became again, in 1998, a principal focus of the Brown camp's hatred. Deeply upset by the ruling out of the Euro in the autumn of 1997, and fed up with the relentless hostility of Brown and his entourage since the leadership election in mid-1994, Mandelson finally gave up all attempts to try to build bridges.[105] According to one Brown aide, 'He never even tried.'[106] A senior official who worked with Mandelson in 1997/98 recalled that 'Peter was always stirring things up, as the conversation was always about him and Gordon, Gordon and Tony and Tony and Gordon'.[107] Dislike of Mandelson among the Brown camp reached a new peak when, in the July 1998 reshuffle, he was promoted to Trade and Industry, a department always viewed with suspicion by the Treasury. Brown had assumed that Blair would consult him over appointments, and he did so in May 1997, when Brown had several of his parliamentary 'ultra-loyalists' placed in key departments. These included Henderson, who became Europe Minister at the FCO, while other allies such as Geoffrey Robinson, Nick Brown and Nigel Griffiths were given key jobs. At first, Blair was thought to have been slow to see how Brown had constructed a network of loyalists across Whitehall: as always, he was reluctant to ascribe manipulative motives to Brown.[108]

Patronage, the power to 'hire and fire', was one Prime Ministerial weapon Blair knew Brown could not touch. Blair believed in meritocracy and was eager to promote the most able,[109] but loyalty was also important, and he resolved to use the reshuffle of July 1998 to stamp his authority on the government.[110] In addition to the Mandelson promotion, he took other decisions to deflate Brown. These included effectively demoting Nick Brown from the politically sensitive post of Chief Whip to Minister of Agriculture, placing the Blairite Byers in the Treasury as Brown's number two ('We knew what he was doing,' said one Brown supporter) and shifting Griffiths, Doug Henderson and Tom Clarke.[111] One change Blair shied away from that July was sacking Robinson as Paymaster General. Many Blairites felt that this should have been one of the easiest decisions. Robinson had caused embarrassment by being evasive over his offshore interests, which earned him several rebukes from the Standards and Privileges Committee.[112] Yet he was close to Brown and so became embroiled in their power struggle. Blair sent for Robinson, but he failed to emerge, apparently confused as to whether the Prime Minister wanted to see him in the Commons or at Number 10.[113] Richard Wilson was then dispatched to the Treasury to track Robinson down. Brown intervened: 'He should not go,' he snapped. 'He's done nothing wrong.'[114] That evening, pungent words were spoken between Brown and Blair, in which the former mixed pleas for Robinson's retention with warnings of dire consequences of his dismissal. The next day, Blair told his officials, somewhat sheepishly, that he had changed his mind over sacking Robinson.[115] Brown only managed to save his old friend for another five months, when as part of the afterburn of the first Mandelson resignation, out went Robinson and Whelan too (according to Brown, this was Blair's fourth attempt to sack Whelan).[116]

The reshuffle, albeit blunted by Robinson remaining, proved the high point of Blair's toughness against Brown and marked a further step in the inevitable distancing of their relationship. Blair always shied away from personal confrontations: the reshuffle had taken a lot out of him, and he did not want to repeat the experience. Brown vowed to seek revenge, and bided his time. Balls took over much of Whelan's media management, the Brown court closed in further and became even more entrenched. The cold war now was fought on so many overlapping fronts that it is hard to discern any overall pattern.

Two constant sources of aggravation between Number 10 and the Treasury were the Budget and public spending rounds, as they have been for many governments. One official insisted that Brown and Blair worked far closer on these issues than most Prime Minister–Chancellor teams in the recent past: 'They used to spend hours closeted together discussing the key messages.'[117] Yet the Treasury still caused intense frustration by refusing to confirm the details of the Budget until the eleventh hour.[118]

The 1999 Budget in particular caused 'absolute rage' in Number 10 because of Brown's secrecy. Blair had used his weapon of patronage to thwart Brown: now Brown was retaliating by withholding information, a critical weapon in the Chancellor's armoury.[119] 'We had to hold back the details,' said one Brownite, 'because we knew that if Number 10 disagreed they would leak the information in such a way that we would be forced to back down.'[120] On public expenditure, Blair and Brown were united over the two-year freeze in 1997–99, and Blair gave staunch support during the jibing from the party over the cuts in lone parents' benefits. Number 10 considered Blair had bent over backwards to be supportive, in contrast to Smith's standoffish attitude towards Brown in 1992–94.[121]

Differences emerged when choices presented themselves after the spending freeze. They disagreed on whether to invest in education and in health, and over Brown's favoured option of spending the money on tax credits.[122] (Blair later would complain that Brown had 'mucked up' his first term by his 'tax credit obsession'.[123]) Through the strength of the relationship between Heywood, David Miliband and Balls, one Number 10 official felt that his side had far more involvement in determining spending allocations than had been the case under the Conservatives.[124] However, although involved, Blair did not always prevail. Number 10 noticed that Brown distributed money to ministers who were his allies or those pursuing policies he believed in, like Darling, Harman, Liddell and Prescott (now an ally, and on whom he knew his succession hinged), rather than to Blairites like Blunkett, Byers, Hoon, Irvine and Straw.[125] Cook, in neither camp, lost out doubly: when he went to complain to Blair during the first spending round that the Foreign Office was being treated unfairly, he did receive some more money, but the Treasury spun the story to make out that Brown had triumphed over him.[126] Blunkett, in particular, had a difficult time with Brown and they had several flaming rows. Brown was not seen as sympathetic to his education agenda: Blairites speculated it was because it was the Prime Minister's priority.[127] Some claim that Number 10 did not fully appreciate what Brown had been doing, and how far some ministers had lost out.[128] The new three-year planning cycles for public spending left the Treasury with far more control than Number 10, who became little more than broker for disgruntled ministers. Yet even this role was performed rarely, as ministers learned that going to Number 10 tended only to make Brown more stubborn, as happened to Cook. Neither did Blair's aides fully realise at first that by determining how much money each department was to receive in the 2000 comprehensive spending review, Brown was effectively shaping the next manifesto, as policy commitments, without the money to enact them, were meaningless.

To voices within Number 10 who wanted Blair to be tougher with his Chancellor – Campbell, Powell, Hunter and Morgan – were added those of some of his Cabinet ministers.[129] Blair, throughout the first term, however, remained reluctant to confront Brown again: 'I know you all want me to have a row with Gordon, but I'm going to do it my way,' he would say.[130] Some Treasury mandarins too wanted Blair to be more emphatic with Brown, but the discontented officials were on the wane, while others were enjoying the power and excitement Brown had brought to the Treasury. Blair managed to win some arguments, as over insisting on higher minimum wage rates than Brown wanted.[131] But such were small beer. On most of the significant differences in the first term Brown carried the day.[132]

Number 10 also distrusted the way that Brown would 'cosy up' to the unions. The union bosses had felt since the days of the closed shop, OMOV and Clause IV that Blair wanted them marginalised, a view apparently confirmed by Blair's deliberately standoffish approach to them after 1997. Brown believed this approach was a mistake. From 1997, helped in particular by Whelan and Sue Nye, he began to build up a strong union base both in and outside Parliament.[133] These efforts continued well after Whelan departed, and were intensified in the second term, when Bill Morris of the TGWU became a key ally. Similar dismay was caused in Number 10 by reports of Brown setting out to win friends in business, giving hospitality to back-benchers and junior ministers and phoning MPs who had been sacked or who were disgruntled.[134] Number 10 also monitored and viewed with suspicion Brown's and Balls' friends in the media, who included Routledge (*Mirror*), William Keegan (*Observer*), Kevin Maguire (*Guardian*) and, after his departure, Whelan, although in fact Brown's cultivation of such a group differed not at all from Blair and Campbell's network in Fleet Street.

Rather than engage in such politicking, Number 10 felt that Brown should have been more ready to support the Prime Minister in difficulties. 'There was always a feeling that, during a crisis, Gordon was conspicuous by his absence.'[135] 'Gordon's disappearing acts' were how they came to be known.[136] Brown felt, on his side, that Number 10 shut him out of major events and only involved him if it suited them. He was thus hurt not to have been asked to play any role over Diana's funeral arrangements: typical of Blair, he oozed remorse when told of Brown's pique, and offered him the Chairmanship of the Diana Memorial Fund afterwards as a sop.[137] Nor did he figure in the Good Friday Agreement triumph, though he took an interest in Northern Ireland. On Kosovo, Brown was not persuaded of the case for involvement, and was then 'deeply shocked' when he learned that Blair had proposed to Clinton that the British pay one-third of the cost of the operation. Brown eventually supported what Blair was doing on Kosovo, but with 'grave reservations'.[138] The detached attitude Brown adopted during the fuel protests in late 2000 led to 'serious anti-Brown commentary in Number 10', which recurred during the foot and mouth crisis, when Blair's camp felt the Chancellor did little other than protest at the financial consequences.[139]

Blair's preference for taking direct control in crises suited Brown in one way, as it removed him from the scene and left him a freer hand. What Brown achieved in the first term was to carve out a vast empire for himself in Whitehall. He was helped by devices such as the public service agreements, which gave him a great say over government departments. Number 10 believed that Brown cherry-picked the best government initiatives to announce himself, thus conveying the impression that he was the driving force in the government. 'Gordon kept Blair out of quite a lot of domestic policy in the first term,' said one senior official, 'and it created great tension about what the Prime Minister's role in domestic policy was.'[140] Brown's exceptional mastery of detail contrasted with Blair's more broad-brush approach. Officials listening to their calls in Number 10 would note how much more acute was Brown's grasp of the facts: 'The Chancellor was really up to speed,' said one. 'I had the feeling often that TB was being dragged along and couldn't really be switched on.'[141] Yet according to one close observer, the paradox of Brown's success in dominating domestic policy was that he actually took 'little interest in large swathes of the domestic agenda: he certainly had no distinct view on public services, health, crime, education or the environment'.[142] It was power, not policy, that drove Brown in these areas. He was determined to show that he, not Blair, was in charge. Indeed, Brown had another attribute, a fanatical desire to succeed. One official told Keegan, 'Every battle has to be won. If not, the Chancellor is terribly angry. He lives life on the edge of a volcano.'[143]

As the General Election approached, Brown and Balls looked back and considered what they had done since 1997. They saw that the achievements of the government, above all economic prosperity, welfare reform and sound foundations for the future, were all due to their own efforts. They did not feel that nearly enough credit had been given from Number 10 for Brown being, they believed, the most successful Labour Chancellor in history, and for avoiding the crises that had plagued Labour governments in the past. The delivery of growth and economic stability was, Brown and Balls believed, justifiably, their own work and achievement, not Blair's. They had also saved Blair from jeopardising their whole future by taking Britain into the Euro. They saw Blair's personal achievements as essentially ephemeral or ill-considered or, in the case of the Millennium Dome, which Brown made known he 'hated', both.[144]

In the run-up to the 2001 election, hostilities calmed. Brown was pleased with his achievements to date and believed that, with Blair leaving half-way through the second term, he and Balls would be well placed to introduce the policies they had long planned. With Mandelson out of the way following his second resignation in January 2001, Brown was able to run the General Election very much on his own lines.[145] Election timing provided a major difference with Blair, marked by a particularly unpleasant scene during which Balls exploded during a meeting in Number 10, shouting at Blair that delay was a serious mistake.[146] Brown fought successfully to have the election campaign based on his economic record, over Blair's wish to base it on entry into the Euro and reform of public services. As one of Brown's supporters put it, 'The campaign was chaired by Gordon, fought to Gordon's agenda and on his record as Chancellor. It was his victory. What particularly pleased him was to win it this time around without any input from Mandelson.'[147] When the majority of 167 was announced Brown felt, after long years of anguish, that he was fully vindicated. He felt his moment had all but arrived.

Love's Labour's Lost, 2001–05

Instead of stabilising after four years of productive work, marred by mutual suspicion and periodic bloody spats, the Blair–Brown relationship now deteriorated badly. Discussions had taken place deep in the Blair bunker about moving Brown after the General Election, possibly to the Foreign Office. Blair was determined to make progress on the Euro and public service reform, neither of which Brown was committed to. A reshuffle would remind Brown in the most public way possible who was boss.[148] They calculated that Brown would turn the offer down and go to the back benches, and would bide his time there before challenging for the leadership. The debate turned on whether he would attract enough support to make the threat credible, or whether he would sink without trace. Voices were divided. Blair finally ruled that, with Brown's success at the Treasury since 1997, neither the party nor the country would understand why he wanted to move him. Brown would stay in his job.[149] Another, less draconian, plan was also debated, to carve up the Treasury, leaving Brown effectively a European-style Minister of Finance, while appointing a separate Chief Secretary to oversee public expenditure and report directly to the Prime Minister. Brown was predictably angry about this possibility, and made it clear to Blair that he would never accept it. Again, the plan was dropped, and the Treasury was left as it was, where under Brown in the second term it acquired even greater hegemony over the rest of Whitehall.[150]

One decision taken within Number 10 engendered substantial bitterness in Brown's camp. This was the decision not to promote Yvette Cooper, Balls' talented wife, to Minister of State rank after the election. Brown's camp viewed it as 'mean, nasty, unnecessary and demeaning. It was politics at its cruellest, clear revenge for Ed overstepping the mark.'[151] 'Total nonsense,' shot back one Number 10 aide, who stressed that Cooper was still young and did not yet merit promotion: Blair was only too happy to promote able Brownites like Douglas Alexander and Wilf Stevenson when the time was right. Either way, the Brownites perceived the decision as the opening salvo for the new session from the Blair camp. Blair had indeed decided that he would learn from his mistakes and say 'no' to Brown more often in the second term. Blairite Cabinet ministers had also decided that, if Brown was to remain as Chancellor, they would not let him interfere in their departments as much as he had in the first term.[152]

The atmosphere between Number 10 and the Chancellor's office was particularly tense in the few weeks between the election and the summer recess. Over the holidays, Brown went to Cape Cod in New England as usual and simmered, as he often did when relaxing.[153] He felt he had done everything humanly possible to win the election and had confidently expected to receive word from Blair of a precise date for a handover. Instead, all that emerged from Number 10 was a plan to carve up the Treasury empire that he had so carefully and effectively husbanded. Brown's patience was running out: 'When is that man going?' he asked repeatedly. Brown pondered on his future all holiday, and returned to Britain determined to have it out with Blair.[154] A series of acrimonious exchanges took place culminating with Brown reportedly thumping the table and shouting at Blair, 'When are you going to move off and give me a date?', and 'I want the job now!'[155]

It dawned on Brown that autumn that Blair was not making plans to retire in 2003/04, or, if he was, he was not prepared to share his thoughts with him.[156] Some senior party figures, like Neil Kinnock, think that Brown's angry outbursts made Blair determined to stay on longer than he might have initially intended.[157] Blair in fact had never settled in his mind on seven years and studiously avoided giving any precise date, despite hints emanating from his lieutenants, soon after the 1997 election, that he might go half-way through the second term. Soon after Blair arrived at Number

10, seven years might have seemed easily long enough; but once he was fully into the job, and after slower progress than expected was made in the first term, he realised how long it would take to make an impact. He then revised any hazy notions he once had, and began to think in terms of standing down soon after a third historic election victory.[158]

Blair was not the only one in his family to have grown tired of Brown's antics. Cherie had resented him for a long time and could not forgive what she saw as his unacceptable treatment of her husband. She played an increasingly important part after 2001 in raising the temperature: 'That bloody man,' was how she was reported to describe him.[159] Brown had never found her easy and had been 'greatly offended' by the peremptory way she had insisted on taking over the Chancellor's flat above Number 11 and 12 Downing Street, leaving him the much smaller flat above Number 10 (which in fact he rarely used).[160] Brown was upset by Cherie's continuing coldness towards his partner, Sarah Macaulay, whom he had married in 2000. A perceived snub by Cherie to Sarah at the fireworks party to celebrate the Golden Jubilee in 2002 caused particular hurt.[161]

Anji Hunter's exit in late 2001 further damaged the Blair–Brown relationship, because together with Sue Nye, she had played a key role in smoothing over tensions.[162] With the departure of David Miliband, Jeremy Heywood became Number 10's sole policy link with the Treasury other than Blair himself. The politics of Adonis, Miliband's successor, were not congenial to Brown and Balls, any more than the majority of his policy team in Number 10 were. To the Brown team, they were not only pumping out the wrong prescriptions, but their methods were exacerbating friction in the party.[163] Consequently, the Heywood–Balls nexus became absolutely crucial, especially as their principals communicated less and less with each other. Much of the detail of the 2003 spending round was determined solely by these two advisers. Balls was the only figure in the Treasury who fully knew Brown's mind: Heywood was the only person in Number 10 to whom he would speak, and who knew Blair's mind best on economic policy.[164] Their negotiations were extremely tough, but the two managed to maintain a robust relationship despite the continued hostility of some in the Brown camp, who insisted that Heywood could not be fully trusted.[165]

From the autumn of 2001 Brown began to make life extremely difficult for Blair. As the second term advanced, Blairites openly briefed that Brown was trying to make things so intolerable that Blair would quit out of desperation.[166] To Blair's circle, Brown's obsessive talk of seven years was self-delusion or 'madness', and they began to raise the 'character' question. Was Brown in fact rounded enough to be the next Prime Minister? Was he too obsessive, not a team player, too insecure and defensive and unable to accept contrasting viewpoints? Would he be able to sustain trusting relations with overseas leaders, notably the US President? Would he commend himself to all the very different types and groups necessary to maintain Labour's broad appeal? Yet another worry was what Brown might do to rubbish Blair's legacy of modernising the Labour Party. Blair came under heavy pressure from his aides to take Brown on, as he had in July 1998. He was steadying himself for a confrontation with Brown in early January 2002, but then Brown's newborn baby, Jennifer, died. Blair's heart melted, the fondness and love again flowed, and he even became concerned for a time that the loss might seriously unsettle Brown's equilibrium. He thus resolved to postpone the confrontation until a better time. It never came. At the funeral service, the Blair camp were taken aback to see sitting in the pews their arch-enemy, Paul Dacre, editor of the *Daily Mail*.[167] Even in tragedy differences simmered below the surface.

Brown's lack of support for Blair's international coalition-building after 9/11 and during the Afghanistan war disappointed Number 10 ('No reason why it should: part of their agreement was that Gordon left Tony a free hand on foreign policy,' said one Brown supporter).[168] When Blair focused again on domestic policy in the early months of 2002, it soon became clear that the two men were now determined to pursue very different aims. Brown had no intention of allowing any progress to be made on the Euro, but bided his time on it. Public services provided the main battleground. Neither he nor Balls accepted that public service reform should be such a high priority for the second term, arguing that there was no coherent or acceptable plan.[169] Differences over Blair's 'choice' agenda – which were never as fundamental as was believed at the time – now exacerbated the increasingly open power struggle between the two men. Foundation hospitals saw the first major battle. Initially, in the spring and early summer of 2002, Balls and Heywood held what Number 10 at least judged constructive discussions. But the accord was shattered by press reports in August, thought to have been briefed by Mandelson, which portrayed Brown as a 'consolidator', not a transformer.[170] It looked to the Brown team like a Number 10-sanctioned attack on the Chancellor. This provoked a Treasury memo, criticising foundation hospitals, viewed in Number 10 as 'incendiary',[171] which was sent to all Cabinet ministers in a way that made Number 10 believe it had been deliberately intended to leak.[172] Here was the Chancellor intentionally seeking to rubbish one of the policies personally associated with the Prime Minister. The episode marked a watershed in relations with the Treasury, and showed that the second term would be played by very different rules from the first.[173] 'The sense was that Gordon was playing to the PLP,' said one Number 10 aide. 'It showed that he wanted no ownership of the public service reform agenda.'[174] The episode highlighted a leitmotif of the Blair–Brown relationship: the propensity for their supporters to poison and undermine trust. But it also revealed a real ideological divide between both men. The clearest exposition of Brown's views came in February 2003 in his speech to the Social Market Foundation, in which he questioned the extension of market principles across the public services. It was viewed correctly as a tightly coded attack on Blair's stance on foundation hospitals and his whole 'choice' agenda.

Brown's offensive was also seen as a deliberate attack on the Health Secretary, the Blairite Milburn. A pattern was discerned where Brown would be hostile to any minister whom he feared might be a possible rival for the crown. Prescott had been an early target after 1994, then Cook in the first term. In the second term, other potential successors aired in the press were Byers and Blunkett, and perhaps even Clarke. A Mary Ann Sieghart article in *The Times*, in which she discussed the merits of 'skipping a generation' by missing out Brown, caused great alarm: her closeness to Blair led to certainty in the Brown camp that she was voicing Blair's own thoughts on the succession.[175] This came on top of an earlier article by Sieghart in April 2002 about Brown and child benefit, thought by the Treasury to have been briefed by Number 10, which had caused a major row at the time.[176]

Feelings over the succession became very raw. Jealousy of Blunkett's standing with Blair lay partly behind the row over asylum in the summer of 2002. Blair's confidential August memo made it clear this had now become one of his two main priorities. Brown wanted the focus on the run-up to the next election to be on the economy and the NHS, and 'he thought it crazy that Blair was hanging on about asylum and crime'.[177] Brown's concern was rather with the *causes* of crime, especially poverty, which he wanted the government to take far more seriously. The initiative at the time, however, was not with him. Blair determined to step up the pace of his public service reform, and to challenge Brown for resisting fresh thinking. Notes from this period also show Blair beginning to identify Brown as a principal culprit for more not having been achieved in the first term.[178] Number 10 in particular viewed the October 2002 party conference as a victory for Blair. As one insider, who sounds like Campbell, told Rawnsley, 'We've dealt with all that Gordon bollocks that he's the lord of the domestic agenda.'[179]

Number 10's irritations with Brown now moved into a new arena – his silence over the mounting tension on Iraq. This rose to a 'peak of tension' in Number 10 in early 2003 because 'Gordon was not prepared to stand up and be counted'.[180] Brown, although no fan of Bush, was still an ardent Americaphile. He nevertheless had serious misgivings about the war. He thought Blair had signed up too early to the Bush agenda, and he was critical of Blair for not consulting him or his colleagues properly.[181] As one of his supporters said, 'Gordon didn't want or like the war, but thought he had to go along with it.'[182] Some argued this amounted to putting self-interest ahead of principle on arguably the most important decision taken by a British government since Suez, nearly fifty years before. But it was not as simple as that: not only did Brown want to avoid splitting the party, but also his strong pro-American sentiments left him very reluctant to urge a break with the US, even with the Republican Bush in the White House.[183] After Brown made his speech backing the war ('We should all give Tony Blair . . . our full support'[184]) tension with Blair eased.[185] Brown, however, was very careful: he always phrased his support in narrow terms, referring only to the need to tackle Saddam's WMD. He never made the moral case.

Brown could have halted British involvement in the war by turning Labour MPs against it in the crucial vote. He did not: and in one sense it was now his war as well as Blair's. But Number 10 was under no illusions – even the rump still well-disposed to Brown said he was only 'biding his time'.[186] Blairites reasoned that Brown had made a calculation, as the then Chancellor Harold Macmillan did over Suez in 1956, that to refuse to support and pay for the war would risk him being seen at home and abroad as the assassin, and that would jeopardise the succession.[187] Opinions within Brown's court differed over support for Blair over Iraq, but caution won through, and it was considered better for Brown to succeed Blair because the Iraq war backfired than to precipitate a crisis by challenging Blair directly over it, as had Cook and Short, when the war might yet turn out to be a success.[188] Was this the moment, some asked, when Brown's caution lost him the crown?[189]

The summer of 2003 saw no let-up in the firefight between Blair and Brown, with the focus on public sector reform and the Euro.[190] On the former, Brown viewed the big increases he achieved in NHS spending as a huge moral victory against Blair – ironically because it was Blair's pre-emptive strike on the *Breakfast With Frost* programme that launched the wave of high increases in health spending.[191] On the Euro, Brown remained firmly opposed. Blair was keen in public, but not keen enough to stake his political future on a campaign to win round the sceptics. Brown sensed weakness and won a victory in ruling out the Euro in June 2003, technically until another review in a year's time, but in reality for the remainder of the Parliament.[192] Some Europhiles in Number 10 were so furious that they again debated whether, on the back of the post-Iraq 'Baghdad bounce', Blair should fire Brown. 'Some were adamant that Gordon had to resign. Eventually the argument prevailed that if he did go, no new Chancellor would be in a position suddenly to announce that he would go all-out for the Euro, so we'd be back where we started.'[193] The pro-European majority among Blair's advisers suspected Brown of being cynical and playing politics over the Euro, denying Blair something he wanted, while also winning him admirers among the Eurosceptic press, principally the *Mail* and *Sun*, which would be useful for him in the future. Indeed, few things Brown did so angered Number 10 as his growing relationship with the *Mail*, *Sun* and even Murdoch's guru, Irwin Stelzer.[194] Campbell, whose relationship with Brown had never fully recovered after the 'psychological flaws' remark, had become utterly disenchanted with Brown. Powell had lost any last vestiges of respect, and Morgan, who earlier had had a lot of time for Brown, had become repelled by his behaviour.[195]

Blair and Brown separately took stock over their 2003 summer holidays. Both men acknowledged the relationship was now at an all-time low. While they debated with their camps what to do, the temperature was kept up by inflammatory sniping from supporters, notably Whelan, with a full-frontal assault on Campbell in the *Mail on Sunday* at the end of August.[196] Reports seeped out that summer of Brown's rage and rudeness to Blair, which had shocked those who had newly joined Downing Street.[197] Even old hands could not believe how openly contemptuous and disrespectful Brown had become. In September, Blair decided that his by-now irregular meetings with Brown would be terminated indefinitely.[198] His mounting frustration over the last nine years had now turned to anger, his affection to coldness. The question he asked increasingly was whether Brown really was of the right cast to become Prime Minister of Great Britain?[199]

Brown had a different take on events. As he reflected that August, he concluded that Blair's attempts to develop a radical policy agenda were doing nothing but scoring 'own goals'. Through focusing on foundation hospitals, Brown believed Blair was detracting attention from the massive new investment being made in the health service. Similarly, because of the disputes over tuition fees, the good news of greater funding for primary education was being crowded out. Reform of the House of Lords was going nowhere and policy on immigration confused. This was the product, Brown deemed, of a man devoid of strategy, planning or clear ideas, who made up policy on the hoof. Brown felt his own achievements, such as reducing child and pensioner poverty, meanwhile, were constantly being downplayed because 'redistribution' did not fit Blair's image for the government.[200] He considered he had bailed Blair out over Iraq, and kept the government on course at home during the year that Blair had spent on foreign affairs.[201] Blair's support in the party, media and country, he noted, was beginning to crumble, and the 'trust' issue was rising in prominence. Was this the moment to pounce?

Brown thus planned to deliver a *coup de théâtre*, his speech to the party conference in Bournemouth in October 2003. According to one associate, 'What Gordon was saying to the world was "I'm here, I'm ready, I've won." It had been the speech he'd been planning to give ever since he became Chancellor. He'd won on the battlefield of ideas, policy, personality and even publicity. He saw himself as palpably stronger than a shrunken and weakened Prime Minister. This was his moment.'[202] Another close aide said: 'Gordon's greatest worry was not that he wouldn't take over – he never doubted that – but that he would inherit a shell of a party that has effectively been destroyed by Blair, a wasteland. He was reaching out to the party's heartland, to the unions, and alerting them.'[203] In direct parody of Blair's soundbite 'We are best when we are at our boldest' from the year before, about which Brown was said to be 'livid', Brown began his speech saying, 'We are best when we are Labour.'[204] Brown basked in the applause of the believers. But it soon became clear that all was not going to plan.

To Number 10, Brown had overplayed his hand. They thought his speech at best 'crass and clumsy', and at worst 'treacherous'.[205] Reports filtered back to the Blair camp that Yvette Cooper had been actively whipping up support at the conference against foundation hospitals,[206] while Nick Brown was said to have been mobilising opposition to tuition fees.[207] Rumours were also heard that Blair's heart scare in October was being played up by Brown's acolytes. Brown protested that he was not responsible for the actions of his supporters: Number 10 was not so sure. Blair, as Brown accepts, has an extraordinary resilience and ability to bounce back from the most inauspicious circumstances. He re-wrote several passages of his conference speech at the last moment in the light of what Brown had said, and delivered one of the strongest speeches of his career. Blair's team were pleased with its impact and felt that he had 'seen off the challenge within the week'.[208] The Brown camp's line of defence – 'Gordon helped Tony raise his act in response and provoked his best speech for a long time' – seems a bit limp.[209]

Blair then considered his options. He thought about his future. He thought about his legacy. Brown had made it clear that he would not only block his plans for the second term, but he would actively work, with the party, the unions and media, to advance his own position at Blair's expense. But what could Blair do? Brown had made it clear again that, if moved, he would 'withdraw from the government', sparking a massive crisis with entirely unpredictable consequences.[210] Besides, Blair had no other successor groomed.[211] So he fell back on two resorts: his ace, his power to decide when he would quit, thus keeping Brown on tenterhooks; and his use of patronage deliberately to humiliate Brown. In early November, he denied Brown a position on the NEC, a body Brown had been anxious to influence in the run up to the election campaign, and which he alleged he had asked Blair three times to join. Blair's action was described as 'toxically dangerous', and the worst crisis in their long years of tension.[212] The move hit Brown very hard, just as Number 10 had intended, and even his joy at the birth of his son, John, on 18 October, was not sufficient to raise him from his unusually dark and hostile mood for long.[213]

Brown's camp insist that he was not on the verge of resigning,[214] but so low was he that the thought passed through his head. His conference speech had not set a bandwagon rolling, the moment of Blair's vulnerability had passed, and there seemed no immediate prospect of the party rising against him. He was running out of options, but so too was Blair, who had lost much of his fight, in part due to worries about his health. Prescott now intervened, making it clear that, whatever deficiencies there might be in a Blair premiership, he would not countenance any attempt to end it forcibly.[215] When the three met over dinner in Admiralty Arch on 6 November 2003, they talked over possible scenarios for the succession and Blair aired his thoughts on standing down the following autumn. Blair needed Brown's loyalty to advance his domestic agenda, while Brown realised that he needed Blair's support if he was to be elected his successor and avoid the risk of inheriting a divided party.[216] For a while it seemed a truce had been forged.

The succession of Michael Howard to the Tory leadership in November 2003 gave Blair and Brown a common sense of purpose. After Hague and Duncan Smith, the Tory party had a leader whom both men respected – and feared – for his potential to re-ignite the embers of his party. 'Blair is obsessed with Howard,' said one. 'He thinks he could win.'[217] Brown meanwhile was reported to be 'besotted' by his newly-born son, John: after being deprived of a family for so long, his associates discerned a new mellowness in the Iron Chancellor.[218] Friends asserted that Brown had always been a warm and sociable figure, but years of frustration had concealed it from the world at large.

Yet before long, relations again deteriorated over claims and counter-claims of the 2004 handover. Brown had left the dinner at Admiralty Arch with the firm belief that Blair had pledged to go in 2004, and that he would publically back him as his favoured successor. Not true, say the Blair camp, who claim it is nonsense to say that any firm date had been given.

The furthest Blair would have gone, they assert, was to talk in general terms about stepping down in 2004 as long as he felt content with his achievements and was confident that his successor, Brown, would build on them.

By mid-2004, after the June elections gave hope of a third land-slide, and after the continued turbulence in Iraq, Blair needed to justify why he now wanted to fight on until after the general election. He realised that Brown would never willingly support his agenda, and came to see him not as the perpetuator but as the potential underminder of his legacy.[219] Brown's 'disloyalty' thus became the reason for his '*volte face*': 'Brown hasn't delivered' became the mantra of the Blair camp. In September, he signalled his new resolve by bringing Brown's arch rival, Alan Milburn, back into the Cabinet to oversee preparations for the election. Blair's announcement that he would stay on as leader for the election and serve a full third term followed, taking Brown by surprise. In January 2005, Robert Peston's book may have offered little substantially new, but it provided further and very detailed evidence of the continuing cycle of hatred and suspicion that had begun in 1994 between the Blair and the Brown camps. Blair had been outwitted by Brown in not only his first but also his second term. Blair resolved that, if he were to see his legacy entrenched, he would have to deal once and for all with the 'Brown problem', which had dogged his entire premiership. Brown equally has resolved in private to deal with his 'Blair problem', but only after the election in 2005 has been safely won. 'Co-existence' in the future would no longer be tenable.

The Impact of Gordon Brown

Blair and Brown were a team whose qualities and skills were perfectly matched in terms of character, interests and beliefs, and who had every hope of creating the most enduring political marriage since Stanley Baldwin and Neville Chamberlain bestrode the Tory party in the inter-war years. Blair and Brown have been bound together for as many years as them, constituting the longest-serving senior political partnership in post-war British politics. But why did it not wholly fulfil its potential?

When the relationship was at its most harmonious, as during 1983–94, it achieved the most, i.e., planning the replacement of a moribund party with New Labour. Still potent during 1994–97, they masterminded the election victory, though differences prevented them, especially Blair, planning fully what they would achieve in government in the long term. Even when the relationship became difficult, during 1997–2001, they still agreed on broad swathes of policy and they achieved much together, concluding with the second election victory. Yet it is no coincidence that most of the government's achievements were down to their separate efforts, the Good Friday Agreement, Kosovo, and improvements to education for Blair; and the strong economy and welfare reform for Brown. In 2001–05, when their relationship was at its worst, the achievement overall was much less, with a government drawn in almost opposite directions by the two men, and pulled asunder as a result. Brown's achievements, above all economic growth and stability, suffered less from the disharmony in the second term than Blair's, who felt far more thwarted than he had before. Brown's reservations over Iraq went unheard by a Prime Minister who had learned to do without his old mentor's judgement. The creative tension of the early years had become destructive.

One can best understand their relationship by looking at the four factors which provide the analytical framework for this book: circumstances, individuals, ideas and interests. Circumstances were vital to understanding the ups and downs. It was Brown's enduring bad fortune that Smith died at the very moment when his own stock was at its lowest. This gave rise to the canon of faith among his supporters that he had been cheated of his inheritance, and to a belief about a precise date given for a handover. Brown's governing passion was his desire to become Prime Minister. Not a day of his life passed when he did not think of this ultimate prize. The belief that he had been initially robbed in 1994, and then repeatedly thwarted of his inheritance since, constantly tugged at and undermined the very fabric of his relationship with Blair.

With different character traits, Brown might have been able to live with the disappointment. While Blair was born with an easy-going personality, strong nerves and physique, capable of springing back from adversity, Brown's, although not without a warm and sociable side, was more given to brooding, introspection and suspicion. Brown's defenders say these traits stemmed from his anger at being denied his inheritance: Blairites were not so sure. For Brown, loyalty was central, and if he felt betrayed or let down, it could take years to rebuild trust. Both men changed inwardly after 1997. Both became more convinced of their own rightness, Blair above all in foreign affairs, Brown domestically. Constantly embittered by what he saw as the injustice meted out to him, Brown did not grow in the generosity and tolerance that might have been expected in a leader in waiting. 'If Gordon had treated Tony with more respect,' said one close associate of both men in April 2004, 'I think there's a strong likelihood he would be Prime Minister by now.'[220] But Blair was soon to decide to work actively to block Brown's most cherished of ambitions.

Differences in their ideas were important, if less so perhaps than other factors. Both men were wedded to New Labour, and in this sense, there was more that united them than divided them. Brown, however, was always more doctrinaire, committed to ameliorating inequality and to the traditional values of Labour. Although he believed in competition, flexible labour markets encouraging entrepreneurship and approved of much of the American capitalist model, Brown always put his 'poverty' agenda above Blair's 'choice' agenda. Blair, on domestic policy at least, was more flexible and pragmatic, was never much attached to the party, and was more willing to adopt fresh thinking in the light of new circumstances to maintain the party's broad appeal. While both were ardent Americanists and keen Europeans, Blair became more fixated on the Euro as the way forward for political reasons, while Brown drifted away from it for economic ones. The difference in their outlook was masked as long as they were united in a common target, defeating the Tories. Once in power, differences of emphasis began to emerge. Brown was willing to take tough decisions that provoked the left, as over the cutbacks in lone parents' benefits, but they were decisions to a greater end, building the long-term platform for the welfare government he wanted to run. Blair was instinctively in favour of tactical shifts that would be popular with the electorate: Brown had his sights set more firmly on the long-term strategy. But what, Blairites asked, *were* his long-term policies, on education, crime, transport, defence and foreign affairs? Was he a broad enough thinker for the top job? In the second term, policy differences were greatly exacerbated by Brown's frustration with Blair's failure to give him a date for when he would stand down. Most Prime Ministers have differences with their Chancellors. For much of the time, they were no worse between Blair and Brown than with many incumbents of these two top jobs; but between 2001 and 2003, they were far worse. In late 2004, relations broke down completely.

The interests behind Blair and Brown, finally, caused much more damage to their relationship. On Blair's side, chief *agent provocateur* was Mandelson, whom Brown, by his unrelenting hostility, made into the very enemy he initially thought him to be. The Brownites then latched on to Mandelson as the target for their ire: 'The canker at the heart of the Labour Party,' was how Ed Balls described him to a friend.[221] They found him divisive, a stirrer and utterly untrustworthy. In 1997, most of Blair's staff in Number 10, both official and political, were well disposed to Brown: within five years, many were hostile. On Brown's side, Balls constantly fanned the flames and remained suspicious and instinctively hostile towards much that Blair tried to do. It was telling that Brown's closest aide was Balls, a policy man, whilst Blair's was Campbell, a communications man. Whelan, while serving Brown, and after, also remained a controversial figure. 'Brown was very unlucky that his two closest aides were characters who amplified his paranoia,' said one close observer. 'If other Brown aides, such as Ed Miliband, Wilf Stevenson and Douglas Alexander, had enjoyed such influence on Brown, the story would have been substantially different.'[222] Neutral observers worried that Brown's unwillingness to rule through a more emollient and larger court augured badly for the future if he was to be in Number 10. The peacemakers, Anji Hunter, Sue Nye and David Miliband, fell steadily away, and until Prescott banged the table, there was no one of sufficient weight to intercede.

In a broader sense, both men finally were representative of their national interests: Brown remained a quintessential Scot, with a very different worldview and comprehension of the electorate to the Englishman Blair. Much of their difficulty in understanding each other stemmed from their different upbringings.

The achievement of New Labour before and after 1997 would not have been possible without Blair and Brown's unique relationship. Its achievements outweigh the negatives: indeed, to the world outside, unaware of the real work going on deep in the bowels of the government, the conflict between both gladiators was often all they saw, and hence the impression was given that the relationship was far more destructive before 2001 than it was. Yet one can only speculate how much more Blair would have accomplished since 1997 had not so much time, emotional energy and goodwill been consumed as their relationship deteriorated. Its poison seeped into almost every office and corridor in Whitehall and Westminster, and regularly blunted the progress made by the government. Attaching blame is pointless. Brown's character was what made him the economic and strategic genius that he is. When combined with his sense that he had been cheated and that for eleven years he had to play second fiddle to a lesser man, Blair found him almost impossible to manage. Brown's achievements were almost undimmed by the shadow the relationship cast, while Blair felt hemmed in and often unable to realise his ambitions. Brown felt himself to be the loser, but from 1997–2005 in terms of policy achievement, it was Blair who lost out far more.

Conclusion

Everything and nothing has happened in the nine months since the first edition of this biography was published in June 2004. New pronouncements, new scandals and muddles, and old faces returning have all been the major stories. Relations between Blair and Brown plumbed new depths; but we have had eight years of hearing that their relationship has been at an 'all time low'. This time round, Ed Balls and other Brown supporters have fed another book, by Robert Peston, which talks about further betrayals and Brown's increasingly distinctive agenda. The Blair camp's initial reaction was that Brown had damaged himself, but that having 'thrown his toys out of his pram', he would now stay onside at least until the General Election, if no longer. Some flirted with getting their own back via a friendly author (I was deemed too unsound) but they consoled themselves with the knowledge that Alastair Campbell's diaries, when published, would reveal facts about Brown that they believed would darken his name irrevocably.

The nine months since June 2004 have seen the resignation of another Blair confidant, David Blunkett, amid further questions about integrity and Blair's judgement. Meanwhile, Blair's personal agenda remains largely unfulfilled, with a final end to the Arab–Israeli conflict, alleviation of poverty in Africa, an improved relationship with the EU and enduring improvements in the public services remaining elusive. Above all the war in Iraq, so personally identified with Blair, remains the largest question mark over his premiership. It was his war, and it will be the principal yardstick on which he will be judged. So, many events have happened since the first edition, but all have followed a predictable pattern, and none were novel. Blair tells us repeatedly that, this time round, his third term really will be radical. When the first edition was published, he was at the lowest point in his standing. In the spring of 2005, he rides high. But none of this makes me want to alter one iota the conclusions I reached in the first edition.

Two groups objected to the first edition. Some Blair aides were annoyed that Blair did not emerge as they would have liked, and felt that the help they gave me should have resulted in more favourable copy. I think they chunter too much. In the book, I played straight with my sources, avoided salacious details and steered away from eye-catching headlines. I wanted it to be a serious book, not one that would play any part in the 'book war', which has raged for over eight years among New Labour's highest echelons. Some aides also disliked the tone of the book, which implied that Blair's premiership was effectively over. Yet it remains to be seen whether Blair will be able to entrench the agenda he has at last defined, or whether he would have been better off to have left of his own volition in 2004. Finally we know what Blairism is, but how far he will be able to achieve it remains to be seen.

The second group who viewed the first edition unfavourably were reviewers in the press. Some on the left, puzzlingly, saw the book as a Blair apologia, while some others in the right wing press found it difficult to understand the structure of the book, which they considered 'gimmicky', and either did not comprehend, or like, the conclusions I reached. A reviewer in *The Times* wrote that 'all we hear in Seldon's vast researches and thin conclusions is a puzzled scratching of the head.'

At the risk of further upsetting Blair's aides, and possibly the *Times* reviewer, my rewritten conclusion to this edition draws together even more emphatically what we have learnt during the preceding 700 pages, through considering both Blair's defining character traits and his likely place in history. My conclusions on Blair were all implicit (and often explicit) in the first edition. Readers may not agree with the verdicts, but none can now say they don't know where I stand. More than anything, Blair's premiership to date emerges from the book as a tale of vast un-fulfilled potential. Despite promises of radical reform, Blair squandered numerous opportunities during his first term through excessive caution and the failure to articulate a distinctive agenda; only well into his second did he finally work out what he wanted to accomplish at home, while abroad his idealism bordered on hubris. With the size of his parliamentary majorities, the strong economy, a subdued Labour movement and his undoubted political skills, he could have achieved so much more. The way Blair chose to conduct policy during the Iraq war has left a deep mark on his premiership, and it delayed still further the fulfilment of his personal agenda. Eight years after entering Downing Street, Blair is not without his achievements, yet Blairism, which should by now amount to a substantial and coherent body of policy, is still largely rhetoric and good intentions.

Ten defining traits

• *Influence of key individuals*

Tony Blair has been influenced to an exceptional degree by the ideas, encouragement and stimulus he has drawn from important individuals throughout his life. This distinctive facet of Blair's character gave rise to the unconventional design for this book, with even-numbered chapters devoted to twenty of these crucial individuals.

Unlike Clement Attlee or Margaret Thatcher, Blair was not a Prime Minister moved by ideology. On the contrary, he is the supreme pragmatist. Neither, like David Lloyd George or John Major, were Blair's politics forged through life experience. Blair's decision to enter politics and join the Labour Party owes almost everything to the influence of his closest friends and associates.

Surprisingly, Blair had no significant mentors among the teaching staff at either school or university. His mother gave him his enduring self-belief and confidence, but she died when he was just twenty-two. The figure who opened his mind to the world of politics was the Australian student-cum-priest Peter Thomson. Cherie Booth channelled his energies and his ambition to become a Labour politician, Derry Irvine schooled his intellect, transformed him from a middling to an accomplished barrister and gave him connections across the Labour Party, but it was Gordon Brown who groomed the naïve young MP and hardened him into a capable and ambitious leader.

At critical moments in his life, Blair was fortunate enough to come across individuals who, whatever their personality flaws, were masters in their field, such as Peter Mandelson and Alastair Campbell. Without their contributions, he would never have become the figure he did. Blair became adept at drawing on individuals for as long as they were useful to him, and then parting with them in often difficult circumstances.

Women have been central figures in Blair's life. His mother, more than anyone, formed his character. The two longest enduring relationships in his life have been with Cherie, who has steadied him and remained single-mindedly ambitious for him throughout, and Anji Hunter. No friend of Cherie, Hunter was described by one Number 10 insider as 'the person who understands Tony better than anyone. No one reads him so well: he never makes an important move without consulting her.' The greatest influence on the content and style of his premiership, however, was yet another woman, Margaret Thatcher, whose importance has been little acknowledged. Without understanding Blair's key relationships, his personality is incomprehensible. He is, in significant part, the sum of these relationships.

• *Cumulative influence of major events*

He is also the sum of certain key events in his life. The second organising theme of the book encompasses these major turning points, which again number twenty. Blair did not have the bold, life-changing experiences early in his life that forged many political leaders. Instead, he has been like a cautious rock climber, testing each foothold and ensuring he felt secure before pressing on upwards. His life has thus been punctuated by key 'staging posts'. For all his outward displays of confidence, on the inside Blair has been racked by self-doubt. Not until 2003–4 did he gain full confidence in his own powers. Before then he was haunted by the prospect of failure and often full of doubt about his own credentials as a leader and his ability to achieve enduring change.

The most remarkable fact about Tony Blair's days at school and university was his fecklessness and his relative lack of achievement. The death of his mother in June 1975 was the first serious crisis he faced. It sobered him and gave him a gravity that he had hitherto lacked, as well as shaking his assumption that his life would work out for the best, with little or no effort on his part. But his subsequent progress in law and politics was modest. It was his chance acquisition of the Labour nomination in the high profile by-election at Beaconsfield in 1982 that embedded his taste for politics, and led him to realise that he could be a figure of substance within the Labour party.

After the inevitable defeat at Beaconsfield, Blair was well placed when Sedgefield, a safe Labour seat, became available just in time to contest the 1983 election. Once in the Commons, he recognised that he was inexperienced and ill prepared for parliamentary life, but built his confidence and his reputation deftly step by step, such as through the closed-shop episode in December 1989.

By 1992 at the latest, Blair began to see himself as a future leader of the party, while his experience as shadow Home Secretary (1992–1994), with his tough stance on crime, proved that he was capable of striking a chord with the nation at large. After he became leader in 1994, the debate over Clause IV established his dominance over the Labour Party, but the internal battles and the close final vote inclined him to caution. Moreover, he doubted his ability to be Prime Minister.

With the scale of his victory in May 1997, which stunned him, and his handling of events in the week following the death of Princess Diana in August, his doubts about himself began to fade. His apprehension over the conduct of foreign policy, about which he knew little, began to diminish after his success in forging the Good Friday Agreement in April 1998, over which he dealt at length with the Irish Taoiseach and the American President. His grit and determination during the Kosovo conflict in 1999, during which he contemplated resignation, gave rise to his belief that he could operate at the highest international level, even in the face of widespread scepticism.

Taking control of events at home, such as during the fuel crisis in 2000 and the foot and mouth crisis in 2001, confirmed Blair's belief that he alone, assisted by his close team in Number 10, could solve any problem. His self-belief, which became increasingly hubristic, could be seen in his attempt to command the world stage after 9/11 and in his grandiloquent pronouncements, notably in his highly charged speech to the 2001 Labour Party Conference. This confidence in his own judgement and that of his team led directly to his decisions to follow American policy over Iraq after 2002. But when Iraq failed to unfold as hoped, and domestic problems threatened his tenure as Prime Minister, his self-confidence again deserted him. In late 2003 and early 2004, he seriously contemplated resigning within the following few months. The final 'turning point' I identify in this book is his decision to remain as Prime Minister, above all because he was determined to see his policies come to fruition at home and abroad. But why in early 2005, after eight years, was his personal agenda so largely unfulfilled?

• *No clear idea of what he wanted to do with power*

The principal answer to why Blair's personal achievements appear so hollow is that he was so tardy in deciding what he wanted to do with power. When elected Labour party leader in 1994, he had accumulated a random series of ideas and thoughts on policy. These included a commitment to the idea of 'community', a belief that individuals should have responsibilities as well as rights, and a belief that democracy, if it was to operate properly, required individuals to have a direct say, whether over trade union policy or decisions within the Labour Party. But none of this amounted to anything like a coherent policy platform.

During the leadership election in 1994, it therefore suited Blair to say that he would reserve his policy positions until after the contest. Yet even after his clear-cut victory, the development of a policy platform before 1997 fell victim to the need to avoid any commitment that might prove vulnerable to attack by the Conservatives or alienate the right wing press and other vested interests. Election victory was all that mattered: the radicalism, he promised, would come later. But once in Number 10, he again worked hard to avoid controversial policies to ensure that business, the media and other powerful interests were all kept on side. So he shunned radical decisions that he could have forced through early on while his political capital was still at its height, most obviously electoral reform or entry to the single currency. Brown was not in favour of the latter, nor was much of business, and the logic of the economics counted against it. Blair pulled back: nothing would be allowed to prejudice an historic second victory.

So he reconciled himself to delaying the fulfilment of his still inchoate personal agenda until after the 2001 election. But his plans to think deeply about policy for a second term were sidetracked even before the election by the foot and mouth crisis, while soon after the election came 9/11 and the distractions of international diplomacy. Only in 2002 did his views on the public services begin to crystallise around the ideas of diversity and choice, and incentives in place of uniform provision. His openness to new and controversial ideas (for the Labour party) was a strength, yet many of his ideas were inherited from Thatcher and Major, and he had arguably waited far too long before developing them. Late too was his zeal for progress in Africa, the Middle East peace process and the environment (principally climate change). Like most Prime Ministers, including Harold Macmillan, Harold Wilson and John Major, he found it impossible to 'control' events, and very hard once in power to devise and implement successful policies.

Blair's lack of considered policy-making extends to foreign policy. The 'doctrine of the international community' (which advocated intervention in sovereign states on humanitarian grounds), was devised by Blair and his inner circle on the wing; almost literally, on a flight to the US in April 1999. The entire conduct of the war in Iraq and its aftermath was similarly based upon faulty and rushed decision-making amongst a tired and too narrow inner circle. The damage done by his preferred style of leadership is the next trait to be discussed.

• *Decision-making among a tight-knit, informal group*

Tony Blair has never been a man who has liked or felt the need to consult widely. From his days gathering in huddles in the boys' studies at Fettes, and the gang that assembled around Peter Thomson in Oxford, to the tight-knit group of barristers in Derry Irvine's chamber, he prefers to relate to small, defined groups. As an MP and shadow minister, Blair's core base was not his fellow MPs elected in 1983, but his office and the group that he gathered around him, with Gordon Brown and then Anji Hunter at its heart. Blair had little time or respect for the shadow cabinet, the NEC or indeed the Parliamentary Labour Party. Once he became leader in 1994, power again swirled around the leader's office: each major decision was taken by Blair's inner circle, which included the increasingly restless Brown, as well as Mandelson, Campbell and Hunter.

Once in Number 10, the tight command structure of the opposition leader's office was simply transferred into government, and centred on the 'den', Blair's small office in Number 10. Some officials were accepted into the bosom of the den, including John Holmes, David Manning and Jeremy Heywood. But many top officials, including Cabinet Secretaries Robin Butler and Richard Wilson, were held at bay. Some Prime Ministers have been able to operate effectively in a crisis with a very small team, such as Winston Churchill during the Second World War. But those around Churchill, notably Alan Brooke, Edward Bridges, Norman Brook, Lord Cherwell and Max Beaverbrook, were of a far higher calibre than those who crouched around Blair's sofa. Blair was not comfortable in the company of most intellectuals, while others in his team like Campbell were contemptuous of them. Instead, the dominant culture in the 'denocracy' was to agree with the conventional Blairite wisdom: counter-vailing viewpoints were not welcomed.

Blair's aides would openly boast that they believed the catchphrase 'results, not procedures' to be the defining characteristic of New Labour's style of government. Indeed it was. Contempt for old Labour, for the civil service, for John Major's government, or for any inherited wisdom or indeed anything historic, was the dominant presumption in Blair's inner circle. Even world opinion could be cast aside over Iraq. They did things in their own way. And for a while, the formula appeared to work.

Neither Blair, however, who came to the premiership historically young and inexperienced, nor any of his intimates, had any practice in managing large organisations. It was only late in the first term that Blair began to realise that achieving the right structures and management presented the keys to improving public services. Much of the second term was spent putting new structures in place, as well as in resurrecting some of the apparatus that he had himself disbanded after 1997.

Blair's style of governing, which I term the 'denocracy' in this book (after his Downing Street 'den'), was increasingly criticised during his premiership, notably by Robin Butler himself: 'there is too much central control,' Butler declared in late 2004, 'and there is too little of what I would describe as reasoned deliberation which brings in all the arguments.' Fellow Cabinet Secretaries Robert Armstrong and Richard Wilson also expressed concern at the decline in cabinet government and the formal procedures for conducting business that they had known all their working lives. They believe that a series of shambolic decisions, notably over Iraq, underlines the danger in abandoning convention.

Although Blair, by 2005, has undoubtedly learnt much about managing bureaucracies, he has shown little sign, despite frequent promises, of a move towards a more consultative style of leadership. Blair believes that progress in his second term was hampered because ministers were ineffective and failed to champion his emerging radical agenda. But Blair himself must shoulder much of the blame. He monitored ministers remorselessly, so if their policies were unsuccessful, he was in part responsible. He did not always pick wisely, lauding Estelle Morris as Education Secretary, who was clearly overawed by her task. Stephen Byers was perhaps the most conspicuously unsatisfactory of all his favoured ministers: his antipathy to his civil servants and his obsession with style over substance epitomised New Labour at its worst.

• *Blair the historian*

Blair was thus contemptuous of many of the traditions and conventions that had underpinned Britain for many years. Blair, as Roy Jenkins reluctantly had to admit, knew very little history, so he set about trying to teach him. The history Blair absorbed may have lacked subtlety, but it had immense potency over his thinking. Blair sees Britain as a conservative-leaning country that will periodically tolerate progressive centre-left governments. Like Philip Gould, he had been struck by the idea that the twentieth century had been the 'Conservative century'. Tory governments, he reasoned, could rule from the right and be re-elected: but Labour governments could never rule from the left and secure re-election. He thus believed, in his own words, that his supreme role was 'to hug the centre ground'. If he let taxes and spending rise more than the public would stand, if he pushed the European agenda too far, paid too much attention to alleviating poverty or helping minorities, or tinkered with the constitution more than was deemed necessary, then the party would suffer at the polls. From this perspective, as Steve Richards has argued, his position on Iraq becomes much clearer. He thought it would be far more dangerous not to support Bush, and alienate not just the

Administration but the right wing press in Britain, and be outflanked by the Tories, than to opt for the stance he did. If Blair's understanding of history illuminates one facet of his character, another is revealed in his role as barrister-actor.

● *Blair the barrister-actor*

Tony Blair's training at university and in the first eight years of his working life was in the law. Much of the barrister has remained with him ever since. He has an extraordinary ability to focus on one subject and to test it to breaking point, while his remarkable skill in presenting his case often wins converts to his argument. He can talk his way out of almost any position, however unfavourable. These are all valuable assets for any Prime Minister, but they are not sufficient to be a good Prime Minister.

The problem is that he has often been too successful in convincing others, as well as himself of a particular course of action, without stepping back and seriously considering the alternatives. Winning the argument has often been more important to him than the truth or otherwise of what is at stake. His struggle to convince the public of the validity of taking action against Saddam Hussein on the basis of his WMD capacity sees this trait at its most single-minded. This quality makes Blair a brilliant debater, but it often poses questions about his underlying principles.

Despite a limited acting career at school and university, Blair developed into an actor of exceptional subtlety and impact. Friends early on in his life noted that he was always much more comfortable delivering his own words on stage than reciting those of a playwright. And so it has remained throughout his life. He has been at his most powerful when making impromptu speeches, as in Scotland during the Clause IV debate when his teleprompter failed, responding in the Trimdon churchyard to Diana's death (a more moving performance than his strained recitation from Corinthians during the funeral) or when delivering his most powerful conference speeches, as in 1995 or 2001, when he felt entirely comfortable with his text.

His skill as an actor is in greatest play when taking questions before an audience, when he displays his almost limitless belief in his ability to persuade. His charm with people of all ages has been used to great effect in winning converts, amongst whom number national leaders, to his cause. The downside of this skill is that substance can lose out to style. The steady and highly damaging erosion of public trust over the course of his premiership owed much to his projection of an image of goodness and plausibility. When it was seen that he had feet of clay, disillusion and cynicism set in. He hates being disliked, especially on moral grounds. Aside from the old left, he was not comfortable making enemies until deep into his second term: primarily, he has wanted to conciliate.

● *Blair as conciliator*

Tony Blair baulks at personal confrontation and has gone a long way to avoid it. He is most comfortable when he feels on the same wavelength as his interlocutors. He dislikes sacking or disappointing people and has used different associates, sometimes Anji Hunter, at other times officials like Richard Wilson, to do the deed. He displayed visible discomfort when challenged by Ken Follett about why Blair had briefed against him in 1995, or by Sharon Storer over the state of the NHS during the 2001 election campaign.

He has found it particularly hard to stand up to powerful figures, whether Rupert Murdoch or Margaret Thatcher (both of whom he was anxious not to offend), or Presidents Bill Clinton and George W. Bush, and, as a result, he failed to achieve as much as he could out of these relationships. Indeed, for all his claims to the contrary, it is hard to see that he had much effect at all in changing the thinking of Clinton or Bush, yet he (and some of his aides) were too caught up in the intoxication of the relationships to see the truth. Nowhere, however, was his dislike of conflict more clearly seen than in his relationship with Gordon Brown. Blair managed to face up to some of Brown's most loyal supporters, like Charlie Whelan, and sacked or failed to promote others to his government. But he failed utterly to stop the steady seepage of bile and contempt from the Brown camp that began as early as 1994. He may well consider his pulling back from moving Brown out of the Treasury in 2001, or demoting him thereafter, to be the biggest missed opportunity of his premiership. Only in 2004 did he take Brown head on, by refusing to stand down that autumn. The consequences of that decision have yet to be seen.

Blair's great strength as a conciliator has been in bringing together people of diverse outlooks, whether Protestants and Republicans in Northern Ireland, or former Conservative voters into Labour's big tent. He does not harbour grudges, so could readily welcome Ken Livingstone back into the Labour fold in early 2004, despite having demonised him for years before. But he also exaggerates greatly his powers of conciliation, believing he could reconcile the EU to Bush's Iraq policy in 2003, or broker peace himself between Israelis and Palestinians. His courage and absence of physical fear help explain his willingness to take such risks.

• Courage and physical stamina

All Prime Ministers have to be tough, but Tony Blair has an exceptional constitution. Although his mother died at the age of fifty-two and his father had a stroke aged forty, he himself has enjoyed mostly good health. His main concern has been his heart, which has resulted in two significant hospital visits in October 2003 and October 2004, and which was a principal factor behind his thinking about standing down in 2004. He has often looked tired, but in early 2005 showed little outward sign of the permanent fatigue that afflicted other long serving Prime Ministers such as Harold Macmillan and Margaret Thatcher.

He paces himself carefully, always trying to be asleep before midnight, takes regular holidays and tires, and bores, easily. However, he is capable of sustained energy when the moment demands it. Never were his stamina and determination more seen than in the final negotiations for the Good Friday Agreement, or in his punishing travel schedule after 9/11, or during the run up to the Iraq war, when he knew he was taking enormous risks, not only in Iraq, but also with the chance of retaliation against British civilian targets. His ability to bounce back from setbacks, such as the row over his children's schooling, the Ecclestone affair, the Mandelson resignations, or his low point in early 2004 is remarkable. Having to adjust from being such a widely admired figure early in his first term to being such an unpopular one by the end of his second term has been exceedingly painful, but he has accommodated himself to it. One aide considers him to possess a 'Zen' personality, almost preternaturally calm. Very little gets to him, attacks on his family and his personal integrity being the two main exceptions. His religious faith is one explanation of this gift.

• Religious and moral convictions

Underpinning Blair's life is his moral and religious belief. He conceptualises the world as a struggle between good and evil in which his particular vocation is to advance the former. Many of the causes he has espoused, whether tackling poverty or AIDS in Africa, or spreading lasting peace in Northern Ireland or in the Middle East, stem from his desire to make the world a better place. His religious and moral conviction lay behind his thinking on Kosovo and Iraq and helps explain why he has been far more decisive and radical on the international stage than in domestic policy. In his eyes, the choice between good and evil is often much clearer abroad than in his struggles at home.

His is not an exclusively Christian theology. He sees the opportunity of being godly and good as available to all humans and considers his own role as the promoter of good on earth as uniquely important. To overlook the importance of religion in Blair's life is to misunderstand him completely. Equally, his very strong moral world view has made it difficult for him to listen to others who have contrasting points of view where they cut across his own sense of rectitude. This has often made him intransigent and unwilling to embrace heterodox viewpoints. Perhaps surprisingly, he has often listened closely to those of no obvious religious belief, such as Campbell, Gould, Hunter and Mandelson. His is a very personal theology, allowing him to discount the view of the most senior religious authorities on earth, including the Pope and the Archbishop of Canterbury, when their own judgements contradict his own. When his religious or moral principles come into play, he has a will of steel.

• *Luck*

All successful leaders need their measure of luck; Tony Blair, however, has been a far luckier premier than most. His string of good fortune began at the outset of his political career. He found a safe seat in 1983, which made possible his meteoric rise through the Labour party. Had the death of John Smith come earlier, or perhaps later, Gordon Brown would have been the clear favourite to succeed Smith. He came to power when disenchantment with the Conservatives had set in, most particularly after Black Wednesday in September 1992. The country and the media were disillusioned with the Conservatives and eager for a fresh face offering new ideas. Like Mrs Thatcher, he did not face powerful opposition leaders: William Hague, Iain Duncan Smith and, more surprisingly, Michael Howard, offering him little challenge. The economy was strong throughout his first and second term. Luck has been a leitmotif of Tony Blair's premiership and it has been his skill to exploit it to the full.

Blair's place in history

Assessing Blair's place in history is difficult in part because he never laid out a clear set of objectives by which he could be judged. Nor has sufficient time elapsed to allow us to view Blair's time in office with perspective. Indeed, at the time of writing, he remains in Number 10. As has been shown throughout the book, Blair has travelled 'agenda-lite': he only began to formulate his platform on foreign policy in 1999 and on domestic policy in 2002–03. Before, in place of a personal manifesto, he offered sweeping statements, such as his claim in 1997 that he would lead 'one of the great, radical, reforming governments of our history'. He was not speaking idly: he believed he could remodel Britain as he had remodelled the Labour party. But the country proved more resistant to his overtures. By late 2000, he was thus protesting that the aim of his first term had been merely to prove that Labour could manage the country and economy responsibly, thereby 'laying the foundations' (a key phrase) for future reform. He would not squander this second term as he had the first. But he was again to be thrown off course. The rhetoric, however, did not soften. By 2003 he was promising to 'remould' the post-1945 Attleean consensus, which had been based on an all-knowing state and a passive citizen, into a new Blairite settlement, rooted in economic prosperity and reformed public services offering choice to active consumers. At last, in 2004–05, as the sun was beginning to set on his premiership, he had found the agenda that had eluded him for so long.

Lack of perspective is a serious factor when assessing Blair's overall impact. Yet the thrust of his policy at home and abroad for the remainder of his premiership, bar unforeseen events, is now clearly established. The difficulty comes in evaluating the impact of his policies. In education, health and the alleviation of poverty, it will take some years before one can assess how enduring and effective the changes have been. Even then, we will never know for certain how far government policy, or other factors, was responsible for any improvements. One historian, Martin Gilbert, has suggested that when the official government documents are released, Blair and Bush's relationship may emerge as of similar significance to the partnership between Churchill and Roosevelt during the Second World War. While it is true that it will be many years before historians will be able draw definitive conclusions on the wisdom of Blair's policy on Iraq, it is false to assert that the release of new documents will result in startlingly new appraisals. We already know, principally from interview evidence, much of the history of the Blair government. One would be wrong to think that the documents (which are far from infallible themselves), for all the fanfare that will greet them, will substantially revise the established picture of the Blair premiership.

So while contemporary biography, as with all contemporary history, is bound to be imperfect, it is still of value. It is also arguably more important to have a fair-minded assessment of Blair now, while he is still Prime

Minister, than after he has been retired for several years, when any assessment will be academic. And, in another sense, all history is contemporary history. Biographies and other historical accounts will always reflect the predominant concerns of the age in which they are written. So I do not think one should worry unduly about the status of contemporary biography, so long as it is rooted in the facts and aims to be balanced.

Even if Blair manages to stay in office, as he hopes, until 2008, the key question about his premiership will be, his election victories notwithstanding, why did he not achieve more? The spotlight will fall in particular on the second term; the first term and the three years that preceded it provide important clues. The combination of Blair's failure to formulate a clear policy platform, his limited understanding of how Whitehall worked and his impatience with managing change proved major handicaps. His obsessive fear of a Tory revival or an implosion of New Labour dictated excessive caution. Even at the end of his first term, Blair had little idea about what he would do in the second, beyond improving public services and securing a new place for Britain in the European Union, as well as showing that a Labour government could work with a Republican administration. One Number 10 aide admitted in early 2005, 'soon after the 2001 General Election, Tony Blair realised he had made a mistake in not formulating a proper strategy for the second term to put into the manifesto.' The second term was not without its achievements, above all in laying down structures in health, welfare, education and crime prevention, on which Blair hopes to build in the third term. But overall, progress has been, at best, modest.

Blair has himself reflected on the reasons why he has not achieved more so far. A first line of defence is to blame Cabinet ministers. Blair's impatience with them can be seen echoed by David Blunkett, when he told his biographer Stephen Pollard that Patricia Hewitt 'cannot think strategically', and that education policy under Charles Clarke had 'gone soft'. One aide told Pollard that when Blunkett's team arrived at the Home Office, it was 'worse than any of us had imagined possible. God alone knows what Jack [Straw] did for four years.' In the first term Blair asserts that he had to restrain ministers, many of whom wanted to spend more than he and Brown felt prudent; in the second term he became frustrated that his ministers were not sufficiently zealous. He determined after the 2001 election that he would keep the ministers in charge of the four key departments (Health, Transport, Home Office and Education) in place throughout the second term. But all four (Milburn, Byers, Blunkett and Morris) were to resign after personal difficulties. In private, Blair would criticise even this handpicked vanguard. In Number

10, Blair could rely on his Principal Private Secretary, Jeremy Heywood, and Blairite thinkers such as Andrew Adonis and Simon Stevens in the Policy Directorate. In Cabinet, however, he lacked a broad support base. He now contrasts his lot unfavourably with Thatcher who, for all her initial battles with the 'wets', was able in her second term to lead a cabinet of true believers. Blair by 2005 came to regret 'rowing back' too far from the policies pursued by the Tories in his first term, even though there was considerable continuity in policy between Thatcher's then Major's government and his own. Blair was perhaps late to accept that another major factor holding back his achievements was Gordon Brown, who he found increasingly obstructive.

Blair's analysis has some validity, but he was at least in part to blame if his ministers, including Brown, did not do what he wanted. His mishandling of Brown has been one of his principal flaws. Life was bound to be difficult when Brown and his aides believed Blair had become leader illegitimately in 1994, that he had promised him that he would retire before the end of the second term, and when, quite early on, they became contemptuous of him as a leader. Policy differences came to the fore in the second term when Blair fell upon his own market-based agenda and Brown realised that he was at last up against a man who possessed some domestic policies of his own, and policies moreover that differed markedly from his.

Some in Blair's camp blame the relative lack of achievement on the time he spent on international diplomacy, particularly Iraq. Blair's intense commitment to foreign affairs in the second term did not, however, distract him significantly from his priority domestic areas of health, education and law and order. He continued with his regular 'stock takes' with these ministers throughout moments of even the highest tension. What did give were the subordinate areas of concern: the European Union, the environment, local government, House of Lords reform, pensions and regional policy. Blair's preoccupation with foreign policy and his fatigue also help explain a series of gaffes and reversals, such as the muddle over the abolition of the Lord Chancellor's office in June 2003.

So what has Blair himself achieved since he became leader of the Labour Party in 1994? Education is the domestic area in which his personal impact has been felt most profoundly, though indicatively his policies have owed much more to Tory precedent than to past Labour thinking or practice. In his first term great attention was given to primary education, above all through the development of a literacy strategy (foreshadowed by initiatives put in place by the Tories), complemented by a new numeracy strategy. In secondary education, Blair's two principal initiatives were specialist schools, which developed rapidly in the second term, and academies, which he hoped to expand significantly in the third term. The origin of both specialist schools and academies lies in the City Technology College (CTC) initiative introduced by the last Conservative government, which funded comprehensives to become language, sport, or technology based colleges. Blair's personal imprimatur can be seen elsewhere in education, such as in the retention of 164 grammar schools, league tables and school inspections, all of which had been championed by the Tories. In higher education, Blair's input can be seen in the eye-catching announcement that 50 per cent of school leavers would attend higher education and in his hope that 'top-up fees' (again originally a Conservative proposal) would bring new revenues to the cash-starved university sector.

Blair's priority on education delivered some positive results. The primary sector improved, particularly in the first term, while specialist schools appeared to out-perform non-specialist schools in GCSE passes and other benchmarks. The extra funds for secondary schools in the second term improved their fabric substantially and meant that by 2005, some state schools were ahead of independents in key areas such as Information and Communications Technology (ICT). But the state sector lagged behind in most other respects, while Labour's hope that the independent sector would wither away, because parents would switch to the state sector, came to nothing as numbers opting for independent schools steadily rose. Top-up fees meanwhile look unlikely to make more than a marginal impact on Britain's under-funded universities, though it will be some years before the effects feed through and can be fully assessed.

In health, progress was slight in the first term and too much weight was given to announcements about increased funding, which often failed to stand up to scrutiny. However, to the consternation of the Treasury, Blair finally resolved that NHS spending should match the EU average, a significant break with the traditional Labour thinking which was to run a lean health service. Orthodox Labour thinking again held that public sector employees should be paid the same regardless of performance. Well into the second term, as his 'choice and diversity' agenda came into effect, Blair defied the traditionalists by introducing pay incentives and rewards. A third change has been a renewed focus on public health and the targeting and measuring of outcomes. Underlying these reforms has been a determination to devolve power from government to service providers and consumers. Again, it was only in the second term that Blair began to focus on reforming the structures of the NHS, as seen in his foundation hospitals initiative. Modest improvements began to be seen by 2005. Blair now believes he has got the mechanics right, and expects to see very significant change in the third term. As with top-up fees, Blair again outflanked the Tories: by moving into their territory, he made it difficult for them to mount a principled attack.

In contrast to signs of improvement in health and education, transport has been an embarrassing failure. As with health, Labour faced an under-funded and demoralised public service. But this time solutions proved elusive. It is telling that the most radical departure in transport policy came from Blair's one-time nemesis Ken Livingstone, who, as the first elected Mayor of London, introduced congestion charging. In his third term, Blair plans that reform will be far more market driven, although whether these ideas will overcome opposition from within his own party remains to be seen. Again, the promise is of 'jam tomorrow'.

Before he became leader, Blair's boldest re-education of Labour occurred during his time as shadow Home Secretary with a shift towards thinking about the victims of crime, rather than its socially deprived perpetrators. Philip Gould's focus group reports repeatedly stressed the electorate's concern with crime and their disappointment at the govern-ment's perceived inaction. Yet in the first term, anxious not to upset traditional Labour voters, the judiciary and liberals by introducing overly authoritarian measures, he left policy largely to the Home Secretary, Jack Straw. Only in the second term, with David Blunkett in Straw's post from 2001 to 2004, did Blair move the agenda decisively in an authoritarian direction though a series of criminal justice, penal reform and asylum measures. Announcements have included the establishment of a national DNA database, devolution of power to police command units, the concentration of resources on the worst 10 per cent of offenders and the establishment of an FBI-style police organisation, the Serious Organised Crime Agency (SOCA). There was disappointment in Number 10 that these changes were not greeted with more acclaim. But they went too far for liberals while still falling short of what the right wing press wanted to see. Yet by acting decisively in an area of traditional Tory strength, in a manner unparalleled by any previous Labour government (with the possible exception of Callaghan's policies as Home Secretary from 1967–70), Blair wrong-footed the Conservatives once again. While overall reported crime has been falling under Labour, violent crime, firearms offences and anti-social behaviour have been on the increase. So again the verdict is mixed, with the improvements insufficient to satisfy the government-raised expectations of greater security at home.

Progress in the Northern Ireland peace process, by contrast, may well be seen as one of Blair's unequivocal achievements as Prime Minister, albeit one where he built again significantly on the record of John Major. Lengthy negotiations saw his personal qualities – of charm, persistence and flexibility as well as his moral outlook on the world – deployed to best effect. He sensed very early on in his premiership that this was an area where he could make a real difference. And his perseverance and stamina were rewarded with the Good Friday Agreement of 1998. He then devoted exceptional time to acting as midwife to the process for the rest of his first term and indeed during his second. Despite ongoing difficulties, Blair's achievement rests with the Good Friday Agreement breakthrough and his patience in keeping the peace process edging forward over the following seven years. Although Northern Ireland is not entirely at peace, the level of violence has decreased dramatically. In 2004, only four people died as a result of the troubles – the lowest annual figure since the 1960s. Here then is a real area of Blairite success.

All previous Labour governments have been hit by an economic crisis in their second or third year of office (such as in 1931, 1947, 1967 and 1976). Blair's government has broken the mould: the stewardship of the economy from 1997 to 2005 ranks as one of the most effective periods of economic management by a government in British history. Labour was, of course, most fortunate to inherit a strong economy, yet eight years on, New Labour has entrenched a reputation as being more trustworthy on the economy than the Tories. Ultimately, credit for New Labour's economic achievement is due to Gordon Brown, but some is due to Tony Blair, not the least for appointing and retaining Brown, and giving him backing (albeit often under duress) for his policies.

Blair's governments devoted considerable effort to welfare reform and tackling inequality. In the first term came Sure Start, welfare to work and a tranche of new tax credits aiming at making work pay. In the second term the effort, with which Blair was closely connected personally, was more technocratic and centred around the creation of the Department of Work and Pensions (DWP). Blair finally recognised, as he did in Health, that the correct structures had to be put in place before enduring reform could occur. Whereas in the first term Brown drove much of the welfare agenda, in the third term Blair has decreed it will be more market based and driven by him. A report in early 2005 showed that, whereas the real income of the poorest 20 per cent did not increase from 1977 to 1996, it has grown by a quarter since. One million children and 600,000 pensioners have been removed from poverty. This improvement is partly due to factors independent of government action, but is also the fruit of deliberate policy. The gap between rich and poor has therefore stopped widening since Labour came to power, although improvements have been concentrated amongst children and the elderly, the two groups targeted by the government. The overall achievement falls a long way short of the early rhetoric: Britain has not become a more equal society under New Labour, but it has at least stopped becoming more unequal in certain areas.

Blair came to power with the broad hope that he would modernise the constitution and enhance the quality of democratic life in Britain. The first term saw some significant change, largely driven by Derry Irvine. Reforms included devolution for Scotland and Wales, limited reforms to the House of Lords and the incorporation of the European convention on human rights into UK law. Nevertheless, Blair's long flirtation with electoral reform came to nothing after the proposals of the Jenkins commission were shelved in 1998. Contrary to expectations, Blair took little personal interest in the constitutional reform agenda, which owed far more to the legacy of his predecessor as leader, John Smith.

If the constitutional reforms of the first term lacked overall coherence, this was still truer of the second term, where change was often piecemeal and poorly executed. In 2005, the long awaited Freedom of Information Act was finally implemented, but many of its original provisions had been watered down. To the disappointment of many, attempts at a comprehensive settlement for the House of Lords stalled, while Blair increasingly gave the impression that he hoped the whole issue would go away. The proposals for reform of the Lord Chancellor's department and the creation of the Department for Constitutional Affairs aroused a considerable storm in parliament and amongst the judiciary, giving the impression of ineptitude and incoherence. The three planned regional assemblies have been abandoned: the first was rejected in a referendum, which led to plans for the other two being dropped. Yet these were John Prescott's initiatives and Blair was not unduly perturbed when they came to nothing.

Throughout the second term, a debate took place in Number 10 about how much Blair should be advocating further constitutional change. The Conservatives won the argument and Blair was dissuaded from making even a single speech on constitutional reform. As the 2005 election beckoned, Blair began to think increasingly about conceiving of constitutional reform from the local government level up, which would include devolving more power to local bodies and pushing forward with elected mayors, rather than top down. Overall, however, the dominant impression is of a lack of strategic and intellectual grip on constitutional reform in the second term, which offered Brown the opportunity to declare that he had a major constitutional reform agenda of his own, with significant measures designed for 'democratic renewal', and to rebuild trust with the electorate – an implicit criticism of Blair. Unsurprisingly, Blair responded by saying that reform would be a key theme of his third term.

Blair's vulnerability on governance extends beyond institutional reform. Early on Blair pledged to lead a government that was 'whiter than white', based on principle and integrity, utterly unlike anything offered, he said, by the sleaze-ridden Tories. Thus Blair aroused expectations of a moral quality in government, which many hoped would lead to enhanced levels of participation. However, the excitement of 1997 soon evaporated after a series of irregularities over how Blair chose to conduct his government. These included an obsession with media management, recurrent questions over Blair's integrity (which began with the Ecclestone affair and reached a climax with the failure to unearth WMD in Iraq) and a widespread impression of hypocrisy. The Hutton and Butler inquiries shone a piercing light on Blair's decision to govern through his 'denocracy', while since 1997 Parliament has emerged as a largely ineffective scrutineer of government activities. It is one of the black marks hanging over his premiership (unless he can, as he says, rebuild trust in his promise-heavy third term). Blair's period as Prime Minister saw a significant erosion of public trust in politicians and falling participation in general elections (turnout was 78 per cent in 1992, 72 per cent in 1997 and just 59 per cent in 2001).

Tony Blair has remodelled the Labour party's organisation, policy and presentation more profoundly than any leader in history. The changes began with Neil Kinnock after 1983 and were continued by John Smith from 1992. Blair, along with fellow New Labour architects Brown, Mandelson, Campbell, Gould and Hunter, completed the transformation, taking it further than either Kinnock or Smith would have done. Blair in particular was responsible for increasing the number of party members, extending 'one member one vote' and establishing the National Policy Forum, which undermined the role of the annual party conference in policy making and reduced the power of the NEC. Blair was the first leader in Labour history who did not owe his status as leader to his parliamentary colleagues, and this fact gave him a critical advantage. The prolonged intra-party fighting of the 1970s and 1980s also provided him with the perfect pretext to insist upon a large measure of central control and loyalty that the party would never have accepted in the past.

Blair put more distance between the leadership and the trade unions than any of his predecessors: the unions have remained a comparatively minor force throughout his premiership. Most extraordinary of all has been Blair's success in securing party backing for the most belligerent foreign policy pursued by any Prime Minister since Anthony Eden over Suez in 1956, and at home for an economic, social and law and order policy that has had far more in common with Conservativism than with past Labour policy. In both style and policy, Blair has not looked to his own party for a role model. Instead, he has turned to Margaret Thatcher, who exerted throughout a powerful grip on his thinking. He sees himself as quite different from the four Labour Prime Ministers who preceded him (MacDonald, Attlee, Wilson and Callaghan). The Labour party might not love Tony Blair, but it has certainly respected his exceptional election-winning ability (albeit achieved with never more than 43.2 per cent of the popular vote). Blair has made little secret of his lack of affection for the old Labour Party, but he sees himself as the custodian of New Labour and feels personal responsibility for its well-being. Party membership may have halved since Blair became Prime Minister, and its base weakened significantly in local elections in 2003 and 2004, but he is determined that his time as leader will become the model for the twenty-first century. Critics argue that Blair has undermined, perhaps fatally, the institutional structures of the traditional Labour party and made it overly dependent on an all powerful leader. Establishing the Blairite Labour party as a credible and responsible governing force may yet, however, prove one of his most enduring challenges.

Before he became Prime Minister, Blair had little experience and had given little thought to foreign or defence policy. His biggest concern prior to 1997 was to convey the impression that, if elected, Labour would guard the country's interests, and leave behind the party's image of being weak and pacifist on the world stage.

On one point Blair was absolutely clear before he became leader: building a closer relationship with the European Union would be an absolute priority. He was contemptuous of the lack of vision and vacillations of Thatcher and Major, and believed that he alone had the vision and skills to carve out a qualitatively new and better relationship with the EU than had existed before. He invested considerable time in his first term in establishing close links with key EU leaders, arousing expectations that Britain would at last cease to be Europe's awkward partner. Entry into the single currency would be at the heart of the new relationship and he naïvely believed that this would be relatively straightforward once in office. He soon realised that he had under-estimated the thrust of the economic argument, the assaults of the Eurosceptic press and the intransigence of Gordon Brown. He resolved that entry would be a second term project. But the obstacles only became more pronounced. He was no more successful after 2001 than he had been in 1997. Blair was never a diehard Europhile. He originally believed that British membership of the single currency was fundamental to forging a new relationship with the EU, and would be considered one of his more significant achievements. But he came to see the costs of entry as heavily outweighing any likely gains. When Britain ducked entry for a second time, disillusionment amongst Europhiles at home and among EU partners grew. Despite this, Blair's standing with EU leaders remained high until 2002, when his decision to support America over Iraq began to exact a heavy cost. Although Blair's reputation never fully recovered, some of the old magic returned in December 2004 when he helped drive the EU to the consensus that talks should be held leading to the eventual admission of Turkey. Blair believes, however fancifully, that in fifteen years' time the world will be far more impressed by his role in imaginatively extending the EU into the Muslim sphere, than by the earlier bickering over the decision to invade Iraq.

Blair's next crucial and possibly final European test will come with the referendum on the EU constitution expected in either the spring or summer of 2006. In April 2004, Blair had resented being bounced into his pledge to hold a referendum, although the logic of his private discussions was already pointing in that direction. Since then, the constitution has been criticised in much of the EU for being overly influenced by the British. A defeat in 2006 could finally unpick Blair's entire EU ambition (as well, perhaps, as his premiership). Overall, one must conclude in 2005 that Blair's European policy has failed to achieve the objectives he set. Yet again, Blair hopes that the glory will lie ahead.

In Blair's first term, he was deeply concerned by humanitarian abuses, as in Kosovo, but it was only in his second term that he began to turn his mind seriously to the problems of the environment, Africa and world poverty. In his October 2001 Party Conference speech, he foresaw a new global consensus that would deliver an end to poverty in Africa, halt global warming and foster a just resolution of the Israeli–Palestinian conflict, with two independent states living in 'equal partnership'. He and Jonathan Powell believed that major world events like 9/11 could be used to shake up the kaleidoscope of settled opinions and lead to fresh opportunities for real change. His quest to alleviate poverty and tackle AIDS in Africa is deeply felt, for all the accusations that it is mere grandstanding. His trips to Africa in February 2002 and October 2004 allowed him to see these problems first hand, while in February 2004 he established his own Africa commission, which included both Bob Geldof and Gordon Brown, to investigate options for reform.

On the environment, Blair's principal concern has been climate change. He remains a strong proponent of the Kyoto protocol and Britain remains on course to meet the Kyoto targets, even if his pleas for the US to take the issue more seriously have fallen on deaf ears. Blair plans to use the British presidency of the EU and of the G8 in 2005 to make progress on the environment, but critics question how effective Blair's late conversion to these issues, as enunciated in his speech at Davos in January 2005, will prove. New Labour's record in practice, they assert, belies Blair's new image as an environmental warrior. Reducing VAT on home heating in 1997 and abolishing the automatic escalator on petrol duties in 2000 might have played well in the country, but encouraged more, not less pollution.

Blair's foreign policy will be defined by his response to 9/11 and the subsequent war in Iraq. Immediately after 9/11, Blair felt that his hour had arrived as he battled hard to build an international coalition against al-Qaeda in Afghanistan. He never tired of telling the world that the struggle was not with Islam, but with those terrorists who wanted to destroy democracy. He spoke almost messianically about a better world emerging from the rubble of the Twin Towers. He sought to realise this vision in Africa and the Middle East: in the latter he was content to deal with the PLO, whom he deemed 'biddable' terrorists, much like the IRA.

But then, from early to mid-2002 at the very moment that public and establishment opinion began to urge caution in following the Bush administration, he stuck ever more determinedly to his favoured course of action. He was a man on a train who noticed through his window stations whistling by and was unable to get off, even if he or his advisers had wanted to, which they did not. He believes that Iraq and nihilistic terrorism are the most important issues any Prime Minister has faced in a generation. Even if all eventually works out well in Iraq, the issue will still have compromised his major objective of establishing a new, settled relationship with the EU. It has damaged Britain's relationship with the Muslim world, and may do so for generations. It also divided his party, disrupted his second term and eroded his greatest asset – public trust.

Blair's error over Iraq was less his decision to confront Saddam after twelve years of evading the UN, which history might well judge kindly. Rather, it was his failure to realise his potential as an independent and critical friend of the US. If Blair had only one historic decision to make in his premiership, it was to restrain Bush from attacking Iraq in March 2003, and ensure that diplomatic pressure was used to find a multilateral solution to whatever threat Saddam Hussein posed. By letting America in effect act alone, the unprecedented outpouring of sympathy for the US from across the world evaporated and turned to suspicion and hostility. Blair also singly failed to achieve his objectives for British support for America, especially progress in the Middle East peace process, while he still possessed real leverage over the Bush administration. He stood by while the UN was marginalised and diminished. Blair made a grave error in accepting flawed intelligence on weapons of mass destruction too readily, thus sending his country to war on a false prospectus. He also failed to ensure that the US had a credible plan for post-war Iraq that would restore law and order swiftly and counter potential insurgents. As with Eden over Suez, he was convinced his decisions were right and would be vindicated by history.

By early 2005, Blair was increasingly upbeat. In November, George W. Bush had been re-elected President, just a few days before the death of Yasser Arafat. Hopes rose of a fresh start for the Middle East as Bush, with Blair's prompting providing impetus, pledged to 'spend the capital of the United States' to advance the peace process. Yet Blair has managed to extract fine words from Bush before. Whether, this time, real action will follow remains to be seen. The elections in Iraq in January 2005 went more smoothly than many feared, but the road to a stable government, made more difficult by the repeated mistakes of the Anglo-American Coalition authority, remains long and uncertain. Even if an established state emerges, and the country avoids further loss of life, the question will remain of whether Saddam could have been removed by other means, keeping the international coalition intact, without the loss of trust over Iraq's alleged weapons of mass destruction, and without the loss of an estimated 100,000 lives in the two years after March 2003. From the perspective of spring 2005, the decision to support America so uncritically over Iraq may yet work out well for Blair, resulting in a triumphant vindication of his vision on the world stage in the face of so much scepticism at home and abroad. But if Iraq becomes a quagmire, the Israeli–Palestinian conflict remains unsolved, and terrorism increases, it will be seen as the most vain and foolish decision taken by a British Prime Minister since Suez in 1956.

Blair has now had eight years as Prime Minister, the maximum duration allowed to an American President, and longer than almost all his predecessors in Downing Street. Yet in spite of landslide election victories and little meaningful opposition at home, Blair's place in history appears still undecided. In the 2001 conclusion to a volume of essays on the first Blair government, *The Blair Effect*, I wrote that 'the edifice may prove more difficult to erect than the foundations have been to lay. Blair has succeeded in remodelling his party; he has yet to reform his country. The future and the ultimate verdict of history on Blair and New Labour are wide open.'

Four years on, the judgement still stands: it is the lack of personal achievement rather than its extent and quality that remains to date the defining characteristic of the Blair premiership. The assault on poverty aside, which was Brown's agenda, almost everything Blair has done personally – in education, health, law and order and Northern Ireland – has also been an extension of Conservative policy between 1979 and 1997. Blair, the Pollyanna Prime Minister, believes that the glory will come in the years ahead and his place in history amongst the pantheon of great national leaders will be secured. He believes that another full term in office will define his entire premiership. He wants to be seen as a model leader for the twenty-first century: flexible, imaginative and humane. He will expect to entrench his reform agenda on the public services and see tangible results felt by the country at large. Abroad, he believes we will see the emergence of a stable democracy in Iraq, real progress in the longstanding conflict between Israel and Palestine and continued action against the proliferation of nuclear weapons, international terrorists and the rogue states who support them. He will also cement a new relationship with the EU.

Without such progress, however, intra-party battles at home, and continuing difficulties in the Middle East and in the EU, will damage his standing further the longer he stays at Number 10. Blair remains in office waiting for his policies at home and abroad to be vindicated. He will then search for a break in the clouds that will allow him to leave on a high note. But the clouds, which darkened profoundly during his second term, may not part. And his final freedom as Prime Minister, the ability to decide the moment of his own departure, might yet be seized from him, as it has from almost all his predecessors at Number 10.

Acknowledgements

This book took eighteen months to research and three months to write, for most of which time, bar one term's sabbatical, I was Head Master of Brighton College. More than many books, therefore, it has depended on a great deal of support. School teaching is a wonderful job, but unlike those whose jobs are in the media or in academic life, it does not bring you into daily contact with figures in politics: thus my need for help was all the greater.

My principal debt has been to my outstanding research team. First on board for a year was Chris Ballinger of Brasenose College, Oxford, who laid down much of the groundwork. From the summer of 2003, a new team was assembled. Peter Snowdon focused on domestic policy; Daniel Collings, who was based at Harvard, specialised on US research and foreign chapters; while Elizabeth Jones held the team and the project together from Brighton with her incisive and orderly mind. This team proved formidably bright and hard-working, and no strangers to fourteen-hour days, seven days a week. Towards the end we were joined by John Hales and Matthew Teller. To our joy, Lewis Baston also came on board for the final stages. It was my good fortune to bring them all together (from the four schools at which I have taught) and they will all go far in life. The project had many days when the task seemed simply overwhelming given the time available. Never in my life have I attempted something so difficult or been so stretched. Without their good humour and strength, the book would have gone under. Critical also were Julia Harris, who typed every single word, and Enid Jones, who typed up many of the interview transcripts. They were both extraordinarily tenacious and dedicated.

Among friends and academics, my chief debt is to Dennis Kavanagh, one of the three figures to whom I have dedicated this book. He was quite extraordinarily encouraging, perceptive and knowledgeable, and I don't think I could have written the book without him.

This biography was unauthorised. Initially Number 10 said it would be supportive and encouraging; then it changed its mind and tried to discourage people from seeing me. Then, when it became clear that just about everybody *was* seeing me, including many in the building, it changed its attitude again to one of turning a blind eye. Having written an authorised biography of a Prime Minister, I have found my 'unofficial' status preferable from every point of view. Almost everyone close to Tony Blair agreed to talk, many on more than one occasion, but my 'unofficial' status meant that I was not burdened by a responsibility to them. This has allowed me simply to tell the truth as I saw it.

I have taken great pains to ensure I played fair with all my sources, keeping identities confidential when requested to do so, and ensuring that all citations, references and facts were fully checked. If I have failed to act in accordance with this understanding, I would be surprised, and I apologise unreservedly.

The book is based on 600 interviews, backed up by some 200 written submissions or commentaries. Many of those who helped have preferred to remain anonymous. Civil servants, especially those still serving, were particularly reluctant to be named: they were by a mile the most valuable witnesses – more objective, detailed and analytical than politicians. My warmest appreciation goes to all my interviewees and correspondents. I would like to single out a tiny cross-section: Cathy Ashton, Peter Brookes, John Burton, Sean Creighton, Dr Brian Crosby, Susan Crosland, John Carr, Alan Haworth, Louise Hayman, Lady Jenkins, Lance Price, Robert Philp, Glenys Thornton, Paul Trippett and Phil Wilson. Many experts and commentators who have written on the period gave generously of their time, including Kamal Ahmed, Matthew d'Ancona, Tom Baldwin, James Blitz, Adam Boulton, Andy Grice, Michael Gove, Ian Hargreaves, Tony Howard, Will Hutton, Simon Jenkins, George Jones, Nicholas Jones, Trevor Kavanagh, David Hughes, John Kampfner, William Keegan, Peter Kellner, Martin Kettle, John Lloyd, Don Macintyre, David McKittrick, Andy McSmith, Andrew Marr, James Naughtie, Peter Oborne, Matthew Parris, Robert Peston, Andrew Rawnsley, John Rentoul, Peter Riddell, Paul Routledge, John Sergeant, David Seymour, Mary Ann Sieghart, Jon Sopel, Peter Stothard, Ivan Stoyanov, David Walker, Simon Walters, Alan Watkins, Philip Webster, Martin Westlake, Michael White and Patrick Wintour.

At Brighton College, I am indebted to Robert Seabrook QC, my then chairman of governors, for willingly granting me the sabbatical; then to Robert Skidelsky, his successor, and Bob Alexander, the College President, and all the other governors. Among colleagues, I am particularly grateful to Simon Smith, who took over the school in the autumn term in 2003 with conspicuous success and who was extraordinarily understanding throughout; to the outstanding teaching body who have cheerfully supported me all the way through, and, within my own office, to Angie Moore, Mary Anne Brightwell, and Debra Lewis. Brighton College is justly regarded as a superb and pioneering school, and it is because of all these figures who work in and for it.

At Simon & Schuster I would like to thank Andrew Gordon, who has been remarkably understanding of an ever-changing schedule and expanding project, and extremely fast in both the editing and turnaround of the book. My thanks also to Edwina Barstow for her help editorially and hunting down the forty chapter pictures. This is the first book I have written with an agent, and I would like to thank Sonia Land, Alex Lea and Roland Baggott. An interesting experience!

Another novelty was writing the book in association with a television production company. Thanks to all at Diverse, especially Leonie Jameson, Alison Cahn, Ben Watt, Liz Seymour and Sian Bundrid. Also to Gary Clarke for his camera work. Finally, thanks to Nick Hornby for his humour and patience with my incredibly busy schedule. Making three hours of television was an additional burden which I often felt I could have done without, but which I ultimately concluded was worthwhile, and helped me to see a more rounded Tony Blair.

At research institutes, archives and libraries I would like to thank Felix Dare and Ellie Harris for their assistance in providing video material; Alexia Lindsay, Archivist, Fettes College; the British Library of Political and Economic Science; the Bodleian Library, Oxford; Brasenose College, Oxford; the Neil Kinnock Archives at Churchill College, Cambridge; Collingdale newspaper library; Darlington Library; Durham City Library; the Kennedy School of Government Library, Harvard University; the Labour History Archive Study Centre; John Rylands University Library, Manchester; Nuffield College, Oxford; Newlands Preparatory School, Seaford; Trinity College, Melbourne; and Westminster Reference Library. Thanks also to the British Academy for their help with my research costs. I am very grateful.

Many people have read part of or indeed all of the book. Again I will not name them all, but Lewis Baston, Chris Ballinger, Daniel Collings, Dennis Kavanagh, Peter Kellner, Peter Riddell, Steve Richards and Mary Ann Sieghart have been quite exceptionally generous with their time and insights.

I tried out my early views of this book on a number of audiences, including at Tel Aviv University, Harrow and Tonbridge schools,

Varndean Sixth Form College and the Brighton Festival, with my own students at Brighton College and at Dorset House Prep School. I learned much from them all.

Particular thanks go to James Dahl, Christopher Everett, David Raeburn and Jonathan Smith for stimulating conversations, not least on Greek tragedy. My debt as ever goes to my colleagues at the Centre for Contemporary British History (formerly the Institute of Contemporary British History) for their inspiration and support. This body, over its seventeen years of existence, has shaped the course of its field of interest more profoundly than many historical institutions five times its size and income.

Finally, I would like to thank my wonderful wife, Joanna, and three children, Jessica, Susannah and Adam, especially for letting our house in Brighton be taken over for a year by the research team, monopolising the computers in 'the den'. There was much more 'denocracy' than democracy in Marine Square. My writing books has succeeded in killing off what little interest in politics my family once had, which has made their love and support all the more remarkable. As with all my writing, any profits will be given to educational charities.

Notes

1: Father's Stroke

1 The 'psychologically disturbed'
   Blair thesis probably has its clearest
   expression in Leo Abse (2001 and
   2003), and Channel 4, 'Inside the
   Mind of Tony Blair', 28.10.03.
2 It has been the conventional
   wisdom that his father's stroke and
   disappointed expectations for his
   career are what drove young Tony
   Blair to decide on a career in
   politics: Stothard (2003), p.191.
3 Lynda Lee Potter, *Daily Mail*,
   26.10.96.
4 Interview.
5 *Daily Mail*, 26.10.96.
6 Interview.
7 Interview, James Fenton, 05.10.03.
8 *Daily Mail*, 26.10.96.
9 Ibid.
10 *The Chorister*, July 1966, which
   confirmed the achievements at the
   prep school in his final year,
   1965–66, do not show Blair widely
   excelling. For such a small school,
   one might have expected him to
   have been more conspicuous. There
   is a record of only one performance
   in a play: he was a soldier in
   Dorothy Sayers' *The Man Born to be
   King*. He did produce his first known
   published writing during these
   years – 'A. Blair, Lower 6th, 12 years
   11 months' published the following
   poem:

A STORY OF ROMANCE
1. This is the story of romance.
How they loved is quite by chance;
The one, Montgomery, is very
   romantic;
The other, Elizabeth, is slightly
   pedantic.
2. How often they used to wander in
   the Park.
Not coming home till it was dark,
Montgomery always wanted to elope,
But Elizabeth said that was too much

to hope.
3. Montgomery said too long they had
   tarried,
That sooner or later they'd have to
   get married,
But Elizabeth as pedantic as ever,
Said, 'as for marrying', she wished to
   never.
4. She explained that there were
   banns to be cried
and the licence to be got,
And without those things done, marry,
   they
certainly could not.
Montgomery soon gave up in despair
—
Pedants and romance don't make a
   pair.

Printed in *The Chorister*, the school
magazine for 1965/66, with thanks to
Dr Brian Crosby for bringing it to
my attention.
11 Interview, Brian Crosby, 11.10.03.
12 Dr Crosby's private video of Tony
   Blair opening the Pre-Prep
   Department, The Chorister School,
   22.10.93.
13 *The Australian Magazine*,
   15–16.03.97.
14 *Observer*, 29.04.03
15 Interview.
16 Private correspondence.
17 Interview, Michael Gascoigne,
   18.07.03.
18 Interview.
19 *The Chorister*, 1965/66, p.7.
20 Interview, Alastair Singleton,
   25.09.03.
21 Interview, Andrew Gordon-Clark,
   26.09.03.
22 Letter from David McMurray,
   former English master at Fettes, to
   the author, 30.12.03.
23 Stothard (2003), p.91.
24 Interviews.
25 Interview, Robert Harris, 23.10.03.
26 *Fettesian*, April 1968. The reviewer
   wrote: 'Blair emerged as a somewhat

youthful Antony, but nevertheless a very promising actor who should prove indispensable for school productions in the next few years.'

27 'He was not a great actor. His Stanhope was okay, good for a house play. But Fettes had a good reputation for drama, school plays, musicals, productions on the Edinburgh Fringe. It was not a big figure in school drama': Interview.

28 Interview.

29 Interview.

30 Interview.

31 Interview. To Andrew Rawnsley, he had praise for the staff who taught him English Literature, History and Drama: *Observer*, 02.10.94.

32 Interview.

33 Interview.

34 Roberts went on to become Headmaster of Worksop College and then set up his own small publishing company in Devon, producing poetry books.

35 Interview.

36 Interview.

37 Interview.

38 Private correspondence.

39 Interview.

40 Ronald Selby-Wright had also helped to arrange – with Jack Mackenzie-Stuart – for Blair to spend the week after his 'A' levels at a boys' camp. Selby-Wright became part-time Chaplain at Fettes in the late 1950s and ran the Canongate Boys' Club in the city. He was adept at helping those who had fallen out of line or, as he liked to see it, had been 'misjudged' by their schoolmasters: Private correspondence.

41 Interview.

42 'Why was he not made even a House prefect? On reflection, I suspect it may have been because, while we all knew what he was against, we had little idea of what he was for. Equally it would have been hard in those days to imagine him saying no as was occasionally demanded of a prefect even in those times': Letter, David McMurray to author, 19.07.03.

43 'I think that compared to a lot of Fettesians he knew that life could be tough for people; and he definitely had a streak of anti-materialism that went far deeper than most people's – it wasn't just a fashionable line': Private correspondence.

44 Rentoul (2001), p.17.

45 Ten pupils at Tonbridge School were given suspended expulsions, and a further thirty were suspended for the final week of the summer term. The anger at Tonbridge was aimed mostly against the CCF, and was inspired in part by the film *If*, written by former Tonbridge School pupils.

46 Interview.

47 Interview.

48 Interview, Hugh Kellett, 19.09.03.

49 Interview, David McMurray, 18.07.03.

50 Interview, Alastair Singleton, 25.09.03.

51 Interview.

52 Interview.

53 Interview.

54 Interview, Alastair Singleton, 25.09.03.

55 Interview.

2: Father and Mother

1 Rentoul (2001), pp.3–14; Sopel (1995), pp.1–15.

2 In his diaries, Lord (Paddy) Ashdown recalls a conversation with Blair about his family background over dinner on 12.11.95. Blair said of his roots, 'Of course, all my ancestors were Irish, and pretty rabble-rousing at that': Ashdown (2000), p.358.

3 *Daily Record*, 07.03.96; Rentoul (2001), p.8.

4 Rentoul (2001), p.8.

5 Interview.

6 Speech in Cape Town, 08.01.99, quoted in Rentoul (2001), p.6.

7 Rentoul (2001), p.7.

8 Leo Blair, quoted in Rentoul (2001), p.8.

9 Interview.

10 Rentoul (2001), p.6.

11 Sopel (1995), p.8.

12 Quoted in Lynda Lee-Potter interview, *Daily Mail*, 26.10.96.

13 Tony Blair to Lesley White, *Sunday Times*, 20.04.97.

14 Interview.

15 Rentoul (2001), p.8.

16 Quoted in Sopel (1995), p.7.

17 'He was always very cheerful and charming at lunch in college [University College, Durham]. He was delightful company and warm to

young people,' remembers one:
Interview, Alan Piper, 15.10.03.
18 Interview.
19 Bill Blair, *Observer*, 27.04.03.
20 Ibid.
21 Interview.
22 One friend from his gap year in
London recalled, 'I know he did talk
about his dad a bit. His dad had had
a stroke fairly recently, so I
remember Tony going up to
Durham, fairly often, and it was
clear to me that he held his dad in
very high esteem': Interview.
23 Interview, Peter Thomson, 12.10.03.
24 *Daily Mail*, 26.10.03.
25 Ibid.
26 *Sunday Times*, 20.04.97.
27 Interview, Tim Allan, 10.09.03.
28 Interview.
29 *Sunday Times*, 20.04.03.
30 Interview.
31 Interestingly, in conversation with
Valerie Grove (*Daily Telegraph*,
09.04.03), he mentions his father but
not his mother in response to her
question 'Who have you learned
most from in life?' The others he
mentions are Peter Thomson, Eric
Anderson and Derry Irvine.
32 Stothard (2003), p.191.

3: Oxford and Loss of Mother

1 A principal reason why 'Oxbridge'
students in the early 1970s took gap
years was that the vast majority had
a 'seventh' term at school to sit
Oxbridge entrance exams, so only
left school in December, too late to
join university immediately.
2 Alan Collenette, who knew him best
in this year, says he cannot recall
what Tony Blair's intention was for
his gap year, beyond broadening his
experience: Interview, Alan
Collenette, 11.09.03.
3 Indeed, Cherie Blair claimed in a
speech at a reception for the
homeless charity Centrepoint on
23.02.04 that Blair had slept on a
park bench near Euston station in
London in 1971: *Sunday Mirror*,
29.02.04.
4 Interview, Chris Blishen, 20.08.03.
5 Letter, Alan Collenette to author,
10.9.03.
6 Ibid.
7 *Daily Mail*, 15.10.00.
8 Interview, Adam Sieff, 27.09.03.
9 Interview, Theo Sloot, 09.09.03.

10 Interview.
11 Interview, Adrian Friend, 03.09.03.
12 Interview.
13 One wrote: 'I may be biased, but
Tony is a very, very nice man. This
will not surprise anyone who knows
Tony well, but even with the
extraordinary weight of
responsibilities that he carries
constantly, he always makes time to
see me if I am in London.'
14 Interviews.
15 Interview.
16 Rentoul (2001), p.43.
17 Interview.
18 BBC Radio 4, *Desert Island Discs*,
23.11.96.
19 *Daily Mail*, 26.10.96.
20 Interview, Andrew Rawnsley,
02.10.94.
21 David Brayshaw, *Daily Telegraph*,
06.05.03.
22 *Cherwell*, 29.11.73.
23 Interview, Revd Nicholas Lowton,
01.10.03.
24 Adam Sharples to Mark Ellen,
Observer, 27.04.03.
25 *Daily Mail*, 26.10.96.
26 Countless words have been written
and broadcast about this band. One
of the most informative articles is by
Richard Pendlebury, *Daily Mail*,
22.11.94.
27 BBC Radio 4, *Desert Island Discs*,
23.11.96.
28 Interview, James Moon, 12.09.03.
29 Interview.
30 *Cherwell*, 29.11.73.
31 Tony Blair, *Saga Magazine*, 05.05.03.
32 Marc Palley, quoted in *Sunday Times*,
13.06.94.
33 Interview, Sally Brampton, 23.11.03.
34 Interview, Anthony Whitestone,
02.06.03.
35 Interview, Hector Smith, 04.09.03.
36 Interview, David Aaronovitch,
13.10.03.
37 *Cherwell*, 08.11.73.
38 Colin Meade, *Daily Telegraph*,
06.05.03.
39 Interview, David Gardner, 03.09.03.
40 Interview, Geoff Gallop, 09.04.03.
41 Interview, Laura Mackenzie,
05.09.03.
42 Interview.
43 Interview, Geoff Gallop, 09.04.03.
44 *New Statesman*, 13.07.94.
45 Samuel Brittan, *New Statesman*,
07.02.99.
46 See, for example, Leo Abse (2001),
pp.98–105.

47 Sarah Hale, 'Professor Macmurray on Mr Blair: The Strange Case of the Communication Guru that Never Was', *Political Quarterly*, pp.191–7; also Nick Cohen, *New Statesman*, 01.07.02: 'Maybe he did read Macmurray once. If he did, he shows every sign of having forgotten every word.'
48 Interview, Geoff Gallop, 09.04.03.
49 Ian Hargreaves, *New Statesman*, 31.05.96.
50 Interview, Peter Thomson, 12.10.03.
51 Interview, Bishop Graham Dow, 19.07.03.
52 *Independent*, 22.05.94.
53 Interviews, Laura Mackenzie, 05.09.03; David Gardner, 03.09.03.
54 Interview, David Fursdon, 26.09.03.
55 Interview.
56 Rentoul (2001), pp.43–4.
57 Blair, quoted in Martin Jacques interview, *Sunday Times*, 17.07.94.
58 Interview, Matthew d'Ancona, 13.11.03.
59 Interview, Laura Mackenzie, 05.09.03.
60 Interview, Alan Judd, 20.07.03.
61 Interview, Delia Rothnie, 22.01.04.
62 In an interview with Andrew Rawnsley, Blair said, 'I really regret having read Law as an academic subject. Law only came alive to me when I started to practise it – being given practical problems in people's lives and finding solutions to them': *Observer*, 02.10.94.
63 Interview, Lord Jenkins, 05.11.02.
64 Geoff Gallop, *Sunday Times*, 19.07.92.
65 Interview, Lord Jenkins, 05.11.02.
66 Letter, Marc Palley to author, 08.10.03.
67 *Oxford University Calendar*, 1975–76, pp.668–9.
68 Jon Sopel and Richard Shears, *Daily Mail*, 27.01.96.
69 Tony Blair, *Daily Mail*, 26.10.96.
70 Ibid.
71 Interview.
72 *Daily Mail*, 26.10.96.
73 Ibid.
74 *Durham Advertiser*, 10–11.07.75.
75 Bill Blair, *Observer*, 27.04.03.
76 Interview.
77 Interview.
78 Sopel (1995), p.39.
79 Mary Ann Sieghart, *The Times*, 29.04.03.

4: Peter Thomson

1 Ian Hargreaves, *New Statesman*, 31.05.96; McSmith (1996), pp.299–300.
2 McSmith (1996), pp.299–300.
3 *Guardian*, 11.12.95.
4 Thomson quoted in the *Evening Standard*, 18.07.94.
5 *New Statesman*, 31.05.96.
6 Interview, David Fursdon, 26.09.03.
7 Interview, Peter Thomson, 12.10.03.
8 Interview.
9 *New Statesman*, 31.05.96.
10 Interviews, David Gardner, 03.09.03; Nicholas Lowton, 17.07.03.
11 Jon Sopel and Richard Shears, *Daily Mail*, 27.01.96.
12 Interview, Charles Leadbetter, 01.10.03.
13 Interview, David Gardner, 03.09.03.
14 Interview, Peter Thomson, 12.10.03.
15 *The Times Magazine*, 30.9.95.
16 Ibid.
17 Interview, Peter Thomson, 12.10.03.
18 Jill Sargeant, *Reuter News*, 19.05.97.
19 Ian Hargreaves, *New Statesman*, 31.05.96.
20 Ibid.
21 Interview.
22 Interview, Peter Thomson, 12.10.03.
23 Interview, Charles Leadbetter, 01.10.03.
24 *Daily Mail*, 27.01.96.
25 Ibid.
26 Interview, Martin Kettle, 04.03.03.
27 Interview, Charles Leadbetter, 01.10.03.
28 Keith Dovkants, *Evening Standard*, 18.07.94.
29 Interview, Peter Thomson, 12.10.03.
30 Interview.

5: Commits to Labour

1 BBC TV, 'Happy Birthday Mr Prime Minister', 30.04.03.
2 Rentoul (2001), pp.52–7.
3 Interview.
4 Rentoul (2001), p.56.
5 Blair to Andrew Rawnsley, *Observer*, 02.10.94.
6 Interview, Jeremy Irwin Singer, 12.09.03.
7 *Observer*, 02.10.94.
8 Letter, Marc Palley to author, 08.10.03.
9 Lord Falconer, quoted in McDougall (2001), p.65.
10 Interview, Sandy Pringle, 28.08.03.
11 Interview, Sean Creighton, 24.03.04.

12 Interview; Letter, Sean Creighton to author, 07.04.04.
13 Interview, David Fursdon, 26.09.03.
14 Interview, Geoff Gallop, 09.04.03.
15 The Blairs attended their first meeting of the Queensbridge Ward Branch, Hackney South CLP on 6 November 1980: Minutes of the Queensbridge Ward Branch, 06.11.80, provided by Baroness (Glenys) Thornton.
16 Katie Kay, *Observer*, 27.04.03.
17 Ibid.
18 Interview.
19 Minutes of the Queensbridge Ward Branch, 03.09.81, provided by Baroness Thornton.
20 Interview, Baroness Thornton, 25.11.03.
21 Interview, Charles Clarke, 02.03.04.
22 Interview; Letter, Neil Kinnock to author, 14.04.04.
23 John Burton recalled Blair's disillusionment with the party in London when he arrived in Sedgefield three years later; Blair colourfully put it to Burton that, 'The loony left were harming the party in London. They were throwing each other off balconies at meetings and through plane glass windows. When I came along here [Sedgefield] I thought – good God, these are normal people – they like the football just as much as the politics': Interview, John Burton, 07.07.03.
24 Interview, Baroness Thornton, 25.11.03.
25 Interview, John Carr, 02.09.03.
26 Interview.
27 McSmith (1996), p.303.
28 Interview, Alan Haworth, 10.10.03; Interview.
29 Interview, Anthony Howard, 02.10.03.
30 Interview, Lord Bragg, 10.09.03.
31 Blair's own written account (for an Australian political journal) of his 1982 lecture to Murdoch University in Perth, Australia, shows a certain animosity to those in the Labour movement who had defected to the SDP. 'They are strange mould-breakers: Roy Jenkins, Shirley Williams, David Owen, Bill Rodgers. If anything, they are the failed representatives of the old mould . . . The SDP rank-and-file are made up largely of middle-aged and middle-class erstwhile Labour members, who have grown too fat and affluent to feel comfortable with Labour': quoted in Rentoul (2001), p.69.
32 Interview, Charles Clarke, 02.03.04.
33 Interview, Margaret Hodge, 24.02.04.
34 Interview, Baroness Thornton, 25.11.03.
35 Rentoul (2001), p.67.
36 The motion was lost by 5 votes to 3: Minutes of the Queensbridge Ward Branch, 06.11.80, provided by Baroness Thornton.
37 Minutes of the Queensbridge Ward Branch, 05.02.81, provided by Baroness Thornton; John Rentoul, *Independent*, 02.10.94.
38 Anthony Blair, 'Second-Class Justice', *Spectator*, 18.08.79. The second appeared in August 1980: Anthony Blair, 'Whose Interest Should Prevail?', *Spectator*, 09.08.80.
39 Interview.
40 Interview, Lord Pendry, 15.10.03.
41 Interview.
42 For an appraisal of this government, see Anthony Seldon and Kevin Hickson (eds, 2004).
43 Interview, Sandy Pringle, 28.08.03.
44 Interview.
45 Interview, Patrick Wintour, 20.10.03.
46 Tony Blair was shortlisted as a local council candidate on 3 December 1981: Minutes of the Queensbridge Ward Branch, 03.12.81, provided by Baroness Thornton.
47 Interview, John Carr, 02.09.03.
48 Tony Blair, who apologised for his absence, was one of three names not selected from the shortlist of six: Minutes of the Queensbridge Ward Branch Selection Meeting, 04.02.82, provided by Baroness Thornton.
49 Interview, David Seymour, 20.10.03.
50 Interview, Lord Pendry, 15.10.03.
51 Rentoul (2001), p.82.
52 *South Bucks Observer*, 08.04.82, quoted in Rentoul (2001), p.84.
53 Ibid.
54 Lord Hattersley, BBC TV, 'Happy Birthday Mr Prime Minister', 30.04.03.
55 Interview, Alan Haworth, 10.10.03.
56 'I was very impressed with him when I went to speak for him at Beaconsfield and I thought then that he would make a future leader': Interview, Denis Healey, 17.11.03.
57 Interview, Lord Holme, 04.11.03.
58 'He was an immensely confident

and lucid performer': Interview, Lord Hattersley, 11.11.03.
59 Interview.

6: Cherie Blair

1 Interview, James Blitz, 04.11.03.
2 Philip Larkin, 'This be the verse', *High Windows*.
3 McDougall (2001), p.27.
4 Ibid, p.28.
5 Interview, John Carr, 02.09.03.
6 Ibid.
7 Interview.
8 Quoted in McDougall (2001), p.64.
9 Sopel (1995), pp.43–4; Rentoul (2001), pp.52–3.
10 Interview, David Fursdon, 26.09.03.
11 Tony Blair, quoted in McDougall (2001), p.65.
12 Gale Booth, quoted in McDougall (2001), p.66.
13 Interview.
14 Egar (1999), p.58.
15 Interview.
16 Cherie said of George Carman QC, 'George was not always larger than life and could be quite subdued at times, particularly when his personal life was unhappy, but he was always kind and helpful to me': quoted in Dominic Carman, *No Ordinary Life* (2002), p.120.
17 McDougall (2001), p.79.
18 Interview, James Hughes-Onslow, 09.04.03.
19 Canon Anthony Phillips, quoted in McDougall (2001), p.80.
20 Interview, John Carr, 02.09.03.
21 McDougall (2001), p.97.
22 Ibid., p.101.
23 Tony Blair, *Daily Mail*, 26.10.96.
24 Interview.
25 McDougall (2001), p.106.
26 Interview.
27 Interview.
28 Interview.
29 Interview.
30 Interview.
31 Interview.
32 *Sunday Times*, 08.10.95; Cherie Booth QC was appointed to sit as a Recorder in June 1999.
33 Ibid.
34 Interview.
35 Interview.
36 Interview.
37 Interview.
38 Stothard (2003), p.14.
39 *Independent*, 19.12.00. Paddy Ashdown also wrote in his diary in November 1995, 'Our relationship [with the Blairs] is now very friendly and relaxed. The presence of Cherie added greatly to this. She and Jane seem to get on well together': Ashdown (2000), p.360.
40 *Scotsman*, 08.05.02; Interview.
41 Interview.
42 John Rentoul said of Cherie's clashes with Brown in 1992, 1994 and 1998, 'Cherie was more aggressive towards Gordon than Tony allowed himself to appear': Rentoul (2001), p.225.
43 Private correspondence.
44 Interview; Linda McDougall, *Sunday Times*, 23.06.02.
45 See Chapter 35.

7: Sedgefield

1 Rentoul (2001), p.92.
2 Ibid., p.72.
3 Interview, Geoff Gallop, 09.04.03.
4 *The Australian Magazine*, 15–16.07.95; Interview, Geoff Gallop, 09.04.03.
5 Tony Blair, lecture delivered at Murdoch University, Western Australia, 1982. Typed transcript kindly supplied by the Hon. Dr Geoff Gallop, MLA.
6 Sopel (1995), pp.55–6.
7 Interview.
8 See, for example, Sopel (1995), pp.64–71; Rentoul (2001), pp.92–109.
9 Interview, John Carr, 02.09.03.
10 Sedgefield had been a constituency until 1974, and was re-created with different boundaries in time for the 1983 General Election.
11 Interview.
12 Rentoul (2001), pp.99–100.
13 Interview, John Burton, 07.07.03.
14 According to one account, Blair turned up almost an hour late. Blair said, 'I borrowed a car, put on a good grey suit, my best, got lost three or four times on the way': quoted in Proud (2003), p.102.
15 Interview, Peter Brookes, 28.07.03.
16 Interview, John Burton, 07.07.03.
17 Proud (2003), p.103.
18 Interview, Paul Trippett, 28.07.03.
19 Philip Wilson was not present at the first meeting with Blair. By bizarre coincidence, on the very day Blair met Burton and the others, Wilson had spoken on a motion drafted by Cherie Booth at the annual

conference of the CPSA, the public service union, in Brighton: Interview.
20 Interview, Peter Brookes, 28.07.03.
21 Interview, John Burton, 07.07.03.
22 Interview, Peter Brookes, 28.07.03.
23 Interview, Philip Wilson, 24.07.03.
24 Interview, John Burton, 07.07.03.
25 Rentoul (2001), p.106.
26 Interview, Peter Brookes, 28.07.03.
27 Interview, Ken Cameron, 24.09.03.
28 Interview, Lord Hattersley, 11.11.03.
29 *Northern Echo*, 6.6.83.
30 Interview, Peter Brookes, 28.07.03.
31 Proud (2003), p.125.

8: John Burton

1 Interview, John Burton, 07.07.03.
2 Interview, Nick Ryden, 18.07.03.
3 Interview, John Burton, 07.07.03.
4 John Burton in Perryman (1995), p.66.
5 *Scotland on Sunday*, 24.07.94, quoted in Rentoul (2001), p.13.
6 *New Statesman*, May 1997 Special Edition.
7 Interview, Keith Proud, 16.07.03.
8 John Burton in Perryman (1995), p.63.
9 Interview.
10 Interview, Philip Wilson, 24.07.03.
11 Philip Webster, *The Times*, 02.10.91.
12 Nicholas Timmins, *Independent*, 29.05.92.
13 Tony Blair in Perryman (1995), p.63.
14 Peter Hetherington, *Guardian*, 28.05.94 and 22.06.94.
15 Interview, Philip Wilson, 24.07.03.
16 Tony Blair in Perryman (1995), p.73.
17 *New Statesman*, May 1997 Special Edition.
18 Ibid.
19 *Independent*, 13.04.02.
20 Interview, Martin Kettle, 04.03.03.
21 Interview, Nick Ryden, 18.07.03.
22 *Mirror*, 26.01.96.
23 Tony Blair in Perryman (1995), p.66.
24 Blair said, 'There is no doubt at all that he was one of the principal architects of New Labour. He formed my own thinking to a significant degree ... He was one of the four or five most influential people on me': quoted in Proud (2003), p.22.
25 Interview, John Burton, 07.07.03.
26 Interview, Paul Trippett, 28.07.03.
27 Interview, John Burton, 07.07.03.
28 According to Burton, Blair's relations with Skinner markedly improved

after that episode: Interview, John Burton, 07.07.03.
29 *Guardian*, 27.07.95.
30 Ibid., 14.05.03.
31 Private correspondence.

9: The Closed Shop

1 Interview, Bryan Gould, 08.07.03.
2 Interview.
3 Interview, Lord Sawyer, 13.09.03.
4 Interview.
5 Interview, Peter Kellner, Baroness Ashton, 11.10.03.
6 Interview, Chris Smith, 04.02.03.
7 Interview, Neil Kinnock, 03.09.03.
8 McSmith (1996), p.309.
9 Interview.
10 Rentoul (2001), p.118.
11 Interview.
12 Rentoul (2001), p.114.
13 Ibid, p.115.
14 Interview, Lord Hattersley, 11.11.03.
15 McSmith (1996), pp.313–15.
16 For example, in the Channel 4 drama, *The Deal*, 28.09.03.
17 Interview, Dave Nellist, 18.10.03.
18 McSmith (1996), pp.310–11.
19 Rentoul (2001), p.118.
20 Alan Clark, then a junior minister at the Department of Employment, who took the legislation through committee, noted in his diary on 8 December 1983 that Blair and Brown were the 'two bright boys' on Labour's team: Clark, *Diaries* (1993), pp.53–4.
21 Interview, Lord Hattersley, 11.11.03.
22 Kinnock offered Brown a position in the Scottish or Social Security front-bench teams, but Brown told Kinnock that 'he wasn't ready' to join the front bench. In fact, Kinnock appointed Brown a front-bench spokesman on trade and industry in November 1985: Routledge (1998), pp.130–1.
23 Interview, David Seymour, 20.10.03.
24 Interview.
25 Interview, David Seymour, 20.10.03.
26 Interview.
27 Interview, Arnab Banerji, 19.02.04.
28 Letter, Tony Blair to 'economic advisory group', 25.03.85. Archived at The Labour History Archive and Study Centre, John Rylands University Library of Manchester.
29 Ibid.
30 Ken Coutts presented the paper on 'Protection and Devaluation' at Trinity College, Cambridge

(20.10.85) and Nick Sharman and Denis Turner tackled 'Industrial Policy Issues' in London (17.02.86). Meeting agendas are available at The Labour History Archive and Study Centre.

31 Interview, Lord Hattersley, 11.11.03.
32 Rentoul (2001), p.120.
33 Interview.
34 Interview.
35 Interview.
36 *Guardian*, 24.06.87.
37 Interview, Neil Kinnock, 03.09.03.
38 Ibid.
39 Ibid.
40 Interview.
41 Interview, Philip Wilson, 24.07.03.
42 *Guardian*, 14.06.88.
43 Peter Mandelson, quoted in Macintyre (2001), p.218.
44 Interview, Bryan Gould, 08.07.03.
45 Interview, Neil Kinnock, 03.09.03.
46 Interview, Rhodri Morgan, 25.09.03.
47 Interview.
48 Interview.
49 Interview, Jon Cruddas, 23.09.03.
50 Interview, Neil Kinnock, 03.09.03.
51 Interview.
52 Interview, Jon Cruddas, 23.09.03.
53 McSmith (1996), p.322.
54 Interview.
55 Interview.
56 Rentoul (2001), p.195.
57 Interview, John Monks, 11.11.03.
58 Interview, John Edmonds, 14.10.03.
59 Westlake (2001), p.446.
60 Interview, Jon Cruddas, 23.09.03.
61 Interview, Colin Byrne, 07.01.04.
62 *Guardian*, 19.12.89.
63 NEC Minutes, 24.01.90, The Labour History Archive and Study Centre.
64 Interview, Mike Craven, 09.10.03.
65 Interview, Neil Stewart, 26.08.03.
66 Interview.
67 Westlake (2001), p.447.
68 Interview, Neil Kinnock, 03.09.03.
69 Rentoul (2001), p.155.
70 Interview, David Aaronovitch, 13.10.03.

10: Neil Kinnock

1 I am indebted to Martin Westlake for telling me about Kinnock's acting of Osborne; Westlake (2001), p.30.
2 Blair said in his 2003 Labour Party conference speech of Neil Kinnock: 'I remember when our journey to government began; here in this hall

in 1985, with Neil Kinnock, here with us today. And, of course today it seems, absurd, doesn't it? Militant, Arthur, all that nonsense. But I tell you. At the time, I remember up there, where the MPs used to be penned in, getting to my feet in the middle of his speech, the hall split asunder, my heart pounding, wondering if this was the beginning or the end': 30.09.03, quoted on the *Guardian Unlimited* website.
3 Westlake (2001), pp.623–5.
4 Rosen (2001), p.122.
5 Interview, Martin Westlake, 17.11.03.
6 Correspondence with author, Neil Kinnock, 23.02.04.
7 Interview, Bryan Gould, 08.07.03.
8 Ibid.
9 Interview, Neil Kinnock, 03.09.03.
10 Interview, Bryan Gould, 08.07.03.
11 Interview; Westlake (2001), pp.445–8.
12 Letter, Neil Kinnock to Blair, 17.04.90, Box 5/18 KNNK, Kinnock Archives, Churchill College, Cambridge.
13 Interview; Correspondence with author, Neil Kinnock, 23.02.04.
14 Interview.
15 Interview, Andy McSmith, 02.09.03.
16 Interview, Andrew Graham, 21.10.03.
17 Interview, Robin Cook, 18.11.03.
18 McSmith (1994), pp.233–45; Interview, Andy McSmith, 02.09.03.
19 McSmith (1994), p.233.
20 Westlake (2001), p.550.
21 Interview; *Guardian*, 13.04.92.
22 Private correspondence.
23 Macintyre (1999), pp.216–21.
24 Interview.
25 Interview, Gerald Kaufman, 10.09.03.
26 Private correspondence.
27 The view of Peter Kellner, in Rosen (2001), p.340.
28 Interview, Neil Kinnock, 03.09.03.
29 *Observer*, 04.02.01; Correspondence with author, Robert Harris, 18.11.03.
30 Interview.
31 Interview, Neil Kinnock, 03.09.03.
32 Westlake (2001), pp.629–30.
33 Interview.
34 Westlake (2001), p.687.
35 Interview, Peter Kellner, 11.10.03.
36 Interview.
37 Interview.
38 Quoted by Kellner in Rosen (2001),

p.337; Westlake (2001), p.680.
39 See Note 2.
40 Interview.
41 Steve Richards, *New Statesman*, 20.11.99.
42 Interview, Margaret Beckett, 16.10.03.
43 Interview, Charles Clarke, 02.03.04.

11: United States Visits

1 Private correspondence; Blair's Bar work had previously taken him to Nashville, Tennessee, in 1982.
2 *Daily Mail*, 04.05.95.
3 *Observer*, 14.04.96.
4 The itinerary for 'Mr Anthony Blair', 03.08–02.09.86, State Department files.
5 Naughtie (2001), pp.215–16.
6 Sopel (1995), p.144.
7 Interview, Michael White, 11.03.04.
8 Scott (2000), p.4.
9 Interview.
10 Interview.
11 Interview.
12 Rentoul (2001), p.195.
13 Walker (1996), pp.154–5; Gould (1996), pp.162–8.
14 Interview, Lord Renwick, 07.04.03.
15 Interview.
16 Interview, Bruce Reed, 11.09.03.
17 Private correspondence.
18 Blumenthal (2003), p.301.
19 Interview, Elaine Kamarck, 18.09.03.
20 *Guardian*, 11.01.93.
21 McSmith (1996), p.330.
22 Interview, John Edmonds, 10.14.03.
23 Jonathan Freedland, *Washington Post*, 25.04.93.
24 John Prescott, *Guardian*, 31.12.92.
25 *Evening Standard*, 06.01.93.
26 Rentoul (2001), pp.195–7; Macintyre (1999), p.241.
27 Interview, Stan Greenberg, 21.11.03.
28 Interview.
29 Interview, Martin Walker, 01.10.03.
30 Gould (1998), p.177.
31 Blumenthal (2003), p.302.
32 Tony Blair, *Evening Standard*, 15.11.93.
33 Rentoul (2001), p.198.
34 Interview.
35 Gould (1998), p.177.
36 *Sunday Times*, 20.11.94.
37 Colin Brown, *Independent*, 04.01.93.
38 Gerald Baker, *Financial Times*, 29.05.97.
39 Interview, Larry Summers, 03.09.03.
40 *Observer*, 24.07.97.

41 Etzioni (2003), p.325.
42 *The Times*, 20.11.03; see also Foley (2000), p.4.

12: Philip Gould

1 *Yorkshire Post*, 15.12.98.
2 Rosen (2001), pp.227–9.
3 *Guardian*, 15.12.98.
4 *Sunday Times*, 29.08.99.
5 Gould (1998), pp.184–5.
6 Letter, Dennis Kavanagh to author, 21.11.03.
7 Correspondence with author, Peter Mandelson, 31.03.04.
8 Butler and Kavanagh (1997), p.62.
9 Dennis Kavanagh, 'Lord Gould', unpublished paper.
10 Correspondence with author, Peter Mandelson, 31.03.04.
11 Dennis Kavanagh, 'Lord Gould', unpublished paper; Butler and Kavanagh (1997), pp.60–7.
12 Interview, Philip Gould, 22.10.03.
13 Rosen (2001), p.228.
14 Anne McElvoy, *Independent*, 22.07.00.
15 Gould (1998), p.184.
16 Ibid, p.195.
17 Ludlam and Smith (2002), p.28.
18 Gould (1998), pp.186–7.
19 David Hare, *New Statesman*, 25.10.96.
20 Gould (1998), pp.163–4.
21 Interview.
22 Interview, Philip Gould, 22.10.03.
23 Interview.
24 Patricia Hewitt and Philip Gould, 'Lessons from America', *Renewal*, Vol. 1, No. 1, January 1993.
25 Interview, Philip Gould, 22.10.03.
26 Gould (1998), pp.181–2.
27 Ibid., p.200.
28 Interview.
29 Gould (1998), pp.211–14.
30 Interview, Philip Gould, 06.11.03.
31 Interview.
32 Jones (2001), p.19; *New Statesman*, 25.10.98.
33 Hennessy (2001), pp.484–5.
34 Dennis Kavanagh, 'Lord Gould', unpublished paper.
35 Interview.
36 Interview.
37 Interview.
38 Macintyre (2000), p.156; Correspondence with author, Peter Mandelson, 31.03.04.
39 Letter, Dennis Kavanagh to author, 21.11.03.
40 Interview.

41　Anne McElvoy, *Independent*, 22.07.00.
42　Interview, Philip Gould, 22.10.03.
43　Interview.
44　*Sunday Times*, 12.06.94.

13: *General and Leadership Elections, 1992*

1　Macintyre (1999), p.261.
2　Interview, Charles Clarke, 02.03.04.
3　Interview.
4　Interview.
5　Private correspondence.
6　Westlake (2001), p.517.
7　Interview.
8　Private correspondence.
9　Interview, Robin Cook, 18.11.03.
10　Interview.
11　Private correspondence.
12　*The Times*, 12.02.92.
13　Private correspondence.
14　Interview, Neil Kinnock, 03.09.03.
15　Westlake (2001), p.571.
16　Interview, Roz Preston, 25.09.03.
17　Interview.
18　Interview.
19　Interview, Robert Harris, 23.10.03.
20　Interview.
21　Interview, Roz Preston, 25.09.03
　　The poll was conducted by MORI and published in *The Times* on 01.04.92. It showed Labour on 42% and the Conservatives on 35%.
22　Interview, John Burton, 07.07.03.
23　Ibid.
24　Interview, Philip Wilson, 24.07.03.
25　Interviews, Clive Russell, 09.09.03; Paul Trippett, 28.07.03.
26　Interview.
27　Interview, Roz Preston, 25.09.03.
28　Rentoul (2001), pp.178–9.
29　Macintyre (1999), pp.263–8.
30　Routledge (1998), p.163.
31　Interview.
32　Interview.
33　Macintyre (1999), p.267.
34　Interview, Robert Harris, 23.10.03.
35　Robert Harris, *Sunday Times*, 08.03.92.
36　Interview.
37　Routledge (1998), p.164.
38　Interview, Andrew Graham, 21.10.03.
39　Routledge (1998), p.164.
40　Interview.
41　Quoted in Macintyre (1999), p.264.
42　Interview.
43　Interview.
44　Interview, Gerald Kaufman, 10.09.03.

45　Interview.
46　McSmith (1994), pp.263–79.
47　Rentoul (2001), pp.184–5.
48　McSmith (1996), p.326.
49　Interview, Margaret Beckett, 16.10.03.
50　Interview.
51　Private correspondence.
52　Interview.
53　Lord Hattersley, quoted in Rentoul (2001), p.184.
54　Interview.
55　Private correspondence.
56　Interview.
57　Letter, Roz Preston to author, 11.01.04.
58　Melanie Phillips, *Guardian*, 29.06.91.
59　Interview, Martin Jacques, 19.09.03.
60　Ibid.
61　*Marxism Today*, October 1991; *The Times*, 29.09.91.
62　Martin Jacques, *Sunday Times*, 12.07.92.
63　Ibid.; Interview, Martin Jacques, 19.09.03.
64　Tony Blair, 'Drawing on Inner Strength', *Guardian*, 30.06.92.
65　Interview, James Purnell, 22.07.03.
66　Interview, Barbara Amiel, 18.09.03.
67　*Sunday Times Magazine*, 19.07.92.
68　Macintyre (1999), p.269.
69　Rentoul (2001), pp.186–7.
70　Private correspondence.
71　Interviews, Gerald Kaufman, 10.09.03; Lord Hattersley, 11.11.03.
72　Letter, Neil Kinnock to author, 22.09.03.
73　Interview, Roz Preston, 25.09.03.
74　McSmith (1996), p.330.
75　Interview.
76　Correspondence with author, Peter Mandelson, 31.03.04.
77　Interview.
78　*Sun*, 03.03.93, quoted in Rentoul (2001), p.200.
79　Interview, Tim Allan, 05.08.03.
80　Patrick Wintour and Michael White, *Guardian*, 01.03.93.
81　Interview.
82　*Independent*, 07.10.93.
83　Interview, Tim Allan, 05.08.03.
84　*Daily Telegraph*, 26.06.93. The speech was given at Alloa on 25 June 1993.
85　Will Self, *Independent Magazine*, 03.06.95, quoted in Rentoul (2001), p.249.
86　Interview.
87　*Guardian*, 12.09.92.
88　*Renewal*, Vol. 1, No. 4, October 1993;

Fabian Review, Vol. 105, No. 5, September/October 1993.
89 BBC TV, *On the Record*, 17.01.93.
90 Interview, Neal Lawson, 23.09.03.
91 *The Times*, 04.03.96.
92 Interview, Lord Butler, 25.02.03.
93 Interview.
94 McSmith (1996), p.328.
95 Interview.
96 *Financial Times*, 27.09.93.
97 Worcester and Mortimer (1999), p.98.

14: Peter Mandelson

1 Interview, Don Macintyre, 28.02.03. The best book on Mandelson is Macintyre's biography (1999). A less sympathetic but still insightful book is Routledge (1999).
2 Anderson and Mann (1997), pp.362–7.
3 Rentoul (2001), pp.131–2.
4 See Mandelson and Liddle (1996).
5 Anthony Howard, *Sunday Times*, 17.01.99.
6 Private correspondence.
7 Macintyre (1999), pp.88–91.
8 Mandelson to Andrew Billen, *Observer*, 25.02.95.
9 *Guardian*, 25.01.85.
10 Mandelson to Julian Langdon, *Guardian*, 21.12.95.
11 *New Statesman*, 08.03.96.
12 Private correspondence.
13 Interview, Peter Mandelson, 16.10.03.
14 Private correspondence.
15 Interview; Anderson and Mann (1996), p.365.
16 Private correspondence.
17 Interview, Peter Mandelson, 29.03.04.
18 *Independent*, 17.04.99.
19 Private correspondence.
20 Andy McSmith, *Observer*, 29.09.96.
21 Interview, Colin Byrne, 15.08.03.
22 Interview, Peter Mandelson, 02.03.04.
23 Interview.
24 Interview, Peter Mandelson, 02.03.04.
25 Interview, Clive Russell, 20.08.03.
26 Interview.
27 Interview, Richard Stott, 03.11.03.
28 Interview.
29 Interview, Robin Cook, 18.11.03.
30 Interview, Tim Allan, 26.06.03.
31 Interview, Clive Russell, 20.08.03.
32 Interview.
33 Interview.

34 Routledge (1998), p.196.
35 Interview, Clive Russell, 20.08.03.
36 Interview.
37 Interview.
38 Interview.
39 Interview, Peter Mandelson, 02.12.03.
40 Macintyre (1999), p.321.
41 Ibid.
42 Interview.
43 Private correspondence.
44 Interview.
45 Private correspondence.
46 Interview, Mark Adams, 21.07.03.
47 Interview.
48 Interview.
49 Interview.
50 Interview.
51 Interview.
52 Interview.
53 Interview.
54 Macintyre (1999), p.500.
55 Rawnsley (2000), p.221–2.
56 *Evening Standard*, 22.12.98: the article was written by Peter Kellner and set the media ball rolling on that day. Interview; see also *Guardian*, 22.12.98.
57 Correspondence with author, Lance Price, 11.11.03.
58 Macintyre (2000), p.505.
59 Diary, Lance Price, 23.12.98.
60 Interview.
61 BBC TV, *Tabloid Tales*, 08.05.03.
62 Macintyre (1999), pp.509–10; Rentoul (2001), pp.468–70.
63 *Independent*, 17.04.99.
64 Anthony King, *Evening Standard*, 12.01.99.
65 Interview.
66 See Chapter 35 for the details of this episode.
67 Interview.
68 Kevin Maguire, *Mirror*, 17.04.99.
69 Interview.
70 Interview.
71 Mandelson to Steve Crawshaw, *Independent*, 17.10.99.
72 Private correspondence.
73 Hennessy (2001), p.496.
74 Interview.
75 Hennessy (2001), pp.498, 527.
76 For the full details of the story see Jones (2001), pp.265–82.
77 *The Times*, 09.02.01.
78 Private correspondence.
79 *Hansard*, 18.01.01, Col. 351.
80 *The Times*, 23.01.01.
81 Private correspondence.
82 Private correspondence.
83 *The Times*, 09.02.01.

84 Philip Webster, *The Times*, 09.02.01: this is a very well-sourced article, apparently heavily informed by Campbell.
85 Interview.
86 *Evening Standard*, 23.01.01.
87 Interview.
88 Interview.
89 *The Times*, 09.02.01.
90 BBC TV, *Tabloid Tales*, 08.05.03.
91 *Daily Mail*, 24.01.01; *Sun*, 24.01.01; Jones (2001), p.278.
92 Interview, Philip Webster, 20.08.03.
93 Interview.
94 *Guardian*, 25.01.01.
95 Private correspondence.
96 Interview.
97 Interview.
98 Interview.
99 Interview.
100 Andrew Grice, *Independent*, 21.04.03.
101 Interview.
102 Interview.
103 Interview, Robin Cook, 18.11.03.
104 Mandelson and Liddle (2002), pp.ix–xlix.
105 Andrew Rawnsley, *Observer*, 25.05.03.
106 Interview, Dennis Kavanagh, 08.11.03.
107 Interview, Peter Mandelson, 02.03.04.
108 Interview.
109 Private correspondence.
110 Interview.
111 Interview.
112 Interview, Peter Mandelson, 30.04.03.

15: Leadership Election, 1994

1 Interview, Andy McSmith, 02.09.03.
2 Interview, Lance Price, 30.08.03.
3 Interview, Andrew Rawnsley, 02.04.03.
4 Interview.
5 Interview, Anthony Howard, 02.10.03.
6 Interview.
7 Interview, Tim Allan, 05.08.03.
8 Interview.
9 Interview.
10 Interview, Alan Haworth, 10.10.03.
11 Interview, Margaret Beckett, 16.10.03.
12 Private correspondence.
13 Interview, Peter Kellner, Baroness Ashton, 11.10.03.
14 Interview.
15 Interview, John Edmonds, 14.10.03.
16 Interview. Murray Elder had known Brown since nursery school. See Naughtie (2001), pp.253–4.
17 Interview, Andy McSmith, 02.09.03.
18 Interview, Baroness Jay, 15.10.03.
19 Interview.
20 Interview, John Carr, 02.09.03.
21 Interview.
22 A detailed account of the OMOV debate can be found in Rentoul (2001), pp.207–18.
23 Jon Cruddas agreed that the vote would not have been won without the Prescott intervention: Interview, Jon Cruddas, 17.09.03.
24 Interview, John Monks, 11.11.02.
25 *Sunday Times*, 03.10.93.
26 Interview, Neal Lawson, 23.09.03.
27 Toby Helm, *Sunday Telegraph*, 28.12.93, quoted in Rentoul (2001), p.208.
28 Interview.
29 Interview, Andy McSmith, 02.09.03.
30 Interview, Peter Kellner, Baroness Ashton, 11.10.03.
31 Rentoul (2001), p.217.
32 Interview.
33 Interview, Richard Stott, 21.11.02.
34 Interview.
35 Interview.
36 Interview, Alan Haworth, 10.10.03.
37 Francis Elliott, Colin Brown, *Sunday Telegraph*, 01.12.02; Rentoul (2001), pp.217–18; Interview, Lord Hattersley, 11.11.03.
38 Interview.
39 *Sunday Times*, 04.05.97.
40 Ashdown (1997), p.259.
41 Interview.
42 Interview, Tim Allan, 05.08.03.
43 Interview.
44 Interview, James Purnell, 22.07.03.
45 Gordon Brown, BBC TV, *The Wilderness Years*, 18.12.95.
46 Interview.
47 Interview.
48 Interview.
49 Interview.
50 Interview.
51 Interview, Sarah Sands, 21.10.03; *Daily Telegraph*, 30.01.03.
52 Interview, Sarah Baxter, 17.10.03.
53 Interview.
54 *Evening Standard*, 12.05.94.
55 Interviews, Sarah Baxter, 17.10.03; Sarah Sands, 21.10.03.
56 Seldon (1997), pp.461–2.
57 Interview, William Hague, 09.09.03.
58 Interview, Robin Cook, 25.02.03.
59 Interview, Gerald Kaufman, 10.09.03.
60 Whatever its qualities as a drama, it

was far too short on fact to be taken seriously: 'As history, it is balls,' wrote Robert Harris, *Sunday Times*, 19.09.03.

61 Interview, Andy McSmith, 02.09.03.
62 Interview, Philip Webster, 20.08.03; *The Times*, 13.05.94.
63 Interview, Ian Hargreaves, 23.11.03.
64 Rentoul (2001), p.226.
65 Interview, Lord Hollick, 19.02.04.
66 Interview, John Carr, 02.09.03.
67 Interview.
68 Interview.
69 Interview.
70 Private correspondence.
71 Gould (1998), p.195.
72 Rentoul (2001), p.230.
73 Interview.
74 Interview.
75 Interview, Margaret Beckett, 16.10.03.
76 Charlie Whelan, quoted in Routledge (1998), p.194.
77 Interview.
78 Interview.
79 Ibid.
80 Rentoul, pp.228–9.
81 Macintyre (1999), pp.286–306; Gould (1998), pp.195–9.
82 Naughtie (2001), p.64.
83 Private correspondence.
84 Interview.
85 Interview.
86 Interview, Gerald Kaufman, 10.09.03.
87 Interview, Nick Ryden, 18.07.03.
88 Interview.
89 Interview.
90 Interview; Rentoul (2001), p.236.
91 Interview.
92 Philip Webster, *The Times*, 30.05.94.
93 Routledge (1998), pp.204–5.
94 Interview.
95 A good account is Colin Brown and Matthew d'Ancona, *Sunday Telegraph*, 08.06.03.
96 Interview.
97 *Guardian*, 06.06.03.
98 Private correspondence.
99 Interview.
100 Interview.
101 Interview.
102 *The Times*, 02.06.94.
103 Interview, Robin Cook, 25.02.03.
104 McSmith (1996), p.279.
105 Interview, Jack Straw, 11.11.03.
106 Interview, Peter Kilfoyle, 16.07.03.
107 Interview, Lord Bragg, 10.09.03.
108 Interview, Lord Levy, 16.09.03.
109 Tony Blair Campaign Committee: income and expenditure report, Labour Party Archives.
110 Interview; Nick Cohen and Paul Routledge, *Independent on Sunday*, 02.10.94.
111 Rentoul (2001), pp.359–60.
112 Barry Cox, quoted in Rentoul (2001), pp.359–60.
113 Correspondence with author, John Carr, 06.01.04.
114 Interview, James Purnell, 22.07.03.
115 Rentoul (2001), p.240.
116 Interview, James Purnell, 22.07.03.
117 Interview, John Edmonds, 14.10.03.
118 Interview.
119 Private correspondence.
120 Patrick Wintour, *Guardian*, 22.07.94.
121 Quoted in Rentoul (2001), p.246.

16: Derry Irvine

1 Interview, Tim Allan, 05.08.03.
2 Howard Dawber has written a very good brief account of his life for Rosen (2001), pp.302–4; Egan (1999) is useful if over-critical.
3 Andrew Grice, *Sunday Times*, 23.11.97.
4 Rentoul (2001), p.54.
5 Interview.
6 Interview.
7 *Independent*, 11.04.97.
8 Egan (1999), p.17.
9 Quoted in Egan (1999), p.57.
10 David Altaras, quoted in Egan (1999), p.107.
11 Sopel (1995), p.41.
12 Maggie Rae, quoted in Egan (1999), p.62.
13 Interview.
14 Interview.
15 Interview.
16 Interview.
17 Interview.
18 Interview.
19 Interview.
20 *Observer*, 11.05.97.
21 Robert Harris, *Sunday Times*, 04.05.97.
22 Interview.
23 Diary, 03.05.95: Ashdown (2000), p.310.
24 *New Statesman*, 06.12.96.
25 Interview, Rhodri Morgan, 25.09.03.
26 Interview.
27 Interview, Lord Robertson, 18.09.03.
28 Interview.
29 Interview, Ron Davies, 25.09.03.
30 *New Statesman*, 06.12.96.
31 *Sunday Times*, 06.04.97.
32 Diary, 04.09.94: Ashdown (2000), p.275.

33 Don Macintyre, *Independent*, 11.04.97.
34 Interview.
35 Interview, Ron Davies, 25.09.03.
36 Interview.
37 Vernon Bogdanor in Seldon (2001), pp.139–56.
38 Interview.
39 Interview.
40 *Scotsman*, 24.02.01.
41 Interview.
42 Letter, Dennis Kavanagh to author, 06.12.03.
43 Frances Gibb, *The Times*, 16.04.02.
44 Interview; Private correspondence.
45 Michael Beloff QC, *Sunday Telegraph*, 25.01.04.
46 Melanie Phillips, *Daily Mail*, 08.01.03.
47 Interview.
48 Interview.
49 Interview.
50 Interview.
51 David Cracknell et al., *Sunday Times*, 15.06.03; Colin Brown, *Sunday Times*, 15.6.03; Nicholas Watt and Clare Dyers, *Guardian*, 13.06.03.
52 Interview.
53 Lord Alexander, *Financial Times*, 13.06.03.
54 *Sunday Times*, 15.06.03.
55 Interview.

17: *Clause IV*

1 Interview, Stan Greenberg, 21.11.03.
2 Interview, Alan Haworth, 10.10.03.
3 Interview, Lord Levy, 16.09.03.
4 Interview.
5 Interview.
6 Don Macintyre, *Independent*, 11.09.94.
7 Interview, Lord Sawyer, 13.09.03.
8 Interview, Alan Haworth, 10.10.03.
9 Interview.
10 Interviews.
11 Interview.
12 Interview.
13 Interview, Lord Sawyer, 13.09.03.
14 Interview, Alan Haworth, 10.10.03.
15 Interviews.
16 Interview.
17 Interview, David Hill, 14.01.03.
18 Seldon (2001), p.593.
19 Speech to Fabian Society on the 50th anniversary of the 1945 General Election victory, 05.07.95.
20 Rentoul (2001), p.253.
21 Ibid., p.254; Fielding (2003), pp.74–8; Taylor (1997), pp.168–91.
22 Interview, Philip Wilson, 24.07.03.

23 Tony Blair, 'Forging a New Agenda', *Marxism Today*, October 1991.
24 Interview, Barbara Amiel, 18.09.03.
25 Archer Committee (1993).
26 Interview, Jack Straw, 11.11.03; Jack Straw to Anne McElvoy, *The Times*, 22.4.95.
27 Will Hutton, *Renewal*, Vol. 1, No. 3, quoted in Taylor (1997), p.169.
28 BBC TV, *Breakfast With Frost*, 12.06.94.
29 Interview, Peter Kellner, 11.10.03.
30 Interview.
31 Interview, Elaine Kamarck, 18.09.03.
32 Interview.
33 Interview, Tim Allan, 05.08.03.
34 Alastair Campbell in Gould (1998), p.215.
35 Interview, Colin Fisher, 09.12.03.
36 Macintyre (1999), pp.315–16.
37 Interview.
38 Gould (1998), pp.215–19.
39 Rentoul (2001), p.255.
40 Private correspondence.
41 Interview.
42 Interview, Colin Fisher, 09.12.03.
43 Interview, Peter Mandelson, 16.10.03.
44 Gould (1998), p.218.
45 Macintyre (1999), pp.314–15.
46 Gould (1998), pp.219–20.
47 Alastair Campbell in Gould (1998), p.222.
48 Interview.
49 *The Times*, 22.04.95.
50 Brown (1997), pp.285–94; Fielding (2003), p.76.
51 Gould (1998), p.221.
52 Ibid.
53 Interview.
54 Interview, John Edmonds, 14.10.03.
55 Interview.
56 Interview.
57 Interview.
58 Interview, Peter Hain, 22.09.03.
59 Interview, John Monks, 11.11.02.
60 Interview, Ken Cameron, 24.09.03.
61 Private correspondence.
62 Interview.
63 *Financial Times*, 05.10.94.
64 Interview.
65 Rentoul (2001), p.256.
66 *Herald* (Glasgow), 07.10.94.
67 Interview.
68 *Guardian*, 07.10.94.
69 Fielding (2003), p.74.
70 Anne McElvoy, *The Times*, 22.04.95.
71 Private correspondence.
72 Sally Morgan in Gould (1998), p.228.

73 Interview.
74 Gould (1998), p.224.
75 *The Times*, 26.01.95.
76 Interview, Margaret McDonagh, 17.09.03.
77 *Guardian*, 01.05.95, quoted in Rentoul (2001), p.262.
78 Kampfner (1999), pp.101–3.
79 Interview; *New Statesman*, 27.01.95.
80 Mandelson and Liddle (1996), p.54; *Guardian*, 09.02.95.
81 Gould (1998), p.226.
82 Interview.
83 Interview.
84 Interview.
85 Interview.
86 Don Macintyre and John Rentoul, *Independent*, 06.03.95.
87 Interview, Lord Robertson, 18.09.03.
88 Ibid.
89 *Sunday Times*, 30.04.95.
90 *The Times*, 22.04.95.
91 Interview, Tony Benn, 02.04.03.
92 Tudor Jones, in Brivati and Heffernan (2000), p.317.
93 John Williams, *Mirror*, 01.05.95.

18: Eric Anderson

1 Henry Porter, *Daily Telegraph*, 04.10.94.
2 Private correspondence.
3 Dimbleby (1994), pp.74–5.
4 Interviews.
5 Interviews.
6 Interview, Alastair Singleton, 25.09.03.
7 Interview, Nick Ryden, 18.07.03.
8 Interview.
9 Interview, Lord Jenkins, 05.11.02.
10 Interview.
11 Private correspondence.
12 *Independent*, 19.01.97.
13 BBC Radio 4, *Desert Island Discs*, 23.11.96.
14 *Guardian*, 28.11.96.
15 Anderson in the *Daily Record*, 24.03.98.
16 *The Times*, 15.10.97.
17 Press Association, 14.10.97.
18 *Scotsman*, 24.11.97.
19 *Financial Times*, 10.02.98.
20 Interview, Lord Hattersley, 11.11.03.
21 Interview, Sir Michael Boyce, 14.04.04.

19: General Election, 1995–97

1 Diary, 20.06.96: Ashdown (2000), p.440.
2 Private correspondence.

3 Seldon (1997), p.134.
4 See Seldon and Hickson (2004).
5 *Observer*, 27.04.97.
6 Interview.
7 Private correspondence.
8 *New Statesman*, 29.07.94.
9 Interview.
10 Private correspondence.
11 Interview.
12 Private correspondence.
13 Interview, Gavyn Davies, 01.12.03.
14 Interview.
15 Interview, Andrew Graham, 21.10.03.
16 *New Statesman*, 04.10.96.
17 See Hutton (1995), Kay (1993) and Kay (1996).
18 Interview, Will Hutton, 05.09.03.
19 *Herald* (Glasgow), 09.01.96.
20 Interview.
21 Interview, Will Hutton, 05.09.03.
22 Interview.
23 Interview, John Kay, 10.11.03.
24 Interview.
25 *New Statesman*, 04.10.96.
26 Philip Webster, *The Times*, 28.09.94.
27 *Financial Times*, 23.05.95; *Independent*, 23.05.95.
28 Keegan (2003), p.148; Private correspondence.
29 Interview.
30 Interview, Conor Ryan, 02.12.03.
31 Interview, Nick Pearce, 24.10.03.
32 Interview.
33 Interview.
34 Interview.
35 Interview, Michael Barber, 05.08.03.
36 Diary, 29.01.96: Ashdown (2000), p.383.
37 *Independent*, 29.01.96.
38 Kavanagh and Seldon (1999), p.242.
39 Interview, Lord Renwick, 02.12.03.
40 Interview, Lord Burns, 16.10.03.
41 Interview, Lord Renwick, 02.12.03.
42 Interview.
43 Hugo Young, *Guardian*, 01.04.97.
44 Martin Jacques and Stuart Hall, *Observer*, 13.04.97.
45 Charles Leadbetter, *New Statesman*, 30.08.96.
46 Interview.
47 Interview; Private correspondence.
48 *Observer*, 10.09.95.
49 Quoted by Kavanagh in Seldon (2001), p.6.
50 Martin J. Smith, in Brivati and Heffernan (2000), p.145.
51 Interview.
52 Private correspondence.
53 Interview.
54 Interview, Lord Sawyer, 13.09.03.

55 Interview, Jon Cruddas, 17.09.03.
56 Private correspondence.
57 Rentoul (2001), p.268.
58 *Observer*, 10.09.95.
59 Interview, Helen Liddell, 10.07.03.
60 Interview, Margaret McDonagh, 17.09.03.
61 Interview.
62 Interview.
63 Rentoul (2001), p.271.
64 Jones (2000), p.22.
65 Interview, Lord Sawyer, 13.09.03.
66 Interview, Jon Cruddas, 17.09.03.
67 Interviews.
68 Interview, Ken Follett, 03.10.03.
69 David McKie, *Guardian*, 30.01.95.
70 Interview, John Carr, 02.09.03.
71 Interview.
72 *Sun*, 09.04.92; Interview; for a discussion of the press for the 1997 election from a Tory perspective, see Seldon (1997), pp.706–13.
73 Interview.
74 Interview.
75 Interview.
76 Interview, Richard Stott, 03.11.03.
77 Ibid.
78 Interview, Irwin Stelzer, 18.10.03.
79 Letter, Jane Reed to author, 06.11.03.
80 Interview, Alison Clark, 05.11.03.
81 Interview.
82 *The Times Magazine*, 30.09.95.
83 *Guardian*, 17.07.95.
84 Interview.
85 Interview, Irwin Stelzer, 18.10.03.
86 Interview.
87 Interview, Irwin Stelzer, 18.10.03.
88 Interview, Trevor Kavanagh, 20.10.03.
89 Interview, Irwin Stelzer, 18.10.03.
90 Interview, Trevor Kavanagh, 20.10.03.
91 Private correspondence.
92 Butler and Kavanagh (1997), p.160.
93 Interview.
94 Interview.
95 Interview.
96 Interview, Mary Ann Sieghart, 12.02.03.
97 Interview, Sir Peter Stothard, 26.02.03.
98 Seldon (1997), p.710.
99 Interview.
100 Interview.
101 Interview.
102 Interview, Paul Dacre, 09.10.03.
103 Interview, David Seymour, 20.10.03.
104 Interview.
105 *Observer*, 10.09.95.
106 Seldon (1997), p.708.
107 Letter, Charles Moore to author, 19.10.03.
108 Interview.
109 Interview.
110 Henry Porter, *Guardian*, 17.07.95.
111 Interview, Paul Johnson, 02.12.03.
112 The best source is Butler and Kavanagh (1997).
113 Interview.
114 Interview.
115 Interview, Paul Routledge, 24.02.03.
116 Interview.
117 Interview, Charlie Whelan, 10.11.03.
118 Robert Harris, *Sunday Times*, 04.05.97.
119 Interview.
120 Private correspondence.
121 Interview, Tim Allan, 05.08.03.
122 Interview, Charlie Whelan, 10.11.03; Interview.
123 Lynda Lee-Potter, *Daily Mail*, 17.04.98.
124 Interview, Lord Butler, 25.02.03.
125 Interview.
126 Interview.
127 Interview.
128 Interview.
129 Interview.
130 Interview.
131 Interview.
132 Letter, Alastair Campbell to author, 30.07.97, in Seldon (1997), p.722.
133 Interview.
134 Robert Harris, *Sunday Times*, 04.05.97.
135 Hugo Young, *Guardian*, 01.05.97.
136 Proud (2003), p.144.
137 Robert Harris, *Sunday Times*, 04.05.97.
138 Interview, John Major, 09.04.03.
139 Ibid.
140 Interview, John Burton, 07.07.03.
141 Interview, Tim Allan, 10.09.03.
142 Interview, Margaret McDonagh, 17.09.03.
143 Interview, John Major, 09.04.03.
144 Private correspondence.

20: Roy Jenkins

1 Robert Harris, *Daily Telegraph*, 06.01.03; John Kampfner, *Daily Express*, 06.01.03.
2 Paddy Ashdown, BBC TV, 'Happy Birthday Mr Prime Minister', 30.04.03.
3 Interview, Lord Jenkins, 05.11.02.
4 Diary, 14.07.93: Ashdown (2000), pp.228–9.
5 Interview, Lord Lester, 05.12.03.
6 Diary, 01.12.93: Ashdown (2000),

pp.242–4.
7   Interview, Lord Ashdown, 15.01.04.
8   Interview.
9   Diary, 04.09.94: Ashdown (2000), pp.275–8.
10 Martin Kettle, *Guardian*, 07.01.03; Interview, Lord Holme, 04.11.03.
11 Diary, 03.05.95: Ashdown (2000), pp.310–14.
12 Interviews, Lord McNally, 22.10.03; Lord Holme, 04.11.03.
13 Letter, Lady Jenkins to author, 27.09.03.
14 Private correspondence.
15 Diary, 14.11.95: Ashdown (2000), p.360.
16 Diary, 12.12.95: Ashdown (2000), p.366.
17 Diary, 24.10.95: Ashdown (2000), p.346.
18 Interview, Lady Jenkins, 17.09.03; Letter, Lady Jenkins to author, 27.09.03.
19 Diary, 17.01.96: Ashdown (2000), p.380.
20 Diary, 29.01.96: Ashdown (2000), p.383.
21 Naughtie (2001), p.158.
22 Diary, 03.05.95: Ashdown (2000), pp.310–14.
23 Macintyre (2000), pp.389–98.
24 Private correspondence.
25 Diary, 02.05.96: Ashdown (2000), p.424.
26 Diary, 20.06.96: Ashdown (2000), pp.439–40.
27 Private correspondence.
28 Diary, 08.05.96: Ashdown (2000), pp.424–9.
29 Diary, 04.12.96: Ashdown (2000), pp.484–6.
30 Interview, Robert Harris, 23.10.03; the biography is John Wilson's book (1973).
31 Ashdown (2000), p.459.
32 Diary, 05.09.96: Ashdown (2000), pp.456–8.
33 Letter, Lady Jenkins to author, 27.09.03.
34 Interview.
35 Diary, 20.01.97: Ashdown (2000), pp.509–10.
36 Macintyre (2000), p.394.
37 Interview.
38 Diary, 01.05.97: Ashdown (2000), pp.555–8.
39 Interview, Robert Harris, 23.10.03.
40 Diary, 02.05.97: Ashdown (2000), pp.558–9.
41 Macintyre (2000), p.395.
42 Interview, Lord Holme, 04.11.03.

43 Naughtie (2001), p.158.
44 *Guardian*, 01.10.97.
45 Naughtie (2001), p.172; Jackie Ashley, *New Statesman*, 12.01.01.
46 Interview.
47 Private correspondence.
48 David Lipsey, in Jefferys (2002), p.111.
49 Interview.
50 Diary, 03.07.98: Ashdown (2002), p.233.
51 Interview, Lord Oakeshott, 12.11.03.
52 Diary, 29.10.98: Ashdown (2002), p.316.
53 Andrew Adonis and Patrick Wintour, *Observer*, 21.09.97.
54 Interview.
55 Interview.
56 Macintyre (2000), p.393.
57 Interview, Lord Holme, 04.11.03.
58 Private correspondence.
59 Interview, Chris Patten, 10.10.03.
60 Interview, Lord Oakeshott, 12.11.03; Naughtie (2001), p.274.
61 Robert Harris says, though, that he remained on warm terms and indulgent towards him: *Daily Telegraph*, 06.01.03.
62 Private correspondence.
63 Roy Jenkins, *Evening Standard*, 27.04.00.
64 Polly Toynbee, *Guardian*, 28.03.03.
65 Diary, 13.11.96: Ashdown (2000), p.477.

21: Death of Diana

1   *Guardian*, 08.09.97.
2   Interview, Michael Gove, 09.07.03.
3   Interview, Elaine Kamarck, 18.09.03.
4   Blair to Piers Morgan, *Mirror*, 29.07.97.
5   Interview.
6   BBC TV, 'Cabinet Confidential', presented by Michael Cockerell, 07.11.01.
7   *Independent*, 09.08.97.
8   *Northern Echo*, 11.09.97.
9   Interview.
10 *Northern Echo*, 08.08.97.
11 *Independent*, 09.08.97.
12 *The Economist*, 09.08.97.
13 Ibid.
14 *Mirror*, 08.08.97.
15 *The Economist*, 09.08.97.
16 *Sunday Times*, 31.08.97.
17 Interview.
18 Morton (1998), p.286.
19 Margaret Driscoll, *Sunday Times*, 07.09.97.

20 Rawnsley (2001), p.60.
21 *Sunday Times*, 07.09.97.
22 Ibid.
23 Rawnsley (2001), p.60.
24 *Sunday Times*, 07.09.97.
25 Lacey (2002), p.5.
26 Interview, John Burton, 07.07.03.
27 Interview, Philip Wilson, 24.07.03.
28 Lacey (2002), p.355.
29 *Independent on Sunday*, 14.09.97.
30 Interview.
31 *Sunday Times*, 07.09.97.
32 Rawnsley (2001), p.64.
33 Lacey (2002), p.358.
34 *Sunday Times*, 07.09.97.
35 Interview.
36 Lacey (2002), pp.5–7.
37 Rawnsley (2001), p.68; Lacey
     (2002), pp.12–13.
38 Interview.
39 Stephen Castle, *Independent on
     Sunday*, 14.09.97.
40 Simon Heffer, *New Statesman*,
     28.08.98.
41 Interview.
42 Rentoul (2001), p.341.
43 Martin Jacques, *European*, 01.10.97.

22: Alastair Campbell

1   Interview, Philip Gould, 22.10.03.
2   Jayant Chauda in Rosen (2000),
     p.102.
3   Campbell to Valerie Grove, *The
     Times*, 09.09.94.
4   Alastair Campbell, *Daily Mirror*,
     10.06.94.
5   Campbell to Bill Hagerty, *The Times*,
     12.06.00.
6   Private correspondence.
7   Interview, Joe Haines, 27.10.03.
8   Gould (1998), p.183.
9   Interview, Richard Stott, 03.11.03.
10 Interview, David Seymour, 20.10.03.
11 Oborne (1999), p.88.
12 *Sunday Mirror*, 11.09.88.
13 Oborne (1999), p.106.
14 Quoted in Seymour and Seymour
     (2003), p.186.
15 Interview, Neil Kinnock, 03.09.03.
16 Campbell to Valerie Grove, *The
     Times*, 09.09.94.
17 Interview.
18 Interview, Joe Haines, 27.10.03.
19 Interview, Tim Allan, 26.06.03.
20 Interview.
21 Oborne (1999), p.108.
22 Interview, Andy McSmith, 02.09.03.
23 Stothard (2003), p.43.
24 Routledge (1998), p.206.
25 Private correspondence.

26 Oborne (1999), p.108.
27 Interview, Andrew Grice, 03.09.03.
28 Interview, Philip Webster, 03.09.03.
29 Interview, Andy McSmith, 02.09.03.
30 Interview.
31 Gould (1998), p.213.
32 Ibid., p.214.
33 Oborne (1999), p.109.
34 Interview, Neil Kinnock, 03.09.03.
35 Gould (1998), pp.214–15.
36 Interview, Nicholas Jones, 09.04.03;
     Jones (1999), p.44.
37 Interview, Michael Brunson,
     06.02.03.
38 Diary, 03.05.95: Ashdown (2000),
     p.314.
39 Gould (1998), p.219.
40 Jones (2001), pp.211–13.
41 *Today*, 06.10.94.
42 *Daily Mail*, 16.01.95.
43 Interview.
44 Gould (1998), p.216.
45 Interview.
46 Private correspondence.
47 Letter, Dennis Kavanagh to author,
     06.12.03.
48 Kavanagh and Seldon (1999), p.254;
     Oborne (1999), pp.215–18.
49 Interview.
50 Jones (2001), p.80.
51 Kavanagh and Seldon (1999), p.258.
52 Quoted in Hennessy (2001), p.486.
53 Diary, 02.09.98: Ashdown (2002),
     p.249.
54 *Daily Mail*, 08.06.00.
55 Diary, 09.06.00, Lance Price.
56 Jones (1999), pp.224–30.
57 Bill Hagerty, *The Times*, 12.06.00.
58 Interview, Tim Allan, 22.01.03.
59 Interview, Michael White, 22.01.03.
60 Interview.
61 Mary Ann Sieghart, *The Times*,
     14.07.00.
62 Interview.
63 Interview.
64 Rosen (2000), p.102.
65 Kavanagh and Seldon (1999), p.259.
66 Interview.
67 Interview.
68 Interview.
69 Interview, Lance Price, 30.08.03.
70 Interview.
71 Rawnsley (2000), pp.245, 448–51.
72 Kavanagh and Seldon (1999), p.283.
73 Interview.
74 Interview.
75 Interview.
76 Interview, Helen Liddell, 10.07.03.
77 Interview.
78 *The Times*, 10.01.04.
79 Interview.

80 Interview.
81 Stothard (2003), p.44.
82 Interview, Paul Dacre, 09.10.03.
83 Interview.
84 *Spectator*, 09.03.02.
85 Interview.
86 Interview.
87 *Observer*, 27.07.03.
88 *Sunday Telegraph*, 31.08.03.
89 Interview.
90 Oral Evidence, Foreign Affairs
    Select Committee, 25.06.03.
91 *Sunday Times*, 29.06.03.
92 Diary, 04.07.03, Alastair Campbell.
    Submitted as evidence to the
    Hutton Inquiry.
93 Lord Hutton, 'Report of the Inquiry
    into the Circumstances Surrounding
    the Death of Dr David Kelly',
    28.01.04, Chapter 12.
94 Diary, 06.07.03, Alastair Campbell.
    Submitted as evidence to the
    Hutton Inquiry.
95 Lord Hutton, 'Report of the Inquiry
    into the Circumstances Surrounding
    the Death of Dr David Kelly',
    28.01.04, Chapter 12.
96 *Guardian*, 29.01.04.
97 *The Times*, 10.01.04.
98 Interview; *The Times*, 10.01.04.
99 *Observer*, 31.08.03.
100 Michael White, *Guardian*, 26.01.99.
101 *The Times*, 12.05.00.
102 Interview.
103 *Daily Mirror*, 03.07.00.
104 *The Times*, 11.01.04.

23: The Euro Decision

1   Diary, 21.10.97: Ashdown (2002),
    p.104.
2   Interview.
3   Interview, Bryan Gould, 08.07.03;
    Interview.
4   *Renewal*, Vol. 1, No. 4, October 1993.
5   Diary, 04.09.94: Ashdown (2000),
    p.276.
6   Brivati and Heffernan (2000), p.344.
7   Diary, 06.11.95: Ashdown (2000),
    p.354.
8   *Irish Times*, 05.09.95.
9   Interview, Lord Renwick, 02.12.03.
10 Interview, Sir John Kerr, 26.09.03.
11 Interview.
12 *Sun*, 17.04.97.
13 Ibid., 22.04.97; Rentoul (2001),
    p.312.
14 In May 1997 Doug Henderson had
    been appointed to the Foreign
    Office as Minister of State with
    responsibility for European affairs.

15 Interview, Lord Simon, 06.11.03.
16 Ibid.
17 Ibid.
18 Rawnsley (2001), pp.74–5.
19 Interview, Tim Allan, 26.06.03.
20 Rawnsley (2001), p.75.
21 Interview.
22 Interview.
23 Interview.
24 Interview.
25 Stephens (2001a), p.72.
26 Rawnsley (2001), p.75; Rentoul
    (2001), p.335.
27 Stephens (2001a), p.69.
28 Interview, Robert Cooper, 04.09.03.
29 Interview.
30 Interview, Sir John Kerr, 26.09.03.
31 Kampfner (1999), pp.113–15.
32 Interview.
33 Interview.
34 *Sunday Times*, 31.08.97.
35 Pym and Kochan (1998), pp.133–7.
    Their book provides the best single
    account of the October episode.
36 Robert Peston, *Financial Times*,
    26.09.97.
37 Interview, Robert Peston, 16.10.03.
38 Private correspondence.
39 Keegan (2003), p.307.
40 Paul Eastham, *Daily Mail*, 13.10.97.
41 Tony Bevins, *Independent*, 14.10.97.
42 Pym and Kochan (1998), pp.138–9.
43 Ibid., p.140.
44 Interview, Philip Webster, 24.09.03.
45 Ibid.
46 *The Times*, 18.10.97.
47 Interview, Philip Webster, 24.09.03.
48 Interview.
49 Interview, Philip Webster, 24.09.03.
50 Interview.
51 Interview.
52 *The Times*, 18.10.97.
53 Interview.
54 Interview, Charlie Whelan, 10.11.03.
55 Pym and Kochan (1998), p.148.
56 Rawnsley (2001), p.86.
57 Interview.
58 Interview.
59 Interview.
60 Keegan (2003), p.303.
61 Interview, Tim Allan, 05.08.03.
62 Interview.
63 Private correspondence.
64 Interview, Sir Alan Budd, 05.12.03.
65 Interview, Lord Simon, 06.11.03.
66 Rawnsley (2000), p.86.
67 Interview.
68 Naughtie (2001), p.367.
69 Interview.
70 Stephens (2001a), p.72.
71 Ibid., p.70.

72 Interview.
73 Interview.
74 Interview, Andy Neather, 20.10.03.
75 Interview, Sir John Kerr, 26.09.03.
76 Interview.
77 Interview.
78 Interview, Simon Buckby, 03.11.03.
79 Interview.
80 *Hansard*, 23.02.99, Col. 179.
81 Interview, David Clark, 20.08.03.

24: Jonathan Powell

1 Rachel Sylvester, *Daily Telegraph*, 05.05.01.
2 Lord Falconer, *Daily Telegraph*, 05.05.01.
3 *New Statesman*, 20.11.98; *Independent*, 27.09.03.
4 *Daily Telegraph*, 05.05.01.
5 *New Statesman*, 20.11.98.
6 *Daily Telegraph*, 05.05.01.
7 Interview.
8 Interview.
9 Interview, Lord Renwick, 02.10.03.
10 Interview, Elaine Kamarck, 18.09.03.
11 Interview, Bruce Reed, 18.09.03.
12 *Sunday Times*, 01.06.97.
13 Naughtie (2001), pp.212–13.
14 Interview.
15 Interview, Elaine Kamarck, 18.09.03.
16 Interview.
17 Interview, Lord Renwick, 02.10.03.
18 *Sunday Times*, 01.06.97.
19 Interview, Lord Powell, 14.04.03.
20 *Daily Telegraph*, 05.05.01.
21 Private correspondence.
22 Interview, Lord Renwick, 02.10.03.
23 Interview.
24 Interview.
25 Interview.
26 Interview.
27 Kavanagh and Seldon (1999), pp.252–3.
28 Interview, Alex Allan, 11.04.03.
29 Interview.
30 Interview.
31 Interview.
32 Rawnsley (2001), p.28.
33 Interview.
34 Interview.
35 Interview.
36 Kampfner (2003), p.100.
37 Interview, Sir John Kerr, 15.09.03.
38 Interview.
39 Interview.
40 *Daily Telegraph*, 05.05.01.
41 Ibid.
42 Interview.

43 Interview.
44 Interview.
45 Private correspondence.
46 *The Times*, 15.04.02.
47 Philip Webster, *The Times*, 15.04.02.
48 Rawnsley (2001), pp.436–8.
49 *Guardian*, 23.02.02.
50 *The Times*, 15.04.02.
51 *Daily Telegraph*, 05.05.01.
52 Ibid.
53 Stothard (2003), p.8.
54 *Daily Telegraph*, 05.05.01.
55 Diary, 21.10.97: Ashdown (2002), p.108.
56 Diary, 18.03.96: Ashdown (2000), p.409.
57 Quoted by Rachel Sylvester, *Daily Telegraph*, 05.05.01.
58 *Daily Telegraph*, 05.05.01.
59 *Belfast Telegraph*, 04.06.01.

25: Good Friday Agreement

1 Interview, Lord Renwick, 02.12.03.
2 Stephens (2004), p.149.
3 Interview.
4 Stephens (2004), p.147.
5 Interview, Lord Williams of Mostyn, 02.04.03.
6 BBC TV, 'Endgame in Ireland', 26.06.01.
7 Interview, Mo Mowlam, 02.12.03.
8 O'Leary (2001), p.450.
9 Diary, 12.11.95: Ashdown (2000), p.355.
10 Interview.
11 Interview, Anthony Lake, 10.09.03.
12 Ibid.
13 Interview.
14 Interview.
15 Interview.
16 Interview, Sir John Chilcot, 10.09.03.
17 Interview.
18 Interview.
19 Interview, Anthony Lake, 10.09.03.
20 Interview, George Mitchell, 03.12.03.
21 Interview, James Steinberg, 02.10.03.
22 *Guardian*, 17.05.97.
23 Interview, David Hill, 14.01.03.
24 Private correspondence.
25 Interview.
26 Interview.
27 Rawnsley (2001), p.126.
28 Interview, Mark Adams, 21.07.03.
29 Interview.
30 Interview, Sir John Chilcot, 10.09.03.
31 Rawnsley (2001), p.123.

32 Interview, Sir John Holmes, 01.04.03.
33 Interview, Sir Christopher Meyer, 02.06.03.
34 Interview, Mo Mowlam, 02.12.03.
35 Private correspondence.
36 Rawnsley (2001), p.125.
37 Interview.
38 Interview, David McKittrick, 05.12.03.
39 Interview.
40 Interview.
41 Private correspondence.
42 BBC TV, 'Endgame in Ireland', 26.06.01.
43 O'Leary (2001), p.455.
44 BBC TV, 'Endgame in Ireland', 26.06.01.
45 Mitchell (1999), p.153.
46 Ibid., pp.152–81.
47 Ibid., p.166.
48 Interview.
49 Interview, George Mitchell, 03.12.03.
50 Rawnsley (2000), p.130; Interview.
51 BBC TV, 'Endgame in Ireland', 26.06.01.
52 Mitchell (1999), p.171.
53 Rawnsley (2000), p.132.
54 Ibid., p.136.
55 Private correspondence.
56 Private correspondence.
57 Interview.
58 Interview.
59 Interview.
60 Interview, James Steinberg, 02.10.03.
61 Interview.
62 Private correspondence.
63 Private correspondence.
64 Interview, Sir John Holmes, 01.04.03.
65 Interview.
66 Interview.
67 BBC TV, 'Endgame in Ireland', 26.06.01.
68 Stephens (2004), p.151.
69 Interview.

26: Bill Clinton

1 Sarah Baxter, *The Nation*, 25.11.96.
2 Andrew Rawnsley, *Observer*, 13.11.94.
3 Interview, Sandy Berger, 04.04.03.
4 Blumenthal (2003), pp.305–6.
5 Interview, Anthony Lake, 10.09.03.
6 Interview, Sidney Blumenthal, 12.09.03.
7 Interview, Sir John Kerr, 26.09.03.
8 John Carlin, *Independent*, 14.04.96.
9 Interview, Sir John Kerr, 26.09.03.
10 Interview, Larry Summers, 30.09.03.
11 R. W. Apple, *New York Times*, 13.04.96.
12 Blumenthal (2003), p.306.
13 Interview, Sir John Kerr, 26.09.03.
14 Interview.
15 Interview.
16 Rodham Clinton (2003), p.423.
17 Christopher Hitchens, *The Nation*, 13.05.96.
18 *New York Times*, 13.04.96.
19 Michael Elliott, *Observer*, 14.04.96.
20 Riddell (2003), p.71.
21 Interview, Elaine Kamarck, 18.09.03.
22 Interview.
23 Interview, Anthony Lake, 10.09.03.
24 Martin Kettle, *Guardian*, 15.02.98.
25 *The Times*, 03.05.97.
26 Ibid.
27 Riddell (2003), p.79.
28 Interview, Michael Waldman, 30.09.03.
29 Interview, Sandy Berger, 03.04.03.
30 Rodham Clinton (2003), p.425.
31 Interview, Melanne Verveer, 29.10.03.
32 Interview, Alex Allan, 11.04.03.
33 Interview, Sir Christopher Meyer, 09.04.03.
34 Ibid., 02.06.03.
35 Interview.
36 See Blair (1998); Finlayson (1999).
37 See Sheehy (1999).
38 Interview, Melanne Verveer, 29.10.03.
39 Interview, James Steinberg, 02.10.03.
40 Rodham Clinton (2003), p.425.
41 Ibid., pp.427–8.
42 Interview, Melanne Verveer, 29.10.03.
43 Interview, Joseph Nye, 16.10.03.
44 Interview.
45 Interview, Anthony Giddens, 31.08.03.
46 Interview.
47 Interview, Sir Christopher Meyer, 02.06.03.
48 Interview.
49 Diary, 26.01.98: Ashdown (2002), p.159.
50 Interview.
51 *Guardian*, 09.02.98.
52 Interview.
53 *Washington Post*, 08.02.98.
54 'Toast at Official Dinner', State Department, United States Government. Released at the request of the author under the

Freedom of Information Act, 25.02.04.

55 Martin Kettle, *Guardian*, 15.02.98.

56 'China Issues', State Department, United States Government. Released at the request of the author under the Freedom of Information Act, 25.02.04.

57 'Libya/Lockerbie' and 'Status of the Northern Ireland Peace Process', State Department, United States Government. Released at the request of the author under the Freedom of Information Act, 25.02.04.

58 Interview, Anthony Giddens, 31.08.03.

59 Interview, Elaine Kamarck, 18.09.03.

60 *Sunday Times*, 08.02.98.

61 Blumenthal (2003), p.395.

62 Interview, Larry Summers, 03.09.03.

63 Interview, Joseph Nye, 16.10.03.

64 Diary, 04.03.98: Ashdown (2002), p.177.

65 *Guardian*, 07.2.98.

66 Interview.

67 Riddell (2003), p.85.

68 Interview, Sir Christopher Meyer, 02.06.03.

69 Peter Riddell says Clinton's role in Northern Ireland was 'much exaggerated': Riddell (2003), p.86.

70 Interview, Sandy Berger, 03.04.03.

71 Interview.

72 Interview.

73 Interview.

74 *Washington Post*, 21.09.98.

75 Interview.

76 Interview.

77 Interview, Sir Christopher Meyer, 01.10.03.

78 Interview.

79 Interview.

80 Interview.

81 Interview.

82 Private correspondence.

83 Riddell (2003), p.2.

84 Blumenthal (2003), pp.740–1.

85 Riddell (2003), p.2.

86 Interview, Sir Christopher Meyer, 02.06.03.

87 Interview, Melanne Verveer, 29.10.03.

88 Interview.

89 Interview.

90 Private correspondence.

91 Interview, Bruce Reed, 12.09.03.

92 Interview.

93 Interview.

94 Interview.

95 *The Times*, 18.12.00.

96 Interview.

97 *Sunday Times*, 05.03.00.

98 Interview, Anthony Giddens, 31.08.03.

99 Stephens (2004), p.137.

100 *Guardian*, 03.10.02.

27: Kosovo

1 Freedman (2001), p.291.

2 Interview, Lord Guthrie, 24.07.03.

3 Interview, Lord Renwick, 02.12.03.

4 Interview, Lord Guthrie, 24.07.03.

5 Ibid.

6 Interview.

7 Interview.

8 Interview.

9 Interview.

10 Interview, Sir Christopher Meyer, 02.06.03.

11 Interview.

12 Diary, 15.11.97: Ashdown (2002), p.127.

13 *Hansard*, 19.11.97, Col. 323.

14 Interview, Sandy Berger, 03.04.03.

15 *Independent*, 22.02.98.

16 Interview, Sandy Berger, 03.04.03.

17 Interview.

18 Cook (2003), p.206.

19 *Washington Post*, 26.02.98.

20 Interview.

21 *Independent*, 25.02.98.

22 Interview.

23 Private correspondence.

24 *Independent*, 16.11.98.

25 Kampfner (2003), p.30.

26 *Independent*, 16.11.98.

27 Kampfner (2003), p.31.

28 Interview, Sandy Berger, 03.04.03.

29 Ibid.

30 Ed Vulliamy, Patrick Wintour and David Sharrock, *Observer*, 20.12.98.

31 *Observer*, 20.12.98.

32 Interview.

33 *Observer*, 20.12.98.

34 Kampfner (2003), pp.31–3.

35 Interview.

36 Interview, Sandy Berger, 03.04.03.

37 Interview, Lord Guthrie, 24.07.03.

38 Interview, Lord Renwick, 02.12.03.

39 Interview.

40 Interview, David Clark, 20.08.03.

41 Ivo Daalder, 'War in Europe', *Frontline* (WGBH Boston), 2000.

42 Interview.

43 Albright (2003), pp.402–5.

44 Interview, James Steinberg, 02.10.03.

45 Ibid.

46 Interview.

47 Interview, Sandy Berger, 03.04.03.
48 Kampfner (2003), p.43.
49 *Hansard*, 23.03.99, Col. 161.
50 Kampfner (2003), pp.43–5.
51 Ibid., p.44.
52 Interview.
53 Kampfner (2003), p.14.
54 Diary, 27.03.99, Lance Price.
55 Interview.
56 Andrew Rawnsley, *Observer*, 08.09.02.
57 Interview.
58 Diary, 04.04.99, Lance Price.
59 Interview.
60 Interview.
61 Interview.
62 *Hansard*, 23.03.99, Col. 170.
63 Private correspondence.
64 Interview, Lord Robertson, 18.09.03.
65 Interview.
66 Interview.
67 Tony Blair, 'War in Europe', *Frontline* (WGBH Boston), 2000.
68 Oborne (1999), pp.204–7.
69 Interview, Lord Robertson, 18.09.03.
70 Diary, 18.04.99, Lance Price.
71 Interview, Sandy Berger, 03.04.03.
72 Halberstam (2001), p.462.
73 Clark (2001), p.xxxiv; Riddell (2003), pp.108–10; Halberstam (2001), pp.461–2.
74 Kampfner (2003), pp.50–3.
75 Interview.
76 *Washington Post*, 23.04.99.
77 Interview.
78 Interview.
79 Interview, James Steinberg, 02.10.03.
80 *Financial Times*, 23.04.99.
81 Interview, Sir Christopher Meyer, 02.06.03.
82 Interview.
83 Interview, James Steinberg, 07.04.04.
84 Interview.
85 Diary, 23.04.99, Lance Price.
86 Interview, Sir Christopher Meyer, 02.06.03.
87 Albright (2003), p.415.
88 Private correspondence.
89 Ivo Daalder, 'War in Europe', *Frontline* (WGBH Boston), 2000.
90 Interview.
91 Rawnsley (2001), p.274.
92 Kampfner (2003), p.55.
93 Interview.
94 Riddell (2003), p.113.
95 Rawnsley (2001), p.282.
96 Interview, Lord Guthrie, 24.07.03.
97 Interview.
98 Interview.
99 Interview, Lord Guthrie, 24.07.03.
100 Diary, 07.05.99, Lance Price.
101 Interview.
102 *Financial Times*, 17.05.99.
103 Interview.
104 Interview.
105 Interview.
106 Interview.
107 Interview.
108 Interviews.
109 Interview, Lord Robertson, 18.09.03.
110 Private correspondence.
111 Interview.
112 Kampfner (2003), pp.58–60.
113 Interview, Sandy Berger, 03.04.03.
114 Kampfner (2003), pp.58–60.
115 Freedman (2001), pp.300–1.
116 Private correspondence.
117 Freedman (2001), pp.299–300.
118 Interview, Lord Robertson, 18.09.03.

28: John Prescott

1 Rawnsley (2000), p.295.
2 Brown (1997), p.11.
3 Anderson and Mann (1997), p.150.
4 Ibid.
5 Ibid., pp.150–1.
6 Ibid., p.151.
7 Ibid., p.157.
8 Interview, Mike Craven, 09.10.03.
9 Interview.
10 Interview.
11 Quoted in Anderson and Mann (1997), pp.159–60.
12 Interview, Mike Craven, 09.10.03.
13 Interview.
14 Interview.
15 Interview.
16 Interview.
17 Interview.
18 Interview.
19 Interview.
20 Interview.
21 Interview, Lord Sawyer, 13.09.03.
22 *Guardian*, 26.08.96.
23 Interview, Mike Craven, 09.10.03.
24 Interview.
25 Rawnsley (2001), p.19.
26 Interview.
27 Interview.
28 Interview.
29 Interview.
30 Interview.
31 Diary, 18.02.98: Ashdown (2000) p.169.
32 Anthony Seldon, Politics Conference, Westminster Central Hall, 29.01.98.
33 Interview.
34 Interview.

35 *Independent*, 03.07.99.
36 Interview.
37 Rawnsley (2001), p.303.
38 Patrick Wintour, *Observer*, 11.07.99.
39 Interview.
40 Thanks to Michael Perrott for sourcing this reference.
41 Interview.
42 Interview. See also Francis Elliott and Colin Brown, *Sunday Telegraph*, 09.11.03.
43 Interview.
44 Steve Richards, *Independent*, 18.01.02.
45 Don Macintyre, *Independent*, 17.03.03.

29: 'Scars on My Back'

1 Steve Richards, *New Statesman*, 01.05.98.
2 Kavanagh and Seldon (1999), p.274.
3 Interview.
4 Rentoul (2001), p.379.
5 Interview.
6 Interview.
7 Interview.
8 Interview.
9 Interview.
10 Interview.
11 Interview, Frank Field, 28.10.03.
12 Interview.
13 Patrick Wintour, *Observer*, 02.08.98.
14 Diary, 27.07.98, Lance Price.
15 Interview.
16 Interview.
17 Interview.
18 Kavanagh and Seldon (1999), p.274.
19 Interview.
20 Interview.
21 *The Times*, 28.01.98.
22 *Observer*, 17.01.99.
23 Rachel Sylvester, *Independent*, 18.07.99.
24 Interview.
25 Interview.
26 Interview.
27 Private correspondence.
28 Private correspondence.
29 Private correspondence.
30 *Guardian*, 07.07.99.
31 Interview.
32 Interview.
33 Interview.
34 Interview.
35 Riddell (2001), p.27.
36 Interview.
37 Interview, Andrew Grice, 03.09.03.
38 Interview.
39 Interview.
40 Seldon (2002), pp.97–137.

41 Peter Riddell, *The Times*, 28.4.04.
42 Interview.
43 Interview.
44 Smithers in Seldon (2001), p.424.
45 Interview, Michael Barber, 05.08.03.
46 Interview.
47 Interview.
48 Private correspondence.
49 Rentoul (2001), p.547.
50 Interview.
51 Interview.
52 Interview.
53 *The Times*, 17.01.00.
54 See, for example, the front-page splash 'Billions promised by Blair to cure NHS', *Herald* (Glasgow), 17.01.00.
55 Rentoul (2001), p.548.
56 Interview.
57 Interview.
58 Interview.
59 Interview.
60 Seldon (2001), p.599.
61 Interview, Andrew Grice, 03.09.03.
62 *Daily Telegraph*, 08.12.01.
63 Interview.
64 Interview.
65 Interview.
66 Interview.
67 Interview, Lord Burns, 05.11.03.
68 Interview.
69 Interview, David Miliband, 09.09.03.
70 Interview.
71 Peter Riddell, *The Times*, 01.01.01.
72 Interview, Jonathan Haslam, 18.07.03.

30: Margaret Thatcher

1 *Guardian*, 24.10.84.
2 Interview, Ron Davies, 25.09.03.
3 Interview, Lord Powell, 14.04.03.
4 *Financial Times*, 01.06.87.
5 Naughtie (2002), p.265.
6 Interview.
7 Interview, Tim Allan, 10.09.03.
8 *Sun*, 02.04.97.
9 *Financial Times*, 01.06.90.
10 Rentoul (2001), p.271.
11 See Chapter 13.
12 Martin Jacques, quoted in Foley (2000), p.199.
13 Philip Gould, quoted in Foley (2000), p.199.
14 Gould (1998), p.53.
15 Interview, Simon Walters, 27.08.03.
16 Matthew Symonds, *Independent*, 22.06.94.
17 *The Times*, 06.07.94.
18 *Observer*, 02.10.94.
19 Interview, Richard Stott, 03.11.03.

20 Major (1999), p.607.
21 Seldon (1997), pp.735–8.
22 Rentoul (2001), pp.276–8.
23 Interview, John Major, 09.04.03.
24 Private correspondence.
25 Seldon (1997), pp.252–5, 290–1, 560–3.
26 Interview.
27 Interview, Julian Seymour, 24.06.03.
28 Interview.
29 Andrew Grice, *Sunday Times*, 23.04.95.
30 Andrew Grice and Michael Prescott, *Sunday Times*, 28.05.95.
31 *The Times*, 17.07.95.
32 Philip Gould had drawn Blair's attention to the 'Conservative Century' idea as articulated in Seldon and Ball (1994); Gould (1998), pp.24, 239.
33 *New York Times*, 03.04.96.
34 Interview, Julian Seymour, 24.06.03.
35 Rentoul (2001), p.277.
36 Interview.
37 Interview.
38 Interview, Lord Powell, 14.04.03.
39 *The Times*, 08.03.97.
40 *Evening Standard*, 13.03.97.
41 Interview, Sir Peter Stothard, 26.02.03.
42 Wyatt (2000), p.721.
43 Interview, Julian Seymour, 24.06.03.
44 *Scotland on Sunday*, 25.05.97.
45 Letter, Lord Powell to author, 19.4.04.
46 Naughtie (2002), p.265.
47 *Sunday Times*, 25.05.97.
48 Foley (2002), p.200.
49 Interview.
50 Interview.
51 Interview, Simon Jenkins, 10.12.03.
52 Interview.
53 Interview.
54 Interview.
55 Interview.
56 Interview, Lord Powell, 14.04.03.
57 *Express on Sunday*, 18.05.03.
58 Interview.
59 Interview.
60 Correspondence with author, Dennis Kavanagh, 23.01.04. This is an excellent example of what political scientists call 'spatial leadership'.
61 Interview.

31: General Election, 2001

1 *Independent on Sunday*, 04.01.01.
2 Private correspondence.
3 Interview.
4 Interview.
5 Interview.
6 Interview.
7 Interview.
8 Interview.
9 Interview.
10 *Independent on Sunday*, 04.01.01.
11 Interview.
12 Private correspondence.
13 Private correspondence.
14 Interview.
15 Interview.
16 *Sunday Times*, 17.09.00.
17 Interview.
18 Diary, 14.09.00, Lance Price.
19 *Guardian*, 12.09.00.
20 Diary, 14.09.00, Lance Price.
21 Interview.
22 Diary, 14.09.00, Lance Price.
23 Interview.
24 *Sunday Times*, 17.09.00.
25 Private correspondence.
26 Interview.
27 Interview.
28 Interview.
29 Interview.
30 McConnell and Stark (2002), pp.664–81.
31 Interview.
32 *The Times*, 04.05.01.
33 Interview.
34 Interview.
35 Interview.
36 Interview, Adam Boulton, 10.07.03.
37 Interview.
38 Diary, 21.03.01, Lance Price.
39 Diary, 22.03.01, Lance Price.
40 *Independent*, 24.03.01.
41 Interview.
42 Diary, 25.03.01, Lance Price.
43 Interview.
44 Interview.
45 Interview.
46 Andrew Rawnsley, *Observer*, 08.04.01.
47 Diary, 02.04.01, Lance Price.
48 Interview.
49 Interview.
50 Interview.
51 Interview.
52 Interview.
53 Interview.
54 Interview.
55 Interview.
56 Interview.
57 Interview.
58 Robert Harris, *Sunday Times*, 10.06.01.
59 Interview.
60 Interview, James Purnell, 08.09.03.
61 Hugo Young, *Guardian*, 26.04.01.

62 *Guardian*, 17.05.01.
63 Private correspondence.
64 Interview.
65 Interview.
66 *Guardian*, 09.05.01.
67 *Daily Telegraph*, 14.05.01.
68 Interview.
69 Interview.
70 *Guardian*, 17.05.01.
71 *Independent*, 17.05.01.
72 Interview.
73 Interview.
74 Interview.
75 *Guardian*, 26.05.01.
76 William Rees-Mogg, *The Times*, 28.05.01.
77 Interview.
78 *Sunday Times*, 10.06.01.
79 Norris (2001), p.5.
80 Interview.
81 Simon Sebag Montefiore, *Sunday Times*, 10.06.01.
82 Robert Harris, *Sunday Times*, 10.01.01.
83 *Guardian*, 09.06.01.
84 Interview.
85 Private correspondence.
86 Interview.
87 Interview.
88 Interview.
89 Interview.
90 Peter Oborne, *Daily Telegraph*, 08.06.01.
91 Interview.
92 *The Times*, 11.06.01.

32: Anji Hunter

1 Interview; Private correspondence.
2 Allan Laing, *Herald* (Glasgow), 24.03.01.
3 Interview.
4 Interview.
5 Interview.
6 Private correspondence.
7 Geoffrey Levy, *Daily Mail*, 05.08.94.
8 Interview.
9 Interview.
10 Interview.
11 Private correspondence.
12 Private correspondence.
13 Private correspondence.
14 John Rentoul, *New Statesman*, 18.10.96.
15 Private correspondence.
16 Rachel Sylvester, *Daily Telegraph*, 31.03.01.
17 Private correspondence.
18 Interview, Mark Adams, 21.07.03.
19 Interview.
20 Interview.
21 Interview.
22 Interview.
23 Interview.
24 *Daily Telegraph*, 31.03.01.
25 Diary, 06.06.00, Lance Price.
26 Ibid.
27 Kampfner (2003), p.54.
28 *Guardian*, 27.09.99.
29 Interview.
30 *Daily Telegraph*, 31.03.01.
31 Interview.
32 Private correspondence.
33 Private correspondence.
34 Private correspondence.
35 Naughtie (2002), p.238.
36 Julia Langdon, *Observer*, 01.04.01.
37 Interviews.
38 Interview.
39 Interview.
40 Interview.
41 Interview.
42 Interview.
43 Private correspondence.
44 Private correspondence.
45 Interview.
46 Interview.
47 Tom Baldwin, *The Times*, 09.11.01.
48 Interview.
49 Interview.
50 Interview.
51 Interview.
52 Interviews.
53 Geoffrey Levy, *Daily Mail*, 22.06.02.
54 Private correspondence.
55 Interview.
56 Kampfner (2003), p.111.
57 Andrew Grice, *Independent*, 9.11.01.
58 *The Times*, 09.11.01.
59 Interview.
60 Interviews.
61 Alice Thompson, *Daily Telegraph*, 18.07.02.
62 Interview.
63 *The Times*, 10.01.04.

33: 9/11 and Aftermath

1 Interview.
2 Tony Blair, 'Campaign Against Terror', *Frontline* (WGBH Boston), 2002.
3 *Independent on Sunday*, 16.09.01.
4 *Observer*, 16.09.01.
5 Interview.
6 Interview.
7 Interview.
8 Interview.
9 Interview.
10 Private correspondence.
11 Kampfner (2003), p.112.
12 *The Times*, 31.07.02.

13 Interview.
14 Interview.
15 *Independent on Sunday*, 16.09.01.
16 Kampfner (2003), p.111.
17 Interview.
18 Tony Blair, 'Campaign Against Terror', *Frontline* (WGBH Boston), 2002.
19 Clarke (2004), p.18.
20 Interview.
21 Kampfner (2003), pp.112–13.
22 Ibid., p.112.
23 Riddell (2003), p.150.
24 Ibid., p.149.
25 *Sunday Times*, 16.09.01.
26 Interview.
27 Interview.
28 Private correspondence.
29 *The Times*, 12.09.01.
30 Tony Blair, 'Campaign Against Terror', *Frontline* (WGBH Boston), 2002.
31 Interview.
32 Kampfner (2003), pp.115.
33 Interview.
34 Riddell (2003), p.150.
35 Interview.
36 Interview.
37 Interview.
38 Interview.
39 Interview.
40 Tony Blair, 'Campaign Against Terror', *Frontline* (WGBH Boston), 2002.
41 Clarke (2004), p.24.
42 Kampfner (2003), pp. 115–16; Riddell (2003), pp.151–2; Bob Woodward and Dan Balz, *Washington Post*, 28.10.02.
43 Interview.
44 Tony Blair, 'Campaign Against Terror', *Frontline* (WGBH Boston), 2002.
45 Kampfner (2003), p.118; Riddell (2003), pp.150–1; Michael Cockerell, *Sunday Times*, 08.09.02.
46 Tony Blair, 'Campaign Against Terror', *Frontline* (WGBH Boston), 2002.
47 Private correspondence.
48 Riddell (2003), p.157.
49 *Hansard*, 14.09.01, Col. 618.
50 *Guardian*, 15.09.01.
51 Woodward and Balz, *Washington Post*, 01.03.02.
52 Kampfner (2003), p.116.
53 Daalder and Lindsay (2003), p.103.
54 Interview.
55 See Woodward (2004), pp.25–6.
56 Interview, Richard Armitage, 04.04.03.
57 Private correspondence.
58 Interview.
59 Michael White, *Guardian*, 19.09.01.
60 Interview.
61 Tony Blair, 'Campaign Against Terror', *Frontline* (WGBH Boston), 2002.
62 Ed Vulliamy, *Observer*, 23.09.01.
63 Letter, Tony Blair to St Thomas' Church, New York, made available by St Thomas' Church, New York.
64 Andrew Grice, *Independent*, 21.09.01; Private correspondence.
65 Kampfner (2003), p.120.
66 Sir Christopher Meyer, 'Blair's War', *Frontline* (WGBH Boston), 2003.
67 *Observer*, 23.09.01.
68 Riddell (2003), p.160.
69 Private correspondence.
70 Tony Blair, 'Campaign Against Terror', *Frontline* (WGBH Boston), 2002.
71 Riddell (2003), p.161.
72 Interview.
73 Interview.
74 Interview.
75 *Independent on Sunday*, 30.09.01.
76 Michael White, *Guardian*, 09.10.01.
77 Interview.
78 *Observer*, 30.09.01.
79 *Independent on Sunday*, 30.09.01.
80 Michael White, *Guardian*, 03.10.01.
81 *Independent*, 03.10.01.
82 Richard Gwyn, *Toronto Star*, 07.10.01.
83 Anatole Kaletsky, *The Times*, 04.10.01.
84 *Independent*, 05.10.01.
85 Kampfner (2003), p.124.
86 Ibid., pp.124–5.
87 Interview, Sir Roderic Lyne, 15.01.04.
88 Ibid.
89 *Daily Telegraph*, 26.09.01.
90 Interview.
91 Interview, Lord Guthrie, 24.07.03.
92 Tony Blair, 'Campaign Against Terror', *Frontline* (WGBH Boston), 2002.
93 *Daily Telegraph*, 06.10.01.
94 *Guardian*, 06.10.01.
95 Philip Webster and Eben Black, *Sunday Times*, 07.10.01.
96 *The Times*, 08.10.01.
97 Interviews.
98 *Guardian*, 31.10.01.
99 Ibid.
100 Interview.
101 Interview.
102 Interview, Sir John Kerr, 15.09.03.
103 Tony Blair, 'Campaign Against

Terror', *Frontline* (WGBH Boston), 2002.
104 Ibid.
105 Andy McSmith, *Daily Telegraph*, 11.10.01.
106 *Guardian*, 11.10.01.
107 Kamal Ahmed, *Observer*, 14.10.01.
108 Interview; *The Times*, 31.01.01; Kampfner (2003), p.135.
109 Joe Murphy, *Sunday Telegraph*, 04.11.01.
110 Simon Jenkins, *The Times*, 02.11.01.
111 *Guardian*, 02.11.01.
112 Interview.
113 Patrick Wintour, *Guardian*, 02.11.01.
114 Akgül (2002), p.16.
115 Private correspondence.
116 Private correspondence.
117 James Blitz, *Financial Times*, 06.11.01; Riddell (2003), pp.166–7.
118 Riddell (2003), p.167.
119 Kampfner (2003), p.138.
120 Interview.
121 Interview.
122 Interview.
123 Interview, Robert Cooper, 04.09.03.
124 *Guardian*, 09.11.01.
125 *The Times*, 08.11.01.
126 *Guardian*, 09.11.01.
127 Tony Blair, 'Campaign Against Terror', *Frontline* (WGBH Boston), 2002.
128 Interview.
129 Sir Christopher Meyer, 'Blair's War', *Frontline* (WGBH Boston), 2002.
130 *Daily Telegraph*, 20.12.01.
131 Philip Webster, *The Times*, 20.12.01.
132 Private correspondence.
133 Interview.
134 Private correspondence.
135 Private correspondence.
136 Interview.
137 Stothard (2003), p.7.
138 Private correspondence.
139 Private correspondence.
140 Interview.

34: God

1 Correspondence with author, Dennis Kavanagh, 05.01.04.
2 Matthew d'Ancona, *Sunday Telegraph*, 07.04.96; for a discussion of Christianity and the Labour Party, see Dale (2000).
3 Interview, Bishop Graham Dow, 19.07.03.
4 Interview, Matthew d'Ancona, 13.11.03.
5 Interview, Geoff Gallop, 09.04.03.
6 Interview, Alastair Singleton,

25.09.03.
7 Interview.
8 Interview.
9 Chris Bryant, *Guardian*, 11.10.97.
10 *Guardian*, 11.10.97.
11 Private correspondence.
12 *Observer*, 04.10.92.
13 Michael Prescott, *Sunday Times*, 04.10.92.
14 See, for example, *Guardian*, 01.03.93.
15 *Herald* (Glasgow), 20.3.93.
16 Interview, Chris Bryant, 30.01.04.
17 Tony Blair, *Independent*, 22.03.93.
18 Interview, Chris Bryant, 30.01.04.
19 *Guardian*, 01.03.93.
20 Chris Bryant, *Guardian*, 11.10.97.
21 Interview, James Blitz, 01.04.04.
22 Interview, Matthew d'Ancona, 13.11.03.
23 The first *Private Eye* 'St Albion Parish News' appeared on 16.05.97.
24 *Vanity Fair*, June 2003.
25 Kamal Ahmed, *Observer*, 04.05.03.
26 Matthew d'Ancona, *Sunday Telegraph*/CSM Joint Fringe Meeting, Labour Conference, 29.09.03.
27 Interview, Matthew d'Ancona, 13.11.03.
28 Interview, Lord Carey, 17.09.03.
29 Stothard (2003), p.106; Michael Gove, *The Times*, 06.05.03.
30 Interview.
31 Proud (2003), p.120.
32 Interview.
33 Interview, Chris Bryant, 30.01.04.
34 Interview.
35 *Daily Record*, 06.03.98, quoted in Rentoul (2001), p.350.
36 Interview, Chris Bryant, 30.01.04.
37 Rentoul (2001), p.352.
38 Smith (1996), p.68.
39 Rentoul (2001), p.352.
40 Michael White, *Guardian*, 05.03.98.
41 Letter, George Carey to Tony Blair, 05.03.98; Private Papers.
42 Interview.
43 *Independent*, 22.08.98.
44 Agence France-Presse, 24.02.03.
45 Interview.
46 Kampfner (2003), p.275.
47 *Sunday Times*, 23.02.03.
48 Matthew d'Ancona, *Sunday Telegraph*, 23.02.03.
49 Interview.
50 *Irish Times*, 24.02.03.
51 Interview.
52 Matthew d'Ancona, *Sunday Telegraph*, 23.02.03.
53 Letter, Carey to Blair, 19.10.94;

Private Papers.
54 Letter, Carey to Blair, 30.08.96;
   Private Papers.
55 Letter, Carey to Blair, 18.03.97;
   Private Papers.
56 Letter, Carey to Blair, 15.11.00;
   Private Papers.
57 Interview, Lord Carey, 17.09.03.
58 Letter, Carey to Blair, 08.06.01;
   Private Papers.
59 Interview, Bishop Graham Dow,
   19.07.03.
60 *The Times*, 17.09.97; Private
   correspondence.
61 Private correspondence.
62 Interview.
63 Private correspondence.
64 Private correspondence.
65 *Sunday Times*, 02.07.00.
66 Simon Jenkins, *The Times*, 24.07.02.
67 Rowan Williams, *New Statesman*,
   25.09.98.
68 Andrew Rawnsley, *Observer*,
   28.07.02.
69 *The Times*, 20.04.04; *Guardian*,
   22.04.04.
70 *The Times*, 04.01.00.
71 *Muslim News*, March 2000.
72 *The Times*, 10.03.00.
73 Kampfner (2003), p.74.
74 *Guardian*, 30.03.01.
75 Letter, Carey to Blair, 12.03.01;
   Private Papers.
76 *Guardian*, 12.10.01.
77 Kamal Ahmed, *Observer*, 03.08.03.
78 John Rentoul, *Independent*, 03.08.03.
79 Paul Vallely, *Independent*, 02.07.00.
80 Hugo Young, *Guardian*, 29.06.00.
81 Interview, Graham Dale, 05.02.04.
82 Interview.
83 Interview, Graham Dale, 05.02.04.
84 Interview.
85 Nicholas Watt, *Guardian*, 07.07.00.
86 A. N. Wilson, *Sunday Telegraph*,
   07.10.01.
87 Minette Marrin, *Daily Telegraph*,
   06.10.01.
88 Interview, Clare Short, 10.12.03.
89 Interview, Patrick Wintour, 20.10.03.
90 Interview, Sir John Kerr, 15.09.03.
91 *Sunday Telegraph*, 18.03.01.
92 Stothard (2003), p.189.
93 Peter Oborne, *Spectator*, 05.04.03.
94 *Herald* (Glasgow), 23.09.00.
95 Anne Applebaum, *Sunday Telegraph*,
   18.03.01.
96 Matthew d'Ancona, *Sunday
   Telegraph*, 18.03.01.

35: 'Cheriegate'

1 Private correspondence.
2 Private correspondence.
3 Rawnsley (2000), p.92.
4 Private correspondence.
5 Rawnsley (200), pp.93–4.
6 Baston (2000), p.201.
7 *Sun*, 12.11.97.
8 Rawnsley (2001), pp.91–104;
   Macintyre (2000), pp.431–6.
9 Quoted in Rawnsley (2001), p.99.
10 *Guardian*, 17.11.97.
11 Interview.
12 Anne McElvoy and Colin Brown,
   Independent on Sunday, 17.02.02.
13 Interview.
14 Andrew Rawnsley, *Observer*,
   17.02.02.
15 Matthew d'Ancona, *Sunday
   Telegraph*, 17.02.02.
16 Interview.
17 *Sunday Telegraph*, 17.02.02.
18 Seldon (1997), p.131.
19 Interview, Mark Adams, 21.07.03.
20 Interview, Robert Seabrook,
   22.11.03.
21 Stephens (2004), p.31.
22 Interview.
23 Interview; Jo Dillon, *Independent on
   Sunday*, 12.05.02.
24 Interview.
25 Interview.
26 *Mirror*, 29.07.97.
27 Interview.
28 Interview.
29 Interview.
30 Interview.
31 Interview.
32 Stephens (2004), p.34.
33 *Herald Sun* (Melbourne), 26.04.03.
34 Stephens (2004), p.33.
35 Jo Dillon, *Independent on Sunday*,
   23.06.03.
36 Interview.
37 Private diary, 18.11.99.
38 Private correspondence.
39 Interview, David Seymour, 20.10.03.
40 Petronella Wyatt, *Spectator*, 20.07.02.
41 Interview.
42 Linda McDougall, *Sunday Times*,
   23.06.02.
43 Interview.
44 Interview.
45 *The Times*, 08.12.02.
46 Interview.
47 Stephens (2004), p.196.
48 Interview; *The Times*, 10.07.02.
49 Mary Liddell, *Observer*, 23.06.02.
50 Private correspondence.
51 McDougall (2001), p.135.
52 Private correspondence.
53 Interview.

54 Interview.
55 Interview.
56 Interview.
57 Interview.
58 Interview.
59 Interview.
60 Interview.
61 Interview.
62 Private correspondence.
63 Interview.
64 Interview, David Hughes, 17.07.03.
65 Interview.
66 Interview.
67 Mary Ann Sieghart, *The Times*,
    11.12.02.
68 Interview.
69 Interview.
70 Interview.
71 *Sunday Telegraph*, 08.12.02.
72 Interview.
73 Francis Elliott and Colin Brown,
    Sunday Telegraph, 08.12.02.
74 *Guardian*, 06.12.02.
75 *The Times*, 07.12.02.
76 Interview.
77 Interview.
78 Interview.
79 Interview.
80 Interview.
81 Interview.
82 Interview.
83 Interview.
84 *Guardian*, 10.12.02.
85 *Independent*, 11.12.02.
86 Kevin Maguire, *Guardian*, 13.12.02.
87 Letter to *The Times*, 08.12.02.
88 Sarah Sands, *Daily Telegraph*,
    12.12.02.
89 *Scotsman*, 12.12.02.
90 *Guardian*, 15.12.02.
91 William Rees-Mogg, *The Times*,
    05.01.03.
92 Alex Mitchell, *Sun-Herald* (Sydney),
    07.03.04; *Sunday Telegraph*, 07.03.04.
93 *Independent on Sunday*, 07.03.04.
94 For a savage attack on the values of
    Blair and Blair-ism, see Cohen
    (2003).
95 Mary Ann Sieghart, *The Times*,
    11.12.03.
96 Philip Stephens, *Financial Times*,
    16.12.03.
97 Interview; *The Times*, 11.12.03.
98 Interview.
99 Stothard (2003), p.73.
100 Interview.
101 Interview.
102 Interview.
103 BBC TV, *The Conman, His Lover and
    the Prime Minister's Wife*, 20.02.03;
    Francis Elliott, *Sunday Telegraph*,

25.05.03.
104 Interview.
105 Private correspondence; Stephens
    (2004), p.36.
106 Kamal Ahmed, *Observer*, 25.05.03.
107 Stothard (2003), p.73.
108 Interview, Philip Webster, 03.09.03.
109 Interview.
110 Private correspondence.
111 Interview.

36: Charles Falconer

1   Don Macintyre, *Independent*,
    09.09.00.
2   Chris Nayler, in Rosen (2001),
    p.191.
3   Interview, Jeremy Irwin-Singer,
    12.09.03.
4   *Independent*, 09.09.00; *Guardian*,
    11.12.99.
5   Interview.
6   Rachel Sylvester, *Independent*,
    25.10.98.
7   McDougall (2001), p.191.
8   Interview.
9   Interview.
10 Don Macintyre, *Independent*,
    25.10.98.
11 Interview.
12 Interview.
13 Interview.
14 *Independent*, 25.10.98.
15 Michael White and Ewen
    MacAskill, *Guardian*, 05.01.99.
16 Justin Cartwright, *Guardian*,
    11.12.99.
17 Interview.
18 Rawnsley (2001), p.220.
19 Interview.
20 Andrew Rawnsley, *Observer*,
    10.09.00.
21 Jackie Ashley, *New Statesman*,
    20.11.00.
22 Interview.
23 Naughtie (2002), p.257.
24 Rachel Sylvester, *Daily Telegraph*,
    06.05.02.
25 Interview.
26 Interview.
27 Jackie Ashley, *Guardian*, 17.06.02.
28 Interview.
29 Interview.
30 Jo Dillon, *Independent on Sunday*,
    25.05.03.
31 Interview.
32 Interview.
33 Interview.
34 Interview.
35 Interview.
36 Interview.

37 Interview.
38 Patrick Wintour, *Guardian*, 14.06.03.
39 Interview.
40 David Cracknell and Eben Black, *Sunday Times*, 15.06.03.
41 Interview.
42 *Observer*, 15.06.03.
43 Interview.
44 *Sunday Times*, 15.06.03.
45 Interview.
46 Interview.
47 *Guardian*, 14.06.03.
48 *The Times*, 05.03.04.
49 Peter Riddell, *The Times*, 10.03.04.
50 Colin Brown, *Sunday Telegraph*, 27.07.03.

37: Iraq

1 'A National Security Strategy for a New Century', White House, December 1999.
2 Stothard (2003), p.64.
3 See Mann (2004) for the best account of the 'Vulcans' and their importance to George W. Bush and the US as a whole.
4 Mann (2004), p.xvi.
5 Daalder and Lindsay (2003), pp.13–16.
6 Interview, John Bolton, 03.12.03.
7 Daalder and Lindsay (2003), p.16.
8 Suskind (2004), p.86.
9 Woodward (2004), pp.21–2.
10 Ibid., p.14.
11 *Houston Chronicle*, 01.08.01.
12 Interview, Sir Christopher Meyer, 09.04.03.
13 Woodward (2004), p.25.
14 Clarke (2004), p.31.
15 *Vanity Fair*, May 2004.
16 Clarke (2004), p.30.
17 Woodward (2004), pp.25–6.
18 *Vanity Fair*, May 2004.
19 Correspondence with author, Sir Christopher Meyer, 01.05.04.
20 Woodward (2004), pp.1–3.
21 Interview.
22 Daalder and Lindsay (2003), p.131; *Vanity Fair*, May 2004.
23 Riddell (2003), pp.89–95; Clare Short, *New Statesman*, 05.01.04; Interview.
24 Interview.
25 Interview, Robert Cooper, 04.09.03; Johann Hari, *Independent on Sunday*, 23.11.03.
26 See Cooper (2003). His preface says 'the twenty-first century may be worse' than the previous worst periods in European history.

27 Interview.
28 Interview, Jack Straw, 11.11.03.
29 *The Times*, 08.04.02.
30 Interview, Sir Christopher Meyer, 02.06.03.
31 *Independent*, 24.02.01.
32 Interview.
33 *Guardian*, 11.11.97.
34 Stephens (2004), p.211.
35 Interview.
36 Letter, Blair to Carey, 30.03.02; Private Papers.
37 Stephens (2004), p.210.
38 Stothard (2003), p.42.
39 Private correspondence.
40 Matthew d'Ancona, *Sunday Telegraph*, 14.04.02.
41 *Washington Post*, 08.04.02.
42 Hugo Young, *Guardian*, 11.04.02.
43 Letter, Blair to Carey, 30.03.02; Private Papers.
44 Tony Blair statement, 11.09.01.
45 Interview.
46 Interview, Sir Christopher Meyer, 11.03.04.
47 Interview.
48 Interview.
49 Interview.
50 Interview.
51 Interview.
52 *Financial Times*, 12.03.02.
53 Cook (2003), p.115.
54 Ibid., p.116.
55 *Time*, 31.03.03.
56 Daalder and Lindsay (2003), pp.132–6.
57 Interview.
58 Kampfner (2003), p.168.
59 Interview.
60 Private correspondence.
61 Interview.
62 Stephens (2004), p.212.
63 Riddell (2003), pp.195–200.
64 Interview.
65 *The Times*, 07.04.03.
66 Cook (2003), p.135.
67 Kampfner (2003), pp.167–9.
68 Interview.
69 Kampfner (2003), p.168.
70 Ibid., p.169.
71 *Time*, 09.03.98.
72 Interview.
73 Private correspondence.
74 Interview.
75 Interview.
76 Private correspondence.
77 *Vanity Fair*, May 2004.
78 Interview, Sir Christopher Meyer, 11.03.04.
79 Kampfner (2003), p.193.
80 Interview.

81 Daalder and Lindsay (2003), p.135.
82 Woodward (2004), p.163.
83 Interview.
84 Woodward (2004), p.161.
85 Private correspondence.
86 Speech, Dick Cheney, 26.08.02.
87 Stephens (2004), pp.214–19.
88 Interview; Kampfner (2003), p.196.
89 Interview.
90 Interview.
91 Interview.
92 Woodward (2004), p.178.
93 Cook (2003), p.205.
94 Interview.
95 Interview.
96 Interview.
97 Interview.
98 Private correspondence.
99 Stephens (2004), p.217.
100 Kampfner (2003), p.233; Riddell
     (2003), p.212.
101 Interview, Geoff Hoon, 03.11.03.
102 Woodward (2004), p.183.
103 Interview, Jeremy Greenstock,
     26.02.04.
104 Kampfner (2003), p.200.
105 Interview.
106 Interview.
107 Interview.
108 Interview.
109 Interview.
110 Kampfner (2003), p.198.
111 See Chapter 33.
112 Kampfner (2003), pp.165–7.
113 Interview.
114 Interview.
115 Interview.
116 Interview.
117 *The Times*, 11.09.02.
118 Patrick Wintour, *Guardian*, 11.09.02.
119 Cook (2003), p.203.
120 Powell and Scarlett, 17.09.02
     (19.41): CAB/11/0069, PRO.
121 Powell, Campbell and Manning,
     17.09.02 (13.36): CAB/11/0053,
     PRO.
122 Campbell and Scarlett, 17.09.02:
     CAB/11/0066, PRO.
123 Stephens (2004), pp.220–1.
124 *Jerusalem Post*, 26.09.02.
125 *Financial Times*, 25.09.02.
126 Cook (2003), pp.212–13.
127 Ibid., p.202.
128 Interview.
129 Interview.
130 Interview.
131 Cook (2003), p.312.
132 *Sunday Times*, 07.03.04.
133 For more on the Hutton Inquiry see
     Chapter 22.
134 Kampfner (2003), pp.204–12.

135 Private correspondence.
136 Testimony to the Senate Armed
     Services Committee, David Kay,
     28.01.04.
137 Riddell (2003), p.215.
138 Interview.
139 Private correspondence.
140 The words of arch-hawk Richard
     Perle, quoted in *Vanity Fair*, May
     2004.
141 Interview.
142 Interview.
143 Interview.
144 Riddell (2003), p.220.
145 Interview, Jeremy Greenstock,
     26.02.04.
146 Kampfner (2003), p.215.
147 Interview.
148 Interview.
149 Interview.
150 Riddell (2003), p.220.
151 Interview, John Bolton, 03.12.03.
152 Interview.
153 Interview.
154 See Woodward (2004), pp.222–6, for
     a detailed account of this debate.
155 Julian Coman and David Wastell,
     Sunday Telegraph, 10.11.02.
156 Quoted in Riddell (2003), p.223.
157 Interview, Sir Christopher Meyer,
     02.06.03.
158 *Foreign Affairs*, September/October
     2003.
159 Interview.
160 Quoted in Kampfner (2003), p.230.
161 Interview, Sir Christopher Meyer,
     01.10.03.
162 Woodward (2004), pp.234–5.
163 Ibid., p.240.
164 Interview.
165 Woodward records Bush telling
     Powell that he made up his mind
     that the US would have to go to war
     on 13.01.03: Woodward (2003),
     pp.269–71.
166 Interview.
167 Interview.
168 Interview, Jeremy Greenstock,
     26.02.04.
169 Private correspondence.
170 Interview.
171 *Vanity Fair*, May 2004.
172 Interview.
173 Kampfner (2003), p.256.
174 Interview.
175 Interview.
176 *The Times*, 23.1.03.
177 Interview.
178 *Wall Street Journal*, 30.01.03.
179 Interview, Sir Roderic Lyne,
     15.01.04.

180 Private correspondence.
181 Woodward (2004), pp.296–7.
182 Private correspondence.
183 Interview.
184 *Observer*, 16.02.03.
185 Interview.
186 Interview.
187 Interview.
188 Daalder and Lindsay (2003), p.144.
189 Private correspondence.
190 Interview.
191 Interview.
192 Interview, Jeremy Greenstock, 26.02.04.
193 Interview.
194 Woodward (2004), pp.343–45.
195 Stothard (2003), p.23.
196 Kampfner (2003), pp.287–8.
197 Stothard (2003), p.14.
198 Interview.
199 Interview.
200 Stephens (2004), p.226.
201 Interview.
202 Cook (2003), p.320.
203 Interview.
204 Interview, Jack Straw, 11.11.03.
205 Woodward (2004), p.338.
206 Interview.
207 Interview, Nigel Sheinwald, 24.11.03.
208 Private correspondence.
209 Interview.
210 Interview.
211 Kampfner (2003), p.292.
212 Interview.
213 Interview.
214 Interview, Sir Peter Stothard, 03.03.04.
215 Interview.
216 *Independent on Sunday*, 29.02.04.
217 Woodward (2004), p.365.
218 Interview.
219 *Guardian*, 26.04.03.
220 Interview, Jack Straw, 11.11.03.
221 Interview, John Burton, 07.07.03.
222 Stothard (2003), p.96.
223 Ibid., p.98.
224 Woodward (2004), p.399.
225 Stothard (2003), p.189.
226 Cook (2003), p.270.
227 Stothard (2003), p.186.
228 Interview.
229 Interview.
230 Interview.
231 Interview, Jack Straw, 11.11.03.
232 Tim Hames, *The Times*, 07.04.03.
233 Tom Baldwin, *The Times*, 10.04.03.
234 Interview.
235 Blair spoke on 05.03.04 in Sedgefield justifying the war: Philip Webster, *The Times*, 06.03.04.
236 Andrew Turnbull, evidence to the House of Commons Select Committee on Public Administration, 04.03.04.
237 Interview.
238 Private correspondence.
239 Private correspondence.
240 Interview.
241 Interview.
242 Blix (2004), pp.69, 271.
243 *Sunday Times*, 21.03.04.
244 *New Yorker*, 21.11.03.
245 Interview.
246 Interview.
247 Interview.
248 Interview.

38: George W. Bush

1 Interview, Sir John Kerr, 15.09.03.
2 Interview.
3 Interview.
4 Interview.
5 Interview.
6 Interview.
7 Interview.
8 Interview.
9 Kampfner (2003), p.81.
10 Interview.
11 Interview, Sir Christopher Meyer, 01.10.03.
12 Cook (2003), p.104.
13 Andrew Grice, *Independent*, 15.12.00.
14 Interview.
15 Interview.
16 Interview.
17 Cook (2003), p.104.
18 Interview, Robin Cook, 18.07.03.
19 Interview, Sir Christopher Meyer, 29.03.04.
20 See Rice (2000).
21 Interview, Sir Christopher Meyer, 02.06.03.
22 Interview.
23 Interview.
24 Interview.
25 Interview, John Bolton, 03.12.03.
26 Interview.
27 Stephens (2004), p.191; Kampfner (2003), pp.81–2; Riddell (2003), p.135.
28 Interview, Sir Christopher Meyer, 02.06.03.
29 Interview.
30 Interview.
31 Interview.
32 Riddell (2003), p.136.
33 Letter, Peter Kellner to author, 31.03.04.
34 Interview.
35 Interview.

36 Interview.
37 Interview.
38 Interview.
39 Interview.
40 Interview.
41 Interview.
42 Interview.
43 Interview.
44 Interview.
45 Interview.
46 Stephens (2004), p.155.
47 Kampfner (2003), p.102.
48 Interview, Sir Roderic Lyne, 15.01.04.
49 Interview.
50 Riddell (2003), p.142.
51 Interview.
52 Michael White, *Guardian*, 20.07.01.
53 Stephens (2004), p.196.
54 Interview.
55 Interview.
56 Interview.
57 Interview.
58 Interview.
59 David Margolick, *Vanity Fair*, June 2003.
60 Interview, Sir Peter Stothard, 02.04.04.
61 See Stothard (2003).
62 Interview.
63 Private correspondence.
64 Interview.
65 *Vanity Fair*, June 2003.
66 Interview, Sir Peter Stothard, 02.04.04.
67 Stothard (2003), p.70.
68 Ibid., p.161.
69 Ibid., p.206.
70 Interview.
71 Interview.
72 Interview.
73 Interview.
74 Speech, George W. Bush, 24.06.02.
75 Interview.
76 *New York Times*, 07.03.02.
77 Interview.
78 Interview.
79 Private correspondence.
80 Interview, Sir Christopher Meyer, 01.10.03.
81 Karen de Young, *Washington Post*, 06.04.02.
82 Interview.
83 Stothard (2003), pp.46–50.
84 Interview, John Bolton, 03.12.03; Interview.
85 Stothard (2003), p.207.
86 Jason Beattie, *Scotsman*, 09.04.03; Kampfner (2003), p.319.
87 Stothard (2003), p.226.
88 Interview.

89 *Guardian*, 16.04.04.
90 Interview.
91 *Guardian*, 26.04.04.
92 Philip Webster, *The Times*, 18.07.03.
93 Private correspondence.
94 Interview.
95 Interview, John Bolton, 03.12.03.
96 *Observer*, 18.04.04.
97 Private correspondence.
98 Andrew Sullivan, *Sunday Times*, 16.11.03.

39: The 'Wobble', 2004

1 Private correspondence.
2 Interview.
3 Interviews.
4 Interview, Baroness Jay, 15.10.03.
5 Interview.
6 Mary Ann Sieghart, *The Times*, 31.07.03.
7 Interview.
8 Interview; the idea of a 'delivery unit' had also been floated in a Policy and Innovation Unit publication on 'Better Policy Design and Delivery', published in autumn 2000; Private correspondence.
9 Interview.
10 Interview.
11 Interview.
12 Interview.
13 Interview.
14 Interview.
15 Private correspondence.
16 Interview.
17 Private correspondence.
18 Interview.
19 Interview.
20 Interview.
21 See Kavanagh and Seldon (1999).
22 Brian Groom, *Financial Times*, 09.07.01.
23 *The Times*, 12.02.02.
24 Private correspondence.
25 Andrew Rawnsley, *Observer*, 01.07.01.
26 Stephens (2004), pp.178–9.
27 Don Macintyre, *Independent*, 28.12.01.
28 Private correspondence.
29 Interview.
30 Interview.
31 *Sunday Times*, 10.03.02.
32 Interview.
33 Private correspondence.
34 Interview.
35 Interview.
36 Interview.
37 Interview.
38 Interview.

39 *Scotsman*, 02.10.10.
40 Peter Riddell, *The Times*, 14.11.02.
41 Andrew Rawnsley, *Observer*, 24.11.02.
42 Interview.
43 Interview.
44 Keegan (2003), p.322.
45 Correspondence with author,
    Stephen Wall, 04.02.04.
46 Interview.
47 Interview.
48 Interview.
49 Stephens (2004), pp.182–6.
50 Keegan (2003), p.327.
51 Interview.
52 Interview.
53 Interview.
54 Interview.
55 Interview.
56 Patrick Wintour and Michael White,
    Guardian, 10.06.03.
57 Keegan (2003), p.328.
58 Interview.
59 Interview.
60 Interview.
61 Interview.
62 Interview.
63 Interview.
64 Interview.
65 Hugo Young, *Guardian*, 08.07.03.
66 Steve Richards, *Independent on
    Sunday*, 07.09.03.
67 Peter Riddell, *The Times*, 03.07.03.
68 Interview.
69 Interview.
70 Interview.
71 Interview.
72 Interview.
73 Interview.
74 Private correspondence.
75 Interviews.
76 Interview.
77 Private correspondence.
78 Interview.
79 Interview.
80 Seldon (1997), p.626.
81 Interview.
82 Interview.
83 Interview.
84 Interview.
85 Interview.
86 Interview.
87 Interview.
88 Interview.
89 Interview.
90 Interview.
91 Interview.
92 Interview.
93 Interview.
94 Interview.
95 *The Times*, 29.01.04.
96 'Political Survey Trends Index',
    available at www.mori.com
97 Peston (2005), p.338.
98 Interview.
99 Peston (2005), p.338.
100 Interview.
101 Interview.
102 Interview.
103 *Sunday Times*, 25.04.04.
104 *Hansard*, 20.04.04, Col. 157.
105 *Guardian*, 16.09.04.
106 Interview.
107 *Independent*, 27.12.04.
108 *The Times*, 15.05.04.
109 Interview.
110 Interview.
111 Interview.
112 Interview.
113 *The Times*, 29.09.04.
114 *Guardian*, 29.09.04.
115 *Observer*, 03.10.04.
116 Peston (2005), p.349.
117 Interview.

40: Gordon Brown

1   *The Times*, 27.11.02.
2   Olga Wojtas, *THES*, 25.07.03.
3   Routledge (1998), p.111.
4   Ibid., p.114.
5   Interview.
6   Interview.
7   Interview.
8   Interview.
9   Interview, Gavyn Davies, 01.12.03.
10 Naughtie (2002), p.50.
11 Jason Allardyce, *Sunday Times*,
    25.04.04.
12 Interview, Neil Kinnock, 03.09.03.
13 Interview, Gerald Kaufman,
    10.09.03.
14 Gould (1998), p.186.
15 Interview.
16 Interview.
17 Interview.
18 Interview.
19 Interview.
20 Interview.
21 Interview.
22 Interview.
23 Interview.
24 Interview.
25 Interview.
26 Interview.
27 Gould (1998), pp.191–3.
28 Interview.
29 Interview.
30 Interview; Private correspondence.
31 Interview.
32 Interview.
33 Interview, Andrew Graham,
    21.10.03.

34 Interview, Robin Cook, 03.03.04.
35 Interview.
36 Interview.
37 Interview.
38 Interview.
39 Mary Ann Sieghart, *The Times*, 27.11.02.
40 Interview.
41 Interview; Private correspondence.
42 Interview.
43 Interview.
44 Interview.
45 Interview.
46 Naughtie (2003), pp.82–3.
47 Interview; Private correspondence.
48 Interview.
49 Interview.
50 Interview.
51 Interview.
52 Interview.
53 Keegan (2003), p.148; Interview.
54 Philip Stephens, *Financial Times*, 30.07.96.
55 Interview.
56 Interview, Jonathan Freedland, 08.05.03.
57 Private correspondence.
58 Interview.
59 Interview.
60 Interview.
61 Interview.
62 Interview.
63 Interview.
64 Interview, Michael White, 22.01.03.
65 Interview, Gavyn Davies, 01.12.03.
66 Keegan (2003), p.171.
67 Interview.
68 Private correspondence.
69 Interview.
70 Interview.
71 Private correspondence.
72 Private correspondence; Rawnsley (2000), p.155.
73 Private correspondence.
74 Interviews.
75 Interview.
76 Private correspondence.
77 Interview.
78 Interview.
79 Interview.
80 Interview.
81 Private correspondence; Interview.
82 Private correspondence.
83 Private correspondence.
84 Private correspondence.
85 Interview.
86 Interview.
87 Interview.
88 Interview.
89 Interview, Charlie Whelan, 10.11.03.
90 Interview.
91 Private correspondence.
92 Interview.
93 Private correspondence.
94 Interview.
95 Interview.
96 Janet Bush, *The Times*, 28.01.98.
97 Interview.
98 Interview.
99 Interview.
100 Michael White, *Guardian*, 20.01.98; Private correspondence.
101 Private correspondence.
102 Interview.
103 Interview.
104 Interview.
105 Interview.
106 Private correspondence.
107 Interview.
108 Interview.
109 Private correspondence.
110 Interview.
111 Rawnsley (2001), pp.164–6.
112 Peter Riddell, *New Statesman*, 04.03.99.
113 Private correspondence.
114 Interview.
115 Interview.
116 Interview.
117 Private correspondence.
118 Interview.
119 Interview.
120 Private correspondence.
121 Interview.
122 Interview.
123 Interview.
124 Private correspondence.
125 Interview.
126 Interview.
127 Interview.
128 Interview.
129 Interview.
130 Interview.
131 Keegan (2003), pp.193, 261.
132 Interview.
133 Interview.
134 Interview.
135 Private correspondence; Interview.
136 Rawnsley (2001), p.413.
137 Interview.
138 Interview.
139 Interview; Private correspondence.
140 Interview.
141 Interview.
142 Private correspondence.
143 Keegan (2003), p.288.
144 Interview; Andrew Rawnsley, *Observer*, 05.03.00.
145 Interview.
146 Interview.
147 Interview.
148 Interview.

149 Interview.
150 Interview.
151 Interview.
152 Interview; David Cracknell, *Sunday Times*, 09.12.01.
153 Interview.
154 Interview.
155 Interviews.
156 Interview.
157 Interview, Neil Kinnock, 03.09.03.
158 Interview.
159 Interview.
160 Interview.
161 Interview.
162 Interview.
163 Interview.
164 Interview.
165 Interview.
166 *Sunday Telegraph*, 19.01.03.
167 Interview.
168 Interview.
169 Interview.
170 Interview; *The Times*, 07.08.02; *Sunday Times*, 11.08.02.
171 Interview.
172 Interview.
173 Interview.
174 Interview.
175 Mary Ann Sieghart, *The Times*, 26.04.02.
176 Ibid.; Interview.
177 Interview.
178 Interview.
179 Andrew Rawnsley, *Observer*, 06.10.02.
180 Interview.
181 Interview.
182 Interview.
183 Private correspondence.
184 *Guardian*, 14.02.03.
185 Interview.
186 Stothard (2003), p.33.

187 Interview.
188 Interview.
189 Interview.
190 Interview.
191 Interview.
192 Interview.
193 Interview.
194 Interview.
195 Interview.
196 Charlie Whelan, *Mail on Sunday*, 31.08.03.
197 Interview.
198 Interview.
199 Interview.
200 Cook (2003), p.121.
201 Interview.
202 Interview.
203 Interview.
204 Michael Gove, *The Times*, 02.12.03.
205 Interview.
206 Interview.
207 Michael Gove, *The Times*, 02.12.03.
208 Interview.
209 Interview.
210 Interview.
211 Private correspondence.
212 Matthew d'Ancona, *Sunday Telegraph*, 09.11.03.
213 Interview.
214 Private correspondence.
215 Interview.
216 Philip Webster, *The Times*, 26.02.04; Mary Ann Sieghart, *The Times*, 06.02.04.
217 Interview.
218 Interview.
219 Interview.
220 Private correspondence.
221 Private correspondence.
222 Private correspondence.

Bibliography

Biographies and Memoirs

Abse, Leo, *The Man Behind the Smile: Tony Blair and the Politics of Perversion* (London: Robson Books, 1996)

Albright, Madeleine, *Madam Secretary* (New York: Miramax, 2003)

Ashdown, Paddy, *The Ashdown Diaries, Volume 1: 1988–1997* (London: Allen Lane, 2000)

——, *The Ashdown Diaries, Volume 2: 1997–1999* (London: Allen Lane, 2001)

Beckett, Francis and Hencke, David, *The Blairs and their Court* (London: Aurum Press, 2004)

Benn, Tony, *Free at Last: Diaries, 1991–2001* (London: Arrow, 2002)

Blix, Hans, *Disarming Iraq: The Search for Weapons of Mass Destruction* (London: Bloomsbury, 2004)

Booth, Tony, *Stroll On: An Autobiography* (London: Sidgwick & Jackson, 1989)

Bower, Tom, *Gordon Brown* (London: HarperCollins, 2004)

Brown, Colin, *Fighting Talk: The Biography of John Prescott* (London: Simon & Schuster, 1997)

Brown, Gordon and Naughtie, James (eds), *John Smith: Life and Soul of the Party* (Edinburgh: Mainstream, 1994)

Brunson, Michael, *A Ringside Seat: The Autobiography* (London: Hodder & Stoughton, 2000)

Carman, Dominic, *No Ordinary Man: A Life of George Carman* (London: Hodder & Stoughton, 2002)

Clark, Alan, *Diaries: In Power* (London: Weidenfeld & Nicolson, 1993)

——, *The Last Diaries: In and Out of the Wilderness* (London: Orion, 2003)

Clarke, Richard, *Against All Enemies: Inside America's War on Terror* (New York: The Free Press, 2004)

Cook, Robin, *Point of Departure* (London: Simon & Schuster, 2003)

Dimbleby, Jonathan, *The Prince of Wales* (London: Little, Brown, 1994)

Drower, George M. F., *Kinnock* (Woodham Ferrers: Publishing Corporation, 1994)

Dyke, Greg, *Greg Dyke: Inside Story* (London: HarperCollins, 2004)

Egan, Dominic, *Irvine: Politically Correct?* (Edinburgh: Mainstream, 1999)

Etzioni, Amitai, *My Brother's Keeper: A Memoir and a Message* (Lanham: Rowman & Littlefield, 2003)

Gould, Bryan, *Goodbye to All That* (London: Macmillan, 1995)

Hamilton, Nigel, *Clinton: An American Journey* (London: Century, 2003)

Jones, Eileen, *Neil Kinnock* (London: Robert Hale, 1994)

Kampfner, John, *Robin Cook: The Biography* (London: Gollancz, 1999)

Keegan, William, *The Prudence of Mr Gordon Brown* (Chichester: Wiley, 2003)

Lacey, Robert, *Monarch: The Life and Reign of Elizabeth II* (New York: The Free Press, 2002)

Langdon, Julia, *Mo Mowlam: The Biography* (London: Warner Books, 2001)

Macintyre, Donald, *Mandelson and the Making of New Labour* (London: HarperCollins, 1999)

Major, John, *The Autobiography* (London: HarperCollins, 1999)

McDougall, Linda, *Cherie: The Perfect Life of Mrs Blair* (London: Politico's, 2001)

McSmith, Andy, *John Smith: A Life, 1938–1994* (London: Mandarin, 1994)

Morgan, Kenneth O., *Callaghan: A Life* (Oxford: OUP, 1997)

Morton, Andrew, *Diana: Her True Story in Her Own Words* (London: Michael O'Mara, 1998)

Mowlam, Mo, *Momentum* (London: Hodder & Stoughton, 2002)

Oakley, Robin, *Inside Track* (London: Bantam Press, 2001)

Oborne, Peter, *Alastair Campbell: New Labour and the Rise of the Media Class* (London: Aurum, 1999)

——, *Alastair Campbell* (London: Aurum Press, 2004)

Pimlott, Ben, *Harold Wilson* (London: HarperCollins, 1992)

Pollard, Stephen, *David Blunkett* (London: Hodder & Stoughton, 2004)

Proud, Keith, *The Grit in the Oyster: The Biography of John Burton of Trimdon* (Newcastle: Northern Echo, 2003)

Radice, Giles, *Diaries 1980-2001: The Political Diaries of Giles Radice* (London: Weidenfeld & Nicolson, 2004)

Rentoul, John, *Tony Blair: Prime Minister* (London: Warner Books, 2001)

Robinson, Geoffrey, *The Unconventional Minister: My Life Inside New Labour* (London: Michael Joseph, 2000)

Rodham Clinton, Hillary, *Living History* (New York: Simon & Schuster, 2003)

Routledge, Paul, *Gordon Brown: The Biography* (London: Simon & Schuster, 1998)

——, *Mandy: The Unauthorised Biography of Peter Mandelson* (London: Simon & Schuster, 1999)

Scott, Derek, *Off Whitehall: A View from Downing Street by Tony Blair's Advisor* (London: I.B. Tauris, 2004)

Seldon, Anthony, *Major: A Political Life* (London: Weidenfeld & Nicholson, 1997)

Sergeant, John, *Give Me Ten Seconds* (London: Macmillan, 2001)

Short, Clare, *An Honourable Deception?* (London: Free Press, 2004)

Sopel, Jon, *Tony Blair: The Moderniser* (London: Bantam Books, 1995)

Stephens, Philip, *Tony Blair: The Making of a World Leader* (New York: Viking, 2004)

Walker, Martin, *The President We Deserve: Bill Clinton: His Rise, Falls, and Comebacks* (New York: Crown, 1996)

Westlake, Martin, *Kinnock: The Biography* (London: Little, Brown, 2001)

Wyatt, Woodrow, *Journals, Volume One* (ed. Sarah Curtis; London: Macmillan, 1998)

——, *Journals, Volume Two* (ed. Sarah Curtis; London: Macmillan, 1999)

——, *Journals, Volume Three* (ed. Sarah Curtis; London: Macmillan, 2000)

Monographs

Anderson, Paul and Mann, Nyta, *Safety First: The Making of New Labour* (London: Granta Books, 1997)

Barrett Brown, Michael and Coates, Kevin, *The Blair Revolution: Deliverance for Whom?* (London: Spokesman, 1996)

Baston, Lewis, *Sleaze: The State of the Nation* (London: Channel 4 Books, 2000)

Blackburn, R. and Plant, R. (eds), *The Labour Government's Constitutional Reform Agenda* (Harlow: Longman, 1994)

Blair, Tony, *Change and National Renewal* (London: Labour Party, 1994)

——, *New Britain: My Vision of a Young Country* (London: Fourth Estate, 1996)

Blumenthal, Sidney, *The Clinton Wars: An Insider's Account of the White House Years* (New York: Viking, 2003)

Brivati, Brian and Bale, Tim, *New Labour in Power: Precedents and Prospects* (London: Routledge, 1997)

Brivati, Brian and Heffernan, Richard, *The Labour Party: A Centenary History* (London: Macmillan, 2000)

Budge, Ian, et al, *The New British Politics* (Harlow: Longman, 2001)

Butler, David and Butler, Gareth, *British Political Facts, 1900–2000* (London: Macmillan, 2000)

Butler, David and Kavanagh, Dennis, *The British General Election of 1992* (London: Macmillan, 1992)

——, *The British General Election of 1997* (London: Macmillan, 1997)

——, *The British General Election of 2001* (London: Macmillan, 2001)

Clarke, Peter, *A Question of Leadership: From Gladstone to Blair* (London: Penguin, 1999)

Coates, David and Lawler, Peter (eds), *New Labour into Power* (Manchester: MUP, 2000)

Cohen, Nick, *Pretty Straight Guys* (London: Faber and Faber Ltd., 2004)

Colebatch, Hal, *Blair's Britain* (London: Claridge Press, 1999)

Cooper, Robert, *The Breaking of Nations: Order and Chaos in the Twenty-first Century* (New York: Atlantic, 2003)

Crewe, Ivor; Gosschalk, Brian, and Bartle, John, *Political Communications: Why Labour Won the General Election of 1997* (London: Macmillan, 1997)

Daalder, Ivo, and Lindsay, James, *America Unbound: The Bush Revolution in Foreign Policy* (Washington DC: Brookings Institution Press, 2003)

Draper, Derek, *Blair's Hundred Days* (London: Faber & Faber, 1997)

Driver, Stephen and Martell, Luke, *New Labour: Politics after Thatcherism* (Cambridge: Polity, 1998)

Fairclough, Norman, *New Labour, New Language?* (London: Routledge, 2000)

Fielding, Steven, *The Labour Party: Continuity and Change in the Making of 'New' Labour* (Basingstoke: Palgrave Macmillan, 2003)

Foley, Michael, *John Major, Tony Blair, and a Conflict of Leadership: Collision Course* (Manchester: MUP, 2002)

——, *The British Presidency* (Manchester: MUP, 2000)

Foote, Geoffrey, *The Labour Party's Political Thought: A History* (London: Macmillan, 1997)

Franklin, Bob, *Tough on Soundbites, Tough on the Causes of Soundbites: New Labour and News Management* (London: Catalyst, 1998)

Gamble, Andrew and Wright, Tony, *The New Social Democracy* (Oxford: Blackwell, 1999)

Geddes, Andrew and Tonge, Jonathan (eds), *Labour's Landslide: The British General Election, 1997* (Manchester: MUP, 1997)

Giddens, Anthony, *The Third Way and Its Critics* (Cambridge: Polity, 2000)

——, *The Third Way: The Renewal of Social Democracy* (Cambridge: Polity, 1998)

Goodman, Geoffrey (ed.) and Blair, Tony, *The State of the Nation* (London: Orion, 1997)

Gould, Philip, *The Unfinished Revolution: How the Modernisers Saved the Labour Party* (London: Little, Brown, 1998)

Halberstam, David, *War in a Time of Peace: Bush, Clinton and the Generals* (New York: Scribner, 2001)

Hay, Colin, *The Political Economy of New Labour: Labouring Under False Pretences?* (Manchester: MUP, 1999)

Heffernan, Richard, *Defeat from the Jaws of Victory: Inside Neil Kinnock's Labour Party* (London: Verso, 1992)

———, *New Labour and Thatcherism: Exploring Political Change* (London: Macmillan, 1999)

Hennessy, Peter, *The Prime Minister: The Office and Its Holders Since 1945* (London: Allen Lane, 2000)

Hutton, Will, *The Stakeholding Society: Writings on Politics and Economics* (Cambridge: Polity Press, 1998)

———, *The State We're In* (London: Jonathan Cape, 1995)

Jefferys, Kevin (ed.), *Leading Labour: From Keir Hardie to Tony Blair* (London: I. B. Tauris, 1999)

———, *Labour Forces: From Ernest Bevin to Gordon Brown* (London: I. B. Tauris, 2002)

Jones, Nicholas, *Election '97* (London: Cassell, 1997)

———, *Soundbites and Spin Doctors* (London: Cassell, 1995)

———, *Sultans of Spin* (London: Victor Gollancz, 1999)

———, *The Control Freaks* (London: Politico's, 2001)

Jones, Tudor, *Remaking the Labour Party: From Gaitskell to Blair* (London: Routledge, 1996)

Kampfner, John, *Blair's Wars* (London: The Free Press, 2003)

Kavanagh, Dennis and Seldon, Anthony, *The Powers Behind the Prime Minister: The Hidden Influence of Number Ten* (London: HarperCollins, 1999)

Kay, John, *Foundations of Corporate Success: How Business Strategies Add Value* (Oxford: OUP, 1993)

———, *Why Firms Succeed* (Oxford: OUP, 1996)

Kilfoyle, Peter and Parker, Ian, *Left Behind: Lessons from Labour's Heartland* (London: Politico's, 2000)

King, Anthony, et al., *New Labour Triumphs: Britain at the Polls* (London: Chatham House, 1998)

Leonard, Dick (ed.), *Crosland and New Labour* (London: Macmillan, 1999)

Lipsey, David, *The Secret Treasury* (London: Viking, 2000)

Little, Richard and Wickham-Jones, Mark (eds), *New Labour's Foreign Policy: A New Moral Crusade?* (Manchester: MUP, 2000)

Ludlam, Steve and Smith, Martin, *New Labour in Government* (London: Macmillan, 2002)

Macmurray, John, *The Personal World: John Macmurray on Self and Society*, selected and introduced by Philip Cornford (Edinburgh: Floris Books, 1996)

Mandelson, Peter and Liddle, Roger, *The Blair Revolution: Can New Labour Deliver?* (London: Faber & Faber, 1996)

Mandelson, Peter, *The Blair Revolution Revisited* (London: Politico's, 2002)

Mann, James, *Rise of the Vulcans: The History of Bush's War Cabinet* (New York: Viking, 2004)

Marquand, David, *The Progressive Dilemma: From Lloyd George to Tony Blair* (London: Phoenix Giant, 2nd edition 1999)

McSmith, Andy, *Faces of Labour: The Inside Story* (London: Verso, 1997)

Micklethwait, John and Wooldridge, Adrian, *The Right Nation: Why America is Different* (London: Penguin, 2004)

Naughtie, James, *The Accidental American: Tony Blair and the Presidency* (London: Macmillan, 2004)

———, *The Rivals: Blair and Brown – The Intimate Story of a Political Marriage* (London: Fourth Estate, 2002)

Norris, Pippa and Gavin, Neil (eds), *Britain Votes 1997* (Oxford: OUP, 1997)

Norris, Pippa (ed.), *Britain Votes 2001* (Oxford: OUP, 2001)

Perryman, Mark (ed.), *The Blair Agenda* (London: Lawrence & Wishart, 1998)

Peston, Robert, *Brown's Britain* (London: Short Books, 2005)

Philip, Robert, *A Keen Wind Blows: The Story of Fettes College* (London: James & James, 1998)

Post, Jerrold (ed.), *The Psychological Assessment of Political Leaders: With Profiles of Saddam Hussein and Bill Clinton* (Ann Arbor: The University of Michigan Press, 2003)

Powell, Martin (ed.), *New Labour, New Welfare State? The 'Third Way' in British Social Policy* (Bristol: The Policy Press, 1999)

Pym, Hugh and Kochan, Nick, *Gordon Brown: The First Year of Power* (London: Bloomsbury, 1998)

Ramsay, Robin, *The Rise of New Labour* (Harpenden: The Pocket Essential, 2002)

Rawnsley, Andrew, *Servants of the People: The Inside Story of New Labour* (London: Penguin, 2001)

Riddell, Peter, *Hug Them Close: Blair, Clinton, Bush and the 'Special Relationship'* (London: Politico's, 2003)

——, *Parliament under Blair* (London: Politico's, 2000)

Rose, Richard, *The Prime Minister in a Shrinking World* (Cambridge: Polity, 2001)

Rosen, Greg, (ed.), *Dictionary of Labour Biography* (London: Politico's, 2001)

Seldon, Anthony (ed.), *The Blair Effect: The Blair Government, 1997–2001* (London: Little, Brown, 2001)

Scott, Andrew, *Running On Empty: 'Modernising' the British and Australian Labour Parties* (Annandale: Pluto Press, 2000)

Smith, Martin J. and Spear, Joanna, *The Changing Labour Party* (London: Routledge, 1992)

Stelzer, Irwin, *Neo-conservatism* (London: Atlantic Books, 2004)

Stothard, Peter, *Thirty Days: A Month at the Heart of Blair's War* (London: HarperCollins, 2003)

Suskind, Ron, *The Price of Loyalty* (New York: Simon & Schuster, 2004)

Taylor, Gerald, *Labour's Renewal: The Policy Renewal and Beyond* (London: Macmillan, 1997)

—— (ed.), *The Impact of New Labour* (London: Macmillan, 1999)

Toynbee, Polly and Walker, David, *Did Things Get Better?* (London: Penguin, 2001)

——, *Did Things Get Better II* (London: Bloomsbury, 2005)

White, Stuart (ed.), *New Labour: The Progressive Future?* (Basingstoke: Palgrave, 2001)

Williams, John and Stoddart, Tom, *Victory: With Tony Blair on the Road to a Landslide* (London: Bookman, 1997)

Woodward, Bob, *Bush at War* (New York: Simon & Schuster, 2003)

——, *Plan of Attack* (New York: Simon & Schuster, 2004)

Worcester, Robert, and Mortimer, Roger, *Explaining Labour's Landslide* (London: Politico's, 1999)

Journal Articles

Akgül, Deniz Altinbas, 'The European Union Response to September 11' (*Review of International Affairs*, Vol. 1, No. 4, 2002)

Applebaum, Anne, 'Tony Blair and the New Left' (*Foreign Affairs*, Vol. 76, No. 2, 1997)

Barr, Nicholas, 'Towards a "Third Way"? Rebalancing the Role of the State' (*New Economy*, Vol. 5, No. 2, 1998)

762

Blair

Blair, Tony, 'Leading the Way' (London: Institute for Public Policy Research, 1998)

——, 'The Third Way: New Politics for the New Century' (London: Fabian Society, 1998)

Burrough, Bryan; Peretz, Evgenia; Rose, David, and Wise, David, 'The Path to War' (*Vanity Fair*, May 2004)

Campbell, Alastair, 'Beyond Spin: Government and the Media' (London: Fabian Society, 1999)

Campbell, Colin, and Rockman, Bert, 'Third Way Leadership, Old Way Government: Blair, Clinton, and the Power to Govern' (*British Journal of Politics and International Relations*, Vol. 3, No 1, 2001)

Commentary, 'From Thatcher to Blair' (*Political Quarterly*, Vol. 70, No.1, 2001)

Finlayson, Alan, 'Third Way Theory' (*Political Quarterly*, Vol. 70, No. 3, 1999)

——, 'Elements of the Blairite Image of Leadership' (*Parliamentary Affairs*, Vol. 55, 2002)

Freeden, Michael, 'The Ideology of New Labour' (*Political Quarterly*, Vol. 70, 1999)

Gray, Andrew and Jenkins, Bill, 'New Labour, New Government? Change and Continuity in Public Administration and Government, 1997' (*Parliamentary Affairs*, Vol. 51, No. 2, 1998)

Hale, Sarah, 'Professor Macmurray and Mr Blair: The Strange Case of the Communication Guru That Never Was' (*Political Quarterly*, Vol. 73, No. 2, 2002)

Harris, Michael, 'New Labour: Government and Opposition' (*Political Quarterly*, Vol. 70, No. 1, 1999)

Hennessy, Peter, 'The Blair Style and the Requirements of Twenty-first-century Premiership' (*Political Quarterly*, Vol. 71, No. 4, 2000)

Hewitt, Patricia, and Gould, Philip, 'Lessons from America' (*Renewal*, Vol. 1, No. 1, Jan 1993)

Kenny, Martin and Smith, Martin, '(Mis)understanding Blair' (*Political Quarterly*, Vol. 68, No. 3, 1997)

Kramer, Steven, 'Blair's Britain after Iraq' (*Foreign Affairs*, Vol. 82, No. 4, 2003)

Labour Party, 'New Labour: Because Britain Deserves Better' (Labour Party Manifesto, 1997)

——, 'Ambitions for Britain' (Labour Party Manifesto, 2001)

Margolick, David, 'Blair's Fiftieth Birthday' (*Vanity Fair*, June 2003)

McConnell, Alan, and Stark, Alastair, 'Foot-and-Mouth 2001: The Politics of Crisis Management' (*Parliamentary Affairs*, No. 55, 2002)

Richards, Steve, 'The Odd Couple' (*Prospect*, October 2003)

Rubin, James, 'Stumbling into War' (*Foreign Affairs*, Vol. 82, No. 5, 2003)

Stephens, Philip, 'The Blair Government and Europe' (*Political Quarterly*, Vol. 70, No. 1, 2001)

Unpublished Papers and Documents

Tony Blair Lecture at Murdoch University, Western Australia, 1982. Transcript provided by the Hon. Dr Geoff Gallop, MLA.

Correspondence and minutes from shadow Cabinet meetings, 1989–92, Neil Kinnock Archives, Churchill Archives Centre, Churchill College, Cambridge.

Minutes of Hackney South Constituency Labour Party Meetings, 1980–83, provided by Baroness Thornton.

Minutes of Sedgefield Constituency Labour Party Meetings, 1983–87, provided by John Burton.

Policy papers and minutes of shadow Cabinet meetings, 1985–92, The Labour History Archive and Study Centre, John Rylands University Library of Manchester.

Private diary, Lance Price, 1998–2001.

Private diary, Lord Jenkins of Hillhead, 1995–97.

Records of the International Visitor Program, 1986–92, US Department of State.

Internal papers from US Department of State, 1995–2003, released to the author under US Freedom of Information Act.

Index

Page references in **bold** denote chapter/major section devoted to subject.